Resources for Teaching

Literature and Its Writers

An Introduction to Fiction, Poetry, and Drama

PREPARED BY

Ann Charters
University of Connecticut

Samuel Charters

William E. Sheidley
University of Southern Colorado

Susan C. W. Abbotson
University of Connecticut

Bedford Books ⩕ BOSTON

For information, write: Bedford Books, 75 Arlington Street, Boston, MA 02116 (617-426-7440)

ISBN: 0–312–13804–0

Cover Design: Hannus Design Associates

Cover Art: Vanessa Bell, *Leonard Sidney Woolf,* oil on canvas, 1940. By courtesy of the National Portrait Gallery, London.

Acknowledgment

Tobey Hiller, "the closing of the south park road." Copyright © 1996 by Tobey Hiller. Reprinted by permission of the author.

PREFACE

We have organized this manual into three sections — Fiction, Poetry, and Drama — to correspond with *Literature and Its Writers*. For individual stories, poems, and plays, we offer brief critical analyses and suggest ways to discuss the work in class. Like the questions that follow, these commentaries aim to promote a lively exchange of responses and perceptions without insisting on any particular interpretation or critical methodology. Among the Topics for Writing are questions we call "Connections," assignments that ask students to link selections in the anthology. These questions were designed to promote critical thinking and to provide both stimulating topics for writing assignments and material for fruitful class discussions. Instructors will readily see ways to rephrase, restructure, and reapply these assignments to suit their purposes and their students' needs. Some writing topics may serve equally well as discussion questions, and vice versa.

The lists of Suggested Reading that conclude many of the entries are neither exhaustive nor highly selective. They simply cite interesting and, when possible, readily available criticism that proved useful in preparing this manual or that contains information and approaches to the stories that could not be incorporated in the commentaries. Thanks are due to the authors mentioned, to whose insights and scholarship these resources are generally indebted.

In the section on Fiction, the commentaries, questions, and topics for writing were prepared by Ann Charters and William Sheidley, with additional help from Samuel Charters, Martha Ramsey, and Robert Gaspar. Samuel Charters wrote the commentaries, questions for discussion, and topics for writing in the Poetry section, and Susan Abbotson prepared the section on Drama. Suzy Johnson and David Wasser also contributed comments on the introductory material. For ease of access, you will find the hundreds of works of fiction and poetry in the first two sections organized alphabetically by author, while in the third section the nineteen plays are organized chronologically by author, to suggest the historical development of this genre. There is no discussion of works in the commentaries and casebook sections of *Literature and Its Writers*, because we believe these works speak for themselves.

The last section of this manual is the Appendix of Audiovisual Resources, which lists a wide range of materials that discuss either individual authors and works or literary genres. At the end of the Appendix is a Directory of Distributors.

Ann Charters
University of Connecticut

Samuel Charters

CONTENTS

Contents

Part Two   Poetry

Contents

Contents

Part Three   *Drama*

INTRODUCTION

NOTES ON TEACHING LITERATURE AND COMPOSITION

If you have not had a lot of experience teaching literature to first-year college students, I offer the following notes in the hope that they may assist you in planning your course. My most vivid memory of the first freshman English course I taught more than thirty-five years ago is an incident that turned out to be the most embarrassing moment in my teaching career. During a particularly long-winded, soft-spoken student's reply to a question I asked the class, I fell asleep. I don't know what made me return to consciousness after a few seconds of restful slumber in the stuffy New Hampshire college classroom — perhaps an instinct that the silence around me was unnatural. I woke up to find fifty eyes of various shades of blue, brown, gray, and hazel staring at me expectantly, more amused than shocked. I was so rattled that I don't remember whether I apologized for my mindless absence from the classroom, but I do recall that I felt like an idiot when I had to ask my student to repeat her answer. She made short work of it this time. I vowed to myself that I would never be inattentive in a classroom again, and the experience hasn't repeated itself, at least up to now.

I nodded off while teaching my first freshman English class because I was so anxious about being prepared that I had stayed up too late the night before creating my lesson plan. I had crammed so many ideas into my outline for that single fifty-minute class that it would probably have taken me the next two weeks to cover them. That's my first advice: Besides getting enough sleep to stay alert in front of your students, try to plan each class realistically. Even though you may fear the dead silence of a classroom, you will discover that your students can and will voice their ideas. Just give them time.

Also do what you can to keep the classroom well ventilated and check that all the students can hear you and one another during your first discussion. Then settle in and enjoy the business and the pleasures of teaching. As Stuart Sherman wrote in "Time in Teaching, Teaching in Time" (*Academe,* September/October 1996), "Teachers perform the strange magic of doing something important while doing nothing tangible (and I suspect that this is why they generally prefer the airy enchantments of the classroom to the physical labor of paper-marking)." Here are some further ideas to consider if you are beginning to teach a literature and composition course to freshmen.

Planning and Writing a Syllabus

Before you plan the semester, find out if your English Department has set goals for students to meet in freshman classes. These usually stress departmental policy concerning class attendance and taking roll and stipulate a minimum number of pages of writing and revision from each student. Often there is also a sample syllabus or a file of syllabi used previously by other instructors teaching the course. These can help you plan your semester.

Distribute a syllabus describing only the first few weeks of the semester when you meet for your first class. You needn't plan the syllabus for the entire course right away (unless your institution requires that you do so). Tell your students that you will provide them with additional syllabi as you go along. This way you won't find yourself committed to unrealistic reading or writing assignments if you discover after meeting your class that they are proceeding at a different rate than you had imagined when you began planning the course. Remember to include your office hours, office location, and telephone number on the syllabus.

Tell your students at the start of the semester how you will arrive at their final grade. They should be clear about the relative importance of class attendance, participation in discussions and group work, homework, essays, research papers, poem memorization, oral reports, quizzes, midterms, and final exams. State in the syllabus the percentage of the grade represented by each of the activities in the course. Consider including collaborative group work whenever feasible: peer assessment of essays and papers, literary research and oral presentations to the class, and similar activities encourage students to take on some of the responsibility for the learning process.

Planning Essay Assignments

Focus attention on the writing assignments early in the semester by passing out guidelines for essay preparation along with your first syllabus. Such a guide might look something like the following.

Your Name and Course Number
Subject: First Paper

Date Paper is Due and Topic of Essay

General Guidelines for Preparing the Paper:

- State the number of words or pages, typed or word-processed and doubled-spaced. Stipulate margins and type size as well.

- Suggest the importance of a descriptive title for the paper, which, if possible, should relate to the student's critical thinking about the subject. The student should use the title as a tool to help the reader focus on the topic.

- Remind students of the need to proofread essays carefully for spelling errors, punctuation, and factual details (accurate titles, authors' names, names of characters, quotations, and so forth).

- Assign specific pages in the Appendix to Literature and Its Writers to help students get started. Emphasize the importance of developing a thesis or central idea that is clearly stated in the opening paragraph of each essay.

Teaching Students to Read Literature

Take time in an early class meeting to discuss how students should be reading their assignments. Assign and review Chapters 5, 16, and 24, on reading, thinking, and writing about short fiction/poetry/drama (the order will depend on your approach). Emphasize the importance of reading slowly and reading twice, so that students begin to notice the way that writers use language, as well as what they are saying. Demonstrate how you would read a text if you were doing a homework assignment. Tell students what the American poet Robert Hass has said about reading literature: "Reading is a gymnasium for the imagination where people can work out, get ready for the shocks of existence."

Teaching Critical Thinking and Writing

Assign student writing every time the class meets. Probably the most frequent problem encountered by new instructors is neglecting to allow sufficient time during the semester to help students with their essays. Discussing the stories, poems, and plays you've assigned becomes so absorbing that too little class time is left to assist students in developing their writing skills.

One of the most immediate ways to integrate composition and writing practice into an introductory literature course is to conclude your first meeting by asking students to produce a writing sample in the last fifteen or so minutes of class. You might ask them to consider the fiction, poetry, and drama they've read either in or out of class and list the three works they've enjoyed (or disliked) the most, citing their reasons why. This exercise helps you to get to know your students and allows them to see the difference between expressing their personal taste and exercising their critical skills.

Student writing throughout the semester can continue on a relatively informal basis in addition to the finished essays. Consider, for example, asking students to write a sentence or a paragraph demonstrating their critical thinking about each reading assignment. These written statements can become the basis for class discussion about the literature, or you could require that students keep journals of their responses. They'll probably start out writing summaries without much thought in them: "I felt sad about the lonely old man when I read Sherwood Anderson's story 'Hands.'" After a few class meetings, however, you can insist that they write about their assignments *as literature,* using their newly acquired critical vocabulary. When you help them recognize the difference between summary and critical analysis, their earlier sentence might read, "Told as a series of flashbacks, the narrative structure of Anderson's story underscores the static, 'going nowhere' life that Wing Biddlebaum lives as a lonely recluse in Winesburg, Ohio."

Challenge students to pack into heir single sentence as much information about the work as they can. You can also ask them to write *two* different sentences in their journals expressing ideas about each assignment — the first one before class discussion and the second one after. If you prefer to assign specific questions for homework to help students focus their thinking, you will find questions for discussion after each entry in this manual, as well as topics for longer writing assignments.

Organizing Your Course

Plan to devote four weeks to each literary genre if your course runs for fourteen weeks. This allows you to introduce the class to your aims and get to know them a little during the first week and to use the last week for oral reports, discussion of research papers, and a general course summary that will help students prepare for the final exam. Of course, if you don't give a final exam or include oral reports, or if you assign only short essays instead of a longer research paper, your final week can take a different direction. Allow time during each four-week period to work with student writing about these genres. Incorporate peer discussion and reviews into class time to involve students in the process of evaluating and improving their essays.

Here are five approaches to using *Literature and Its Writers* to help you plan the semester.

FORMAL

With this method you assign the introductory chapters on fiction, poetry, and drama at the beginning of each of the weeks devoted to the specific genre. You go over these pages in the classroom, clarifying the definitions of concepts important to each genre (plot, character, setting, point of view, style, and theme in short fiction; the poet's means; the elements of drama, and so on) and discussing the examples of stories, poems, and plays in these introductory chapters. Then you assign individual works to explore aspects of these formal elements (that is, any story of your choice to illustrate the importance of setting in short fiction, or Washington Irving's "Rip Van Winkle" if you want to develop the idea addressed in the opening chapter of the text of the difference between the folktale and a literary story, emphasizing the uniqueness of literary language). This is a somewhat traditional approach, but it gives you and your students a clear idea of what you're up to. You can teach the different genres in the order in which they are presented in *Literature and Its Writers,* or you can introduce them in a different order. Many instructors begin the course with short fiction, because students find it easiest to read. Other instructors prefer to start with poetry, because it is the oldest literary form, followed by drama and fiction. Still others teach poetry last, after fiction and drama, so that they won't run out of class time in the middle of a long dramatic work.

HISTORICAL

Here you might want to mix the genres to stress the origins and development of literature in the Western tradition. You could investigate literature's role as a record of historical and ideological change and the continuing significance of this record to our culture. You could begin with the selections of epic poetry, move on to classical Greek drama and Shakespeare, read the Augustan and Romantic poets, and continue into modernism with James Joyce, Ernest Hemingway, T. S. Eliot, and Samuel Beckett. Or you could proceed in the opposite direction, beginning with contemporary poetry, drama, and fiction and tracing a line back to the classics. A major drawback to this approach is that the end of the semester will probably occur long before you've worked your way back to Sophocles and Homer. Be prepared to make radical revisions in your syllabus as the semester progresses. Or you might decide as you plan the course that you want to structure it exclusively as a survey of recent literature, or that you're most intrigued by the thought of developing the concept of canon revision by pairing traditional literary icons with alternate cultural statements (for instance, teaching the excerpt from Homer's *Iliad* along with Alhaji Fabala Kanuteh's African epic).

THEMATIC

You could devise a course in which the assigned reading illustrates important themes — for example, "Nature and Consciousness," in which you could read such authors as Leslie Marmon Silko, Percy Bysshe Shelley, and Susan Glaspell, or "Social Problems of Our Time," where the writing could include work by James Baldwin, Lawrence Ferlinghetti, and Marsha Norman. The possibilities are endless, depending on your interests.

WRITERS' CASEBOOKS

Literature and Its Writers contains casebooks on three fiction writers, four poets, and two playwrights. A week or more spent on the literary work and commentaries of each author could be a satisfying and well-defined way to proceed through the semester. The commentaries could serve as models of different types of student writing, and related works of literature could be assigned from the anthology. For example (and this is not meant to imply that this is the only choice of writers or use of the commentaries), students could also read the stories of southern writers Richard Wright, William Faulkner, and Eudora Welty while they are studying the work of Flannery O'Connor; they could read poems by Elizabeth Barrett Browning and Christina Rossetti in addition to those of Emily Dickinson; they could read a recent short play by August Wilson along with the Lorraine Hansberry play and commentaries.

INTERTEXTUAL

You could organize a course around the way different writers have responded to and developed the literary tradition. Washington Irving's "Rip Van Winkle" as a response to J. C. C. Nachtigal's folktale "Peter Klaus the Goatherd" can lead to a discussion of Sandra Cisneros's allusion to Rip Van Winkle in "The Monkey Garden." Other examples of writers' responses to one another include Leslie Marmon Silko's re-imagining a Native American story, John Steinbeck's rewriting of D. H. Lawrence, and Joyce Carol Oates's revision of Katherine Anne Porter. Studying poetry, you might trace instances of quotation, paraphrase, imitation, parody, allusion, address, and tribute. For drama, you could read Shakespeare's *Hamlet* and the excerpt from Tom Stoppard's *Dogg's Hamlet*, as well as the plays by Tennessee Williams and Christopher Durang, or you could consider how elements of a classic Nō play like *Kantan* are reflected in a recent short work by David Henry Hwang.

Emphasizing Critical Thinking

Regardless of how you organize the course, you might want to introduce students to the usefulness and limitations of different critical methods — "close reading," reader response, feminism, Marxism, Freudianism, deconstruction —

to help them understand stories, poems, and plays. We have selected commentaries that follow specific critical methods to serve as examples. When teaching poetry, remind the students that they should read every assigned poem through to the end, even if they don't completely understand it. Although they may not get every word, they will often find that the poem has made a strong emotional impression on them.

Always allow sufficient time, if possible, for students to reflect on their reading after the class has discussed an assignment. Refer back to the work read for the previous class and ask if there are further questions or insights to share about that work before taking on the next one. The story writer John Cheever reminds us that "the basic test" of literature is "Is it interesting?" And "interest" connotes "suspense, emotional involvement and a sustained claim on one's attention."

During the first weeks of the semester, consider giving a brief paraphrase of the story, poem, or play before asking students to discuss the work. This minimizes the loss of precious time while unprepared students mumble vague and halting answers to the question "What is this story/poem/play about?" It will also head off student embarrassment in the classroom if the content of the work has been grossly misunderstood. Critical thinking and sound interpretation depend on a clear understanding of the text. A brief paraphrase by the instructor before opening up the work for questions will start everyone off on equal ground and allow the class to go on to more interesting matters. If students have brought in a written homework assignment based on what they now see is a faulty understanding of a work's content, give them the opportunity to revise their paper before turning it in. This will help them to sharpen their critical thinking and to get more writing practice. You might also want to include occasional quizzes in class to check if students are keeping up with the reading.

In this manual you will find interpretive essays clarifying each selection in *Literature and Its Writers* and scores of discussion questions and writing topics. They have been designed to challenge students' understanding and to lead them to a more thoughtful appreciation of each writer's literary strategies. And this, at least in my experience, is what literature and composition courses are all about.

Ann Charters
University of Connecticut

PART ONE

FICTION

JACK AGUEROS

Dominoes (p. 32)

The action of this story erupts as suddenly as does the murderous street fight Agueros describes. What begins as a game of dominoes between four Puerto Rican men in New York City deteriorates into open warfare between two of the players whose cultural background has instilled in them the belief that their destiny lies in being *macho*. As Wilson explains the philosophy to Alma, "Men who are real men can live their lives any way they like — because their destiny is clear. To be a *macho* is the destiny." With his large hands wrapped around the other's throat, Paco intends to strangle Ebarito, who in turn pulls out a pair of scissors and stabs Paco a dozen times between the ribs. Ebarito survives with his vocal chords permanently damaged, while Paco staggers off to a fire hydrant and crumples "into a pile like a pneumatic tire that had a blow out." Alma, hysterical, screaming over Ebarito's body on the sidewalk, doesn't even realize her Uncle Paco is dead. Her grief is misdirected, Agueros tells the reader: "She screamed at everyone. She screamed at no one."

While Agueros is careful to sketch in the individual personalities of the four domino players in order to motivate the action, he does so without sentimentality or sensationalism. Ebarito can't play the game as skillfully as the other three players, and he is unable to concede defeat gracefully, although he knows he should. He tries to cheat instead, and he gets caught immediately. Tito is kinder but weak, unlike Wilson and Paco, best friends, who both left Puerto Rico at sixteen to join the merchant marine. Agueros shows sympathy for their poverty-stricken background: Wilson and Paco had been "country boys suddenly [placed in the merchant marine] with mean men and dangerous work and thirty years at sea always looking to see who was standing behind you."

Poverty and hardship have toughened both men, but Agueros is critical of the lessons their difficult lives have taught them. His placement of Alma in the story provides a moral frame of reference to contrast with the amorality of the other characters' brutal behavior. The orderly game of dominoes, explained as Paco taught it to Alma, is another steadfast reference point, a contrast to the impulsive and destructive behavior the men display when not playing the game.

Questions for Discussion

1. "Dominoes seemed to Alma a ridiculous game." Explain how to play it, and analyze its appeal for Paco, Wilson, Tito, and Ebarito.
2. Why do Wilson and Paco break into laughter at Wilson's response to Alma after she asks him, "What is the fate for a woman?"
3. Why does Wilson keep Tito from stopping the fight between Paco and Ebarito?

4. What is the effect of Agueros's organization of the story into sections paralleling the doubled numbers ranging from six to zero (blank) on the face of the dominoes?

Topics for Writing

1. Instead of using Agueros's omniscient point of view, rewrite the story from the first-person point of view of Alma or one of the other characters.
2. Analyze the social and cultural background of the Puerto Rican community in New York City as it appears in "Dominoes."

Suggested Readings

Agueros, Jack. *Correspondence Between the Stonehaulers.* Brooklyn: Hanging Loose, 1991.

———. *Dominoes and Other Stories from the Puerto Rican.* Willimantic, CT: Curbstone, 1993.

WOODY ALLEN

The Kugelmass Episode (p. 38)

Like most works of fiction based on impossible or unlikely suppositions, "The Kugelmass Episode" entertains us with the device on which it is grounded. Rather than developing the intellectual puzzles of science fiction, however, Allen mainly offers gently satiric jokes made possible by the incongruities arising from his donnée. When her class notices that on page 100 "a bald Jew is kissing Madame Bovary," the teacher in South Dakota, without consulting her desk copy, blames the problem on a mass-media stereotype, drug-crazed students; a professor at Stanford sees in the incredible instability of the text a confirmation of a mindless academic cliché: "Well, I guess the mark of a classic is that you can reread it a thousand times and always find something new." Thus we transform what is unfamiliar into bricks for the wall of presupposition that barricades us from the truth. Meanwhile, Allen delights in collapsing the distance between "good literature" and everyday banality. Emma admires Kugelmass's leisure suit; he thrills her with black panties and designer slacks; and, like every other good-looking girl who goes to New York, she dreams of a career on the stage.

But the fantasy on which Allen bases his tale has deeper roots. Like Faust, Kugelmass dreams of transcending human limitations, of living for a while free from the constraints of time and ordinary causation. He abandons human science and philosophy, here represented by his shrink, and turns to magic. Although Persky resembles an auto mechanic more than Mephistopheles, he offers an equally dangerous and meaningful temptation to Kugelmass. If the professor lacks the poetry and grandeur of his Faustian predecessors, he is motivated by parallel desires. Bored with his life and unable to love the people he shares it with (who can blame him?), he bargains for something he expects will be better. Appropriately, given the diminished scale of modern heroism, he signs away not his soul but merely a "double sawbuck." As happens especially with Marlowe's Dr. Faustus, for his reward Kugelmass gets only what he is capable of imagining. Emma Bovary as he experiences her talks and acts like any woman he could have picked up at

Elaine's — exactly what he wanted, and what he turns her into by bringing her out of the novel and into the Plaza Hotel.

After the near disaster of his affair with Emma, Kugelmass swears off philandering, but of course he has not learned his lesson. When he asks Persky to use the wondrous machine to send him for a date with "The Monkey" of Philip Roth's *Portnoy's Complaint*, Kugelmass reveals the utter emptiness of spirit that hides behind his glib pop-culture romanticism, and it is fitting that he ends up scrambling through a desert inhabited by predatory words without meaning.

The intellectual and moral universe that Kugelmass inhabits even before his final translation is no less devoid of meaning. Allen's fantasy shows how the sophistication of modern life can drain the spirit out of human language, desires, and relationships. Kugelmass claims to have "soul," but his needs are quoted from advertisements in *The New Yorker*. The language of commercial psychology debases even his dreams, whose imagery is thirdhand and probably phony: "I was skipping through a meadow holding a picnic basket and the basket was marked 'Options.'" Kugelmass picks his mistress as from a menu; he decides to plunge into the supernatural (but for exceedingly *natural* reasons) more easily than he chooses between red and white wine (as if those were the only possibilities); significantly, he is most comfortable minimizing the importance of what he is doing: "'Sex and romance,' Kugelmass said from inside the box. 'What we go through for a pretty face.'"

Through the fantastic device of Persky's box, Allen achieves the small dislocation necessary to reveal that remark of Kugelmass's as a pitifully inadequate cliché. The story is full of such instances, and the technique embodies its larger vision. We choose the things we say to describe our lives to ourselves because they have been purged of discomforting truths. Allen shows that these statements are illusions. Kugelmass regards his life as a novel that has turned out badly. Rather than seeking to understand why he has come to a second marital dead end burdened with financial obligations and bored with his family, he tries to escape from the present and reenact the past. He wants only to enter *Madame Bovary* before page 120, and he dreams of starting life over in Europe, selling the (long defunct) *International Herald Tribune* "like those young girls used to."

The story leaves us with an implicit question: What redemption is possible for Kugelmass and the culture — our culture — that he represents? Is there an alternative to the Hobson's choice between desperation and meaninglessness?

WILLIAM E. SHEIDLEY

Questions for Discussion

1. Comment on the situation of Kugelmass as described in the first two paragraphs. Do you think his circumstances are unusual? Where should we lay blame for his predicament?
2. Kugelmass "had soul." What does that term seem to mean in this context?
3. Interpret Kugelmass's dream. Is it profoundly symbolic?
4. How effective is Dr. Mandel? Why does Kugelmass need a magician?
5. Discuss Persky. What might be Allen's basis for this character? How important is Persky to the story?
6. What factors enter into Kugelmass's choice of a mistress? What does this event suggest about his attitude toward literature? toward women?

7. Explore the implications of this quip: "She spoke in the same fine English translation as the paperback."
8. Review the first conversation between Kugelmass and Emma. Has Kugelmass really been transported into *Madame Bovary*? Does it resemble the novel as you read it or as you imagine it to be?
9. What does Allen achieve by noting the effect of the sudden appearance of the Kugelmass episode in the novel on various readers?
10. "By showing up during the correct chapters, I've got the situation knocked," Kugelmass says. Consider the implications of that idea. Would you like to live only certain chapters of your life?
11. Why does Emma want to come to New York? Why does Kugelmass want to take her there? Are the ensuing problems entirely the result of her being a character in a novel?
12. As Persky struggles to repair his box and Emma consumes "Dom Pérignon and black eggs," Kugelmass becomes more and more agitated. Finally, he contemplates suicide ("Too bad this is a low floor") or running away to Europe to sell the *International Herald Tribune*. How serious is he? Explain why those ideas accord with his character.
13. Why does it take Kugelmass only three weeks to break his resolution, "I'll never cheat again"?
14. *Portnoy's Complaint* examines, among other things, masturbation and adolescent sexual fantasies. What does it imply about Kugelmass that he chooses that book for his next adventure?
15. Do you think the ending of the story is appropriate? Why should Allen choose a remedial Spanish grammar for Kugelmass's hell rather than, say, a book in which adulterers are punished or in which none of the characters is a good-looking young woman?

Topics for Writing

1. Analyze how Allen crosses the border between life and art in "The Kugelmass Episode" and in his film *The Purple Rose of Cairo*.
2. Discuss the theme of meaningless language in "The Kugelmass Episode."
3. Study the use of language in Allen's story. List familiar phrases. What are their sources? Examine the conversations between characters. How much communication is taking place?
4. People often wish aloud for something they know to be impossible or speak of what they would do *if only*: "If only I had her looks and his money." "If only I were in charge." Imagine a character — yourself or someone you know, perhaps — whose impossible wish comes true. Then what? Follow Allen's lead by using the device to express the truth in a surprising new way.
5. **CONNECTIONS** Compare and contrast the responses to marvels in Allen's "The Kugelmass Episode" and García Márquez's "A Very Old Man with Enormous Wings."

Related Play

Woody Allen, Two Monologues from *Annie Hall* and *Manhattan*, p. 1897.

Suggested Readings

Gianetti, L. "Ciao, Woody." *Western Humanities Review* 35 (1981): 157–61.
Jacobs, Diane. *Magic of Woody Allen*. London: Robson, 1982.

Reisch, M. S. "Woody Allen: American Prose Humorist." *Journal of Popular Culture* 17 (1983): 68–74.

Rose, L. "Humor and Nothingness." *Atlantic* 255 (1985): 94–96.

Shechner, Mark. "Woody Allen: The Failure of the Therapeutic." In *From Hester Street to Hollywood.* Ed. Sarah B. Cohen. Bloomington: Indiana UP, 1983. 231–44.

"Woody Allen on the American Character." *Commentary* 76 (1983): 61–65.

Dorothy Allison

Lupus (p. 47)

Allison's title and the footnotes she has placed at the beginning of her story will help most students find an entrance into it, but her imaginative treatment of her subject may be difficult for some readers to follow. Class could begin with a discussion of the elements of fiction in "Lupus," so that students understand how the author's choice of the form of her story helps to shape its meaning. "Lupus" is told by a first-person narrator as a series of flashbacks. The first flashback is presented as the opening of the story, as the narrator sits drinking iced tea on her older cousin Temple's dilapidated porch during a hot August afternoon. The narrator has returned to the small town of Greenville, Georgia, to visit her favorite cousin, Temple, who lives there with her two unmarried daughters, Maryat and Claire. Temple has been widowed for twenty-five years since the death, apparently from lupus, of her beloved husband Robert in 1959. A short time later, her third daughter died while still a baby. Temple has been unable to recover from her sense of guilt that she is responsible for her husband's death. As she tells the narrator, "Nobody in his family had it, but Granny said we'd had a cousin with it, so maybe it had come through me."

As the two women talk through the afternoon, the narrator intersperses references to a series of important events in Temple's life, which occur as undramatized flashbacks throughout the two women's conversation. We are given references to Temple's marriage, her loss of her mother as a child of seven, her memory of the narrator as a "string bean" little girl, her economic struggle and bouts of depression since becoming a widow, when she blamed herself for passing on the disease of lupus to her husband and daughters. Midway in the conversation, Temple asks the narrator if she has read the stories of Flannery O'Connor, the Georgia author who was afflicted with lupus. This serves as a transition for the narrator to tell Temple about her experiences in northern cities since leaving Georgia. Temple's response is to give her own news, that she is in poor health, suffering from diabetes and high blood pressure. Obsessed with thoughts of disease, Temple confides two recurring dreams. In the first one, she dreams of throwing herself and her two girls in front of one of the semi-trucks that screech past her house. In the second, she dreams of walking alone through the town of Greenville as it burns down. Her troubled dreams are the climax of the story.

In the falling action of the plot, the narrator imagines Temple — obsessed with her thoughts of illness and painful death — continuing to live on with her daughters on her porch. The narrator concludes with a paragraph about her memories of her beloved cousin. She identifies with Temple as a proud nonconformist like herself, but one who chose to stay in the provincial Georgia community.

Questions for Discussion

1. Analyze how the description of Temple's house and yard foreshadow the events to come in the narrative.
2. Discuss how the author's description of Temple and her daughters makes you sympathetic or unsympathetic to them.
3. How does the narrator feel about Temple? What is the effect of her description of her dreams of "pulling her [Temple] into my neck, sucking her throat, and licking her eyes"?
4. Does Temple reciprocate the narrator's feelings?
5. Why doesn't Temple respond to the narrator's description of what it's like to live in cities that she's never seen?
6. Why is Temple so obsessed with lupus?
7. Why is the narrator so obsessed with Temple?
8. Which of these two obsessions is the central conflict of the story?
9. How is the lack of narrative resolution of these conflicts reflected in the form Allison has chosen to tell this story?

Topics for Writing

1. What is lupus? Is it an inherited or contagious disease, as Allison suggests in her short story? Write a paper in which you research the medical facts about lupus and relate these facts to the way Allison describes it in her short fiction. Is Allison using lupus as a metaphor as well as a medical condition in the story?
2. **CONNECTIONS**   Although Allison refers to two Flannery O'Connor stories in "Lupus," Allison's story is closer in its subject matter and narrative approach to Sherwood Anderson's "Hands" than it is to O'Connor's short fiction. Compare and contrast "Lupus" and "Hands," analyzing how Anderson's commentary on "Form, Not Plot, in the Short Story" relates to both stories.

Related Story

Flannery O'Connor, A Good Man Is Hard to Find, p. 558.

SHERWOOD ANDERSON

Hands (p. 54)

Anderson's story "Hands" might be called a portrait. Like a formal painted portrait, it depicts Wing Biddlebaum not only as he exists at a given moment but also in conjunction with certain props in the background that reveal who he is by recalling his past and defining his circumstances. The focal image of the portrait is Wing's hands, around which the other elements of the picture are organized and to which they lend meaning. Further, the story depends for a portion of its effect on a series of painterly tableaux, from the sunset landscape with berry pickers with which it begins to the silhouette of Wing as a holy hermit, saying over and over the rosary of his lonely years of penance for a sin he did not commit.

In keeping with this achronological narration (which William L. Phillips has shown may in part result from Anderson's thinking his way through the story as he wrote it), neither Wing nor George Willard experiences any clear revelation or makes any climactic decision. Wing never understands why he was driven out of Pennsylvania, and George is afraid to ask the questions that might lead them both to a liberating understanding of Wing's experience.

The reader, however, is not permitted to remain in the dark. With the clear understanding of how the crudity and narrow-minded suspicion of his neighbors have perverted Wing's selfless, "diffused" love for his students into a source of fear and shame comes a poignant sorrow for what is being wasted. Wing's hands may be the pride of Winesburg for their agility at picking strawberries, but the nurturing love that they betoken is feared by everyone, including George, including even Wing himself, whose loneliness is as great as his capacity to love — from which, by a cruel irony, it arises.

WILLIAM E. SHEIDLEY

Questions for Discussion

1. Define Wing Biddlebaum's relationship to his community as it is implied in the first paragraph. To what extent is the impression created here borne out?
2. Why does Wing hope George Willard will come to visit? Does George ever arrive?
3. Wing's name, which refers to his hands, was given to him by "some obscure poet of the town," and telling the full story of those hands "is a job for a poet." What connotations of "wings" are appropriate? Why is "Wing" a better name for Biddlebaum than, say, "Claw," or "Hook," or "Picker"?
4. Could Wing himself have been a poet? Why does he tell his dreams only to George?
5. Why did the people of the town in Pennsylvania nearly lynch Adolph Myers? Why was he unable to defend himself?
6. Are the people in Ohio any different from those in Pennsylvania? Explain. What about George Willard? Evaluate his decision not to ask Wing about his hands.
7. What other hands do we see in the story? Compare them with Wing's.
8. Explain the implications of our last view of Wing. What is the pun in the last line?

Topics for Writing

1. Write an essay analyzing the crucifixion of Wing Biddlebaum.
2. Consider Anderson's comments in "Form, Not Plot, in the Short Story" (included in Chapter 7, p. 730) as a key to his art in "Hands."
3. After reading the story once, jot down your response, including your feelings about Wing, George, the townspeople, and the narrator. Also write, in one or two sentences, a summation of the story's theme as you understand it. Then reread the paragraphs in the order they would have followed had Anderson told the story in chronological order. Would your responses differ? Would the story have an identical theme? Explain.
4. Anderson claimed to have written this story at a sitting and to have published it without rearrangements or major additions or deletions of material. Imitating his process, write a vignette about a person unknown to you whom you see in a photograph. Start with the scene in the photo and end with the same, interpolating previous incidents and background information as they occur to you.

Related Commentary

Sherwood Anderson, Form, Not Plot, in the Short Story, p. 730.

Suggested Readings

Anderson, David, ed. *Critical Essays on Sherwood Anderson*. Boston: G. K. Hall, 1981.

Anderson, Sherwood. *A Story Teller's Story*. Cleveland: The UP of Case Western Reserve, 1968.

———. *The Portable Sherwood Anderson*. New York: Viking, 1972.

———. *The Teller's Tales*. Introduction by Frank Gado. Schenectady, NY: Union College P, 1983.

Burbank, Rex. *Sherwood Anderson*. Twayne's United States Authors Series 65. New York: Twayne, 1964. 64–66.

Crowley, John W., ed. *New Essays on "Winesburg, Ohio."* New York: Cambridge UP, 1990.

Joselyn, Sister Mary. "Some Artistic Dimensions of Sherwood Anderson's 'Death in the Woods.'" *Studies in Short Fiction* 4 (1967): 252–59.

Phillips, William L. "How Sherwood Anderson Wrote *Winesburg, Ohio*." *The Achievement of Sherwood Anderson*. Ed. Ray Lewis White. Chapel Hill: U of North Carolina P, 1966. 62–84, esp. 74–78. Originally published in *American Literature* 23 (1951): 7–30.

Rideout, Walter B., ed. *Sherwood Anderson*. Englewood Cliffs, NJ: Prentice, 1974.

Scheick, William J. "Compulsion toward Repetition: Sherwood Anderson's 'Death in the Woods.'" *Studies in Short Fiction* 11 (1974): 141–46.

Townsend, Kim. *Sherwood Anderson*. Boston: Houghton, 1987.

White, Ray Lewis. *"Winesburg, Ohio": An Explanation*. Boston: Twayne, 1990.

Margaret Atwood

Happy Endings (p. 59)

Atwood's story can be read profitably in conjunction with Grace Paley's "A Conversation with My Father." In both, the authors use humor to suggest a certain impatience with the traditional short-story form. Both stories can be read as "metafictions," fictions that comment on the art of telling stories. Atwood's piece is harsher than Paley's in its insistence that happy endings are impossible in stories; Atwood tells us clearly that death is "the only authentic ending" to everyone's story. Paley, in contrast, clearly values both her relationship with her dying father and her own imagination, allowing (even half-jokingly) her fictional heroine the possibility of rehabilitation after her drug addiction and a valued place in society as a counselor in a center for young addicts.

The first time students read "Happy Endings," they may miss the way Atwood connects the stories from "A" to "F." "B" is the first unhappy ending (as Atwood warns us in the third sentence), with the "worst possible scenario" worked out in John and Mary's love affair. Atwood's vocabulary here is deliberately harsh and unromantic, unlike the sentimental clichés of the "A" scenario.

As Atwood continues her permutations of the couples' possible relationships, her stories get shorter and more perfunctory. Her language becomes more elemental, preparing the reader for her summary dismissal of all plots, since they all end in death. In the final three paragraphs, Atwood drops any pretense that she is telling stories and directly addresses her readers, revealing that her true subject is not the emotional life she is creating for her characters but her awareness of the elements of fiction. She defines plot as "what" or "just one thing after another." Then, like the instructor's manual of a short-story anthology, she leaves the rest up to her reader: "Now try How [character] and Why [theme.]"

Questions for Discussion

1. Atwood's authorial presence is the strongest element in "Happy Endings." Does this make the text closer to an essay than a short story? Explain.
2. How does Atwood elicit your curiosity, so that you continue to read this short story? Would you say that she has proven that plot is the most essential element in a story? Is there also an underlying, coherent theme to "Happy Endings"?
3. Would the story still be effective if Atwood omitted her direct address to the reader ("If you want a happy ending, try A")? Explain.

Topics for Writing

1. Rewrite the story by inventing additional outcomes for John and Mary's relationship.
2. Ray Bradbury, in his book *Zen in the Art of Writing: Essays on Creativity* (Capra, 1990), writes, "The writer must let his fingers run out the story of his characters, who, being only human and full of strange dreams and obsessions, are only too glad to run. . . . Remember: *Plot* is no more than footprints left in the snow after your characters have run by on their way to incredible destinations. *Plot* is observed after the fact rather than before. It cannot precede action. It is the chart that remains when an action is through." Apply Bradbury's analysis to "Happy Endings."

Suggested Readings

Atwood, Margaret. *Murder in the Dark.* Toronto: Coach House, 1983.
———. *Second Words.* Toronto: Anansi, 1982.
Grace, Sherrill E., and Lorraine Weir. *Margaret Atwood: Language, Text and System.* Vancouver: U of British Columbia P, 1983.
Rigney, Barbara Hill. *Margaret Atwood.* Totowa, NJ: Barnes, 1987.
Stouck, David. *Major Canadian Authors.* Lincoln: U of Nebraska P, 1988.

Isaac Babel

My First Goose (p. 62)

The narrator in this story is an outsider, a lonely and hungry intellectual who wins a meal and the acceptance of the Cossacks by killing the old peasant woman's goose. He does it roughly, demonstrating that he will "get on all right" at the front. The act is portrayed partly as a rape, partly as a crucifixion. The quartermaster tells him, "you go and mess up a lady, and a good lady too, and you'll have the boys patting you on the back," and that is what he does, trampling her goose under his boot and plunging his sword into it while she repeats, "I want to go and hang myself," and he says, "Christ!" But the narrator recoils from his self-debasement: The night that enfolds him resembles a prostitute; the moon decorates it "like a cheap earring." Lenin says there is a shortage of everything, and though Surovkov believes that Lenin strikes straight at the truth "like a hen pecking at a grain," the narrator uses the spectacles of his learning to discern "the secret curve of Lenin's straight line," the hidden purpose of the speech. The narrator, too, has taken an apparently bold and forthright step in killing the goose, but the secret curve of his straight line has been to gain acceptance by the Cossacks and a share of *their* dinner, which reminds him of his home. As he sleeps with his new friends he dreams of women, just as he saw female beauty in the long legs of Savitsky. But in taking his first goose he has messed up a good lady and stained his heart with bloodshed, and his conscience is not at peace.

Questions for Discussion

1. Describe Savitsky. What is the narrator's attitude toward him? Why does Babel begin the story with this character, who never reappears?
2. What advice does the quartermaster give? Does the narrator follow it?
3. Why are the narrator's "specs" an object of derision? Who else in the story wears glasses?
4. Why does the Cossack throw the narrator's trunk out at the gate?
5. When the narrator first tries to read Lenin's speech, he cannot concentrate. Why?
6. How does the narrator win the respect of the Cossacks?
7. Discuss the difference between Surovkov's understanding of Lenin's speech and the narrator's.
8. Explain the last sentence. What is the narrator's feeling about himself? about the situation he is in?
9. "Lenin writes that there's a shortage of everything." Of what is there a particular shortage in the story?

Topics for Writing

1. Write an essay analyzing the function of sexual imagery in "My First Goose."
2. Explain why the narrator stains himself in "My First Goose."
3. What is the effect of Babel's extreme brevity in "My First Goose?" Describe the way it is achieved.
4. Before beginning to read "My First Goose," write your prediction of what its subject might be on the basis of its title alone. Write a second guess as well. After reading the story, review your predictions. To what extent were the expectations aroused by the title — even if they were not confirmed — relevant to an understanding of Babel's narrative?

Suggested Readings

Carden, Patricia. *The Art of Isaac Babel.* Ithaca, NY: Cornell UP, 1972. 97, 100, 110, 130–31.

Falen, James E. *Isaac Babel: Russian Master of the Short Story.* Knoxville: U of Tennessee P, 1974. 142–45.

JAMES BALDWIN

Sonny's Blues (p. 65)

The marvel of this story is the way the narrator — Sonny's older brother — narrows the physical and emotional distance between himself and Sonny until Sonny's plight is revealed and illuminated in a remarkable moment of empathy and insight. This story of drug addiction in the inner city's black ghetto is as valid today as it was when it was written. By juxtaposing the two brothers — a straight high school math teacher and a heroin-addicted blues pianist — Baldwin makes it possible for readers to enter the world of the story regardless of their racial background or their opinions about drugs. The author doesn't judge Sonny's plight. Instead, through the brother, he helps us understand it, sympathize with it, and transcend it in a brief shared experience of Sonny's inspired musical improvisation.

This is a long story, and its plot consists mostly of flashbacks, more "told" than "shown" in the reminiscences of Sonny's older brother. Yet the power of Baldwin's sympathy for his characters and his eloquent style move the reader along. Baldwin captures the African American culture of strong family allegiances in the face of American racism. Both Sonny and his brother are trying to survive, and we respect them for their courage.

One of the ways to discuss the story is through an analysis of the narrator's growing sympathy for Sonny. Baldwin tells us that the narrator thinks, after the death of his little daughter, Grace, from polio, "My trouble made his real." This realization motivates the first scene with the two brothers in which Baldwin begins to build the bridge between them. Separately they watch three sisters and a brother hold a revival meeting on the sidewalk opposite the narrator's apartment, and after they hear the gospel music, the silence between Sonny and his brother begins to give way to shared sound. The scene leads directly to the two brothers going to the bar where Sonny plays and creates an opportunity for the narrator (and the reader) to enter Sonny's world and satisfy his anguished need to share his music with someone who will listen to it and understand.

Questions for Discussion

1. Analyze the following speech, in which Sonny explains to his brother how he has survived (however tenuously) the experience of racism in America:

   "It's terrible sometimes, inside," he said, "that's what's the trouble. You walk these streets, black and funky and cold, and there's not really a living ass to talk to, and there's nothing shaking, and there's no way of getting it out — that storm inside. You can't talk it and you can't make love with it, and when you finally try to get with it and play it, you realize *nobody's* listening. So *you've* got to listen. You got to find a way to listen."

   How does this explanation make Sonny a sympathetic character?

2. Discuss Baldwin's comment on the blues Sonny plays with Creole and the two other musicians at the end of the story:

   Creole began to tell us what the blues were all about. They were not about anything very new. He and his boys up there were keeping it new, at the risk of ruin, destruction, madness, and death, in order to find new ways to make us listen. For, while the tale of how we suffer, and how we are delighted, and how we may triumph is never new, it always must be heard. There isn't any other tale to tell, it's the only light we've got in all this darkness.

Baldwin's subject is the music, of course, but he is also talking about other forms of creation. What might they be?

Topics for Writing

1. Chinua Achebe describes Baldwin as having brought "a new sharpness of vision, a new energy of passion, a new perfection of language to battle the incubus of race" in his eulogy titled "Postscript: James Baldwin (1924–1987)" (*Hopes and Impediments*, 1990). How does "Sonny's Blues" embody these qualities?

2. **CONNECTIONS** Baldwin's commentary "Autobiographical Notes" (p. 732) states that he found it difficult to be a writer because he was forced to become a spokesman for his race: "I have not written about being a Negro at such length because I expect that to be my only subject, but only because it was the gate I had to unlock before I could hope to write about anything else." Yet Baldwin's depiction of the life lived by African Americans is unique and very different from Richard Wright's or Ralph Ellison's, Toni Cade Bambara's or Alice Walker's accounts. Compare and contrast "Sonny's Blues" with a story by one or more of these writers to describe how each finds his or her own way to dramatize what Baldwin calls "the ambiguity and irony of Negro life." Could "Sonny's Blues" be set in an Italian American or Jewish American family?

Related Commentary

James Baldwin, Autobiographical Notes, p. 732.

Suggested Readings

Bloom, Harold, ed. *James Baldwin.* New York: Chelsea House, 1986.

Burt, Nancy, ed. *Critical Essays on James Baldwin.* Boston: G. K. Hall, 1986.

Campbell, James. *Talking at the Gates: A Life of James Baldwin.* New York: Viking, 1991.

Chametzky, Jules, ed. *A Tribute to James Baldwin: Black Writers Redefine the Struggle.* Amherst: U of Massachusetts P, 1989.

Kinnamon, Kenneth, ed. *James Baldwin.* Englewood Cliffs, NJ: Prentice, 1974.

Macebuh, Stanley. *James Baldwin: A Critical Study.* New York: Third, 1973.

Pratt, Louis H. *James Baldwin.* Twayne's United States Authors Series 290. Boston: Twayne, 1978.

Standley, F. L., ed. *Conversations with James Baldwin.* Jackson: U of Mississippi P, 1989.

Toni Cade Bambara

The Lesson (p. 89)

Relationships are an organizational key to this story. "The Lesson" is narrated by Sylvia, one of a group of eight African American children living in an uptown slum in New York City who are "treated" by their neighborhood guide Miss Moore to an educational visit to the F.A.O. Schwarz toy store at Fifth Avenue and Fifty-seventh Street. The group consists of four girls (Sylvia and her best friend, Sugar, and the relatively affluent Mercedes and her friend Rosie Giraffe) and four boys (Big Butt [Ronald], Junebug, Little Q.T., and Flyboy).

The "lesson" of the story is learned first by Sugar and then by Sylvia. All along Sylvia has assumed Sugar to be her ally, sharing her hostility to all adults as authority figures and to the idea of education. There's a suggestion of foreshadowing when the girls pay the taxicab driver outside F.A.O. Schwarz and Sugar steps in when Sylvia can't figure out the 10 percent tip on the 85-cent fare — "Give him a dime." (This is a taxi fare from twenty-five years ago, when the story was written.) But Sugar plays dumb as usual in her next appearance in the story, when she asks Miss Moore outside the toy store, "Can we steal?"

After the children learn about the high prices of the luxury toys at F.A.O. Schwarz, they return to their homes uptown. Sugar's remark to Miss Moore before they disperse reveals that the afternoon's lesson in economics hasn't been wasted: "this is not much of a democracy if you ask me. Equal chance to pursue happiness means an equal crack at the dough, don't it?" Bambara doesn't tell us whether Sugar intends to begin studying hard in school or to begin dealing drugs (this is the early 1970s), but the blinders formed by her life in the inner-city ghetto have fallen away, and she's clearly dissatisfied with her customary smart-aleck role. In her first response Sylvia is dumbfounded by her friend's betrayal, but within a few minutes she awakens to a sense of rivalry: "But ain't nobody gonna beat me at nuthin." Again Bambara leaves the lesson unspecified, and the reader must imagine *how* Sylvia intends to win the new game she's playing.

Questions for Discussion

1. What is the effect of the inner-city language in the story?
2. Is Sylvia a reliable or an unreliable narrator?
3. How does Bambara evoke a sense of sympathy for the people enduring the poverty and filth in Sylvia's neighborhood through her descriptions of the relationship of the winos and the newly arrived families from the South?
4. Describe the eight children and their relationships within the neighborhood group. How dependent is Sylvia on her friend Sugar?
5. Who is Miss Moore? Why does she personify the hostile force of "education" to the ghetto children?
6. Why does Sylvia keep the four dollars' change from the taxi fare? What does she do with the money? Is this a convincing ending to the story?

Topics for Writing

1. Write a story using a special dialect that you have learned from your family or friends.

2.   **CONNECTIONS**   Compare and contrast the authors' uses of African American speech in this story and in Richard Wright's "The Man Who Was Almost a Man." Analyze the different ways the two writers keep the dialect from distracting readers and causing them to lose interest in the stories.

Suggested Readings

Bambara, Toni Cade. *The Sea Birds Are Still Alive: Stories*. New York: Vintage, 1982.

Bell, Roseann P., Bettye J. Parker, and Beverly Guy-Sheftall, eds. *Sturdy Black Bridges: Visions of Black Women in Literature*. New York: Anchor, 1979.

Butler-Evans, Elliot. *Race, Gender, and Desire: Narrative Strategies in the Fiction of Toni Cade Bambara, Toni Morrison, and Alice Walker*. Philadelphia: Temple UP, 1989.

Cartwright, Jerome. "Bambara's 'The Lesson.'" *Explicator* 47.3 (Spring 1989): 61–63.

Evans, Mari, ed. *Black Women Writers (1950–1980): A Critical Evaluation*. New York: Anchor, 1984. 41–71.

Giddings, P. "Call to Wholeness from a Gifted Storyteller." *Encore* 9 (1980): 48–49.

Lyles, Lois F. "Time, Motion, Sound and Fury in *The Sea Birds Are Still Alive*." *College Language Association Journal* December 36.2 (1992): 134–44.

Morrison, Toni. "City Limits, Village Values: Concepts of the Neighborhood in Black Fiction." In *Literature and the Urban Experience: Essays on the City and Literature*. Ed. Ann Chalmers Watts and Michael C. Jaye. New Brunswick: Rutgers UP, 1981.

Tate, Claudia, ed. *Black Women Writers at Work*. New York: Continuum, 1983. 12–38.

Vertreace, Martha M. "A Bibliography of Writings about Toni Cade Bambara." In *American Women Writing Fiction: Memory, Identity, Family, Space*. Ed. Mickey Pearlman. Lexington: U of Kentucky P, 1989.

———. "Toni Cade Bambara: The Dance of Character and Community." In *American Women Writing Fiction: Memory, Identity, Family, Space*. Ed. Mickey Pearlman. Lexington: U of Kentucky P, 1989.

JORGE LUIS BORGES

Everything and Nothing (p. 96)

Borges's description of William Shakespeare's life is a sketch rather than a short story. None of the elements of fiction is developed in the Argentinian author's three brief paragraphs, with the exception of his theme. Long after we finish the sketch, it remains with us as a highly provocative and original explanation of the essential quality of Shakespeare's genius.

Borges organizes his sketch chronologically, dividing Shakespeare's life according to the standard biographical convention into his youth, maturity, and old age. As we begin to read, the title and opening sentences veil the identity of Borges's subject. Shakespeare could be everyman until Borges mentions that "he learned the small Latin and less Greek" he was taught as a youth; then the alert reader, who recognizes Ben Jonson's description of the playwright, becomes aware that the subject of "Everything and Nothing" is Shakespeare.

Playing with the elusive nature of identity, Borges continues to develop his central idea. This young man without a center cannot fall in love, so "he let himself be initiated by Anne Hathaway one long June afternoon." He is not passive — he actively seeks his fate by moving to London, where he "hit upon the profession to which he was predestined," acting. He is honest in his writing, revealing the split between his body and his soul, and this transparently honest self-expression Borges takes to be the key to his genius: "His passages on the fundamental identity of existing, dreaming, and acting are famous."

Students reading this sketch can disagree with Borges's reading of Shakespeare's genius, but they might be interested to learn that Borges's theory is perhaps our most reasonable explanation of the English playwright's final years of retirement in Stratford. How else to explain the great author's "arid" final will and testament, written without a "trace of emotion and of literature"? Borges concludes his sketch by revealing the name of his subject so there will be no doubt in the reader's mind of his identity. Then, finally, he confounds us by imagining a conversation between Shakespeare and God, in which God has the last word. Who else, in Borges's labyrinthian universe, could have it?

Questions for Discussion

1. Explain Borges's choice of his title for the sketch. Why is it appropriate?
2. Summarize the events of Shakespeare's life to which Borges refers in "Everything and Nothing."
3. Why does Borges call Shakespeare's creation of plays "that controlled hallucination"?
4. Paraphrase God's final words to Shakespeare.

Topics for Writing

1. **CONNECTIONS** Compare and contrast the explanations of Shakespeare's genius in Borges's sketch and in John Keats's letter to his brothers George and Thomas Keats on 21 December 1817.
2. Write a short story dramatizing the first two sentences of Borges's sketch, imagining the conversation between the young Shakespeare and his Stratford friend.

Related Play

William Shakespeare, *Hamlet, Prince of Denmark*, p. 1474.

Related Commentary

John Keats, From a Letter to George and Thomas Keats, 21 December 1817, p. 2048.

Suggested Readings

Agheana, Ion Tudro. *The Meaning of Experience in the Prose of Jorge Luis Borges*. New York: P. Lang, 1988.
Alazraki, Jaime, ed. *Critical Essays on Jorge Luis Borges*. Boston: G. K. Hall, 1987.
Borges, Jorge Luis. *The Book of Fantasy*. New York: Carroll and Graf, 1990.
———. *The Book of Sand*. New York: NAL–Dutton, 1979.
———. *Dreamtigers*. Austin: U of Texas P, 1984.
———. *A Personal Anthology*. New York: Grove Weidenfeld, 1961.
Christ, Ronald J. *The Narrow Act: Borges's Art of Allusion*. New York: New York UP, 1969.

Lindstrom, Naomi. *Jorge Luis Borges: A Study of the Short Fiction.* Boston: Twayne, 1990.

McMurray, George R. *Jorge Luis Borges.* Modern Literature Monographs. New York: Ungar, 1980.

Stabb, Martin S. *Borges Revisited.* Boston: Twayne, 1991.

Raymond Carver

Cathedral (p. 98)

"Cathedral" is a story about alienation, isolation, and the cure for both. The narrator is an insecure, jealous man, more dead than alive — a man who has constructed a virtual prison in which he exists emotionally detached from his wife and cut off from any active participation in what makes life worth living. He anesthetizes his pain with drink and marijuana while making comments that reveal his feelings of inferiority, confusion, and resentment.

When the story opens, the narrator's tone is anecdotal and familiar ("this blind man, an old friend of my wife's, he was on his way to spend the night . . . I wasn't enthusiastic about his visit"); at the conclusion, however, his tone has become one of awe ("'it's really something,' I said"). We are aware that he has undergone an important transformation, an almost mystical experience that comes to him at an unexpected moment from an unexpected source and literally frees him from the prison his life had become. Despite his jealousy of blind Robert, and his professed resistance to the other's intrusion, the narrator unwittingly makes a friend of the blind man and in the process comes to understand something about himself. As he begins, ironically, to see through Robert's eyes, to experience the world through Robert's perceptions, his own horizons are expanded ("my eyes were still closed. I was in my house. I knew that. But I didn't feel like I was inside anything"). Robert contradicts every stereotypical idea the narrator holds about the blind, and with his commanding presence, his vitality, his sensitivity, and his engagement with life, he forces the narrator to see.

Contrasts abound between Robert and the narrator and between their respective relationships with the narrator's wife. The blind man is infinitely more alive than the narrator ("I don't have any blind friends," the narrator tells his wife; "you don't have *any* friends," she replies. "The blind man was also a ham radio operator. He talked in his loud voice about conversations he'd had with fellow operators in Guam, in the Philippines, in Alaska, and even in Tahiti. He said he'd have a lot of friends there if he ever wanted to go visit those places"). Robert and the narrator's wife (whom the narrator never calls by name but refers to, significantly, as "my wife") have a special and long-lasting friendship that involves a level of intimacy conspicuously absent from the narrator's marital relationship, the cause of much jealousy and resentment. An underlying tension is constantly present in the conversations between the couple, but with Robert the woman is a different person: "I saw my wife laughing as she parked the car. I saw her get out of the car and shut the door. She was still wearing a smile. Just amazing." We infer from this observation that she does not laugh much with her husband. His wife and Robert approach the house, "talking all the way." Earlier the narrator had commented, "right then my wife filled me in with more detail than I cared to know." Talking and the emotional sharing that results have played a vital role in the enduring relationship between the woman and the blind man; they are obviously not an integral part of the marital relationship.

"I want you to feel comfortable in this house," the wife says to her friend. "I am comfortable," Robert replies. Oddly, it is the narrator who is uncomfortable, and this discomfort prompts his pathetic attempts to feel superior to the blind man. Offering him marijuana, the narrator observes, "I could tell he didn't know the first thing." But soon he grudgingly acknowledges, "it was like he'd been doing it since he was nine years old," and the dynamics of the relationship slowly begin to change. After his wife falls asleep, the narrator offers to take Robert up to bed, but Robert declines. The narrator politely responds with "I'm glad for the company," then realizes, "and I guess I was." They watch television together, Robert telling his host, "whatever you want to watch is okay. I'm always learning something. Learning never ends. It won't hurt me to learn something tonight," but it is the narrator, not the blind man, who will learn something important tonight. The image of the two men's hands tracing the cathedral together is dramatic, striking, and poignant. Robert asks him if he is religious, and the narrator realizes that he truly does not know how to talk to Robert, but the difference now is that he begins to care that he doesn't ("I guess I don't believe in it. In anything. Sometimes it's hard. You know what I'm saying?" "Sure, I do," Robert answers. "Right," the narrator replies).

As the two men's hands trace the cathedral, we are reminded of the time when Robert touched the woman's face. Perhaps the connection that has been forged between the men will influence the marriage as well. The narrator's awkward and inadequate attempts at conversation with Robert are a form of engagement, and his hand speeding across the page drawing windows and arches and buttresses is truly a liberating experience. Inspired by the man who cannot see, he has literally drawn himself out of the prison to which his own limited perceptions had restricted him.

Questions for Discussion

1. Is the narrator a sympathetic protagonist? Does our opinion of him change as the story progresses?

2. What does the narrator learn from his encounter with Robert? Do you believe that there will be a significant change in his outlook from this point on?

3. What is the significance of Carver's choice of a cathedral as catalyst for the narrator's learning experience? What added dimension does this symbol bring to our understanding of the story? Can you tie it to any previous detail?

4. Contrast the author's tone and the narrator's mood at the opening of the story with the tone and mood at the end. How does the change in style reflect the change that has occurred in the narrator?

5. What is the narrator's attitude toward his wife? What kind of marriage do they have, and what evidence do you find to support your conclusion? Is the narrator's jealousy of Robert irrational?

6. What are the primary emotions displayed by the narrator throughout, and how can we understand them in terms of the life he leads? What are some adjectives you would use to characterize him? What role does alcohol play in his life?

7. What is it about Robert that unsettles the narrator? How do his appearance and bearing resist every stereotypical image the narrator has about blind people, and why is this so upsetting?

Topics for Writing

1. For Carver, salvation lies in human contact and connection. Comment critically.
2. Create a conversation between the narrator and his wife after Robert's departure.
3. Discuss "Cathedral" as a story about "the blind leading the blind."

Related Commentaries

Raymond Carver, The Ashtray, p. 821.
Raymond Carver, Creative Writing 101, p. 818.
Raymond Carver, On Writing, p. 815.
Tom Jenks, The Origin of "Cathedral," p. 829.

Suggested Readings

See page 22 of this manual.

RAYMOND CARVER

Errand (p. 109)

Raymond Carver's story may be instructively compared with the excerpt from Henri Troyat's biography of Anton Chekhov describing Chekhov's death (included with other commentary in the Carver Casebook in this anthology). In addition to providing a considerable amount of factual background about Chekhov and the last years of his century, this comparison may shed light on a question that could conceivably be asked by students in the course: What is the difference between a short story and an essay?

In comparing the fiction and nonfiction descriptions of Chekhov's last days, students will notice that Carver has based a good deal of his story on Troyat's biography of Chekhov, which Carver read and enjoyed. A knowledgeable and highly skilled literary biographer, Troyat wrote prose that (even in translation) moves briskly along almost like a short story, since Troyat eliminates editorial digressions and commentary in his desire to dramatize his account of Chekhov's last illness.

Carver has absorbed Troyat's style in addition to information about the people and places involved in Chekhov's death. The pace of the narrative is calm and unhurried, the tone unassuming and authoritative. To make "Errand" complete unto itself as a short narrative, Carver includes information about Chekhov's life — the hemorrhage he suffered while dining with Suvorin, his marriage to the actress Olga Knipper — found in earlier pages in Troyat's biography. These details provide the reader with the background necessary to appreciate the context of the story.

Perhaps most significant, Carver, unlike Troyat, invents details in telling the story of Chekhov's death. "Errand" contains the fictional character of the blond young man who works at the hotel. He brings up the bottle of champagne that Doctor Schwöhrer has ordered for Chekhov in the middle of the night. Later in the morning, the young man reappears at the door of the suite with a vase containing three yellow roses to announce to Olga Knipper that breakfast will be served that day in the garden of the hotel because of the heat wave.

Carver ingeniously introduces this fictional character by having Doctor Schwöhrer summon him from the hotel kitchen by using the telephone in Chekhov's room. This would have been a newfangled gadget in 1904, and the doctor's meticulous way of following the "instructions for using the device" makes his action believable to the reader, thus preparing the way for a fictional rather than a historical character to enter the story. Carver then tells us everything we need to know to accept the "lie": First we visualize the appearance of the young man, who was awakened from sleep and who dressed so hastily that his jacket is carelessly buttoned. Then we see what he sees when he brings his tray into Chekhov's hotel suite, and hear what he hears — the "dreadful, harrowing sound" of the dying writer's "ratchety breathing."

With the young man's reappearance in the concluding paragraphs of the story, Carver's imagination sets to work dramatizing the way that Chekhov's widow entrusts the waiter with the precious errand of notifying the mortician of Chekhov's death. Olga Knipper was an actress, and her way of explaining the errand is an actress's visualization technique: "If it would help keep his movements purposeful he should imagine himself as someone moving down the busy sidewalk carrying in his arms a porcelain vase of roses that he had to deliver to an important man." Chekhov, of course, is the precious "porcelain vase of roses," but to keep the story from veering off into sentimentality, Carver must keep imagining. He succeeds by balancing the widow's beautiful image of the precious vase with the prosaic fact of the champagne cork in the last paragraph of the narrative. The young servant, totally alive and believable as he functions in the story, has been superbly trained in this elegant Swiss hotel to do his duty. "He leaned over. Without looking down, he reached out and closed it into his hand."

Questions for Discussion

1. Why does Carver begin "Errand" with an account of Chekhov's meeting with Alexei Suvorin in 1897, four years before the writer's death?
2. Why does Carver allow Leo Tolstoy to appear in this story?
3. What have you learned about the difference between Tolstoy and Chekhov from this fictionalized encounter? (Refer to Tolstoy's commentary on Chekhov's "The Darling" in this anthology.)
4. What do Chekhov's efforts to minimize the seriousness of his tuberculosis tell you about him?
5. How effective was the medical treatment of tuberculosis at the turn of the century, judging from Doctor Schwöhrer's prescription for Chekhov's diet?
6. Why does Doctor Schwöhrer try to muffle "the festive explosion" when he uncorks the champagne? Why does he push the cork back into the bottle after he pours three glasses of the wine? Why does the champagne cork reappear in the story?

Topics for Writing

1. Write a short story based on an incident you have read in a biography of a famous person.
2. **CONNECTIONS** Write an essay comparing and contrasting Carver's treatment of death and dying with Tolstoy's in "The Death of Ivan Ilych."

(text pp. 117–126)

Related Commentaries

Raymond Carver, The Ashtray, p. 821.
Raymond Carver, Creative Writing 101, p. 818.
Raymond Carver, On "Errand," p. 823.
Raymond Carver, On Writing, p. 815.
Henri Troyat, Chekhov's Last Days, p. 826.

Suggested Readings

See page 22 of this manual.

RAYMOND CARVER

What We Talk About When We Talk About Love (p. 117)

The scarcely veiled animosity between Dr. Mel McGinnis and his wife, Terri, gives tension to this story of three married couples. Through Mel's thoughts and experiences, Carver is investigating the nature of married love. Like the naive boy in Sherwood Anderson's classic short story "I Want to Know Why," Mel insists on asking an impossible question: What is the nature of love? What is the meaning of sharing?

The three pairs of lovers represent different stages of marriage. At one end of a spectrum are Laura and Nick (the narrator), married only a year and a half, still infatuated, glowing with the power of their attraction for each other.

At the other end of the spectrum are the old married pair in the hospital whom Mel and the other doctors have patched up after a catastrophic highway accident. Glad to learn his wife has survived, the old man — as Mel tells the story — is depressed, not because of their physical suffering but because he can't see his wife through the eye holes in his bandages. As Mel says, "Can you imagine? I'm telling you, the man's heart was breaking because he couldn't turn his goddamn head and *see* his goddamn wife."

Between the two extremes of perfect love, Mel and Terri are veterans (four years married to each other), who are past the bliss of their first attraction and not yet two halves of a whole because they've survived the long haul together. Each has been married before, and each is obsessed with the earlier partner. First Terri talks too much about her sadistic ex-husband, Ed; then Mel reveals that he hates his first wife because she kept their kids. Terri says, "She's bankrupting us." The talk appears to ramble, but Carver keeps it under control by sticking to his subject — specific examples of the different varieties of love — and organizing the four friends' conversation by chronicling the stages of their drunkenness as they go through two bottles of gin in the afternoon.

The passing of time is brilliantly described, paralleling the waxing and waning stages of love. When the story opens, sunlight fills the New Mexico kitchen where the four friends with their gin and tonics are talking around the table. Midway, when the narrator is beginning to feel the drinks, he describes the sun like the warmth and lift of the gin in his body. "The afternoon sun was like a presence in this room, the spacious light of ease and generosity." As the conversation wears on and Mel tells Terri to shut up after she's interrupted one too many times, the light shifts again, the sunshine getting thinner. The narrator is a shade drunker, and his gaze fixes on the pattern of leaves on the windowpanes and on the Formica kitchen counter, as if he's staying alert by focusing deliberately on the edges of the objects around him: "They weren't the same patterns, of course." Finally, mysteriously, the light drains out of the room, "going back through the window where it had come from." The alcoholic elation has evaporated. At the end of the story, the couples sit in darkness on their kitchen chairs, not moving. The only sound the narrator hears is everyone's heart beating, separately.

The person we know least about is the narrator, Nick. Perhaps Carver deliberately echoes the name of Nick Adams, Hemingway's autobiographical narrator in his stories of initiation; or Nick Carraway, the narrator of Fitzgerald's *The Great Gatsby*. The role of Carver's Nick in the story is also like that of Marlow in Conrad's "Heart of Darkness," as Nick voyages through the conversation of Mel and Terri into the deep, uncharted waters of the heart. But this Nick is also a participant, through the gin and the sunlight, in the feelings of his troubled, overworked doctor friend.

Questions for Discussion

1. As the story opens, what is the setting in time, place, and situation?
2. How would you describe Terri? What type of person is Mel?
3. What was Terri's experience with her first husband, Ed? In what way was Mel involved in this experience? How does Terri's view of Ed contrast with Mel's view of him? What does this contrast reveal about the character of Mel and Terri's relationship?
4. In the discussion about Ed, what do we discover about the couple with whom Mel and Terri are socializing? What is their relationship both to each other and to Mel and Terri? Compare and contrast their marriage with Terri and Mel's.
5. What is the point of view in this story? Who is the narrator? How reliable is he?
6. Does Mel view his first wife in the same way he does Terri? What are we told about his first wife?
7. What are some of the questions about love that Carver raises through his characters? Does he offer any answers to these questions?
8. A third couple is introduced in the story. What astonishes Mel about their relationship?
9. What changes in the setting, if any, can you identify over the course of the story? In what way does the setting mirror Carver's message about the stages of love?
10. What does each of the couples represent? What is the significance of the last paragraph?

Topics for Writing

1. Write an essay discussing theme and characterization in "What We Talk About When We Talk About Love."
2. Explore the question posed by the title of this story: What does Carver (and the reader) talk about when he (and we) talks about love?
3. Think about married couples you know and discuss what their views on love might be as well as the quality of their relationships.
4. **CONNECTIONS** Compare and contrast the types of love in Carver's story and in Joyce's "The Dead."

Related Commentaries

Raymond Carver, The Ashtray, p. 821.
Raymond Carver, Creative Writing 101, p. 818.
Raymond Carver, On Writing, p. 815.
Arthur M. Saltzman, A Reading of "What We Talk About When We Talk About Love," p. 1539.

Suggested Readings

Adelman, Bob. *Carver Country — The World of Raymond Carver.* New York: Scribners, 1991. A photographic essay with quotations from Carver's writing.
Carver, Raymond. "The Art of Fiction LXXVI." Interview. *Paris Review.* 88 (Summer 1983).
————. *Fires: Essays, Poems, Stories.* Santa Barbara, CA: Capra, 1983.
————. *Where I'm Calling From: New and Selected Stories.* New York: Atlantic Monthly, 1988.
Gentry, Marshall B., and William A. Stull, eds. *Conversations with Raymond Carver.* Jackson: UP of Mississippi, 1990.
Halpert, Sam, ed. *When We Talk About Raymond Carver.* Layton, UT: Gibbs Smith, 1991.
Simpson, M. "Art of Fiction: Raymond Carver." *Paris Review* 25 (1983): 193–221.
Stull, W. L. "Beyond Hopelessville: Another Side of Raymond Carver." *Philological Quarterly* 64 (1985): 1–15.
Troyat, Henri. *Chekhov.* Trans. Michael Henry Heim. New York: Dutton, 1986.

JOHN CHEEVER

The Swimmer (p. 127)

One way to reconstruct a naturalistic time scheme for the story so that Neddy's "misfortunes," the awareness of which he seems to have repressed, can be dated with regard to the other events in the narrative, is to imagine a gap in time that is covered by the line "He stayed in the Levys' gazebo until the storm had passed." The authoritative point of view in the opening paragraphs seems to preclude placing the misfortunes before Neddy begins his swim, while the gathering clouds and circling de Haviland trainer assert the continuity of the first phase of his journey. After the storm, however, signs of change appear, and it is possible to reconcile Neddy's subsequent encounters with the proposition that he is continuing his swim on another day or days under quite different circumstances. Before the storm, he visits the Grahams and the Bunkers, who greet him as the prosperous and popular Neddy Merrill described at the beginning of the story, but after the storm Neddy visits only the empty houses of the Lindleys and the Welchers; the public pool where any derelict may swim; the peculiar Hallorans, who mention his troubles; the Sachses, who have problems of their own and refuse him a drink; the socially inferior Biswangers, who snub him; and his old mistress Shirley, who implies that this call is not the first he has paid in this condition.

But Cheever is not interested in a realistic time scheme. If he were, he would not have burned the 250-page novel version of the story (mentioned in the headnote) that presumably filled in the blanks. Instead, he has constructed the story so Neddy's recognition of his loss strikes the reader with the same impact it has on Neddy. By telescoping time, Cheever thrusts us forward into a state of affairs that exists only as a dim cloud on the horizon on the day the story begins and at first seems to be entirely taking place.

What accounts for the reversal in Neddy's life? Surely it is possible to tax Neddy for irresponsibility and childishness in turning his back on his friends and family and so casually setting off on an odyssey from which he returns far too late. Neddy's own view of his adventure is considerably more attractive. The only member of his society who seems free from a hangover on this midsummer Sunday, Neddy simply wishes to savor the pleasures of his fortunate life: "The day was beautiful and it seemed to him that a long swim might enlarge and celebrate its beauty." Although he has been (or will be) unfaithful to his wife with Shirley Adams, and although he kisses close to a dozen other women on his journey, Neddy does not construe his departure as infidelity to Lucinda. Rather, to swim the string of pools across the suburban county is to travel along "the Lucinda River." As "a pilgrim, an explorer, a man with a destiny," Neddy plunges into this river of life aware of the gathering storm on the horizon but regarding it with pleasurable anticipation. When it finally breaks over the Levys' gazebo, he savors the exciting release of tension that accompanies the arrival of a thunder shower, but with the explosion of thunder and the smell of gunpowder that ensues, Neddy finds his happy illusions, his world of "youth, sport, and clement weather," lashed by a more unpleasant reality, just as the "rain lashed the Japanese lanterns that Mrs. Levy had bought in Kyoto the year before last, or was it the year before that?"

What Neddy now confronts, though he tries gamely to ignore it, are the twin recognitions that his youth is not eternal and that the pleasant society of the "bonny and lush . . . banks of the Lucinda River" is unstable, exclusive, and cruel. Grass grows in the Lindleys' riding ring, the Welchers have moved away, and the sky is now overcast. Crossing Route 424 in his swimming suit, Neddy is subjected to the ridicule of the public, and at the Recreation Center he finds that swimming does not convey the same sense of elegance, pleasure, and freedom that it does in the pools of his affluent friends. The validity of the society Neddy has previously enjoyed is called further into question by the very existence of the self-contradictory Hallorans, whose personal eccentricity is matched by their political hypocrisy. Neddy's visits to the Biswangers and to Shirley Adams complete the destruction of his illusions, but it is Eric Sachs, disfigured by surgery and (with the loss of his navel) symbolically cut off from the human community, who embodies the most troubling reflection of Neddy's condition. "I'm not alone," Shirley proclaims, but Neddy is, and as this man who "might have been compared to a summer's day" recognizes that his summer is over, it is not surprising that for "the first time in his adult life" he begins to cry. While the reader may relish Cheever's indictment of a society whose values have so betrayed Neddy, it is hard not to feel some admiration for a man who, by executing his plan to swim the county through the now icy autumn waters, has indeed become a legendary figure, an epic hero of a sort.

WILLIAM E. SHEIDLEY

Questions for Discussion

1. Who is referred to by the word "everyone" in the opening sentence? Who is not?
2. How does Neddy Merrill relate to the world in which he moves? Why does he decide to swim home?

3. Why does Neddy name his route "the Lucinda River"? The Levys live on "Alewives Lane." Alewives are a kind of fish that swim upriver to spawn. Is there a sexual component to Neddy's journey?

4. Is the storm that breaks a surprise? How does Neddy feel about the beginning of the rain?

5. What differences can be noticed between what Neddy experiences before and after the storm? How might they be explained?

6. What new elements enter the story when Neddy crosses Route 424? Why do the drivers jeer at him?

7. Before he dives into the unappealing public swimming pool, Neddy tells himself "that this was merely a stagnant bend in the Lucinda River." How characteristic is this effort to assuage his own doubts and discontents?

8. Based on what the Hallorans, the Sachses, the Biswangers, and Shirley Adams say to Neddy, what is the truth about himself and his life of which he is unaware?

9. Cheever has his hero discover the season by observing the stars. What effect does that choice among various possibilities have on our attitude toward Neddy?

10. It is not difficult to say what Neddy has lost. What has he gained?

Topics for Writing

1. Explain why Neddy Merrill talks only with women.
2. Analyze the characters Rusty Towers, Eric Sachs, and Neddy Merrill.
3. Write an essay discussing Neddy Merrill's voyage of exploration and discovery.
4. Evaluate Cheever's attitude toward the swimmer.

Related Commentary

John Cheever, Why I Write Short Stories, p. 736.

Suggested Readings

Cheever, John. *The Journals of John Cheever.* New York: Knopf, 1991.
Cheever, Susan. *Home before Dark.* Boston: Houghton, 1984.
Coale, Samuel. *John Cheever.* New York: Ungar, 1977. 43–47.
Collins, R. G., ed. *Critical Essays on John Cheever.* Boston: G. K. Hall, 1982.
O'Hara, James E. *John Cheever: A Study of the Short Fiction.* Boston: Twayne, 1989.
Waldeland, Lynne. *John Cheever.* Boston: Twayne, 1979.
Writers at Work. Fifth Series. New York: Penguin, 1981. Interview with John Cheever by Annette Grant. Fall 1976.

ANTON CHEKHOV

The Darling (p. 136)

One of the liveliest discussions about a short story in this anthology could be started by a class debate based on the contradictory interpretations of "The Darling" by Leo Tolstoy and Eudora Welty included in Chapter 7 (pp. 801 and 811). Tolstoy was convinced that Chekhov was misguided in satirizing women's tendency to depend on men for meaning and direction in their lives. In Tolstoy's view, Chekhov had allowed himself to become a women's rights advocate under the pernicious influence of his "liberated" wife, the actress Olga Knipper. Welty, in contrast, reveals the subtle emotional tyranny of the protagonist, Olenka. In Welty's interpretation, the schoolboy shows us at the end of the story that men want their "space" too. Students could be assigned Tolstoy's or Welty's interpretation and asked to support or refute it. Certainly neither interpretation is unassailable.

Other critical perspectives can also be applied to this provocative story. A feminist reader could argue that Olenka has been handicapped by her environment: Uneducated for a profession, she can have no ideas or life of her own. A psychological interpretation could concentrate on the darling's early, possibly traumatic fixation on her father and his long mortal illness just as she reaches manageable age. A formalist approach might look closely at the words the schoolboy uses as he cries out in his sleep: "I'll give it you! Get away! Shut up!" Welty assumes that the boy is dreaming of Olenka. He could just as well be dreaming of his teacher at school, other students fighting with him in the schoolyard, or his own mother, who appears to have abandoned him. He could even be repeating the cruel words his mother might have said to drive him away from her before she left him with Olenka.

The English short story writer H. E. Bates interpreted the story yet another way. Comparing Chekhov's technique with Maupassant's, Bates writes, "Both like to portray a certain type of weak, stupid, thoughtless woman, a sort of yes-woman who can unwittingly impose tragedy or happiness on others. Maupassant had no patience with the type; but in Olenka, in 'The Darling,' it is precisely a quality of tender patience, the judgment of the heart and not the head, that gives Chekhov's story its effect of uncommon understanding and radiance."

Bates saw Chekhov as subtle: His

> receptivity, his capacity for compassion, are both enormous. Of his characters he seems to say, "I know what they are doing is their own responsibility. But how did they come to this, how did it happen? There may be some trivial thing that will explain." That triviality, discovered, held for a moment in the light, is the key to Chekhov's emotional solution. In Maupassant's case the importance of that key would have been inexorably driven home; but as we turn to ask of Chekhov if we have caught his meaning aright, it is to discover that we must answer that question for ourselves — for Chekhov has gone. . . . Both [Maupassant and Chekhov] knew to perfection when they had said enough; an acute instinct continually reminded them of the fatal tedium of explanation, of going on a second too long. In Chekhov this sense of impatience, almost a fear, caused him frequently to stop speaking, as it were, in mid-air. It was this which gave his stories an air of remaining unfinished, of leaving the reader to his own explanations, of imposing on each story's end a note of suspense so abrupt and yet refined that it produced on the reader an effect of delayed shock.

Questions for Discussion

1. How does Chekhov characterize Olenka at the beginning of the story?
2. Why does he have the "lady visitors" be the first ones to call her a "darling"?

3. Olenka "mothers" each of her husbands. Could she have been both a good wife and a good mother if she had had children of her own? Why or why not?

Topics for Writing

1. Interpret Sasha's words at the end of "The Darling." Identify the person to whom he is talking and find details in the story that justify your interpretation.
2. Continue "The Darling," supposing that the "loud knock at the gate" is a message from Sasha's mother, who wants him to join her in Harkov.

Related Play

Anton Chekhov, A Monologue, p. 1661.

Related Commentaries

Anton Chekhov, Technique in Writing the Short Story, p. 738.
Leo Tolstoy, Chekhov's Intent in "The Darling," p. 801.
Eudora Welty, Plot and Character in Chekhov's "The Darling," p. 811.

Suggested Readings

See page 28 of this manual.

ANTON CHEKHOV

The Lady with the Pet Dog (p. 145)

Anna Sergeyevna comes to Yalta because she wants "to live, to live!" Gurov begins his affair with her because he is bored and enjoys the freedom and ease of a casual liaison. At the outset both are undistinguished, almost clichés — a philandering bank employee escaping from a wife he cannot measure up to, a lady with a dog and a "flunkey" for a husband. By the end of the story, however, after having been captured and tormented by a love that refuses to be filed away in memory, the two gain dignity and stature by recognizing that life is neither exciting nor easy; and, by taking up the burden of the life they have discovered in their mutual compassion, they validate their love.

Chekhov develops the nature of this true love, so ennobling and so tragic, by testing it against a series of stereotypes that it transcends and by showing a series of stock expectations that it violates. Anna Sergeyevna reacts differently from any of the several types of women Gurov has previously made love to, and Gurov finds himself unable to handle his own feelings in the way he is accustomed to. Anna Sergeyevna proves neither a slice of watermelon nor a pleasant focus of nostalgia. Most important, as the conclusion implies, she will not remain the secret core of his life, bought at the price of falsehood and suspicion of others.

In observing the evolution of the lovers, the reader is led through a series of potential misconceptions. We may want to despise Gurov as a careless breaker of hearts, but it is clear that he has one of his own when he sees Anna Sergeyevna as a Magdalene. Later, when Gurov is tormented by his longings for Anna Sergeyevna, we are tempted to laugh the superior realist's laugh at a romantic fool: Surely when

Gurov arrives at S——, disillusionment will await him. And in a sense it does. Just as there was dust in the streets at Yalta, the best room in the hotel at S—— is coated with dust; reality is an ugly fence; and even the theater (where *The Geisha* is playing) is full of reminders of how unromantic life really is. But Anna Sergeyevna has not, as Gurov supposes at one point, taken another lover, nor has she been able to forget Gurov.

The antiromantic tone is but another oversimplification, and the story comes to rest, somewhat like Milton's *Paradise Lost,* at a moment of beginning. The lovers' disillusionment about the nature of the struggle they face creates in them a deep compassion for each other, which finds its echo in readers' final attitude toward them as fellow human beings whose lives are like our own and who deserve a full measure of our sympathy. Or perhaps they draw our pity; surely their fate, which Chekhov so skillfully depicts as probable and true, inspires tragic fear. Gurov and Anna Sergeyevna have met the god of love, and Chekhov awes us by making him seem real.

WILLIAM E. SHEIDLEY

Questions for Discussion

1. Why does Gurov call women "the inferior race"?
2. At the end of section I, Gurov thinks that there is "something pathetic" about Anna Sergeyevna. Is there? What is it?
3. Why is Anna Sergeyevna so distracted as she watches the steamer docking and its passengers debarking?
4. How does Anna Sergeyevna differ from other women Gurov has known, as they are described in the paragraph that ends "the lace on their lingerie seemed to him to resemble scales"? Compare this passage with the paragraph that begins "His hair was already beginning to turn gray."
5. In view of what follows, is it appropriate that Gurov should see Anna Sergeyevna as a Magdalene?
6. What is the function of the paragraph that begins "At Oreanda they sat on a bench not far from the church"?
7. What "complete change" does Gurov undergo during his affair with Anna Sergeyevna at Yalta? Is it permanent?
8. Explain Gurov's remark at the end of section II: "High time!"
9. Why is Gurov enraged at his companion's remark about the sturgeon?
10. Discuss the possible meanings of the objects Gurov encounters in S——: the broken figurine, the long gray fence, the cheap blanket, and so on.
11. Seeing Anna Sergeyevna enter the theater, Gurov "understood clearly that in the whole world there was no human being so near, so precious, and so important to him." What is Chekhov's tone in this statement?
12. Explain Anna Sergeyevna's reaction to Gurov's arrival. Why does she volunteer to come to Moscow?
13. Discuss the implications of Gurov's "two lives" as Chekhov explains them in section IV. Do you agree with the generalizations about the desire for privacy with which the paragraph ends? Relate these ideas to the story's ending.
14. What will life be like for Gurov and Anna Sergeyevna? Anna has previously said, "I have never been happy; I am unhappy now, and I never, never shall be happy, never!" Is she right?

Topics for Writing

1. Write an essay describing Chekhov's characterization of the wronged spouse in "The Lady with the Pet Dog."
2. Discuss the meaning of the three geographical locales in "The Lady with the Pet Dog."
3. On your first reading of the story, stop at the end of each section and write down your judgment of Gurov and Anna Sergeyevna and your prediction of what will happen next. When you have finished reading, compare what you wrote with what turned out to be the case and with your final estimate of the protagonists. To the extent that your initial impressions were borne out, what points in the text helped to guide you? To the extent that you were surprised, explain what led you astray. What might Chekhov have wanted to accomplish by making such misconceptions possible?

Related Commentaries

Anton Chekhov, Technique in Writing the Short Story, p. 738.
Vladimir Nabokov, A Reading of Chekhov's "The Lady with the Little Dog," p. 775.

Suggested Readings

Bates, H. E. *The Modern Short Story*. Boston: The Writer, 1972.
Eekman, Thomas, ed. *Critical Essays on Anton Chekhov*. Boston: G. K. Hall, 1989.
Friedland, Louis S., ed. *Anton Tchekhov's Letters on the Short Story, the Drama, and Other Topics*. Salem, NH: Ayer, 1965.
Kramer, Karl D. *The Chameleon and the Dream: The Image of Reality in Chekhov's Stories*. The Hague: Mouton, 1970. 171.
Matlaw, Ralph E., ed. *Anton Chekhov's Short Stories*. New York: Norton, 1979.
Meister, Charles W. *Chekhov Criticism, 1880 through 1986*. New York: St. Martin's, 1990.
Pritchett, V. S. *Chekhov: A Spirit Set Free*. New York: Random, 1988.
Rayfield, Donald. *Chekhov: The Evolution of His Art*. New York: Barnes, 1975. 197–200.
Smith, Virginia Llewellyn. "The Lady with the Dog." In *Anton Chekhov's Short Stories: Texts of the Stories, Backgrounds, Criticism*. Ed. Ralph E. Matlaw. New York: Norton, 1979. Excerpted from Smith, *Anton Chekhov and the Lady with the Dog* (New York: Oxford UP, 1973). 96–97, 212–18.
Troyat, Henri. *Chekhov*. Trans. Michael Henry Heim. New York: Dutton, 1986.

KATE CHOPIN

The Story of an Hour (p. 158)

Does the O. Henryesque trick ending of this story merely surprise us, or does Chopin arrange to have Louise Mallard expire at the sight of her unexpectedly still living husband in order to make a thematic point? Students inclined to groan when Brently Mallard returns "composedly carrying his gripsack and umbrella" may come to think better of the ending if you ask them to evaluate the doctors' conclusions about the cause of Mrs. Mallard's death. Although Richards and Josephine take "great care . . . to break to her as gently as possible the news of her husband's death," what actually kills Mrs. Mallard is the news that he is still alive. The experience of regeneration and freedom that she undergoes in the armchair looking out upon a springtime vista involves an almost sexual surrender of conventional repressions and restraints. As she *abandons herself* to the realization of her freedom that *approaches to possess her*, Mrs. Mallard enjoys a hitherto forbidden physical and spiritual excitement. The presumption that she would be devastated by the death of her husband, like the presumption that she needs to be protected by watchful, "tender" friends, reduces Mrs. Mallard to a dependency from which she is joyful at last to escape. Chopin best depicts this oppressive, debilitating concern in what Mrs. Mallard thinks she will weep again to see: "the kind, tender hands folded in death; the face that had never looked save with love upon her, fixed and gray and dead." Although had she lived Mrs. Mallard might have felt guilty for taking her selfhood like a lover and pridefully stepping forth "like a goddess of Victory," Chopin effectively suggests that the guilt belongs instead to the caretakers, the "travel-stained" Brently, the discomfited Josephine, and Richards, whose "quick motion" to conceal his error comes "too late."

WILLIAM E. SHEIDLEY

Questions for Discussion

1. In view of Mrs. Mallard's eventual reactions, evaluate the efforts of Josephine and Richards to break the news of her husband's death gently.
2. What purpose might Chopin have in stressing that Mrs. Mallard does not block out the realization that her husband has died?
3. What might be the cause or causes of the "physical exhaustion that haunted her body and seemed to reach into her soul" that Mrs. Mallard feels as she sinks into the armchair?
4. Describe your reaction to the view out the window the first time you read the story. Did it change on a second reading?
5. Mrs. Mallard's face bespeaks repression. What has she been repressing?
6. Discuss the imagery Chopin uses to describe Mrs. Mallard's recognition of her new freedom.
7. What kind of man is Brently Mallard, as Mrs. Mallard remembers him? In what ways does he resemble Josephine and Richards?
8. Describe your feelings about Mrs. Mallard as she emerges from her room. Is the saying "Pride goeth before a fall" relevant here?
9. In what way is the doctors' pronouncement on the cause of Mrs. Mallard's death ironic? In what sense is it nonetheless correct?

Topics for Writing

1. Discuss the imagery of life and the imagery of death in "The Story of an Hour."
2. Write a paper analyzing "The Story of an Hour" as a thwarted awakening.
3. Describe the tragic irony in "The Story of an Hour."
4. On a second reading of "The Story of an Hour," try to recall how you responded to each paragraph or significant passage when you read it the first time. Write short explanations of any significant changes in your reactions. To what extent are those changes the result of knowing the story's ending? What other factors are at work?
5. Can falsehood be the key to truth? Narrate a personal experience in which your own or someone else's reaction to misinformation revealed something meaningful and true.

6. How long is a turning point? Tell a story covering a brief span of time — a few minutes or an hour — in which the central character's life is permanently changed. Study Chopin's techniques for summarizing and condensing information.

Related Commentary

Kate Chopin, "How I Stumbled upon Maupassant," p. 740.

Suggested Readings

Bender, B. "Kate Chopin's Lyrical Short Stories." *Studies in Short Fiction* 11 (1974): 257–66.

Chopin, Kate. *The Complete Works of Kate Chopin.* Baton Rouge: Louisiana State UP, 1970.

Dimock, Wai-chee. "Kate Chopin." In *Modern American Women Writers.* Ed. Elaine Showalter et al. New York: Collier, 1993.

Fluck, Winifred. "Tentative Transgressions: Kate Chopin's Fiction as a Mode of Symbolic Action." *Studies in American Fiction* 10 (1982): 151–71.

Miner, Madonne M. "Veiled Hints: An Affected Stylist's Reading of Kate Chopin's 'Story of an Hour.' " *Markham Review* 11 (1982): 29–32.

Seyersted, Per. *Kate Chopin: A Critical Biography.* Baton Rouge: Louisiana State UP, 1969. 57–59.

Skaggs, Peggy. *Kate Chopin.* Boston: Twayne, 1985.

Toth, Emily. *Kate Chopin.* New York: Morrow, 1990.

SANDRA CISNEROS

The House on Mango Street (p. 161)
Hairs (p. 162)
My Name (p. 162)
The Monkey Garden (p. 163)
Mango Says Goodbye Sometimes (p. 165)

THE HOUSE ON MANGO STREET, HAIRS, AND MY NAME

Cisneros opens her collection *The House on Mango Street,* with these three stories, and they are so short that, read together as a unit, they can serve the student well as an introduction to the author's narrative approach. Cisneros credits Jorge Luis Borges's *Dreamtigers* as an important influence on her choice of form in *The House on Mango Street.* Like Borges in "Everything and Nothing" (p. 96), a short piece from *Dreamtigers,* Cisneros works within short narrative forms, writing sketches rather than stories. Where Borges develops an idea about Shakespeare as his theme, Cisneros dramatizes emotions in her sketches. These emotions belong to the young narrator as she tells about her experiences of economic hardship and social marginalization within a Mexican American family. The economic and social realities of her life are difficult, but the emotional security she finds within her tightly knit family appears to have given her the strength to survive the difficulties she faces and enables her to speak in the positive tone of her stories.

"The House on Mango Street" starts in a voice that suggests muted protest, foreshadowing our awareness of the narrator's developing strength of character. In the opening paragraph, the narrator names the various streets her family has lived on as they moved from apartment to apartment during her early childhood. Her memories center on the difficult living conditions in the different rental apartments — for example, broken water pipes and a hostile landlord "banging on the ceiling with a broom" if the six members of her family made too much noise. Her parents have told their four children that they would eventually own their own home, and this promise gives them hope. Cisneros's book begins when the family has achieved its dream of home ownership. Then the author takes the difference between the American dream and its economic and social reality as the subject of her book.

Students should be aware that Cisneros and her young narrator are not identical. Cisneros has chosen the persona of a young girl to tell her stories, and this choice of first-person point of view adds considerable poignancy to her narratives. Reading "The House on Mango Street," we are aware that the (imaginary) narrator's naiveté is part of the emotional effect of what she tells us. We become emotionally involved in the story through her shy pride at moving into her "own" house on Mango Street, and through her confusion after she realizes that the dream house her parents have promised her isn't at all what she dreamed it would be.

We understand how important the house is to the narrator when she tells us about the apartment on Loomis where the family lived before moving to Mango Street. There a nun from her school made her "feel like nothing" by tactlessly wondering how her young pupil could live in a building that had been so brazenly burglarized. Yet among the descriptive details of the way the Loomis building looked, the narrator discloses that her father had nailed wooden bars on the windows of the family's third-floor apartment so that she and her brother Carlos and sister Nenny and the baby Kiki wouldn't fall out. The significance of this detail doesn't weigh as heavily on the narrator as her memory of her shame before the nun, but we register the father's concern for his young children's safety. There is little character description in Cisneros's stories, but the essential details giving coherence to the narrative are there.

"Hairs" describes the narrator's perception of the different types of hair within her immediate family. Reading her description as metaphor, we can understand each character's personality traits. Once again the reader is shown the importance of the family's emotional support to the narrator's sense of well-being. Her father's "hair is like a broom" (that is, he is an industrious man, working hard to support his family). Her hair "is lazy" (that is, she is still an irresponsible child, with a mind of her own). The baby Kiki "has hair like fur" (the child narrator perceives the demanding little sister as more animal than human). The longest description is of the mother's hair, as the narrator's relationship with her mother is central to the girl's sense of emotional security. Her hair "is the warm smell of bread before you bake it," complete sustenance and acceptance, the staff of life itself.

"My Name" follows "Hairs" as the narrator places herself in the center of this third sketch. The reader learns that her name is "Esperanza," but only midway through the sketch. She is named after her great-grandmother, giving us a sense of the girl's pride in the continuity and longevity of her family. The name means "hope" in Spanish, and it has a faintly old-fashioned ring, reminiscent of the Puritans' tradition of naming their daughters "Hope," "Faith," and "Charity."

Now the Mexican, not the English, are the immigrants to the New Land, and Cisneros's stories are the literature of this new cultural wave, as Hawthorne's were to readers in the United States in the preceding century.

THE MONKEY GARDEN AND MANGO SAYS GOODBYE SOMETIMES

In the three earlier stories, Cisneros introduces the setting, plot, and characters of her narrative. Esperanza's family background is central to these introductory sketches, but as she begins to grow up on Mango Street, she spends more time with her friends. Then she discovers that the strongest sense of conflict in her life can come from her own feelings.

"The Monkey Garden" begins abruptly with a statement of the absence of the monkey. This is odd, as the monkey is featured in the story's title. There are more highly developed characters and action in the plot of this story, but ironically the sense of absence is at the narrative's emotional center. Esperanza experiences happiness playing as a tomboy with her young friends in the monkey garden. She thinks she has found the Garden of Eden, where she and her neighborhood gang can escape the complexities of the adult world. It contains treasure ("Nenny found a dollar and a dead mouse") and perfect peace ("Eddie Vargas laid his head beneath a hibiscus tree and fell asleep there like a Rip Van Winkle").

Conflict is introduced into the plot when Esperanza discovers that her friend Sally would rather flirt with the boys than continue to play in the garden. The narrator experiences peer pressure to exchange the innocence of childhood for the sexual knowledge of adolescence. The girl is so reluctant to leave her earthly paradise that she tries to imagine suicide as a way to quell her anger about what is happening to her. She learns that willing death is not as easy as it appears in the books she has read. At the end of the story she is left with a headache and an undefined sense of loss: "My garden that had been such a good place to play didn't seem mine either."

Cisneros's first-person narrator has attempted, all unknowingly, to turn Washington Irving's "Rip Van Winkle" into its opposite statement. Her immature heroine is unaware that responsible, productive adult life is elsewhere than in the garden. When little Eddie Vargas falls asleep, she presents it as a positive act — he and the others playing in the garden are free in paradise, "Far away from where our mothers could find us." But life intervenes, and our brief time on earth is no paradise, as both Irving and Cisneros show us in their different ways.

In the sketch "Mango Says Goodbye Sometimes," Cisneros creates a humorous meditation on storytelling through her young narrator's explanation of why she makes up stories. Esperanza is a survivor. She tells stories for at least ten reasons:

1. for companionship ("The mailman says, here's your mail.")
2. for self-dramatization ("She trudged up the wooden stairs.")
3. for pleasure ("I like to tell stories.")
4. to express rebellion ("I'm going to tell you a story about a girl who didn't want to belong.")
5. to keep memory alive ("We didn't always live on Mango Street.")
6. to comfort herself in the face of perceived adversity ("I put it down on paper and then the ghost does not ache so much.")

7. to free herself from the pain of the past ("Mango says goodbye sometimes.")
8. to create something tangible that gives her the sense of belonging to a larger community ("One day I will pack my bags of books and paper.")
9. to impress others ("Friends and neighbors will say, What happened to that Esperanza?")
10. to help others trapped by a similarly harsh experience of life ("I have gone away to come back. For the ones I left behind and for the ones who cannot out.").

Questions for Discussion

1. How does your awareness of the author's background help you to understand her stories in *The House on Mango Street*?
2. What clues does Cisneros give you to help you understand that she has created a fictional narrator in these five stories?
3. How does Cisneros's choice of a first-person narrator shape the way she tells her stories?
4. Why is the image of bread appropriate for the smell of Esperanza's mother's hair? What feelings does it suggest to the reader?
5. What clues does the narrator give us to help us sense a continuing passage of time between the stories "My Name" and "The Monkey Garden"?
6. Why does the reference to "Rip Van Winkle" seem appropriate in "The Monkey Garden"?
7. What is the role of the monkey in "The Monkey Garden"?
8. What is the effect of Cisneros's repetition of lines from her opening story "The House on Mango Street" in her concluding story "Mango Says Goodbye Sometimes"?

Topics for Writing

1. **CONNECTIONS** Compare and contrast the themes in Irving's "Rip Van Winkle" and Cisneros's "The Monkey Garden."
2. **CONNECTIONS** Compare and contrast the narrative approach in Borges's "Everything and Nothing" with any one of Cisneros's stories.
3. Summarize one of the commentaries in the Cisneros casebook.
4. Write a sketch of your earliest memories of the home(s) you lived in as a young child.

Related Story

Jorge Luis Borges, Everything and Nothing, p. 96.

Related Commentaries

Sandra Cisneros, Straw into Gold, p. 823.
Ellen McCracken, On Cisneros's "The House on Mango Street," p. 835.
Julian Olivares, The House as Symbol, p. 842.
Mark Zimmerman, U.S. Latino Literature: History and Development, p. 844.

Stephen Crane

The Open Boat (p. 166)

Crane's story fictionalizes an actual experience. A correspondent himself, Crane happened to be aboard the *Commodore* when it went down, and he included in his newspaper report of the event this passage (as quoted by E. R. Hagemann):

> The history of life in an open boat for thirty hours would no doubt be instructive for the young, but none is to be told here now. For my part I would prefer to tell the story at once, because from it would shine the splendid manhood of Captain Edward Murphy and of William Higgins, the oiler, but let it suffice at this time to say that when we were swamped in the surf and making the best of our way toward the shore the captain gave orders amid the wildness of the breakers as clearly as if he had been on the quarter deck of a battleship.

It is good that Crane did not write "at once" but let his experience take shape as a work of art that, instead of celebrating the "splendid manhood" of two or four individuals, recognizes a profound truth about human life in general — about the puniness of humankind in the face of an indifferent nature and about the consequent value of the solidarity and compassion that arise from an awareness of our common fate. Crane's meditation on his experience "after the fact" enables him to become not simply a reporter but, as he puts it in the last line of the story, an *interpreter* of the message spoken to us by the world we confront.

Crane portrays the exertions of the four men in the boat without glamorizing them. His extended and intimate account of their hard work and weariness wrings out any false emotion from the reader's view of the situation. By varying the narrative point of view from a coolly detached objective observer to a plural account of all four men's shared feelings and perceptions to the correspondent's rueful, self-mocking cogitations, Crane defeats our impulse to choose a hero for adulation, at the same time driving home the point that the condition of the men in the dinghy — their longing, their fear, and their powerlessness before nature and destiny —reflects our own. By the end, what has been revealed is so horrible that there can be no triumph in survival. The good fortune of a rescue brings only a reprieve, not an escape from what awaits us. Billie the oiler drowns, but there is no reason it should have been he, or only he. His death could be anybody's death.

Crane's narration builds suspense through rhythmic repetition, foreshadowing, and irony. We hear the surf periodically: Our hopes for rescue are repeatedly raised and dashed; night follows day, wave follows wave, and the endless struggle goes on. The correspondent's complaint against the cruelty of fate recurs in diminuendo, with less whimsy and self-consciousness each time.

These recurrences mark the men's changes in attitude — from the egocentric viewpoint they start with, imagining that the whole world is watching them and working for their survival, to the perception of the utter indifference of nature with which the story ends. Some stages in this progression include the men's false sense of security when they light up the cigars; their isolation from the people on shore, epitomized by their inability to interpret the signal of the man waving his coat (whose apparent advice to try another stretch of beach they nonetheless inadvertently follow); their experience of aloneness at night; their confrontation with the hostility of nature in the shark; and, finally, their recognition that death might be a welcome release from toil and suffering. They respond by drawing together in a communion that sustains them, sharing their labor and their body heat, huddled together in their tiny, helpless dinghy. Even their strong bond of comradeship, however, cannot withstand the onslaught of the waves. When the boat is swamped, it is every man for himself: Each individual must face death alone. Because of the fellowship that has grown up among them, however, when Billie dies, each of the others feels the oiler's death as his own. The reader, whom Crane's narrative has caused to share thirty hours at sea in an open boat, may recognize the implication in what is spoken by "the sound of the great sea's voice to the men on shore."

WILLIAM E. SHEIDLEY

Questions for Discussion

1. Contrast the imagery and the tone of the first paragraph with those of the second. Why does Crane continually seek to magnify nature and to belittle the men who are struggling with it? Find other instances of Crane's reductive irony and discuss their effects.
2. How does Crane convey the men's concentration on keeping the boat afloat?
3. Explain Crane's use of the word "probably" in the first paragraph of section II.
4. Why does the seagull seem "somehow gruesome and ominous" to the men in the boat? Compare and contrast the seagull with the shark that appears later.
5. Comment on the imagery Crane uses to describe changing seats in the dinghy (stealing eggs, Sèvres).
6. What is it that the correspondent "knew even at the time was the best experience of his life"? Why is it the best?
7. What is the purpose of Crane's understatement in the line "neither the oiler nor the correspondent was fond of rowing at this time"?
8. What is the effect on the reader of the men's lighting up cigars?
9. Discuss the meaning of the correspondent's question "Was I brought here merely to have my nose dragged away as I was about to nibble the sacred cheese of life?"
10. What do you think the man waving a coat means? Why is it impossible for him to communicate with the men in the boat?
11. "A night on the sea in an open boat is a long night," says Crane. How does he make the reader feel the truth of that assertion?
12. At one point the correspondent thinks that he is "the one man afloat on all the oceans." Explain that sensation. Why does the wind he hears sound "sadder than the end"? Why does he later wish he had known the captain was awake when the shark came by?
13. Why does the correspondent have a different attitude toward the poem about the dying soldier in Algiers from the one he had as a boy?
14. Examine the third paragraph of section VII. How important are the thoughts of the correspondent to our understanding of the story? What would the story lose if they were omitted? What would the effect of this passage have been if Crane had narrated the story in the first person? If he had made these comments in the voice of an omniscient third-person narrator?
15. Define the correspondent's physical, mental, and emotional condition during his final moments on the boat and during his swim to the beach.

16. Characterize and explain the tone of Crane's description of the man who pulls the castaways from the sea.
17. Why does Crane make fun of the women who bring coffee to the survivors?

Topics for Writing

1. Consider Crane's handling of point of view in "The Open Boat."
2. Discuss the importance of repetition in Crane's narrative.
3. Analyze imagery as a key to tone in "The Open Boat."
4. After reading the story once rapidly, read it again with a pencil in hand, marking every simile and metaphor. Then sort them into categories. What realms of experience does Crane bring into view through these devices that are not actually part of the simple boat-sea-sky-beach world in which the story is set? Why?
5. Write an eyewitness account of some experience you have undergone that would be suitable for newspaper publication. Then note the changes you would make to turn it into a fictional narrative with broader or more profound implications — or write that story.

Related Commentary

Stephen Crane, The Sinking of the *Commodore*, p. 741.

Suggested Readings

Adams, Richard P. "Naturalistic Fiction: 'The Open Boat.' " *Stephen Crane's Career: Perspectives and Evaluations.* Ed. Thomas A. Gullason. New York: New York UP, 1972. 421–29. Originally published in *Tulane Studies in English* 4 (1954): 137–46.

Cady, Edwin H. *Stephen Crane.* Twayne's United States Authors Series 23. Rev. ed. Boston: Twayne, 1980. 150–54.

Colvert, James B. *Stephen Crane.* New York: Ungar, 1987.

Follett, Wilson, ed. *The Work of Stephen Crane.* New York: Knopf, 1925.

Fryckstedt, O. W., ed. *Stephen Crane: Uncollected Writings.* Uppsala: Studia Anglistica Upsaliensia, 1963.

Hagemann, E. R. " 'Sadder than the End': Another Look at 'The Open Boat.' " In *Stephen Crane in Transition: Centenary Essays.* Ed. Joseph Katz. DeKalb: Northern Illinois UP, 1972. 66–85.

Johnson, Glen M. "Stephen Crane." In *American Short-Story Writers, 1880–1910. Dictionary of Literary Biography,* vol. 78. Detroit: Gale, 1989.

Katz, Joseph, ed. *The Portable Stephen Crane.* New York: Viking, 1985.

Kissane, Leedice. "Interpretation through Language: A Study of the Metaphors in Stephen Crane's 'The Open Boat.' " In *Stephen Crane's Career: Perspectives and Evaluations.* Ed. Thomas Gullason. New York: New York UP, 1972. 410–16. Originally published in *Rendezvous* (Idaho State U) 1 (1966): 18–22.

Knapp, Bettina L. *Stephen Crane.* New York: Ungar, 1987.

Stallman, R. W. *Stephen Crane: A Critical Bibliography.* Ames: Iowa State UP, 1972.

———. *Stories and Tales/Stephen Crane.* New York: Vintage, 1955.

Wolford, Chester L. *Stephen Crane: A Study of the Short Fiction.* Boston: Twayne, 1989.

RALPH ELLISON

Battle Royal (p. 185)

In the headnote to his comments on "Battle Royal" reprinted in Chapter 7 (p. 744), Ellison is quoted expounding on the importance of "converting experience into symbolic action" in fiction. One of the major triumphs of "Battle Royal" (and of *Invisible Man* as a whole) is Ellison's success in the realistic rendering of experiences that are in themselves so obviously significant of larger social, psychological, and moral truths that explication is unnecessary. From the small American flag tattooed on the nude dancer's belly to the "rope of bloody saliva forming a shape like an undiscovered continent" that the narrator drools on his new briefcase, Ellison's account of the festivities at the men's smoker effectively symbolizes the condition of blacks in America while remaining thoroughly persuasive in its verisimilitude. Both the broader structure of the evening and the finer details of narration and description carry the force of Ellison's theme. The young blacks are tortured first by having the most forbidden of America's riches dangled before them, then by being put through their paces in a melee in which their only victims are their fellows and the whites look on with glee, and finally by being debased into groveling for money (some of it counterfeit) on a rug whose electrification underlines their own powerlessness. In one brief passage, the nightmare of such an existence appears in a strange subaqueous vision of primitive life: "The boys groped about like blind, cautious crabs crouching to protect their midsections, their heads pulled in short against their shoulders, their arms stretched nervously before them, with their fists testing the smoke-filled air like the knobbed feelers of hypersensitive snails."

Because his actual experience forms itself into such revealing images, the narrator's dream of his grandfather seems all the more credible as a statement of his position. He dreams that the message on his briefcase says "Keep This Nigger-Boy Running" — not far from "You've got to know your place at all times." The narrator's grandfather knew his place and played his role, but he never believed a word of it. It is this assurance of an inner being quite different from the face he turned toward the world that makes him so troubling to his descendants. In his effort to please the white folks and in so doing to get ahead, the narrator seeks alliance rather than secret enmity with his antagonists. As a result he subjects himself to the trickery and delusions the white community chooses to impose on him. Dependent for his sense of himself on his ability to guess what they want him to do, the narrator finds himself groping in a fog deeper than the swirls of cigar smoke that hang over the scene of the battle royal. When the smoke clears and the blindfold comes off, he will recognize, as he puts it at the start, that he is invisible to the whites and may therefore discover his own identity within himself.

The first episode of a long novel does not accomplish the narrator's enlightenment, but it constitutes his initiation into the realities of the world he must eventually come to understand. Ellison says (in his commentary on p. 744) that the battle royal "is a ritual in preservation of caste lines, a keeping of taboo to appease the gods and ward off bad luck," and that "it is also the initiation ritual to which all greenhorns are subjected." This rite of initiation bears a revealing relation to the primitive initiation ceremonies known to anthropologists. The battle royal, for example, separates the boys from their families, challenges them to prove their valor, and subjects them to instruction by the tribal elders in a sort of men's house.

The boys are stripped and introduced to sexual mysteries. But the hazing of women that is a frequent feature of such initiations is not carried on here by the boys but by the gross elders, whose savagery is barely under control; the ritual ends not with the entry of the initiates into the larger community but with their pointed exclusion; and the sacred lore embodied in the narrator's recital of his graduation speech makes explicit the contradictions inherent in the society it describes. To cast down his bucket where he is forces him to swallow his own blood. The narrator is delighted with the scholarship to "the state college for Negroes" that he wins by toeing the line and knowing his place, and he does not object that the "gold" coins he groveled for are fraudulent. His education in the meaning of his grandfather's troubling injunctions will continue, but the reader has already seen enough to recognize their validity.

WILLIAM E. SHEIDLEY

Questions for Discussion

1. In the opening paragraph the narrator says, "I was naïve." In what ways is his naiveté revealed in the story that follows?
2. Why does the narrator feel guilty when praised?
3. What is the message to the narrator behind the suggestion "that since I was to be there anyway I might as well take part in the battle royal"? Explain his hesitation. What is the most important part of the evening for the whites?
4. Who is present at the smoker? Discuss the role of the school superintendent.
5. What techniques does Ellison use to convey to the reader the impact that seeing the stripper has on the boys?
6. What does the stripper have in common with the boys? Why are both a stripper and a battle royal part of the evening's entertainment?
7. During the chaos of the battle, the narrator worries about how his speech will be received. Is that absurd or understandable?
8. Does the deathbed advice of the narrator's grandfather offer a way to handle the battle royal?
9. Why does Tatlock refuse to take a dive?
10. Explain the narrator's first reaction to seeing the "small square rug." In what sense is his instinct correct?
11. What is the meaning of the electric rug to the whites? What do they wish it to demonstrate to the blacks?
12. Explain Mr. Colcord's reaction when the narrator tries to topple him onto the rug.
13. Analyze the narrator's speech. What is the implication of his having to deliver it while swallowing his own blood?
14. Why is the school superintendent confident that the narrator will "lead his people in the proper paths"?
15. Why does the narrator stand in front of his grandfather's picture holding his briefcase? Who gets the better of this confrontation?

Topics for Writing

1. Make a study of seeing and understanding in "Battle Royal."
2. Analyze the role of sex, violence, and power in "Battle Royal."
3. Write an essay exploring the battle royal and black experience in America.
4. Describe the "permanent interest" of "Battle Royal." (See Ellison's commentary in Chapter 7, p. 744.)

5. Examine the blonde, the gold coins, and the calfskin briefcase in "Battle Royal."
6. Select a passage of twenty or fewer lines from this story for detailed explication. Relate as many of its images as possible to others in the story and to the general ideas that the story develops. To what extent does the passage you chose reflect the meaning of the story as a whole?
7. Recall an experience in which you were humiliated or embarrassed. What motives of your own and of those before whom you were embarrassed put you in such a position? Narrate the incident so that these underlying purposes become evident to the reader.
8. Write a description of a game or ceremony with which you are familiar. What set of principles or relationships (not necessarily malign) does it express?

Related Commentary

Ralph Ellison, The Influence of Folklore on "Battle Royal," p. 744.

Suggested Readings

Blake, Susan L. "Ritual and Rationalization: Black Folklore in the Works of Ralph Ellison." *PMLA* 94 (1979): 121–26, esp. 122–23.

Horowitz, Ellin. "The Rebirth of the Artist." In *Twentieth-Century Interpretations of "Invisible Man."* Ed. John M. Reilly. Englewood Cliffs, NJ: Prentice, 1970. 80–88, esp. 81. (Originally published in 1964.)

O'Meally, Robert G. *The Craft of Ralph Ellison.* Cambridge, MA: Harvard UP, 1980. 12–14.

Vogler, Thomas A. "*Invisible Man*: Somebody's Protest Novel." *Ralph Ellison: A Collection of Critical Essays.* Ed. John Hersey. Englewood Cliffs, NJ: Prentice, 1974. 127–50, esp. 143–44.

Louise Erdrich

The Red Convertible (p. 196)

The story takes place in 1974, when Henry Junior comes back to the Chippewa Indian reservation after more than three years as a soldier in Vietnam. He is mentally disturbed by his experiences in the war, and, as his brother Lyman (who narrates the story) says laconically, "the change was no good."

Erdrich has structured her story in a traditional manner. It is narrated in the first person by Lyman, who uses the past tense to describe the finality of what happened to his brother and the red Oldsmobile convertible they once shared. The plot moves conventionally, after a lengthy introduction giving the background of the two brothers and their pleasure in the car. They are Indians who work hard for what they earn, but they also enjoy their money. As Lyman says, "We went places in that car, me and Henry." An atmosphere of innocence pervades this part of the story. They enjoy sightseeing along the western highways, going when and where they please, spending an entire summer in Alaska after they drive home a female hitchhiker with long, beautiful hair.

The story moves forward chronologically (although it is told as a flashback after the opening frame of four paragraphs), organized in sections usually several paragraphs long. Its structure is as loose and comfortable as the brothers' relationship. Then, midway, the story darkens when Henry goes off to Vietnam. For three sections, Lyman describes Henry's disorientation after the war. Then Henry fixes the convertible, the boys get back behind the wheel, and it seems briefly as if the good times are again starting to roll. But Henry feels internal turmoil similar to that of the flooded river they park alongside. The story reaches its climax when Henry suddenly goes wild after drinking several beers, deteriorating into what he calls a "crazy Indian." Lyman stares after him as he jumps into the river, shouting, "Got to cool me off!" His last words are quieter, "My boots are filling," and then he is gone.

The last paragraph of the story is its final section, Lyman describing how he drove the car into the river after he couldn't rescue Henry. It has grown dark, and he is left alone with the sound of the rushing water "going and running and running." This brings the story full circle, back to the beginning, where Lyman told us that now he "walks everywhere he goes." His grief for his brother is as understated as the rest of his personality. Erdrich has invented a natural storyteller in Lyman. We feel his emotional loss as if it were our own.

Questions for Discussion

1. In the opening paragraph, Lyman says that he and Henry owned the red convertible "together until his boots filled with water on a windy night and he bought out my share." When does the meaning of this sentence become clear to you? What is the effect of putting this sentence in the first paragraph?

2. Also in the opening paragraph, Erdrich writes: "his youngest brother Lyman (that's myself), Lyman walks everywhere he goes." If Lyman is narrating this story, why does he name himself? Does speaking of himself in the third person create any particular effect?

3. What is the function of the third section of the story? Why does the narrator tell us about their wandering, about meeting Susy? What associations does the red convertible carry?

4. Watching Henry watching television, Lyman says, "He sat in his chair gripping the armrests with all his might, as if the chair itself was moving at a high speed and if he let go at all he would rocket forward and maybe crash right through the set." How would you describe the diction in this sentence? What effect does the sentence's length — and its syntax — create? What is the tone? What does this line, and the paragraphs around it, tell you about Lyman's reaction to Henry's change?

5. Where do Lyman and Henry speak directly to each other in this story? Where do they speak indirectly? How do they communicate without speech? Describe how Erdrich presents the moments of emotion in this story.

6. Why is Lyman upset by the picture of himself and his brother? When does the picture begin to bother him? Do we know if it's before or after Henry's death? Does it make a difference to our interpretation of the story? What burden of memory does this picture carry?

7. Consider the tone of the final paragraph, in which Lyman is describing how he felt when he gave his car to his dead brother. Look at the diction surrounding the red convertible here: It plows into the water; the headlights "reach in . . . go down, searching"; they are "still lighted." What attribute does the diction give the car? How is the car different now from the way it's

been in the rest of the story? Does this transformation of the car invoke a sense of closure in the story?

8. The closing sentence says, "And then there is only the water, the sound of it going and running and going and running and running." How does this statement comment on the relationship between the two brothers?

Topics for Writing

1. Write an essay considering brotherhood in "The Red Convertible."
2. Discuss Erdrich's use of setting to determine tone.
3. Rewrite the story from the third-person point of view.
4. **CONNECTIONS** Compare and discuss Lyman's initiation into maturity with that of Julian in Flannery O'Connor's "Everything That Rises Must Converge."

Suggested Readings

Erdrich, Louise. "Excellence Has Always Made Me Fill with Fright When It Is Demanded by Other People, but Fills Me with Pleasure When I Am Left to Practice It Alone." *Ms.* 13 (1985): 84.

———."Where I Ought to Be: A Writer's Sense of Place." *New York Times Book Review* 28 July 1985: 1+.

Howard, J. "Louise Erdrich." *Life* 8 (1985): 27+.

WILLIAM FAULKNER

A Rose for Emily (p. 204)

Few stories, surely, differ more on a second reading than does "A Rose for Emily," which yields to the initiate some detail or circumstance anticipating the ending in nearly every paragraph. But Faulkner sets the pieces of his puzzle in place so coolly that the first-time reader hardly suspects them to fit together into a picture at all, until the curtain is finally swept aside and the shocking secret of Miss Emily's upstairs room is revealed. Faulkner makes it easy to write off the episodes of the smell, Miss Emily's denial of her father's death, the arsenic, and the aborted wedding (note the shuffled chronology) as the simple eccentricities of a pathetic old maid, to be pitied and indulged. The impact of the final scene drives home the realization that the passions of a former generation and its experience of life are no less real or profound for all their being in the past — whether we view them through the haze of sentimental nostalgia, as the Confederate veterans near the end of the story do, or place them at an aesthetic distance, as the townspeople do in the romantic tableau imagined in section II.

In his interviews with students at the University of Virginia (excerpted in Chapter 7 on p. 748), Faulkner stressed Miss Emily's being "kept down" by her father as an important factor in driving her to violate the code of her society by taking a lover, and he expressed a deep human sympathy for her long expiation for that sin. In the narrative consciousness of the story, however — the impersonal "we" that speaks for the communal mind of Jefferson — Miss Emily Grierson is a town relic, a monument to the local past to be shown to strangers, like the graves of the men slain at the battle of Jefferson or the big houses on what long ago, before they put the sidewalks in, was the "most select street." Because all relics are to a degree symbolic, one should not hesitate to take up the challenge found in Faulkner's ambiguous claim that "the writer is too busy . . . to have time to be conscious of all the symbolism that he may put into what he does or what people may read into it" (quoted in the headnote on p. 204). Miss Emily, for example, may be understood to express the part of southern culture that is paralyzed in the present by its inability to let go of the past, even though that past is as dead as Homer Barron, and even though its reality differed from the treasured memory as greatly as the Yankee paving contractor — "not a marrying man" — differs from the husband of Miss Emily's desperate longings. Other details in Faulkner's economical narration fit this reading: the prominence of Miss Emily's iconic portrait of her father; her refusal to acknowledge changing laws and customs; her insistence that the privilege of paying no taxes, bestowed on her by the chivalrous Colonel Sartoris, is an inalienable right; her dependence on the labors of her Negro servant, whose patient silence renders him an accomplice in her strange crime; and, not least, her relationship of mutual exploitation with Homer, the representative of the North — a relationship that ends in a morbid and grotesque parody of marriage. In this context, the smell of death that reeks from Miss Emily's house tells how the story judges what she stands for, and the dust that falls on everything brings the welcome promise of relief.

But Faulkner will not let it lie. Seen for what she is, neither romanticized nor trivialized, Miss Emily has a forthright dignity and a singleness of purpose that contrast sharply with those representatives of propriety and progress who sneak around her foundation in the dark spreading lime or knock on her door in the ineffectual effort to collect her taxes. And as the speechless townsfolk tiptoe aghast about her bridal chamber, it is Miss Emily's iron will, speaking through the strand of iron-gray hair that lies where she has lain, that has the final word.

WILLIAM E. SHEIDLEY

Questions for Discussion

1. The story begins and ends with Miss Emily's funeral. Trace the chronology of the intervening sections.
2. Emily is called "a fallen monument" and "a tradition." Explain.
3. Why does the narrator label Miss Emily's house "an eyesore among eyesores"?
4. Define the opposing forces in the confrontation that occupies most of section I. How does Miss Emily "vanquish them"?
5. Discuss the transition between sections I and II. In what ways are the two episodes parallel?
6. Apart from her black servant, Miss Emily has three men in her life. What similarities are there in her attitudes toward them?
7. Why is Homer Barron considered an inappropriate companion for Miss Emily?
8. Consider Faulkner's introduction of the rat poison into the story in section III. What is the narrator's avowed reason for bringing it up?
9. At the beginning of section IV, the townspeople think Emily will commit suicide, and they think "it would be the best thing." Why? What is the basis of their error regarding her intentions?
10. Why do you think Miss Emily gets fat and develops gray hair when she does?
11. Why does Miss Emily's servant disappear after her death?

12. Describe Miss Emily's funeral before the upstairs room is opened. In what way does that scene serve as a foil to set off what follows?
13. Discuss the role of dust in the last few paragraphs of the story.
14. Why does Faulkner end the story with "a long strand of iron-gray hair"?

Topics for Writing

1. Contrast the various attitudes toward the past in "A Rose for Emily."
2. Discuss the meaning of time and Faulkner's handling of chronology in "A Rose for Emily."
3. Construct a profile of Emily Grierson. Is she a criminal, a lunatic, or a heroine?
4. Explain the title of "A Rose for Emily."
5. Consider the relationship between "A Rose for Emily" and the history of the South.
6. What can you discern about the narrator of "A Rose for Emily"?
7. Were you surprised by the story's ending? On a second reading, mark all the passages that foreshadow it.
8. Imitate Faulkner by telling the events that lead up to a climax out of chronological order. What new effects do you find it possible to achieve? What problems in continuity do you encounter?

Related Commentary

William Faulkner, The Meaning of "A Rose for Emily," p. 748.

Suggested Readings

See page 44 of this manual.

WILLIAM FAULKNER

That Evening Sun (p. 211)

"That Evening Sun" is one of a handful of American short stories that have been so frequently anthologized and discussed that they almost define the style and the method of American short fiction. For the instructor the question may not be so much presenting the story for its literary qualities, but in seeing how well the story still relates to the political and social attitudes of students today, more than sixty years since it was first published. It isn't as acceptable now for a white writer to deal with themes of African American life, and for many feminists there can be questions about a white male author's presentation of a black woman's experience. Does the story still have the powerful effect on its readers that it had in the harsh years of the Great Depression and the cruelest decades of legalized segregation?

The answer is that the narrative device that gave the story so much of its first impact still is as effective today. By weaving through the story the uncomprehending chorus of children's voices, Faulkner succeeds in making the brutal violence of the story frighteningly real. There is no more desperate moment in American literature than when Nancy's attempt to keep the children amused in her lonely cabin ends with the broken popcorn popper. The reader's realization that the children don't understand what is happening only sharpens the effect. For women readers the story perhaps will reflect some of their own emotions and responses as the society is ready now to listen to the stories of battered wives and of women threatened by lovers or friends. The terror that is stalking Nancy is no different from the fear that a woman feels when she knows that a restraining order issued by a distant judge won't protect her from the rage of a disturbed ex-husband.

From the perspective of sixty years, it is also possible to see the racial dimensions of the story in a different way. Perhaps part of what gave Faulkner his great international reputation — and his Nobel Prize — was an understanding that what he was describing was the bitter reality of life for any underclass. The black underclass outside the white neighborhoods of this southern town has been forced into the way of life of the peasants of the older European societies. Faulkner's Nancy could have been a servant in a renter's cottage outside the manor walls in nineteenth-century England, or a woman forced outside the social framework — as she would be by her unwed pregnancy — in any European small town before World War I. Faulkner's story still forces us to face this very real inhumanity in a world we realize has not left this legacy of violence behind.

Questions for Discussion

1. Compare the ages of the children with the responses to Nancy's fear. How much more awareness do the older children have?
2. How does Faulkner describe the small town's ability to help someone like Nancy?
3. Why is Jesus still able to go free, despite the awareness of the children's father of what is happening?

Topics for Writing

1. Faulkner describes the uneasy boundary where the white and the black societies of this small town meet. What are the real effects of this boundary?
2. Compare the situation Nancy faces with a similar situation today.
3. The children's father acts in a way that he would consider sympathetic and protective but would be considered paternalistic today. Discuss his character and role in the story.

Suggested Readings

Basset, John E. *Vision and Revisions: Essays on Faulkner.* West Cornwall, CT: Locust Hill, 1989.

Bloom, Harold. *William Faulkner.* New York: Chelsea House, 1986.

Blotner, Joseph. *Faulkner: A Biography.* New York: Random, 1991.

Brooks, Cleanth. *A Shaping Joy.* New York: Harcourt, 1971.

Gwynn, Frederick, and Joseph Blotner, eds. *Faulkner in the University.* Charlottesville: U of Virginia P, 1959.

Hall, Donald. *To Read Literature: Fiction, Poetry, Drama.* New York: Holt, 1981. 10–16.

Heller, Terry. "The Telltale Hair: A Critical Study of William Faulkner's 'A Rose for Emily.' " *Arizona Quarterly* 28 (1972): 301–18.

Hoffman, Frederick J. *William Faulkner, Revised.* Boston: Twayne, 1990.

Howe, Irving. *William Faulkner: A Critical Study.* 2nd ed. New York: Vintage, 1962. 265.

Leary, Lewis. *William Faulkner of Yoknapatawpha County.* Twentieth-Century American Writers. New York: Crowell, 1973. 136.

Millgate, Michael. *The Achievement of William Faulkner.* New York: Random, 1966.

GABRIEL GARCÍA MÁRQUEZ

A Very Old Man with Enormous Wings (p. 224)

The word "allegories" in the headnote presents a challenge to readers of this story, and the inevitable failure of any simple scheme of interpretation to grasp fully the mystery at its heart, reflects García Márquez's central theme exactly. Like the crabs, which come into the human world from an alien realm, the "flesh-and-blood angel" constitutes an intrusion of something strange and unfathomable into the comfortable world of reality as we choose to define it. Everybody, from the "wise" woman next door to the pope, takes a turn at trying to find a slot in which to file the winged visitor, but no definition seems satisfactory, and even Pelayo and Elisenda, whom the angel's presence has made wealthy, spend their money on a house "with iron bars on the windows so that angels wouldn't get in." When at last the old man flies away, Elisenda feels relief, "because then he was no longer an annoyance in her life but an imaginary dot on the horizon of the sea."

In discussing how he receives artistic inspiration, García Márquez says, "There's nothing deliberate or predictable in all this, nor do I know when it's going to happen to me. I'm at the mercy of my imagination." Without intending to limit the story's implications, one might associate the angel with this sort of unpredictable intrusion of the visionary and wonderful into everyday life. As an old man with wings, the angel recalls the mythical symbol of the artist, Daedalus, except that his wings are "so natural on that completely human organism that [the doctor] couldn't understand why other men didn't have them too." Bogged down in the mud, the angel seems less an allusion to Daedalus's son, the overreacher Icarus, than a representation of the difficulty of the artistic imagination in sustaining its flight through the unpleasant circumstances of this "sad" world. True artists are often misunderstood, ill treated, and rejected in favor of more practical concerns or of the creators of ersatz works that flatter established prejudices. Just so, nobody can understand the angel's "hermetic" language, and when he performs his aggressively unpractical miracles, no one is delighted. Exploited by his keepers, to whom he brings vast wealth, the angel receives as royalties only his quarters in the chicken coop and the flat side of the broom when underfoot. Popular for a time as a sideshow attraction, the angel is soon passed over in favor of the horrible "woman who had been changed into a spider for having disobeyed her parents," a grotesque and slapdash creation of the lowest order of imaginative synthesis, whose "human truth" gratifies both sentimentality and narrow-mindedness. But the artistic imagination lives happily on eggplant mush, possesses a supernatural patience, and though functionally blind to the bumping posts of ordinary reality, ever again takes wing. The angel has, perhaps rightly, appeared to his human observers "a cataclysm in repose," but near the end, as he sings his sea chanteys under the stars, he definitely comes to resemble "a hero taking his ease," preparing to navigate the high seas beyond the horizon.

WILLIAM E. SHEIDLEY

Questions for Discussion

1. Why are there crabs in the house? Is it for the same reason the old man with enormous wings has fallen in the courtyard? What other associations does the story make between the old man and the crabs?
2. Pelayo first thinks the old man is a nightmare. What other attempts are made to put this prodigy into a familiar category?
3. How does the old man differ from our usual conceptions of angels? What is the essential difference?
4. Explain Father Gonzaga's approach to the angel. What implications — about the angel and about the church — may be derived from his failure to communicate with him effectively?
5. Comment on the angel's career as a sideshow freak. Who receives the benefit of his success? Why does he fall? Compare what he has to offer with what the spider-woman has. What reasons might people have to prefer the latter?
6. Why do you think the angel tolerates the child patiently?
7. What are the implications of the angel's examination by the doctor?
8. How do we feel as the angel finally flaps away at the end? Does Elisenda's response adequately express the reader's?

Topics for Writing

1. Consider the ordinary and the enormous in "A Very Old Man with Enormous Wings." (Consider the etymological meaning of "enormous.")
2. Is García Márquez's fallen angel a fairy tale, a myth, or an allegory?
3. Recharging the sense of wonder: How does García Márquez make the reader believe in his angel?
4. Read the story aloud to a selected spectrum of people (at least three) of various ages and educational levels. Tabulate their responses and opinions, perhaps in an interview. Combining this evidence with your own response to the story, try to define the basis of its appeal.
5. Select a supernatural being from a fairy tale or other familiar source (the cartoons involving talking animals that wear clothes and drive cars might be worth considering), and imagine the being as a physical reality in your own ordinary surroundings. Write a sketch about what happens.
6. **CONNECTIONS** Compare "A Very Old Man with Enormous Wings" with other presentations of the supernatural (Hawthorne's, for example).

Suggested Readings

Bell-Villada, Gene H. *García Márquez: The Man and His Work.* Chapel Hill: U of North Carolina P, 1990.

Byk, John. "From Fact to Fiction: Gabriel García Márquez and the Short Story." *Mid-American Review* 6.2 (1986): 111–16.

Fau, Margaret Eustella. *Bibliographic Guide to Gabriel García Márquez, 1979–1985.* Westport, CT: Greenwood, 1986.

García Márquez, Gabriel. *Collected Stories.* New York: Harper, 1984.

———. *Strange Pilgrims: Twelve Stories.* New York: Knopf, 1993.

McMurray, George R. *Gabriel García Márquez.* New York: Ungar, 1977. 116–19.

McNerney, Kathleen. *Understanding Gabriel García Márquez.* Columbia: U of South Carolina P, 1989.

Morello Frosch, Marta. "The Common Wonders of García Márquez's Recent Fiction." *Books Abroad* 47 (1973): 496–501.

Oberhelman, Harley D. *Gabriel García Márquez: A Study of the Short Fiction*. Boston: Twayne, 1991.

Ortega, Julio. *Gabriel García Márquez and the Powers of Fiction*. Austin: U of Texas P, 1988.

Williams, Raymond L. *Gabriel García Márquez*. Boston: Twayne, 1984.

Zhu, Jingdong. "García Márquez and His Writing of Short Stories." *Foreign Literatures* 1 (1987): 77–80.

CHARLOTTE PERKINS GILMAN

The Yellow Wallpaper (p. 230)

Gilman wrote "The Yellow Wallpaper" between 1890 and 1894, during what she later recalled were the hardest years of her life. She had left her first husband and child to live alone in California after a nervous breakdown, and she was beginning to give lectures on freedom for women and socialism while she kept a boardinghouse, taught school, and edited newspapers. During this time, her husband married her best friend, to whom Gilman relinquished her child. The emotional pressures and economic uncertainties under which Gilman lived contributed to the desperate tone of this story.

Early readers of "The Yellow Wallpaper" compared it with the horror stories of Edgar Allan Poe (William Dean Howells said it was a story to "freeze our . . . blood" when he reprinted it in 1920 in *Great Modern American Stories*). Like Poe's homicidal narrators, Gilman's heroine tells her story in a state of neurotic compulsion. But she is no homicidal maniac. Unlike Poe, Gilman suggests that a specific social malady has driven her heroine to the brink of madness: the bondage of conventional marriage.

Her husband is her physician and keeper, the father of her beloved but absent child, the money earner who pays the rent on the mansion where she is held captive for her "own good." When she begs to get away, he replies practically, "Our lease will be up in three weeks, and I can't see how to leave before." Insisting that he knows what is best for her, he believes that the cure for her mysterious "weakness" is total rest. The husband is supported in his view by the opinion of the foremost medical authority on the treatment of mental illness, Dr. S. Weir Mitchell, a name explicitly mentioned in the story. Gilman had spent a month in Dr. Mitchell's sanitorium five years before. In her autobiography she later reported that she almost lost her mind there and would often "crawl into remote closets and under beds — to hide from the grinding pressure of that profound distress."

Gilman transferred the memory of her physical debilitation and "absolute incapacity" for normal (read "conventional") married life into her heroine's state in "The Yellow Wallpaper." The story dramatizes Gilman's fear while living with her first husband that marriage and motherhood might incapacitate her (as it apparently had Gilman's mother) for what she called "work in the world." She felt imprisoned within her marriage, a victim of her desire to please, trapped by her wedding ring. Gilman left her husband, but in "The Yellow Wallpaper" her heroine is sacrificed to the emotional turmoil she experiences.

As a symbolic projection of psychological stress, "The Yellow Wallpaper" has resemblances to Kafka's "The Metamorphosis," although it is more specific in its focus on social injustice to women. Like Gregor Samsa, Gilman's heroine is victimized by the people she loves. The yellow wallpaper surrounding her is "like a bad dream." It furnishes the central images in the story. The reader can use it like a Rorschach test to understand the heroine's experience of entrapment, confinement, and sacrifice for other family members. Like Gregor Samsa, she regresses to subhuman behavior as a self-inflicted punishment following her psychological rebellion — the wallpaper's bad smell, its bars and grid, its fungus and toadstools, and its images of the creeping (dependent, inferior) woman. But unlike Gregor Samsa, Gilman's heroine thinks she is freed from the "bad dream" by telling her story, not to a "living soul," but to what she calls (nonjudgmentally) "dead paper."

Telling her story enables her to achieve her greatest desire — the symbolic death of her husband. The story ends, "Now why should that man have fainted? But he did, and right across my path by the wall, so that I had to creep over him every time!" The central irony of the story, however, is that by the time she realizes the twisted ambition fostered by obediently following "like a good girl" her passive role as a conventional member of the "weaker sex," she has been driven insane.

Questions for Discussion

1. Why have the narrator and her husband, John, rented the "colonial mansion"? What is its history, and what is the reaction of the heroine to this estate? Does she feel comfortable living in the house?

2. Give a description of John. Why does the heroine say that his profession is "*perhaps* . . . one reason I do not get well faster"? How does the narrator view her husband? Does she agree with John's diagnosis and treatment? Who else supports John's diagnosis? What effect does this have on the heroine?

3. What clue does the narrator's repeated lament, "what can one do?" give us about her personality? Describe other aspects of the woman's personality that are revealed in the opening of the story. What conflicting emotions is she having toward her husband, her condition, and the mansion?

4. How would you characterize the narrator's initial reaction to, and description of, the wallpaper?

5. Describe the narrator's state after the first two weeks of residence. Has John's relationship with his wife changed at all?

6. Who is Jennie? What is her relationship to the narrator, and what is her function in the story?

7. How has the narrator changed in her description of the wallpaper? Is it fair to say that the wallpaper has become more dominant in her day-to-day routine? Explain.

8. By the Fourth of July, what does the narrator admit about the wallpaper? What clues does Gilman give us about the education of the narrator and her increasingly agitated state? Is she finding it more and more difficult to communicate? Explain.

9. As the summer continues, describe the narrator's thoughts. What is her physical condition? Is there a link between her symptoms and psychological illness?

10. How does the narrator try to reach out to her husband? What is his reaction? Is this her last contact with sanity? Do you think John really has no comprehension of the seriousness of her illness?

11. Why do you think Gilman briefly changes the point of view from first person singular to the second person as the narrator describes the pattern of the wallpaper? What effect does the narrator say light has on the wallpaper?

12. Who does the narrator see in the wallpaper? How have her perceptions of John and Jennie changed from the beginning of the story?

13. Abruptly the narrator switches mood from boredom and frustration to excitement. To what does she attribute this change? How does John react to this? What new aspects of the wallpaper does she discuss?

14. By the final section of the story, what is the narrator's relationship to her husband? to Jennie? to the wallpaper? How has the narrator's perspective changed from the start of the story? What change do we see in her actions?

15. Identify what has driven the narrator to the brink of madness. How does she try to free herself from this element? What is her greatest desire? What is the central irony of the story?

Topics for Writing

1. **CONNECTIONS** Compare and contrast the husband-wife relationship and its outcome in Gilman's "The Yellow Wallpaper" and Henrik Ibsen's play "A Doll's House."

2. **CONNECTIONS** Compare and contrast the monologue in Gilman's "The Yellow Wallpaper" with that in Poe's "The Cask of Amontillado" or "The Tell-Tale Heart."

3. **CONNECTIONS** Compare and discuss the concept of marriage in Gilman's "The Yellow Wallpaper," Carver's "What We Talk About When We Talk About Love," and Walker's "Roselily."

Related Commentaries

Sandra M. Gilbert and Susan Gubar, A Feminist Reading of Gilman's "The Yellow Wallpaper," p. 749.

Charlotte Perkins Gilman, Undergoing the Cure for Nervous Prostration, p. 752.

Suggested Readings

Bader, J. "The Dissolving Vision: Realism in Jewett, Freeman, and Gilman." In *American Realism; New Essays*. Ed. Eric J. Sundquist. Baltimore: Johns Hopkins UP, 1982. 176–98.

Delaney, Sheila. *Writing Women: Women Writers and Women in Literature, Medieval to Modern*. New York: Schocken, 1983.

Feminist Papers: From Adams to de Beauvoir. Ed. Alice S. Rossi. New York: Columbia UP, 1973.

Hanley-Peritz, J. "Monumental Feminism and Literature's Ancestral House: Another Look at 'The Yellow Wallpaper.' " *Women's Studies* 12.2 (1986): 113–28.

Hill, Mary A. "Charlotte Perkins Gilman: A Feminist's Struggle with Womanhood." *Massachusetts Review* 21 (1980): 503–26.

———. *Charlotte Perkins Gilman: The Making of a Radical Feminist, 1860–1896.* Philadelphia: Temple UP, 1980.

Lane, Ann J. "Charlotte Perkins Gilman: The Personal Is Political." In *Feminist Theorists*. Ed. Dale Spender. New York: Pantheon, 1983.

Nies, Judith. *Seven Women*. New York: Viking, 1977. 127–45.

Shumaker, C. " 'Too Terribly Good to Be Printed': Charlotte Gilman's 'The Yellow Wallpaper.' " *American Literature* 57 (1985): 588–99.

SUSAN GLASPELL

A Jury of Her Peers (p. 243)

Students will most likely profit from reading both Glaspell's story and her play, *Trifles,* included in Part Three of this anthology, along with Leonard Mustazza's commentary "Generic Translation and Thematic Shift in Glaspell's *Trifles* and 'A Jury of Her Peers.'" Class discussion can be based on the similarities and differences between the play and the short story. Mustazza finds Glaspell's story "a much more interesting, resonant, and disturbing [work] than the slighter drama from which it derives." You might begin in the classroom by asking if students agree or disagree with his judgment, expressed at the conclusion of his essay.

Mustazza bases his argument on the fact that when Glaspell converted her play into a short story, it became twice as long. This enabled her to do more than present the theme of *Trifles* in short story form. She was able to include another dimension in "A Jury of Her Peers" when she dramatized the separateness of Mrs. Hale (from whose point of view the story is told) and Mrs. Peters (the sheriff's wife) at the beginning of the story. The story becomes more substantial than the play because Glaspell develops her characterization of these two women more fully; over the course of the narrative she shows how Mrs. Hale wins over Mrs. Peters to her opinion that Minnie Wright should not be punished for killing her husband. As Mustazza summarizes his thesis, "'A Jury of Her Peers' is much more concerned with the separateness of the women themselves and their self-injurious acquiescence in male-defined roles."

Questions for Discussion

1. Why does Glaspell begin her story in Mrs. Hale's kitchen?
2. Why is Glaspell's choice of point of view particularly important in this story?
3. When do you first become aware of the conflict between the female characters' feeling about Mrs. Wright and the male characters' approach to justice?
4. Why is Sheriff Peters so concerned with finding a motive for the crime?
5. Why were the women invited to accompany the men to the Wright farmhouse?
6. What does the strangled canary symbolize?

Topics for Writing

1. Summarize Leonard Mustazza's commentary in a hundred words.
2. **CONNECTIONS** Compare and contrast Glaspell's play and short story in order to defend your opinion about which you prefer. You may agree or disagree with Mustazza's commentary.
3. **CONNECTIONS** Compare and contrast the little girl Sylvia in Sarah Orne Jewett's "A White Heron" with Mrs. Hale in "A Jury of Her Peers." What qualities of independence do they share? How have their characters been shaped by their lives in remote rural settings in the United States?

Suggested Readings

See pp. 335–336 of this manual.

Nadine Gordimer

The Kindest Thing to Do (p. 260)

In the headnote to this Gordimer story, the author tells us that a short story expresses "the life-giving drop — sweat, tear, semen, saliva — that will spread an intensity on the page; burn a hole in it." In "The Kindest Thing to Do" Gordimer has taken a brief moment in an adolescent's life, when she has to kill a living creature for the first time, and describes it so intensely that it can burn a hole in an attentive reader's consciousness.

The setting of the story is a prosperous white family's home in South Africa on a drowsy Sunday afternoon. Because of the daughter's carelessness, the family dog, Micky, has mangled an injured dove. The mother insists that the daughter put an end to its suffering because she has been too engrossed in her book to check that the dog was with her. Reluctantly, considering herself a murderer, the girl batters the dove to death with her sandal. Then, to her surprise, she takes on a "dark knowledge." She learns that she possesses "the will to kill" within herself. She thinks, "I could kill anything now. . . and the words seemed light and easy."

Gordimer has developed this early story in a style reminiscent of Katherine Mansfield's interior monologue in "Miss Brill." The image of the dove becomes a symbol of the daughter's lost innocence, or what Mansfield would have called "the state of the soul." Approaching what Willa Cather described as "the major forces of life through comparatively trivial incidents," Gordimer has given us a poignant rite of passage.

Questions for Discussion

1. How does Gordimer's choice of a dove seem appropriate in the story? Would the symbolic interpretation be different if the author had chosen another kind of bird — for example, a sparrow or a hawk?
2. Why is it ironic that the family dog is the only character with a name ("Micky") in this story? What does it suggest about the family?
3. What is the importance of the South African setting to this story?
4. Why does the mother insist that her daughter kill the wounded bird? What is the mother trying to teach her daughter?
5. How does the ending of the story continue to develop its theme?
6. Why is the title of the story ironic?

Topics for Writing

1. Analyze the symbolism of the sun as Gordimer uses it in the story.
2. Explain the significance of the literary references in this story to Carroll's *Through the Looking-Glass* and Petrarch's "Laura in Death."
3. **CONNECTIONS** Compare and contrast Gordimer's "The Kindest Thing to Do" with Isaac Babel's "My First Goose" or Katherine Mansfield's "Miss Brill."

Suggested Readings

Clayton, Cherry, ed. *Women and Writing in South Africa: A Critical Anthology.* Marshalltown: Heinemann Southern Africa. 1989, 183ff.

Cooke, J. "African Landscapes: The World of Nadine Gordimer." *World Literature Today* 52 (1978): 533–38.

Eckstein, B. "Pleasure and Joy: Political Activism in Nadine Gordimer's Short Stories." *World Literature Today* 59 (1985): 343–46.

Gordimer, Nadine. *Jump and Other Stories*. New York: Farrar, 1991.

Gray, S. "Interview with Nadine Gordimer." *Contemporary Literature* 22 (1981): 263–71.

Heywood, Christopher. *Nadine Gordimer*. Windsor, Ontario: Profile, 1983.

Hurwitt, J. "The Art of Fiction: Nadine Gordimer." *Paris Review* 25 (1983): 83–127.

Jacobs, J. U. "Living Space and Narrative Space in Nadine Gordimer's 'Something Out There.'" *English in Africa* 14(2) (Oct. 1987): 31–43.

Lazar, Karen. "Feminism as 'Piffling'? Ambiguities in Some of Nadine Gordimer's Short Stories." *Current Writing* 2(1) (Oct. 1990): 101–16.

Mazurek, Raymond A. "Nadine Gordimer's 'Something Out There' and Ndebele's 'Fools' and Other Stories: The Politics of Literary Form." *Studies in Short Fiction* 26(1) (Winter 1989): 71–79.

Newman, Judie. *Nadine Gordimer*. New York: Routledge, 1988.

Ross, Robert L., ed. *International Literature on Major Writers*. New York: Garland, 1991. 762ff.

Smith, Rowland, ed. *Critical Essays on Nadine Gordimer*. Boston: G. K. Hall, 1990.

Smyer, R. I. "Africa in the Fiction of Nadine Gordimer." *Ariel* 16 (1985): 15–29.

Trump, Martin. "The Short Fiction of Nadine Gordimer." *Research in African Literature* 17.3 (Fall 1968): 341–69.

Nathaniel Hawthorne

The Hollow of the Three Hills (p. 264)

This story may serve to illustrate what Hawthorne called his "inveterate love of allegory." At first reading some students will suppose it to be a realistic story about a séance carried out during the hour of sunset in a deserted quarry by an "old withered woman" for a desperate younger woman described by Hawthorne merely as "the lady." Other students who read more carefully will suspect that Hawthorne had more in mind than a vivid description of the old woman's incantations and her supplicant's subsequent hallucinations of the sounds of her parents' grief, her husband's despair, and her dead child's funeral. Theme is Hawthorne's concern in this didactic story.

The opening paragraph with its romantic description of the deserted land-scape is like a stage backdrop for the allegory. In due course it will be followed by three more long paragraphs describing the ruined lives of the lady's parents, husband, and child, — the consequences of her breaking what the husband describes as "her holiest vows." She has broken God's commandments — she has not honored her parents, nor has she been faithful to her marriage vows or devoted her life to her child. Hawthorne shows us the results of her "unnatural" actions — dishonor, remorse, and death.

Questions for Discussion

1. What is the plot of this story?

2. Is Hawthorne being ironic when he calls the younger woman "the lady"? How would you define a "lady"? Judging from this tale, what is Hawthorne's definition of the word? In what way is the fictional character still a "lady," despite the way she has lived her life? Do you think the manner of her death is honorable or dishonorable?

3. Why doesn't Hawthorne describe the appearance of the lady? Why does the old woman insist that the younger woman kneel and then draw her cloak over the younger woman's face?

4. What moral lesson is Hawthorne attempting to teach the reader in this story?

5. In "Young Goodman Brown" Hawthorne dramatized the consequences of a Faustian pact made between the Devil and Goodman Brown. In "The Hollow of the Three Hills" a similar bargain is struck between the old woman (witch) and the lady — the protagonists gain supernatural knowledge at the cost of their souls. What are some important differences between the two stories? What do these differences suggest about Hawthorne's view of the basic psychological natures of men and women?

Topics for Writing

1. **CONNECTIONS** Compare and contrast "Young Goodman Brown" and "The Hollow of the Three Hills" in their presentation of male and female protagonists.

2. **CONNECTIONS** Discuss how Hawthorne and Poe each use their description of the settings to foreshadow the deaths of the lady in "The Hollow of the Three Hills" and of Fortunato in "The Cask of Amontillado."

3. **CONNECTIONS** Compare and contrast "The Hollow of the Three Hills" with the lyrics to the Eagles' song "Hotel California."

4. In his review of Hawthorne's short fiction, Poe singled out "The Hollow of the Three Hills" for particular praise:

> *The Hollow of the Three Hills* we would quote in full, had we space; — not as evincing higher talent than any of the other pieces, but as affording an excellent example of the author's peculiar ability. The subject is commonplace. A witch subjects the Distant and the Past to the view of a mourner. It has been the fashion to describe, in such cases, a mirror in which the images of the absent appear; or a cloud of smoke is made to arise, and thence the figures are gradually unfolded. Mr. Hawthorne has wonderfully heightened his effect by making the ear, in place of the eye, the medium by which the fantasy is conveyed. The head of the mourner is enveloped in the cloak of the witch, and within its magic folds there arise sounds which have an all-sufficient intelligence. Throughout this article also, the artist is conspicuous — not more in positive than in negative merits. Not only is all done that should be done, but (what perhaps is an end with more difficulty attained) there is nothing done which should not be. Every word *tells*, and there is not a word which does *not* tell.

Analyze Hawthorne's use of sound, rather than visual, imagery in the story.

Related Commentaries

Edgar Allan Poe, The Importance of the Single Effect in a Prose Tale, p. 787.

Suggested Readings

See page 56 of this manual.

NATHANIEL HAWTHORNE

Young Goodman Brown (p. 268)

Teaching "Young Goodman Brown," you should encourage students to read the Appendix, "Writing about Literature" (p. 2081), which has student essays developing different ideas about Hawthorne's short story.

Students often need help recognizing stories that are not intended to be read as realistic narrative. Some readers tend to take every word in the story literally; Hawthorne, however, meant "Young Goodman Brown" to be a moral allegory, not a realistic story. While most students will be able to recognize the use of symbolism, you might have to introduce them to the idea of allegory, in which the entire story is an extended metaphor representing one thing in the guise of another.

An allegory is a story that has a dual meaning — one in the events, characters, and setting, and the other in the ideas they are intended to convey. At first, "Young Goodman Brown" holds our interest on the level of the surface narrative. But the story also has a second meaning, which must be read beneath, and concurrent with, the surface narrative. This second meaning is not to be confused with the theme of the story — all stories have themes, but not all stories are allegories. In an allegory, the characters are usually personifications of abstract qualities (faith) and the setting is representative of the relations among the abstractions (Goodman Brown takes leave of his "Faith" at the beginning of the story).

A story is an allegory only if the characters, events, and setting are presented in a logical pattern so that they represent meanings independent of the action described in the surface story. Most writers of allegorical fiction are moralists. In this moral allegory, Hawthorne is suggesting the ethical principle that should govern human life. The *unpardonable sin* for Hawthorne is a "want of love and reverence for the Human Soul" and is typified by the person who searches the depths of the heart with "a cold philosophical curiosity." The result is a separation of the intellect from the heart, which is fatal in relationships among human beings, as shown in what happens to Goodman Brown when he returns to Salem village at the end of the story.

Questions for Discussion

1. When is a careful reader first aware that Hawthorne intends this story to be read as a moral allegory?
2. One of the characters in a Hawthorne story says, "You know that I can never separate the idea from the symbol in which it manifests itself." Hawthorne's flat characters — such as Deacon Gookin, Goody Cloyse, and the minister — represent social institutions. Why does Hawthorne include them in the story?
3. On page 269 Hawthorne writes, "But the only thing about him that could be fixed upon as remarkable was his staff, which bore the likeness of a great black snake, so curiously wrought that it might almost be seen to twist and

wriggle itself like a living serpent. This, of course, must have been an ocular deception, assisted by the uncertain light." What is the assertion contained in the first sentence? What effect do the words "might almost" have on that assertion? Why does Hawthorne immediately qualify the first sentence in the second? On page 274, Hawthorne writes: "Either the sudden gleams of light flashing over the obscure field bedazzled Goodman Brown, or he recognized a score of the church members of Salem village famous for their especial sanctity." Discuss the function of this sentence and find others like it throughout the story. What is their cumulative effect?

4. Why is it important that most of the action in this story takes place in the forest? Looking through Hawthorne's story, isolate the particular words that are associated with the woods. Consider the paragraph on page 273 that begins "And, maddened with despair." List the characteristics of forests that are responsible for this long literary tradition. Consider, too, whether the idea of wilderness remains static throughout history. In the late nineteenth century, with industrialization such a potent force, would people have conceived of the forest in the same way the early settlers did? Why or why not?

5. Where does this story take place (besides in the forest)? On page 269 a man addresses the protagonist saying, "You are late, Goodman Brown. . . . The clock of the Old South was striking as I came through Boston, and that is full fifteen minutes agone." What does this detail — that the traveler was in Boston fifteen minutes ago — mean to our interpretation of the story?

6. On page 275, "the dark figure" welcomes his listeners to "the communion of your race." What is usually meant by the word "communion"? How is it meant here? What does the speaker mean by the phrase in which he uses it? What kinds of powers does the "sable form" promise the crowd? Discuss the kinds of knowledge that will henceforth be accessible to his listeners' senses. Who is speaking in this passage on page 276: "Herein did the shape of evil dip his hand and prepare to lay the mark of baptism upon their foreheads, that they might be partakers of the mystery of sin, more conscious of the secret guilt of others, both in deed and thought, than they could now be of their own"? How does this sentence guide your judgment of young Goodman Brown in the closing paragraph of the story? How does the sable figure's sermon comment on the closing paragraph?

7. How much time does this story cover? Where do the first seven paragraphs take place? How many paragraphs are set in the forest? What do the final three paragraphs address? What might be some reasons for the story to be built this way?

Topic for Writing

1. Show how knowledge of seventeenth-century New England history and Puritan theology can enhance a reading of the story.

Related Commentaries

Herman Melville, Blackness in Hawthorne's "Young Goodman Brown," p. 768.
Edgar Allan Poe, The Importance of the Single Effect in a Prose Tale, p. 787.

Suggested Readings

Arvin, Newton. *Hawthorne.* Russell and Russell, 1961.

Bloom, Harold. *Nathaniel Hawthorne.* New York: Chelsea House, 1990.

Cowley, Malcolm, ed. *Portable Hawthorne.* New York: Penguin, 1977.

Crowley, J. Donald, ed. *Centenary Edition of the Works of Nathaniel Hawthorne.* Columbus: Ohio State UP, 1974. Vol. IX, *Twice-Told Tales;* Vol. X, *Mosses from an Old Manse;* Vol. XI, *The Snow Image and Uncollected Tales.*

Ferguson, J. M., Jr. "Hawthorne's 'Young Goodman Brown.' " *Explicator* 28 (1969): Item 32.

Fetterley, Judith. *The Resisting Reader.* Bloomington: Indiana UP, 1978.

Gallagher, Edward J. "The Concluding Paragraph of 'Young Goodman Brown.' " *Studies in Short Fiction* 12 (1975): 29–30.

McIntosh, James, ed. *Nathaniel Hawthorne's Tales.* New York: Norton, 1987.

Newman, Lea Bertani. *A Reader's Guide to the Short Stories of Nathaniel Hawthorne.* Boston: G. K. Hall, 1979.

Robinson, E. Arthur. "The Vision of Goodman Brown: A Source and Interpretation." *American Literature* 35 (1963): 218–25.

Von Frank, Albert J., ed. *Critical Essays on Hawthorne's Short Stories.* Boston: G. K. Hall, 1991.

Whelan, Robert E. "Hawthorne Interprets 'Young Goodman Brown.' " *Emerson Society Quarterly* 62 (1971): 3–6.

BESSIE HEAD

Looking for a Rain God (p. 277)

Bessie Head's narrative about the tragic effects of drought on an African farm family suggests the desperation of human beings living in extreme poverty. We are told that the story occurs in 1965, but it could have happened at any time after the white settlers' religion and law had been established in Botswana (formerly Rhodesia).

The narrative tone of "Looking for a Rain God" resembles the seriousness of J. C. C. Nachtigal's transcription of "Peter Klaus the Goatherd," another literary tale based on an oral tradition of storytelling (see text p. 3). Closer to our own time, Head's narrative does not contain a miracle. If anything, that is the point of her story.

Questions for Discussion

1. How does Head organize the plot of her story? Does she primarily tell, or show, as a narrator?
2. Why doesn't Head give more details about the characters in the story?
3. What is the effect of the two little girls' voices engrossed in their game, scolding each other in "an exact imitation of their mother"?
4. Why is it so hard for the grandfather to remember the exact ritual for appeasing a rain god?
5. Why doesn't Head describe the ritual killing of the little girls?

Topics for Writing

1. **CONNECTIONS**   Compare and contrast the different themes in "Looking for a Rain God" and Nachtigal's "Peter Klaus the Goatherd."
2. Write a book report on Bessie Head's *The Collector of Treasures and Other Botswana Village Tales* (1977), the volume in which this story appeared.

Suggested Readings

Head, Bessie. *The Collector of Treasures and Other Botswana Village Tales.* London: Heinemann, 1977.

————. *Tales of Tenderness and Power.* Portsmouth, NH: Heinemann International, 1990.

ERNEST HEMINGWAY

Hills Like White Elephants (p. 281)

Hemingway wrote this story in May 1927, while on his honeymoon in the Rhône delta with his second wife, Pauline. According to his biographer Kenneth Lynn, the story was a dramatization of a fantasy he had about his first wife, Hadley: "[I]f only the two of them had not allowed a child to enter their lives they would never have parted." Throughout his biography, Lynn interprets the fiction in terms of Hemingway's relationships. How much this approach sheds light on the fiction each reader must judge.

This story is an early example of a minimalist technique. Characterization and plot are mere suggestions, and it is possible for some young readers to finish the story for the first time with no idea that the couple are discussing an abortion. The setting Hemingway chooses for the couple's conversation is more richly developed. The symbolism of the "two lines of rails" at the station (the choice either to end the pregnancy or have the child); the fields of grain and trees along the Ebro River, which the girl sees on the other side of the station (fertility, a settled life) compared with the barren hills, long and white like white elephants (something considered unlucky, unwanted, and rejected); the bar and the station building (the temporary escape offered by alcohol, the sense of people in transit) — one can interpret these details in perfect harmony with the couple's emotional and physical dilemma.

The man's bullying of the girl drives the story. His ignorance about abortion and his insensitivity to what she is feeling or will have to endure physically ("It's not really anything. It's just to let the air in") are not presented as weakness. They are simply part of his insistence on persuading Jig to do what he wants her to do. The girl is also worthy of discussion. Her vulnerability is idealized, yet she is not stupid. Without the suggestion of her intelligence, there would be no story.

Hemingway regarded "Hills Like White Elephants" as one of his best stories, reserving a prominent place for it in his second collection, *Men Without Women*, published in the fall of 1927. Lynn states that in choosing this title for the book, Hemingway meant to suggest "that the alienation of women from men (as well as vice versa) was one of his themes."

Questions for Discussion

1. In what ways could you categorize this story as a minimalist work?
2. What do we know about the man? About the girl? Why isn't Jig called "a woman" in the story?
3. What is a "white elephant"? How does this expression suit the story?
4. What do you think will happen to this couple after the story ends?
5. Read the story aloud in class, assigning two students the roles of the man and the girl. Is the story as effective read as dialogue as it is on the page as a literary text?

Topic for Writing

1. Rewrite the story in a different setting to discover the importance of the railroad station and the Spanish landscape in "Hills Like White Elephants."

Suggested Reading

Baker, Carlos, ed. *Ernest Hemingway: A Life Story.* New York: Macmillan, 1976.

———. *Ernest Hemingway: Selected Letters 1917–1961.* Scribner, 1981.

Beegel, Susan F., ed. *Hemingway's Neglected Short Fiction: New Perspectives.* Ann Arbor, MI: UMI Research Press, 1989.

Benson, Jackson. *The Short Stories of Ernest Hemingway: Critical Essays.* Durham, NC: Duke UP, 1975.

———., ed. *New Critical Approaches to the Short Stories of Ernest Hemingway.* Durham, NC: Duke UP, 1990.

Brenner, Gerry, and Earl Rovit. *Ernest Hemingway. Rev. ed.* Boston: Twayne, 1990.

Flora, Joseph M. *Ernest Hemingway: A Study of the Short Fiction.* Boston. Twayne, 1989.

Hays, Peter L. *Ernest Hemingway.* New York: Continuum, 1990.

Lynn, Kenneth S. *Hemingway.* New York: Simon, 1987.

Reynolds, Michael S., ed. *Critical Essays on Ernest Hemingway's "In Our Time."* Boston: G. K. Hall, 1983.

ZORA NEALE HURSTON

Sweat (p. 285)

"Sweat" is interesting for the modern reader on many levels. For the student familiar with the regional authors of the previous generation — writers such as Sarah Orne Jewett and Kate Chopin — the style of the story will be familiar. The story is set in a small, isolated community; the central figure is an older woman; and the story is concerned with her personal tragedy. As in most regional stories, the line of the horizon is the boundary of the action. In "Sweat" there is no suggestion that there is a world beyond the limits of the small town and the woman's cabin on a dirt road just on the outskirts. The carefully rendered dialogue is written in the colloquial speech favored by the regionalists, and, as in their work, the descriptions of the house and the dirt roads set the scene with precise detail.

For the student who has read such contemporary black women writers as Alice Walker and Toni Morrison, the theme of the story will also be familiar. Hurston presents the same bitter anger and despair between black men and women in the rural South that Walker and Morrison present later. Hurston is perhaps even more important as a precursor of current openness than she is as a writer who is simply continuing an older, regional literary style.

In reading a story like "Sweat" it is useful to forget Hurston's studies in black folklore, which in fact were done *after* the story was published. At this point in her career she was part of a very sophisticated and socially conscious movement that was attempting to give the black minority in the United States a literary voice. Unlike many of the writers of a generation before who modeled their work on Maupassant, Hurston is much closer to the French realist Émile Zola, whose grim novels of small-town life in the French provinces were widely read in the United States at this time. There is in his work, as in Hurston's, an uncompromising hardness, and he would have approved of Hurston's heroine as she creeps back in the shadows to let her husband die of the rattlesnake bite he had intended for her. It is a description that Alice Walker would appreciate.

Questions for Discussion

1. Why doesn't Delia go to the sheriff when her husband terrorizes her with the snake?
2. Why is it this "other" woman of Sykes's who finally drives Delia to try to do something to save what is left of her life?
3. What will happen to Delia now that her husband is dead?
4. Why didn't people in the community try to help Delia when they learned of her husband's open infidelities?
5. Why does Delia decide to go to a different church?
6. Why is her husband still permitted to take part in church services, even though he is not trying to hide his "sinful ways"?
7. Will there be any investigation into the circumstances of Delia's husband's death?

Topics for Writing

1. **CONNECTIONS** Compare the description of Delia's situation in "Sweat" with Nancy's situation in Faulkner's "That Evening Sun." How do the different authors resolve their plots?
2. Discuss the role of the white families in the small town in making it possible for Delia to eke out her hard living. What could the community have done to make her life better?
3. Discuss the social attitudes that accept Delia's husband's right to brutalize her physically and emotionally.

Related Commentaries

Zora Neale Hurston, What White Publishers Won't Print, p. 758.
Alice Walker, Zora Neale Hurston: A Cautionary Tale and a Partisan View, p. 807.

Suggested Readings

Edwards, Lee R. *Psyche as Hero: Female Heroism and Fictional Form.* Middletown, CT: Wesleyan 1984.
Gates, Henry Louis, ed. *Black Literature and Literary Theory.* New York: Methuen, 1984.
Hemenway, Robert. *Zora Neale Hurston: A Literary Biography.* Urbana: U of Illinois P 1977.

Howard, Lillie P. *Zora Neale Hurston*. Boston: Twayne, 1980.

Hull, Gloria T. *Color, Sex, and Poetry: Three Women Writers of the Harlem Renaissance*. Bloomington: Indiana 1987.

Hurston, Zora Neale. *The Gilded Six-Bits*. Minneapolis: Redpath 1986.

———. *I Love Myself When I Am Laughing . . . and Then Again When I Am Looking Mean and Impressive*. Ed. Alice Walker. Old Westbury, NY: Feminist Press, 1979.

———. *Mules and Men*. Westport, CT: Greenwood 1969.

Lupton, Mary Jane. "Zora Neale Hurston and the Survival of the Female." *Southern Literary Journal* 15.1 (Fall 1982): 45–54.

Washington, Mary Helen, ed. *Invented Lives: Narratives of Black Women, 1860–1960*. Garden City, NY: Anchor 1987.

Yates, Janelle. *Zora Neale Hurston: A Storyteller's Life*. Staten Island, NY: Ward Hill 1991.

WASHINGTON IRVING

Rip Van Winkle (p. 296)

Class discussion of this story could center on a statement found in Chapter 2, "The Elements of Fiction: A Storyteller's Means": You might say that the difference between the treatment of the plot in the two versions [of J. C. C. Nachtigal's "Peter Klaus the Goatherd" and Washington Irving's "Rip Van Winkle"] is that Nachtigal's folktale tends to *summarize* the action, while Irving's short story *develops* it.

One of the ways that Irving developed the tale was to add more details about the protagonist's wife. In "Rip Van Winkle," Dame Winkle henpecks her husband so mercilessly that he runs off to hunt squirrel in the Catskill Mountains in order to avoid her. Feminist readers have criticized Irving for his unflattering portrait of Rip's wife. On further reflection, you can see that Irving paid a substantial price for his humorous tone in the story — including the verbal irony in his portrait of Dame Winkle. It forced him to sacrifice the tragic undertones suggested in Nachtigal's transcription of the folktale.

Questions for Discussion

1. In what ways did Irving rewrite Nachtigal's folktale to make it an American story?
2. Why did Irving begin his tale with the poem by Cartwright (an unidentified poet) and the cumbersome explanation of the origin of the tale in Diedrich Knickerbocker's papers?
3. What different kinds of humor are present in "Rip Van Winkle"?
4. Do you think any less (or any more) of Irving's story after reading "Peter Klaus the Goatherd"? How important is evidence of an author's originality in judging the success or failure of a literary work?
5. Do you think the portrait of Dame Winkle is fair or unfair? How essential is her role in Rip's story?

Topics for Writing

1. **CONNECTIONS** Compare and contrast the plots in "Peter Klaus the Goatherd" and "Rip Van Winkle."

2. Investigate and report on other mythical stories about a human being's encounter with the spirit world.

Related Story

J. C. C. Nachtigal, Peter Klaus the Goatherd, p. 3.

SHIRLEY JACKSON

The Lottery (p. 308)

The interpretive suggestions in the headnote should guide students toward a recognition of the main themes of "The Lottery." The near universality of the ritual sacrifice of year gods and scapegoats in primitive cultures to ensure fertility, the continuation of life, and the purgation of society has been a common assumption since the publication of James G. Frazer's *The Golden Bough*. Jackson does not explore the transmutations of these old ceremonies in the accepted religious practices and psychological mechanisms of modern humanity; rather, she attempts to shock her readers into an awareness of the presence of raw, brutal, and superstitious impulses within us all. A fruitful approach for class discussion might involve exploring how the story achieves its impact. Jackson's comments (included in Chapter 7 on p. 762) provide incontrovertible documentation of the power of "The Lottery" to stir the dark instincts dwelling below the surface of the civilized psyche, perhaps the same regions from which the story emerged fully formed — as Jackson claims — in the mind of the writer. No wonder readers, from the author's agent on, have found "The Lottery" disturbing.

But they have also found it compelling, fascinating, and irresistible, and the reason may have partly to do with Jackson's technical skill. For the inattentive first reader, the natural suspense of any drawing, contest, or lottery provides strong motivation to hurry through to the ending, and when the realization of what is at stake comes, it strikes with redoubled force because of the reader's increased velocity. For the more careful reader, or for the reader already aware of the ending, the subtle foreshadowing — the boys are gathering stones, the box is black, Tessie Hutchinson "clean forgot what day it was" — triggers an uncomfortable double awareness that also urges haste, a haste like that spurs Mr. Summers's final, horrible remark, "All right, folks. . . . Let's finish quickly," and the cries of "Come on" and "Hurry up" by other villagers.

Jackson has succeeded in gaining the reader's vicarious participation in the lottery. Even the backwoods New England quaintness of the setting draws not the kind of condescending laughter that would distance the reader but the warm sentimental indulgence we reserve for the cutest Norman Rockwell illustrations. Little boys are being little boys as they pick up the stones, the villagers are walking clichés, and even Tessie Hutchinson, singled out from the rest by her tardiness, is tardy for the most housewifely of reasons. (How different the story would be if she appeared nervous and flustered, a few moments ahead of, say, a disheveled Steve Adams!) The reader is drawn to sink into this warm bath of comfortable stereotypes, illusions intact. Totally off guard against the possibility that the good hearts of these neighborly folks might beat in time with an ancient and brutal rhythm, that superstitious fears of hunger and death might easily outweigh feelings of friendliness and compassion, the reader may well recoil from any previous fascination and, in an effort to deny involvement, recoil from the story, too. Except that we do not reject it; "The Lottery" continues to exert such power over the imagination of its readers that it clearly must be providing a catharsis for instincts similar to those that move the villagers to pick up stones.

WILLIAM E. SHEIDLEY

Questions for Discussion

1. What associations does the word "lottery" have for you? Are they relevant to the story?
2. Comment on the ending of the first paragraph.
3. On what other occasions might the people of the village gather in the way they do for the lottery? Mr. Summers is in charge of "civic activities." Is the lottery one of these? Explain.
4. Discuss the degree to which the tradition of the lottery has been kept. Why does no one want to make a new box? Why is the whole institution not abandoned?
5. Examine the character of Tessie Hutchinson. She claims that her fate is not *fair*. Is there any reason why she should be singled out? Is she a tragic heroine? Consider her cry, "There's Don and Eva. . . . Make *them* take their chance!"
6. On your first reading, when did you begin to suspect what happens at the end of the story? How soon might it become evident? What are the most important hints?
7. One reason the ending can surprise a reader is that the villagers never speak directly of what they are about. Why not? Are they ashamed? afraid?
8. Comment on the conversation between the Adamses and Old Man Warner. What is the implication of Steve Adams's last appearance in the story?
9. Does the rhyme "Lottery in June, corn be heavy soon" adequately explain the institution of the lottery? What other reasons might people have for such behavior? What is the social function of a scapegoat?
10. After her family has received the black spot, Tessie complains, but Mrs. Delacroix tells her, "Be a good sport, Tessie." Comment on this choice of words.
11. Discuss the reaction of the Hutchinson family. Why does the lottery single out a family first, then a victim?
12. Old Man Warner says, "People ain't the way they used to be." Are they? What does he mean?
13. Why are the people in such a hurry to "finish"?
14. What is the implication of "someone gave little Davy Hutchinson a few pebbles"?

Topics for Writing

1. Discuss Jackson's techniques for building suspense in "The Lottery."
2. Write an essay exploring the usefulness of stereotypes in "The Lottery."
3. Examine the behavior of groups of people with which you are familiar. Can you find actual instances of formal or informal practices similar to the one described in "The Lottery" — even though they may not lead to such a brutal finale? Have you or has anyone you know been made a scapegoat? Write an essay showing how one such case reflects and confirms the implications of Jackson's story.

4. **CONNECTIONS**   Compare and contrast Jackson's "The Lottery" and Bessie Head's "Looking for a Rain God."

Related Commentary

Shirley Jackson, The Morning of June 28, 1948, and "The Lottery," p. 762.

Suggested Reading

Freidman, Lenemaja. *Shirley Jackson.* Boston: Twayne, 1975. 63–67.

SARAH ORNE JEWETT

A White Heron (p. 315)

Jewett portrays Sylvia, whose very name associates her with the woodland, as torn between the natural world in which she is so fully at home and the first stirrings of the "great power" of love in her "woman's heart." Her project of pleasing the young hunter and winning the treasure of his gratitude, in the form of ten dollars, leads her out of her shyness and into the heroic adventure of climbing the great pine tree. As a result of her efforts, Sylvia grows within herself. The reader worries that she may be tempted into betraying the white heron and thus into surrendering something essential to her own integrity, but Sylvia, in her vision from the top of the tree and her face-to-face meeting with the heron, has gained the perspective necessary to hold firm.

Jewett's rich evocation of the landscape and the emotional intensity with which she narrates the climactic action contribute to the story's deeper resonances. If Sylvia recalls the woodland goddess Diana — and similarly guards her chastity — she also resembles those heroes and heroines of myth and folklore who must go to some symbolic world-navel or towering height in quest of wisdom, or who must suffer an initiation that involves mastering their fear of the (sometimes phallic) *other* and reintegrating their identities in order to cope with this fear. Sylvia rejects the destructive gun and mounts the pine tree, "a great main-mast to the voyaging earth," electing the fecund life of a natural world she is still discovering over the destructive promises of the "ornithologist," whose grounds are populated with dead, stuffed birds. While the narrator ends fretting over Sylvia's having consigned herself to loneliness and love-longing, nothing in the story suggests that she would be better off having sold herself for ten dollars and a whistle.

Students may find it easier to approach the story through its autobiographical dimensions. According to Eugene Hillhouse Pool, who builds on F. O. Matthiessen's early study, Jewett remained childlike and single all her life, treasuring the love of her father, who used to take her on long rambles through the countryside when she was a girl. According to Pool, "As Sylvia elects to keep her private and meaningful secret, so is she choosing for Miss Jewett too. . . . She chooses, psychologically, to remain a child, with Sylvia." But if Jewett chose to remain a child, it is a child in terms she met in reading Wordsworth, whom she admired: as one privy to the indwelling spirit of the natural world.

The imagery that surrounds Sylvia is uniformly associated with *mother* nature until she ventures up the tree and meets the heron. Her adventure enables her to reject assertively the young man and the advancing modern world of science and machinery with which he is associated. This is a step forward from her original strategies of withdrawal and concealment. The antinomy, however, is not resolved. The only perfect marriage in the story is between the nesting herons, and Jewett offers no key to a satisfactory union between the world of nature and the civilization that threatens to despoil it.

WILLIAM E. SHEIDLEY

Questions for Discussion

1. Jewett is known as a local colorist. To what extent is the locale of this story its subject? To what extent does the story transcend its specific Maine setting?
2. Discuss the presentation of the cow Sylvia is driving as the story opens. What does her "loud moo by way of explanation" actually explain?
3. Comment on the men, apart from the hunter, mentioned in the story. Is the absence of men from Sylvia's world a significant factor in the story?
4. As a child in town, Sylvia has the reputation of being "afraid of folks." Is she? Does she have reason?
5. Explain Sylvia's reaction when she hears the hunter's whistle. Why does Jewett briefly switch to the present tense here? Does she do so elsewhere?
6. Comment on the omniscient-narrative point of view in this story. How is it controlled? What does the narrative voice contribute?
7. Describe the character and appurtenances of the young hunter, and contrast them with those of Sylvia. How important are his evident gentleness and good intentions?
8. How does Jewett charge the pine tree and Sylvia's climb to the top of it with special meaning? What does Sylvia see up there that she has never seen before?
9. What do Sylvia and the heron have in common?
10. Analyze the last paragraph. What has Sylvia lost? What has she preserved? What has she gained?

Topics for Writing

1. Research elements of folk and fairy tale in "A White Heron."
2. Analyze Sylvia's nighttime excursion as a journey into the self.
3. Examine maternal and sexual imagery in "A White Heron."
4. Consider "A White Heron" as a rejection of modern industrial society.

Suggested Readings

Brenzo, Richard. "Free Heron or Dead Sparrow: Sylvia's Choice in Sarah Orne Jewett's 'A White Heron.' " *Colby Library Quarterly* 14 (1978): 36–41.

Cary, Richard. *Sarah Orne Jewett*. Albany, NY: New Collections UP, 1962.

Donovan, Josephine L. *Sarah Orne Jewett*. New York: Ungar, 1980.

Hovet, Theodore R. "America's 'Lonely Country Child': The Theme of Separation in Sarah Orne Jewett's 'A White Heron.'" *Colby Library Quarterly* 14 (1978): 166–71.

———." 'Once Upon a Time': Sarah Orne Jewett's 'A White Heron' as a Fairy Tale." *Studies in Short Fiction* 15 (1978): 63-68.

Keyworth, Cynthia, et al. *Master Smart Woman: A Portrait of Sarah Orne Jewett*. Belfast, ME: North Country, 1988.

Nagel, Gwen, ed. *Critical Essays on Sarah Orne Jewett.* Boston: G. K. Hall, 1984.

Pool, Eugene Hillhouse. "The Child in Sarah Orne Jewett." *Appreciation of Sarah Orne Jewett.* Ed. Richard Cary. Waterville, ME: Colby College P, 1973. 223–28, esp. 225. Originally published in *Colby Library Quarterly* 7 (1967): 503–09.

Westbrook, Perry D. *Acres of Flint: Sarah Orne Jewett and Her Contemporaries.* Rev. ed. Metuchen, NJ: Scarecrow, 1981.

Charles Johnson

Menagerie, A Child's Fable (p. 323)

Despite the subtitle of "Menagerie" ("A Child's Fable"), Johnson's interest in psychology, philosophy, religion, history, and folk and popular culture contributes such a wealth of references to people, ideas, images, and events in this story that it jumps out of the category of Children's Literature to become a story for adults (or precocious children). Yet Johnson's writing is so clear, steady, and lucid that his references, far from seeming obscure, explain themselves with little fuss or fanfare. Of course a flighty aerobic dance teacher would own a flirtatious little female poodle. Of course a cruel pet shop owner with a heart condition would live alone and fail to show up one fine Monday morning. By the time readers finish "Menagerie," there's a good chance they will have emphathized so closely with the narrator Berkeley, the German shepherd, that they will feel that they are also on his intellectual wavelength: "Not the smartest, but steady."

Children's stories with fabulous talking animals that dramatize a moral are not unusual (Aesop's fables come immediately to mind), but adult stories "peopled" with talking animals instead of human beings are rare indeed. Johnson's irrepressible sense of humor — and his unwavering moral sense — underpin the narrative, but it is his ability to create realistic "human" characters in the bodies of dog, monkey, turtle, fish, rabbit, and Siamese cat that holds our interest.

Take Monkey, for example. We're told right from the start that Berkeley didn't care "a whole lot" for him, and then we're shown his uninhibited wickedness: He is "a comedian always grabbing his groin to get a laugh, throwing feces, or fooling with the other animals." He's the Freudian amoral id in action, doing just as he pleases, totally devoid of any higher instincts of conscience, justice, or gratitude, entirely capable of biting the hand that feeds him. Tortoise, on the other hand, is at the other extreme, so repressed by his dizzying week of freedom after escaping from his cage that "he hadn't spoken in a year."

"Menagerie, A Child's Fable" is included in Johnson's collection of what he calls "tales and conjurations," *The Sorcerer's Apprentice.* (*Webster's Dictionary* defines "conjuration" as the act of conjuring, or practicing magic; the word also has a second meaning, "a solemn appeal.") Johnson uses as an epigraph a quotation from chapter 23 of Herman Melville's *The Confidence Man:* "It is with fiction as with religion; it should present another world, and yet one to which we feel the tie." "Menagerie" presents a fictional world that has such clear ties to our own muddled state of humanity that students should understand the allegory without much explanation. If they need help interpreting the chaos of the last scene, a suggestion that they watch the evening news on television or read the front page of their local newspaper might help to illuminate Johnson's meaning for them.

Questions for Discussion

1. When do you become aware that the story will be narrated solely from the point of view of the animals in the pet shop?
2. What is the larger point Johnson is making when he tells us that Berkeley mistakes the gunfire on television for the real thing?
3. What is the basic conflict in the story?
4. How does Johnson make you sympathetic to some of the animals and hostile to others?
5. Is Monkey right in saying that Berkeley is being a fascist by keeping the animals locked up? In what ways is Monkey smarter than Berkeley? In what ways is Monkey less intelligent?
6. Why is Berkeley unsympathetic to Rabbit's organization of the females into a radical group hostile to the males? What does Berkeley suggest to smooth relations between the sexes? Why does his rational suggestion fall upon deaf ears?
7. Why does Berkeley fret over the idea that "truth was decided in the end by those who could be bloodiest in fang and claw"? How does this idea reflect Darwin's theory of evolution? Does Monkey's use of the store owner's gun challenge nineteenth-century evolutionary theory?
8. Why does Johnson give Tortoise the last grim word in the story?

Topics for Writing

1. Create a story in which animals who think and speak and interact are the only characters.
2. Write an essay in which you discuss the implications of Johnson's fable as a moral allegory.
3. Rewrite "Menagerie" as a comic strip.

Suggested Reading

Johnson, Charles. *The Sorcerer's Apprentice.* New York: Penguin, 1987.

JAMES JOYCE

Araby (p. 331)

The rich texture of imagery and allusion that Joyce weaves into "Araby" may delight the sophisticated reader, but for the classroom instructor it represents a temptation comparable to the one brought to mind by the apple tree in the "wild garden" mentioned in the second paragraph. Students should not be asked to contemplate the story's symbolism until they grasp its plot. To begin class discussion of "Araby" with the question "What happens?" may well be to discover that, for a novice reader, no meaningful action seems to have been completed. When the confusion arising from this sense of anticlimax is compounded by the difficulties presented by the unfamiliarity of florins, bazaars, hallstands, and other things old and Irish, "Araby" may strike students as pointless and unnecessarily obscure.

Once it is seen, however, that the narrator's disappointment at the bazaar resolves the tension built up by his attraction to Mangan's sister and his quest to fetch her a symbol of his love, the many specific contrasts between the sensuous and romantic world of the narrator's imagination and the banal and tawdry world of actual experience become meaningful keys to understanding what has happened. The opposition between fantasy and reality continues throughout: "Her image accompanied me even in places the most hostile to romance." The story's pivotal paragraph ends with the narrator cooling his forehead against the window in one of the empty upper rooms, staring out not really at Mangan's sister but at "the brown-clad figure cast by my imagination." Before this moment, his excited fancy has transformed the "decent" and somewhat dilapidated neighborhood of North Richmond Street into a fitting backdrop for such a tale as one might find in a yellow-leaved romance. Mangan's sister, kissed by lamplight, becomes in his view a work of art like a painting by Rossetti. The narrator's soul luxuriates in a dream of exotic beauty soon to be possessed by means of a journey to Araby: "I imagined that I bore my chalice safely through a throng of foes." But after the protracted visit from the tedious Mrs. Mercer and the even longer delayed return of the narrator's uncle with the necessary coin, the limitations of the romantic imagination begin to emerge. The "chalice" is replaced by a florin, held "tightly in my hand"; the quest is made by "third-class carriage"; and the bazaar itself, its potential visionary qualities defeated by failing illumination, turns out to be an ordinary market populated by ordinary shop girls from no farther east than England. At Araby, what matters is not purity of heart but hard cash.

The pitiful inadequacy of the narrator's two pennies and sixpence to master "the great jars that stood like eastern guards" at the door of the bazaar stall completes his painful disillusionment, but Joyce allows his hero one last Byronic vision of himself "as a creature driven and derided by vanity." When the lights go out in Araby, its delusive magic collapses, and the bazaar becomes as "blind" as North Richmond Street. Well might the narrator's eyes burn, for they have been working hard to create out of intractable materials a much more beautiful illusion than Araby. This imaginative power cannot be entirely vain, however, since in the mind that tells the story it is capable of evoking experiences like those described in the story's third paragraph, against which even the hoped-for transports of Araby would have paled.

WILLIAM E. SHEIDLEY

Questions for Discussion

1. Why does the narrator want to go to the bazaar?
2. Why does he arrive so late?
3. Why doesn't he buy anything for Mangan's sister?
4. Enumerate the activities taking place at Araby. To what extent do they sustain its "magical name"?
5. What had the narrator expected to find at Araby? What was the basis of his expectation?
6. Define the narrator's feelings for Mangan's sister. To what extent is she the cause of those feelings? What, as they say, does he *see* in her?
7. What purpose might Joyce have had in choosing not to mention the object of the narrator's affections until the middle of the third paragraph? Describe the context into which she is introduced. In what ways is she part of the world of North Richmond Street?
8. What is the role of the narrator's uncle in the story? What values and attitudes does he represent? Are they preferable to those of the narrator?

Topics for Writing

1. Make a study of light, vision, and beauty in "Araby."
2. Compare "Araby" and the quest for the Holy Grail.
3. Analyze the function of nonvisual sense imagery in "Araby."
4. Explore Joyce's control of tone in "Araby."
5. On a second reading of the story, keep two lists. In the first record ideas, images, and allusions that suggest contexts remote from the immediate situation, jotting down associations that they bring to mind. In the second list note anything mentioned in the story with which you are unfamiliar. Look some of these items up. Then write an informal paragraph or two showing to what extent tracking Joyce's mind in this fashion helped you to understand and enjoy the story.
6. Using the first three paragraphs of "Araby" as a model, write a recollection of the way you spent your evenings at some memorable period of your childhood. Use specific sensory images to evoke the locale, the activities, and the way you felt at the time.
7. Narrate an experience in which you were disappointed. First show how your erroneous expectations were generated; then describe what you actually encountered in such a way that its contrast with your expectations is clear.

Suggested Readings

See page 71 of this manual.

JAMES JOYCE

The Dead (p. 335)

"The Dead" is an apprehension of mortality. Joyce's carefully detailed scrutiny of the party, with all its apparent vivacity, serves only to reveal the triviality, transience, and emptiness of what passes for life in Dublin. The story involves a series of supersessions. Miss Ivors's friendliness is superseded by rigid politics, and she departs. Her kind of fervor is superseded by the "hospitality" of the dinner table that Gabriel feels so good about and that he celebrates in his speech. That conviviality, however, is exposed as mostly hypocritical, as each person reveals a selfish preoccupation — including Gabriel, who uses his oration to reassure himself after his self-esteem has been wounded by Miss Ivors. The long evening, however, generates in the heart of Gabriel a strong surge of love for Gretta that supersedes his selfishness. It is edged with jealousy and self-contempt, Gabriel's habitual weaknesses; nonetheless, the reader feels for a while that out of the waste of the soiree at least this rejuvenation has been salvaged. But Gabriel is longing for something just as dead as Michael Furey, and Gretta's devastating disclosure of a dead lover's power over her mind brings the "thought-tormented" Gabriel to his final recognition of the predominance of death. Like the monks of Mount Melleray, all people in Ireland, dead or alive — from the aged Aunt Julia on down — seem to be sleeping in their coffins.

While Gabriel's vision is triggered by the revelation of a dead man's sway over the emotions of his wife and of his consequent power to thwart Gabriel's desire, it is supported by the pervasive imagery of snow, chill, and death that comes to fulfillment in the last paragraph. The snow has been falling intermittently throughout the story. Gabriel is blanketed with it when he arrives on the scene, and images of cold and dampness pervade the narration. Last year "Gretta caught a dreadful cold"; Bartell D'Arcy has one this year. The girl in the song he sings holds her death-cold infant in a soaking rain. Not only are the physical descriptions of some characters so vivid that one almost sees the skulls beneath the flesh; even the warm, lively, cheerful elements of the story contribute to the final impression of morbidity. The Misses Morkan are giving what may be their final dance. The alcoholic antics of Mr. Browne and Freddy Malins consist only of ersatz good humor. And Gabriel himself, on whom everyone depends, can barely sustain his nerve and perform his function as master of the revels, keeper of order, and sustainer of life.

In the moribund and sterile world presided over by his three spinster aunts, Gabriel is called upon to play a role not unlike that of a year god at this Christmas season. (The party probably takes place on Epiphany, January 6.) From the outset he is willing, but in three sequential encounters he fails. Each failure strikes a blow at his naïveté, his self-confidence, and his sense of superiority. His first two defeats are followed by accomplishments (handling Freddy, his performance at dinner), but their effect on him is cumulative. Gabriel's cheerful banter with the pale, pale Lily does not suit her, as one who has been hurt in love, and his Christmas gift of a coin can do little to ease her "great bitterness." Afterward, his pretensions to take care of people are subjected to merciless ridicule in the "goloshes" passage. With Miss Ivors, Gabriel is more circumspect than with Lily, but that does not prevent him from being whipsawed between her political hostility and her personal affection. This confusing interaction not only causes Miss Ivors to abandon the company and Gabriel in his speech to reject the entire younger generation of Ireland, but it also sets the stage for Gabriel's ultimate failure with Gretta. Gretta's favorable response to Miss Ivors's plan for a trip to Galway now seems to Gabriel a betrayal, and the association of this trip with Gretta's love for the long-dead Michael compounds the feelings of alienation and self-contempt that Miss Ivors's disapproval fosters in him.

Gabriel's failures and self-doubts should not diminish him unduly in the reader's eyes: Joyce portrays him as aesthetically sensitive, charitable, and loving. The "generous tears" he sheds out of sympathy for Gretta's sorrow may not redeem anyone in a world devoted to death, but they are the distillation of a compassion quite opposite to the self-serving hypocrisy that has passed for friendly conversation at the Misses Morkan's ball. By the end of the story Gabriel no longer feels superior to his compatriots. He recognizes that when Aunt Julia dies his speechifying will be useless. He turns his mind away from the past and toward a future in which, as he feels his old identity fade and dissolve, at least the theoretical possibility of growth and change exists. The ambiguity of Gabriel's much-debated "journey westward" reflects the uncertainty of any future, but Gabriel's readiness to embrace it represents a major step forward from his rejection of Miss Ivors's proposition in favor of recycling of the European continent.

WILLIAM E. SHEIDLEY

Questions for Discussion

1. Contrast the mood of the first paragraph with that of the second. Why does Joyce move from anticipation to rigidity?
2. Why are the Misses Morkan so eager for Gabriel to arrive?

3. What is the basis of Gabriel's error with Lily?
4. Explain Gabriel's hesitation to quote Browning.
5. What does Gabriel's interest in galoshes reveal about him?
6. Comment on the men present at the dance besides Gabriel. Why does Joyce limit his cast so narrowly?
7. Discuss the reception of Mary Jane's "Academy piece."
8. What does Miss Ivors want from Gabriel? Why is he so upset by his conversation with her? Why does she leave early? Figuratively, what does she take with her when she goes?
9. Explain Gabriel's longing to be out in the snow. Is Gabriel "thought-tormented"?
10. Explain the irony of Julia's singing "Arrayed for the Bridal" to Mary Jane's accompaniment. What, in this regard, is the effect of the subsequent conversation?
11. Comment on the relevance of the dinner-table conversation to the themes of the story.
12. Why is Gabriel so cheerful when carving and when proposing his toast? Is he justified? Why does he imagine people standing in the snow before he begins to speak?
13. What is the effect of Joyce's ending the tribute to the Misses Morkan with a glimpse of Freddy conducting the singers with his fork?
14. Comment on Gabriel's anecdote about "the never-to-be-forgotten Johnny." Can it be read as a summation in a minor key of the party now ending? of the life of the Morkan family? of their society?
15. Discuss the scene in which Gabriel watches Gretta listening to D'Arcy. What is Gabriel responding to? What is Gretta responding to? What do they have in common? Trace their moods as they proceed to the hotel.
16. Why is Gabriel so humiliated when he learns that Michael Furey is dead? What other effects does this revelation have on him? Explain what he realizes in the last section of the story.
17. Discuss the final paragraph. What does its poetic beauty contribute to the story? What is our final attitude toward Gabriel?

Topics for Writing

1. Discuss the relationship between Gabriel Conroy and women in general.
2. Would you say "The Dead" is a Christmas story? Why or why not?
3. Comment upon Gabriel Conroy's death wish.
4. Consider Gabriel Conroy as a failed redeemer.
5. Explore habit and hypocrisy in "The Dead."
6. After your first reading of the story, scan it again, marking the following: all references to cold, dampness, and snow; all references to death, illness, or people dead at the time of the story; all references to warmth, light, fire, and the like; all references to youth, young people, children, and the like. Catalog your findings and write a paragraph on the importance of these elements in the story.
7. For a specific occasion, plan and compose an after-dinner speech with several headings like Gabriel's. Then analyze your speech, explaining what you were trying to accomplish for your audience — and for yourself. Compare your intentions with Gabriel's.

Related Commentaries

Richard Ellmann, A Biographical Perspective on Joyce's "The Dead," p. 746.
Frank O'Connor, Style and Form in Joyce's "The Dead," p. 780.

Suggested Readings

Anderson, Chester G. *James Joyce*. New York: Thames and Hudson, 1986.

Attridge, Derek, ed. *The Cambridge Companion to James Joyce*. New York: Cambridge UP, 1990.

Beck, Warren. *Joyce's "Dubliners": Substance, Vision, and Art*. Durham, NC: Duke UP, 1969. 303–60.

Beckett, Samuel, et al. *An Examination of James Joyce*. Brooklyn, NY: Haskell, 1974.

Benstock, Bernard, ed. *Critical Essays on James Joyce*. Boston: G. K. Hall, 1985.

Brugaletta, J. J., and M. H. Hayden. "Motivation for Anguish in Joyce's 'Araby.'" *Studies in Short Fiction* 15 (1978): 11–17.

Cronin, E. J. "James Joyce's Trilogy and Epilogue: 'The Sisters,' 'An Encounter,' 'Araby,' and 'The Dead.'" *Renascence* 31 (1979): 229–48.

Ellmann, Richard. *James Joyce. New and Revised Edition*. New York: Oxford UP, 1982.

Levin, Harry. *James Joyce: A Critical Introduction*. New York: New Directions, 1960.

Loomis, C. C., Jr. "Structure and Sympathy in 'The Dead.'" *Twentieth Century Interpretations of "Dubliners."* Ed. Peter K. Garrett. Englewood Cliffs, NJ: Prentice, 1968. 110–14. Originally published in *PMLA* 75 (1960): 149–51.

Mason, Ellsworth, and Richard Ellmann, eds. *The Critical Writings of James Joyce*. Ithaca, NY: Cornell UP, 1989.

Morrissey, L. J. "Joyce's Narrative Struggles in 'Araby.'" *Modern Fiction Studies* 28 (1982): 45–52.

Riquelme, John P. *Teller and Tale in Joyce's Fiction: Oscillating Perspectives*. Baltimore: Johns Hopkins UP, 1983.

Roberts, R. P. "'Araby' and the Palimpsest of Criticism, or Through a Glass Eye Darkly." *Antioch Review* 26 (1966–67): 469–89.

San Juan, Epifanio, Jr. *James Joyce and the Craft of Fiction: An Interpretation of "Dubliners."* Rutherford, NJ: Fairleigh Dickinson UP, 1972. 209–23.

Scott, Bonnie. *James Joyce*. Atlantic Highlands, NJ: Humanities Press International, 1987.

Stone, H. "'Araby' and the Writings of James Joyce." *Antioch Review* 25 (1965): 375–410.

FRANZ KAFKA

The Metamorphosis (p. 366)

This story admits the broadest range of explications — biographical, psychoanalytical, religious, philosophical. Here is one way it might be read: As the sole supporter of his family after the collapse of his father's business, Gregor Samsa has selflessly devoted himself to serving others. Bringing home "good round coin which he could lay on the table for his amazed and happy family" has given him great satisfaction, and his only ambition has been to send his sister, "who loved music, unlike himself," to study at the Conservatorium. After his metamorphosis, Gregor can no longer justify his existence by serving others. Instead, he must come to terms with himself *as* himself, an alien being whose own nature and needs are perhaps only by a degree more strange to Gregor than those of the human Gregor Samsa would have been, if somehow he had confronted them rather than deferring to the version of himself projected by the supposed needs of his family.

Kafka simultaneously traces Gregor's painful growth to self-willed individuality and the family's liberation from dependence upon him, for the relationship of dependence and exploitation has been crippling to both parties. Gregor learns what food he likes, stakes his sticky claim to the sexually suggestive picture of the woman with the fur muff (which may represent an objectification of his libido), and, no longer "considerate," at last *comes* out, intruding his obscene existence upon the world out of a purely self-assertive desire to enjoy his sister's music and to be united with its beauty. With this act Gregor has become fully himself; his death soon after simply releases him from the misery of his existence.

It is also a final release of the family from dependence and from the shame and incompetence that it entails. As an insect, Gregor becomes quite obviously the embarrassment to the family that they allowed him to be when he was human. Step by step they discover their ability to support themselves — taking jobs, coping with what is now merely the troublesome burden of Gregor, and learning finally the necessity of escaping from the prison that his solicitousness has placed them in. Gregor's battle with his father strangely transmutes the Oedipal conflict. It is triggered by Gregor's becoming a being for whom there is no longer room in the family, just as if he were a youth growing to sexual maturity, but the result is that the father, who has previously been reduced to a state of supine inertia by Gregor's diligent exertions, returns to claim his full manhood as husband and paterfamilias.

Emerging from their apartment, "which Gregor had selected," the family members grow into an independent purposiveness that Gregor himself is never able to attain. The story may be said to end with a second metamorphosis, focused in the image of Grete stretching her young body — almost like a butterfly newly emerged from her cocoon. Gregor, left behind like the caterpillar whose demise releases her, is denied all but a premonitory glimpse of the sexual and reproductive fulfillment for which his sister seems destined.

WILLIAM E. SHEIDLEY

Questions for Discussion

1. Describe the effect of Kafka's matter-of-fact assertion of the bizarre incident with which the story begins. Are you very interested in how it came to pass? How does Kafka keep that from becoming an issue in the story?
2. What are Gregor's concerns in section I? To what degree do they differ from what would matter to him if he had *not* been transformed into an insect?
3. When Gregor is trying to get out of bed, he considers calling for help but then dismisses the idea. Why?
4. What seems most important to the members of Gregor's family as he lies in bed? Is it his health?
5. Describe the reaction of Gregor's parents to their first view of the metamorphosed Gregor. What circumstances in ordinary life might elicit a similar response?
6. Discuss the view from Gregor's window.
7. Trace Gregor's adaptation to his new body. In what ways do the satisfactions of his life as an insect differ from the satisfactions of his life as a traveling salesman?

8. When Gregor's father pushes him back into his room at the end of section I, Kafka calls it "literally a deliverance." Comment on the possible implications of that description.
9. Describe Grete's treatment of Gregor in section II. Is Gregor ill?
10. What are Gregor's hopes for the future? Is there anything wrong with those hopes?
11. For a time, Gregor is ashamed of his condition and tries to hide from everyone. In what way might this be called a step forward for him?
12. Discuss the conflicting feelings Gregor has about the furniture's being taken out of his room. Why does he try to save the picture? What might Kafka's intention be in stressing that it is on this occasion that Grete calls Gregor by his name for the first time since his metamorphosis?
13. "Gregor's broken loose." What does Gregor's father do? Why? Explain the situation that has developed by the end of section II.
14. How does the charwoman relate to Gregor? Why is she the one who presides over his "funeral"?
15. Compare the role of the lodgers in the family with that of Gregor. Have they supplanted him? Why does Gregor's father send them away in the morning?
16. Why does Gregor, who previously did not like music, feel so attracted to his sister's playing? What change has taken place in his attitude toward himself? What might Kafka mean by "the unknown nourishment he craved"?
17. Comment on Grete's use of the neuter pronoun "it" to refer to Gregor.
18. What is the mood of the final passages of the story?

Topics for Writing

1. Write an essay describing how Kafka gains the reader's "willing suspension of disbelief."
2. Consider Gregor Samsa's metamorphosis as a triumph of the self.
3. Analyze Kafka's "The Metamorphosis" as a study of sublimated incest.
4. Consider Kafka's use of apparently symbolic images whose complete meaning seems impossible to state in abstract terms — the apples, the fur muff, or the hospital beyond the window, for example. Write a vignette in which symbolic objects play a role without becoming counters in a paraphrasable allegory. Some examples of symbols: a candle, a cup, the sea, broken glass, ants.
5. **CONNECTIONS** Compare and discuss Tolstoy's "The Death of Ivan Ilych" and Kafka's "The Metamorphosis" as two studies of dying.

Related Commentaries

Jane Smiley, Gregor: My Life as a Bug, p. 798.
John Updike, Kafka and "The Metamorphosis," p. 804.

Suggested Readings

Anderson, Mark. *Reading Kafka*. New York: Schocken, 1990.
Canetti, Elias. *Kafka's Other Trial: Letters to Felice*. New York: Schocken, 1988.
Greenberg, Martin. "Kafka's 'Metamorphosis' and Modern Spirituality." *Tri-Quarterly* 6 (1966): 5–20.
Gross, Ruth V., ed. *Critical Essays on Franz Kafka*. Boston: G. K. Hall, 1990.
Kafka, Franz. *The Diaries of Franz Kafka*. New York: Schocken, 1988.
———. *The Metamorphosis*. Trans. and ed. Stanley Corngold. New York: Bantam, 1972. (Contains notes, documents, and ten critical essays.)

Levi, Primo. "Translating Kafka." In *The Mirror Maker*. New York: Schocken, 1989.

Moss, Leonard. "A Key to the Door Image in 'The Metamorphosis.'" *Modern Fiction Studies* 17 (1971): 37–42.

Nabokov, Vladimir. *Lectures on Literature*. New York: Harcourt, 1980. 250–83.

Pascal, Roy. *Kafka's Narrators: A Study of His Stories and Sketches*. New York: Cambridge UP, 1984.

Pawel, Ernst. *The Nightmare of Reason: A Life of Franz Kafka*. New York: Farrar, 1984.

Spann, Meno. *Franz Kafka*. Boston: Twayne, 1976.

Tauber, Herbert. *Franz Kafka: An Interpretation of His Works*. Brooklyn, NY: Haskell, 1969.

Taylor, Alexander. "The Waking: The Theme of Kafka's 'Metamorphosis.'" *Studies in Short Fiction* 2 (1965): 337–42.

Wolkenfeld, Suzanne. "Christian Symbolism in Kafka's 'The Metamorphosis.'" *Studies in Short Fiction* 10 (1973): 205–7.

JAMAICA KINCAID

Girl (p. 400)

Kincaid's one-paragraph story is a dialogue between a mother and a daughter, consisting mostly of the mother's litany of advice about how to act in a ladylike manner. Students might enjoy reading it aloud. The West Indian prose rhythms are subtly beautiful, and the humor of the mother's advice is revealed in the audible reading process for anyone who has missed it by scanning too quickly. The conflict between the girl and her mother is evident in the mother's fears that her daughter will grow up to be a "slut." Everything the mother says is twisted in light of that fear. The daughter wonders, *"But what if the baker won't let me feel the bread?"* And the mother replies, "You mean to say that after all you are really going to be the kind of woman who the baker won't let near the bread?" The following speech rhythm is reminiscent of James Joyce's interior monologues. In fact, we are not amiss to ask whether the mother is actually speaking to her daughter in the story, or whether the daughter has internalized her mother's voice and written it down for us to read to the accompaniment of our own laughter.

Questions for Discussion

1. What are the major subjects in this litany of advice? What kind of life do they describe?

2. The title of the story is "Girl," yet the girl seems to have only two lines of her own — one a protest and the other a question. Why might the author have decided to call the story "Girl" rather than "Mother" or "Woman" or "Advice" or "Memory"?

3. Identify and discuss Kincaid's use of humor in "Girl." What contribution does it make to the story?

4. What is the effect of fairly precise household rules alternating with comments such as "on Sundays try to walk like a lady and not like the slut you are so bent on becoming"? String together the lines that admonish the potential slut. What do we think of the mother? What connection is there between the subjects the mother is speaking of and the idea of a slut? Why does it keep popping up from the most innocuous of items? What does this

refrain make us think of the daughter? Is the "slut" refrain a joke or is the author making a suggestion about the construction of self?

5. Some of the advice seems like it could never have been spoken, only inferred: "this is how you smile to someone you don't like too much; this is how you smile to someone you don't like at all; this is how you smile to someone you like completely." Throughout the whole piece, do you think the mother is speaking to her daughter? What other possibilities could underlie the story's composition?

6. Toward the end of the paragraph the kind of advice changes: "this is how to make a good medicine to throw away a child before it even becomes a child," says the mother. Surely she's not speaking to a young girl here. In the final line, the mother calls her a "woman," the only direct address in the story; earlier the listener has been addressed as a potential slut and been told she's "not a boy." What's the difference between the advice that precedes and follows the reference to aborting a child? Which is more concrete? More abstract? Why does the advice change because of the listener's age? What kinds of knowledge is her mother able to offer?

Topics for Writing

1. Analyze Kincaid's use of humor to indicate conflict in "Girl."
2. Expand the story through the use of descriptive prose. Is the result more or less effective than Kincaid's original?
3. Write a short story in which you use only dialogue.

Suggested Reading

Kincaid, Jamaica. *At the Bottom of the River.* New York: Vintage, 1985.
———. Interview. *New York Times Book Review* 7 Apr. 1985: 6+.

D. H. LAWRENCE

The Rocking-Horse Winner (p. 402)

Lawrence's masterful technical control wins the reader's assent to the fantastic premise on which the story is built; without that assent, the thematic statement the story propounds would lack cogency. Rather than confronting us boldly with his improbable donnée, as Kafka does in "The Metamorphosis," Lawrence edges up to it. The whispering voices in the house that drive Paul to his furious rocking begin as a thought in the mother's mind and then become a figure of speech that crystallizes imperceptibly into a literal fact — or rather, into an auditory hallucination heard by the children that expresses their perception of their mother's unquenchable need for funds. Paul's ability to pick a winner by riding his rocking horse to where he is lucky requires even more circumspect handling. Like the family members, we learn about it after the fact, putting together bits of information to explain a set of peculiar but at first not at all implausible circumstances — Paul's claim ("Well, I got there!"), his familiarity with race horses, Bassett's reluctance "to give him away" to Oscar, Paul's giving Oscar a tip on a long shot that comes in a winner, and only then, with Oscar's skepticism always preempting that of the reader, the revelation of how much he has won. It is not until the very end that we, with his astonished mother, actually witness Paul in the act of receiving revelation — just as he slips beyond the world of everyday probability for good and into the uncharted supernatural realm from whence his "luck" seems to emanate.

Although no explanation, supernatural or otherwise, is necessary to account for good fortune at the race track, Lawrence persuades the reader that Paul's success is caused by his exertions and therefore has a moral meaning. In Paul's household the lack of love is perceived as a lack of money and the lack of money is attributed to a lack of luck. Because luck is by definition something that happens *to* one, to blame one's troubles on luck is to deny responsibility for them and to abandon any effort to overcome them. As the event makes clear, Paul's mother will never be satisfied, no matter how much money falls her way, because no amount of money can fill the emptiness left by the absence of love. The "hard little place" in her heart at the beginning of the story has expanded until, at the end, she feels that her whole heart has "turned actually into a stone." Paul sets out by the force of will to redefine luck as something one can acquire. He places belief before evidence and asserts, "I'm a lucky person. . . . God told me," and then makes good on his promise by riding his rocking horse to where luck comes from. " 'It's as if he had it from heaven,' " Bassett says, "in a secret, religious voice."

In his single-minded devotion to winning money for his mother at the racetrack by riding his rocking horse (which W. D. Snodgrass has likened to masturbation as Lawrence understood it), Paul diverts his spiritual and emotional forces to material aims, and Lawrence symbolically represents the effect of this *materialization* in the process of petrification by which the mother's heart and Paul's blue eyes, which have throughout the story served as an emblem of his obsession, turn to stone. At the end Oscar states the case with epigrammatic precision: Hester's son has been transformed into eighty-odd thousand pounds — a tidy sum, but of course it will not be enough.

WILLIAM E. SHEIDLEY

Questions for Discussion

1. How is Paul's mother portrayed at the outset? Does Lawrence suggest that she is blameworthy? Why or why not?
2. Explain the family's "grinding sense of the shortage of money." Why do the voices get even louder when some money becomes available? What would it take to still the voices?
3. Discuss the implications of Paul's confusing *luck* with *lucre*. How accurate is his mother's definition of luck? What would constitute true good luck for him?
4. Explain Paul's claim to be lucky. In what sense is he justified? In what sense is he very unlucky?
5. What function do Oscar and Bassett play in the story, beyond providing Paul with practical access to the racetrack and the lawyer?
6. "Bassett was serious as a church." Is this a humorous line? Does it suggest anything beyond the comic?
7. What is the effect on the reader of the episode in which Oscar takes Paul to the track and Paul's horse Daffodil wins the race?
8. Explain the mother's response to her birthday gift. What is its effect on Paul? Why?
9. Before the Derby, Paul does not "know" for several races. Can this dry spell be explained? What brings it to an end?

10. Analyze Paul's last words in the story. What does he mean by *"get there"*? Where, in fact, does he go? Is *absolute* certainty possible? How? Why is Paul so proud to proclaim that he is lucky to his mother? Finally, comment on her reaction.

11. Evaluate Oscar's remarks, which end the story. Was Paul a "poor devil"? In what senses?

Topics for Writing

1. Describe the handling of the supernatural in Lawrence's "The Rocking-Horse Winner."
2. Explore the religious theme of "The Rocking-Horse Winner."
3. Consider luck, will, and faith in "The Rocking-Horse Winner."
4. Analyze the realistic elements and the social theme of Lawrence's supernatural tale.
5. Consider luck, lucre, and love in "The Rocking-Horse Winner."
6. Look up a newspaper story about some unexplained phenomenon — perhaps a ghost or a poltergeist — and work it into a narrative whose meaning is finally not dependent on an interest in the supernatural.

Related Commentary

Janice H. Harris, Levels of Meaning in Lawrence's "The Rocking-Horse Winner," p. 754.

Suggested Readings

See page 79 of this manual.

D. H. Lawrence

Odour of Chrysanthemums (p. 413)

Because of its unusual vocabulary and emotional complexity, this can be a difficult story for many students to understand. Before they read it, their attention should be directed to the first paragraph of the headnote, which suggests an approach. Elizabeth Bates, the protagonist, is bitter because she feels trapped in her marriage. She is caught between her attempt to relate to her husband and her struggle to break free from her marital bondage. Her husband drinks away most of the meager wages he earns at the coal mine, leaving her to tend the children in a dark, squalid cottage she calls a "dirty hole, rats and all." She is fiercely protective of their two children — daughter, Annie, and young son, John. There is another baby on the way. Consumed with anger toward her husband, Elizabeth channels her love and tenderness toward her children. She feels herself "absolutely necessary for them. They were her business."

Recognizing the pattern of Lawrence's use of symbolism in the story may be one of the best ways to approach it. In the opening paragraph, Elizabeth's emotional situation is prefigured in the image of the nameless woman forced back into the hedge by the oncoming train. The female-male opposition in the story is symbolized here: marriage and home (the hedge) versus the mine and the pub (the train). A little later on, Lawrence has Elizabeth comment explicitly on the symbolism implied in the title of the story. When her young daughter is charmed to see her mother wearing the chrysanthemums — "You've got a flower in your apron" (pregnancy = flowering), Elizabeth tells her that she's speaking nonsense. To the mother, the flowers are not beautiful anymore. Most emphatically she does not treasure them as a hardy symbol of fertility in her otherwise bleak existence. To her, they are a symbol of death: "It was chrysanthemums when I married him, and chrysanthemums when you were born, and the first time they ever brought him home drunk, he'd got brown chrysanthemums in his button-hole."

Ironically, near the end of the story, when Elizabeth lays out her dead husband on the parlor floor, she smells "a cold, deathly smell of chrysanthemums in the room." One of the miners coming in with the stretcher knocks the vase of flowers to the floor, and she mops up the spilled water. In this action she is a servant of death, "her ultimate master" at the end of the story.

For most of the story, however, her master is her husband. The word "master" is the common name for husband among the village wives, but Elizabeth has refused to submit to her destiny. The line between female and male is clearly drawn in her world, where the sight of twelve children living at home on a miner's salary is not uncommon. But Elizabeth feels herself apart from the other housewives and miners. She judges everyone she comes in contact with, except herself. Then, as she begins to wash the naked body of her dead husband, she feels herself "countermanded. She saw him, how utterly inviolable he lay in himself. She had nothing to do with him. She could not accept it."

The final scene of "Odour of Chrysanthemums," the description of the mother and the wife laying out the body of the dead man, is one of the most unforgettable moments in Lawrence's fiction. The physicality of the dead man is unmistakable, and it affects the two women differently. Now Elizabeth fully accepts the reality of her individuality, her separate existence in the world. Before, she felt herself apart as an emotional defense against her disappointment with her marriage. Now she knows "the utter isolation of the human soul." The husband she hated existed only in her mind. With his death, she is free to ask, "Who am I? What have I been doing? . . . What wrong have I done? . . . There lies the reality, this man." The story ends with her horrified by the distance between her and her husband's corpse. Yet she is at peace.

Questions for Discussion

1. "Odour of Chrysanthemums" is set in the kind of mining village Lawrence grew up in. The first four paragraphs "pan in" on the social world of the story, establishing a relationship among the industrial landscape, wild nature, and human beings. Read the opening carefully, noting the diction of the passage, and try to state Lawrence's vision of the relationship among these elements.

2. Note how Elizabeth Bates appears on the scene merely as "a woman." How does the author go on to establish a closer relationship to her? What is she like when we first meet her? Describe the world she inhabits.

3. When Elizabeth sets out to find Walter, she notes "with faint disapproval the general untidiness" of the Rigleys. Consider the use of dialect in this passage. Who uses it? Can you determine Elizabeth's relationship to her neighbors and her class position? Might it be connected to her general satisfaction with her marriage?

4. In section I the family awaits Walter Bates's return from the mines — and yet his presence seems to haunt the family. What influence does even his absence exert on his wife and children?

5. Elizabeth's mother-in-law arrives, and the two women discuss Walter. How does Lawrence subtly and comically establish their relationship to each other and to Walter?

6. Miners stripped down to work underground; half-naked, white Walter is strangely beautiful as he is brought home. Her husband's body is a revelation to Elizabeth: "And she knew what a stranger he was to her." Try to explain the epiphany Elizabeth undergoes; what does she now understand about her marriage?

7. Lawrence said of literary symbols, "You can't give a symbol a meaning anymore than you can give a cat a 'meaning.' Symbols are organic units of consciousness with a life of their own, and you can never explain them away because their value is dynamic, emotional, belonging to the sense-consciousness of the body and soul, and not simply mental. An allegorical image has a *meaning*" (from an essay that appears in *Dragon of Apocalypse: Selected Literary Criticism*, ed. Anthony Beal [New York: Viking, 1966]). Trace the meaning that chrysanthemums take on in each stage of this story. Is it possible to give them a "full" meaning? According to Lawrence, are the flowers symbolic or allegorical?

8. Given the portrait of the social world in the story and the portrayal of this unhappy marriage, how might the two be related? Is Lawrence explicit about the relationship or might you like to argue with him about the causes of feeling in it?

9. One of the difficulties in understanding "Odour of Chrysanthemums" is its vocabulary. Consult a good dictionary to discover the meanings of words such as "gorse," "coppice," "hips," "spinney," "cleaved," "whimsey," "reedy," "pit-pond," "alders," "tarred," "pit-bank," "headstocks," and "colliery." How does this increase your understanding of Lawrence's story?

Topics for Writing

1. Analyze light and dark imagery in "Odour of Chrysanthemums."
2. Discuss the use of sound and silence in "Odour of Chrysanthemums."
3. **CONNECTIONS** Compare the isolation and alienation of marriage in Lawrence's "Odour of Chrysanthemums" and Steinbeck's "The Chrysanthemums."

Related Commentaries

D. H. Lawrence, Draft Passage from "Odour of Chrysanthemums," p. 765.
Jay Parini, Lawrence's and Steinbeck's "Chrysanthemums," p. 786.

Suggested Readings

Boulton, J. T., ed. *The Letters of D. H. Lawrence.* New York: Cambridge UP, 1989.
Clayton, J. J. "D. H. Lawrence: Psychic Wholeness through Rebirth." *Massachusetts Review* 25 (1984): 200–21.
Harris, Janice. *The Short Fiction of D. H. Lawrence.* New Brunswick, NJ: Rutgers UP, 1984.
Hyde, G. M. *D. H. Lawrence.* New York: St. Martin's, 1990.
Jackson, Dennis, and Felda Jackson, ed. *Critical Essays on D. H. Lawrence.* Boston: G. K. Hall, 1988.

Kalnins, M. "D. H. Lawrence's 'Odour of Chrysanthemums': The Three Endings." *Studies in Short Fiction* 13 (1976): 471–79.

Lawrence, D. H. *The Portable D. H. Lawrence.* New York: Penguin, 1977.

Meyers, Jeffry. *D. H. Lawrence: A Biography.* New York: Knopf, 1990.

Olson, Charles. *D. H . Lawrence and the High Temptation of the Mind.* Santa Barbara, CA: Black Sparrow, 1980.

Rice, Thomas Jackson. *D. H. Lawrence: A Guide to Research.* New York: Garland, 1983.

Rose, S. "Physical Trauma in D. H. Lawrence's Short Fiction." *Contemporary Literature* 16 (1975): 73–83.

Sager, Keith. *D. H. Lawrence: Life into Art.* Athens: U of Georgia P, 1985.

San Juan, E., Jr. "Theme versus Imitation: D. H. Lawrence's 'The Rocking-Horse Winner.'" *D. H. Lawrence Review* 3 (1970): 136–40.

Schneider, Daniel J. *The Consciousness of D. H. Lawrence: An Intellectual Biography.* Lawrence: U of Kansas P, 1986.

———. *D. H. Lawrence: The Artist as Psychologist.* Lawrence: UP of Kansas, 1984.

Shaw, M. "Lawrence and Feminism." *Critical Quarterly* 25 (1983): 23–27.

Snodgrass, W. D. "A Rocking Horse: The Symbol, the Pattern, the Way to Live." In *D. H. Lawrence: A Collection of Critical Essays.* Ed. Mark Spilka. *Twentieth-Century Views.* Englewood Cliffs, NJ: Prentice, 1963. Originally published in *The Hudson Review* 11 (1958).

Squires, Michael, and Keith Cushman. *The Challenge of D. H. Lawrence.* Madison: U of Wisconsin P, 1990.

Widmer, Kingsley. *The Art of Perversity: D. H. Lawrence's Shorter Fictions.* Seattle: U of Washington P, 1962. 92–95, 213.

CLARICE LISPECTOR

The Smallest Woman in the World (p. 427)

Julia Alvarez's commentary on this story in Chapter 7 of the text can provide students with an approach to Lispector's narrative. Another idea that sheds light on Lispector's theme has been provided by the critic Giovanni Pontiero, who recognized that Lispector's characters — like the smallest woman in the world — are "free from psychological conflicts, [so] they show a greater participation in what is real, the greater space that includes all spaces." This is perhaps Little Flower's possession of "the most perfect feeling," her knowledge that "not to be devoured is the secret goal of a whole life."

Questions for Discussion

1. Lispector has framed the beginning and ending of her story by setting it "in the depths of Equatorial Africa," where the French explorer Marcel Pretre has discovered the smallest woman in the world. In the middle of the story, Lispector dramatizes the responses of the "civilized world" to the newspaper reports of Little Flower. How does Lispector keep our interest in the story despite her unconventional organization of her plot?

2. In the fifth paragraph, Lispector refers to "the heart of Africa," which the white explorer has penetrated to find Little Flower. What is Lispector's view of "the heart of Africa" in this story? How does it compare to conventional views of Africa, as in Joseph Conrad's story "Heart of Darkness"?

3. What kinds of humor do you find in "The Smallest Woman in the World"?
4. Why do the people reading about Little Flower in the newspaper react so differently to her? What is Lispector trying to show about our so-called civilized life?
5. How does Lispector shape the conclusion of her story by giving the last word to "one old lady, folding up the newspaper decisively"?

Topics for Writing

1. **CONNECTIONS** Compare and contrast "The Smallest Woman in the World" with Gabriel García Márquez's "A Very Old Man with Enormous Wings" as examples of magical realism.
2. Summarize Julia Alvarez's commentary on Lispector's story (p. 727). How did it help you to understand the story?

Related Commentary

Julia Alvarez, On Lispector's "The Smallest Woman in the World," p. 727.

KATHERINE MANSFIELD

Miss Brill (p. 432)

This is Mansfield's most-often anthologized story, and students in the classroom may have read it in high school surveys of English literature. Some will find Mansfield's tone a trifle arch and mannered, but most will probably suspend their disbelief in her literary approach and can enjoy her poignant, skillful sketch of the lonely spinster on her Sunday outing in the French park.

The setting of the story in the Jardins Publiques is mentioned in the opening sentence, but students may not remember this detail. Mansfield carefully builds her portrait of Miss Brill as the English outsider, carefully registering the nationality of others in the park ("an Englishman and his wife," children dressed as "little French dolls"). Miss Brill lives in France and makes her living as an English teacher; she feels shy "telling her English pupils how she spent her Sunday afternoons." Yet in her isolation, she could be any older person passing the time in a public park, without the solace of family living nearby or the companionship of a pet. Her fur piece is her pet, but it is no more alive than she is to the young lovers sitting at the other end of her park bench. Her active mind suggests that she is a performer on a stage, and she is quite happy to act a minor part. But when the young lovers mock her fur piece, comparing it to a fried fish, she is crushed. Not even her customary frugal treat of a slice of honey-cake has the power to comfort her.

Questions for Discussion

1. Why is Miss Brill's identity as an Englishwoman important in this story?
2. How does Mansfield suggest a first-person narrator in the story, despite her choice of third-person narration?
3. Discuss the brilliant paradox of this story, in which Mansfield brings us into intimate contact with the feelings of her protagonist while dramatizing Miss Brill's isolation from the world.

4. Analyze the escalating progression of incidents in the plot that sustain the drama of Miss Brill's story. What actually occurs, and what does Miss Brill *think* occurs, during her afternoon in the park?
5. Why does Miss Brill find such solace in thinking that she is in a play? Could she have taken some comfort if it had been possible for her to know that she was actually a character in a story by Katherine Mansfield?
6. How much of Miss Brill's feeling of isolation is a factor of her age? What other aspects of her personal situation contribute to her sense of isolation?
7. What do the fur piece and the slice of honey-cake (with and without an almond) symbolize for Miss Brill?

Topics for Writing

1. **CONNECTIONS** Compare and contrast the thoughts and actions of the central characters in "Miss Brill" and the dramatic monologues by Robert Browning ("My Last Duchess," p. 970) and Randall Jarrell ("Next Day," p. 972).
2. Write a sketch in which you present the interior monologue of a character coming to the realization of an important truth about his or her life.

Suggested Readings

Boddy, Gill. *Katherine Mansfield: The Woman and the Writer.* New York: Penguin, 1988.

Fullbrook, Kate. *Katherine Mansfield.* Muskogee: Indiana UP, 1986.

Hanson, Clare, ed. *The Critical Writings of Katherine Mansfield.* New York: St. Martin's, 1987.

Kobler, Jasper F. *Katherine Mansfield: A Study of the Short Fiction.* Boston: Twayne, 1990.

Mansfield, Katherine. *Journal of Katherine Mansfield.* New York: Ecco, 1983.

O'Sullivan, Vincent, and Margaret Scott, eds. *The Collected Letters of Katherine Mansfield.* New York: Oxford UP, 1987.

Rohrberger, Mary H. *The Art of Katherine Mansfield.* Ann Arbor, MI: UMI, 1977.

GUY DE MAUPASSANT

The Necklace (p. 436)

"The Necklace" has long been one of the most popular of Maupassant's stories, and one of the most interesting aspects of the story is this popularity, since artistically it is far from his best. The story is little more than an anecdote. Mme. Loisel, a woman from the lower middle class, is deeply dissatisfied with her station in life. As she sits down to dinner with her husband — a "little clerk at the Ministry of Public Instructions" — she thinks of "dainty dinners, of shining silverware, of tapestry which peopled the walls with ancient personages and with strange birds in the middle of a fairy forest."

Her husband, sensing her unhappiness, gets a ticket for a grand ball, and, when she is miserable at not having a fine dress, he gives her money he has been saving for a gun and a shooting holiday with his friends. When she is still unhappy at not having jewels, he suggests she borrow some from a wealthy friend, Mme.

Forestier. Mme. Loisel borrows what she thinks is a diamond necklace, is a great success at the ball, but loses the necklace on the way home.

Too ashamed to tell the friend what has happened, the couple borrow money to buy a diamond necklace like the one that was lost. They return the necklace and slowly repay the loan. After ten years, during which the wife has become "the woman of impoverished households — strong and hard and rough," she accidentally meets Mme. Forestier and learns that she had lent her only a paste copy of a diamond necklace. Mme. Loisel and her husband have destroyed their lives for nothing.

Unlike in his finest stories, Maupassant here stays on the surface of the characters. Mme. Forestier and Mme. Loisel's husband are only faintly sketched; they seem to exist merely to act out roles. The anecdote itself is so implausible that a single question — why didn't Mme. Forestier notice that a different necklace had been returned to her? why did M. Loisel allow his life to be destroyed without a protest? — would bring it to earth. But most readers are willing to suspend their disbelief.

When we place the story in the time it was written, its themes stand out even more sharply. On its most obvious level this is one of the tales of moral instruction that were so widespread in nineteenth-century popular literature. Mme. Loisel's dreams of clothes and jewels represent the sin of vanity, and someone who has such dreams must be punished. The punishment inflicted on the woman and her husband is memorably out of proportion to their sin, the better to serve as a warning to those reading the story for moral instruction.

A second theme, which may be less obvious to the contemporary reader, is that Mme. Loisel has dreamed of moving to a higher social level. French society was rigidly structured, and Mme. Loisel's ambitions represented a threat, however vague, to the story's privileged audience. They would, of course, want to see her punished for this ambition.

These facts help to explain why the story was so widely read when it was written — but for today's readers other factors seem to be at work. For example, to one young student the necklace became the symbol for everything the world of adults represents. Perhaps it is the story's weaknesses — its implausible simplicities, the lack of definition of its minor characters, the trite obviousness of Mme. Loisel's yearning, and the pious cruelty of her punishment — that make it possible for other generations to give "The Necklace" their own interpretation.

Questions for Discussion

1. Do we use anecdotes like "The Necklace" to point out moral lessons today? What other examples of this kind of moral instruction can you think of in popular literature?
2. How did an evening at a ball offer Mme. Loisel a chance to present herself in a new guise?
3. What do we learn from the story about the structure of French society at the time "The Necklace" was written?
4. What symbols for wealth and station could be used in a story like Maupassant's that was written for today?

Topics for Writing

1. Analyze the symbolic implications of the necklace.
2. Consider the contrast between the lives of Mme. Loisel and her friend Mme. Forestier.

Related Commentary

Kate Chopin, How I Stumbled upon Maupassant, p. 740.

Suggested Readings

Fusco, Richard A. "Maupassant and the Turn of the Century American Short Story." *Dissertation Abstracts International* 51.5 (Nov. 1990): 1612A.
James, Henry. *Tales of Art and Life.* Schenectady, NY: Union College P, 1984.
Lohafer, Susan, ed. *Short Story Theory at a Crossroads.* Baton Rouge: Louisiana State UP, 1989. 276–98.
Los Angeles Public Library Staff. *Index to the Stories of Guy de Maupassant.* Boston: G. K. Hall, 1970.
McCrory, Donald. "Maupassant: Problems of Interpretation." *Modern Languages: Journal of the Modern Language Association* 70.1 (Mar. 1989): 39–43.
Poteau-Tralie, Mary L. "Voices of Authority: The Criminal Obsession in Guy de Maupassant's Short Works." *Dissertation Abstracts International* 52.4 (Oct. 1991): 1353A.
Traill, Nancy Helen. "The Fantastic for the Realist: The Paranormal Fictions of Dickens, Turgenev, and Maupassant." *Dissertation Abstracts International* 50.9 Mar. 1990): 2891A.
Troyat, Henri. *Maupassant.* Paris: Flammarion, 1989.

HERMAN MELVILLE

Bartleby, the Scrivener (p. 443)

Many students have trouble reading this story because they cannot accept what they consider the weirdness of Bartleby's character. On first reading, the story seems to yield this interpretation. Shortly after it appeared in the November and December issues of *Putnam's Monthly Magazine* in 1853, for example, Richard Henry Dana Sr. wrote to Melville's friend Evert Duyckinck saying that he admired the skill involved in creating the character of Bartleby because "the secret power of such an inefficient and harmless creature over his employer, who all the while has a misgiving of it, shows no common insight." Dana's interpretation will probably also be the way 99 percent of present-day college students will respond to the story, sharing his lack of sympathy for Bartleby.

The question is: Did Melville intend the readers of his story to feel this way? Why did he conclude his tale with the lines "Ah, Bartleby! Ah, humanity!"?

Most sympathetic literary critics see this story as Melville's attempt to dramatize the complex question of an individual's obligation to society. Like the dead letters that Bartleby burned in his previous job after they were no longer needed, his life ends when he is no longer useful to his employer. What standards should we use to judge someone's worth? How should we view those who no longer accept the world they are offered?

Questions for Discussion

1. How does the narrator's viewpoint affect your feelings toward Bartleby? What details particularly influence you one way or the other?
2. Do your feelings toward Bartleby change when the narrator reveals Bartleby's previous job in the Dead Letter Office?
3. How does Melville's humorous description of the two other clerks in the law office relieve his heavy presentation of the Wall Street setting? How do these minor characters set off each other, the lawyer, and Bartleby?
4. Do you ever feel like saying "I would prefer not to" in reply to figures of authority? What do you do when you feel a bit of Bartleby in you?

Topics for Writing

1. Explicate the paragraph beginning "For the first time in my life a feeling of overpowering stinging melancholy seized me." A close reading of this passage may bring you closer to realizing the complexity of Melville's portrayal of the lawyer's relationship to Bartleby.
2. Analyze the conclusion of the story. How can Bartleby's life be compared to a dead letter?
3. This story has an unusually prolonged and discursive exposition before the title character is introduced. Also, Melville doesn't motivate his behavior until the end of the story, after he is dead and the lawyer finds out about his previous job. Breaking the customary rules of starting a short story with a brief exposition and motivating the characters as they are introduced, Melville might be accused of writing a poorly structured tale. Argue for or against this accusation, remembering that the short-story genre was in its infancy when Melville wrote "Bartleby, the Scrivener."
4. Read the excerpt from Melville's review of Hawthorne's *Mosses from an Old Manse* (p. 768), discussing what Melville calls "the power of blackness" in Hawthorne's tales. Can you find the same "power of blackness" in Melville's description of Bartleby's situation?

Related Commentary

J. Hillis Miller, A Deconstructive Reading of Melville's "Bartleby, the Scrivener," p. 770.

Suggested Readings

Boswell, Jeanetta. *Herman Melville and the Critics: A Checklist of Criticism.* Metuchen, NJ: Scarecrow, 1981.

Budd, Louis J., and Edwin H. Cady, eds. *On Melville.* Durham, NC: Duke UP, 1988.

Dillingham, W. B. *Melville's Short Fiction, 1853–1856.* Athens: U of Georgia P, 1977.

Fogle, R. H. *Melville's Shorter Tales.* Norman: U of Oklahoma P, 1960.

Freeman, John. *Herman Melville.* Brooklyn, NY: Haskell, 1974.

Higgins, Brian. *Herman Melville: A Reference Guide, 1931–1960.* Boston: G. K. Hall, 1987.

Inge, M. Thomas, ed. *Bartleby the Inscrutable: A Collection of Commentary on Herman Melville's Tale "Bartleby the Scrivener."* Hamden, CT: Shoe String, 1979.

McCall, Dan. *The Silence of Bartleby.* Ithaca, NY: Cornell UP, 1989.

Melville, Herman. *Correspondence.* Evanston, IL: Northwestern UP, 1991.

———. *"Pierre," The Piazza Tales, and Uncollected Prose.* New York: Library of America, 1984.

Vincent, H. P., ed. *"Bartleby the Scrivener": Melville Annual for 1965.* Kent, OH: Kent State UP, 1967. Includes Henry Murray's "Bartleby and I," 3–24.

Whitehead, Fred A. "Melville's 'Bartleby the Scrivener': A Case Study." *New York State Journal of Medicine* 90 (Jan. 1990): 17–22.

LORRIE MOORE

How to Become a Writer (p. 470)

Students reading this humorous story may regard it as a mirror reflecting a "sitcom" version of themselves. It is as familiar as an empty Diet Coke can. The setting of the story is both nonexistent and omnipresent: parents on the verge of divorce, a son in the armed services, a kid sister who's good with little kids. Life swirls around, full of plot action, and what's a crazy girl who wants to become a writer to do? The answer for this affluent family: Advance one painless step — go on to college.

The girl attends college as a child psychology major. Nothing much happens there except a fateful accident: A computer erroneously assigns the girl to a creative writing class instead of "The Ornithological Field Trip" on Tuesdays and Thursdays at 2 P.M. So begins her apprenticeship to her craft, for which she shows more enthusiasm than talent. She apparently never reads short fiction, yet she tries very hard to write it. After graduation, she flirts briefly with the idea of law school before settling for slow starvation at home. Her kind, divorced mother is resigned: "Sure you like to write. Of course. Sure you like to write."

Moore's decision to tell the story in the second person gives her narrative its sense of immediacy. Her sense of humor does the rest, as she carves and serves up her tender victim, a sacrifice to the creative spirit that lives within us all.

Questions for Discussion

1. What is the irony involved in the girl's inability to find good plots for her stories, in the light of her parents' troubled marriage and her brother's military service in Vietnam?
2. Judging from the girl's behavior in her writing classes, does she show any talent? Are creative writing classes in college a good place to find out if one can write?
3. What does Moore gain by organizing her story chronologically?
4. Do you think that the fragments the girl keeps in a folder can be developed into good stories?
5. How does the detail the girl notices about her date at the end of the story suggest that she might have the talent to become a writer after all?

Topic for Writing

1. Moore's story is a gold mine of possibilities for writing other stories. For example, experiment with the point of view of her narrative — rewrite it in the first or the third person. Or develop her fragments into short stories of your own — humorous if possible, tragic if not.

Suggested Reading

Moore, Lorrie. *Self-Help.* New York: Knopf, 1985.

Bharati Mukherjee

A Father (p. 476)

Mukherjee has written a powerful story about the effect of the psychological pressures of assimilation on an immigrant family who have uprooted their life in Bombay to begin again in a Detroit suburb. The three members of the Bhowmick family — father, mother, daughter — have found good jobs and economic security in the United States, but their emotional relationships have floundered and their future together seems grim. Mukherjee is making a complex statement about her characters' situation. This family is so dysfunctional that it is likely they would have been miserable together if they had stayed in India, but their dislocation as immigrants has probably aggravated their situation beyond repair.

A large part of the story's power is that Mukherjee has chosen to narrate it from the point of view of the father, Mr. Bhowmick, an unsympathetic character who is described in the concluding paragraph as beating the stomach of his unwed pregnant daughter, Babli, with a rolling pin in order to abort her test-tube baby. Mukherjee's choice of narrative point of view is handled so skillfully that most readers will be surprised by the ending of the story, yet they will discover on a second reading that the presumably "objective" narration contains a multitude of details about Mr. Bhowmick that foreshadow his action at the end of the story.

In the opening paragraph we are told that Mr. Bhowmick was "a naturally dutiful, cautious man," neutral adjectives that suggest the father's conservatism without giving it negative connotations. He worships at the shrine of the Hindu goddess Kali-Mata, "the patron goddess of his family, the goddess of wrath and vengeance." Most students won't think twice about the implications of Mr. Bhowmick's religion, even after reading that the statue of the goddess, standing in the homemade wooden shrine he has constructed for her in his bedroom, wears "a garland strung together from sinners' chopped off heads." Mukherjee's story contains many examples of irony. For example, Mr. Bhowmick becomes the instrument of Kali-Mata when he acts to abort his daughter's child, whose "chopped-off" head symbolically joins the others on the goddess's garland.

Mukherjee supplies the motivation of Mr. Bhowmick's action when we learn that he has never loved his wife, his partner in a marriage arranged for him in India. We are told that "at twenty-six Mr. Bhowmick had given up on truth, beauty, and poetry and exchanged them for two years at Carnegie Tech" in Pittsburgh, a wedding gift from his father-in-law. Mr. Bhowmick blames his wife for forcing him to leave India to go back to live permanently in the United States. He scorns her and his daughter for their enthusiastic participation in American culture after the family has settled in Detroit — good careers, their own credit cards, shopping malls, K-Mart clothes, women's magazine fashion tips about costume jewelry. Yet Mukherjee presents him as a complex, rounded character, not a caricature or a stereotype: Mr. Bhowmick has made a life for himself in Detroit. He prides himself on being able to adapt to the new land, making "small trade-offs between new-world reasonableness and old-world beliefs." Yet his wife and daughter have adjusted so much better than he: "The women in his family were smarter than him. They were cheerful, outgoing, more American somehow." Mr. Bhowmick is unable to deal with his jealousy of them.

Repressing his anger at his wife and daughter has made Mr. Bhowmick ill. He has "sick-in-the-guts sensations that came over him most mornings" — ailments that drugstore remedies can't soothe. Ironically, his wife serves him a breakfast of French toast guaranteed to aggravate his upset stomach, yet he never reveals his gastric trouble to her, just as he never tells her about his discovery that Babli is pregnant. Living with the example of her parents' conventional but unloving marriage, Babli allows her anger to explode when they are forced to deal with the situation of her pregnancy at the end of the story. "Who needs a man?" she "hisse[s]" at them. "You should be happy — that's what marriage is all about, isn't it? Matching bloodlines, matching horoscopes, matching castes, matching, matching, matching."

Questions for Discussion

1. Mukherjee refers to traditional Hindu religious and social practices (such as arranged marriages) throughout the story. What are these practices, and what do they suggest about Hindu values?
2. Why is the goddess Kali-Mata important to Mr. Bhowmick?
3. Why does Mr. Bhowmick admire his wife "for having the nerve" to give up her traditional religion and become an agnostic, "which as a college boy in backward Bihar he too had claimed"? Why did his values change after his marriage?
4. What was Mrs. Bhowmick's response to Indian culture on her return to Bihar after two years in Pittsburgh to live with her mother-in-law? Why did Mr. Bhowmick refuse to support his wife's behavior?
5. Irony is one of the ways that Mukherjee suggests that her point of view is different from Mr. Bhowmick's perspective. For example, explain the irony in Al Stazniak's question to his Indian neighbor: "Everything okay?"
6. How is Babli's pregnancy her response to her father's values and her feelings of cultural dislocation as a transplant to the United States?
7. What are the feelings between Mrs. Bhowmick and Babli? Are they presented as flat or rounded, static or dynamic characters? In what ways is this mother-daughter relationship sympathetic? In what ways is it an antagonistic relationship? How do the two women exemplify different generational responses to American culture?

Topics for Writing

1. **CONNECTIONS** Compare and contrast the protagonist in "A Father" with the mother Mrs. Chan in David Henry Hwang's short play *As the Crow Flies*.
2. **CONNECTIONS** Compare and contrast the protagonist in "A Father" with the father in another short story you have read this semester (for instance, Kafka's "The Metamorphosis," Grace Paley's "A Conversation with My Father," or Alice Munro's "Walker Brothers Cowboy").
3. Analyze the connection between the role of the goddess Kali-Mata and the description of the daughter, Babli, in Mukherjee's story.
4. Explicate "A Father" to show the conflict between Mr. Bhowmick's adherence to traditional values and his feelings of cultural dislocation in the United States.

ALICE MUNRO

Walker Brothers Cowboy (p. 485)

"Walker Brothers Cowboy" is set during the Depression, and it is the Depression itself that determines and motivates the Tuppertown lives that Munro describes. The father in the story has lost his fox farm, and the family has been forced to move to an unfriendly neighboring town while the father works as a door-to-door salesman of household items manufactured by a company called Walker Brothers.

Munro's story is set in a specific time, and her narrator devotes much of the early part of the story to describing the setting. Details of her mother working on a dress made of the family's old clothes and the description of the encounter with the tramp reinforce the sense of economic hardship, but some of the strongest details are the names of the shops and the description of neighbors sitting out, "men in shirt-sleeves and undershirts and women in aprons — not people we know but if anybody looks ready to nod and say 'Warm night,' my father will nod too and say something the same."

The events of the story are slight. The narrator and her younger brother go with their father as he sells his products. At one of the houses he visits, someone empties a chamber pot on him from a second-story window. Although he laughs about it in front of his children, the father is obviously disturbed. Then he takes the children off his route to visit a woman he knew and loved when he was younger.

The slight events of the story are conveyed with poignant restraint and affection by the narrator, an adult who represents the incidents of that afternoon through the eyes of her younger self. The author's intent is to fix a life at a moment and in a place, and her story brilliantly succeeds.

Questions for Discussion

1. When did the Depression take place, and what was its effect on the lives of people such as those the author portrays?
2. Describe some of the details and incidents of the walk the narrator takes with her father that set the story in its time and place.
3. Why does the father describe himself as a "Walker Brothers Cowboy"?
4. Do men like this father still travel the backroads of the United States selling products like Walker Brothers medicines and household supplies? What has happened to this kind of job?
5. What does Munro tell us of the lives of women like the friend the father takes his children to visit?

Topics for Writing

1. Find another example of writing about the Depression years and compare it with "Walker Brothers Cowboy."
2. Comment on the following passage from the story, which describes the girl's mother and her attitude toward their new life:

    No bathroom with a claw-footed tub and flush toilet is going to comfort her, nor water on tap and sidewalks past the house and milk in bottles, not even the two movie theatres and the Venus Restaurant and Woolworths so marvellous it has live birds singing in its fan-cooled corners and fish as tiny as finger nails, as bright as moons, swimming in its green tanks. My mother does not care.

3. The critic Michiko Kakutani writes that Munro's characters "never completely dispose of their pasts. Unlike so many characters in contemporary fiction, they do not assume that they can continually reinvent themselves, that they can always start over tabula rasa. They tend to stay in touch with ex-lovers, distant family members, childhood friends; they acknowledge, however reluctantly, the ways in which their pasts have shaped their futures." How does this comment apply to "Walker Brothers Cowboy"?

Suggested Readings

Bardolph, Jacqueline, ed. *Short Fiction in the New Literature in English: Proceedings of the Nice Conference of the European Association for the Common Wealth Literature and Language Studies.* Nice: Faculté des Lettres et Sciences Humaines de Nice, 1989. 141–51.

Blodgett, E. D. *Alice Munro.* Boston: Twayne, 1988.

Carrington, Ildiko de Papp. *Controlling the Uncontrollable: The Fiction of Alice Munro.* DeKalb: Northern Illinois UP, 1989.

Hanson, Clare, ed. *Rereading the Short Story.* New York: St. Martin's, 1989. 65–85.

Jansen, Reamy. "Being Lonely: Dimensions of the Short Story." *Crosscurrents* 39.4 (Winter 1989–90): 391–401, 419.

MacKendrick, Louis K., ed. *Probable Fictions: Alice Munro's Narrative Acts.* Downsview, ONT: ECW, 1983.

Martin, W. R. *Alice Munro: Paradox and Parallel.* Edmonton: U of Alberta P, 1987.

Miller, Judith. *The Art of Alice Munro: Saying the Unsayable: Papers from the Waterloo Conference.* Madison: U of Wisconsin P, 1984.

Nischik, Reingard M., ed. *Modes of Narrative: Approaches to American, Canadian, and British Fiction.* Wurzburg: Konigshausen, 1990. 110–18, 141–52.

Rasporich, Beverly J. *Dance of the Sexes: Art and Gender in the Fiction of Alice Munro.* Edmonton: U of Alberta P, 1990.

Stich, K. P., ed. *Reflections: Autobiography and Canadian Literature.* Ottawa: U of Ottawa P, 1988. 176.

JOYCE CAROL OATES

Heat (p. 496)

In Oates's comments on this story, she states that the "formal challenge of 'Heat' was to present a narrative in a seemingly acausal manner, analogous to the playing of a piano sans pedal; as if each paragraph, or chord, were separate from the rest. For how otherwise can we speak of the unspeakable, except through the prism of technique?"

The "unspeakable" — the sex crime involving the murder of the twins Rhea and Rhoda Kunkel by their simpleminded nineteen-year-old neighbor Roger Whipple — is never directly described, but Oates understands that leaving it to readers' imaginations is the most effective way to handle the scene. The tension in Oates's narrative gains intensity from her indirection as a storyteller. Always clear, her voice brings the reader to the edge of the suggested gothic horror depiction — she believes that the gothic genre is "a fairly accurate assessment of modern life" — and then she steps carefully back: "What had been done to them, the lower parts of them, didn't show in the caskets."

Rhea and Rhoda join the other portraits of adolescent girls that Oates has created; as the critic Ellen G. Friedman has recognized, Oates "has perhaps the largest gallery of adolescent girls of any contemporary writer." Their doubling as twins reflects Oates's interest in the themes of twins and the double as developed in the series of thrillers she has written under the pseudonym Rosamond Smith. In "Heat," the doubling of the victims subtly informs the reader that the situation is somehow askew, as suggestive as a portrait from the 1950s by the brilliant American photographer Diane Arbus.

"Heat" is narrated in the first person by one of the twins' schoolmates, about eleven years old, like the twins. Her perspective is limited by her age, but it is similar to the twins, so we learn a good deal about their families and games, including the twins' pleasure in stealing six dollars from their grandmother's purse. The narrative jumps to the future, when the narrator is in the tenth grade, and then to a description of her adultery after her marriage, before returning in the final paragraphs to the twins' murders. Oates's skillful control of the progression of her story highlights the obsessive quality of the narrator's memory, surfacing after all these years in the story: "I wasn't there, but some things you know."

Questions for Discussion

1. What part does the heat of the summer play in the story?
2. Would the story be less effective if it had been about the murder of one girl and not twin sisters? What dimension does Oates add by making the sisters twins?
3. Why did the twins steal six dollars from their grandmother? What did they intend to do with the money?
4. Were the twins likable girls?
5. What is the relationship of the narrator to the twins?
6. How does the incident under the Kunkels' veranda help to foreshadow the murders?
7. What is added to the story by the narrator's description of her adultery years after the murders?
8. Why is the narrator obsessed with the murders?

Topics for Writing

1. In *On Writers and Writing,* John Gardner wrote that in her fiction Oates "avoids analysis in a way that seems intentional, fragmenting the world . . . by a use of close, almost myopic examination followed by startling cuts — to another character, another era — that disorient the reader like the kick of a mule. . . . [She produces] an image of history, personal or public, as a track of machine-gun wounds. Value affirmations are as fleeing as destructions, and often as grotesque." Analyze the narrative structure of "Heat" in relation to Gardner's description.
2. **CONNECTIONS** Compare and contrast "Heat" with Katherine Anne Porter's story "He." (The link between them is suggested by Oates's use of the surname "Whipple," the surname of the family in Porter's story.)

(text pp. 505–517)

Related Story

Katherine Anne Porter, He, p. 601.

Suggested Readings

See page 95 of this manual.

JOYCE CAROL OATES

Where Are You Going, Where Have You Been? (p. 505)

Pointing to Oates's remark that she usually writes "about real people in a real society" should help to keep discussion away from premature allegorization or mythologizing, which — for all its eventual value and interest — smothers the story's impact by diverting attention from its realism. Her further observation that she understands Connie to be "struggling heroically to define personal identity in the face of incredible opposition, even in the face of death itself," may suggest how to go about answering the main question the story poses when considered in naturalistic terms: Why does Connie go out to Arnold Friend?

Connie's life as Oates depicts it takes place in two realms. Within her home and family Connie feels condemned and rejected, and she returns the disapproval. Outside these familiar precincts lies a world defined by movies, the drive-in restaurant, and the ever-present popular music. It is *not* the music of Bob Dylan, as Tom Quirk assures us, but the comparatively mindless, sentimental, and romantic music against which in the early 1960s Dylan stood out in such bold contrast. Connie's idea of the world into which, at the age of fifteen, she is beginning to make her first tentative forays is shaped by these songs and occupied by *boys*: boys who can be snubbed with impunity, boys who merge into one undifferentiated and safe blur in her mind, boys who offer hamburgers and "the caresses of love." And that love is "not the way someone like June would suppose but sweet, gentle, the way it was in movies and promised in songs." To these boys Connie presents herself as undifferentiated *girl*, and she is concerned that she look attractive to them.

The world, however, is occupied not only by frank and tentative boys but also by determined and deceitful men, by evil as well as by innocence, by hypocrisy, perversion, and violence — an exponent of all of which Connie attracts in Arnold Friend. Although in the course of their interview Connie sees through his disguise, the impoverishment of her world provides her no way to resist his advances. Her home offers no refuge, her father does not come when she needs him (he has always been essentially absent anyway), and she is unable to manipulate the telephone because of her panic. Meanwhile, Arnold, who presents himself in the guise of a movie hero, a teenage "boy," and her lover, offers to take charge of her. He places his mark upon her and gives her a role to play in a world of his devising. Because she is cut off from her past and has no idea of a future, she is at his mercy in determining what to do in the present. Like her cultural cousin, Vladimir Nabokov's Lolita, sobbing in Humbert's arms, she simply has nowhere else to go. Not only does Arnold show Connie that she is desired, he also provides her a way to be "good": By going with him she will save her undeserving family from getting hurt. Connie does not so much decide to go out to Arnold as she watches an alien being that Arnold has called into existence in her body respond to his desires. The final ironic horror, of course, is that she will be raped and murdered and buried in the desert not as brown-eyed Connie but as the imaginary "sweet little blue-eyed girl" of Arnold's sick imagination.

Oates acknowledges that her inspiration for the story came in part from reading about an actual case, and Tom Quirk has demonstrated at length the degree to which the circumstances of "Where Are You Going, Where Have You Been?" seem to be derived from an article in *Life* (4 Mar. 1955) by Don Moser entitled (in a reference to some lyrics from a popular song) "The Pied Piper of Tucson." Even some of the most apparently allegorical details, such as Arnold's trouble with his boots, which has been attributed to his having cloven hooves or wolf paws, reflect the facts about Charles Schmid, a wiry gymnast of twenty-three who stuffed things in his boots, wore makeup, and drove around Tucson in a gold car playing the hero to a group of high school kids until he was arrested for the rape and murder of three young girls. Quirk's argument that Oates followed the magazine article's theme in relating this horror in the "golden west" to the emptiness of "the American dream" points out an important dimension of the story, and his emphasis keeps the real horror of the incident in focus.

Gretchen Schulz and R. J. R. Rockwood are aware of the *Life* article, but they focus instead on another acknowledged source of Oates's inspiration, the folktale. Their discussion of the story's allusions to and affinities with "The Pied Piper of Hamelin," "Cinderella," "Little Red Riding Hood," and other tales suggests why "Where Are You Going, Where Have You Been?" is such a disturbing work. Their article offers detailed interpretations of the psychological crises Connie passes through, based on psychoanalytic interpretations of the meaning and developmental function of the analogous tales. (They use Bruno Bettelheim as their chief authority.) But whereas folktales most often smooth the passage of their readers through Oedipal conflicts and reintegration of the childhood identity into the adult by working through to a happy ending, "Where Are You Going, Where Have You Been?" taps these powerful psychic forces in the reader only to pour them out on the sand.

WILLIAM E. SHEIDLEY

Questions for Discussion

1. Define Connie's relationships with her mother, sister, and father. What is missing from this family? Why does Connie wish "her mother was dead and she herself was dead and it was all over"?

2. What are Connie's "two sides"? Is Connie's case unusual for a girl her age in our society? In what ways is she atypical? What about June?

3. The girls enter the drive-in with "faces pleased and expectant as if they were entering a sacred building," and the popular music in the background seems "like music at a church service." Explore the drive-in religion further. What are its creeds, its mysteries? Is it a true religion? a guide to the good life? Does Connie believe in anything else?

4. Discuss the similarities between Eddie, who rotates on a counter stool and offers "something to eat," and the emblem of the drive-in on its bottle-top roof. What else does Eddie offer? Compare Eddie with Arnold Friend as we first see him at the drive-in.

5. What does Oates accomplish by returning briefly to Connie's relationship with her family before narrating what happens "one Sunday"?

6. Discuss Connie's daydreams, in which "all the boys fell back and dissolved into a single face that was not even a face, but an idea, a feeling, mixed up with the urgent insistent pounding of the music," and in which she associates sunbathing with the "sweet, gentle" lovemaking "in movies and promised in song." What is the source of the sexual desire reflected in these dreams? What is its object?

7. Asbestos was formerly used as a nonflammable insulating material. Trace the images of heat and fire associated with it in the story.

8. Compare Connie's gentle breathing as she listens to the "XYZ Sunday Jamboree" with her breath "jerking back and forth in her lungs" when she tries to use the telephone at the climax of the story.

9. Why does Connie whisper "Christ. Christ" when she hears a car coming up the driveway? Does the effort to see Arnold Friend as a Christ figure find further substantiation in the text? Does it yield any meaningful insights?

10. Where does Connie stand during the first part of her conversation with Arnold? Is Oates's blocking of the scene realistic? symbolic?

11. Describe Arnold's car and clothing. What purpose is served by his transparent disguise? Why does it take Connie so long to penetrate the disguise?

12. Does Arnold have supernatural knowledge about Connie, her family, and her friends? Can his apparent clairvoyance about the barbecue be explained in naturalistic terms?

13. Account for Connie's idea that Arnold "had driven up the driveway all right but had come from nowhere before that and belonged nowhere and that everything about him and even the music that was so familiar to her was only half real." Explain why that idea is important to our understanding of what happens to Connie.

14. Why does Connie's kitchen seem "like a place she had never seen before"? How has Arnold succeeded in making Connie feel cut off from her past and unprotected in her home? What is the implication of "the echo of a song from last year" in this context?

15. What is the role of Ellie in Arnold's assault on Connie?

16. Arnold implies that Connie can protect her family from harm by coming with him. How important a factor is this in his winning her over to his will?

17. Examine the passage in which Connie tries to telephone her mother and then collapses in panic and hysteria. Notice its associations with sex and birth. What is taking place in Connie at this moment?

18. Arnold asks rhetorically, "What else is there for a girl like you but to be sweet and pretty and give in?" In what sense is this true?

19. Explain Connie's feeling that she is watching herself go out the door. What has caused this split in her consciousness?

Topics for Writing

1. Discuss Arnold Friend's obvious masquerade, and why it succeeds.

2. Comment on popular music and religion in "Where Are You Going, Where Have You Been?"

3. Read the story once while bearing in mind that it is "based on fact" — something very much like this is known to have actually happened. After finishing the story, write a personal essay giving your reaction. What does this account imply about human nature? About the society reflected in the story?

4. Reread the story with an eye to its allusions to folktales and fairy tales with which you are familiar. Arnold's "coach" has a pumpkin on it; Connie is nearly asleep when he awakens her; he has big teeth; and so forth. What are the tales alluded to about? Is this story a fairy tale, too?

5. Select an item from the news that grips your imagination and ask yourself why it does. Does it have affinities with folktales or myths? Does it suggest disturbing ideas about human nature and society? Write a narrative of the event, perhaps from the point of view of one of the participants, that incorporates these larger implications.

6. **CONNECTIONS** Compare technique and theme in Oates's "Where Are You Going, Where Have You Been?" and Jackson's "The Lottery."

7. **CONNECTIONS** Compare and contrast Arnold Friend and The Misfit in Flannery O'Connor's "A Good Man is Hard to Find."

8. **CONNECTIONS** Study the allusions to religion in the story. How would Flannery O'Connor have handled this material?

Suggested Readings

Bloom, Harold. *Joyce Carol Oates*. New York: Chelsea House, 1981.

Friedman, Ellen G. "Joyce Carol Oates." In *Modern American Women Writers*. Ed. Elaine Showalter. New York: Macmillan, 1991.

Gardner, John. *On Writers and Writing*. Reading, MA: Addison-Wesley, 1994. 75.

Gillis, Christina Marsden. " 'Where Are You Going, Where Have You Been?': Seduction, Space, and a Fictional Mode." *Studies in Short Fiction* 18 (1981): 65–70.

Johnson, Greg. *Understanding Joyce Carol Oates*. Columbia: U of South Carolina P, 1987.

Oates, Joyce Carol. *New Heaven, New Earth*. New York: Vanguard, 1974.

———. *(Woman) Writer: Occasions and Opportunities*. New York: NAL-Dutton, 1989.

Milazzo, Lee. *Conversations with Joyce Carol Oates*. Jackson: UP of Mississippi, 1989.

Pearlman, Mickey, ed. *American Women Writing Fiction: Memory, Identity, Family, Space*. Lexington: U of Kentucky P, 1989. 9–44.

Plimpton, George. *Women Writers at Work: The Paris Review Interviews*. New York: Penguin, 1989.

Quirk, Tom. "A Source for 'Where Are You Going, Where Have You Been?' " *Studies in Short Fiction* 18 (1981): 413–19.

Rozga, Margaret. "Threatening Places, Hiding Places: The Midwest in Selected Stories by Joyce Carol Oates." *Midwestern Miscellany* 18 (1990): 34–44.

Schulz, Gretchen, and R. J. R. Rockwood. "In Fairyland, without a Map: Connie's Exploration Inward in Joyce Carol Oates's 'Where Are You Going, Where Have You Been?' " *Literature and Psychology* 30 (1980): 155–67.

Urbanski, Marie Mitchell Olesen. "Existential Allegory: Joyce Carol Oates's 'Where Are You Going, Where Have You Been?' " *Studies in Short Fiction* 15 (1978): 200–03.

Wegs, Joyce M. " 'Don't You Know Who I Am?': The Grotesque in Oates's 'Where Are You Going, Where Have You Been?' " *Journal of Narrative Technique* 5 (1975): 66–72.

Wesley, Marilyn Clarke. "Transgression and Refusal: The Dynamic of Power in the Domestic Fiction of Joyce Carol Oates." *Dissertation Abstracts International* 49.11 (May 1989): 3365A.

Winslow, Joan D. "The Stranger Within: Two Stories by Oates and Hawthorne." *Studies in Short Fiction* 17 (1980): 263–68.

TIM O'BRIEN

The Things They Carried (p. 518)

In "The Things They Carried," O'Brien has found a brilliant solution to one of the most common problems a writer faces: how to find a new way to approach a subject that has been written about many times before. His subject is men at war, a topic that has occupied writers since remotest antiquity. The earliest epic in the European tradition is Homer's account of the siege of Troy, and the earliest griot narratives from the empires of Africa recount battles fought along the banks of the Niger River.

The Vietnam War has been treated in a stream of stories, books, articles, studies, and debates. O'Brien's innovation is to tell us directly not about the soldiers, or about the meaningless war they find themselves in, but about the things they are carrying on their shoulders and in their pockets. This simple device is startling and effective. The things his "grunts" are carrying are one way to identify them, to bring them to life, and the author also tells us about the things they carry under different circumstances.

This use of the small detail to illuminate the whole picture would not be as effective if it were limited to a simple description of what each of the men is carrying. But as he discusses the items — their use, their importance to the assignment the men are carrying out, and the significance of each thing to each man — O'Brien tells us about the war itself, and the soldiers' attitudes toward what they are doing. By presenting each of these objects as a microcosm of the reality of the war, the author makes the experience more comprehensible. He has found a dimension that shows us the soldiers as human beings, and that is the most important task for a writer who wants to make us face this cruel reality again.

Questions for Discussion

1. What is the effect of O'Brien's use of abbreviations and acronyms: R & R, SOP, M & Ms, USO, Psy Ops, KIA?
2. When the author writes, "Afterward they burned Than Khe," what is he telling us about the attitude of the men toward the people in the villages around them?
3. Why is it important to specify the weight of the equipment each man is carrying?
4. Does the language of the soldiers sound "real"? Do the descriptions of the weapons have the feeling of reality?
5. Why does the lieutenant burn the letters he has been carrying?

Topics for Writing

1. Soldiers from both sides are fighting the war, but the author only tells us about the men from one side. Why doesn't he describe the North Vietnamese soldiers?
2. Discuss the attitudes toward the war in the United States as they are reflected in the attitudes of the soldiers in "The Things They Carried."
3. Stories about men at war usually emphasize heroism and heroic acts; these are completely absent in this story. What has caused this change in attitude?

Suggested Readings

Bonn, Maria S. "A Different World: The Vietnam Veteran Novel Comes Home." In *Fourteen Landing Zones: Approaches to Vietnam War Literature.* Ed. Philip K. Jason. Iowa City: U of Iowa P, 1992.

Calloway, Catherine. "Pluralities of Vision: *Going After Cacciato* and Tim O'Brien's Short Fiction." In *America Rediscovered: Critical Essays on Literature and Film of the Vietnam War.* Ed. Owen W. Gilman, Jr. New York: Garland, 1990.

———. "Tim O'Brien (1946–): A Primary and Secondary Bibliography." *Bulletin of Bibliography* (50.3 Sept. 1993): 223–29.

FLANNERY O'CONNOR

Everything That Rises Must Converge (p. 532)

"Everything That Rises Must Converge" is one of O'Connor's most powerful stories. Although they are emotionally linked as closely as Siamese twins, Julian and his mother are in such fundamental disagreement that only death can bring their souls together, since "everything that rises must converge." O'Connor goes to great lengths to spell out the differences between mother and son. They are so extreme that humor is the one thing that makes them bearable to the sensitive reader. Julian asserts that "true culture is in the mind." His mother says, "It's in the heart." He insists that "nobody in the damn bus cares who you are." She replies, "I care who I am." She always looks on the bright side of things. He glories in scenting out impending disasters. He tells himself he isn't dominated by his mother. She knows he's both financially and emotionally dependent on her, and she gets him to do whatever she asks.

Contrasts and opposites rule this unlikely pair, but the world they inhabit is also in a state of opposition to their sense of themselves. Blacks no longer know their place in the back of the bus; mother and son are exiled from the destroyed family mansion; Julian wants to be a writer after his college education, but he's selling typewriters instead. The only constant is his mother's ridiculous hat. It reappears on the head of the black lady sitting with her little son next to Julian and his mother on the bus. This sight amuses his mother, who hasn't lost her sense of humor, her spirit refusing to be worn down by the remarks and behavior of her critical, hostile son. As a character she is partially redeemed (despite her racial bigotry) by her humor and her fundamental generosity. In contrast, Julian is damned by his sense of pride.

O'Connor makes certain of this damnation by subtly shifting the point of view to Julian's mental outlook during his journey on the bus, when he withdraws "into the inner compartment of his mind where he spent most of his time." He will be alone there, feeling smugly superior to his mother, until he realizes that he has lost her, at which time he will be forced to include her in his emotional state by entering "the world of guilt and sorrow."

Students may enjoy discussing the humor in this story as well as O'Connor's sublime ear for the ridiculous in her characters' speech. "Everything That Rises Must Converge" also lends itself well to different critical perspectives. Because O'Connor wrote from a Christian orientation, the religious implications of the narrative can be traced: the references to Saint Sebastian, or the black mother's threat to her little boy, "Quit yo' foolishness . . . before I knock the living Jesus out of you!" Or O'Connor's quiet comment about "guilt and sorrow" at the end. Students who are budding social historians, psychologists, or feminists can also find abundant material in this story to explore from their orientations.

Questions for Discussion

1. O'Connor writes that Julian's mother's eyes, "sky-blue, were as innocent and untouched by experience as they must have been when she was ten." Again, when she turns her eyes, now a "bruised purple," on Julian, he gets an "uncomfortable sense of her innocence." What are we to make of her innocence? How do we reconcile this attribute with her racism?

2. Julian seems to hate almost everything about his mother. Does she hate anything about her son? Why does he despise her? Why does she love him?

3. The idea of family mansion implies family ties. How do family ties appear in this story? Does the "decayed mansion" mean more to Julian or to his mother? What does it mean to him? to her?

4. What point of view controls "Everything That Rises Must Converge"? At which points in the story do we have the most intimate access to Julian's thoughts?

5. Describe Julian's relationships with people other than his mother. Consider the paragraphs beginning "He began to imagine" and "He imagined his mother." Who would he like to be friends with and why? Does his acknowledgment of his mother's racism imply positive things about Julian's own character?

6. On page 537 we discover that Julian's mother doesn't think Julian knows "a thing about 'life,' that he hadn't even entered the real world" yet. Does the narrator agree with her? Discuss this sentence and the closing sentence of the story together. What does this imply about the characteristics that belong to "real life"?

7. After his mother's stroke, Julian looks "into a face he had never seen before." What is different about her face now? What metaphor is O'Connor sustaining behind the description of the literal differences brought on by neurological devastation?

8. O'Connor, a devout Catholic, said her stories were meant to be more like parables than true to life. What elements of this story are Christian? Is the preoccupation central to this story available only to Christians?

Topics for Writing

1. Compare and contrast the two mothers and the two sons in the story.
2. Analyze the symbolism of the hat at the convergence of two apparent opposites — the two mothers.
3. Discuss the role of pride and the response to charity in Julian and the black mother.
4. Write an examination of the changing social order between the generations of Julian's mother and Julian.
5. Explore the role of irony in "Everything That Rises Must Converge."

Related Commentaries

Wayne C. Booth, A Rhetorical Reading of O'Connor's "Everything That Rises Must Converge," p. 867.

Robert H. Brinkmeyer, Jr., Flannery O'Connor and Her Readers, p. 859.
Flannery O'Connor, From Letters 1954–1955, p. 847.
Flannery O'Connor, Writing Short Stories, p. 849.
V. S. Pritchett, Flannery O'Connor: Satan Comes to Georgia, p. 857.

Suggested Readings

See page 103 of this manual

FLANNERY O'CONNOR

Good Country People (p. 543)

In the world of Flannery O'Connor's fiction, characters are seldom who we think they are or even who they think they are. "Good Country People" provides an intriguing twist on the archetypal theme: Events and people are seldom as simple as they seem.

O'Connor revels in the idiosyncrasies of personality, peopling this story with three strong characters in Joy (Hulga), Mrs. Hopewell, and Manley Pointer, as well as an interesting subsidiary character, Mrs. Freeman, with her "special fondness for the details of secret infections, hidden deformities," and "assaults upon children." O'Connor's choice of names figures prominently. Joy changes her name to Hulga to symbolize her sense of her own ugliness. Mrs. Hopewell continually hopes well of things, blathering a stream of banal platitudes that reveal her own lack of depth. The name Manley Pointer strikes the reader as almost humorously phallic and predatory-sounding, given the surprising turn of events in the storage barn.

We don't see how "right" the details of this story are until we reach its sardonic conclusion, Pointer going Hulga's intellectual atheism one better, disappearing with her leg in his "Bible" valise, Mrs. Hopewell in her ignorance commenting on "that nice dull young man." Looking back, we see the clever meticulousness of Pointer's con — the feigned heaviness of his satchel, his feigned simplicity (as in mistaking the name of the house for its owner), the rube suit. It turns out that this specimen of "good country people" reads people better than the highly educated Hulga or the self-aggrandizing Mrs. Hopewell.

The experience of losing her artificial limb to the perverted Manley Pointer is the loss of a certain kind of virginity for Hulga, and however harrowing the experience, we sense that it will be a valuable one. Prior to her victimization, we feel mainly revulsion for Joy/Hulga. We sympathize with her hunting accident, but O'Connor highlights the unpleasant abrasiveness of her personality; clearly Hulga's psyche, as well as her body, has been damaged. Hulga's low self-esteem is exacerbated by her mother's implications of Hulga's abnormality, which focus on her intellectualism as much as on her disfigurement. For all Mrs. Hopewell's assertions that "it takes all kinds to make the world go 'round," she resents her daughter's interest in philosophy (female education is for a "good time") as well as Hulga's individuation: "It seemed to Mrs. Hopewell that every year she grew less like other people and more like herself."

In this multifaceted story of moral blindness, Hulga experiences a physical intimacy with Pointer that forces her into a new mode of reacting and out of her customary detached intellectualism: "Without the leg she felt entirely dependent on him. Her brain seemed to have stopped thinking altogether and to be about some other function that it was not very good at." However dastardly Pointer's actions, he forces Hulga to feel and acknowledge her emotions for the first time. We go away from the story feeling that Hulga will be a changed (and humbled) person — a person less presumptuous and closer to psychic wholeness.

Questions for Discussion

1. What does Mrs. Hopewell mean by "good country people"?
2. Why does Joy change her name to Hulga?
3. In what ways do you expect Joy/Hulga will change after her experience in the barn with Manley Pointer?
4. Discuss O'Connor's choice of names for the characters in this story.
5. Is Manley Pointer a believable character? Have you encountered people who are entirely other than they seem? What is Pointer really interested in? Why does he carry off Hulga's leg?
6. Discuss the dramatic function of Mrs. Freeman and her two daughters.
7. Discuss the effects on characterization of O'Connor's choosing to give Joy a Ph.D. in philosophy and an artificial leg. How do these details predispose our expectations?

Topics for Writing

1. Discuss the function of Christianity in "Good Country People."
2. **CONNECTIONS** Compare "Good Country People" with "Everything That Rises Must Converge." What similarities and differences do you find among mother, son or daughter, and stranger in these stories? What can you infer from this comparison about Flannery O'Connor's attraction to certain types of characters?

Related Commentaries

Robert H. Brinkmeyer, Jr., Flannery O'Connor and Her Readers, p. 859.
Dorothy Tuck McFarland, On "Good Country People," p. 864.
Flannery O'Connor, From Letters 1954–1955, p. 847.
Flannery O'Connor, Writing Short Stories, p. 849.

Suggested Readings

See page 103 of this manual.

FLANNERY O'CONNOR

A Good Man Is Hard to Find (p. 558)

O'Connor's comments (included in Chapter 8, p. 854) direct attention to the climax of her story and suggest how she intended the central characters to be viewed and what she meant the story to imply. Students may benefit, however, from struggling at first to interpret the text unassisted by authorial explanation. The effort should reveal dimensions of O'Connor's art that might otherwise be overlooked.

The grandmother's reawakening to reality, which leads to her gesture of grace as she reaches out to The Misfit as one of her own children, may be triggered by the violence of the murders going on just offstage and the extremity of her own case, but her conversion has been carefully prepared for. Throughout the story this old woman longs in various ways to go back *home* — to Tennessee, to the days of her youth, to the mansion with the imaginary secret panel, which is as much in heaven as it is down a hilly back road in Georgia. Death is seldom far from her thoughts, though for a long time she does not apprehend its reality. Her initial worries about The Misfit are disingenuous, but encountering him or returning to east Tennessee come to the same thing in the end. On the road, the grandmother dresses up in nice clothes so that "anyone seeing her dead on the highway would know at once that she was a lady," observes a graveyard, and remembers her mansion at a town named Toombsboro. The Misfit and his men approach in a "hearse-like automobile"; the family awaits them in front of the woods that "gaped like a dark open mouth." The grandmother is at odds with present times. She squabbles with the children (whose behavior even the reader may find unusually improper); easily upstages the cabbage-headed, slacks-wearing woman who is their mother; joins Red Sammy in deploring the state of world affairs; and disastrously deludes Bailey by smuggling the cat into the car. But she loves the world as well, in a selfish, childish way. She *will* have the cat along; she admires the scenery (including a picturesque "pickaninny" for whose poverty she is not yet ready to feel compassion); she wishes she had married Mr. *E. A.* Teagarden, who courted her with watermelon and would have supplied all her worldly needs from the proceeds of his Coca-Cola stock; and she even makes a play for Red Sammy, the only tycoon in sight.

These desires may be misdirected, but just as it takes very little to upset the valise, release the cat, flip the car off the road, and carry the story into an entirely new set of circumstances, so, under the intensifying presence of death, it takes only a moment for the grandmother's selfish love for and alienation from the world to flip over into the selfless love that leads her to open her heart to The Misfit. After all, she at least rationalizes bringing the cat to protect it; she supportively asserts that Red Sammy is "a good man" in face of his own cynicism and despair; and she offers the same praise to The Misfit from the moment she recognizes him. Without a doubt the grandmother's motive in insisting that The Misfit is "a good man" and in urging him to pray is to divert him from his evident intention and so to save her skin. But as the bullets ring out in the background and the grandmother's maternal instincts burst forth in her repeated cries of "Bailey Boy!" she begins to act charitably in spite of herself. She offers The Misfit one of Bailey's shirts, listens to his confession (although she is the one who is about to die), and when he *is* wearing Bailey's shirt, she reaches out to him in his anguish. A good man *is* hard to find; Jesus may have been the only one who was intrinsically good. But when she loves and pities the radically fallen Misfit, the grandmother becomes for the moment a *good woman* through her Christ-like action, as The Misfit himself acerbically recognizes.

As O'Connor mentions in her commentary, The Misfit has evoked widely differing responses from readers and critics, who have associated him with the devil, the modern agnostic existentialist, or "the prophet he was meant to become," in O'Connor's own phrase. Perhaps The Misfit's daddy provides the best way of distinguishing him from the rest of the characters with his remark, "It's some that can live their whole life out without asking about it and it's others has to know why it is, and this boy is one of the latters." Unlike O'Connor, whose vision of the world was grounded in *belief*, The Misfit wants to *know*. With Faustian presumption, he seeks to comprehend the divine mysteries in terms of his own intellect and demands a kind of justice in life that he can understand. When he cannot find the answers to his questions, but only the implication of inexplicable guilt (like Original Sin) in the punishment he receives, The Misfit sees the world not as the charming place it has appeared to the grandmother but as a prison whose empty sky resembles the blank walls of his cell in the penitentiary. In his own calculus of guilt, The Misfit feels he has been excessively punished, and he seems to be going about the world committing crimes in order to right the balance. His most perverse principle, "No pleasure but meanness," is sustained surprisingly well by the world O'Connor portrays. (Is *this* the reason for the story's lack of anything or anyone to admire and its unremittingly ironic tone?) But it gives way after he has been touched by the grandmother to his first true prophecy: "It's no real pleasure in life" — no *real* pleasure in *this* life, though true goodness sometimes appears in those made conscious of death.

William E. Sheidley

Questions for Discussion

1. What is the grandmother's reason for bringing up The Misfit at the beginning of the story?
2. Describe "the children's mother." Why does O'Connor make her such a nonentity?
3. What about John Wesley and June Star? What would have been the result had O'Connor characterized them as something other than totally obnoxious?
4. Discuss the grandmother's reasons for her fatal decision to bring Pitty Sing on the trip.
5. Why does the grandmother dress so nicely for the trip?
6. Compare the grandmother's response to the scenery and the trip with that of the children. What does O'Connor accomplish by means of this distinction?
7. Just before the stop at The Tower, the grandmother reminisces about her old suitor, Edgar Atkins Teagarden. Specify the connections between the two episodes.
8. What tower might O'Connor have had in mind in choosing the name for Red Sammy's establishment? Why is there a monkey in a chinaberry tree feasting on fleas posted outside The Tower? What do we learn about the world at Red Sammy's?
9. Contrast The Tower with the mansion the grandmother awakens to remember "outside of Toombsboro."
10. What factors cause the accident? Consider its meaning as a consequence of the grandmother's choices and desires.
11. Describe the manner in which The Misfit arrives on the scene. What effect does his appearance have on the reader?
12. The grandmother's response to The Misfit's remark that "it would have been better for all of you, lady, if you hadn't of reckernized me" is "You wouldn't shoot a lady, would you?" Evaluate her question.

13. To what extent is the grandmother correct in her praise of The Misfit? In what ways is he a gentleman?
14. Describe the grandmother's reaction to Bailey's departure. Is her response consistent with her previous behavior?
15. Define The Misfit's experience of the world. To what extent can his criminality be blamed on the conditions of his life? Does The Misfit feel any more free outside the penitentiary than in it?
16. How can the logic of The Misfit's position that "the crime don't matter . . . because sooner or later you're going to forget what it was you done and just be punished for it" be attacked? To what extent does The Misfit's description of himself apply to everyone? Bear in mind that the whole family is being punished with death for no ascertainable crime.
17. Explain how, to The Misfit, "Jesus thown everything off balance."
18. What is the effect of O'Connor's comparing the grandmother to "a parched old turkey hen crying for water"?
19. Does The Misfit do or say anything to deserve the grandmother's gesture of concern?
20. Explain The Misfit's final evaluation of the grandmother: "She would of been a good woman . . . if it had been somebody there to shoot her every minute of her life."
21. Contrast The Misfit's "No pleasure but meanness" with his last words in the story.

Topics for Writing

1. What is the function of tone in O'Connor's story?
2. Describe techniques of characterization in "A Good Man Is Hard to Find."
3. Write a parable or short tale designed to illustrate a religious or philosophical truth. Following O'Connor's example, portray your characters ruthlessly as embodiments of what you want them to represent.
4. **CONNECTIONS** Compare and contrast O'Connor's "A Good Man Is Hard to Find" and Tolstoy's "The Death of Ivan Ilych."
5. **CONNECTIONS** Comment on the relationship between the grandmother and The Misfit in "A Good Man Is Hard to Find" and the relationship between Connie and Arnold Friend in Oates's "Where Are You Going, Where Have You Been?"

Related Commentaries

Robert H. Brinkmeyer, Jr., Flannery O'Connor and Her Readers, p. 859.
Flannery O'Connor, The Element of Suspense in "A Good Man Is Hard to Find," p. 854.
Flannery O'Connor, From Letters 1954–1955, p. 847.
Flannery O'Connor, Writing Short Stories, p. 849.

Suggested Reading

Asals, Frederick. *Flannery O'Connor: The Imagination of Extremity.* Athens: U of Georgia P, 1982. 142–54.
Brinkmeyer, Robert H., Jr. *The Art and Vision of Flannery O'Connor.* Baton Rouge: Louisiana State UP, 1989.
Browning, Preston M., Jr. *Flannery O'Connor.* Crosscurrents/Modern Critiques. Carbondale: Southern Illinois UP, 1974. 54–59.

Burke, John J. "Convergence of Flannery O'Connor and Chardin." *Renascence* 19 (1966): 41–47, 52.

Church, Joseph. "An Abuse of the Imagination in Flannery O'Connor's 'A Good Man Is Hard to Find.'" *Notes on Contemporary Literature* 20.3 (May 1990): 8–10.

Clark, Beverly Lyon, and Melville J. Friedman, eds. *Critical Essays on Flannery O'Connor.* Boston: G. K. Hall, 1985.

Esch, Robert M. "O'Connor's 'Everything That Rises Must Converge.' " *Explicator* 27 (1969): Item 58.

Feeley, Sister Kathleen. *Flannery O'Connor: Voice of the Peacock.* New Brunswick, NJ: Rutgers UP, 1972.

Gatta, John. *"The Scarlet Letter* as Pre-Text for Flannery O'Connor's 'Good Country People.'" *Nathaniel Hawthorne Review* 16.2 (Fall 1990): 6–9.

Giannone, Richard. *Flannery O'Connor.* Boston: Twayne, 1988.

Grimshaw, James A. *The Flannery O'Connor Companion.* Westport, CT: Greenwood, 1981.

Hendin, Josephine. *The World of Flannery O'Connor.* Ann Arbor, MI: Books Demand UMI, 1986.

Kane, Patricia. "Flannery O'Connor's 'Everything That Rises Must Converge.' " *Critique: Studies in Short Fiction* 8 (1965): 85–91.

McDermott, John V. "Julian's Journey into Hell: Flannery O'Connor's Allegory of Pride." *Mississippi Quarterly* 28 (1975): 171–79.

Maida, Patricia Dinneen. "Convergence in Flannery O'Connor's 'Everything That Rises Must Converge.' " *Studies in Short Fiction* 7 (1970): 549–55.

Martin, W. R. "The Apostate in Flannery O'Connor's 'Everything That Rises Must Converge.' " *American Notes and Queries* 23 (1985): 113–14.

Nisly, P. W. "Prison of the Self: Isolation in Flannery O'Connor's Fiction." *Studies in Short Fiction* 17 (1980): 49–54.

Ochshorn, Kathleen G. "A Cloak of Grace: Contradictions in 'A Good Man Is Hard to Find.'" *Studies in American Fiction* 18.1 (Spring 1990): 113–17.

O'Connor, Flannery. *The Habit of Being.* Letters edited and with an introduction by Sally Fitzgerald. New York: Farrar, 1979.

———. *Mystery and Manners.* New York: Farrar, 1969.

Orvell, Miles. *Invisible Parade: The Fiction of Flannery O'Connor.* Philadelphia: Temple UP, 1972.

Paulson, Suzanne. *Flannery O'Connor: A Study of the Short Fiction.* Boston: Twayne, 1988.

Petry, Alice Hall. "Miss O'Connor and Mrs. Mitchell: The Example of 'Everything That Rises.'" *The Southern Quarterly: A Journal of the Arts in the South* 27.4 (Summer 1989): 5–15.

Pyron, V. " 'Strange Country': The Landscape of Flannery O'Connor's Short Stories." *Mississippi Quarterly* 36 (1983): 557–68.

FRANK O'CONNOR

Guests of the Nation (p. 570)

O'Connor's story draws exceptional power from its concern with a betrayal of the most primitive basis of human society, the host-guest relationship. The English prisoners, billeted with their guards in a cottage so thoroughly rooted in the land that its occupant still bears traces of indigenous paganism, earn the status of guests and come to feel at home. Belcher's contributions to the household chores call attention to the simple satisfactions of the peaceful, cooperative labor that is disrupted by the war, and Hawkins's learning Irish dances implies the underlying brotherhood of men, in contrast to which the scruples of "our lads" who "at that time did not dance foreign dances on principle" seem absurd — and ominous. The futility of Hawkins's debates with Noble on theology calls further into question the reality of the issues that divide the English from the Irish, and his international socialist politics provide a hint that there are issues of at least equal importance that would not polarize the two pairs of men but unite them against a common enemy.

The inhumanity of the conflict that orders Belcher and Hawkins to be executed by their "chums," their brothers, appears clearer for O'Connor's skillful portrayal of the prisoners as distinct from each other, individualized and consistent in their personalities. Further, by opening the story with a plunge into what seems an ongoing state of affairs, O'Connor shows that it is the war that interrupts the natural friendly interaction among the men rather than their fellowship interrupting a "normal" condition of bitter hostility between the English and the Irish. Even Jeremiah Donovan, who eventually brings down the cruel warrant and carries it out, forms part of the circle around the card table and scolds Hawkins for poor play "as if he were one of our own."

Bonaparte, the narrator, embraces the Englishmen as comrades and chafes at his official duties as their guard. With Noble, he imagines that the brigade officers, who also "knew the Englishmen well," will treat them as men rather than as enemies. But when the moment of decision arrives, Noble's resistance only extends to accepting the secondary role of gravedigger, and Bonaparte, though he hopes the prisoners will run away, finds himself powerless to aid them. Belcher and Hawkins are most fully themselves at the moment of their deaths, Hawkins talking on about his larger cause, Belcher finally revealing the fullness of his loving and generous nature. To Bonaparte and Noble the execution conveys a shock of revelation that changes the world for them. As Noble prays with the old woman in the doorway of the cottage — now become a shrine to the communion that took place within it, the only holy place in a world that seems to Noble composed entirely of the grave of his friends — Bonaparte, made profane in the literal etymological sense ("outside the shrine") and figuratively as well by his participation in the killing, feels himself cast out, alone, cut off from all atonement.

WILLIAM E. SHEIDLEY

Questions for Discussion

1. Describe and explain the pacing of the story. Contrast the movement of sections II and III with that of section IV.
2. What is the effect of the abrupt beginning of the story? Why does O'Connor introduce the characters before specifying that they are prisoners and guards in a war?
3. Why does O'Connor trouble to introduce the message from Mary Brigid O'Connell about her brother's socks?
4. Distinguish between the two Englishmen. Are they more different from the Irishmen or from each other?
5. Explore the significance of the old woman's superstitions about Jupiter Pluvius and "the hidden powers." Compare her interest in religion with that of Noble and Hawkins.

6. Why is Bonaparte so shocked when he learns what may happen to the hostages?
7. What is the relevance to the story of Hawkins's political beliefs? Do we think less of him when he volunteers to become a traitor and join the Irish cause?
8. What is the effect of Belcher's last-minute confidences? of his apparently sincere repetition of the word *chum* throughout his ordeal?
9. Discuss Bonaparte's role in the execution. Is he culpable? Does he feel guilty?
10. Define the symbolic implications of the final scene. Why do Noble and Bonaparte have contrasting visions? Do their visions have anything in common? Why does Bonaparte burst out of the cottage where Noble and the old woman are praying?

Topics for Writing

1. What is the meaning of the old woman and her cottage in "Guests of the Nation"?
2. Summarize the conflict and the action of this story on personal, public (national, historical, political), and eternal (philosophical, religious, mythical) levels. Could these levels be reconciled so that the polarities of value would be parallel?
3. **CONNECTIONS** Compare and contrast O'Connor's "Guests of the Nation" and Isaac Babel's "My First Goose" — introductions to war.

Related Commentary

Frank O'Connor, Style and Form in Joyce's "The Dead," p. 780.

Suggested Readings

Bordewyk, Gordon. "Quest for Meaning: The Stories of Frank O'Connor." *Illinois Quarterly* 41 (1978): 37–47, esp. 38–39.
Matthews, James. *Voices: A Life of Frank O'Connor.* New York: Atheneum, 1983.
O'Connor, Frank. *The Lonely Voice: A Study of the Short Story.* Cleveland: World, 1963.
Prosky, Murray. "The Pattern of Diminishing Certitude in the Stories of Frank O'Connor." *Colby Library Quarterly* 9 (1971): 311–21, esp. 311–14.
Steinman, Michael. *Frank O'Connor at Work.* Syracuse, NY: Syracuse UP, 1990.
Tomory, William. *Frank O'Connor.* Boston: Twayne, 1980.

TILLIE OLSEN

I Stand Here Ironing (p. 579)

One way to begin discussing this story is to look at the ending. "I will never total it all," the narrator affirms and then pronounces the summary whose inadequacy she has already proclaimed. The summarizing passage clarifies and organizes the impressions the reader may have gleaned from the preceding monologue. It is so clear that if it stood alone or came first in the story the validity of its interpretation of Emily could hardly be doubted. But since it follows her mother's "tormented" meditations, the summary seems incomplete in its clinical precision and must give way to a final paragraph of comparatively obscure and paradoxical requests focused in the startling but brilliantly adept image of the "dress on the ironing board, helpless before the iron," which links the story's end to its beginning and directs attention to the true central character.

What is mainly missing from the summary is the love and understanding that Emily's mother feels for her daughter as a result of living through the experiences bracketed by the orderly generalizations. Just as much as Emily, her mother has been the victim "of depression, of war, of fear." By virtue of having had to cope with those circumstances, she can respect Emily's response to them. Doing so enables her to counter the suggestion that "she's a youngster who needs help" with "Let her be." A good deal of the help Emily and her mother have received so far has put them in separate prisons — as when Emily was incarcerated at the convalescent home — and cut them off from love. To let Emily alone is at least to allow her some freedom to grow at her own slow pace.

Her mother is tempted to blame herself for the deficiencies in Emily's childhood, since she learned things about being a mother with her second family that she did not know with Emily. But her consideration of a characteristic incident early in the narrative suggests a crucial qualifying factor: When she placed Emily in nursery school at the age of two, she did not know what she was subjecting her daughter to, "except that it would have made no difference if I had known. . . . It was the only way we could be together, the only way I could hold a job." As much a victim of rigid and unfavorable economic and historic circumstances as her daughter, Emily's mother can speak her concluding line with feeling. In pleading that Emily somehow be made to know "that she is more than this dress on the ironing board, helpless before the iron," Emily's mother asks that her daughter be spared a condition to which she herself has been subjected. But Emily's mother, unlike Whistler's, does not sit for her portrait passively in a rocking chair; she stands there wielding the iron, controlling the very symbol of the circumstances that have not yet flattened her, painting her own self-portrait, and calling for help not in adjusting Emily to the world but in making the world a place in which Emily can thrive.

WILLIAM E. SHEIDLEY

Questions for Discussion

1. Who is "you" in the first sentence? What is the mother's first response to the request to unlock the mystery of Emily? Does her position change?
2. Does Emily's mother feel guilty about how she has cared for Emily? Why? What factors have affected her dealings with her daughter?
3. Why is the passage in which Emily throws the clock so effective?
4. Discuss the "help" Emily gets at the convalescent home. How does it compare with the help her mother calls for at the end?
5. Emily has suffered from the absence of her father, the exhaustion of her mother, poverty, asthma and other diseases, sibling rivalry, and unpopularity, among other complaints. What is the effect of these hardships on the young woman she has become? What is the effect of her discovery of a talent?
6. What has her mother learned from Emily?
7. Does Emily's mother love her daughter? How can we tell?

Topics for Writing

1. Compare and contrast Emily's talent and her mother's.
2. Discuss the function of the interruptions in "I Stand Here Ironing."
3. Consider "I will never total it all" — the importance of indeterminacy in Olsen's analysis of Emily.
4. Analyze the politics of "I Stand Here Ironing."
5. Write a summary statement in general terms about the personality of a sibling, relative, or friend you have known closely for a long time. Put it aside and cast your memory back to three or four specific incidents involving your subject. Narrate them briefly but in specific terms. Read over your sketches and compare the personality of your subject as it emerges with what you wrote in your generalized summary. Do you still think your summary is accurate? What are its limitations?

Suggested Readings

Frye, Joanne S. "'I Stand Here Ironing': Motherhood as Experience and Metaphor." *Studies in Short Fiction* 18 (1981): 287–92.
O'Connor, William Van. "The Short Stories of Tillie Olsen." *Studies in Short Fiction* 1 (1963): 21–25, esp. 21–22.

GRACE PALEY

A Conversation with My Father (p. 586)

The story the narrator writes in response to her father's request is so interesting that it is easy to forget for a while that it is only an element within the larger story Paley has to tell. Confronted with the inescapable fact of the father's imminent death, the narrator and her father respond in differing ways because of their differing needs. Both use gallows humor to make the situation less intolerable, as when the father remarks, "It so happens I'm not going out this evening"; but the narrator seeks that refuge much more often, and her father chides her repeatedly for doing so. Things *matter* to a dying man, and it is not surprising that he should prefer the straight line of tragedy — in which failure and defeat are compensated for by a perception of the real value of what has been lost — to the idea of "the open destiny of life," which, by holding out hope of recovery from any disaster, implies that there is nothing indispensable, no absolute loss. A man on his deathbed knows better.

The narrator's first attempt to write a story that suits her father's taste reflects her discomfort with the assignment. Her "unadorned and miserable tale" remains so sketchy that it lacks verisimilitude and conviction, like meaningless statistics on highway deaths or counterinsurgency body counts. Challenged to try again, she partly confirms her father's complaint that "with you, it's all a joke" by writing a brilliantly comic and incontrovertibly realistic version of the story, whose merits even her father has to recognize: "Number One: You have a nice sense of humor." In a few deft strokes, Paley renders an incisive satiric portrait of two contemporary "life-styles," their hypocrisy, and their destructiveness, focused neatly in the competing periodical titles, *Oh! Golden Horse!* (heroin) and *Man Does Live by Bread Alone*. The narrator knows as well as her father how thorough a perversion of true spiritual values is embodied in each of these titles, and she dramatizes her understanding in the destruction of the mother in her story. But she cannot quite "look it in the face," and she ends her tale with one last grim joke: "terrible, face-scarring, time-consuming tears." Her father spies her desperate evasion: "Number Two: I see you can't tell a plain story. So don't waste time." Ironically, the clarity of his disillusioned vision enables the dying man to feel a purer sympathy for the mother in the story than does the narrator herself, although she claims to care so much about her characters that she wants to give them all a second chance. "Poor woman," he says. "Poor girl, born in a time of fools, to live among fools. The end. The end. You were right to put that down. The end." Not necessarily, the narrator argues, and goes on to invent the kind of future for her character that we always imagine for the dying, in the probably misguided effort to ease their anxiety. But her father, as usual, knows better: " 'How long will it be?' he asked. 'Tragedy! You too. When will you look it in the face?' "

WILLIAM E. SHEIDLEY

Questions for Discussion

1. Describe the medical condition of the narrator's father. How important is it to understanding his position in the conversation?
2. Explain the phrase "despite my metaphors" in the first paragraph. What other writerly tactics of the narrator does her father ignore?
3. The narrator says she *would* like to tell a story with the kind of plot she has always despised. Analyze her conflict.
4. What is the point of the first version of the story? What is wrong with it as a piece of fiction?
5. When her father asks for details, the narrator comes up with things he calls jokes. Are they? What makes them jokes rather than facts?
6. Why does the narrator's father consider that "it is of great consequence" whether the woman in the story is married? Is he simply old-fashioned?
7. What does the narrator add to her story in the second version? Does the point of the story remain the same? Does her father get the point?
8. The woman in the story "would rather be with the young." Consider that motivation and its results from the point of view of the narrator and of her father.
9. What techniques does Paley use to satirize the woman's son and his girl-friend?
10. Explain the term "time-consuming" at the end of the inset story.
11. The narrator's father makes three separate responses to the story. Account for each of them. Do they cohere?
12. What does the narrator's father mean by the statement he makes in various forms culminating in his final question?

Topics for Writing

1. Analyze "A Conversation with My Father" as a story about writing.
2. Evaluate the qualities of tragedy versus satire in "A Conversation with My Father."
3. Write your own version of the narrator's story. Start from her first version and elaborate on it as you choose, without necessarily using the material the narrator includes in her second version and subsequent commentary.

4. **CONNECTIONS** Compare and contrast attitudes toward death and life in Paley's "A Conversation with My Father" and Tolstoy's "The Death of Ivan Ilych."

Related Commentary

Grace Paley, A Conversation with Ann Charters, p. 782.

Suggested Readings

See below.

GRACE PALEY

Samuel (p. 589)

The key to Paley's power in this sketch is how she dramatizes the death of an inner-city African American boy on the New York subway. Motion is essential to life. Ask your students to notice the verbs in the opening and closing sentences of each paragraph: "jiggle," "hop," "jiggling," "jumping," "jerk," "grab," "leaned," and so forth. The chronological movement of the plot as it develops in each succeeding paragraph races along like the line of cars itself. Paley has re-created the motion of the subway car as it rockets through the tunnels of the city. We encounter four black boys acting up on the swaying platform between the cars and embarrassing a lady, a watchful man pulling the emergency cord, the little boy Samuel "crushed and killed between the cars," the hysterical response of Samuel's mother, and the birth of a new baby boy to take his place — "but never again" a boy "exactly like Samuel."

Questions for Discussion

1. Why is Paley careful to tell the reader that these four boys had mothers who "all knew that they had gone to see the missile exhibit on Fourteenth Street"?
2. Why does Paley name the four boys? What is the significance of their names?
3. What is the theme of Paley's story before the last paragraph? How does her concluding sentence affect this theme?

Topics for Writing

1. Describe an action leading to the death of one of the participants in a sports event you have seen on television.
2. **CONNECTIONS** Compare and contrast the community of subway riders with the community of school children in Toni Cade Bambara's "The Lesson."

Suggested Readings

Aarons, Victoria. "Talking Lives: Storytelling and Renewal in Grace Paley's Short Fiction." *Studies in Jewish Literature* 9.1 (Spring 1990): 20–35.
Arcana, Judith. "Grace Paley: Life and Stories." *Dissertation Abstracts International* 50.7 (Jan. 1990): 2271A.

Baba, Minako. "Faith Darwin as Writer, Heroine: A Study of Grace Paley's Short Stories." *Studies in American Jewish Literature* 7.1 (Spring 1988): 40–54.

Halfman, Ulrich, and Philipp Gerlach. "Grace Paley: A Bibliography." *Tulsa Studies in Women's Literature* 8.2 (Fall 1989): 339–54.

Isaacs, Neil David. *Grace Paley: A Study of the Short Fiction*. Boston: Twayne, 1990.

Logsdon, Loren, and Charles W. Mayer, ed. *Since Flannery O'Connor: Essays on the Contemporary American Short Story*. Macomb: Western Illinois U, 1987. 93–100.

Lyons, Bonnie. "Grace Paley's Jewish Miniatures." *Studies in American Jewish Literature* 8.1 (Spring 1989): 26–33.

Paley, Grace. *Long Walks and Intimate Talks: Stories and Poems by Grace Paley*. New York: Feminist Press and the City U of New York, 1991.

Taylor, Jacqueline. *Grace Paley: Illuminating the Dark Lives*. Austin: U of Texas P, 1990.

———. "Grace Paley on Storytelling and Story Hearing." *Literature in Performance: A Journal of Literature and Performing Arts* 7.2 (April 1987): 46–58.

Wilde, Alan. "Grace Paley's World, Investing Words." In *Middle Grounds*. Philadelphia: U of Pennsylvania P, 1987.

EDGAR ALLAN POE

The Cask of Amontillado (p. 592)

Poe is the great master of the contrived suspense story, and "The Cask of Amontillado" is a model of narrative compression toward a single effect. Students should understand that Poe had a theory on the short story; its essential points are suggested in his commentary in Chapter 7 on p. 787.

Despite Poe's rational explanation of how a writer should compose a story, his own fiction is directed toward eliciting irrational emotions. Poe's literary style aims at using as many extravagances of character, setting, and plot as he could invent, exploiting the reader's emotional vulnerability to disturbing images of darkness and chaos. The hectic unpredictability of the carnival season, the creepy subterranean wine cellar, and the ancient family crypt with its moldering skeletons all challenge us emotionally and make us want to read further.

In the reading, our own fears become the true subject matter. As in a nightmare, Fortunato finds himself being buried alive, one of the most basic human fears. On a more conscious level, we rely on a social contract to bind us together as a human family, and Montresor's lawlessness plays on our fear that any person can take the law into his or her own hands without being checked by conscience. Poe doesn't have to give us a great number of details about his characters; our imagination draws from the depths of the common human psyche to supply all that we need.

This story is a good example to use in stressing the importance of the students' close reading of a text. It's easy for readers to miss, in the last paragraph, the sentence "My heart grew sick — on account of the dampness of the catacombs." Yet upon this sentence rests the interpretation of Montresor's character: Can we excuse his action on grounds of insanity? Was he insane at the time he buried Fortunato alive, or did he go insane in the half century during which, he tells us, his crime has remained undetected? If the reader has not paid careful attention to that sentence, he or she will have missed an essential detail in understanding the story.

The book *Mysterious New England,* edited by A. N. Stevens (1971), suggests that Poe first heard the anecdote on which he might have based this story when he was a private in the army in 1827. Supposedly, only ten years before, a popular young lieutenant named Robert F. Massie had also been stationed at Fort Independence in Boston Harbor; when Poe was serving there, he saw a gravestone erected to the memory of Lieutenant Massie, who had been unfairly killed in a duel by a bully named Captain Green. As Stevens tells it,

> Feeling against Captain Green ran high for many weeks, and then suddenly he vanished. Years went by without a sign of him, and Green was written off the army records as a deserter.
>
> According to the story that Poe finally gathered together, Captain Green had been so detested by his fellow officers that they decided to take a terrible revenge on him for Massie's death.
>
> Visiting Captain Green one moonless night, they pretended to be friendly and plied him with wine until he was helplessly intoxicated. Then, carrying the captain down to one of the ancient dungeons, the officers forced his body through a tiny opening that led into the subterranean casemate. His captors began to shackle him to the floor, using the heavy iron handcuffs and footcuffs fastened into the stone. Then they sealed the captain up alive inside the windowless casemate, using bricks and mortar that they had hidden close at hand.
>
> Captain Green shrieked in terror and begged for mercy, but his cries fell on deaf ears. The last brick was finally inserted, mortar applied, and the room closed off, the officers believed, forever. Captain Green undoubtedly died a horrible death within a few days.

WILLIAM E. SHEIDLEY

Questions for Discussion

1. How does Poe motivate the behavior of Montresor? Does the story provide any hints as to the "thousand injuries" he has suffered? Are any hints necessary?
2. Why is the setting of the story appropriate?
3. What does Montresor's treatment of his house servants tell us about his knowledge of human psychology, and how does it prepare us for his treatment of Fortunato?
4. How does Poe increase the elements of suspense as Fortunato is gradually walled into the catacombs?

Topics for Writing

(Remind the class that, on p. 2104 of the textbook, is a student paper comparing and contrasting this story with Hawthorne's "Young Goodman Brown.")

1. Montresor doesn't tell his story until a half century after the actual event. Analyze how Poe adapts the flashback technique to affect the reader of "The Cask of Amontillado."

2. Explicate the passage in the story in which Montresor entices Fortunato into the crypt.

Related Commentary

Edgar Allan Poe, The Importance of the Single Effect in a Prose Tale, p. 787.

Suggested Readings

See page 114 of this manual.

EDGAR ALLAN POE

The Tell-Tale Heart (p. 597)

"The Tell-Tale Heart" is a story about what has been called "the demonic self" — a person who feels a compulsion to commit a gratuitous act of evil. Poe wrote explicitly about what he calls this "spirit of perverseness" in his story "The Black Cat," published in 1843, two years before "The Tell-Tale Heart":

> Of this spirit [of perverseness] philosophy takes no account. Yet I am not more sure that my soul lives, than I am that perverseness is one of the primitive impulses of the human heart — one of the indivisible primary faculties, or sentiments, which give direction to the character of Man. Who has not, a hundred times, found himself committing a vile or a silly action, for no other reason than because he knows he should *not*? Have we not a perpetual inclination, in the teeth of our best judgment, to violate that which is *Law*, merely because we understand it to be such?

According to the critic Eric W. Carlson, "The Tell-Tale Heart" was one of Poe's favorite stories. In addition to dramatizing the "spirit of perverseness" in his narrative, Poe combines other elements of the gothic tale (the evil eye, the curse), the psychorealistic (the narrator's paranoia), the dramatic (concentrated intensity of tone, gradually heightened series of dramatic events), and the moral (the compulsion to confess).

Questions for Discussion

1. How would you describe the narrator of the story? How does your description compare or contrast with what he would like to have you believe about him?
2. What disease is the narrator referring to in the first paragraph?
3. What caused the narrator to murder the old man? Was his reason valid?
4. What narrative devices does Poe use to heighten the suspense of the tale? Give examples.
5. Poe believed in the existence of the "spirit of perverseness" within every man. How is this revealed in the story?
6. Do you feel the confession at the end of the tale is necessary? Why? What is Poe's purpose in presenting this confession?

Topics for Writing

1. Discuss the significance of the light and dark imagery in "The Tell-Tale Heart."
2. Consider the effect of premeditation in "The Tell-Tale Heart."
3. Discuss the use of sight and sound as dramatic devices in "The Tell-Tale Heart."
4. Write an essay analyzing the dichotomy between the narrator's view of himself and our view of him in "The Tell-Tale Heart."
5. Explore reality versus illusion in "The Tell-Tale Heart."
6. Rewrite the story from the point of view of the police officers or from the point of view of the old man.
7. Consider the events that might result from the action of this story and write a sequel presenting these developments.

Related Commentary

Edgar Allan Poe, The Importance of the Single Effect in a Prose Tale, p. 787.

Suggested Readings

Adler, Jacob H. "Are There Flaws in 'The Cask of Amontillado'?" *Notes and Queries* 199 (1954): 32–34.

Buranelli, Vincent. *Edgar Allan Poe.* Rev. ed. Boston: Twayne, 1977.

Baudelaire, Charles P. *Baudelaire on Poe: Critical Papers.* University Park: Pennsylvania State UP, 1952.

Carlson, Eric W., ed. *Critical Essays on Edgar Allan Poe.* Boston: G. K. Hall, 1987.

Carlson, Eric W. *Introduction to Poe: A Thematic Reader.* Glenville, IL: Scott, 1967.

Dillon, John M. *Edgar Allan Poe.* Brooklyn, NY: Haskell, 1974.

Fletcher, Richard M. *The Stylistic Development of Edgar Allan Poe.* New York: Mouton, 1974.

Gargano, J. W. "'The Cask of Amontillado': A Masquerade of Motive and Identity." *Studies in Short Fiction* 4 (1967): 119–26.

———. *The Masquerade Vision in Poe's Short Stories.* Baltimore: Enoch Pratt, 1977.

Hammond, J. R. *An Edgar Allan Poe Companion: A Guide to Short Stories, Romances, and Essays.* Savage, MD: B and N Imports, 1981.

Knapp, Bettina L. *Edgar Allan Poe.* New York: Ungar, 1984.

Levin, Harry. *The Power of Blackness: Hawthorne, Poe, Melville.* Columbus: Ohio UP, 1980.

Mabbott, Thomas Olivle, ed. *Collected Works of Edgar Allan Poe.* Cambridge, MA: Harvard UP, 1978.

May, Charles E. *Edgar Allan Poe: A Study of Short Fiction.* Boston: Twayne, 1990.

Muller, John P., and William J. Richardson, eds. *The Purloined Poe: Lacan, Derrida, and Psychoanalytic Reading.* Baltimore: Johns Hopkins UP, 1988.

Pitcher, E. W. "Physiognomical Meaning of Poe's 'The Tell-Tale Heart.' " *Studies in Short Fiction* 16 (1979): 231–33.

Robinson, E. A. "Poe's 'The Tell-Tale Heart.' " *Nineteenth Century Fiction* 19 (1965): 369–78.

Symons, Julian, ed. *Selected Tales.* New York: Oxford UP, 1980.

Tucker, B. D. "Tell-Tale Heart and the Evil Eye." *Southern Literary Journal* 13 (1981): 92–98.

KATHERINE ANNE PORTER

He (p. 601)

"He" is the earlier of two stories in this anthology that are related by subject — both plots are about what happens to a boy or man of subnormal intelligence. The other story is "Heat" by Joyce Carol Oates.

The similarity of the characters' surnames suggests that Porter's story served as the direct inspiration for Oates's narrative. "He" was included in Porter's collection *Flowering Judas,* published in 1930. Like the photographs from the 1930s taken in the American South by Dorothea Lange and Walker Evans for the Works Progress Administration, which can serve as eloquent illustrations of the lives of poor families, Porter's volume describes the poverty-stricken lives of many rural Americans like the Whipple family.

The Whipples' struggle to feed and clothe their family is made more difficult by the fact that their second son is mentally defective. (They have two normal children — their daughter, Emly, and their son Adna.) This boy doesn't have a name. He is referred to as "He" or "Him" or "His," always with a capital "H," signifying His special status in the family. The extraordinary quality of the story is the result of the way it is told. The third-person-singular narration is channeled through the point of view and characteristic language of Mrs. Whipple, who is her son's primary caretaker and who is deeply involved in his welfare. "His" interior life is blocked to us, because he never talks, but Mrs. Whipple tells us everything she thinks and feels and elicits comments from family and neighbors around her; we participate in the tragedy of the boy's life through her responses.

With such a subject, it would be extremely easy for Porter's story to slip into sentimentality given the reader's direct access to Mrs. Whipple's feelings. What makes the story effective is Porter's unflinching honesty in dramatizing the social and economic background of the characters and her brilliant use of Mrs. Whipple's language, both of which keep the narrative solidly positioned on the hard nub of truth. (A generation later Flannery O'Connor took Porter's work as a model for her use of colloquial speech rhythms and dialogue in her short fiction.)

For example, the Whipples' neighbors say behind their backs that it would be much better for the family if the second son died ("'A Lord's pure mercy if He should die,' they said"), yet to their faces "everybody said, 'He's not so bad off. He'll be all right yet. Look how He grows!'"

Mrs. Whipple does the best she can to love and protect her second son. Taking care of Him becomes a way to repel the bad luck visited on the family. His well-being is a sign that she and the family will survive this bad luck as long as He keeps going. She also believes that no matter how badly things go for the family, her good care of her second son is a way to show the world that the Whipples may be whipped, but not beaten. The neighbors who speak ill of her boy really are judging her entire family. As Mrs. Whipple says, "I get sick of people coming around saying things all the time."

Even a visit from her brother's family, whom she loves, isn't a happy occasion. Mr. Whipple resents the fact that must kill a suckling pig for them in order to put on the appearance of doing well. He ruins his wife's pleasure in recollecting the visit by suggesting that the guests were critical of the family: "Who knows what they had in their minds all along?" Mrs. Whipple's response is to defend the way she has cared for her second son: "They can't say He wasn't dressed every lick as good as Adna — oh, honest, sometimes I wish I was dead!"

The family's fortunes continue to slide during the development of the story. Mrs. Whipple says, "We're losing our hold. Why can't we do like other people and watch for our best chances? They'll be calling us poor white trash next." Adna and Emly leave home to take jobs to earn much-needed money, and He gets sick. Even after four months' worth of medical bills, Mrs. Whipple manages to remain optimistic. Her refusal to accept the reality of the situation continues nearly until the end, when He begins to cry as the wagon leaves the Whipple residence on the way to the County Home. When He breaks down, she begins to cry too, and Porter lets us share her internal anguish as she relinquishes her boy: "There was nothing she could do to make up to Him for His life. Oh, what a mortal pity He was ever born."

Questions for Discussion

1. What is Mr. Whipple's educational background? Mrs. Whipple's? How much better educated will Emly and Adna be?
2. What opportunities do the Whipples have to make money and prosper?
3. Why does Mrs. Whipple take her brother's visit so seriously? Why didn't Mr. Whipple want to kill the suckling pig?
4. Why does Mrs. Whipple box His ears? How does she feel afterwards?
5. What is the relationship between Mr. and Mrs. Whipple?
6. Why is Mrs. Whipple so nervous when she sees Him leading the bull? Is this a foreshadowing of His sickness later in the story?

Topics for Writing

1. Describe Mrs. Whipple's personality. Is she a good or an overprotective mother?
2. Analyze how Porter dramatizes the economic hardship of the Whipple family in "He" and makes it an integral part of the story.
3. **CONNECTIONS** Compare and contrast the narrative point of view in "He" with Oates's treatment of the same aspect in "Heat."

Suggested Readings

Bayley, Isabel, ed. *Letters of Katherine Anne Porter.* New York: Atlantic Monthly Press, 1990.

Bruccoli, Matthew J., ed. *Understanding Katherine Anne Porter.* Columbia: U of South Carolina P, 1988.

Demouy, Jane Krause. *Katherine Anne Porter's Women: The Eye of Her Fiction.* Austin: U of Texas P, 1983.

Hendrick, Willene, and George Hendrick. *Katherine Anne Porter.* Boston: Twayne, 1988.

Mooney, Harry J. *The Fiction and Criticism of Katherine Anne Porter.* Rev. ed. Pittsburgh: U of Pittsburgh P, 1990.

Plimpton, George, ed. *Women Writers at Work: The Paris Review Interviews.* New York: Penguin, 1989.

Porter, Katherine Anne. *The Collected Essays and Occasional Writings.* New York: Harcourt, 1970.

———. *Flowering Judas.* New York: Harcourt, 1930, 1958.

Stout, Janis P. *Strategies of Reticence: Silence and Meaning in the Works of Jane Austen, Willa Cather, Katherine Anne Porter, and Joan Didion.* Charlottesville: UP of Virginia, 1990.

Tanner, James T. F. *The Texas Legacy of Katherine Anne Porter.* Denton: U of North Texas P, 1990.

Unrue, Darlene H. *Truth and Vision in Katherine Anne Porter's Fiction.* Athens: U of Georgia P, 1985.

Leslie Marmon Silko

Yellow Woman (p. 609)

This story is told in the first person and presented episodically in several sections. It takes place over two days, beginning the morning Yellow Woman wakes up beside the river with Silva, the stranger she has spent the night with. The story ends at sundown the next day, when she returns to her family in the Pueblo village.

"Yellow Woman" is built on different traditions from those in the cultural background of most American students. Silko writes fiction that preserves her cultural heritage by re-creating its customs and values in stories that dramatize emotional conflicts of interest to modern readers.

As Yellow Woman narrates the story of her abduction and return to her family, the reader comes to share her mood and her interpretation of what has happened. As a girl she was fascinated by the stories her grandfather told her about Silva, the mysterious kachina spirit who kidnaps married women from the tribe, then returns them after he has kept them as his wives. These stories were probably similar to the imaginary tales passed down in an oral tradition whose origins are lost to contemporary American folklorists. Silko has created their modern equivalent, her version of how they might be reenacted in today's world. The overweight, white Arizona rancher is familiar to us, as is the Jell-O being prepared for supper, and we have no difficulty imagining the gunnysacks full of freshly slaughtered meat bouncing on the back of Yellow Woman's horse.

The dreamlike atmosphere Silko creates in "Yellow Woman" makes such realistic details protrude sharply from the soft-focus narrative. Yellow Woman doesn't think clearly. She seems bewitched by the myths her grandfather told her, and her adventure following the man she calls Silva holds her enthralled. At the end she says, "I thought about Silva, and I felt sad at leaving him; still, there was something strange about him, and I tried to figure it out all the way back home." We are not told what — if anything — she does figure out.

Instead, action takes the place of thought in the story. Yellow Woman looks at the place on the riverbank where she met Silva and tells herself that "he will come back sometime and be waiting again by the river." Action moves so swiftly that we follow Yellow Woman as obediently as she follows her abductor, mesmerized by the audacity of what is happening. There is no menace in Silva, no danger or malice in his rape of Yellow Woman. The bullets in his rifle are for the white rancher who realizes he has been killing other men's cattle, not for Yellow Woman — or for us.

117

Questions for Discussion

1. Why is Yellow Woman so eager to believe that she and Silva are acting out the stories her grandfather told her?
2. How does Silko structure the opening paragraphs of the story to help the reader suspend disbelief and enter the dreamlike atmosphere of Yellow Woman's perceptions?
3. Why does Silko tell the story through the woman's point of view? Describe the Pueblo Indian woman we know as Yellow Woman. Is she happy at home with her mother, grandmother, husband, and baby? Why is Yellow Woman's father absent from the story?
4. Are there any limitations to Silko's choice to tell the story through Yellow Woman's point of view? Explain.
5. Why doesn't the narrator escape from Silva when she discovers him asleep by the river as the story opens? What makes her decide to return home the next day?

Topics for Writing

1. Tell the story through a third-person omniscient narration.
2. Compare "Yellow Woman" with Paula Gunn Allen's "Whirlwind Man Steals Yellow Woman."
3. **CONNECTIONS** Compare Silko's "Yellow Woman" and Oates's "Where Are You Going, Where Have You Been?" as rape narratives.

Related Commentaries

Paula Gunn Allen, Whirlwind Man Steals Yellow Woman, p. 726.
Leslie Marmon Silko, Language and Literature from a Pueblo Indian Perspective, p. 793.

Suggested Readings

Allen, Paula Gunn. *The Sacred Hoop: Recovering the Feminine in American Indian Traditions*. Boston: Beacon, 1986.
———, ed. *Spider Woman's Granddaughters: Traditional Tales and Contemporary Writing by Native American Women*. Boston: Beacon, 1989.
Graulich, Melody, ed. *Yellow Woman*. Women, Text, and Contexts Series. New Brunswick, NJ: Rutgers UP, 1993.
Hoilman, Dennis. "The Ethnic Imagination: A Case History." *Canadian Journal of Native Studies* 5.2 (1985): 167–75.
Nelson, Robert M. *Place and Vision: The Function of Landscape in Native American Fiction*. New York: P. Lang, 1993.
Sands, Kathleen Mullen. "Indian Women's Personal Narrative: Voices Past and Present." In *American Women's Autobiography: Fea(s)ts of Memory*. Ed. Margo Culley. Madison: U of Wisconsin P, 1992.
Silko, Leslie Marmon. *Almanac of the Dead*. New York: Simon, 1991.

Hjalmar Söderberg

A Dog without a Master (p. 617)

Söderberg's comment in the headnote that people have always liked this story because "they think it is about a dog" can serve as a useful way to begin class discussion. Many students will skip the headnote and finish the story thinking that it is obviously about a black dog, or even several dogs, and perhaps feel a little puzzled about why they are reading it. The title of the story highlights the central figure, who obviously plays an important role in the narrative. The black dog is literally a dog without a master, of course, but Söderberg also intends him to represent any human being who has lost faith in God.

How does an attentive reader make the mental leap from literal dog to metaphorical dog when thinking about the story? Because the story is a translation into English from the Swedish original, Söderberg's tone of voice is not accessible to us, but the matter-of-fact language of the tale (no pun intended), with its wryly humorous undertone apparent in the opening paragraph, should register with most readers. It seems to beg to be taken literally. The narrator summarizes the young dog's behavior as the years pass in typical canine pursuits, until the penultimate paragraph, when the dog (now old) hears his master's whistle. Now the dog becomes so perplexed he begins to think like a harried human. His doggy mind is filled with questions and a sense of loss. He "stretched his shaggy head toward the sky and howled." Söderberg's repetition of this sentence in his final paragraph should tip off the reader that this is no ordinary dog. This is a remarkably human angst. It is, in fact, a human desire at the end of life for something beyond the self, for a clear sign of a divine presence, which Söderberg withholds from reader and dog alike in this short narrative.

Questions for Discussion

1. What does Söderberg intend by his reference to the New Testament in his second paragraph, when he refers to Christ's driving the moneylenders out of the temple?
2. Söderberg takes one paragraph to describe years of activity as the young dog "got older without noticing." Then he takes roughly the same number of words to describe the old dog's confused response to hearing the sound of his master whistling three times. How does this illustrate the author's skillful construction of his plot?
3. At what point in your reading did you begin to suspect that the story isn't about a dog?

Topics for Writing

1. Analyze the points of comparison between a dog and a human being as Söderberg develops the central metaphor of the story. Do you think that Söderberg intends to ennoble the dog by comparing him to a human being, or is the author suggesting that human beings can never be rational enough to live existentially and transcend their animal nature?
2. **CONNECTIONS** Compare and contrast the use of animals as characters in "A Dog without a Master" and Charles Johnson's "Menagerie, A Child's Fable."

3. **CONNECTIONS** Compare and contrast the different uses of a dog as metaphor in Söderberg's story, the poem "Dog" by Lawrence Ferlinghetti, and "How to Tell a Wolf from a Dog" by Louis Jenkins.

Related Poems

Lawrence Ferlinghetti, Dog, p. 1092.
Louis Jenkins, How to Tell a Wolf from a Dog, p. 961.

Susan Sontag

The Way We Live Now (p. 619)

Most stories by contemporary authors in this anthology are told from a limited-omniscient point of view. Leslie Marmon Silko narrates her story through the perceptions of Yellow Woman; James Baldwin uses first-person narration in "Sonny's Blues"; Lorrie Moore uses a second-person narrator in "How to Become a Writer." Susan Sontag does something very different in "The Way We Live Now." The story chronicles the last months of a man dying of AIDS, but we never learn directly what he sees or feels. Instead, we hear what he is suffering through the comments of his many friends. The end result is a work that deliberately treats its subject the way most people treat AIDS itself — at a distance, through hearsay, with mingled fascination and horror, as something terrible that can only happen to other people.

We never learn the name, occupation, or physical description of the AIDS victim in Sontag's story. Instead, we are told the responses of his friends, like a roll call of potential victims of the virus. These friends — more than twenty-five of them — are also not described, only presented by name as they talk to one another about the sick man. Their names follow one another so rapidly we are not given any explanation of their relationships: Max, Ellen, Greg, Tanya, Orson, Stephen, Frank, Jan, Quentin, Paolo, Kate, Aileen, Donny, Ursula, Ira, Hilda, Nora, Wesley, Victor, Xavier, Lewis, Robert, Betsy, Yvonne, Zack, and Clarice. The first-name basis is fitting, since the majority of the people know one another and inhabit the same world. We are never told what city they all live in, but we assume from the way they talk and their large numbers that they live in New York and are part of its cliques of people active in the arts, literature, and cultural journalism.

The first-name basis of the conversations is also aesthetically appropriate, because for the most part the characters are using the telephone. They repeat the latest gossip they have learned from one another; for all their sophistication, they pass along news of the stages of their friend's illness like the voices of tribal drums alerting the inhabitants of villages in Africa. The reader has the same sense of a closely knit community joined by common interests and means of livelihood. Because the community is left unspecified, the setting and the characters become mythologized into "Anyplace" and "Everyone." Sontag's implication is that we are all participants in this human tragedy. AIDS can happen to anyone.

As we read "The Way We Live Now," our rational impulses function despite the lack of specificity about the central character. The short conversational exchanges function as a literary code that we try to decipher. We attempt to trace relationships (Quentin, Lewis, Paolo, and Tanya have all been lovers of the AIDS victim); we categorize important information about lives outside the main story (Max gets AIDS too, as does Hilda's seventy-five-year-old aunt); we highlight generalizations that suggest a broader social and moral significance to this individual tragedy (the age of "debauchery" is over).

Close readers may even be able to interpret the fragments of conversations to gain psychological insights of use in other contexts. For example, Kate tells Aileen that the sick man is "not judging people or wondering about their motives" (when they come to see him in the hospital); rather, "he's just happy to see his friends." By presenting the numbers of people linked to a specific AIDS victim who appears to be well known and highly regarded in his community, Sontag is making an ironic comment about the isolation of all AIDS victims. Her story is an attempt to write about a taboo subject and encourage compassion toward those suffering from the disease.

Questions for Discussion

1. The story is developed chronologically, from the news of the patient's illness, through his first hospitalization, to his return home and rehospitalization. How does this progression give coherence to the story?
2. How do the relationships suggested among the twenty-five characters in the story give you a sense of the occupation and lifestyle of the central character?
3. Hilda says that the death of the pianist in Paris "who specialized in twentieth-century Czech and Polish music" is important because "he's such a valuable person . . . and it's such a loss to the culture." Do you think Sontag shares Hilda's opinion? Do you? Why or why not?
4. Agree or disagree with Ursula's idea at the end of the story.

Topics for Writing

1. Write a review of Sontag's nonfiction work *AIDS and Its Metaphors*.
2. Choose any five characters in "The Way We Live Now" and invent backgrounds for them.
3. Rewrite the story from the point of view of the AIDS patient, perhaps in the form of his diary.

Related Commentary

David Leavitt, The Way I Live Now, p. 766.

Suggested Reading

Sontag, Susan. *AIDS and Its Metaphors*. New York: Farrar, 1989.

JOHN STEINBECK

The Chrysanthemums (p. 632)

The instinctive life that Elisa Allen loves as she tends her chrysanthemum plants lies dormant under her fingers. She is good with flowers, like her mother before her. Elisa says, "She could stick anything in the ground and make it grow."

But it is December, and Steinbeck tells us it is "a time of quiet and of waiting." The Salinas landscape lies peacefully, but Elisa is vaguely unfulfilled. She begins to transplant her little chrysanthemum shoots, working without haste, conscious of her "hard-swept" house and her well-ordered garden, protected with its fence of chicken wire. Everything in her little world is under control. The tension in the scene is in herself, something she vaguely senses but refuses to face: the difference between her little world and the larger one encompassing it. Elisa is strong and mature, at the height of her physical strength. Why should she lie dormant? She has no fit scope for her powers. Steinbeck suggests the contradiction between her strength and her passivity in his description of the landscape: "The yellow stubble fields seemed to be bathed in pale cold sunshine, but there was no sunshine in the valley now in December." Like Hemingway, Steinbeck uses physical and geographical details to suggest the *absence* of positive qualities in his fictional characters. There is no sunshine in the valley, and the chrysanthemum plants aren't flowering, but what is natural in the annual vegetation cycle is out of kilter in Elisa. She experiences the world as a state of frustration.

Steinbeck has written an understated Chekhovian story in which ostensibly nothing much happens. It is a slice of life as Elisa lives it, sheltered and comfortable, yet — in Henry David Thoreau's words — life lived in a state of "quiet desperation."

The two male characters feel none of Elisa's lack of fulfillment. They live in a male world and take their opportunities for granted. Her husband, Henry Allen, is having a fine day. He's sold his thirty head of steer for a good price, and he's celebrating this Saturday night by taking his wife out to dinner and the movies in town. The traveling man is a trifle down on his luck, but it's nothing serious. He's found no customers this day so he lacks the money for his supper, but he knows a mark when he sees one. He flatters Elisa by agreeing with her and handing her a line about bringing some of her chrysanthemums to a lady he knows "down the road a piece." Elisa springs into action, delighted to be needed. Her tender shoots need her too, but she is not sufficiently absorbed by her gardening. The men do the real work of the world in this story. Gardening is a hobby she's proud of, and her husband encourages her to take pride in it, but she needs to feel of use in a larger dimension. Elisa mistakes this need for the freedom she imagines the transient knows on the road. Steinbeck gives her a clue as to the man's real condition in the state of his horse and mule, which she as a good gardener shouldn't have missed: "The horse and donkey drooped like unwatered flowers."

Instead, Elisa is caught up in her romantic fantasy of his nomadic life. Her sexual tension reduces her to a "fawning dog" as she envisions his life, but finally she realizes the man doesn't have the money for his dinner. "She stood up then, very straight, and her face was ashamed." Ashamed for what reason? Her lack of sensitivity to his poverty? her sexual excitement? her sense of captivity in a masculine world, where apparently only motherhood would bring opportunities for real work? Elisa brings the man two battered pots to fix and resumes talking, unable to leave him or her fantasy about the freedom she thinks he enjoys. He tells her outright that "it ain't the right kind of a life for a woman." Again she misreads the situation, taking his comment as a challenge. Her response is understandable, since she's never had his opportunity to choose a life on the road. She defends her ability to be his rival at sharpening scissors and banging out dents in pots and pans.

When the man leaves, Elisa is suddenly aware of her loneliness. She scrubs her body as rigorously as she's swept her house, punishing her skin with a pumice stone instead of pampering it with bubble bath. Then she puts on "the dress which was the symbol of her prettiness." An odd choice of words. Without understanding her instinctive rebellion against male expectations, Elisa refuses to be a sex symbol. Again she loses, denying herself pleasure in soft fabrics and beautiful colors. When Henry returns, he is bewildered by her mood and unable to reach her. She sees the chrysanthemums dying on the road, but she still can't face the truth about her sense of the repression and futility of her life. Wine at dinner and the idea of going to see a prize fight briefly bring her closer to the flesh and the instinctive life she has shunned outside her contact with her flowers, but they don't lift her mood. She feels as fragile and undervalued as her chrysanthemums. She begins to cry weakly, "like an old woman," as Henry drives her down the road.

Like Lawrence's heroine in "Odour of Chrysanthemums," Elisa is frustrated, cut off from the fullness of life by her physical destiny as a woman in a man's world. Does Steinbeck understand the sexual bias that undermines Elisa's sense of herself? He makes Henry as considerate a husband as a woman could wish for — he takes Elisa to the movies instead of going off to the prize fight himself. Like Hemingway, Steinbeck was sensitive to women's frustration, depicting it often in his fiction, even if he didn't look too closely at its probable causes in the society of his time.

Questions for Discussion

1. Based on Steinbeck's description in the first three paragraphs, how would you characterize the initial tone of the story? What do you associate with Steinbeck's image of the valley as "a closed pot"? In what way does this initial description foreshadow the events of the story?
2. What kind of character is Elisa Allen? What are the physical boundaries of her world? What is Elisa's psychological state at the beginning of the story?
3. Characterize the two men who are part of Elisa's world. In what ways are they similar and different? How does their way of life compare and contrast with the life Elisa leads?
4. What is the role of the chrysanthemums in Elisa's life? What do they symbolize?
5. How does Elisa delude herself about the life of the tinker? What other fantasies does this lead her to indulge in?
6. In what way does the tinker manipulate Elisa to accomplish his goals?
7. When the tinker leaves, a change comes over Elisa. What has she suddenly realized, and what course of action does she adopt?
8. As Elisa, both realistically and symbolically, goes out into the world, has she achieved any resolution of her problem? Why does she end the story "crying weakly — like an old woman"?

Topics for Writing

1. Discuss Steinbeck's use of setting to establish theme in "The Chrysanthemums."
2. Consider the isolation of Elisa Allen.
3. Analyze Elisa's illusions about the tinker and his interest in her as contrasted with reality.
4. Recall a time when you felt threatened and frustrated by events that isolated you. Write a narrative recounting this experience from a third-person point of view.

5. **CONNECTIONS** Compare male versus female societal and sexual roles in Lawrence's "Odour of Chrysanthemums" and Steinbeck's "The Chrysanthemums."
6. **CONNECTIONS** Discuss woman in a man's world: Steinbeck's Elisa and Silko's Yellow Woman.

Related Story

D. H. Lawrence, Odour of Chrysanthemums, p. 413.

Related Commentary

Jay Parini, Lawrence's and Steinbeck's "Chrysanthemum," p. 786.

Suggested Readings

Marcus, Mordecai. "The Lost Dream of Sex and Children in 'The Chrysanthemums." *Modern Fiction Studies* 11 (1965): 54–58.

McMahan, Elizabeth. "'The Chrysanthemums': Study of a Woman's Sexuality." *Modern Fiction Studies* 14 (1968–69): 453–58.

Miller, William V. "Sexual and Spiritual Ambiguity in 'The Chrysanthemums.'" *Steinbeck Quarterly* 5 (1972): 68–75.

Renner, S. "The Real Woman behind the Fence in 'The Chrysanthemums.'" *Modern Fiction Studies* 31 (1985): 305–17.

Sweet, Charles A. "Ms. Elisa Allen and Steinbeck's 'The Chrysanthemums.'" *Modern Fiction Studies* 20 (1974): 210–14.

AMY TAN

Two Kinds (p. 641)

"Two Kinds," which was first published in the February 1989 issue of *The Atlantic Monthly*, is an excerpt from Amy Tan's best-selling book, *The Joy Luck Club.* It is a skillfully written story that will probably pose no difficulty for most students; plot, characters, setting, and theme are immediately clear. The narrator states what she's "learned" from her experience in her final paragraph: She has come to realize that "Pleading Child" and "Perfectly Contented" are "two halves of the same song."

Looking back to her childhood, the narrator appears to be "perfectly contented" with her memories. Her interpretation of her relationship with her mother is presented in a calm, even self-satisfied, way. After her mother's death, she tunes the piano left to her in her parents' apartment: "I played a few bars [of the piano piece by Robert Schumann], surprised at how easily the notes came back to me." The painful memory of her fiasco as a piano student has dissipated. Now she is her own audience, and she is pleased with what she hears. There is no real emotional stress in "Two Kinds"; the girl has had a comfortable life. She has survived her mother and can dispose of her possessions as she likes. She is at peace with her past, fulfilling her mother's prophecy that "you can be best anything."

The mother earned her right to look on the bright side of life by surviving tremendous losses when she left China. Her desire to turn her daughter into a

"Chinese Shirley Temple" is understandable but unfortunate, since it places a tremendous psychological burden on the child. A discussion about this story might center on parents' supporting children versus "pushing" them to succeed in tasks beyond their abilities or ambitions.

Still, the narrator doesn't appear to have suffered unduly from her mother's ambitions for her. By her own account she was more than a match for her mother in the contest of wills on the piano bench. After her wretched performance at the recital, the daughter refuses to practice anymore. When her mother shouts, "Only two kinds of daughters.... Those who are obedient and those who follow their own mind! Only one kind of daughter can live in this house. Obedient daughter!" the girl answers by saying the unspeakable: "I wish I'd never been born! I wish I were dead! Like them [the mother's twin baby girls lost in China]." This ends the conflict, but the narrator goes on to tell us that she was unrelenting in victory: "In the years that followed, I failed her many times, each time asserting my will, my right to fall short of expectations. I didn't get straight *A*s. I didn't become class president. I didn't get into Stanford. I dropped out of college." She tells us that only after her mother's death can she begin to see things in perspective, when she is free to create her version of the past.

Because most students in class will be of the age when they are also asserting their will against parents in a struggle to take control of their lives, they will probably sympathize with Tan's narrator and accept her judgments uncritically. Will any reader take the mother's side?

Questions for Discussion

1. Why is the setting of this story important? What do you learn from it about the experience of Asian immigrants in their first years in the United States?
2. What advantages are offered to the child? What disadvantages?
3. How typical is Tan's story of the mother-daughter conflict? Explain.
4. Explain the meaning of the last paragraph of the story.

Topics for Writing

1. **CONNECTIONS** Compare and contrast the theme of initiation in Ellison's "Battle Royal" and Tan's "Two Kinds."
2. **CONNECTIONS** Analyze the use of dialect in Wright's "The Man Who Was Almost a Man" and Tan's "Two Kinds."
3. **CONNECTIONS** Compare and contrast the mother in Tan's "Two Kinds" with Olenka, the protagonist of Chekhov's "The Darling."
4. **CONNECTIONS** Compare and contrast Tan's "Two Kinds" with Munro's "Walker Brothers Cowboy," in which the narrator does *not* try to justify her actions or her feelings for a parent.

Suggested Readings

Tan, Amy. *The Joy Luck Club*. New York: Ballantine, 1989.
————. "The Language of Discretion." In *The State of the Language*. Ed. Christopher Ricks. Berkeley: U of California P, 1990.

(text pp. 650–690)

Leo Tolstoy

The Death of Ivan Ilych (p. 650)

No one who comes to "The Death of Ivan Ilych" from a direction other than that of *War and Peace* and *Anna Karenina* is likely to share the opinion of some Tolstoy scholars that it is parable-thin in its evocation of life, providing only a transparent surface of detail through which Tolstoy's allegorical intentions are exposed. The story is studded with brilliantly realistic representations of experiences that the reader encounters with a twinge of sometimes embarrassed recognition — Peter Ivanovich's struggle with the pouffe, for example. But it is nonetheless a product of the period following Tolstoy's religious crisis and a story written by one whose explicit theory of art rested on a utilitarian moral didacticism.

The story's effectiveness depends on Tolstoy's avoiding, until the last possible moment, preaching the sermon that, as the headnote suggests, he eventually means to preach. The opening section places us in the shoes of Peter Ivanovich, causing us to sympathize with the desire to look away from death, at the same time that it subjects that desire to a devastating satiric attack. Then, by returning to a long chronological survey of Ivan Ilych's life, Tolstoy forces us to do exactly the opposite of what Peter Ivanovich does: to confront death and its meaning in an extended and excruciatingly matter-of-fact account. What we see is not a life, but a death — or a life viewed as death. For Ivan Ilych's life, as he eventually comes to realize, is a slow but accelerating process of dying. The narration, however, decelerates, so that the reader may expect it to be nearly over around section VI, whereas in fact there are six more (albeit shorter) sections to come, containing a series of painful revelations that burst through the screen Ivan Ilych has built up to hide himself from reality.

Tolstoy tortures the reader just as Ivan Ilych is tortured, so that the precept finally advanced by the story arrives as the answer to the reader's fervent need. Ivan Ilych is not a particularly bad man; and — bad or good — all men, as Gerasim remarks, come to the same spot. Tolstoy makes this recognition virtually intolerable by his vivid rendering of Ivan Ilych's suffering. Then he offers a way out by proposing that one simple motion of the soul toward charity can release the sufferer from his mortal anguish. Tolstoy prepares us for this revelation by stressing the relief Ivan Ilych finds in the kindness of Gerasim, whose health, strength, and repose are bound up with his simple acceptance of sickness and death as necessary parts of life. Some critics have claimed that Tolstoy's art fails to encompass the illumination Ivan Ilych receives at the end, which rests on doctrines extrinsic to the text; but at least it can be said that he avoids sentimental piety by providing for an ironic interpretation when he caps Ivan Ilych's triumphant assertion "Death is finished.... It is no more!" with the paradoxical conclusion "He drew in a breath, stopped in the midst of a sigh, stretched out, and died."

The preoccupations and activities of Ivan Ilych and his peers during Ilych's lifetime in the society portrayed by Tolstoy contrast sharply with those of the unselfish peasant Gerasim. They are directed to no constructive end, serving only to gratify the ego with a sense of power and to hide the fear of death under a surface awareness of pleasure and propriety. Ivan Ilych is never more content than when manipulating the inert objects that are so plentiful in the story — as when decorating his new house — and he does his best to relate to people as he relates to things, insulating himself from true human contact. After he has received his death blow from the quite inert knob of a window frame, however, Ivan Ilych experiences a similar dehumanizing treatment by the doctors, his wife, and his friends, none of whom can bear to face the implications of his evident mortality. As his sickness steadily reduces him to a state of infantile dependency, Ilych comes to recognize first his own powerlessness and then the error in his strategy of living. Finally, as the coffin-womb he has built for himself falls away and he is reborn into the light of spiritual understanding, he sees the fundamental truth he has worked so hard to deny: The feelings of others are as real as his own. At this moment, moved by pity for his wife and son, he at last finds something worthwhile to do; and, in doing it, he attains the sense of ease and "rightness" that has previously eluded him. That the single positive act of Ivan Ilych's life is to die may be seen as either a grim irony or an exciting revelation, depending on the perspective from which the reader views it. But either way the conclusion of the story embodies the kernel of Tolstoy's social theme. As Edward Wasiolek puts it, "Death for Tolstoy now, as the supremely shared experience, is the model of all solidarity, and only the profound consciousness of its significance can bring one to the communion of true brotherhood."

WILLIAM E. SHEIDLEY

Questions for Discussion

1. How does the authorial voice qualify our view of Ivan Ilych's survivors' reactions to his death in section I?
2. Evaluate Peter Ivanovich's view of Ivan Ilych's son when he meets him near the end of section I.
3. Comment on the implications of Ivan Ilych's hanging a medallion bearing the motto *respice finem* (consider your end) on his watch chain.
4. What is wrong with Ivan Ilych's marriage? with his work? with his ambitions?
5. By examining the authorial comments in sections III and IV, define the attitude toward Ivan Ilych that Tolstoy asks the reader to share. Does this attitude change?
6. Consider the opening sentence of section VI. Is this section a low point in the story? If so, what kind of rise ensues?
7. Why does Ivan Ilych find relief in having his legs supported by Gerasim?
8. What is the effect of the shift to the present tense about one-third of the way through section VIII?
9. In section IX, Ivan Ilych complains to God in language similar to that of Job. Compare and contrast their plights.
10. What is the meaning of Ivan Ilych's reversion to childhood shortly before his death?
11. How might Ivan Ilych's dream of the black sack be interpreted?

Topics for Writing

1. Stop after reading section I and write a paragraph or two on the theme and tone of the story as you understand them so far. After reading the rest of the story, write a paragraph evaluating your original response. Write an essay examining the opening section as a story in itself, but one fully understood only after reading sections II–XII.

2. Consider the game of bridge as an epitome of the life Ivan Ilych and his friends try to live.
3. Discuss Tolstoy's use of symbolic, descriptive details in "The Death of Ivan Ilych."
4. Using "The Death of Ivan Ilych" as the basis of your knowledge of society, write a manifesto calling for revolution or reform.
5. Write a sermon, using the demise of Ivan Ilych Golovin as your occasion.

Related Commentary

Peter Rudy, Tolstoy's Revisions in "The Death of Ivan Ilych," p. 790.

Suggested Readings

Christian, R. F. *Tolstoy: A Critical Introduction*. Cambridge: Cambridge UP, 1969. 236–38.
Greenwood, E. B. *Tolstoy: The Comprehensive Vision*. New York: St. Martin's, 1975. 118–23.
Simmons, Ernest J. *Introduction to Tolstoy's Writings*. Chicago: U of Chicago P, 1968. Esp. 148–50.
Wasiolek, Edward. *Tolstoy's Major Fiction*. Chicago: U of Chicago P, 1978. Esp. 165–79.

JOHN UPDIKE

A & P (p. 691)

Although Updike was a precociously successful writer who spent his apprenticeship living in New York City and writing for *The New Yorker*, much of the strength of his writing stems from his ability to take the reader back to the atmosphere of the small town where he grew up. "A & P" showcases this ability. This story about a nineteen-year-old at a checkout counter in an A & P supermarket skillfully sustains the point of view of a teenage boy from a small-town working-class family.

The incident the story describes is slight. What gives "A & P" its substance is the voice of the narrator. He is obviously what the author thinks of as an ordinary teenager, impatient with old people, not interested in his job, and deeply aroused by girls. The longest descriptive passage — almost a third of the story itself — dwells on the body of one of the girls; as the story's slight action unfolds, the bodies of that girl and one of her friends are mentioned several times again. The narrator's adolescent desire and adoration are amusingly played off his clumsy bravado and the idiom of sexist stereotypes he is trying to master. "You never know for sure how girls' minds work (do you really think it's a mind in there or just a little buzz like a bee in a glass jar?)." His view of adult women is no less callow: "We're right in the middle of town, and the women generally put on a shirt or shorts or something before they get out of the car into the street. And anyway these are usually women with six children and varicose veins mapping their legs and nobody, including them, could care less."

It is probably true that when the story was written, in the late 1950s, its attitudes were not considered unusual. Today we have to ask ourselves whether the deplorable sexism is redeemed by the artfulness of the story, the technique Updike brings to constructing his narrator's voice.

Questions for Discussion

1. What does the language of the story tell us about the narrator's social background?
2. Are there any details in the story that place it in a specific part of the United States, or could it be happening anywhere within a few miles of a beach? Explain.
3. Is the boy's discomfort with older people limited to women, or is he also uncomfortable with men? Is there anyone in the store he *is* comfortable with? Explain.
4. Do you think Updike shares the narrator's attitudes?

Topics for Writing

1. Analyze the strengths and limitations of the first-person narrative in "A & P."
2. **CONNECTIONS** Consider "acting like a man": Updike's bag boy in "A & P" and Wright's Dave in "The Man Who Was Almost a Man."
3. **CONNECTIONS** Compare and contrast adolescent narrators in Updike's "A & P" and Joyce's "Araby."
4. **CONNECTIONS** Compare this story with Munro's "Walker Brothers Cowboy." How do the descriptive details in the two stories establish a specific time and place?

Suggested Readings

Cantor, Jay. "On Giving Birth to One's Own Mother." *TriQuarterly* 75 (Spring–Summer 1989): 78–91.

Detweiler, Robert. *John Updike.* Rev. ed. Boston: Twayne, 1987.

Fleischauer, John F. "John Updike's Prose Style: Definition at the Periphery of Meaning." *Critique: Studies in Contemporary Fiction* 30.4 (Summer 1989): 277–90.

Greiner, Donald J. *The Other Updike: Poems, Short Stories, Prose, Play.* Columbus: Ohio UP, 1981.

Luscher, Robert M. "John Updike's Olinger Stories: New Light among the Shadows." *Journal of the Short Story in English* 11 (Autumn 1988): 99–117.

Lyons, E. "John Updike: The Beginning and the End." *Critique* 14.2 (1972): 44–59.

Newman, Judie. *John Updike.* New York: St. Martin's, 1988.

Samuels, C. T. "The Art of Fiction: John Updike." *Paris Review* 12 (1968): 84–117.

Seib, P. "Lovely Way through Life: An Interview with John Updike." *Southwest Review* 66 (1981): 341–50.

Taylor, Charles C. *John Updike: A Bibliography.* Ann Arbor, MI: Books Demand UMI, 1989.

Thorburn, David, and Howard Eiland, eds. *John Updike: A Collection of Critical Essays.* New York: Prentice, 1979.

Updike, John. *Hugging the Shore.* New York: Random, 1983.

———. *Picked-Up Pieces.* New York: Knopf, 1976.

———. *Too Far to Go.* New York: Ballantine, 1979.

Wilhelm, Albert E. "Rebecca Cune: Updike's Wedge between the Maples." *Notes on Modern American Literature* 7.2 (Fall 1983): Item 9.

———. "The Trail-of-Bread-Crumbs Motif in Updike's Maples Stories." *Studies in Short Fiction* 25.1 (Winter 1988): 71–73.

ALICE WALKER

Roselily (p. 697)

This is the story of a black woman, Roselily, on her wedding day. Contrary to what we might expect, however, the tone is not joyful but tense and apprehensive. Roselily is full of doubts, about herself and the man who will soon be her husband. Her motivation to marry this man is not love of him as an individual. In fact, she admits she "does not even know if she loves him." What she does love are some of his qualities and properties, "his sobriety," "his pride," "his blackness," "his gray car," "his understanding of her *condition*," and, most important, his ability to "free her" from her current life. And what of his love for her? Roselily is realistic enough to know that he loves her, but again, she admits, he does not love her because of who she is. She acknowledges that "he will make [an effort] to redo her into what he truly wants." We are left with a picture of a woman trying to escape her past by marrying a man who will "free her" to "be respectable and respected and free" and a man marrying out of an apparent desire to reform.

"Roselily" has as its seminal concept the number *two*. It presents two opposite individuals at a crucial moment in their lives. Yet, as they symbolically fuse their lives into a single relationship, each brings very different experiences and backgrounds to the marriage. Roselily knows only the southern, small-town, country way of life, complete with its provincial religious beliefs and its sense of connectedness with family and community. Her husband is "against this." A northerner from Chicago, his ways are city ways, his religious beliefs are alien and restrictive. Rather than a feeling of community, he knows independence and anonymity.

Roselily wants freedom: "She wants to live for once. But doesn't know quite what that means. Wonders if she has ever done it. If she ever will." She spends the entire ceremony rationalizing that this marriage is the right thing to do, despite the fact that she "feels shut away from" this man. By the last paragraph she is finally able to formulate her feelings: "She feels ignorant, *wrong*, backward." By then, however, it is too late. The ceremony is complete, and "her husband's hand is like the clasp of an iron gate."

The structural framework for "Roselily" is the Christian marriage ceremony. It provides form as well as forward movement for a story that is essentially a stream-of-consciousness remembrance and narrative of the lead character, Roselily, from a third-person point of view. Contrast is the subject of the story. Conflict is the theme.

The title, "Roselily," does more than introduce the heroine. It also foreshadows the scope of the story. The rose becomes a lily. By means of the marriage vows, Roselily changes from a woman who is passionate, natural, and, in the eyes of society, impure and immoral to one who is resurrected and reborn but passionless and dead. For a price, she gains respectability. Now she must decide whether or not the cost is equal to the value. The conflict has not been resolved; it has only been postponed.

Questions for Discussion

1. Walker uses the marriage service to break up Roselily's reflections. What does this particular structure emphasize? What effect does it create?

2. Roselily's first passage opens with her dreaming of "dragging herself across the world. A small girl in her mother's white robe and veil, knee raised waist high through a bowl of quicksand soup." What subjects in these sentences persist throughout this story? Describe the qualities of this girl that reflect Roselily's own representation of herself in this story. Is she helpless, vulnerable, childish, struggling, or play-acting?

3. Why does Roselily spend so much time thinking about her fourth child's father? Do we know as much about the man she is marrying as we do about her ex-lover? What do Roselily's reflections on his character tell us about hers?

4. What does Roselily's fourth child, the one she gave to his father, represent? What kind of a connection does she feel to the child? Can she imagine his future?

5. Part of Roselily's reflections are devoted to wondering "what one does with memories in a brand-new life." What alternatives are open to her? Can she just shut her memories away, or break them off and start again? Consider the question of memory and the burden of the past against her sudden dream of having no children. Roselily's own mother is dead, yet Roselily still feels a connection to her. What are the "ghosts" that Roselily believes in?

6. Much of this story depends on oppositions. "Her husband's hand," Roselily thinks, "is like the clasp of an iron gate." What are the positive and negative qualities of an iron gate? Roselily thinks of "ropes, chains, handcuffs, his religion." What other images does she associate with this man she is marrying? He's going to "free her." How do you reconcile the images of bondage and freedom? Consider the diction in this passage: "A romantic hush. Proposal. Promises. A new life! Respectable, reclaimed, renewed. Free! In robe and veil." Yet suddenly Walker presents "a rat trapped, concerned, scurrying to and fro in her head, peering through the windows of her eyes." What is the difference in the language in both examples? Is one kind of diction stronger than the other? Why?

7. What do you infer about Roselily's feelings from these sentences: "The rest she does not hear. She feels a kiss, passionate, rousing, within the general pandemonium. Cars drive up blowing their horns. Firecrackers go off. Dogs come from under the house and begin to yelp and bark." Look first at the syntax of these sentences. Why do you think they are all short and unconnected to one another? What effect does that create? What is the subject of each sentence? Why might Roselily only be able to receive certain kinds of impressions?

8. How do you interpret the final paragraph of this story? Does this paragraph control your understanding of the story retrospectively? How did you weigh the oppositions until this paragraph? Were Roselily's hopes and fears in equilibrium? Which words carry the heaviest burden of meaning for you? Would the paragraph — and your judgment — be very different without them?

Topics for Writing

1. Contrast Roselily's culture and environment and those of her husband-to-be.

2. Discuss the disparity between Roselily's dreams and her situation.
3. Describe the point of view in "Roselily."
4. Think back in your own life to a time when your thoughts received stimulation from an outside event but were not totally controlled by that event. Try to re-create your thought patterns and structure them into an interesting narrative account.
5. **CONNECTIONS** Compare and contrast the concept of marriage in Walker's "Roselily" and Lawrence's "Odour of Chrysanthemums."

Suggested Readings

Banks, Erma Davis, and Keith Byerman. *Alice Walker: An Annotated Bibliography 1968–1986.* New York: Garland, 1989.

Bell, Roseann P., Bettye J. Parker, and Beverly Guy-Sheftall, eds. *Sturdy Black Bridges: Visions of Black Women in Literature.* New York: Anchor, 1979.

Bloom, Harold. *Alice Walker.* New York: Chelsea House, 1990.

Byerman, Keith, and Erma Banks. "Alice Walker: A Selected Bibliography, 1968–1988." *Callaloo: An Afro-American and African Journal of Arts and Letters* 12.2 (Spring 1989): 343–45.

Byrne, Mary Ellen. "Welty's 'A Worn Path' and Walker's 'Everyday Use': Companion Pieces." *Teaching English in a Two-Year College* 16(2) (May 1989): 129–33.

Cooke, Michael. *Afro-American Literature in the Twentieth Century: The Achievement of Intimacy.* New Haven: Yale UP, 1984.

Davis, T. M. "Alice Walker's Celebration of Self in Southern Generations." In *Women Writers of the Contemporary South.* Ed. Peggy Whitman Prenshaw. Jackson: UP of Mississippi, 1984. 83–94.

Erickson, P. "Cast Out Alone/To Heal/and Re-create/Ourselves: Family Based Identity in the Work of Alice Walker." *College Language Association Journal* 23 (1979): 71–94.

Evans, Mari, ed. *Black Women Writers (1950–1980): A Critical Evaluation.* New York: Anchor, 1984. 453–95.

Mariani, Philomena, ed. *Critical Fictions: The Politics of Imaginative Writing.* Seattle: Bay Press, 1991.

Petry, Alice Hall. "Alice Walker: The Achievement of the Short Fiction." *Modern Language Studies* 19.1 (Winter 1989): 12–27.

Stade, G. "Womanist Fiction and Male Characters." *Partisan Review* 52 (1985): 265–70.

Winchell, Donna Haisty. *Alice Walker.* Boston: Twayne, 1990.

EUDORA WELTY

A Worn Path (p. 701)

Try not to force the Christian or mythological allegories the story supports until you encourage students to savor the beauty of the literal narration. Phoenix Jackson is an embodiment of love, faith, sacrifice, charity, self-renunciation, and triumph over death in herself, quite apart from the typological implications of her name or the allusions to the stations of the cross in her journey. Phoenix transcends her merely archetypal significance just as she transcends the stereotype of old black mammies on which she is built. Welty accomplishes this act of creation by entering fully into the consciousness of her character. There she discovers the little child that still lives within the old woman and causes her to dream of chocolate cake, dance with a scarecrow, and delight in a Christmas toy. Phoenix is right when she says, "I wasn't as old as I thought," but she does not merit the condescension of the hunter's exclamation, "I know you old colored people! Wouldn't miss going to town to see Santa Claus!" Even in her greatest discomfort, lying in the weeds, losing her memory, getting her shoes tied, "stealing" a nickel, or taking one as a handout, Phoenix retains her invincible dignity, an essential component of the single glimpse we receive of her triumphant homeward march, bearing aloft the bright symbol of life she has retrieved through her exertions.

In her comments on the story (included in Chapter 7, p. 809), Welty implies that the meaning of Phoenix's journey is that of any human exertion carried out in good faith despite the uncertainty of the outcome: "The path is the thing that matters." In keeping with this theme, Welty repeatedly shows Phoenix asserting life in the face of death. Her name itself, taken from the mythical bird that periodically immolates itself and rises reborn from its ashes, embodies the idea. (She even makes a noise like "a solitary little bird" in the first paragraph.) Phoenix makes her journey at the time of the death and rebirth of the year; her own skin color is like the sun bursting through darkness; she overcomes discouragement as she tops the hill; she extricates herself from a thorn bush (of which much may be made in a Christian allegorical interpretation); she passes "big dead trees" and a buzzard; she traverses a field of dead corn; she sees a "ghost" that turns out to be a dancing scarecrow; she is overcome by a "black dog" but rescued by a death-dealing hunter whose gun she faces down and whom she beats out of a shiny nickel; and she emerges from a deathlike trance in the doctor's office to return with the medicine her grandson needs to stay alive. Phoenix's strength lies in the purpose of her journey, and her spirit is contagious. The hunter, the woman who ties her shoes, and the doctor's attendant all perform acts of charity toward her, and lest the reader overlook the one word that lies at the heart of Welty's vision, the nurse says "Charity" while "making a check mark in a book."

Questions for Discussion

1. Notice Phoenix's identification with "a solitary little bird." What other birds does she encounter on her journey? Explain their implications.

2. What techniques does Welty use to suggest the laboriousness of Phoenix's trip?

3. Before she crosses the creek, Phoenix says, "Now comes the trial." Does she pass it? How? To what extent is this event a microcosm of the whole story? Are there other microcosmic episodes?

4. What effect do Phoenix's sequential reactions to the scarecrow, the abandoned cabins, and the spring have on the reader's view of her?

5. What is your opinion of the hunter? What conclusion might be drawn from the fact that even though he kills birds and patronizes Phoenix, he helps her in a way he does not know?

6. Interpret the passage that begins with Phoenix bending for the nickel and ends with her parting from the hunter.

7. Describe Natchez as Phoenix perceives it. Is it a worthy culmination for her journey?

8. In her comments reprinted in Chapter 7 (p. 809), Welty remarks that Phoenix's victory comes when she sees the doctor's diploma "nailed up on the wall." In what sense is this moment the climax of the story? What is different about the ensuing action from the action that leads up to this moment? Are there any similarities?
9. How does Phoenix describe her grandson? What is Welty's reason for using these terms?
10. Explain the irony in the way the nurse records Phoenix's visit.

Topics for Writing

1. Explain why many readers think that Phoenix Jackson's grandson is dead.
2. Discuss the symbolism of birds in "A Worn Path."
3. After your first reading of "A Worn Path," write a paragraph giving your opinion of Phoenix Jackson. Then study some symbolic interpretations of the story (such as those by Ardelino, Isaacs, and Keys, cited in Suggested Reading). Reread the story and write another assessment of the central character. Does she bear up under the freight of symbolic meaning the critics ask her to carry? Does her relation to these archetypes help to account for your original response?
4. Read Welty's account of how she came to write "A Worn Path" (p. 809). Following her example, write an account of what you imagine to be the day's experience of someone you catch a glimpse of who strikes your fancy. Use the intimate interior third-person limited-omniscient point of view that Welty employs for Phoenix Jackson.

Related Commentary

Eudora Welty, Is Phoenix Jackson's Grandson Really Dead? p. 809.

Suggested Readings

Ardelino, Frank. "Life out of Death: Ancient Myth and Ritual in Welty's 'A Worn Path.' " *Notes on Mississippi Writers* 9 (1976): 1–9.
Bloom, Harold. *Eudora Welty.* New York: Chelsea House, 1986.
Desmond, John F. *A Still Moment: Essays on the Art of Eudora Welty.* Metuchen, NJ: Scarecrow, 1978.
Isaacs, Neil D. "Life for Phoenix." *Sewanee Review* 71 (1963): 75–81.
Keys, Marilynn. " 'A Worn Path': The Way of Dispossession." *Studies in Short Fiction* 16 (1979): 354–56.
Kieft, Ruth M. *Eudora Welty.* Rev. ed. Boston: Twayne, 1987.
MacNeil, Robert. In *Eudora Welty: Seeing Black and White.* Westport, CT: Greenwood, 1990.
Phillips, Robert L., Jr. "A Structural Approach to Myth in the Fiction of Eudora Welty." *Eudora Welty: Critical Essays.* Ed. Peggy Whitman Prenshaw. Jackson: UP of Mississippi, 1979. 56–67, esp. 60.
Preenshaw, Peggy W., ed. *Eudora Welty: Thirteen Essays.* Jackson: UP of Mississippi, 1983.
Schmidt, Peter. *The Heart of the Story: Eudora Welty's Short Fiction.* Jackson: UP of Mississippi, 1991.
Turner, W. Craig, and Lee Harding, eds. *Critical Essays on Eudora Welty.* Boston: G. K. Hall, 1989.
Welty, Eudora. *The Eye of the Story.* New York: Vintage, 1990.
———. *One Writer's Beginnings.* New York: Warner, 1984.

TENNESSEE WILLIAMS

Portrait of a Girl in Glass (p. 708)

In addition to comparing and contrasting this story with the fuller treatment of characters and theme in Williams's *The Glass Menagerie,* students might also read the stories of two other authors in this anthology — Susan Glaspell and Arthur Miller — that have been treated as plays. (See Glaspell's "A Jury of Her Peers" and *Trifles* and Miller's *Death of a Salesman* and "In Memoriam" included in Part Three of the text.)

In the Appendix, "Writing about Literature," you might also assign the student essay by Steven Silvester (p. 2106) comparing and contrasting Williams's "Portrait of a Girl in Glass" with *The Glass Menagerie.* Silvester analyzes how Williams developed the character of Laura when he adapted his short story for the stage. Pointing out the importance of the book *Freckles* to Laura in the story, Silvester argues that her character is so volatile in the short narrative that, as he says, "we are not quite sure what to make of" her. Your students might find that they prefer the mystery surrounding Laura in the story to the more predictable and consistent Laura in the play.

Questions for Discussion

1. How does "Portrait of a Girl in Glass" reflect Williams's own family life?
2. Which of the characters in the story are sympathetic? Unsympathetic?
3. How does the description of the setting of the family's apartment set the mood for what will happen in the story?

Topics for Writing

1. **CONNECTIONS** Compare and contrast Williams's story and his reworking of his characters, setting, and plot as a play.
2. Find a copy of *Freckles* in the library and write a book report on it as if you were the character Laura in "Portrait of a Girl in Glass."

Related Commentary

Tennessee Williams, *The Glass Menagerie,* p. 1704.

RICHARD WRIGHT

The Man Who Was Almost a Man (p. 716)

Dave Saunders dislikes being laughed at, and his discomfort at becoming an object of amusement for accidentally shooting old Jenny, the mule, precipitates his final step into manhood. Although the anecdote around which Wright builds the story is comical enough, the reader probably should accede to Dave's wish to be taken seriously, for the fate that lies ahead of this young man as he rolls toward his unknown destination atop a boxcar with nothing in his pocket but an unloaded gun is likely to be grim.

At the same time, however, Dave's self-esteem and independence deserve respect. At the beginning of the story he dissociates himself from the field hands and fixes on his ambition to declare his manhood by owning a gun. Throughout the story the idea that *boys* do not have guns recurs, and Dave not only wants a gun but also chafes at being call "boy" by his parents and at being treated as a child. Just before he goes out to master the gun and hop a freight, Dave grumbles, "They treat me like a mule, n then they beat me." His resolution to escape his inferior status will involve not only leaving home but taking potshots at the facade of white society just as he wants to shoot at "Jim Hawkins' big white house" in order "to let him know Dave Saunders is a man." The question Wright leaves hanging for the reader as his story trails off into ellipses is whether Dave has killed the mule in himself or whether he himself, like Jenny, may become the victim of his own wild shots.

William E. Sheidley

Questions for Discussion

1. Explain the pun in the last sentence of the first paragraph.
2. Define our first impression of Dave. What reasons do we have to admire him? to laugh at him? to pity him?
3. What does it take to be a man in the world of the story? Is a gun enough? How does one get a gun?
4. What is ironic about the way Dave gets the money to buy his gun?
5. How is Dave treated by his father? Why does Ma say of the gun, "It be fer Pa"?
6. With the gun under his pillow, Dave feels "a sense of power. Could kill a man with a gun like this. Kill anybody, black or white." What does Dave still have to learn before he can be called a man? How does the story bring it home to him?
7. Explain what happens the first time Dave fires the gun. What does he do differently the next time?
8. Why does Wright describe the death of the mule in such detail?
9. Explain why being laughed at is so painful for Dave. What might enable him to join in and laugh at himself?
10. Comment on the possible implications of Dave's remark "They treat me like a mule, n then they beat me," both within the story and in a broader social and historical context. Does Dave's killing the mule have a symbolic significance?
11. Where might Dave be headed as he hops the Illinois Central? What might he find at the end of his journey?
12. Why is the title not "The Boy Who Was Almost a Man"?

Topics for Writing

1. Examine the tone of Wright's story.
2. Discuss the treatment of Wright's social themes in "The Man Who Was Almost a Man." (See the story's headnote.)
3. Write a sequel to Wright's story, another episode in the life of Dave Saunders — something that happens on the train ride or when he arrives in New Orleans or Chicago or wherever. Try to sustain and develop as many themes and motives already present in Wright's story as you can, but make the material your own by imagining what you think happens, not necessarily what you guess Wright would have written. Decide whether to adopt

Wright's style and point of view or employ a different mode of narration. Remember that the story is set during the Great Depression.

Suggested Readings

Felgar, Robert. *Richard Wright.* Boston: Twayne, 1980.

Hakutani, Yoshinobu, ed. *Critical Essays on Richard Wright.* Boston: G. K. Hall, 1982.

Margolies, Edward. *The Art of Richard Wright.* Carbondale: Southern Illinois UP, 1969.

McCall, Dan. *The Example of Richard Wright.* New York: Harcourt, 1969.

Reilly, John M. *Richard Wright: The Critical Reception.* New York: Burt Franklin, 1978.

Wright, Richard. *Uncle Tom's Children.* New York: Harper, 1989.

PART TWO

POETRY

Helen Adam

I Love My Love (p. 928)

One of the more memorable experiences for audiences at poetry readings in the 1960s and 1970s was hearing Helen Adam read her ballad "I Love My Love." Adam's poem seemed to have come from an almost forgotten time, when poets wrote with ease and confidence, before the anxieties and difficulties of modern life had left their mark on much current verse. Adam and her ballad did in fact come from another period and from another poetic tradition. Although she was often grouped with the American underground poets after World War II — and she was congenially comfortable with them and their lifestyle — Adam was from Scotland, and she was older. She was born in 1909 and began composing ballads when she was two. Her first book was published when she was twelve, and it was a collection of ballads.

She lived for years in San Francisco, where she was a vital creative force in a community of artists, writers, and performers. A reading, she felt, should be a magical performance, and as one reviewer wrote after hearing her perform, "Who has a defense after all against witchcraft?" After a series of artistic and personal difficulties in the 1960s, she had to be hospitalized and was given shock treatments. She eventually moved with her sister to New York City, where she died in 1992.

Questions for Discussion

1. What stylistic elements of "I Love My Love" classify it as a ballad?
2. Analyze the poem for its metric form. What is the term for a line of this length?
3. What phrases indicate that the poem was meant to be performed or read aloud?
4. The poem tells a grim story. Discuss whether it is a story of witchcraft, or if it is a metaphor for excessive love.
5. Is there a significance to the woman's statement at the beginning of the poem that she loves her love with a "capital A," and at the end of the poem that she loves him with a "capital Z"?

Topics for Writing

1. CONNECTIONS   Discuss the similarities and differences between this modern ballad and a traditional ballad like "Barbara Allan" (p. 921).
2. Many traditional ballads focus on a woman who is an evil witch. Analyze this ballad for its elements of witchcraft and sorcery.

ANNA AKHMATOVA

Instead of a Preface (p. 990)
Dedication (p. 990)

Born in southern Russia in 1889, Anna Akhmatova was one of the twentieth century's most outstanding poets. Her early poetry was personal and lyric, but for her the personal became political when she was swept up in the turmoil of the Bolshevik Revolution and her husband was executed as an antirevolutionary in 1921. The short prose selection "Instead of a Preface" describes the years she spent waiting outside a Leningrad prison for news of her son. She survived decades of isolation, persecution, and continual threats of imprisonment. It was only in the years before her death in 1966 that her work was permitted to appear and she was able to accept some of the many honors offered her.

Questions for Discussion

1. Explain the title of "Instead of a Preface."
2. What is Akhmatova suggesting about the woman in the last line of "Instead of a Preface"?
3. How does Akhmatova use images of nature in "Dedication"? To what does she contrast them?

Topic for Writing

1. Ask students to write a two-page essay stating which of Akhmatova's two poems is more effective, and why.

MATTHEW ARNOLD

Dover Beach (p. 1018)

This well-known poem by one of the Victorian era's most important writers has continued to fascinate readers throughout the century and a half since its composition. Although its diction and complex rhyme scheme seem to place it in an older historical context, the poem is in many ways modern. There is no clearly sensed metric form. The first line, "The sea is calm tonight," is a matter of fact statement without any kind of hyperbole. Even with the enjambment of the second line — the phrase as the ear hears it is "the moon lies fair upon the straits" — there is still no sense that we are reading a poem from an era in which a poem's diction and vocabulary were expected to be different from everyday speech. It is only Arnold's use of onomatopoeia in line 11, with its description of the waves streaming up the beach ("Begin and cease, and then begin again"), or the simile of line 23, when the poet writes that religious faith was once like a sea that "Lay like the folds of a bright girdle furl'd," that the modern reader is reminded of the language and technique of the Victorian poets.

The poem is also modern in its disillusionment. The poet, and the woman who has come with him to Dover, are left alone, without solace on a quiet night, as they look out at the sea. It is not a difficult poem for modern readers to understand, although students may be confused by the leap in exposition that occurs after the third verse. To paraphrase the poem and its setting most simply, the poet is watching the sea as it sweeps up the beach on a moonlit night, and the sound seems to him to be filled with sadness. The reason for his sadness — his consciousness of "the turbid ebb and flow of human misery" as he describes it in line 17 — is not fully revealed until the last verse, but the mood weighs on him so heavily that he is reminded of Sophocles, who also heard the sea with this same mood of melancholy. If students have difficulty making this connection, the "it" of line 16 refers to this "eternal note of sadness," and the "it" of line 20 refers to the phrase again, but in this line Arnold has modified the reference by telling the reader that hearing the sound has given him "a thought." The "thought" is clarified in the third verse, when he says that religious belief, "The Sea of Faith," once covered the earth; now, however, as the sea retreats from the beach, the poet hears the sound of faith retreating with it. The use of the phrase "naked shingles" to describe the beach in line 28 is a further extension of the mood of sadness that fills the poem's early lines.

The difficulty for some students comes in the leap Arnold makes from the descriptive passages of the first three verses to the personal outcry of the last verse. What he has left out — to paraphrase the verse he might have written here — is the explanation that the mood of sadness he feels as he listens to the sea has made him conscious that there is no Sea of Faith surrounding him, and if there is no faith, then he and his loved one are left alone in a confused and frightening world, and for that moment they have only each other to cling to. This shift in mood can confuse readers, who become conscious that the last five lines of the poem seem sarcastic and angry. If there is no faith, then nothing, not even military heroism, has any meaning, and human history is simply the dark spectacle of an appalling world "Where ignorant armies clash by night." If students can supply the missing step in their minds, then the poem will become much clearer to them.

Perhaps the most helpful way to introduce students to the poem is to remind them that it was written in the mid-nineteenth century, when discoveries in geology, archaeology, astrology, and genetics had shattered the creation stories that Arnold, as a Christian, had been taught. Charles Darwin's *Origin of Species* was to become the most debated book of its time, and Arnold's poem is in many ways a direct, anguished response to the confusion and uncertainty that he felt at the new world he was facing — a world without religious faith at its center.

Questions for Discussion

1. In what ways do the questions of religious faith that trouble Arnold in this poem still trouble us today?
2. What is Arnold suggesting in the phrase "the folds of a bright girdle furl'd" in line 23?
3. What is Arnold suggesting in the image of "the vast edges drear / And naked shingles of the world" in lines 27 and 28?
4. What is meant in the contrast between the Aegean and "this distant northern sea" in the second verse?
5. What is the significance of the reference to Sophocles in line 15?
6. Is the despair Arnold expresses in the poem justified by the events of the last 150 years?

Topics for Writing

1. "Dover Beach" has a symbolic importance to English readers, and the southern part of England has played an important part in English history. Students might be interested in analyzing this role.
2. At the time Arnold wrote the poem, England and France had been at peace with each other for only thirty-five years, after centuries of intermittent warfare. Students might be interested in explicating the line "ignorant armies clash by night" in terms of this history.
3. It is a complicated and still controversial issue, but students might want to discuss the effect of the scientific discoveries of the nineteenth century on Christian beliefs.
4. **CONNECTIONS**   Many students will want to read "The Dover Bitch" (p. 1269), the parody of "Dover Beach" by contemporary poet Anthony Hecht. They could compare the differences in mood and attitude between the two poems.

Related Commentaries

Anthony Hecht, "The Dover Bitch," p. 1269.
Eric Trethewey, "The Virtue of Arnold's "Dover Beach," p. 1318.

W. H. AUDEN

Miss Gee (p. 1019)
Musée des Beaux Arts (p. 1022)
In Memory of W. B. Yeats (p. 1022)

MISS GEE

Like other young writers before and after him, Auden rebelled against what he perceived as the conformity and emotional repression of his time. The instructor is probably familiar with poems that describe the stultified lives of the middle classes — poems such as Edward Arlington Robinson's "Miniver Cheevy," E. E. Cummings's "'Gay' is the captivating cognomen of a Young woman of cambridge, mass," or T. S. Eliot's "Portrait of a Lady." None of them, however, matches the cruelty of Auden's poem. Poor Miss Gee suppresses all natural feeling, develops a large cancerous tumor, and ends up as a cadaver in an anatomy class at Oxford. As he makes clear in lines 73–74, Auden certainly intends the cancer to symbolize a body that has poisoned itself by denying its natural hungers, and Miss Gee's dream of being pursued by a bull in lines 31–36 is almost a textbook example of a sexual dream. (Auden didn't use the singular for the bull's horns in line 32 simply for the sake of the rhyme.)

Questions for Discussion

1. Like a traditional ballad, the poem is written in a four-line stanza. Why did Auden choose this form?
2. What does Auden mean in line 24 when he writes of Miss Gee living "on one hundred pounds a year"? Were there many women like Miss Gee in England in the 1930s?

3. What is Auden suggesting in lines 35–36 when he describes the bicycle as going "slower and slower / Because of that back-pedal brake"?

Topic for Writing

1. There is still no medical agreement on whether our emotions can cause cancer. Students might want to look at current evidence and discuss it in terms of Auden's suggestion.

MUSÉE DES BEAUX ARTS

The painting by the sixteenth-century Flemish artist Pieter Brueghel the Elder that Auden uses as the theme of his poem is in the Museum of Art in Brussels. The painting's full title is *Landscape with the Fall of Icarus*. In the poem he alludes to Icarus, a figure from Greek mythology who has fascinated writers and artists for centuries. Icarus attempted to fly, using wings of feathers that he fastened to his shoulders with beeswax. Despite his father's warnings not to go too high, he flew too close to the sun, so that the sun's warmth melted the wax, and he fell into the ocean and drowned. The moral of the tale is that a son should listen to his father and not struggle against authority. A larger meaning is that humankind should not attempt to do things for which it was not made, and that challenging the order of the world — in this legend, attempting to fly — will only lead to tragedy.

In the painting that Auden describes, Icarus, who is ostensibly the composition's subject, is almost lost in a corner of the canvas. In the center foreground peasant country life is going on in its ordinary way. A farmer is ploughing, and behind him a shepherd is tending to a scattered flock of sheep. It is only after you look at the painting for several moments, reminding yourself that Icarus must be there somewhere because the painting is named for him, that you notice two naked legs protruding from the ocean in the lower right-hand corner, almost out of sight of the other people in the painting, who are paying no attention to what is happening. There is also a ship on the ocean, but there is no sign that anyone on board has seen anything. Even the ocean seems unconcerned. As Auden says in line 17, "the sun shone / as it had to onto the white legs disappearing into the green / Water."

What Auden is saying in his poem is that the Old Masters knew that despite suffering and tragedy, life goes on. The style of the poem, which is relaxed and conversational, matches Auden's theme, and the details he describes in the first stanzas are as ordinary as the lives depicted in Brueghel's painting. In his ironic comment, even the horse ridden by a torturer is not to be blamed for anything, as it "Scratches its innocent behind on a tree."

Questions for Discussion

1. When Auden uses the term "suffering" in line 1, what is he describing?
2. When he uses the terms "miraculous birth" in line 6 and "dreadful martyrdom" in line 10, what is he referring to?
3. Auden spent most of his early years as a political activist. Does this poem express activist sentiments?
4. In lines 5 and 6 Auden suggests that it is the older generation who is waiting for something miraculous to happen, while young people are unconcerned. Is this a valid description of young people's attitudes today?

Topics for Writing

1. Many painters used fables like the story of Icarus as the subject of their work. Students might be interested in taking this as a subject for further study.
2. **CONNECTIONS** Many other poets — for instance, Lawrence Ferlinghetti in "In Goya's greatest scenes we seem to see" (p. 1094) and "Late Impressionist Dream" (p. 1095) — have described paintings. Students might want to compare Auden's poem with other poems about painting. Another poem that might be an interesting subject for this kind of comparison is Keats's "Ode on a Grecian Urn" (p. 934).
3. Students might want to respond to the poem's suggestion that despite whatever miracles or disasters happen to us, life goes on.

IN MEMORY OF W. B. YEATS

The instructor might want to assign this poem after students have spent some class time discussing the Yeats poems included in Chapter 17. Auden, as students will have surmised from reading "Miss Gee," could be savagely critical of aspects of society that he didn't like, but his admiration and respect for Yeats's work is obvious in this poem written shortly after Yeats's death. The instructor might also include the poem in a discussion of other writing in the "Address and Tribute" section of Chapter 15, which includes poems written as a tribute to another writer.

Questions for Discussion

1. The stanza beginning with line 18 is a complicated description of what happens to writers' work after their death. How would a student explain this stanza, with its conclusion that the work is modified "in the guts of the living"?
2. Many lines and phrases in the poem reflect a politically activist point of view. How would a student summarize Auden's attitudes in such lines as 25–28, 37–38, 60–66, and 75–77?
3. What does Auden mean in line 32, when he speaks of Yeats as "silly like us"?
4. What is Auden suggesting in line 41, when he speaks of poetry as "a mouth"?
5. Is there a contradiction in Auden's assertion, in lines 50–57, that the world will forgive a writer for any political opinions if he or she writes well enough?

Topics for Writing

1. Lines 26 and 27 are a cynical view of daily life for many people. Students might want to discuss Auden's attitudes in this poem and in "Miss Gee."
2. In this poem Auden makes many angry statements about the inadequacies and cruelties of society. Students might analyze these statements and decide, in a paper, whether the statements are inspired by Auden's dark view of the human race or reflect the specific circumstances of the difficult year in European history, 1940, when the poem was written.

(text pp. 891, 1024–1028)

John Berryman

A Professor's Song (p. 891)

Perhaps no American poet was as self-doomed and as self-damned as John Berryman. His suicide at the age of fifty-eight in 1972 seemed the only possible ending for a life of poetic brilliance, helpless alcoholism, intense scholarship, and an untiring interest in women (often women married to other men). For much of his life — after Columbia University and Cambridge University — he taught literature and poetry. He became a professor at the University of Minnesota in 1955 and remained there until his death. His major work was the startlingly original and idiosyncratic collection *77 Dream Songs,* which won every major literary prize in 1964, the year it was published. In the opening lines of "Dream Song #77," he gives a laconic view of himself, as "Henry," setting out to teach one of his classes:

> Seedy Henry rose up shy in de world
> & shaved and swung his barbells, duded Henry up
> and p. a.'d poor thousands of persons on topics of
> > grand
> moment to Henry, ah to those less & none.

Questions for Discussion

1. What class is the professor teaching in Berryman's poem?
2. What is he asking the class to do in the phrase "Troll me the sources of that Song" in line 3?
3. What is he asking the class with the parenthetical question in line 9, "(Red all your eyes, O when?)"?
4. Explain the allusion to Mozart in line 16.
5. Is the professor's garbled description of his lecture a glimpse into his methods as a teacher or into his feelings toward the class?
6. What is the professor suggesting about himself in the phrases "foaming immortal blood" in the last line?

Elizabeth Bishop

The Bight (p. 904)
Sestina (p. 956)
The Fish (p. 1025)
The Armadillo (p. 1027)
One Art (p. 1028)

"The Bight" is analyzed in Chapter 11, and the form of "Sestina" is discussed in Chapter 13. The subject of "Sestina" is clearly Bishop's own childhood. Her father died when she was only eight months old, and after her mother suffered a mental breakdown Bishop was sent to live with her grandmother in Nova Scotia. Her grandmother's father had also died when she was a child, so although Bishop doesn't identify the reason for the grief that is so palpable in the poem, the fact that the child and her grandmother both feel it makes it clear that this is what Bishop is describing.

Bishop's poetry is popular with students because both her subject and the means with which she presents it are clear and immediately understandable. What makes her writing so useful for classroom discussion is that students also have no problem reading a Bishop poem for its technical skill and secondary meanings. On a first reading the class will have no difficulty with "The Fish." The narrator has caught a large ugly fish, and as she pulls it halfway out of the water she sees from the old hooks and lines in its mouth that it has been caught before, but each time it has been strong enough to break free. When she realizes what an event it is for her to have caught a fish like this, she feels a sense of victory fill the air around her, and she lets the fish go.

If Bishop intended any symbolism in letting the fish go, there is no way a student could infer it from the poem; nonetheless, an interesting class discussion could arise from analyzing some of the reasons she might have done so.

If the class has already read the text's analysis of "The Bight," they are conscious of some of the imaginative ways in which Bishop works with diction and imagery. In the first line of "The Fish," the word "tremendous" is unexpected. It seems too momentous a word for the act of fishing to warrant. It does, however, prepare us for the ending of the poem, with its intonation of "rainbow, rainbow, rainbow!" — which is also more dramatic terminology than we'd expect from a simple description of a fish the narrator has caught. When you add the detail that the fish didn't fight at all, it seems that nothing about the fish is what you would expect. Line 7 is a remarkable example of Bishop's ability to compress words for effect. The line is telling us that it's a very big fish that isn't doing anything except grunting, and the narrator tells us this in five words: "He hung a grunting weight." The three adjectives she chooses to describe the fish are equally chosen for effect. She gives us three points of description, almost like a triangulation, and where the three adjectives meet we have the fish, "Battered . . . venerable . . . homely."

Bishop has already managed to tell us so much about the fish that we almost don't need more, but she goes on to a brilliant simile: "his brown skin hung in strips / like an ancient wallpaper." Her description continues as she finds more and more to tell us about the fish, using simile and metaphor to compress and illustrate. She manages, in her description, to show us a fish that is like most other fish, but at the same time she shows us how complex and miraculous a physical body is, and as we read about her fish we can't help being conscious of our own bodies. The fish deserves its medals of old bent hooks and frayed lines, and as you read the final lines there is the consciousness that part of the victory belongs to the fish.

"The Armadillo" is a poem describing a native custom in the countryside of Brazil, where Bishop lived for many years. The natives release small balloons lit with a fire inside. Most of the balloons drift harmlessly into the sky where they burn out, but some get caught in down drafts and start forest fires. Out of this small event Bishop has created a poem of much larger dimensions, ending with a four-line stanza written in a classic lyric style as she envisions the fate of the small creatures endangered by the fire. She personifies them as lifting "a weak mail fist / clenched ignorant against the sky." Once again, as in "The Fish," she suggests at the beginning of the poem what we might expect at the end of it. With "The Armadillo" we can anticipate a classic lyric form because the poem is written in rhymed stanzas. Bishop uses the a-b-a-b rhyme scheme freely, and there is considerable variation in the meter, basically an iambic trimeter, but the poem is constructed like a classic lyric, so she is justified with the self-consciously "literary" diction of the final stanza.

Although it is one of Bishop's later poems, "One Art" has so much of the arch tone and mocking self-irony of poetry written in the 1920s by women poets such as Elinor Wylie or Louise Bogan that it might have been an early poem that she didn't publish until this later date. It is also an exercise in rhyming virtuosity that is similar to many of Wylie's and Bogan's experiments. There are only two rhymes, *aba,* the same sounds occurring in each verse, and the *a* rhyme is repeated in the last line. It is probably no coincidence that one of the rhymes — *master, disaster, fluster, last or,* and so forth — is feminine, and the other — *intent, spent, meant,* and so forth — is masculine.

Questions for Discussion

1. What is similar between the ways the child and her grandmother each feel grief in "Sestina"?
2. In "The Fish," why does some of the narrator's feeling of victory also seem to have been won by the fish?
3. In "The Armadillo," what does the narrator mean in line 35, "a handful of intangible ash"?
4. What is Bishop suggesting with the word "ignorant" in the last line of "The Armadillo"?
5. Although some of the details of "One Art" are very personal — "two cities . . . two rivers" — could this poem also have an emotional meaning for readers? Could they substitute personal details of their own?

Topics for Writing

1. The word "tears" occurs in every stanza of "Sestina." Students might analyze each of the times "tears" appears and how these uses prepare for the phrase "Time to plant tears" in the poem's final stanza.
2. In his novella *The Old Man and the Sea,* Ernest Hemingway describes an old Cuban fisherman who also catches a "tremendous" fish, but he is so determined to bring it back to harbor that he keeps it tied to the side of his boat, even after sharks have stripped it and nothing is left of it but the bones. The class might consider whether Hemingway's fisher performs a masculine act and Bishop's fisher performs a feminine act.
3. **CONNECTIONS** Marianne Moore, whom Bishop regarded as her mentor, also wrote a poem titled "The Fish" (p. 1153). Students could compare and contrast the two poems.
4. **CONNECTIONS** "The Armadillo" is dedicated to the poet Robert Lowell. It would be interesting to compare Bishop's poem with one of Lowell's — for instance, "Skunk Hour" (p. 1147).

Related Commentaries

Julia Alvarez, "Elizabeth Bishop's 'One Art,'" p. 1231.
Elizabeth Bishop, "Efforts of Affection: A Memoir of Marianne Moore," p. 1236.

WILLIAM BLAKE

Song (p. 915)

From Songs of Innocence: Introduction *(p. 1029)*

The Lamb (p. 1030)

Holy Thursday (p. 1030)

The Little Boy Lost (p. 1031)

The Little Boy Found (p. 1031)

From Songs of Experience: Introduction *(p. 1031)*

The Sick Rose (p. 1032)

The Tyger (p. 1032)

London (p. 1033)

A Poison Tree (p. 1033)

The Garden of Love (p. 1034)

I askèd a thief (p. 1034)

Never pain to tell thy love (p. 1035)

It may be helpful to students if the instructor clarifies the connection between Blake's *Songs of Innocence* and *Songs of Experience*. Conceived as a children's book, *Songs of Innocence* (1789) consisted of thirty-one engraved and hand-colored plates, with illustrations of country scenes and floral decorations on every page. Only twenty-one copies are known to exist, so the work probably should be called a kind of art print multiple instead of a book, which suggests that copies went into bookstores and had some public circulation. There is no evidence of a separate publication of *Songs of Experience*. In 1794 Blake added the engraved plates of the new *Experience* poems to the original book and printed the two groups of poems together. Two different poems, "A Little Boy Lost" and "A Little Girl Lost," were added to the group of *Experience* poems. The title page of the complete collection read *Songs of Innocence and of Experience*, and there was a descriptive subtitle: "Shewing the Two Contrary States of the Human Soul." Over the next several years copies were printed and then hand-colored by Blake's wife to fill an order from a subscriber. Only twenty-four copies survive, so it had as small a circulation as the earlier version of the book.

The poems in these two small collections are so different from Blake's complex and difficult "prophetic" books that readers often assume that the *Innocence* and *Experience* poems are an earlier state of his development as a poet. The truth is, however, that before the *Innocence* poems he had already published an undistinguished collection of ordinary verse, followed by several works that many of today's readers consider "difficult," as did the few people who read them in Blake's time. Between the *Innocence* poems and the *Experience* poems Blake published or printed some of these ambitious longer works, again written in a visionary language that is often almost incomprehensible. The simplest explanation for the difference between these poems and the rest of his work is that he was writing the *Innocence* poems, at least in the first group, for children. As he writes in his Introduction to *Songs of Innocence,* "I wrote my happy songs / Every child may joy to hear." It is the quality of childish, innocent joy and childish experience that makes the poems unique.

Students usually have little difficulty reading Blake. During the Haight-Ashbury days of the 1960s, San Francisco rock bands would sometimes recite Blake from the stage, and Beat poet Allen Ginsberg recorded an entire album of his own musical settings of the poems. The "contrary states" that Blake described in the subtitle are the metaphysical contradictions he finds around him. In the book he matches pairs of poems to expose the harsh contrasts between the paradise of mankind living in a natural state — the innocence of childhood — and the despair and constraints of eighteenth-century England.

SONG
FROM *SONGS OF INNOCENCE:* INTRODUCTION
FROM *SONGS OF EXPERIENCE:* INTRODUCTION
THE LAMB
THE TYGER

Although Blake's images in the brief poems of these collections often describe children's play or gardens or creatures of the fields, he could express complex emotions within this seemingly limited imagery. "Song" precedes the first collection by six years, but already has the somber, troubling quality of the *Experience* poems. In the poem a golden winged cherub roams freely through the summer fields, almost like a butterfly, until it meets Cupid, the god of love. It follows Cupid into the god's gardens and experiences Cupid's "golden pleasures." Then when its wings become soaked with dew, it is caught and put in a cage by Phoebus, the god of the sun, who teases it and pulls its golden wings open and laughs at it. The poem's extended metaphor for the loss of freedom is one of Blake's persistent themes.

There are several paired poems in the volumes Blake printed later. In the Introduction to *Songs of Innocence,* he describes himself as a happy piper who responds to a child's laughing wish that he pipe a melody about a lamb. As the "child" vanishes, it asks the piper to write down his songs "In a book that all may read," and the poems that follow are his songs. The Introduction to *Songs of Experience,* on the other hand, is a somber, muffled, portentous call to "Hear the voice of the Bard." In the last verses he cries out to the earth to return, despite the night, as the night's "starry floor" and "watery shore" are still the earth's until sunrise.

One of the most obvious matched pair of poems are "The Lamb" of *Innocence* and "The Tyger" from *Experience.* "The Lamb" is a gentle hymn praising Jesus Christ, and it wouldn't have been out of place in any children's prayer book of the time. If students analyze the meter they will see that the poem can be "sung" as a hymn in which the two lines that open and close each verse function as a chorus. These lines have three accents, and the six interior lines of each verse have four accents. The meter is trochaic throughout. The effect of the contrasting lines is like a softly breathed introductory chorus, followed by a recitative, and then the verse closing with the repeated soft chorus. As a class exercise, students can "perform" the poem, reading the "chorus" line slowly and the interior lines more quickly.

They will immediately hear the effect that Blake intended. The poem's religious theme is echoed in its soft tones, its *l* sounds and the internal alliterations of lines such as "Gave thee clothing of delight / Softest clothing, wooly, bright."

"The Tyger," with its hard accents and its strident, fearful imagery, is clearly something completely different, although there never has been any agreement as to how Blake meant the poem to be read. A collaborative note by two European scholars, John Chalker and Erik Frykman, presents one of the most widely held views: "*The Tiger* expresses a sense of awe in the face of the mysterious and uncontrollable energy of life that the tiger symbolizes, and asks whether it is possible that animals so different as the lamb and the tiger should be the work of the same Creator. As well as symbolizing gentleness and energy, the lamb and the tiger express dual aspects of the personality of Christ." Many of the details of the poem — the "fire of thine eye" in line 6, "twist the sinews of thy heart" in line 10, "What the hammer? what the chain?" in line 13, and "When the stars threw down their spears" in line 17 — also suggest a visceral linking to the language and imagery of Milton's *Paradise Lost,* and if this was Blake's intention, then it is the figure of Satan that the tiger symbolizes. The stars, in this interpretation, would be the fallen angels who have thrown down their weapons after their defeat by God's angels.

Students may have difficulty following "The Tyger," but if they read it closely they will find that it has many parallels with "The Lamb." In "The Lamb" the question is, Does the lamb know who created it? In "The Tyger" the question of lines 3–4 is, Who could have had the power to create something like this tiger? One of the immediate problems is the word "frame." Blake means it in the way that a builder frames a house. A workable and helpful reading of lines 3 and 4 might be, What immortal force or skill could have shaped something of your fearful proportions? The fire in the eyes in line 6 is one of the materials that was brought to the tiger's creation, and the lines that follow ask who this powerful creator might be who could construct such a creature. The image "Could twist the sinews of thy heart?" in line 10 often confuses students, but Blake is using "twist" as a verb describing how the tiger was created, and the heart was made by twisting sinews. The questions in the last line of the stanza, "What dread hand? and what dread feet," are so compressed that they seem cryptic on first reading, but what Blake is asking is, What is the power that could have created that dread hand or foot? Blake doesn't answer the question of the first lines, because it is obvious to him that no other power than God could have created the tiger. It is the same power that created the lamb. Blake's final question, in lines 19–20 is, What did its creator think of the creature it had shaped and brought to life?

Questions for Discussion

1. Does Blake intend a contradiction in lines 7–8 of "The Lamb," when he says that the lamb has such a tender voice that it can make all the valleys rejoice? What does Blake mean here?
2. In "The Lamb" the question is answered about who created the lamb. In "The Tyger" the question is not answered, but Blake's questions about who might be the creator are only rhetorical. How do we know from the poem that Blake is certain of his answer?
3. How would students paraphrase Blake's wondering questions in lines 19–20?
4. What is Blake's meaning in lines 7–8?

5. Is there some similarity in what Blake is describing in the poem to the well-known story of the Frankenstein monster?
6. What is Blake suggesting when he tells us that the creator of the tiger would have to have had almighty power?

HOLY THURSDAY
THE LITTLE BOY LOST
THE LITTLE BOY FOUND

These poems from *Innocence* continue the collection's mood of childish joy, although one describes a gathering of London's workhouse children, and in the "Lost" and "Found" poems the child is frightened and tearful. "Holy Thursday" is a hymnlike celebration of the one day a year that children from the London workhouses are brought to St. Paul's Cathedral for a special service. The meter of the poem is unusual — iambic heptameter, which is seven accents to each line. Several of the lines, however, are punctuated to divide them into units of four and three stresses, which is the familiar meter of popular ballads. The lines that are not divided are heard with the same metrical division. Blake undoubtedly wrote the poem with the longer linear unit to give it a more imposing appearance on the page. It is one of his most sympathetic responses to children's life in the city. He describes them as "these flowers of London town" in line 5, and his sympathy even includes the church functionaries, the "Grey headed beadles," and the men who are responsible for the children's care, the "wise guardians of the poor." This is one of the few moments in Blake's writing where he accepts (or seems to accept) the church and its role in English society.

"The Little Boy Lost" and "The Little Boy Found" seem like simple lyrics of a child's experience of being lost at night on the fen. Because this poem is included in the *Innocence* section, it is followed immediately with the reassuring poem describing the boy, with God's help, being found by his mother. There is an ambiguous note in the poem. When the boy cries out for his father in line 5 of "The Little Boy Lost," "no father was there." In line 4 of "The Little Boy Found," God appears to the boy "like his father in white." Blake is probably suggesting that the boy's father is dead, and it is the father's spirit that has led him to his mother, alone in the night searching for him.

Questions for Discussion

1. Why does Blake use the image of the "Thames' waters" in line 4 of "Holy Thursday"? (This assumes that students are familiar with London's geography.)
2. What is Blake telling us about the children in line 7 of "Holy Thursday"?
3. How would a student paraphrase the last line of "Holy Thursday"?
4. In "The Little Boy Lost" and "The Little Boy Found" there is an intimation that the boy's father is dead and that God has acted through his father's spirit to save the boy. How could students clarify this interpretation through the details in the two poems?
5. What is Blake telling us in the last line of "The Little Boy Lost," "And away the vapour flew"?

THE SICK ROSE
LONDON
A POISON TREE
THE GARDEN OF LOVE

Students will immediately notice how the mood in these poems differs from those of *Innocence*. "The Sick Rose" is clearly a metaphor for something that is eating at the heart of the rose, a symbol of love and joy. There are many interpretations of the poem, but one that perhaps comes closest to Blake's meaning is that the rose here symbolizes sexual love, described as "thy bed / Of crimson joy." Because the worm is described as "dark secret love," it is probably a metaphor for venereal disease, which Blake describes, again in oblique language, in the poem "London."

"London" is one of Blake's most explicitly political poems, and for many readers the London he describes could be any city of our modern world. The word "chartered" in lines 1 and 2 mean for Blake the restrictions that hem in natural life in the city. It refers to the charter of the City of London, which is its basis for governing. In line 8 the term "mind-forged manacles I hear" is Blake's judgment that the chains that bind the people he sees on London's streets were created by the people themselves. The "youthful harlot's curse" in the last line can be taken in two ways — one meaning the curses of a street prostitute as she cries out to a customer, and the other the curse of venereal disease, which at the time was virtually incurable and raged through every level of European and American society. Marriage, Blake suggests in the last two lines of the poem, will bring only sickness and death to the married couple and their child.

"A Poison Tree" is a paradox. The moral is that with a friend you can be open, and any anger between you will dissipate in your open exchange about it. With a foe you nurse your anger until it grows and grows. In Blake's parable, his anger blossoms into a flower, which tempts his foe and kills him when he comes too close. "The Garden of Love" demonstrates the other side of the feelings about churches and priests that Blake presented in "Holy Thursday." This is the same outrage at organized religion's denial of the human right to happiness that he intimates in the image of the "black'ning church" in "London."

Questions for Discussion

1. Although the "invisible worm" in "The Sick Rose" is usually interpreted as venereal disease, are there other possible interpretations?
2. In line 2 of "London," when Blake speaks of "the charted Thames," what is he saying ironically about the river?
3. How would students explain Blake's meaning in line 8, "The mind-forged manacles I hear"?
4. In the third verse is he blaming the church for the plight of the chimney sweeps and the government for the deaths of soldiers in battle?
5. What does he mean specifically in line 15, "the new-born Infant's tear"?
6. In "A Poison Tree" what does Blake mean by "the pole" in line 14?
7. Is the first verse of "The Garden of Love" a metaphor for the poet's childhood or his early manhood?
8. In line 8, is he saying that organized religion is the death of love? Do students have other interpretations?
9. Blake creates an ironic singsong effect in the last two lines of the poem. What are these internal rhymes?

I ASKÈD A THIEF
NEVER PAIN TO TELL THY LOVE

These poems were found in a notebook Blake was using at the time he was writing the *Innocence* and *Experience* poems. They can be most simply read as small parables of the helplessness of the innocent in a cynical world — a world in which people have grown so accustomed to being divided from one another that any attempt to come closer is met with fear and misunderstanding.

Questions for Discussion

1. "I askèd a thief" is rife with ironies, like the thief turning up his eyes at the thought of stealing something. What are some instances of irony?
2. What is Blake saying about religion when he makes an angel the thief and seducer?
3. What is he saying in line 11, when he describes the angel as "still as a maid"?
4. In line 2 of "Never pain to tell thy love" Blake speaks of "Love that never told can be." What does he mean?
5. Why does the lady "trembling, cold, in ghastly fears," leave him as soon as he has told her of his love?
6. Why does the stranger succeed with the lady, saying nothing? Has Blake already suggested why in lines 3–4?

Topics for Writing

1. There was a serious debate in Blake's time over the nature of mankind in a "state of nature" and the corrupting influences of life in cities and towns. This is a theme that was also part of the social revolution of the 1960s, and it would be a useful opening for writing and discussing Blake's work.
2. How "innocent" are the poems of the first section of Blake's book? Students could analyze the contrasts between the paired poems to find out what Blake means by innocence and what he means by experience.
3. The question of whether the poems were written for children could begin a discussion of Blake's use of language and his poetic forms.
4. Students could write an interesting paper describing, step by step, the construction of "The Tyger."
5. More advanced students might want to examine the opening passages of John Milton's *Paradise Lost* to compare Blake's image of the tiger with Milton's descriptions of Satan and the fallen angels.

Related Commentaries

T. S. Eliot, From "William Blake," p. 1256.

ROBERT BLY

The Dead Seal near McClure's Beach (p. 960)

Robert Bly's poetry is challenging and committed, and he is intensely concerned about the environment. He lives in rural Minnesota, but since the worldwide success of his book *Iron John,* which examines the male role in our society, he has spent much of his time leading men's seminars and discussing his ideas at conferences and gatherings. He has been active as a poet since the 1950s, and he has also played a crucial role in American cultural life with his translations of authors as diverse as the Swedish poet Tomas Tranströmer and the Spanish Nobel Prize–winner Juan Ramón Jiménez.

In an introduction to a collection of his prose poems Bly wrote, "When I composed the first of these poems . . . I hoped that a writer could describe an object or a creature without claiming it, without immersing it like a negative in his developing tank of disappointment and desire. I no longer think that is possible."

Questions for Discussion

1. What does Bly mean by the image "A shock goes through me, as if a wall of my room had been taken away"?
2. Is his comment "here on its back is the oil that heats our homes so efficiently" meant ironically? What are the poet's feelings about the seal?
3. Why is Bly telling us about his emotions as he carefully describes the dying seal's appearance each day?
4. "The crown of his head looks like a leather jacket" is a simile and "your innertube race" is a metaphor. Discuss the differences between them. What is the comparison Bly is making with "innertube race"?
5. Bly writes, "Forgive us if we have killed you." Does the poem express any guilt? Why or why not?
6. What is Bly saying about other life on earth with his phrase "ducking under as assassinations break over you"?

Topic for Writing

1. The poem can be read as a larger comment on our exploitation of the earth. A student paper could discuss the poem in these terms.

ANNE BRADSTREET

To My Dear and Loving Husband (p. 1036)
In Reference to Her Children, 23 June 1659 (p. 1036)

Students will find these poems easily comprehensible. The first is a love poem from a wife to her husband; the second is a poem of loving care from a mother to her children. On closer reading, students will find that the poems are very different from each other and that each is written with considerable technical skill and imagination.

"To My Dear and Loving Husband" is an example of what Elizabethan writers called "conceits" — clever and revealing ways of playing with words and ideas — and it ends with a paradox that is reminiscent of the poems of John Donne. The meaning of the first line, of course, is "If ever two people were one, then surely we two are," but Bradstreet catches our attention with her wordplay "then surely we," and she follows it with a similar device in the second line, "then thee." The hyperbole of her description of how much she prizes his love for her and how much she loves him has the extravagance of an Elizabethan drama, and the paradox of the last line — "when we live no more, we may live ever" — is a widely used poetic device asserting that in death there will be life.

Both poems are written in rhyming couplets, but students will notice that for the first, a poem of formal ideas, Bradstreet uses the more formal five-stress line of iambic pentameter. The second is a personal, domestic poem, so she employs the more familiar four-stress line of iambic tetrameter.

"In Reference to Her Children" is also an imaginative technical achievement. The entire poem is an extended metaphor describing herself as a mother bird and her children as her "brood." As she follows the life of each of them she finds a way to describe what is happening to them in terms that also describe the ordinary events of a bird's life. The only hesitation for a modern reader in following the metaphor is her use of the term "dam" to describe herself. The modern connotations of the word are a mother animal, like a horse. Its denotative meaning, however, is simply any kind of mother in the natural world, and because there is no word that specifically describes a mother bird, Bradstreet's use of the term is entirely justified. Students also should notice that Bradstreet is more fortunate than most women of her time: She has given birth to eight children, and all of them are still living.

Questions for Discussion

1. In line 6 of "To My Dear and Loving Husband," "all the riches that the East doth hold," what is Bradstreet referring to?
2. In line 8, "Thy love is such I can no way repay," she is suggesting that she feels her husband's love is a gift to her. How do students respond to this concept of love as a gift?
3. What is the term for the type of rhyme of the last two lines?
4. Is Bradstreet suggesting in these lines that her and her husband's reward for loving each other will be eternal life together?
5. Does the first line of "In Reference to Her Children" refer to the poet's womb? Could the line also be read as referring to her house? Which reading seems more plausible?
6. In her "mournful chirps" in lines 9–12, what is she asking of her son?
7. In line 25, what is she saying about where her daughter has traveled?
8. In lines 59–60, what is she saying about her emotions as a mother?
9. In lines 68–74 she writes of herself as sitting and singing. Does she mean that she is writing poetry, or is she continuing with the poem's bird metaphor, in which she means singing as a bird?

Topics for Writing

1. **CONNECTIONS** The idea expressed in the last line of "To My Dear and Loving Husband" — Bradstreet's assertion that "when we live no more, we may live ever" — is very similar to the idea expressed in John Donne's sonnet "Death, be not proud" (p. 948). Students could compare the poems and analyze how this concept is presented by each poet.
2. Many of the emotions Bradstreet expresses in "In Reference to Her Children" will be familiar to students today. Other emotions may seem to describe a woman's role as mother in ways that no longer represent a woman's life and ambitions. Students could write a paper for class discussion comparing the differences and the similarities between these two views of a woman's role as mother.

Gwendolyn Brooks

We Real Cool (p. 1039)
The Mother (p. 1039)

We Real Cool

"We Real Cool" is an excellent example of a poet's use of a persona. Brooks is not a dropout pool player, but she adopts the voice and the language of street adolescents to make her point that they are leading dead-end lives. The language is as sardonic and unsentimental as the life it describes, even though Brooks has slightly disguised the directness of the statement she is making by ending each line with the first word of the next. The poem uses alliteration and compression, and a responsive class might even try reciting it as an athletic cheer. Repeated over and over, its bitter self-contempt becomes even more obvious. The term "strikes straight" refers to their pool playing.

Questions for Discussion

1. In the phrases "thin gin" and "jazz June" Brooks is using "thin" and "jazz" as verbs. What does she mean?
2. This poem is written in everyday slang, a language that changes continually. Do students recognize the poem's terms and the phrases as language they would have used themselves as adolescents? How would they change the poem to fit it into today's street language?

Topic for Writing

1. Because Gwendolyn Brooks is an African American writer, it will be natural for most readers of the poem to assume that she is describing black adolescents. It would be helpful to the class if a student were to discuss the poem's implications for all adolescent dropouts, and in the discussion it would be interesting to consider whether other vernacular terms could give the poem a specific white identify.

The Mother

In "The Mother" we enter a completely different emotional world. Brooks here is presumably writing in her own voice — or if she has not had the abortions she describes, then she is writing in the voice of a woman very much like herself. Although the first verse is in rhymed couplets, the meter is very free, and in the second verse there is so much emotion that the poet doesn't even retain the regular rhyme; she seems only to snatch at whatever rhyme occurs as she is writing. In "We Real Cool" she keeps an emotional distance from the poem by writing through a persona. In "The Mother" there is no emotional distance at all.

Questions for Discussion

1. What is Brooks referring to with the phrase "wind up the sucking-thumb" in line 7?
2. What does she mean by the images of line 10?
3. What does she mean by the adjective "dim" in lines 11 and 13?

4. What is Brooks suggesting in the paradox of line 21, "in my deliberateness I was not deliberate"? Is the statement that she was not deliberate a possible reason for some of the complicated emotions she expresses in the poem?
5. What is the truth she is trying to express in line 28?
6. Is there any significance in the fact that Brooks placed the title of the poem in lowercase letters?

Topic for Writing

1. Throughout the poem Brooks presents images of the life she has denied the children she didn't have. She also describes what is denied the mother — among other things that she will never neglect or beat these children. A discussion of the things that make up this life she describes, both as mother and child, would be a stimulating subject for a student paper.

Related Commentary

Gary Smith, "On Gwendolyn Brooks's *A Street in Bronzeville*," p. 1316.

STERLING A. BROWN

He Was a Man (p. 926)

Sterling Brown was born in Washington, D.C., in 1901 and died there in 1989. Although his background was middle class and he was educated at Williams College and Harvard University, he never lost his sense of identification with his African American cultural heritage. His father was dean of religion at Howard University, where Brown was to teach for forty years. In 1921 an anthology by Louis Untermeyer opened his consciousness to the new poetry, and he became interested in southern folklore. He taught in Lynchburg, Virginia, before coming to Howard, and it was there that he was able to immerse himself in black folk culture. He began teaching at Howard in 1929, and in the depression years he coordinated the Federal Writers' Project for the Works Progress Administration. He also supervised the crucially important collection of ex-slave narratives that were gathered by dozens of field informants during these years.

Brown's own poetry drew on folk sources in the same way as the writing of Langston Hughes, whom Brown admired and to some extent emulated. "He Was a Man" is written as a ballad in vernacular dialect (it can be sung to the tune of "Frankie and Johnny"), but it is a bitter cry against southern racism.

Questions for Discussion

1. What identifies this poem as a ballad?
2. How does it compare with other ballads presented in the text? What are the differences or similarities?
3. Explain the difference between the refrain in the stanzas at the beginning of the poem and that of the last three.
4. What is Brown saying about the man in lines 16–17?

Topic for Writing

1.   Although the poem has many linguistic similarities to black vernacular
     speech, it was written in a literary folk style. Identify the words and phrases
     that are African American and those that are Anglo-American and discuss
     the differences between them.

ELIZABETH BARRETT BROWNING

How Do I Love Thee? (p. 950)
From *The Cry of the Children (p. 1041)*
From *The Runaway Slave at Pilgrim's Point (p. 1042)*
If thou must love me, let it be for nought (p. 1047)
Belovèd, my Belovèd, when I think (p. 1048)
If I leave all for thee, wilt thou exchange (p. 1048)
I thought once how Theocritus had sung (p. 1049)

Elizabeth Barrett Browning is one of many women poets of the Victorian era
whose work was once highly regarded but was later dismissed as an historical
anachronism. It may not be possible to read the work of Felicia Hemans or Lydia
Sigourney with more than curious interest today, but Barrett Browning's poetry is
being rediscovered. Students should read Angela Leighton's commentary (p.
1283), which discusses how public interest in the romantic story of Barrett
Browning's courtship and marriage to Robert Browning has led to confusion in the
way she is regarded by critics and readers. The continued popularity of her *Sonnets
from the Portuguese* has meant that readers often haven't gone on to read the social
poetry that was the basis for her early fame. Today's readers should remember that
Emily Dickinson considered herself a "secret admirer" of Barrett Browning's
poetry and had a portrait of Barrett Browning on her bedroom wall.

Child labor is as widespread today as it was during Barrett Browning's
lifetime, but most of the abuse of child workers is happening in countries far from
the industrial centers of the United States and Europe. In nineteenth-century
England the factories were in the middle of cities, and the children who were being
forced onto the primitive production lines or into the mines were the children of
people who had been farmers and craftsmen only a generation before. Many
Victorian writers attacked the system of child labor, and most students will have
read a novel by Charles Dickens in which he describes the cruelty and greed of the
system. Barrett Browning's long poem *The Cry of the Children* was widely read
during her lifetime, and although today's students may find the concept of child
labor too distant from their own world, they will respond to the bitterness of stanza
IV, when children speak enviously of Little Alice, a child who has died. When they
looked into her grave they saw no work laid out for her to do, and she doesn't cry
any longer, as she's dead. They are sure that if they could see her face, she would
be smiling. The children's own statement, in lines 39–40, is the sardonic, "It is good
when it happens . . . / That we die before our time."

Although many of the leaders of the American abolitionist movement were men, the large majority of the volunteer workers and many of the most important speakers and writers — for instance, Harriet Beecher Stowe, the author of *Uncle Tom's Cabin* — were women. Barrett Browning was asked to contribute something to an abolitionist Congress, and when she sent off the long poem *The Runaway Slave at Pilgrim's Point* she had some misgivings that it would be too cruel for its audience. Instead, it was reprinted by nearly every abolitionist journal and was also widely read by people who weren't committed to the cause of abolition.

Barrett Browning had never been to the United States when she wrote the poem, and she obviously is confused as to where Plymouth Rock — "Pilgrim's Rock" in the poem — actually lies, but the story of the poem has a ring of authenticity. In the poem a slave woman falls in love with another slave, but when her master becomes aware of this the male slave is beaten and taken away. She is raped by her master and gives birth to his child. When she sees that the baby has a white face she smothers it and flees with the baby's body to Pilgrim's Point. She has been pursued, and the poem is her narrative of what has happened as a search party closes in on her. At the end of the poem the white men stone her to death. The story has some similarities to the plot of the novel *Beloved*, by Nobel Prize–winning African American writer Toni Morrison, in which an escaped slave also murders her child to save the child from being returned to slavery.

You will probably have students who have read at least one poem in *Sonnets from the Portuguese*, which has been used as lovers' gifts since its publication in 1850. If there is any single reason for their continued popularity, it might be that what Barrett Browning depicts are the hesitations and confusions any woman feels before committing herself to marriage. The opening lines of "If I leave all for thee" certainly can be read as a direct reflection of the situation in the poet's own home, but they also reflect anyone's feelings at the thought of what she may have to give up when she marries.

Questions for Discussion

1. In the selection from *The Cry of the Children* the meter is very free and there is considerable use of half-rhyme. Students should scan one of the stanzas and discuss what Barrett Browning has gained by her use of irregular meter and what she might have lost by it.
2. Some of the lines have six strong accents. What do we call this kind of line?
3. In stanza III is the poet saying that the children are longing for death? Why do the children ask the aged "why they weep"?
4. Could *The Runaway Slave at Pilgrim's Point* be called a dramatic monologue? What characteristics of the monologue does the poem present?
5. What does Barrett Browning mean in line 56, "Though my tears had washed a place for my knee"?
6. What is she describing in the phrase "master right" in line 63? How could this apply to a newborn baby?
7. What is Barrett Browning contrasting between the pilgrims and their sons in stanzas XXIX and XXX?
8. Discuss what she means by "Washington race" in line 144.
9. What is the significance of the slave's final cry, "White-men, I leave you all curse-free"?
10. Are Barrett Browning's sonnets English or Italian in form?

11. The sonnets are much more regular metrically than *The Cry of the Children.* The class should discuss whether they think this is due to the subject of the sonnets or the discipline of the sonnet form.

12. In "How Do I Love Thee?" what is the poet describing in line 11, "my lost saints"?

13. The class should discuss the Elizabethan elements of paradox and conceit in the sonnet "If thou must love me, let it be for nought."

14. The class should paraphrase line 10, "Thine own dear pity's wiping my cheeks dry."

15. A class discussion could center on the last two lines of "Belovèd, my Belovèd:" "Atheists are as dull, / Who cannot guess God's presence out of sight."

16. The class should discuss the paradox in lines 11–12 of "If I leave all for thee."

17. What is Barrett Browning alluding to in the phrase "his antique tongue" in line 5 of "I thought once how Theocritus had sung"? What does she mean by the term "mused it" in the same line?

18. What is she referring to as "who" in line 8? What do we call this figure of speech?

19. The class should discuss the poet's meaning in the metaphor of line 11, "drew me backward by the hair."

20. Why does Barrett Browning use two tones of voice in the last lines? (A voice asks "in mastery" and the answer is "silver.")

Topics for Writing

1. *The Cry of the Children* has some of the themes described by Charles Dickens in his novel *Oliver Twist.* An interesting comparison could be made between the two works.

2. Barrett Browning had derived all of her knowledge of the United States from her reading and several lines in *The Runaway Slave at Pilgrim's Point* contain factual errors. Students could discuss these mistakes, and their papers could lead to a class discussion as to whether these errors detract from the poem's effectiveness.

3. When Abraham Lincoln met Harriet Beecher Stowe, the author of *Uncle Tom's Cabin,* he is supposed to have said something like, "So you're the little lady who started the big war!" Students could analyze *A Runaway Slave at Pilgrim's Point* from the perspective of its role in the abolitionist movement.

4. **CONNECTIONS** The sonnet form is difficult to master, but the great sonnet writers also turn their poems into presentations of their own personalities. Students could compare sonnets by William Shakespeare, Barrett Browning, and Edna St. Vincent Millay and discuss each poet's use of the form.

5. *Sonnets from the Portuguese* describes marriage and married love in ways that no longer entirely reflect social attitudes. Students might want to write about the differences and the similarities they find between Victorian and current views of marriage.

6. **CONNECTIONS** Both Barrett Browning's "I thought once how Theocritus had sung" and Ralph Waldo Emerson's "Days" (p. 909) use the image of years passing in procession before the writer. Emerson's poem, in fact, was probably inspired by Barrett Browning's. Students could compare the two poems and refer to the way each writer uses the central image to describe something in his or her life.

ROBERT BROWNING

My Last Duchess (p. 970)

Robert Browning's family was able to support him in his decision to write, and he lived at home or traveled abroad until he married at the age of thirty-four. His early poetry was poorly received by critics, and during the years he was married to Elizabeth Barrett she was much better known as a poet than he was. It was not until the publication of the long dramatic poem *The Ring and the Book* in 1869, eight years after her death, that he began to be considered as a poet in his own right.

"My Last Duchess" has always been popular with students, and some of them may have read it in high school. It is particularly effective read aloud, and as students listen to the poem the skill of Browning's versification becomes more obvious. The poem uses end rhyme throughout, but with so much enjambment that the lines read like a casual conversation in which only one of the voices is heard. Some of the language may cause problems for students, but once they realize that the "plot" of the poem is like a made-for-TV movie, they'll follow it to the conclusion.

The story reveals itself line by line, somewhat in the manner of a story by Edgar Allan Poe. As the poem begins, a nobleman is showing a portrait of his previous wife to a visitor. Looking at the portrait upsets the nobleman because he sees again the expression of joy that the painter has depicted on his wife's face. As the duke talks about her he becomes more and more angry. The smile, he fumes, should have been only for him, but she smiled that way at everyone and at everything pleasant in her life. Almost in disbelief, we listen to him tell the visitor that because she wouldn't stop smiling, he had her killed. Now — and he is all business in the last lines of the poem — we realize that the visitor is an agent working for another nobleman who is offering his daughter to the duke in marriage. As we are left with the realization that the daughter may be the duke's next victim, the duke takes the visitor down to dinner, talking again about his art collection.

Questions for Discussion

1. When do we realize that there is something about the portrait that upsets the duke?
2. Why does he keep the portrait covered behind a curtain?
3. What does he mean by "Who'd stoop to blame" in line 34?
4. What does he say about himself in the words "I choose / Never to stoop" in lines 42–43?
5. What is he telling the agent about a request for a dowry?

Topics for Writing

1. Students might want to develop the idea suggested in the poem that to the duke his wife was simply another possession, like the objects in his art collection.
2. The poem's setting seems to be a place that is not English. It would be interesting to discuss whether Browning would have written the same poem about an English duke.

ROBERT BURNS

To a Mouse (p. 914)
Ae Fond Kiss (p. 931)

Robert Burns was born on a Scottish farm in 1759 and died in Dumfries, a small town in southern Scotland, in 1796. He spent his youth as a farmworker, and much of his poetry was written in his native Scots dialect. His first book was immediately successful, and for a brief time he was lionized by fashionable society in Edinburgh, but he realized that he could only be comfortable in the country, and he married and tried to make a living as a farmer. When this failed he moved to Dumfries and spent the last years of his life tirelessly collecting and editing Scottish folk songs and ballads.

"To a Mouse" is one of Burns's most well-known poems, despite the difficulties most readers experience with the Scots dialect. Burns was conscious of the problems the dialect presented, so he skillfully blended it with standard English, as in the second stanza of the poem, beginning with the line "I'm truly sorry man's dominion." As he writes in the subtitle, the poem describes the poet's breaking up a mouse's nest with his plow. The appeal of the poem is the poet's identification with the mouse and his feelings of uncertainty about his own past and future. The poem contains the famous lines "The best-laid schemes o' mice an' men / Gang aft a-gley," which are usually translated into ordinary English as "The best laid plans of mice and men often go awry."

"Ae Fond Kiss" is an example of Burns's skills of versification. The poem is a simple song, but the love story it tells has roots in our richest fantasies of helpless love and loss. As he writes, "Had we never lov'd sae kindly, / Had we never lov'd sae blindly." The poem is sometimes translated into English, but few readers have difficulty understanding it in its original Scots.

Questions for Discussion

1. "To a Mouse" has a complicated structure, although it reads simply and directly. Scan a verse for its meter and rhyme and discuss why it seems to read easily.
2. What is the meaning of lines 7–10? Is Burns being ironic?
3. What is he saying to the mouse in line 21, "An' naething, now, to big a new ane"?
4. What is the cause of Burns's despair in the final stanza?
5. As the text notes in its discussion of "Ae Fond Kiss," the meter is unbroken throughout its three stanzas. Is this characteristic of a poem meant to be sung?
6. What is the poet saying about his hopes in lines 5–6?
7. Line 7 is written in Scots, and line 8 is written in English. What words or phrases make the differences clear?
8. What is Burns suggesting with the phrase "partial fancy" in line 9?

Topics for Writing

1. Discuss Burns's statement that the mouse is a "poor, earth-born companion, / An' fellow mortal!"

2.   Discuss the four lines beginning with line 39, "The best-laid schemes o' mice an' men."

GEORGE GORDON, LORD BYRON

She Walks in Beauty (p. 916)

Byron's life was so turbulent and so filled with extravagant gestures and disasters that the adjective "Byronic" was coined to describe a dangerously exaggerated lifestyle. At his birth in 1788 it was understood that he would inherit his title, but his father had squandered the family fortune, and Byron spent much of his childhood in poverty in Scotland. He was born with a club foot, and to compensate for his disability he stubbornly made himself into an excellent sportsman and swimmer. He was also handsome and daring, living much of his life in alternating periods of relative calm, when he did his writing, and chaotic excess, which included hundreds of affairs with women of every social class and experimental relationships with young men and boys. His books were enormously successful, despite the scandal over his incestuous relationship with his half-sister, which drove him from England. He died in 1824, at the age of thirty-five, trying to train and lead a small body of soldiers he had assembled at his own expense to fight for Greek independence.

Much of Byron's fame derives from his wildly colorful life, but his writing is even more interesting than that vivid life. His masterpiece is the long narrative poem *Don Juan*, but he wrote drama, satiric verse, and short lyrics such as "She Walks in Beauty." Much of his writing is neoclassical, but the turbulence of his life and the simplicity of his lyric poetry place him in the company of the Romantic poets, and one of his few intellectual and spiritual friendships was with Percy Bysshe Shelley, during the years when they both lived in Italy.

Questions for Discussion

1.   Although the poem is about the woman's physical beauty, Byron also writes of her spiritual beauty. What images or lines describe this spiritual beauty?
2.   What is the term for the comparison in lines 1–2?
3.   What is the poet saying about the woman's appearance in lines 5–6?
4.   What does he mean with the phrase "nameless grace" in line 8? What words would students suggest to describe this grace?

Topic for Writing

1.   CONNECTIONS The admiration Byron feels for the woman he describes in this poem is contradicted by John Donne in his short lyric poem "Song" (p. 887). Compare the two poems in their portrayal of women.

Lorna Dee Cervantes

Poem for the Young White Man Who Asked Me How I, an Intelligent, Well-Read Person, Could Believe in the War between Races (p. 987)

Lorna Dee Cervantes was born in 1940. Her poetry is committed to social issues, balancing her American and Hispanic heritage. She lives in Boulder, Colorado.

Questions for Discussion
1. Why might Cervantes have given her poem such a long title?
2. Why are lines 25–28 put in parentheses?

Topic for Writing
1. Have students write a one-page response to Cervantes's poem, explaining whether she has convinced them that there is a "war between races."

Marilyn Chin

How I Got That Name (p. 1050)
Elegy for Chloe Nguyen (p. 1052)

The subtitle of "How I Got That Name" is "An Essay on Assimilation," and students will find the poem's meaning even clearer if they understand that the subtitle's "essay" is only half-serious. The poem is about Chin's own assimilation, as an Asian American with a difficult family background, into mainstream American life. As the poem also makes clear, her experience as a child of immigrant parents is a classic story of American life, and only the details would need to be changed for the story to fit Jewish immigrants or Haitian immigrants.

In lines 38–39 Chin emphasizes one of the details that is unique about the Asian American experience: "How we've managed to fool the experts / in education, statistics, and demography." Yes, the speaker is saying, we're considered a "model minority," but I'm just as unhappy as anybody else. She is so uncertain about herself and her role in America that in line 71 she declares, "I wait for imminent death." The death, she continues, is only "metaphorical," but the last long verse of the poem is her own wry epitaph.

"Elegy for Chloe Nguyen" is also about the immigrant experience, this time told from the outside, as Chin describes her friend who died at the age of thirty-three. Chloe Nguyen seemed to have many of the things Chin longed for, but in line 25 Chin describes her life as filled with "her hunger, her despair." Chloe's brilliance and comfortable family life couldn't bring her happiness. The final irony is that death will make them both Americans.

Questions for Discussion

1. What does Chin mean by "the resoluteness / of the first person singular" and the following three lines at the beginning of "How I Got That Name"?
2. In line 15, "lust drove men to greatness," is she being sarcastic?
3. What is she saying about her father in line 26?
4. What does she mean when she says, in lines 38–39, that the Asian American minority has "managed to fool the experts"?
5. Line 57, "We have no inner resources," is a cliché. Does Chin mean it satirically here?
6. What does she mean in lines 72–73?
7. Students might discuss what they think has "swallowed her whole" in the last lines of the poem. Is it America, which has finally admitted her into its society? What other suggestions might students have?
8. In "Elegy for Chloe Nguyen," what is Chin saying in lines 6–9 about the contrast between her mother and Chloe's mother?
9. In lines 32–36 in the "Elegy for Chloe Nguyen," what is Chin describing?
10. Is the last line of the poem meant ironically? How would students explain what Chin is saying about her life and Chloe's death?

Topic for Writing

1. To most outsiders, the fact that Asian Americans are a "model minority" and have higher average test scores, education, and income than Anglo-Americans is a mark of unusual success. Students could analyze their response to Chin's assertion in her poems that these facts have no meaning for someone like herself.

Related Commentary

Marilyn Chin, "On the Canon," p. 1249.

AMY CLAMPITT

Fog (p. 882)
The Dakota (p. 944)

Students may be interested to know that Clampitt spent many years in her poetic apprenticeship and that her first book, *The Kingfisher*, didn't appear until 1983, when she was in her fifties. The book was an immediate success, and there were several reprintings in the next two years.

Questions for Discussion

1. In "Fog," what verbs has Clampitt used to describe how the fog has covered over objects around her, such as the lighthouse and the tree branches?
2. What does she mean in lines 8–10, "granite / subsumed, a rumor / in a mumble of ocean"?
3. What is she describing in lines 17–20 when she writes about "last season's rose hips"?

4. In line 23, what does she mean by the adjective "hueless"?
5. What does Clampitt mean by the term "Grief for a generation" in the opening line of "The Dakota"?
6. How would students explain the last four lines of the poem, when Clampitt writes that "Grief / is original"?

Topics for Writing

1. The critic Helen Vendler has written of Clampitt's poetry that "she has the sensibility of a painter and the mind of a contemplative." Students might want to analyze "Fog" in terms of Vendler's description.
2. "The Dakota" is an elegy for the murdered rock musician John Lennon, and in the lines

> Pick up
> the wedding rice, take out
> the face left over from
> the funeral nobody came to

Clampitt alludes to the lyrics of "Eleanor Rigby," one of the songs Lennon wrote with Paul McCartney. Her response to Lennon's death could be contrasted with the song Paul Simon wrote about the same tragic event, "The Late Great Johnny Ace."
3. Students might want to analyze those elements of "The Dakota" that make the poem an elegy by discussing the characteristics of the classical elegy and showing how Clampitt's poem shares these characteristics.
4. **CONNECTIONS** This poem is similar to H.D.'s "Oread" (p. 965). What similarities and dissimilarities do students notice?

LUCILLE CLIFTON

the thirty eighth year (p. 1054)
Reply (p. 1055)

The direct language of Lucille Clifton's poetry should present no difficulties for students. The care and the skill with which she presents her concepts show her long experience as a writer of children's books. Although she has had considerable success as a writer, there is a contradiction in the self-image she presents us in "the thirty eighth year." As she writes in line 41, she finds herself "a perfect picture of / blackness blessed," but, she continues, "I had not expected this / loneliness." She finds that she is an "ordinary woman," and clearly she expected to think of herself as extraordinary.

A letter such as this 1905 query found in the files of W. E. B. Du Bois, an important figure in the development of African American consciousness in the early decades of this century, would be unthinkable today, not because the country is no longer tinged with racism, but because through film, television, and the creative arts African Americans play a very visible role in society. Clifton, however, understands that the letter is a symbol of the country's lingering racism, and her "Reply" asks us once again to realize the African American's common humanity.

Questions for Discussion

1. Is it possible for the reader of "the thirty eighth year" to form a clear picture of Clifton's relationship to her mother? Why or why not?
2. How would a student paraphrase lines 27–30?
3. Clifton seems to associate her loneliness with a concept of "western," the "final Europe in my mind." What is she suggesting here?
4. In "Reply," why does Clifton use the vernacular "he do / she do" instead of "he does / she does"? Why does she repeat it three times at the end of the poem?
5. In the poem's terse phases Clifton presents us with a thumbnail sketch of the events of anyone's life. Are there any phrases that students might add to this list?
6. Clifton is proud of her African American heritage, but in this poem she consistently writes "they" instead of "we." Why does she exclude herself from the poem?

Topics for Writing

1. In lines 9–10 Clifton speaks of her expectation that she would be "more beautiful / wiser in afrikan ways," and she writes in line 35 that her daughters will be fruitful "like afrikan trees." Students might compare this concept of Africa with the concept of Africa expressed in the poetry of such Harlem Renaissance writers as Countee Cullen (especially "Heritage") and Langston Hughes. Students might also compare this concept of Africa with the reality of Africa that we see on nightly television news programs.
2. "Reply" is a political poem, and critics generally agree that political poetry has what could be called "a short shelf life." The poem is meaningful only as long as the political issue it addresses is meaningful. Students might like to write a short paper on whether they think Clifton's poem will have a lasting relevance.

SAMUEL TAYLOR COLERIDGE

Kubla Khan: or, a Vision in a Dream (p. 1056)
Frost at Midnight (p. 1058)

This introduction to "Kubla Khan" — written in 1797, when Coleridge was living in Somerset — is included in the *Bloomsbury Guide to English Literature* (1995) and is a useful way to begin a closer study of this complex and enigmatic poem:

> Coleridge recorded that he fell asleep after reading a description in *Purchas his Pilgrimage* (1613) of the pleasure gardens constructed in Xanadu by the 13th-century Mongol king of China, Khan (king) Kublai. While he was asleep "from two to three hundred lines" came to him, which upon waking he hastened to write down. However he was interrupted by "a person on business from Porlock," and afterwards could recall nothing of the remainder, "with the exception of some eight or ten scattered lines and images." It is difficult to know how much of this account to believe. One element Coleridge suppresses is his addiction to opium, which is certainly relevant to the

hallucinatory clarity of the poem's exotic images. Because of the oddness of Coleridge's account "a visitor from Porlock" has become a byword for any kind of intriguing, possibly evasive, excuse.

Despite its designation "A Fragment" the work is artistically complete. The first three sections rework phrases from the Jacobean travel book to describe a strangely primal landscape. An awesome "mighty fountain" forms the source of the "sacred river" Alph, on the banks of which Kubla has built a "stately pleasure-dome" surrounded by orchards and gardens. After watering the garden the river continues its course, entering "caverns measureless to man" and sinking "in tumult to a lifeless ocean." The clarity and primitiveness of these images gives the poem an archetypal resonance. The river can be seen as the river of life or creativity; the fountain symbolizes birth (of an individual, civilization, poetic inspiration), and the "lifeless ocean" death or sterility. The dome stands for the precarious balance between. It is possible that the final fourth section of the poem, which seems to be a commentary upon the preceding lines, were "the eight or ten lines or images" written after the departure of Coleridge's visitor, if he or she ever existed. The poem ends by imputing magical qualities to the poem itself and its bardic author: "Weave a circle round him thrice, / And close your eyes with holy dread, / For he on honey-dew hath fed, / And drunk the milk of Paradise." (p. 726)

If the reader continues with this explication of elements of the poem, it could be suggested that the terms "honey-dew" and "milk of Paradise" describe opium, which would clarify much of the poem's imagery. This is the opening sentence of the book that Coleridge was reading: "In Xamdu did Cublai Can build a stately Palace, encompassing sixteene miles of plaine ground with a wall, wherein are fertile Meddowes, pleasant Springs, delightful streames, and all sorts of beasts of chase and game, and in the midst thereof a sumptuous house of pleasure." In Coleridge's time, "Can" was the usual spelling of the word, and it was pronounced as it was spelled, so there is a perfect rhyme between "Khan" and "man" in lines 1 and 3.

Questions for Discussion

1. "Kubla Khan" could be described as a rhapsody on a visual theme, which is the imagined pleasure garden. What are some of the visual images Coleridge associates with his theme?
2. What might he be describing in lines 15–16, "As e'er beneath a waning moon was haunted / By woman wailing for her demon lover!"
3. What is he describing as the source of the sacred river?
4. Is there anything in the poem that suggests what he might be comparing with the metaphoric image "caves of ice"? What do students think he means with this image?
5. What is Coleridge saying about this unknown figure in the last two lines?
6. Is there any way to identify the figure from the poem itself?

Topics for Writing

1. In its use of specific details — for instance, "five miles of fertile ground" — that contrast with its imaginative setting, "Kubla Khan" could be described

as poetic science fiction. Students could develop papers around this theme, which could lead to a provocative class discussion.

2. One of the most unusual aspects of the poem is its rhyme, which occurs throughout but not in a regular pattern. Students could analyze the rhymes and describe the way they enhance the poem's musicality.

3. The poem's first five lines are usually admired for their euphony (their musicality). Students could analyze how alliteration, assonance, rhyme, and meter illustrate the musical effect of these lines.

FROST AT MIDNIGHT

This poem is a fireside meditation exemplary of early Romantic poetry. It describes a humble event in everyday language, and it leads the writer to profound thoughts about nature and human life. The baby sleeping beside Coleridge is his son Hartley. The poem is written in blank verse, but the play of thought is so richly imagined that it often seems as though the poem was written in rhyme. The only difficulty for the student will probably be the image of the "film," or coat of soot, on the grate in line 15. Coleridge himself supplied a gloss on the term: "In all parts of the kingdom these films are called *Strangers* and are supposed to portend the arrival of some absent friend."

Questions for Discussion

1. What does Coleridge mean in the image of line 1, "The Frost performs its secret ministry"? Why does he call this ministry "secret"?
2. What is he describing in lines 8–9, when he writes that the quiet around him disturbs his meditation?
3. What does he mean by the phrase "makes a toy of Thought" in line 23?
4. What is he saying about childhood and the city in line 51 to the end of the verse?
5. What is he saying with the word "pent" in line 52? What are its connotative meanings here?
6. What word is used to define the belief, which Coleridge expresses in line 62, that God is present: "Himself in all, and all things in himself"?

Topics for Writing

1. Coleridge's pantheistic beliefs were widespread among artists and intellectuals of his time. Students could compare his belief in nature with the beliefs of other Romantic poets — for instance, Shelley and Keats.
2. The poem could be analyzed for elements that characterize Romantic poetry, referring to William Wordsworth's definition in his Introduction to his *Lyrical Ballads* (p. 1330).

STEPHEN CRANE

War Is Kind (p. 982)

Stephen Crane was known in his brief life for the brilliantly imagined evocation of a young soldier's experience in the American Civil War, *The Red Badge of Courage*, published in 1895, but his bitter antiwar poem "War Is Kind" reflected his changed attitudes a few years later. He was born in New Jersey in 1871, and his career began with considerable promise, but he contracted tuberculosis and died in England in 1900 at the age of twenty-nine.

Question for Discussion

1. Discuss what is going on in stanzas 2 and 4 in comparison with stanzas 1, 3, and 5. Who are the persons in each stanza? How are they presented?

Topic for Writing

1. Have students read some of Crane's other poetry or fiction about war and write a three- to five-page essay discussing his characteristic attitudes and images.

COUNTEE CULLEN

Yet Do I Marvel (p. 951)

Countee Cullen was never able to resolve the contradictions between the divided cultures of European America and African America. A poised, highly educated poet, he was, along with Langston Hughes, one of the most promising writers associated with the Harlem Renaissance in the 1920s, when he — and Hughes — were both in their twenties. Cullen identified with European culture, and Keats was the model for his poetry. Hughes instead turned to cultural activism and the blues. Ironically, Cullen's poem "Heritage" is one of the most poignant statements of the ties the black community feels toward Africa.

Born in New York City in 1903, Cullen was educated at New York University and Harvard University, and after a brilliant debut as a poet, he spent most of his short life teaching junior high school in New York. Feeling that his poetry was suspended between the two cultures, he virtually stopped writing, giving his attention to prose translation and short books with children's themes. He died in 1946.

"Yet Do I Marvel" illustrates the contradictions that Cullen set out to resolve, and in this poem he achieves a masterful balance between his identification with European culture and his African American heritage. The form — a sonnet — and the allusions are European, but the subject is his racial identity.

Questions for Discussion

1. What is the model for his sonnet — English or Italian?
2. What is the meaning of line 4, "Why flesh that mirrors Him must some day die"?
3. Explain Cullen's reference in line 9, "immune to catechism." Why is the word "catechism" a useful allusion in the context of the poem?
4. In line 11, is "slightly understood" meant ironically?

Topic for Writing

1. **CONNECTIONS** Compare Cullen's sonnet with a poem by Langston Hughes and discuss the differences of language and imagery.

(text pp. 890, 951, 1059–1062)

E. E. CUMMINGS

when god lets my body be (p. 890)
goodby Betty, don't remember me (p. 951)
somewhere i have never travelled (p. 1060)
Buffalo Bill 's (p. 1061)
if there are any heavens (p. 1061)
in Just- (p. 1062)

Much of E. E. Cummings's poetry can be confusing. In his need to be continually upsetting to conventional readers, Cummings experimented with typography in ways that often pushed his poems beyond comprehension. It is possible to puzzle out what he means in lines such as these from "XIAPE" (1950):

tw

o o
ld
o

nce upon
n

Too often, however, the poem the reader is left with is simplistic and banal. A more serious problem that Cummings's desire to present himself as a "bad boy" projects into the poetry is his insistence on maintaining social attitudes that are offensive to many readers and certainly will cause problems for most students. Cummings was anti-Semitic and racist, and his view of women was limited to images of mistress or whore. On the one hand, Cummings could create poems of great sensitivity and beauty. Certainly "somewhere i have never travelled" is one of the most beautiful love poems in the English language, and "if there are any heavens" is a moving tribute to Cummings's mother. Students glancing through the table of contents of his collected writing, however, will encounter such titles as "IKEY (GOLDBERG)'S WORTH I'M" and "a kike is the most dangerous," which is certainly one of the most offensive anti-Semitic poems to be found outside of the hate literature of militia groups. African American students will find titles such as "one day a nigger" or "theys so alive/(who is/?niggers)" especially reprehensible.

Cummings's politics presents as many difficulties as his social attitudes. A reader encountering his work as an adolescent finds Cummings's thumbing-of-the-nose toward authority a refreshing sign of youthful high spirits. His antiwar poems of the 1920s, such as "my sweet old etcetera" or "next to of course god america I," and the anti-Americanism of a poem like "POEM, OR BEAUTY HURTS MR. VINAL" seem less startling after the angry writing of the 1960s and 1970s. At the time, however, Cummings's poems were a useful antidote to the unthinking jingoism that was pervasive in America. They are also very funny. Reading more of his writing, however, makes it clear that his view of America is not shaped by compassion or tolerance. He dislikes salesmen, politicians, businessmen, and academics as much as he does minority groups and unfriendly women. The Cummings of much of the poetry is an elitist and a snob, a man who angrily denounces a society that gets up in the morning and goes to work and doesn't have time for his poems about his love affair — many of them chance encounters with prostitutes — or the sunsets and sunrises he finds so breathtaking.

It will also be helpful to the instructor presenting Cummings to a class to realize that many critics, since the publication of Cummings's first book in 1923, have made these same criticisms — that his work is often immature, sentimental, dismissive, and arrogant — just as they have praised the best of his poetry for its sensitivity and technical skill. One aspect of Cummings's writing that has always fascinated readers is its blend of a modern, slangy, jazz-rhythmed style with traditional verse forms. "When god lets my body be" is from Cummings's first collection, *Tulips and Chimneys* (1923), but it expresses the sentiments and uses some of the same imagery as medieval love poetry. Students might read John Donne's "Song" (p. 887) or Robert Herrick's "To the Virgins, to Make Much of Time" (p. 888) to get the feeling of this earlier poetic idiom.

"Goodby Betty, don't remember me" is also from Cummings's first book, but it is in the section titled "Sonnets-Realities," and these poems have fewer allusions to writing from previous centuries, although, again, Cummings combines the freshness of his new language with one of the most traditional forms of verse, the sonnet. The poem is about his brief relationship with a Parisian prostitute, and students have always responded to his images of Paris at dusk.

"Buffalo Bill 's," another poem from the first book, is one of Cummings's most popular poems, and once again there is the contrast between the seriousness of the poem's subject, the death of famed frontier scout and showman William "Buffalo Bill" Cody, and the flippancy of the language. Buffalo Bill isn't dead; he's "defunct." And when Cummings asks the Angel of Death how he responds to the death of someone as heroic as Cody, the question is presented in the unforgettable phrase "how do you like your blueeyed boy / Mister Death." Students will also find it appealing that Cummings, despite his seeming flippancy, expresses a real admiration for Buffalo Bill. Cody rode a "watersmooth-silver / Stallion," and as Cummings remembers the posters of Cody that advertised his Wild West Show, he bursts out, "Jesus / he was a handsome man."

"In Just-" is another poem from Cummings's first book. In it he creates the sudden excitement of a spring day when a balloon seller comes to a place where children are playing and whistles to get their attention. As students will realize as they finish reading the poem, this balloon man is no ordinary street peddler. The "goat footed" figure ushering in spring is the god Pan, who whistles with his syrinx, bound together hollow reeds known as pan pipes, to call up Persephone from the underworld. The names of the children in the poem — "eddieandbill," "bettyandisabel" — could just as easily have been the names of French children or children from anywhere in the world. Students will be able to picture the spring in such phrases as "mud-luscious" and "puddle-wonderful," and the opening image "in Just-/ spring," which means that spring has just arrived, will help students to understand some of the ways that Cummings's best poems are a discovery of the possibilities of language. Students will also notice the use of run-together word phrases in both this poem and "Buffalo Bill 's," with the latter's "onetwothreefourfive pigeonsjustlikethat." This device helps Cummings suggest that sometimes things happen so quickly that you can't really be sure of what you've seen.

For much of his life, Cummings was married to a beautiful model named Marian Moorehouse, and many of his love poems reflect this deep and genuine emotion. "Somewhere i have never travelled" is one of his most affecting love poems, and it is technically one of his most skillful. Students can follow the image of the rose through Cummings's descriptions of how his loved one's fingers can open him, as spring opens "her first rose," to the last image, "the voice of your eyes is deeper than all roses." They should also be able to respond to the use of words like "frail" and "fragility," which suggest the softness of flower petals. Also, they will respond to the care with which Cummings introduces rhyme into the last verse, subtly intensifying the beauty of the poem's language.

In some of his early poems, Cummings wrote contemptuously of the careful, thoughtful middle-class women of Cambridge, Massachusetts, where he'd grown up, but his mother was one of these Cambridge women, and when he wrote "if there are any heavens" for her he dropped his "bad boy" pose and wrote directly and sincerely of his love for her. As in "somewhere i have never travelled," the poem is constructed around the image of a rose, suggesting that heaven, for the poet's mother, will be her garden.

Questions for Discussion

1. Which words and phrases in the poem "when god lets my body be" allude to poetry of the earlier European lyric tradition?
2. What does Cummings mean with the phrase "maidens whom passion wastes"?
3. What visual image does Cummings intend for us to see with the last line of the poem: "With the bulge and muzzle of the sea"?
4. In the poem "in Just-" Cummings uses wide spaces between the words "whistles," "far," and "wee." Why did he leave that space?
5. What other unusual typographical devices does Cummings use in the poem? Do you think they help us to understand what he is writing about?
6. In "Buffalo Bill 's," is Cummings describing William Cody as a frontier scout or as a showman? What tells us this in the poem?
7. What kind of pigeons is Cummings referring to in the line describing Buffalo Bill's shooting abilities?
8. What is the effect of the words that are run together in this same line?
9. Which form of the sonnet has Cummings chosen for "goodby Betty"?
10. What is Cummings describing in the image of line 12, "you exactly paled and curled"?
11. In "somewhere i have never travelled," why do you think Cummings chose the rose for his image of a flower?
12. Why do you think Cummings sets so many of his poems in the spring?
13. Some critics have suggested that "somewhere i have never travelled" is like a sonnet. Why do they make that comparison?
14. In "if there are any heavens" Cummings names other flowers that will be in his mother's garden, but why does he choose a rose — a "blackred" rose — as a symbol for his father's love?

Topics for Writing

1. Students might be interested in discussing several of Cummings's typographical devices and judging their effectiveness in his poetry.
2. The pose of the "bad boy" that Cummings adopts in his poetry has close links to such classic American archetypes as Mark Twain's Tom Sawyer and J. D. Salinger's Holden Caulfield. Students could analyze this persistent American image and try to explain its meaning.

3.   Some of the brashness in Cummings's poems is also reflected in the popular visual arts and the jazz music of the 1920s. It would be an interesting project to compare Cummings's attitudes with the images and forms of the decade's other arts.

4.   One of the criticisms of Cummings is that essentially his work didn't change as he grew older — in other words, he never grew up. Students might find it interesting to compare an early and a late poem to see what, if any, changes occurred in the poet's attitudes.

5.   Students could explicate the flower imagery in "somewhere i have never travelled," and these papers could initiate a class discussion.

H.D. [HILDA DOOLITTLE]

Mid-day (p. 932)
Oread (p. 965)
Orchard (p. 1063)
May 1943 (p. 1064)

In the early poetry of H.D., the reader recognizes the schoolgirl who sat down in a rainstorm, stretched out her arms, and cried, "Beautiful rain, welcome." In "Oread," one of the first poems H.D. wrote as an imagist, she cries out to the sea to engulf the land, and herself with it. Although the poem is only a few lines long, it presents us with a complex series of images. In "The Poetry of Modernity," the English literary historian Linda Ruth Williams analyzed the poem in its imagist context:

> "Oread" is often tendered as the exemplary imagist poem, with the complex of sea, pines and nymph fusing as image. Pound had defined the image as "that which presents an intellectual and emotional complex in an instant of time"; H.D.'s text pares down superfluity to a series of discrete, spare phrases. What the poem "is" is the relation between these phrases, how they build up into an image which does not come from individual key words or vague feelings but from the ways in which the component elements of the poem *relate*. (*Bloomsbury Guide to English Literature* [London: Bloomsbury, 1995], p. 272)

In "Mid-day," written two years later, when she was no longer as closely involved with the original imagist group, H.D. describes how the smallest things in nature, like the sunlight or the crackling of a leaf, overwhelm her. She feels the wind scattering her being, just as it scatters seeds, and she becomes aware of other things around her that have been split or bent, cracked or blackened. But then she sees a poplar tree on a distant hillside and remembers that the poplar is deep-rooted. The poplar is strong enough to withstand the wind that has scattered her, as seeds are scattered in the crevices of the stones. She doesn't make it explicit in the text, but seeds left in the stone crevices can never grow.

In "Orchard" H.D. describes again how she is overwhelmed by the beauty of nature. A ripe pear falls from an orchard tree, and even though the bees fly to the fruit immediately, she is even quicker in lying down before the tree in deference to its beauty. The bees, as she writes in lines 12–15, pay no attention her.

Their hunger is only for the sweetness of the fallen pear. In homage, she brings the tree — "god of the orchard" as she describes it in line 17 — nuts, berries, and fruit, a classic offering to a god of nature.

It will be obvious to students that the surging waves, the poplar tree, and the pear tree are symbols for the poet's own complicated emotions, but it may be difficult to involve the students in this dimension of the poetry, as H.D. has hung so many veils of metaphor between the symbols and her personal situation. When these poems were written she was virtually alone in London, with a small child and an unfaithful husband, and no certainty at all about her future. At the same time, however, students can respond to the idea that these are not poems that *consciously* project the emotions H.D. was struggling to control. These are poems that can be described as coming from the *unconscious*. The imagery of sunlight and trees, swollen fruit, and handfuls of nuts and berries is so distant from the grime and cold of London that the poems have the quality of a dream.

"May 1943" was written more than twenty-five years later, and everything that has happened to the poet in those years, including extensive psychiatric therapy with Sigmund Freud in the mid-1930s, has changed her poetry. The details in this poem *do* reflect the mundane realities of her life in London. It is wartime, and she is struggling with shortages and discomfort. She begins, in line 22, to say that people around her are heroic, then she denies this, "no / no / no," and wonders about herself — "what am I saying?" The reader is left with the feeling that even though she probably would not sit out in a rainstorm now, she would still like to.

Questions for Discussion

1. What is H.D. describing in "Oread" when she writes "pointed pines," "great pines," and "pools of fir"? What is the term for this kind of description?
2. What could students suggest as emotional equivalents for the waves she is asking to splash on "our rocks"?
3. In "Mid-day" H.D. writes, "I am anguished — defeated." What does she mean?
4. In "Orchard" she writes, "spare us from loveliness." How is this related to the line in question 3?
5. What does the poet mean by the phrase "we've grown alike" in line 15 of "May 1943"?

Topics for Writing

1. Students could write a paper discussing how "Oread" fits into the imagist program as outlined in the text (pp. 964–67), using images and lines from the poem as illustrations.
2. Three of the poems discussed include extensive images of nature, used in a very emotional context. Students could analyze these images and make some suggestions as to their symbolic meaning for H.D.
3. **CONNECTIONS** In "Mid-day" some of the imagery is related to images in Percy Bysshe Shelley's "Ode to the West Wind" (p. 935). In his poem he asks the wind to drive his thoughts over the universe, "Like withered leaves," and "Scatter, as from an unextinguished hearth / . . . my words among mankind!" Students could compare and contrast the sections of the two poems that describe the wind as it whirls around each poet.

Related Commentaries

Alicia Ostriker, "The Poet as Heroine: H.D." p. 1291.
Ezra Pound, "On the Principles of Imagism," p. 1297.

EMILY DICKINSON

Students should read the casebook commentaries while they are reading the poems. It can be difficult to picture the elusive Dickinson in her writing, but Thomas Wentworth Higginson's description is helpful in giving her a physical reality. Higginson was even more open in the letters he wrote to his wife shortly after his meeting with Dickinson, responding to an inner resiliency he sensed in the reclusive poet. He quoted Dickinson as saying, "How do most people live without any thoughts? There are many people in the world (you must have noticed them in the street). How do they live? How do they get the strength to put on their clothes in the morning?" She also said to him, "Women talk: men are silent: that is why I dread women."

Thomas H. Johnson was the editor who finally had the opportunity to work with the entire body of Dickinson manuscripts, and his description of his problems deciding on a final version of some of the poems will help the student to understand the way that any poet works. Richard Wilbur discusses some of the underlying themes in the poems, and Linda Gregg responds, as a poet, to Dickinson's use of verbal resources. Galway Kinnell, also writing as a poet, reacts with wry humor to the ways in which Dickinson has been taught in recent years.

Although it is a concept that has not been previously suggested, it might help students if they approach Dickinson's poetry in two different ways. During the years she was writing poetry at a feverish pace, from 1860 to 1863, she produced almost a poem a day, and she kept no other diary. This work could be described as "diary poems" — lyrics that Dickinson used to express, or conceal, her most personal emotions and descriptions of things that were happening in her personal life. These poems are usually loosely written, with irregular meter, uneven stanza length, and rhymes that often stretch even her very elastic consideration of "slant" or near rhyme. The other poems, which could be called her "public" writing, often have a general philosophic theme or a response to nature as their subject, and they tend to be more tightly written, usually in the four-line stanzas of alternating four- and three-stress lines that constituted the commonplace hymnal verse of the time. The poems Dickinson sent to Higginson were generally her "public" poems, and when Helen Hunt Jackson persuaded her to publish a single poem anonymously a few years before her death, the meter and rhyme had been elegantly "smoothed" to current fashion, although there is no way to know if the smoothing was done by Jackson or Dickinson herself.

In early letters to her brother Austin's wife, Susan Gilbert, Dickinson's language was extravagantly emotional, and in a series of passionate letters she wrote a few years later to a "master" (probably Charles Wadsworth), she expresses herself in fervent images. Her poetry, however, is often more guarded, often calculating in its evasions and silences. Dickinson also uses her poetry to debate with herself questions of religious faith and philosophy. So much in her poetry is concealed, but because so much is also told "slant," as she termed it, her work continues to fascinate and challenge her readers.

You love me — you are sure — **(p. 1069)**
I'm "wife" — I've finished that — **(p. 1069)**
I taste a liquor never brewed — **(p. 1070)**
I've nothing else — to bring, You know — **(p. 1070)**
Wild Nights — Wild Nights! **(p. 1070)**

Of these five poems, four could be considered "diary poems," as they clearly are "an overflow of emotion" — as Wordsworth expressed it — and were left in such a rough state that there was no way they could have been considered for publication at the time they were written. It was only when modern readers began to read them as contemporary poems that the irregular rhyme, oblique phrasing, and startling use of metaphor were appreciated. "I taste a liquor never brewed —" is the one "public" poem of the group, and it is written in regular meter and rhyme. The end rhyme of the first and third lines to which an early critic objected, "Pearl" / "alcohol," can be read as one of Dickinson's characteristic slant rhymes.

The dating of 1860 coincides with Charles Wadsworth's visit to Amherst, and if the interpretation of this period in Dickinson's life is correct, the poems relate to her emotional response to their relationship. Dickinson sent Wadsworth "I've nothing else — to bring, You know —" in a packet of other lyrics, and it seems to refer to the poems themselves, the only gift she could offer him. However she intended the poems to be read, their power lies in their imagery and in a poetic form that matches the immediacy of Dickinson's thought. Few poets have written so spontaneously and so directly. A term that Dickinson applied to her poetry was "bolts of melody," and it is a useful description of her technique. If she had used the usual poetic diction and guarded emotional expression of the popular poets of her day, she would have never achieved the lyric extravagance of "I taste a liquor never brewed —" or the abrupt gust of emotion of "Wild Nights — Wild Nights!"

Questions for Discussion

1. In "You love me — you are sure —" Dickinson seems to cast herself in the role of a small girl. What images in the poem would suggest this?
2. What is Dickinson describing with the term "grinning morn" in line 4?
3. What is the term for the metric pauses she indicates by dashes in the middle of some of the lines?
4. Discuss the poem's rhymes and half-rhymes. Is there a pattern to the rhyme?
5. Discuss what Dickinson might mean in "I'm 'wife' — I've finished that —" by using the word "wife" to describe herself. What might she mean by "Czar" and "It's safer so" in lines 3–4?
6. What is she describing with the term "soft Eclipse" in line 6? Why does she use the term "eclipse" for her metaphor?
7. What is she comparing in line 11?
8. Discuss the meter and rhyme scheme of "I taste a liquor never brewed —." Does it vary from its regular metric pattern? Why would Dickinson make any changes in the meter?
9. What is she referring to in line 3, "Vats upon the Rhine"?
10. What use does she make of alliteration in lines 4–6?
11. What is the metaphor she is introducing in lines 7–8, "Reeling . . . From inns of Molten Blue"? How does she develop this metaphor in the stanzas that follow?

12. Why do you think Dickinson didn't use the "correct" rhyme by Thomas Bailey Aldrich, quoted in the headnote?
13. We would use the term *hyperbole* for the poem's last stanzas. Discuss why we would describe them this way.
14. Discuss the use of near rhyme and eye rhyme in "I've nothing else — to bring, You know —."
15. What is the term for the figure of speech of "our familiar eyes" in line 4?
16. Have the class paraphrase Dickinson's meaning in the final four lines of the poem.
17. If we ignore the dashes in scanning the meter of "Wild Nights — Wild Nights!" the poem is written in regular dimeter except for the penultimate line. Why did Dickinson write the line that way?
18. What is the metaphor of the second and third stanzas?
19. What is Dickinson saying with the phrase "Futile — the Winds — / To a heart in port —" in lines 4–5?
20. How would line 9, "Rowing in Eden —," be interpreted?

Topic for Writing

1. Compare "You love me — you are sure —" and "I taste a liquor never brewed —" for their differences in meter and rhyme.

"HOPE" IS THE THING WITH FEATHERS — (p. 1071)
THERE'S A CERTAIN SLANT OF LIGHT, (p. 1071)
I'M NOBODY! WHO ARE YOU? (p. 1072)
AFTER GREAT PAIN, A FORMAL FEELING COMES — (p. 1072)
MUCH MADNESS IS DIVINEST SENSE — (p. 1072)

"'Hope' is the thing with feathers —" is one of Dickinson's most imaginative poems, and one that expresses reassurance. Whatever else has (or has not) happened in Dickinson's life, there is still hope — hope that is everywhere and never asks for anything. "There's a certain Slant of light" is more ambiguous, as it depicts a mood, a sense of depression the poet feels on winter afternoons. There is, however, no ambiguity about the darkness of her mood. One of Dickinson's biographers, Richard B. Sewall, notes that in their editing of the poem, Higginson and Mrs. Todd changed "Heft" to "weight" and

> included the poem in the section [of the 1890 *Poems*] entitled "Nature," even though it would have been more at home in their very next category, "Time and Eternity." Actually, the poem straddles both categories. The New England scene is sharp and clear, while the long, long thoughts it induces control our response to it. But what is the response? Are we left in a bleak, hurtful, hopeless world? When the light goes, are we in utter darkness? . . . I am reminded of the psychologist Carl Jung's phrase as he opposes the powerful, dangerous factors in our lives to the "grand, beautiful, and meaningful": he refers to this opposition as "the terrible ambiguities of immediate experience" (*Psychology and Religion* 55). Here, the poem seems to say, "If in the midst of life we die, it is also true that in the midst of death, we live." The oppressive tunes are "Cathedral," the hurt is "Heavenly," the despair is "imperial," of the "Air." And in this awareness we live more intensely, closer to the divine in our nature. It takes the shock of such awareness — the "look of Death" — to wake us up. (qtd. in

> *Voices and Visions: The Poet in America,* ed. Helen Vendler [New York: Random House, 1987], p. 80)

In early poems written when she was a teenager, Dickinson was often wickedly funny, and in her mature poetry she could still be intentionally humorous. "I'm Nobody! Who are you?" is one of her poems dealing with the themes of fame and adulation, and she dismisses them with the arch comparison of public acclaim with a frog's croak.

"After great pain, a formal feeling comes —" is loosely composed, like the diary poems, and could be an emotional response to a moment of despair. Her comparison with a numb happiness as a "Quartz contentment" is one of her most startling images and sets up the contrast with the despair she is feeling, which is "Lead." The final line of the poem is one of her most deeply unhappy images. The hour of lead — if outlived — is like freezing to death in the snow.

"Much Madness is divinest Sense —" is one of Dickinson's most popular poems. It was included in the first collection of her work in 1890 and has been anthologized many times since then. It is one of her few poems that show a flash of anger — for a moment she lets us glimpse her impatience with the everyday world and its contradictions.

Questions for Discussion

1. What is Dickinson describing in line 3 of "'Hope' is the thing with feathers —": "And sings the tune without the words"?
2. What is she saying in the last two lines?
3. In "There's a certain Slant of light," what does Dickinson mean by "Heft / Of Cathedral Tunes"? Discuss why she might find them oppressive.
4. What can she be referring to with her "Heavenly Hurt" that leaves no scar?
5. What is the term for the figure of speech Dickinson is using in "the Landscape listens" in line 13?
6. What is she suggesting in the juxtaposition of the words "Distance" and "Death" in the last lines?
7. Do we have any idea to whom Dickinson is speaking in "I'm Nobody! Who are you?" Is this an important consideration in our reading of the poem? Why or why not?
8. What does she mean by "they'd advertise" in line 4?
9. Discuss Dickinson's implied comparison in the poem of public life to a bog.
10. "After great pain, a formal feeling comes —" could be classed as a diary poem. What are the elements that would put it in this category?
11. Discuss Dickinson's meaning in the poem, clarifying her comparison between quartz and lead.
12. What does she mean in line 2, "Nerves sit ceremonious, like Tombs"?
13. Are the last two lines a metaphor of her own death?
14. What is the paradox she is describing in the first lines of "Much Madness is divinest Sense —"?
15. Could the poem be considered a statement of a political philosophy? What would that philosophy be?
16. Is this an angry poem, or is it only expressing an ironic observation?

Topics for Writing

1. Describe in a short paper the emotions Dickinson is expressing in "'Hope' is the thing with feathers —."

2. Discuss her images of pain and death in "After great pain, a formal feeling comes —."
3. In "Much Madness is divinest Sense —" discuss the implications of "'Tis the Majority / In this, as All, prevail."

I DIED FOR BEAUTY — BUT WAS SCARCE (P. 1073)

This poem can be grouped with Dickinson's other "public" poetry. Its theme is derived from the last lines of John Keats's "Ode on a Grecian Urn," which also indicates that Dickinson was not as isolated from the main poetic influences of her time as her other poetry suggests. Keats's lines "'Beauty is truth, truth beauty,' — that is all / Ye know on earth, and all ye need to know" are echoed in her whispered conversation between two people who have just died. Of all the Romantic poets, it was Keats that Dickinson read and admired the most. In a later poem she said that she told the truth in her poetry, but that she told it "slant," so it is perhaps not an unconscious choice that she describes herself here as dying for beauty, while the man beside her has died for truth. The final lines also edge closely to another of her themes — her hidden disappointment that she would not have any recognition for her writing, even if this was a resolve she had made herself and to which she held firmly throughout her life.

Questions for Discussion

1. What is the form of the poem? Compare it to "I taste a liquor never brewed —."
2. What does Dickinson mean by the phrase "an adjoining Room" in line 4?
3. What does she mean when she calls death a failure in the second stanza?
4. What is the image she presents in lines 9–10?
5. Is the last line suggesting that the poet's name would be lost after her death? Does she express disappointment in this knowledge?

Topic for Writing

1. **CONNECTIONS** Relate the poem to the last lines of Keats's "Ode on a Grecian Urn" (p. 934).

LOVE — THOU ART HIGH — (p. 1073)
I HEARD A FLY BUZZ — WHEN I DIED — (p. 1074)
IF YOU WERE COMING IN THE FALL (p. 1074)

With its series of metaphors for love — first as a mountain, then a stream, and finally as a mysterious veiled figure — and the parallel structure of the opening lines of each verse, "Love — thou art high —" is one of Dickinson's most formal poems. It also uses a regular six-line stanza, which differs from the poet's usual four-line structure, and she uses the formal poetic diction of "thee" and "thou." With so many stylistic elements borrowed from conventional verse of the time, the poem could be an experiment in the use of these forms. At the same time, however, Dickinson writes with her characteristic imagery and allusive diction. The ending of the poem is one of her familiar linkings of love with eternity.

Many meanings have been suggested for "I heard a Fly buzz — when I died —," among them that the fly represents the spirit of Christ entering her death chamber, or that the fly is the symbol of temporal reality breaking into the poem's spirituality. As with many of Dickinson's poems, there is probably no entirely satisfactory explanation for all of its imagery. Less difficult is "If you were coming in the Fall," a simple, determined expression of love — a love delayed by separation. The poem also uses the image of two insects that often appear in her verse, a fly and a bee.

Questions for Discussion

1. Students should scan the stanzas of "Love — thou art high —" and compare them to Dickinson's usual four-line stanza.
2. Explain the metaphor of the first lines of each stanza.
3. What does she mean by "Ducal" in line 6?
4. What is she suggesting with the term "sovereign summer" in line 11? How does the adjective "sovereign" relate to the term "Ducal" in line 6?
5. What is Dickinson saying about the effect of love in line 15?
6. How in the final lines does she say "love" became a word for eternity?
7. In "I heard a Fly buzz — when I died —," what is happening in the room?
8. What is Dickinson describing in lines 7–8?
9. What does she mean by saying she has signed away her "assignables" in line 11?
10. What could she mean with the color image of the fly's buzz — "With Blue — uncertain Buzz —" — in line 13?
11. There is a humorous tone to the first lines of "If you were coming in the Fall." Is it a humorous poem?
12. What is Dickinson saying with her image of the "Rind" in line 15?
13. What is she saying about her mood in the poem's final lines? Is she describing impatience?
14. Why does she use the term "Goblin bee"?

Topics for Writing

1. **CONNECTIONS** Like Dickinson's poems "I died for Beauty — but was scarce" and "I heard a Fly buzz — when I died —," Christina Rossetti's poem "After Death" (p. 1184) is also about her own death. Compare the three poems.
2. Students could analyze the imagery of the third stanza of "Love — thou art high —."

MINE — BY THE RIGHT OF THE WHITE ELECTION! (P. 1075)

This is one of Dickinson's strongest emotional outbursts and also one of the most difficult of her poems to interpret. It is certainly a diary poem and was not intended for publication. There have been many suggestions as to its meaning, none of them entirely satisfactory. It is known that about this time she began to dress entirely in white, and she wore white until her death. One possible meaning is that the image depicts an imagined wedding ceremony. The poem could also mean that she was now dedicating herself to her consummated love affair with Charles Wadsworth — "the Sign in the Scarlet prison" — and that she was making a decision to remain celibate — "in Veto!" By wearing white she would renounce any possibility of a relationship with someone else, and by this renunciation her love for Wadsworth could continue whole and intact. It would remain hers because she had "elected" to dedicate herself to it, and her decision would be her "Delirious Charter!"

Question for Discussion

1. What does Dickinson mean by "the Grave's repeal" in line 6?

BECAUSE I COULD NOT STOP FOR DEATH — (P. 1075)

Although there is no agreement among other poets about so many of Dickinson's poems, there is no disagreement about this one. In a 1932 essay Allen Tate wrote,

> If the word "great" means anything in poetry, this poem is one of the greatest in the English language. The rhythm charges with movement the pattern of suspended action back of the poem. Every image is precise and, moreover, not merely beautiful, but fused with the central idea. Every image extends and intensifies every other. The third stanza especially shows Miss Dickinson's power to fuse, into a single order of perception, a heterogeneous series: the children, the grain, and the setting sun (time) have the same degree of credibility; the first subtly preparing for the last. The sharp *gazing* before *grain* instills into nature a cold vitality of which the qualitative richness has infinite depth. The content of death in the poem eludes explicit definition. He is a gentleman taking a lady out for a drive. But note the restraint that keeps the poet from carrying this so far that it becomes ludicrous and incredible; and note the subtly interfused erotic motive, which the idea of death has presented to most romantic poets, love being a symbol interchangeable with death. (qtd. in *Emily Dickinson*, ed. Richard B. Sewall [Englewood Cliffs, N.J.: Prentice-Hall, 1964], p. 22)

Questions for Discussion

1. What is the form of the poem? Is the rhyme scheme regular? What half-rhymes does Dickinson use?
2. What term would we use to describe the entire poem?
3. What does Dickinson mean by "My labor and my leisure too" in line 7?
4. What term would we use for the phrase "Gazing Grain" in line 11?
5. What is Dickinson saying about their ride in line 13, "Or rather — He passed us —"?
6. Discuss what she is saying in the fifth stanza, beginning "We paused before a House."
7. Is she suggesting in the last line that eternity is a goal? Does this mean that she wants us to think of eternity as a place rather than a measure of time?

Topics for Writing

1. Discuss the figure of death in the poem.
2. Dickinson mentions or describes death in many poems, including examples in this selection. Compare this poem with any of the others.
3. There are many images of time and its passage in the poem. Analyze and discuss them.

A NARROW FELLOW IN THE GRASS (P. 1077)

This is one of the handful of Dickinson's poems published in her lifetime, but it was printed by her friend Samuel Bowles in his newspaper, the *Springfield*

Republican, without her permission. Dickinson often worked in clusters of poems, and this is one of several poems she wrote about snakes. Despite her unhappiness at seeing the poem in print, it has many of the characteristics of her public poems, even though there is a subtle shift in the poem's metric pattern after the second stanza. It does seem likely that when she wrote it she saw it as something that could be published, as the style and subject matter are similar to popular magazine verse with which she was familiar. What suggests this even more strongly is that she presents herself as a barefoot boy, one of the popular personae for poems of this type.

Questions for Discussion

1. Scan the poem for its metric form and discuss Dickinson's use of rhyme and half-rhyme.
2. What is she saying in line 4?
3. What is she describing in the second stanza? How could this be paraphrased?
4. What reasons might be suggested for her use of the "Boy, and Barefoot" as a persona?
5. What is she saying about the poem's persona in the stanza beginning with line 17, "Several of Nature's People"? Does this seem consistent with Dickinson's own feelings about the natural world?
6. What does she mean by "Zero at the Bone" in line 24?

Topics for Writing

1. Discuss why a barefoot boy would be a popular persona for a poem about nature.
2. Discuss the feeling Dickinson describes as a "transport of cordiality" toward "Nature's people."
3. **CONNECTIONS** Compare this poem with "Snake" by D. H. Lawrence (p. 1144).

I NEVER SAW A MOOR — (P. 1077)

In many of her poems written after the turmoil of the early 1860s, Dickinson's subject is eternity or heaven. This is one of her most direct expressions of her religious faith.

Questions for Discussion

1. Is the meter regular throughout the poem? How would the stanzas be scanned?
2. There are changes in the word order of lines 3 and 7. Why has Dickinson made these changes?
3. Why would she choose a moor as an image?
4. What does she mean by "Checks" in line 8?

Topic for Writing

1. Discuss her concept of God and heaven in the poem.

JOHN DONNE

Song (p. 887)
Death, be not proud (p. 948)
The Good-Morrow (p. 1078)
The Flea (p. 1079)
Good Friday, 1613. Riding Westward (p. 1080)
Thou hast made me (p. 1081)
At the round earth's imagined corners (p. 1081)
Batter my heart, three-personed God (p. 1082)

Anyone who spends a little time with John Donne's poetry soon becomes aware of the contradictions in both his life and in his writing. In his early poetry he writes as "Jack" Donne, a young and passionate adventurer and London man about town. In his later poems and sermons he writes, just as passionately, as Dr. Donne of St. Paul's Cathedral. When the biographer Lytton Strachey described the contradictions of the Elizabethan age in which Donne lived, he found that Donne was a particularly complicated example of these contradictions. Strachey wrote,

> It is above all the contradictions of the age that baffle our imagination and perplex our intelligence. Human beings no doubt cease to be human beings unless they were inconsistent; but the inconsistency of the Elizabethans exceeds the limits permitted to man. Their elements fly off from one another wildly. . . . By what perverse magic were intellectual ingenuity and theological ingenuousness intertwined in John Donne? (qtd. in *Donne*, ed. Sir Herbert Grierson [Oxford: Oxford UP 1933], p. xiii)

In discussing the near hopelessness of Donne's situation — a Catholic in a Protestant country who converted to the Anglican Church and attempted to satisfy the emotional complications of his decision — the critic and editor of Donne's poetry, Sir Herbert Grierson, wrote, "His was a poetic temperament, imaginative, susceptible, impulsive, served by an acute and subtle intellect, and under the influence of diverse elements in his nature he complied with circumstances more than once in his life; but such compliance does not make for peace of mind" (*Donne* xv). If students have difficulty understanding these disparate elements in Donne's writing, they should understand that Donne, and all his later critics, had some of the same difficulties.

SONG

Some students may have difficulties with "Song" that have nothing to do with Donne's contradictory nature. It is a brilliant, imaginative poem that is clearer and more directly comprehensible than much of Donne's other writing. It is also, by contemporary standards, a poem that is sexist and demeaning toward women. In the poem Donne declares that even if someone reading his lines can perform daunting tasks like catching a meteorite or having intercourse with a plant, the reader still won't find — anywhere — a woman who is faithful to her lover. Even if this person comes from a journey of "ten thousand days and nights" to tell him that he knows of a woman who is "true and fair," Donne won't bother to go, even if the woman lives next door. By the time he gets there she will already have been "false, ere I come, to two or three."

Not only is the poem's imagery startling and effective, its structure is as fresh and surprising as it was when the poem was written almost four hundred years ago. The trochaic tetrameter is fairly regular through the first six lines, then it suddenly breaks with two lines of iambic monometer, before returning to the four-beat line to end the stanza. The shift in the meter allows Donne to change the tone of what he is saying as a kind of abrupt aside. By the third verse the tone of these asides has become a sarcastic jeer. There is also subtle modification in the rhymes. The first two couplets of each verse end in masculine rhymes; the third couplets end in feminine rhymes. The poem is an excellent example of the resources and skills of the best Elizabethan poets, but poems are more than examples of rhyme and meter. Readers will have to make their own decisions about the theme that Donne has so skillfully presented.

Questions for Discussion

1. Who is Donne addressing in the poem? Does the reader learn more about who the person might be from what Donne writes later in the poem?
2. Why is he asking this person to perform tasks that are all obviously impossible to do?
3. What is he asking this person about time in line 3?
4. In lines 8 and 9 he asks the person to find a wind that would "advance an honest mind." What does he mean by this?
5. In lines 10–11, what does he tell us about the person he has been addressing?
6. What does he mean by the phrase "Such a pilgrimage were sweet" in line 20?
7. The class might consider whether Donne is truly angry in the poem's final lines, or if he is only cynical and resigned.

Topics for Writing

1. Students, or the entire class, may want to write about or discuss the poem's sexism — perhaps even to defend it as youthful high spirits.
2. Students could paraphrase and suggest modern equivalents to the tasks Donne proposes in the first verse.

THE GOOD-MORROW

In this poem for a new lover, Donne pretends that he cannot believe he and his lover were fully alive until they loved each other. The things they did before they loved were childish, "country" pleasures or simply dreams, and not real. With "Good-Morrow" he says good morning to their "wakening souls." They are so fulfilled in their love that their hemispheres are only east, where the sun rises, and the south, where there is only warmth. There is no "sharp north" or "declining west" in their love.

Questions for Discussion

1. What is Donne suggesting with the words "weaned" and "sucked" in lines 2–3?

2. What is he telling his love in lines 6–7?
3. What does Donne mean in line 10, "For love all love of other sights controls"?
4. Explain the conceit in line 14, "Let us possess one world; each hath one, and is one."
5. In line 15 are the lovers looking into each other's eyes?
6. What is Donne saying about the death of lovers in line 19?

Topics for Writing

1. The images of "sea-discovers," new worlds, maps, and hemispheres reflect the Elizabethans' excitement at the discoveries of the new worlds of America, Africa, and Asia. Students could explicate these references in terms of the discoveries.
2. Donne's rhymes in the poem are subtle and unexpected. It would be interesting for students to discuss the perfect rhymes, the near rhymes, and, in the final three lines, the multiple rhymes.

THE FLEA

The Elizabethan "conceit," an unexpected play of language or context, certainly describes "The Flea," one of Donne's most startling examples of this convention. It is also one of literature's most inept and transparent attempts to get a woman into bed. The poet begins by saying that her denial means little, since a flea has sucked blood from both of them, and their blood is already mingled in the flea's body. Then he begins an involved explanation of why she shouldn't kill the flea, as three lives now are mingled inside it — his and hers and the flea's. Whatever she — and her parents — may feel about it, the flea's body is their marriage bed. When his lady kills the flea and tells him that she doesn't feel any different now that the flea is dead, he tells her that she will feel as little loss when she yields to him.

It might help students if the instructor points out that in the first verse Donne is telling the lady to see the flea, swollen with the blood it has sucked from both of them. The second verse opens with him saying to her, stop, don't kill the flea, as it is their marriage bed. "Cruel and sudden," the words that open the third verse, describe the way the lady kills the flea. If students have not had experience with fleas, they need to know that in order to kill a flea one must squeeze their hard shells between the fingernails, which is why Donne uses the phrase "Purpled thy nail."

Students will probably have as much trouble following his argument as the lady did, but the poem is a brilliant example of Elizabethan wordplay.

Questions for Discussion

1. In the second line Donne tells the lady that what she is denying him is such a little thing. Does he mean this? If he doesn't mean it, why is he using it as an argument with her?
2. In lines 8–9, is he saying that, alas, the lady isn't pregnant?
3. What does he mean in line 10, when he asks her to spare three lives in the flea?
4. What does he mean by the description "living walls of jet" in line 15?
5. What does Donne mean in lines 16–18, that she is committing suicide and sacrilege?

6. What does Donne tell us about the lady's mood in his phrase "Yet thou triumph'st" in line 23?

Topic for Writing

1. Students will find it interesting to paraphrase the poem to follow Donne's argument.

GOOD FRIDAY, 1613. RIDING WESTWARD

With this poem we begin to read Donne's religious work. Grierson wrote that these poems recapture

> the peculiar charm of [Donne's] early love verses at their best, the unique blend of passionate feeling and rapid subtle thinking, the strange sense that his verse gives of a certain conflict between the passionate thought and the varied and often elaborate pattern into which he moulds its expression, resulting in a strange blend of harshness and constraint with reverberating and penetrating harmony. (*Donne* xli)

According to notes on the various manuscripts from which the poem was transcribed, Donne wrote it as a meditation when he was traveling to Wales and sent it back to "Sir H. G.," with whom he had been staying. Although the poem opens with a series of paradoxes that are characteristic of Donne's style, the greatest paradox of the day is that on this Good Friday he is traveling toward the West, while all his thoughts are turned toward the East, where the Crucifixion took place. The seriousness of his thoughts finally overcomes his habit of writing in paradox, and, beginning with line 21, "Could I behold those hands which span the poles," the poem, while still complex in its imagery, becomes an impassioned prayer for the forgiveness of his soul.

Questions for Discussion

1. In the first eight lines of the poem, Donne is explaining why he has to set off on business on Good Friday. What is he saying?
2. In lines 11–12, "There I should see a sun by rising set, / and by that setting endless day beget," how does the reader know that he is referring to Christ?
3. What does he mean by lines 21–22? What is he describing in the phrase "pierced with those holes"?
4. Explain his meaning in the description in line 27, "that flesh which was worn / By God for his apparel."
5. Line 37 has a double meaning. What is Donne saying here?
6. What is Donne asking of God in the last two lines of the poem?

Topic for Writing

1. Donne assumes that anyone reading the poem will be a Christian. A useful topic for a paper could be the question of what meaning, if any, the poem might have for someone who is not a Christian.

DEATH, BE NOT PROUD
THOU HAST MADE ME
AT THE ROUND EARTH'S IMAGINED CORNERS
BATTER MY HEART, THREE-PERSONED GOD

John Chalker and Erik Frykman, in the notes to their anthology of English verse, are helpful in their description of Donne's Holy Sonnets. They write,

> Like his other verse they show an impassioned mind expressing itself in forceful, colloquial terms, with the usual admixture of ingenious imagery. They are pervaded by a tortured sense of sin and unworthiness counterbalanced by the hope of divine mercy. Terror of death is a frequent theme in these sonnets: in the most often quoted of them it is overcome by a triumphant assurance of death's powerlessness. (*An Anthology of English Verse*, ed. John Chalker and Erik Frykman [Stockholm: Almquvist & Wiksell, 1969], p. 245)

Students will notice that the form of the sonnets combines the English and Italian models. The first two quatrains rhyme in the Italian style, *abba/abba*, and the last six lines rhyme in the English style, either *cddc* or *cdcd*, with a new rhyme, *ee*, in the final two lines. Although the sonnets are concentrated and sometimes complex in their imagery, students usually find that with a few moments of discussion they can follow their attitudes and ideas. Perhaps because of their religious themes, or perhaps because Donne was older, the sonnets are less crabbed and difficult than most of his secular verse. They still, however, are filled with paradox.

"Death, be not proud" develops a paradox that was common at the time — that because at death human beings wake to live eternally, it is death that dies: "One short sleep past, we wake eternally / And death shall be no more." In "Thou hast made me" Donne addresses God, saying that if God has made him, will God let the "work," which is Donne's body or physical existence, decay? Donne is weak and running toward death, but the worst for him is that his "old subtle foe," the devil, still tempts him. Only God's grace can save him, drawing Donne's "iron heart" to him like a magnet.

"At the round earth's imagined corners" is a triumphant sonnet of Christian salvation. When the trumpets sound from the corners of the earth, all will rise and "behold God," but Donne asks for a moment more before the trumpets sound. His sins are so heavy he needs to ask for grace before the throngs come to heaven. If God will teach him how to ask for forgiveness, then he will be saved, his pardon as good as if God had sealed it with his blood. The theme of so many of the sonnets is death, but in "Batter my heart, three-personed God" Donne is asking God to hammer at his heart until he gains admittance. Donne has labored to give himself to God, but he still is filled with doubt. This is usually interpreted to mean the doubts that torment many Christians, but it could also be a veiled reference to Donne's difficulties with his divided faith. The sonnet expresses its theme in paradoxes that are as effective as the language of "Death, be not proud." If Donne is to rise and stand, then God must overthrow him. In the powerful final lines he says that he never will be free until God fetters him, and he never will be chaste until God ravishes him.

Questions for Discussion

1. In lines 5–6 of "Death, be not proud," Donne says that rest and sleep are a pleasurable picture of death. What will death itself be like?
2. What is he saying in line 7, with "soonest our best men with thee do go"? Is this similar to the familiar saying "Only the good die young"?
3. What does he mean by calling death a slave in line 9?
4. In "Thou hast made me," is Donne asking for God to make him healthy again, or is he prepared for death?
5. What does he mean in line 4, that his pleasures are "like yesterday"?
6. Is it death he is afraid of, or dying when he's not in a state of grace?
7. With the term "iron heart" in the last line, what is he saying about himself?
8. In "At the round earth's imagined corners," is Donne describing the "final trumpets"?
9. In line 5 he speaks of those who died from the flood and those who will die from the fire. Consider this in the context of the biblical prophecy that the next time God punishes the earth it will be with fire, not with another flood.
10. In line 8 Donne speaks of the "death's woe." Is this a contradiction of the description of death in the other sonnets?
11. What is the meaning of the phrase that ends the sonnet, "seal my pardon with thy blood"?
12. In "Batter my heart, three-personed God," what does Donne mean by "three-personed God"?
13. What does he mean in line 2, with the list of things like "knock" and "breathe" that failed to open his heart?
14. What does he mean in line 5, that he is "to another due"?
15. In line 7 he describes reason as God's viceroy. What does he mean by this?
16. What is the meaning in line 11, of his request that God divorce him?

Topics for Writing

1. **CONNECTIONS** This sequence of Donne's sonnets was written not long after the collection of Shakespeare's sonnets was published. Students could compare the two writers' sonnets.
2. Students could write an extensive paper comparing and contrasting Donne's various uses of paradox in the Holy Sonnets.

RITA DOVE

Wiring Home (p. 952)
Belinda's Petition (p. 1083)
Weathering Out (p. 1083)
Daystar (p. 1084)

Rita Dove's writing is so clear that students should have no difficulty understanding her poetry. "Belinda's Petition" is an early poem, written before Dove's extended visits to Europe, and it has a specific African American theme. "Weathering Out" and "Daystar" are from her Pulitzer Prize–winning sequence of poems about her grandparents, *Thomas and Beulah*, published in 1987. Dove's grandfather died in 1963, and her grandmother died six years later. "Wiring Home" is one of a group of these poems she wrote in the last few years. Students should read Dove's commentary on the sonnet form, "An Intact World" (p. 1252).

Questions for Discussion

1. What does "new born" refer to in line 3 of "Belinda's Petition"?
2. In lines 11–12, is Belinda allowing herself to be ironic?
3. What do lines 1–18 tell the reader about Belinda's religion?
4. Who is Dove describing in the image "Men with Faces like the Moon" in line 19?
5. In "Weathering Out," how do the adjectives describing the trees relate to the poet's own condition?
6. What is she describing in line 6, "navigating in wonder"?
7. What is the meaning of the phrase "she glistened in cocoa butter" in line 14?
8. What do we call the figure of speech Dove uses in the phrase "everything shivered in tinfoil" in line 23? What is she describing?
9. What does Dove mean by the image "pinched armor" in line 7 of "Daystar"?
10. What is she telling us with the image of "her own vivid blood" in line 11?
11. In line 16, why does she tell her daughter that she was building a palace?
12. In the last lines of the poem, is she expressing unhappiness?
13. The sonnet "Wiring Home" has fourteen lines. What other elements of the poem relate it to the traditional sonnet form? Students should consult the discussion of the sonnet in the text (pp. 945–54).
14. What does Dove mean by "Lest the wolves loose their whistles"? If she does not intend for the term "wolves" to be taken literally, what connotations is she suggesting?
15. What is she describing in the image of the "trumpeting kiosk's / tales of odyssey and heartbreak" in lines 8–9?
16. What happened to her as she turned the corner? Why does she use the word "ambushed"?

Topics for Writing

1. In an essay written in the 1980s, Dove stated that poetry by African American writers should have the emotionalism of the black gospel church, and that when the poems are read aloud readers should feel themselves so excited that they would interrupt with cries of "right on." Her own poems, however, are written in a modern European American style that, except for their subject matter, seem to have nothing to do with African American speech or the rhythms of gospel song. Students could examine and discuss this seeming contradiction.
2. Although the story of Dove's grandparents' life in Akron, Ohio, describes an African American man and woman, there are many similarities between their experience and the experience of any young couple living in a strange American city at the same time. Students could discuss the similarities and differences between Dove's grandparents' experience and the experience of their own grandparents.

ROBERT DUNCAN

Song (p. 1085)
My Mother Would Be a Falconress (p. 1086)

The visual image of "Song" is a winter stable, and someone coming to sleep with the animals. Phrases and words like "they sleep in grace" and archaic spellings like "damnd" and "passt" suggest that this is a night in an older time. The night symbolizes the rest that can come with darkness, the rest that can come with death. In contrast to the calm the animals feel, the poet lies in the darkness and feels his body tormented with his confused desires. It is a poem that suggests, obliquely, that Duncan is still struggling to accept his homosexuality.

In "My Mother Would Be a Falconress" there is no longer any sexual confusion. Although Duncan presents his struggle for emotional and sexual freedom as an extended metaphor, imagining himself as a falcon chained to his mother's wrist, the meaning that is partially concealed behind the metaphor is unmistakable. Students should not be misled by the word "gay" in the second line. At the time Duncan wrote the poem the word was not used to describe sexual preference. What Duncan is suggesting in the poem's central metaphor is that, as a homosexual, he is as different from his mother as a hawk is from its master. His final realization of his homosexuality is expressed as a discovery of "the blue hills where the falcons nest." He understands now that there are others like him.

Students should read the commentary on the poem by Samuel Charters (p. 1243). It discusses Duncan's fascination with the medieval period and its elaborate rituals, among them the sport of falconry.

Questions for Discussion

1. In lines 8 and 41 of "My Mother Would Be a Falconress" Duncan writes about the limited distance he feels he can travel from his mother. What is he describing?
2. In the third stanza, beginning with line 13, what is he saying about his life?
3. Line 36 describes a real part of a falcon's training. What is its meaning for Duncan?
4. In lines 47–49 he writes that his mother's pride still "sought in me flight beyond the horizon." What does this suggest?
5. What does he mean in line 54, "It seemd my human soul went down in flames"?

Topics for Writing

1. Students could prepare an interesting paper by reading about the sport of falconry in other sources and comparing the details of the sport with Duncan's poem.
2. Students could explicate the metaphor of the poem and relate it to Duncan's emotional struggle with his mother.

T. S. ELIOT

The Love Song of J. Alfred Prufrock (p. 1088)

Students should read the commentary on the poem by Cleanth Brooks Jr. and Robert Penn Warren (p. 1240). They offer an interesting insight into the character of the poem's protagonist. Students will be surprised to learn that although the poem was not published until Eliot had moved to Europe, it was written while he was still an undergraduate at Harvard College. The poem's mingling of many of Eliot's literary interests — from Renaissance writing to traditional English poetry to the fashionable new poetry of the French symbolists — is so free and spontaneous that some of the poem's images seem as startling to Eliot as they do to modern readers. When he used this method of organization again for the long poem *The Wasteland* a few years later, the new poem achieved worldwide success and made him famous, but it now seems mannered and self-conscious, whereas "Prufrock" still has the brash excitement of fresh discovery.

What Brooks and Warren do not make clear in their analysis is that the poem is not only a maze of allusion but also a maze of quotation, direct and indirect. Students may feel that in some sections it reads like a pastiche or a collage, and their instincts here are right. Except for the passage from Dante that he used as an epigraph to the poem, Eliot chose not to identify the quotes, unlike Marianne Moore, who was writing at the same time and who also used quotations liberally in her work. Eliot's decision *not* to identify the sources of many of the lines of the poem was useful to his reputation. Only literary specialists could identify the quotes, so Eliot was often praised for images and language that he took from other sources. One of the most arresting images of this poem is the despairing cry "I should've been a pair of ragged claws / Scuttling across the floors of silent seas," but it isn't made clear that this image is actually from a poem by Jules Laforgue, a symbolist poet whom Eliot had translated. For most students, however, simply mastering the most obvious details of this long and complex poem will be enough of a challenge in the classroom.

The opening line of the poem poses a question that has never been satisfactorily answered: Who is the "you" Eliot asks to go with him for the evening? In *Modern American Poetry, 1865–1950*, Fred Moramarco has summarized the various interpretations:

> To whom he is speaking in the poem is purposefully ambiguous. It is possibly someone else in the room, most likely a woman he is trying to seduce; it could be to the reader, so that the "you" in the first line — "Let us go then, you and I" — becomes everyone who reads the poem; and it could be to another part of Prufrock himself, so that the poem becomes an internal monolog between two parts of a self — a nervous chat between the Ego and the Id. Each of these interpretations has advocates. It is a measure of the poem's strength that it can be read consistently with any of these three premises in mind. (Alan Shucard, Fred Moramarco, and William Sullivan, *Modern American Poetry, 1865–1950* [Amherst: U of Massachusetts P, 1989], p. 99)

Questions for Discussion

1. The poem is actually a dramatic monologue. What elements place it in this category?
2. At the time the poem was published, the image of line 3 was considered very shocking. Is it still shocking to readers today?
3. What is Eliot describing in line 7, "sawdust restaurants with oyster-shells"? Do places like this exist in our cities today?
4. What does he mean in lines 26–27 "there will be time / To prepare a face to meet the faces that you meet"?
5. What is Eliot telling us with the repetition of the lines "In the room the women come and go / Talking of Michelangelo"?
6. What is he describing in line 39, "Time to turn back and descend the stair"?
7. In line 86, "And in short, I was afraid," what is the narrator afraid of?
8. What is the narrator saying about himself in line 125, "I do not think that they will sing to me"?

Topics for Writing

1. Although the language of the poem is ironic, self-deprecating, and often humorous, the person described in the poem is deeply tragic. Students could analyze the tragedy of the poem.
2. **CONNECTIONS** The melancholy of aging, which Eliot depicted while still so young, is also an important theme in the poetry of William Butler Yeats, a contemporary writer whom Eliot had read. Students could compare the sense of melancholy in Yeats's "The Wild Swans at Coole" (p. 1228) with the despair of Eliot's poem.
3. Many commentators have written about the last three lines of the poem. Students could write their own responses to these lines and compare their interpretations in class discussion.

Related Commentaries

T. S. Eliot, From "Tradition and the Individual Talent," p. 1253.
T. S. Eliot, From "William Blake," p. 1256.
Michael Rubiner, T. S. Eliot Interactive, p. 1301.

RALPH WALDO EMERSON

Days (p. 909)

Emerson was the leading American intellectual of his time: an essayist, poet, and lecturer whose ideas influenced an entire generation of American writers, including Henry David Thoreau, Walt Whitman, and Emily Dickinson. The poem that the reclusive Dickinson permitted to be published in a collection of anonymous writing in 1880 was universally credited to Emerson.

Emerson was born in 1803. Much of his life was spent in Concord, Massachusetts, where he died in 1882. Despite his fame, Emerson was always certain that he could achieve little with his life, and "Days" is an expression of his profound self-doubt. The same mood is reflected in a journal entry written in the spring of 1824, when he had just finished his studies at Harvard and was about to take up his first position as a Unitarian minister:

> I cannot accurately estimate my chances of success, in my profession, & in life. Were it just to judge the future from the past, they would be very low. . . . Thus far the dupe of hope I have trudged on with my bundle at my back, and my eye fixed on the distant hill where my burden would fall. It may be I shall write *dupe* a long time to come & the end of my life shall intervene betwixt me & the release.

Questions for Discussion

1. "Days" is unrhymed, but it is written in regular meter. What is the term for this meter?
2. Describe the scene of the poem.
3. What is Emerson describing in his naming of the gifts the days are offering? What do we call this figure of speech?
4. What does he mean by "morning wishes" in line 8?
5. What does he say about himself in the next line?
6. What is the term for the image of the day's expression in the last line? Is the scorn he sees a metaphor for his own feelings?

Topics for Writing

1. Although "Days" has only eleven lines and is unrhymed, it could be considered a sonnet. Discuss the reasons that it could be called a sonnet.
2. The scene of the poem, which is the description of the days coming to Emerson in his garden, could be called an allegory. Analyze the elements that make the poem an allegory.

LOUISE ERDRICH

Indian Boarding School: The Runaways (p. 984)

Louise Erdrich is of a mixed Native American and European American background, and she has made this a theme of her writing. She was born in Minnesota in 1954 and raised in North Dakota, where her father taught at a Bureau of Indian Affairs boarding school. She is married to writer Michael Dorris, with whom she collaborates on longer fiction.

Questions for Discussion

1. Discuss the images in the poem that suggest movement or flight. What is Erdrich doing by juxtaposing these with other kinds of images?
2. Explicate the long last sentence of the poem.

Topic for Writing

1. **CONNECTIONS** Ask students to explore in a two-page essay the theme of flight and escape in this poem and in Erdrich's story "The Red Convertible" (p. 196).

LAWRENCE FERLINGHETTI

Constantly Risking Absurdity (p. 877)

Two Scavengers in a Truck, Two Beautiful People in a Mercedes (p. 997)

Dog (p. 1092)

In Goya's greatest scenes we seem to see (p. 1094)

Late Impressionist Dream (p. 1095)

CONSTANTLY RISKING ABSURDITY

Ferlinghetti has chosen a trapeze artist's performance as a metaphor for a poet's performance with words. Each must present himself to his audience, and if the poet fails to be convincing and entertaining as he performs on his "eyebeams" over the heads of his audience, he and his little act will appear ridiculous. There above the people's heads he is constantly risking the embarrassment of appearing absurd. Ferlinghetti makes it clear that even though the poet is the performer, his poet's role is modest. There waiting for him is Beauty, and he — a little figure looking like Charlie Chaplin — might be lucky enough to catch her as she leaps. If students have read the E. E. Cummings poem "Buffalo Bill 's," they will notice that, like Cummings, Ferlinghetti has run together words — for instance, "charlie-chaplin" — and certainly his poem has some of Cummings's playfulness and humor.

Questions for Discussion

1. What does Ferlinghetti mean when he writes in line 8 that the poet "climbs to a high wire of his own making"?
2. What is the association between the trapeze artist and Charlie Chaplin?
3. What is Ferlinghetti telling us in line 12, when he writes that the poet's act goes on "to the other side of day"?
4. In lines 16–18, what is he saying about a poet's depiction of reality?
5. To what is he comparing the truth in the metaphor "taut truth" of line 21?

Topics for Writing

1. As a modern poet, Ferlinghetti uses lines of different lengths and patterns in his writing. Some of the lines are written and spaced on the page so that they seem to suggest the "high wire" of a trapeze act. Students might wish to comment on this.
2. Much of the poem is presented in a lighthearted manner, and it seems that there is no larger issue than the risks poets take in presenting their work to an audience. In the final lines, however, Ferlinghetti says that Beauty has leaped into "the empty air / of existence." An interesting paper and class discussion could center on this idea, that our existence is only "empty air."

Two Scavengers in a Truck, Two Beautiful People in a Mercedes
Dog

The contrast Ferlinghetti describes in "Two Scavengers . . ." between rich and poor people passing on the street will present no difficulty to students, who have certainly made many of the same comparisons themselves. They probably would not, however, have made the laconic comment that ends the poem: "as if anything at all were possible / between them / across that small gulf / in the high seas / of this democracy."

"Dog" was intended to be read aloud with a jazz group, so the line spacing is more straightforward than in most of Ferlinghetti's poetry. His dog did urinate on a policeman on one of their walks. Congressman Doyle could be any one of several politicians whose actions have troubled Ferlinghetti, but Doyle specifically was involved with the investigations of the House Un-American Activities Committee.

Questions for Discussion

1. In "Two Scavengers," what would we call the figure of speech that the poet uses in the last lines, "that small gulf / in the high seas / of this democracy"? What are some of the associations he wants us to make with these lines?
2. In his use of the word "reality" in line 2 of "Dog," is Ferlinghetti referring only to a dog's perception of reality, or is this a description of how every creature perceives reality?
3. To what is "without benefit of perjury" alluding in line 53?
4. What does Ferlinghetti mean by his ironic reference to "free enterprise" in line 61?

Topic for Writing

1. **CONNECTIONS** There are certainly similarities between the dog's adventures that Ferlinghetti describes and the adventures of the dog that is described wandering the streets in Hjalmar Söderberg's story "A Dog without a Master" (p. 617). Students might want to compare the poem and the story to clarify each writer's view of life.

In Goya's greatest scenes we seem to see
Late Impressionist Dream

Ferlinghetti studied art in Paris when he was discharged from the service after World War II, and he now spends as much time painting in his studio in South San Francisco as he does writing. He has written many poems about paintings, and a recent collection of these poems, *When I Look at Pictures,* with illustrations of the paintings he describes, has become an international best-seller in museum gift shops. The group of etchings by the Spanish painter Francisco Goya depicting the horrors of the French occupation of Spain during the Napoleonic Wars has become even more relevant in our own century. Other artists have depicted war from the point of view of the leaders or the soldiers involved in battle. Goya's etchings showed what happened to civilians caught behind the lines, and they are a terrifying glimpse into what war would become in the twentieth century, when helpless civilians are considered as much the enemy as the opposing armed forces. As Ferlinghetti makes clear in line 22, "Only the landscape is changed."

"Late Impressionist Dream" is an affectionate description of everything Ferlinghetti loves about impressionist painting and the Paris of those years. He presents it in the context of a dream, perhaps so that he can introduce his friend the writer Jack Kerouac, whose French Canadian background may have inspired the dream.

Questions for Discussion

1. In line 11 of "In Goya's greatest scenes we seem to see," Ferlinghetti uses the term "cement skies." What association does he want us to make with this image?
2. In lines 20–22 he is again making a reference to reality. What is his intention with his statement that the scenes in these paintings still exist?
3. What does Ferlinghetti mean by the term "legionnaires" in line 24? Are they still a factor in today's wars?
4. What is Ferlinghetti describing when he writes "The scene shows fewer tumbrils / but more maimed citizens / in painted cars"?
5. In "Late Impressionist Dream," what historical period is Ferlinghetti describing?
6. Why does he call his dream "Late Impressionist"?
7. What is he describing in lines 9–10, "French intel- / lectuals are indulging in their famous *grande logique*"?
8. What are some of the associations he is making in the poem's last phrase, "the fish / still speak Breton"?

Topics for Writing

1. **CONNECTIONS** There are other examples of poets writing about paintings in the text, among them poems by W. H. Auden, Anne Sexton, and William Carlos Williams. Students could compare these poems and perhaps illustrate them with copies of the paintings that the poets describe.
2. Students could discuss some of the reasons that poets respond so emotionally to the work of painters.

CAROLYN FORCHÉ

The Colonel (p. 989)

Carolyn Forché was born in 1950 and teaches at George Mason University. In the 1970s she worked in El Salvador as a human rights advocate and journalist for Amnesty International. Her anthology *Against Forgetting* (1993) is a major gathering of twentieth-century protest poetry against injustice and inhumanity.

Questions for Discussion

1. What poetic elements strike you about this "prose poem"?
2. Describe the character of the colonel and how it emerges through the poem.

Topic for Writing

1. **CONNECTIONS** Have students compare the emergence of the characters of the colonel and the duke in Robert Browning's "My Last Duchess" (p. 970).

ROBERT FROST

Most students will already have read some of Frost's poetry in high school, and they will be able to discuss some of the themes and backgrounds in the poems. Many aspects of Frost's writing, and Frost himself, are contradictory and elusive, and it will be challenging to the instructor to present a more balanced and perhaps less immediately appealing view of Frost to the class.

The Nobel Prize–winning Irish poet Seamus Heaney has summed up the complicated response of many other poets to Frost in his essay "Above the Brim":

> Among major poets of the English language in this century, Robert Frost is the one who takes the most punishment. "Like a chimpanzee" is how one friend of mine remembers him in the flesh, but in the afterlife of the text he has been consigned to a far less amiable sector of the bestiary, among the stoats, perhaps, or the weasels. Calculating self-publicist, reprehensible egotist, oppressive parent — theories of the death of the author have failed to lay the ghost of this vigorous old contender who beats along undauntedly at the reader's elbow. His immense popular acclaim during his own lifetime; his apotheosis into an idol mutually acceptable to his own and his country's self-esteem, and greatly inflationary of both; his constantly resourceful acclimatization of himself to this condition, as writer and performer — it all generated a critical resistance. (*Homage to Robert Frost* [New York: Farrar Straus & Giroux, 1996] p. 61)

As is well known, Frost set out from the beginning to make himself a success as a writer. As he wrote in a letter in 1913, "There is a kind of success called 'esteem' and it butters no parsnips. I mean a success with the critical few who are supposed to know. But really to arrive where I can stand on my legs as a poet and nothing else I must get outside that circle to the general reader who buys books in their thousands. I may not be able to do that. I believe in doing it — don't you doubt me there. I want to be a poet to all sorts and kinds. I could never make a merit of being caviar to the crowd the way my quasi-friend Pound does."

He felt he deserved success because, as he said in another letter, "to be perfectly frank with you I am one of the most notable craftsmen of my time. . . . I am possibly the only person going who works on any but a worn out theory (principle I had better say) of versification. . . . I alone of English writers have consciously set myself to make music out of what I may call the sound of sense."

Frost, however, faced a problem in his hunger for fame and recognition. The kind of familiar, pastoral poetry he might have wanted to write was already being written by poets who will not be familiar to students but who were much more successful than Frost at the time, among them Vachel Lindsay, Carl Sandburg, and Edgar Lee Masters. In the 1930s Frost had to contend with the enormous success of the populist poet Stephen Vincent Benét. He was also painfully conscious of the work of such modernist poets as T. S. Eliot and Ezra Pound, who were beginning their careers at the same time as he, and his difficulties with Eliot's poetry lingered for most of his life.

Faced with the competition of poets working on either side of him, Frost was left with little room to reach the audience he desired. His strategy was to write with a modernist clarity of diction and syntax, retaining, however, the traditional forms of meter and rhyme, and to strip his work of the sentimental clichés that had stifled late Victorian verse and, indeed, had been the deadening characteristic of his own verse. In his sense of verse structure and verbal nuance, Frost was as good as he said he was, and he carefully constructed a body of work that was narrow in scope but tightly concentrated around a recognizable persona as a crafty New England cracker-barrel sage. Frost's major poems usually were skillfully constructed to present readers with a homily — a "detachable statement," in poet Lawrence Raab's words — that they could take away from the reading. The most famous of Frost's homilies are "Good fences make good neighbors" from "Mending Wall" and "Home is the place where, when you go there, / They have to take you in" from "The Death of the Hired Man." It was, as poet Robert Lowell described it, a "great act."

Students should read the commentaries on Frost and his writing, which include an early interview with Frost and a close reading of one of his major poems, "After Apple-Picking."

THE PASTURE (P. 1099)
MENDING WALL (P. 1099)

Frost liked "The Pasture" very much, and he used it to open several collections. "Mending Wall" is one of his best-known poems, and it has been quoted on occasions as solemn as President John F. Kennedy's inspection of the Berlin Wall, when he recited its first line, "Something there is that doesn't love a wall." As critics immediately noted, the Russians could quote the last line of the poem, "Good fences make good neighbors," to justify the building of the wall. Frost himself was amused by the differing interpretations and said that he should have written the opening lines "for the generality," as he sometimes referred to his readers: "Something there is that doesn't love a wall / Something there is that does."

In an extended discussion of "Mending Wall," Lawrence Raab examines the "riddle" of the opening line:

> "Mending Wall" opens with a riddle: "Something there is . . ." And a riddle, after all, is a series of hints calculated to make us imagine and then name its hidden subject. The poem doesn't begin "I hate walls," or even "Something dislikes a wall." Its first gesture is one of elaborate and playful concealment, a calculated withholding of meaning. Notice also that it is the speaker himself who repairs the wall after the hunters have broken it. And it is the speaker each year who notifies his neighbor when the time has come to meet and mend the wall. Then can we safely claim that the speaker views the wall simply as a barrier between human contact and understanding? (*Touchstones* [Middlebury College Press; University Press of New England, 1996], p. 204)

Most students will immediately identify with the attitude of the poet rather than that of the neighbor, who is presented as "an old-stone savage." When asked by the English novelist Graham Greene what he meant by the phrase "Good fences make good neighbors," Frost replied, "I wish you knew more about it, without my helping you." If they think more closely about what Frost seems to be saying — that it isn't really important to be so concerned about property rights — a few students may come to identify with the more conservative views of the neighbor.

Questions for Discussion

1. Discuss what might be termed the "suspended rhyme" of the last lines of each stanza of "The Pasture" that ties together the overall rhyme scheme. Is it effective?
2. In line 3, Frost has changed the word order for the sake of the rhyme. Would the line have been as effective if it had been left in the normal word order?
3. What is the metric form of "Mending Wall"?
4. What elements of assonance and alliteration can be found in the first line?
5. What does Frost mean by "To each the boulders that have fallen to each" in line 16?
6. What is he suggesting with the term "outdoor game" in line 21?
7. What is he saying in line 24, "He is all pine and I am apple orchard"? What is the term for this figure of speech?
8. Discuss Frost's phrase "Spring is the mischief in me" in line 27.
9. In his use of the word "Elves" in line 36, is Frost being serious, or is this more of his spring mischief?
10. Discuss his description of his neighbor, beginning with line 40. Is this a fair description?

Topic for Writing

1. In a short paper students could discuss the contradiction between the poem's two "detachable statements": "Something there is that doesn't love a wall" and "Good fences make good neighbors."

THE DEATH OF THE HIRED MAN (P. 1100)
FROM THE HILL WIFE (P. 1104)

Although students will probably not be familiar with the poetry of Thomas Hardy, the mood of hopelessness in "The Death of the Hired Man," as well as its diction and approach, have much in common with Hardy's work, which Frost had read with considerable attention. It is one of Frost's less "poetic" poems, and it isn't until line 106 that he allows himself any kind of imaginative use of language. If students find the style of the poem very prosaic, show them that they are correct by illustrating for them how the first section is written as a prose narrative:

> Mary sat musing on the lamp-flame at the table waiting for Warren. When she heard his step, she ran on tiptoe down the darkened passage to meet him in the doorway with the news and put him on his guard.
>
> "Silas is back."
>
> She pushed him outward with her through the door and shut it after her.
>
> "Be kind," she said.
>
> She took the market things from Warren's arms and set them on the porch, then drew him down to sit beside her on the wooden steps.

In this early poem, Frost's iambic pentameter is tightly controlled. His later poems often contained words or phrases inserted to fill out the five-stress meter of each line. The preceding paragraphs could be the beginning of a very credible short story.

(text pp. 1096–1109)

In "The Road Taken" the Nobel Prize–winning poet Derek Walcott comments on the atmosphere of Frost's poems set in New England, among them "The Death of the Hired Man":

> The metronomic rhythm of their dialogue, the inflexible morality, these pinched tragedies in which their narrow lives are seeped can tire attention. Something mean, sour, and embittered, like the late mulch of November soil, rises from the pages and disturbs us with the kind of punishment that a tireless gossip demands of his hearers. This is a mercilessly moral climate that produces attic idiots and witch-hunters. (*Homage to Robert Frost*, p. 106)

Although Frost was fiercely opposed to any intrusion of government agencies into everyday life, the poem can easily be read as a comment on the problems faced in rural America before the enactment of the social legislation of the 1930s, particularly the Social Security Act, which would have given the broken farm laborer of the poem some financial security. As we have said, the strength of a Frost poem is often its homily, and here the phrase with which the reader is left is "Home is the place where, when you have to go there, / They have to take you in."

Questions for Discussion

1. What is the poetic form of "The Death of the Hired Man"?
2. Discuss the social implications of line 24, "'Someone else can.' 'Then someone else will have to.'"
3. What is the reason for the division of lines 39–40?
4. What is the wife suggesting about the old man's mental state in lines 57–60?
5. What is the term for the figure of speech in line 106?
6. What is Frost telling us about the wife's action in lines 112–13?
7. One of the poem's most effective lines is the laconic sentence "It hit the moon" in line 169. What makes the sentence so strong in this context?

Topics for Writing

1. In the selection from *The Hill Wife* Frost describes loneliness from the woman's point of view. Discuss the poem's image of the birds and their effect on the emotions of the wife and her husband.
2. Frost's poems of the New England countryside make no mention of a possible alternative of city life or any suggestion that the two, country and city, might be economically or culturally linked, or even that there is any larger social unit than the isolated farm. Discuss the concept of social isolation that this presents in terms of its effect on the three people of this poem.
3. In lines 76–90 the hired man makes very specific comments on the education and ambitions of his younger co-worker. A paper could explore the attitudes that Silas presents and discuss whether his life would have been better if he had had different ideas when he was younger.

BIRCHES (P. 1105)

If students find this poem difficult to follow, they will be encouraged to learn that Frost composed it using two fragments, and he later confessed being unable to remember where the two were joined. Of all his major poems, it is the least well-constructed, and a closer reading may convince the student that it may have been patched together from several fragments.

It was a joke among Frost's students at his Bread Loaf Writing Program that you always could tell when you were coming close to Frost's farm because all the birch trees along the road were bent down. The poem, however, is better read as a metaphor or allegory than as a simple description of climbing birch trees. It is one of his most complex poems and one of his most sentimental. It is also a poem that displays all his masks.

As they begin to study the poem, students will find that one section detaches itself from the rest — the sixteen-line description of birches in a coating of winter ice, beginning with "Often you must have seen them" in line 5. It is one of his most brilliantly imagined passages, and it fits so uncomfortably with the other segments of the poem that Frost himself breaks it off with a comment by the crusty old farmer persona he was so carefully nurturing: "But I was going to say when Truth broke in / With all her matter-of-fact about the ice-storm." He capitalizes "Truth" to suggest a note of derision for the "factual" description.

In terms of the poem's overall structure, Frost is correct in dismissing his extended descriptive passage, as the poem is about something else, but there is a brilliant clarity to the description. The poem's wordy iambic pentameter almost disguises the imaginative verbal skill of the imagery, but if the lines are rewritten in terms of the imagist credo that Ezra Pound published at about the same time that Frost was writing the poem — "No unnecessary words" — the effect of the imagery is more obvious:

> You must have seen them
> Loaded with ice on a sunny winter morning,
> Clicking upon themselves as the breeze rises,
> Turning many colored as the stir cracks
> And crazes their enamel . . .

The passage ends with the unforgettable simile of the birches bent down and trailing their leaves on the ground, "Like girls on hands and knees that throw their hair / Before them over their heads to dry in the sun."

The subject of the poem is Frost's desire to return to the simplicities of childhood. Although there are darker hints of masturbation and a fierce Oedipal conflict in lines 26–32, Frost ends the poem on a self-satisfied note: "One could do worse than be a swinger of birches." The homily he leaves is the sentence "Earth's the right place for love: / I don't know where it's likely to go better."

Questions for Discussion

1. In his description of fallen birches in lines 1–2, Frost intimates that the concept of a boy swinging on birches is an imagined construct. Is this concept developed in the rest of the poem?
2. In his extended description of the leaves covered with ice, what does he mean by "many colored" in line 8? What are the "heaps of broken glass" in line 12?
3. What is the antecedent of the word "They" in line 14?
4. What is Frost referring to with the phrase "matter-of-fact" in line 22?
5. The class could discuss the Oedipal overtones of lines 28–33.
6. What is Frost saying in line 50, "May no fate willfully misunderstand me"? Could the previous lines be interpreted as a wish for death? What does he mean by "get away from earth awhile?"
7. Why has Frost emphasized "Toward" in line 56?

Topics for Writing

1. "Birches" seems to present a factual description of something Frost remembers from his childhood, but the poem also suggests that this is all a metaphor for a dream of childhood. These contradictions could be the topic of a paper.

2. **CONNECTIONS** Frost's relationship to nature, as expressed in the line "I'd like to go by climbing a birch tree," is the opposite of the relationship the poet Percy Bysshe Shelly expresses in "Ode to the West Wind" in the line "I fall upon the thorns of life! I bleed!" Students could compare these two responses.

FIRE AND ICE (P. 1106)
TO EARTHWARD (P. 1106)

"Fire and Ice" is almost an epigram, but its corrosive cynicism is more strongly weighted than most epigrams. Part of the effect of this poem and "To Earthward" is the concentrated language and the obvious skill with rhyme and meter. In concise lyrics like these, Frost was able to strip away the wordiness and occasional padding of his poems in blank verse. The lines in "Fire and Ice," as is usual in Frost's shorter lyrics, are end-stopped, but "To Earthward" is one of his most ingenious displays of enjambment, often across the gap between the stanzas. Students should scan the poems to understand their metric subtlety. In its passion and yearning, "To Earthward" is as close to the traditional lyric mode as Frost allowed himself to come.

Questions for Discussion

1. Each of these poems mixes lines of unequal length. In "Fire and Ice" it is a mixture of two- and four-stress lines, dimeter and tetrameter; in "To Earthward" the mixture is two- and three-stress lines, dimeter and trimeter. Why does Frost mix the lines? Is there a pattern he follows throughout each poem? What is the effect of the shorter lines?
2. In "To Earthward" the break between the last line of the first stanza and the first line of the next is an enjambment. Where else in the poem does Frost use enjambment?
3. What is he saying with the poem's opening image, "Love at the lips"? What is the term for this figure of speech?
4. What does he mean by the phrase "swirl and ache" in line 9?
5. What is the antecedent of "those" in line 13?
6. Is there a paradox in lines 15–16, "The petal of the rose / It was that stung"? What is Frost saying about love in this phrase?
7. What is he saying in "the aftermark / Of almost too much love"?
8. What does he mean by "The sweet of bitter bark" in line 23?
9. In emotional terms, what is he longing for in the poem's final lines?

Topics for Writing

1. "Fire and Ice" has as its subject the destruction of the world. An African American gospel song also describes the destruction of the world in the lines "God gave Noah the rainbow sign / No more water, fire next time." A topic for a paper could be the concept of the end of the world as described in Frost's poem and in the gospel song.

2.   **CONNECTIONS**   This poem expresses many of the attitudes of the typical carpe diem poem — for instance Andrew Marvell's "To His Coy Mistress" (p. 910) or A. E. Housman's "Loveliest of trees, the cherry now" (p. 884). A paper could analyze these elements in Frost's poem.

3.   **CONNECTIONS**   "To Earthward" expresses some of the melancholy of Ralph Waldo Emerson's "Days" (p. 909), which is also about the failure of the writer to live life to its fullest. Students could compare the two poems in terms of their expression of personal disappointment.

STOPPING BY WOODS ON A SNOWY EVENING (P. 1107)

Students familiar with old popular songs may be interested to know that student waiters at Frost's Breadloaf Conference discovered that this poem can be sung to the familiar melody "Hernando's Hideaway."

There have been many suggestions as to the significance of the repeated final line of the poem. Frost said that he had planned for the poem to have another stanza, but he couldn't think of one, so he brought the poem to a close by repeating the last line he'd written. The poem's rhyme scheme is carefully planned, and this could be the reason for the repeat. If they study the poem, students will find that it has an intricate, interlocked rhyme scheme that calls for the third line of each stanza to set the rhyme for the first two and final lines of the next. The only way Frost could finish the rhyme of his final stanza was to repeat the third line, which would otherwise be left without a rhyme for closure. The poem's regular meter is unusual for Frost, who normally employed subtle shifts of syntax, but there is no interruption in the metric flow.

The setting of the poem seems simple — a man stops his horse in the woods on the year's shortest day, the winter solstice of December 21, and looks into the darkness. There are many ambiguous elements to the poem, however, and readers have noted the implied death wish of the first line of the final stanza. Frost tacitly accepted this interpretation but always insisted that because the man continued on his journey, the poem also expressed a life wish. The poem's homily is the line "But I have promises to keep" and the repeated two final lines, "And miles to go before I sleep."

Questions for Discussion

1.   Students should outline the poem's rhyme scheme and scan its meter.

2.   Why is there a change in word order in the first line?

3.   Discuss the alliteration of the first stanza.

4.   Why does Frost use the adjective "his" to describe the woods? Does he intend some larger meaning?

5.   Is there any significance to the fact that the poem describes something happening on the night of the winter solstice?

6.   In line 12 there seems to be contradiction between the poet's earlier description of the dark, cold night and his description of "easy wind and downy flake." What does he mean by this?

7.   What is the implication of the adjective "lovely" in line 13?

8.   The class should discuss whether they feel this line expresses a wish for death.

9.   To whom has the narrator made his "promises"? Is the poem specific about this?

Topic for Writing

1. This poem could be read as an allegory of human life, with the interpretation that we are only travelers through a world that is often dark and lonely. This interpretation could be the subject of a paper.

THE ROAD NOT TAKEN (P. 1108)

Students who have read the introductory note to Frost's poetry in the text know that the poem was originally written as a joke for his friend Edward Thomas, who never could decide which road he wanted to take and always regretted whichever choice he made. It is more obvious as a joke if students read the two outer stanzas by themselves and read the two inner stanzas separately. It is in these two inner stanzas that Frost depicts his friend trying to decide which road to take, even though, as Frost makes clear, they are just about the same, one of them no less traveled than the other. The homily with which the reader is left is in the last lines, "I took the one less traveled by, / And that has made all the difference," and the muddle of the middle stanzas is quickly forgotten.

One reason the muddle is forgotten is certainly that the last two lines exemplify the persona Frost spent his life shaping — that of the person a little outside, who has gone his own way and who has become a different person because of it. This is what Frost's audiences expected of him, and these two lines of the poem fulfill our expectations.

Questions for Discussion

1. What does Frost mean in lines 2–3, "I could not travel both / And be one traveler"?
2. The class should outline the descriptions of the two roads Frost describes in the poem's two middle stanzas, especially emphasizing the first two lines of the third stanza. Does he contradict these lines with his famous assertion later in the poem that he "took the one less traveled"?
3. What is Frost saying in the phrase "how way leads on to way" in line 14?
4. What is the effect of the dash that ends line 14?

Topics for Writing

1. Part of the reason Edward Thomas didn't understand that the poem was intended as a joke is that the middle two stanzas aren't clearly funny in their attempt to portray his indecisions. A topic for a paper could be a rewriting of these stanzas to make the joke more obvious.
2. The first two lines of the final stanza can be read as a prophecy of Frost's later life. Discuss what this foretells about his future.

AFTER APPLE-PICKING (P. 1108)

Students will find that Philip Gerber's commentary on "After Apple-Picking" discusses the question of whether Frost intended the poem to be read as an allegory of his death.

This is one of Frost's most memorable poems, with a sonority that has some of the quality of Keats's "To Autumn" and an "ice mirror" image and a "nightmare" section that stretch to depths of imagination Frost seldom allowed himself.

Although he vigorously rejected what he called "free verse," some of the poem's strength comes from its technical freedom. It is as close to free verse as Frost could get without stepping over the line. He has resorted to irregular line lengths to emphasize rhyming words, but there is no regular rhyme pattern, and the poem could almost have been written in free verse, as this recasting of the first lines shows:

> My long two-pointed ladder's sticking
> through a tree toward heaven still,
> And there's a barrel that I
> didn't fill with apples beside it,
> and there may be two or three apples
> I didn't pick up on some bough.

Students should discuss the nightmare of lines 18–27 and also look closely at the ice / glass / pane imagery of lines 10–15. This imagery constitutes some of Frost's most ambiguous, and it is highly effective for this very reason. This is one of those moments when he trusted his intuition. As he said in a letter, "You get more credit for thinking if you restate formulae or cite cases that fall easily under formulae, but all the fun is outside: saying things that suggest formulae that won't formulate — that almost but don't quite formulate." If he was pressed to explain images such as these, he always maintained that explaining them would just say the same thing but in words that were not as good.

Questions for Discussion

1. Discuss with the class whether they think the poem is meant as an allegory of Frost's life.
2. What does he mean by "Essence of winter sleep" in line 7?
3. Discuss the possible meanings of the ice / glass / pane imagery in lines 10–17. Why does Frost say he was already on his way to sleep before the melted piece of glass fell from his fingers?
4. Discuss the nightmare of lines 18–27 and Frost's use of imagery: tactile, visual, and aural. The only type of image missing in the section is olfactory, but he has already used it earlier in the poem. Where is the olfactory image?
5. What is Frost suggesting with line 30, "There were ten thousand thousand fruit to touch"? If the poem is an allegory, what could be the meaning of this line and of the opening phrase of the next line, "Cherish to touch"?
6. Discuss what Frost could mean by "trouble" in line 37.
7. Is the sleep he describes in line 38, "This sleep of mine, whatever sleep it is," a metaphor for death? Does the "long sleep" in the penultimate line describe only the woodchuck's hibernation?

Topics for Writing

1. This is a poem of regret and resignation. A paper could analyze the way these emotions are presented in the poem.
2. A paper could take as its topic Frost's nightmare of the apple harvest and describe the ways in which its details take on a nightmarish quality.

ALLEN GINSBERG

America (p. 994)
A Supermarket in California (1007)
From Howl *(p. 1110)*
Sunflower Sutra (p. 1115)

For a discussion of Ginsberg's technical means, the instructor is referred to the section suggesting approaches to his poem *Howl*, and students should read the interview with Ginsberg in Chapter 18 (p. 1260). It should be emphasized in any discussion of Ginsberg's poetry that these are performance pieces, and to experience their whole effect students should hear them read aloud, preferably in one of the many recordings that Ginsberg has made of his poetry over the last forty years.

AMERICA

In "America," despite Ginsberg's claim in the first line that he has done something for his country, the role he plays in the poem is that of an adolescent trying to deal emotionally with the necessity of joining his individuality with a larger social organism. Ginsberg expresses his wariness in a hilarious catalog of the reasons that he shouldn't have to join, and insists he hasn't got much to offer America if he does join. He points out that he's poor, that he smokes marijuana "every chance I get," that he reads the communist writings of Karl Marx, that he has mystical visions. One of the most popular lines at his readings is the adolescent yearning, "When can I go into the supermarket and buy what I need with my good looks?"

In the last lines of the poem his attitude changes. America is threatened by Russia; America needs him. What young person can hold out against being needed? Ginsberg will join, despite the fact that he's nearsighted and psychopathic, even despite the fact that — and like any good stand-up comic, he holds this back to the last — he's gay.

Questions for Discussion

1. What is Ginsberg saying about America in line 9, "When will you take off your clothes?"?
2. What are the more serious implications of line 10?
3. What is Ginsberg saying about the hidden side of America in line 12, "why are your libraries full of tears?"? Is this a comment on the history of America?
4. What is he saying in line 25, "America the plum blossoms are falling"? How is this similar to his other comments on America?
5. What is the specific reference of line 53, "My ambition is to be President despite the fact that I'm Catholic"?
6. The poem is a series of what comedians call "one-liners." The class could discuss what themes hold the seemingly loose material of the poem together.

Topics for Writing

1. The poem is a maze of references to political events and opinions. Students could discuss some of the references in terms of Ginsberg's political vision.

2. Ginsberg writes in many different voices throughout the poem, from his family's colloquial English to the phony Native American dialect of Hollywood films. Students could analyze his reasons for using these voices in the poem.

A SUPERMARKET IN CALIFORNIA

This, like all of Ginsberg's best-known poems, is a skillfully constructed performance piece. It uses a "line breath," as Ginsberg terms it, that reminds the listener of the cadence and breadth of Walt Whitman's lines. The poem describes a night in Berkeley when Ginsberg has been reading Whitman's poetry. He is tired and hungry, so he walks the few blocks from his back garden cottage on Milvia Street to the all-night supermarket on University Avenue. In the poem he brings Whitman to his audience, not as a distant literary figure but as an old man he overhears in the next aisle propositioning the grocery clerks. Ginsberg's readings are a careful balance of poems that are humorous, scandalous, and wryly moving, and in this tribute to Whitman he expresses his feeling of companionship with the "lonely old grubber" and his consciousness that part of what they share is loneliness. He also expresses his ultimate feelings of detachment from the America that we saw him, in the poem "America," finally agreeing to join.

Questions for Discussion

1. What does Ginsberg mean by the phrase "shopping for images" in line 2? What are some of the images he finds in the supermarket?
2. In the second line he speaks of Whitman's "enumerations." What does he mean by this? Does it describe his own writing?
3. Who was García Lorca, and why does Ginsberg mention him here?
4. Why do Ginsberg and Whitman, in line 7, never pass the cashier?
5. What is he describing in line 10, "trees add shade to shade"?
6. What is the contrast he is suggesting in line 11, "past blue automobiles in driveways"?

Topic for Writing

1. Students might want to suggest an answer to the question Ginsberg asks in the last line of the poem.

FROM HOWL

Many students may have heard Ginsberg read *Howl*, and they are aware that it is meant to be, as the title describes, a howl. It is a poem written to be performed, and reading it is like reading a screenplay. What is on the page is only part of the final effect. Students will learn a great deal about Ginsberg's theories of poetry and the poets who have influenced him by reading the interview with him in Chapter 18 (p. 1260). The traditional poetic means discussed in the text have little relevance in a discussion of his writing. With *Howl* we have a new kind of poem.

The meter of *Howl* is best described as the breath. Ginsberg in his interview calls it "continuous breath leading to ecstatic climax." If you shout the poem you will run out of breath at the end of each extended line unit. In the longer line units — three or four printed lines — you will have to take a breath somewhere in the middle. The diction and syntax of the poem are also new, as Ginsberg realized that in a performance piece there is no chance for the audience to look back at a phrase or an image. The line has to affect its audience immediately. There is a centuries-old tradition of oral poetry, but longer oral poems almost always sustain the interest of their listeners through their power as narratives. They tell a story. Ginsberg is essentially delivering, loudly, a philosophical meditation.

To maintain the energy and movement of the poem, Ginsberg uses a nontraditional poetic syntax. Words are interjected for their associative effect. In line 4 he describes the people he is writing about as poor, in tattered clothing, and in bad physical condition, partly the result of drug use. But because this is a howl intended for performance, he achieves a more dramatic effect by simply giving us the crucial words "poverty," "tatters," and "hollow-eyed" and letting the minds of his listeners make the associations as he rushes on. Much of the controversy about *Howl* has centered on its sexual imagery or its descriptions of drug abuse, but the poem's powerful effect on its listeners owes as much to its startling originality as to its shock value.

Howl not only uses words in new ways but uses them in new contexts for new effects. In its nervous burst of energy we can almost hear language being re-invented through free association, allusion, hyperbole, and constant shifts of word forms and sentence order — the elements of diction and syntax discussed in the text. As nouns become verbs and verbs become adjectives, we are able to hear, rather than see, words being shaken in a verbal kaleidoscope. Whatever the moral or social judgment will finally be of *Howl*, there is no poem like it. Along with its uniqueness, it is also howlingly funny. Forty years after its first reading, audiences still find it is as funny as it is frightening, harrowing, and revelatory.

Questions for Discussion

1. In line 2, what are some of the associations of Ginsberg's phrase "negro streets at dawn"?
2. In line 3, what is he suggesting about the universe in the image "starry dynamo in the machinery of night"?
3. Who is he describing in his image of "Mohammedan angels staggering on tenement roofs" in line 5?
4. In line 8, does he mean "rooms unshaven"? What is the name of this figure of speech?
5. What is Ginsberg telling us about these intellectuals in the ironic contrasts of line 17?
6. What image is he conveying to the listener with the phrase "boxcars boxcars boxcars" in line 23? Is this an example of onomatopoeia?
7. What does the image in line 54, "alarm clocks fell on their heads every day for the next decade," tell us about these people? What is the name of this figure of speech?
8. What is Ginsberg saying about jobs on Madison Avenue, with the phrase "buried alive in their innocent flannel suits"? What does "Madison Avenue" symbolize?
9. In line 65, what is Ginsberg telling us about the seriousness of the people having visions?
10. What is the psychiatric treatment he describes in lines 72–73?
11. In line 76, what is it he can't bring himself to say about his mother?
12. In the last lines of the selection, what is Ginsberg telling us about the role of jazz in America?

Topics for Writing

1. Because of the frankness of the poem's language, many students will feel uncomfortable discussing *Howl*. A classroom discussion might instead focus on the social conditions that produced the poem.
2. To help students understand the means Ginsberg used in creating *Howl*, the instructor might take a line like 20, "who vanished into nowhere Zen New Jersey leaving a trail of ambiguous postcards of Atlantic City Hall," and analyze its language in terms of suggestion, association, and allusion. The line could be the scenario for a narrative that students might find helpful to develop.

SUNFLOWER SUTRA

Like all of Ginsberg's poetry, this is meant to be performed, but it is a sutra rather than a howl. As a sutra — a precept or discourse — it is meant to be performed more quietly, but with no less conviction. In its line units Ginsberg uses more euphony than in other poems — it is more consciously musical — at the same time he uses a broader range of comic effects. Some lines are childishly silly, so as to sustain the tone of wonder he wants to convey. The poem's references are to Whitman and Blake, particularly to Blake's poem "Ah Sun-flower," which the instructor might want to read to the class. As a sutra, the poem has a conclusion with which both of the older poets would have agreed — that we are all also a holy part of the universe around us:

Ah Sun-flower

Ah Sun-flower! weary of time,
Who countest the steps of the Sun,
Seeking after that sweet golden clime
Where the traveller's journey is done;

Where the Youth pined away with desire,
And the pale Virgin shrouded in snow,
Arise from their graves and aspire,
Where my Sun-flower wishes to go.
                                        –WILLIAM BLAKE

Questions for Discussion

1. Why does the sunflower stir Ginsberg's memory?
2. What are some of the fuller meanings he has compressed into a few words in line 2, "companion, we thought the same thoughts of the soul, bleak and blue and sad eyed"?
3. What is he telling us about the bums in the phrase "tired and wily" in line 3?
4. What is he contrasting in the images of the sunflower and the locomotive?
5. In line 21 he writes that what he is about to say, "to anyone who'll listen," is a sermon. How does this term describe the last lines of the poem?

Topic for Writing

1. In a short paper, students could discuss the elements of Ginsberg's poem that make it a sutra.

LOUISE GLÜCK

Labor Day (p. 1118)
For My Mother (p. 1118)
Gratitude (p. 1119)
Brown Circle (p. 1119)

The strength of Glück's poetry is its directness and clarity. The images are compressed and burnished, with any distracting elements stripped away. It is this unflinching objectivity that makes it possible for her to express feelings and attitudes that would be difficult for her readers to accept if she began explaining why she has written the poem the way she has — or if she asked us for sympathy. The weekend college date she describes in "Labor Day" was a disaster, but her terse description of it is enough for us to understand her anger. Any pretense of affection in "For My Mother" is stripped away in the first line: "It was better when we were / together in one body." She compresses the thirty years that have passed into the statement that a marsh has grown around the house and that spores — perhaps from the ferns that have grown up — drift among the leafy plants.

"Gratitude" is a lighter poem, and students will respond to Glück's image of a large favor as a large animal lying on the rug where you can never forget it. "Brown Circle" returns to the theme of her unsuccessful relationship with her family. The disappointment she felt with her mother is now part of a larger circle that includes her son. Students are sometimes uncomfortable on a first reading with what seems to be a cold dismissal of the people around her, but as they become more accustomed to her language and her imagery, they will sense the turbulent emotions that lie just beneath the surface of the poems.

Questions for Discussion

1. "Labor Day" begins with regular meter and rhyme, then unravels as the weekend unravels. The class should scan the poem and discuss the point when it begins to lose its formal structure.
2. Why does Glück use the enjambment that ends line 8?
3. What does she mean by calling her date "Johnston-baby"?
4. The only detailed descriptive passage in the poem is in the final lines, when Glück describes the plants in the pasture. What does this tell us about her weekend?
5. In "For My Mother," what is she describing in lines 5–9?
6. What does she mean in lines 12–15: "And then spring / came and withdrew from me / the absolute / knowledge of the unborn"?
7. Glück repeats the phrase "Thirty years" three times in the poem. The class could discuss whether they think this is an expression of her anger at her mother or a subtle means of organizing the poem.
8. What is Glück suggesting in her image of the moon as "stationed . . . / . . . among / the small tin markers of the stars"? Is this image consciously antiromantic?

9. In "Gratitude," what does Glück mean with the last image "the bright sun shining on its tusks"? Is she genuinely upset at the thought of dealing with gratitude, or is she using hyperbole?
10. What is the term for the figure of speech that "Gratitude" presents?
11. What is Glück saying about herself in lines 13–18 of "Brown Circle"?
12. The class should paraphrase her image of her love as a magnifying glass that burns the grass around the flower.

Topic for Writing

1. In the last line of "Brown Circle," when Glück writes that she is helpless to spare her son, she is saying that she can do nothing to change her feelings or actions toward her child. Discuss this attitude with reference to her description about her relationship with her mother in the other poems of the selection.

Thomas Gray

Elegy Written in a Country Churchyard (p. 940)

The poem's social and political attitudes are discussed in Chapter 12. Because of the sympathy for the lives of the common villagers that the poem expresses, students might question whether it is an Augustan or neoclassical poem, as some of its language and sentiments seem closer to the Romantic poetry of a few years later. In a collaborative comment, however, Professors John Chalker and Erik Frykman make it clear that Gray's work is "within the central Augustan tradition in its preoccupation with the large general truths of human nature, its avoidance of overt subjective feeling, its use of elevated diction and personification, and its cultivation of extensive literary reference to enrich the texture of the writing" (*An Anthology of English Verse*, 93).

Although the poem's effect is largely derived from the fact that the villager for whom the elegy is written is nameless and unknown, students will be interested to learn that Gray was moved to write the poem by the death of a friend, Richard West. The writing took Gray eight years to complete. The poem was an immediate success, and the most important literary figure of the time, Samuel Johnson, succinctly summed up the reasons for its popularity. The elegy, he wrote, "abounds with images which find a mirror in every mind and with sentiments to which every bosom returns an echo."

Questions for Discussion

1. Although the poem is written in four-line ballad stanzas, which usually are written in tetrameter, the meter Gray has chosen is iambic pentameter. With regard to the discussion in the text as to the effect of different line lengths and meter, why did Gray write in this longer line?
2. Why would the poem have been less effective if Gray had given a name and a history to the person buried in the cemetery?
3. What ideas in the poem suggest the coming social changes that would culminate in the American and the French revolutions?

4.   To whom is Gray speaking in lines 31 and 32?
5.   In lines 47 and 48 Gray uses the figure of speech of hands playing a harp to describe literary accomplishment. What is the figure of speech called?
6.   What does Gray mean in lines 49 and 50 when he speaks of knowledge as an "ample page / Rich with the spoils of time"?

Topics for Writing

1.   Gray's poem expressed sentiments that for their time seemed revolutionary to many people. Students could analyze these sentiments and explain their significance for the mid-eighteenth century, when the poem was published.
2.   **CONNECTIONS**   In lines 61–72 Gray suggests that the lowly role of the village peasants prevents them from having an effect on history, but he also writes that they won't be tempted to commit the crimes of the rich and powerful. They won't, for example, "wade through slaughter to a throne," as he writes in line 67. Students could discuss Gray's sentiments here and contrast them with the sentiments of writers of the same period — for instance, William Blake, who believed in the essential goodness and innocence of mankind.
3.   The poem is filled with images of nature. Students could use these images in an analysis of the relationship between the physical setting of the poem and the sentiments it expresses.
4.   The famous lines of the stanza beginning with "The boast of heraldry" (line 33) suggest sentiments that lie outside Gray's Christian beliefs. Students might want to explicate the philosophical implications of these lines.

THOMAS HARDY

The Man He Killed (p. 983)

Born in southern England in 1840, Thomas Hardy devoted himself to fiction for nearly fifty years, becoming one of England's most successful novelists. In his fifties, financially secure, he was able to devote himself to lyric poetry. He died in 1928.

Question for Discussion

1.   Discuss the development of the speaker's attitude toward the man he killed.

Topic for Writing

1.   **CONNECTIONS**   In a one- to two-page essay, students can compare Hardy's use of irony with that of Stephen Crane in "War Is Kind" (p. 982).

MICHAEL S. HARPER

Martin's Blues (p. 944)

Michael S. Harper was born in 1938 in Brooklyn, grew up in Los Angeles, and attended Los Angeles State College. The letters of John Keats and the writings of Ralph Ellison were important influences. He teaches at Brown University in Providence, Rhode Island.

Question for Discussion

1. Discuss how Harper uses language to mingle grief and triumph in the poem.

Topic for Writing

1. **CONNECTIONS** Students could write a paper comparing Harper's elegy with Amy Clampitt's "The Dakota" (p. 944).

ROBERT HASS

A Story about the Body (p. 961)

Poet Laureate Robert Hass is a Californian who often uses the California landscape as his theme. He has also written many psychologically insightful prose poems.

Questions for Discussion

1. What do the dead bees represent?
2. Could the bees be interpreted as the woman's comment on the man's love?
3. The poem is titled "A Story about the Body." Could it be interpreted as a comment on each of their bodies, not just his? Could it refer to a collective body? Would any of our bodies respond the same way?
4. What is the significance of the layer of rose petals the woman places over the dead bees?
5. Is the woman's gesture made in anger or in sad resignation?

Topic for Writing

1. So many love poems take as their theme the body of the loved one. Comment on how the injury to the woman's body ends the man's love, and discuss whether it was an honest love.

ROBERT HAYDEN

Those Winter Sundays (p. 1121)
"Incense of the Lucky Virgin" (p. 1121)
A Letter from Phillis Wheatley (p. 1122)

Students may find that poet Robert Huddle's commentary "The 'Banked Fire' of Robert Hayden's 'Those Winter Sundays'" (p. 1271) presents them with more than they need to understand the poem, but the instructor will find much of Huddle's discussion very useful. Hayden was not a productive writer, and in some of his work he seems uncertain of his poetic voice, but "Those Winter Sundays" has become an American classic, and students find much in the poem that touches them.

Like "Those Winter Sundays," "'Incense of the Lucky Virgin'" is a scene from the poor Detroit childhood that Hayden knew so well. Unlike the first poem, however, "'Incense of the Lucky Virgin'" is a harrowing narrative of a woman who gives up hope for herself and her children. She has tried popular street magic — incense and the conqueror root — and prayer and candles, but all of these things have failed to bring back the children's father, and the family is destitute. She dresses the children in their Sunday clothes, but the poem doesn't make clear what happens next, only that the boy was "too quick" for her and ran away. Did she take the children and put them in an institution? Did she kill them? All the poem tells us is "they'll never cry and hunger any more."

The poem has the pitiless narrative style of a medieval ballad and uses phrases ("make haste and shine your shoes") that derive from older ways of speaking. This suggests that the repetition of the last lines of each verse is alluding to the English ballad tradition, which sometimes repeats the last line of each verse as a refrain. The first two lines of a blues song also repeat, however, so some students might decide that it is the blues that is alluded to in the poem's repetitions.

Students should read the selection of Phillis Wheatley's poetry (pp. 1208–1209) before turning to Hayden's "A Letter from Phillis Wheatley." Also useful in reading this poem is Rita Dove's "Belinda's Petition" (p. 1083), which is similar in subject matter and style.

Questions for Discussion

1. In "Those Winter Sundays," what does Hayden mean by the first two words, "Sundays too"?
2. In line 3, what does he mean by "cracked hands"?
3. The emotional center of the poem is the short sentence at the end of line 5, "No one ever thanked him." Discuss what Hayden suggests in this sentence.
4. In line 6, "the cold splintering, breaking," what is Hayden describing?
5. What is Hayden saying about himself in the last verse of the poem? Why does he repeat the question in line 13?
6. Students might discuss what they feel is the reason Hayden repeats the last line of each verse as a refrain in "'Incense of the Lucky Virgin.'"
7. What is the symbolism of lines 9–10?
8. Why does the mother dress the children in their best clothes?

9. Students might discuss whether they think the mother has killed her children.
10. Before a discussion of "A Letter from Phillis Wheatley," students should read the selection of her poetry (pp. 1208–1209). How closely does Hayden's "letter" match Wheatley's own way of writing?
11. In line 20 Hayden's Wheatley describes herself eating alone, "like captive royalty." Is she being ironic? What other meanings can students think of?
12. What is the importance of the signatures she mentions in lines 21–22?
13. Why does she think she should decline the honor of appearing at court?
14. In line 33, what does she mean by "no Eden without its serpent"?

Topic for Writing

1. The question of identity was a complex one for Hayden, who thought of himself as a writer, not an African American writer. As David Huddle points out in his commentary on "Those Winter Sundays," there is nothing in the poem that ties it directly to the African American experience: Hayden describes a normal Sunday experience for every poor family in America. Students could write about the question of racial identity in this poem, and their papers could be used for class discussion.

Related Commentary

Robert Hayden, "On Negro Poetry," p. 1266.

GEORGE HERBERT

Easter Wings (p. 889)

This "shaped verse," as poems written to form a representation of the title are called, is one of the best-known works of a modest clergyman whose mother had been a friend of John Donne. Herbert was born in 1593 and lived until 1633, when he died of tuberculosis while serving as curate of a small rural parish in southern England. His only book, *The Temple*, was published a few months after his death. It is with Donne that Herbert's poetry is most often compared, as they share the Elizabethan penchant for conceit and paradox. Herbert's faith, however, is less troubled than Donne's, and his conception of his relationship with God is direct and trusting. The poem is deceptively simple, but if read aloud with the line lengths carefully observed, it has the rise and fall of a bird's flight. The text is so skillfully presented that the diminution of line lengths — from pentameter to monometer, a foot lost with each line — and then the expansion again back to pentameter — seems entirely natural, even if on first glance the poem seems contrived.

Questions for Discussion

1. Scan the poem and analyze the steps by which Herbert reduces and expands the line lengths.
2. Analyze the first five lines and discuss how they suggest a diminution in the lines by their description of humankind's fall from grace.
3. Compare the two stanzas. What is the denotative meaning of lines 5 and 15 that justifies their short length?

4. What images in the poem continue the concept in the title of "wings"?
5. Lines 10 and 20 say something very similar in images that are only slightly altered. Discuss what Herbert means in the two lines.
6. What is the symbolic meaning of the first line?
7. The second stanza may be read metaphorically as a reference to Herbert's illness. What images in the stanza suggest the physical effects of tuberculosis?
8. If the second stanza does describe his illness, how would the last line be interpreted?

Topic for Writing

1. **CONNECTIONS** Compare Herbert's religious faith as expressed in this poem with the religious faith expressed in John Donne's Holy Sonnets (pp. 948, 1081, 1082).

ROBERT HERRICK

To the Virgins, to Make Much of Time (p. 888)

Herrick was a Londoner, born in the city in 1591, who reluctantly spent his long life in the west of England as a modestly paid clergyman. His consolation seems to have been the hours he spent writing brief verse in the style of Ben Jonson. When the troubled years of the Puritan Commonwealth drove him back to London, he published in 1648 a volume containing 1,200 poems divided into two sections — *Hesperides*, the secular poems, and *Noble Numbers*, the religious poems. Following the restoration of the monarchy in 1660, he returned to his country parish, where he died in 1674 at the age of eighty-three.

The great majority of Herrick's secular poems would have to be classed among the silliest poetry in the English language, but a handful of short lyrics have given him a small but enduring reputation. The poems were ignored during his lifetime but became popular in the sexually repressive Victorian era as a kind of delicate erotica, thanks to poems with titles like "Upon the Nipples of Julia's Breasts."

"To the Virgins, to Make Much of Time" is the classic representative of the carpe diem poem in English. The term means "seize the day," and the meaning is simply "live now, as tomorrow you will die." The Victorians understood that underneath the metaphors of rosebuds and flowers Herrick was telling young women to stop wasting their time and to get married as soon as possible. The Victorians also understood that the loss of virginity was the most important of the poem's suggestions.

Questions for Discussion

1. Herrick's poem contains veiled suggestions of regret and disappointment in his own life. What does he say that implies this?
2. The poem is a quatrain with a rhyme scheme of alternating masculine and feminine rhymes. Is there any implied meaning in this rhyme scheme? Is its use solely for rhythmic effect?

Topics for Writing

1.   **CONNECTIONS**   Compare this poem with Andrew Marvell's "To His Coy Mistress" (p. 910) and discuss the presentation of the carpe diem theme in each poem.

2.   Herrick's statement in the poem that youth is the best age of life has echoes in today's youth culture. Discuss the idea in terms of current attitudes toward clothing, music, and the arts.

TOBEY HILLER

The Poem (or, Alice's Remarks on Reading the Fine Print on the Bottle's Label) (p. 878)

Tobey Hiller is a psychodramatist and psychologist who lives and works in Oakland, California. Her poetry has been published in a number of anthologies, and in 1987 her work won two West Coast poetry contests. Her latest book, *Aqueduct*, was published in 1993.

On the surface Hiller's poem seems to be a humorous joke, beginning with the reference to Lewis Carroll's Alice reading the "fine print" on the label of the bottle of liquid she is about to drink. In some of the lines, poems are described in terms of all the useful, everyday things that they cannot do; other lines suggest things a poem *can* do. At the same time, subtly, Hiller is making us think about all the things we expect to find in poetry. Students will notice the reference in lines 17–18 to Archibald MacLeish's "Ars Poetica" (p. 874). Hiller is saying in the last line that what we are and what we do is mortal and evanescent. It is all only a "flight."

Questions for Discussion

1.   Hiller has used ordinary, conversational diction and syntax in the poem. What is she suggesting by using this kind of language?

2.   Would a consciously intellectual use of imagery and idiom give the poem a stronger effect?

3.   In lines 13–14, what is Hiller asking the poem to do for her children?

Topic for Writing

1.   **CONNECTIONS**   Hiller's images of the things that poetry can and cannot do alternate between the possible and what can only be imagined. Give examples of each kind of image, concluding with a short discussion of what she means by her reference to MacLeish's "Ars Poetica."

Several lines from Hiller's poem "the closing of the south park road" are quoted in Chapter 15. For instructors who wish to consult the entire poem, it is included here. The image from Emily Dickinson to which Hiller alludes is in the last line of Dickinson's poem #1540, "As imperceptibly as Grief." The poem ends, "Our summer made her light escape / Into the beautiful."

the closing of the south park road

happens every year between Thanksgiving and Christmas
just when the light grows lucid, forgiving nothing and

disappearing into beauty,
as Emily says

on these days the air over the water opens into a hard wise body
lying low and immortal over everything it loves

and during this particular light and clocked by leaves darking into mold
the brown newts that live in the park and on Mt. Diablo
appear in droves, emerging from any under,
all shining and sheeny and lacking in corners
as though made from foam spawn
or grown secret as mushrooms
in some place wet and between we'd never imagined
right there in our own backyards
and in the crepuscular folds of the hills

we think of the south park road as ours,
after all we built it

but they cross it as though it's theirs,
clogging its black with their brown insisting bodies,
slicking it with newt travel
faster than snails, leaving no trail, but something more like water
than our flesh is —
they cannot get enough
of whatever it is they're after:
each other, or life, or coupling, or the deepness of a brown and shining
place
the egg place, the smelly meatsweet of mold, those little toes articulate
and too easily smashed

so now this time of year they close the road

before anything is dust
it lies low and immortal in desire's long body
with light riding on its back, and
disappears

–Tobey Hiller

Gerard Manley Hopkins

The Windhover (p. 1124)

Pied Beauty (p. 1124)

Spring and Fall (p. 1125)

Thou art indeed just, Lord (p. 1125)

God's Grandeur (p. 1126)

When Hopkins's writing was first published after World War I, most poetry was still being written in regular meter and rhyme, and there was a stormy controversy over his attempt to create new meters with what he called "sprung rhythm." He intended for each line to have an equal number of stresses, regardless of whether the line could be scanned in a traditional form of meter, like iambic or trochaic. If he thought there would be some uncertainty about where the stress should fall, he wrote it in above the word or syllable.

The poem "Spring and Fall" is written in sprung rhythm, and if the reader follows Hopkins's stress markings, the rhythm he intends — a four-stress line — is clear. The lines he didn't mark can be scanned as trochaic tetrameter, although lines 8, 13, and 14 have shifts of accent. Today, with so much poetry written in open form, it is an interesting question whether Hopkins would have struggled with a concept like sprung rhythm to give his lines more flexibility.

Today Hopkins's poetry seems remarkable not for its metrical innovation but for its ecstatic mysticism. As English literary historian Linda Ruth Williams described his writing, "For Hopkins, poetry exceeds meaning; it is . . . his impulse to communicate with the 'isness' of things, to allow material language to touch the thing itself through a poetic experience of epiphany" (*Bloomsbury Guide to English Literature*, p. 228). Hopkins was a religious mystic, and to modern readers the openness of his poetic forms seems a natural expression of his religious fervor. There is a trance state in Christian worship known as "speaking in tongues," and in "The Windhover," which Hopkins considered one of his most successful poems, the reader does get the sense of a man in an ecstatic trance at the sight of the hawk in the morning air.

"The Windhover" is a difficult poem, and many have attempted to interpret it. Students should read the commentary by Bernard Bergonzi (p. 1235), which might not answer the questions they have about the poem but will certainly illustrate the problems that critics have had interpreting it.

With the exception of "Spring and Fall," all of the poems included here are sonnets. It is almost as though Hopkins chose the strictest form to rein in his ecstatic outbursts. "Pied Beauty" is shorter, but he called its form a "curtal," or shortened sonnet. It has been compressed into roughly two-thirds of the traditional sonnet. The first eight lines become six, and the last six become three and a half. The form gives the poet the opportunity to achieve the drama of the shortened last line.

Questions for Discussion

1. Would Hopkins have experimented with sprung rhythm today?
2. Although "The Windhover" is a difficult poem, students may be able to understand some of Hopkins's way of writing if they paraphrase the less complex lines. How would the class paraphrase the first four lines, continuing to the word "ecstasy" in the beginning of the fifth line?
3. Although much of the poem's imagery will become clear after a careful reading, critics have been unable to agree on the meaning of some of the images. Some critics feel that the word "chevalier" in line 11 is a metaphor for Christ. Can students find anything in the poem that supports or refutes this interpretation?
4. In "Pied Beauty," Hopkins cries out for glory to God for "dappled things." What are the dappled things he names in the next four lines?
5. What does he mean by "All things counter" in line 7?

6. In "Thou art indeed just, Lord" Hopkins uses the phrase "Time's eunuch." Is he referring to himself?
7. In "Pied Beauty," what does Hopkins mean by the line "He fathers-forth whose beauty is past change"?

Topics for Writing

1. Like Emily Dickinson, Hopkins resisted pleas by friends to publish his poetry. Students might want to comment on whether his awareness that he would have to make changes in his poems for publication might have influenced his decision. Students could also suggest the kind of changes Hopkins might have had to make to his poems for them to be acceptable to a late-Victorian audience.
2. In "Pied Beauty," Hopkins catalogues the things for which he wishes to praise God. Students could describe the things in more everyday terms and suggest what a list like this tells us about Hopkins.

A. E. HOUSMAN

Loveliest of trees, the cherry now (p. 884)

When I was one-and-twenty (p. 884)

Oh, when I was in love with you (p. 920)

Alfred Edward Housman was born in England in 1859 and died in 1936. His fame as a poet rests on two slender volumes, the first of which, *A Shropshire Lad*, he published himself in 1896. Shropshire is a rural county in the west of England, and the themes of the poems were inspired by everyday life in Shropshire villages. The book became very popular in England during World War I, and in 1922 *Last Poems* appeared, including the last of the poetry Housman had written in the 1890s and a handful of newer poems. A few additional poems were included in a collected edition a few years after his death. Although it would appear from this small output that Housman lacked a serious commitment to literature, he was, in fact, a leading scholar of Latin poetry, publishing hundreds of articles and editing the works of several Roman poets. His own poems are wryly affectionate, but he was savagely critical of other scholars in his field, and some of his writing consists of vituperative attacks on what he considered "shabby" scholarship.

Because he lived a solitary bachelor's life, he is sometimes considered to have been homosexual. The truth is more complicated. While a student at Oxford, he suddenly realized that an intense friendship he felt for another male student could become physical, and he immediately withdrew from the relationship. He was so disturbed by what he had felt, however, that his Oxford studies suffered, and he failed to pass with distinction. Because of this he was unable to secure a teaching job immediately and was forced to work as a clerk in the London Patents Office for ten years while he produced his scholarly articles and editions in the evenings and on vacations. He finally was given a professorship at London University in 1892, when he was thirty-three, and in 1911 he became a professor at Cambridge University.

Although Housman was a literary scholar, his own work has a deceptive simplicity that reflects the directness and immediacy of the Roman poets, particularly Horace and Catullus, whose work he studied. It was the unsentimental directness of the poetry and the familiarity of his themes that attracted such a large readership during the war. Many of his readers today find that the way of life he described has disappeared from the English countryside, and a strong sense of nostalgia is part of the response to his writing. The poems read effortlessly, but Housman later commented that writing poetry with this deceptive ease was intensely difficult, and that he couldn't sustain the immense effort.

Questions for Discussion

1. "Loveliest of trees" is sometimes described as a "perfect lyric." Students could discuss the poem in terms of its meter and rhyme scheme, examining it to see if there is any use of enjambment or half-rhyme and discussing its occasionally rhythmical irregularities.
2. Although a gentle example of the genre, "Loveliest of trees" is a carpe diem poem. What in the poem places it in this genre?
3. The middle stanza has some of the elements of Elizabethan paradox. How would this stanza be paraphrased?
4. To what is Housman alluding in line 5, "of my three score years and ten"?
5. What elements of irony do students find in "When I was one-and-twenty"?
6. Much of the appeal of Housman's poems in his own time owed to the naturalness of their language. What phrases in "When I was one-and-twenty" related it to this kind of direct spontaneity?
7. What is the speaker saying about himself in "Oh, when I was in love with you"?
8. What metrical elements in the poem relate it to folk ballads?

Topics for Writing

1. **CONNECTIONS** Housman's poetry could in many ways be considered a fulfillment of the poetic ideals Wordsworth expressed in the Introduction to his *Lyrical Ballads* almost a hundred years earlier (see p. 1330). Students could discuss Housman's themes and language in terms of Wordsworth's description of what he was trying to achieve with the "new" Romantic poetry.
2. **CONNECTIONS** Students could compare "Loveliest of trees" with other carpe diem poems in the anthology and discuss why Housman's poem would be included in this category.

LANGSTON HUGHES

For a broader perspective on the poet and his writing, students should read the commentaries in the Langston Hughes casebook, which emphasize Hughes's role as a social poet. Throughout his career he spoke for the African American community, confronting white society for its racism and an economic structure that led to inequality and injustice. Of all the major American writers of his era, Hughes was perhaps the most courageous, and his decision to write in a direct, simple language that spoke *for* as well as *to* the black community cost him the serious critical attention his work deserved. Hughes decided early what he wanted to do with his writing, and he never wavered from his course.

We sometimes forget that the circumstances of a writer's life play a crucial role in the work he or she is able to produce. Hughes was the only important American poet of this period who supported himself by writing, which meant that he wrote many poems and his work often responded to topical questions that interested his Harlem audience. Sometimes he deprecatingly called himself a "folk" poet, but this overlooks his subtle but sure sense of words and their nuance, his sensitivity to vernacular speech, and his sure sense of form. Hughes used a great variety of structures, but always for the purpose of presenting the poem's voice most effectively. His poetry, as his biographer Arnold Rampersad wrote, was always at the service of the black community, and it continued to mirror the African American travail in America — the joys and angers, the disappointments and consolations — but always with a sure and conscious poetic skill and intelligence.

Students will not find many examples of traditional verse forms in Hughes's work, and there are no allusions or references that would not be obvious to most of his readers. His genius lies in his ability to present the voice of the person who is speaking, the poem's persona, in a few deceptively simple lines. His gift to his readers is a world teeming with real people — young, old, rich, poor, angry, happy — whose voices mingle in the rich texture of his poetry.

THE NEGRO SPEAKS OF RIVERS (p. 1129)

Hughes wrote this poem after he'd seen the Mississippi River for the first time, when he was on a train taking him to stay with his father in Mexico. He was nineteen years old, and when the poem was published a year later it attracted immediate attention in the Harlem intellectual community. It is still a poem that is read and loved. At his funeral the audience recited the poem aloud. The poem has an important meaning to many of its readers because it presents in a single haunting image — that of the world's ancient rivers — the concept of the antiquity of the African race, the unique differences between African American and European American cultures, and the spiritual depths that these factors have given to the African American community.

Questions for Discussion

1. How has Hughes's soul "grown deep like the rivers"?
2. In line 5, what does he mean by "dawns were young"?
3. What connection is he making in the phrase "Nile of the Mississippi" in line 7?
4. Why does he include the image of Lincoln in the same line? Is this simply a historical reference, or does the phrase also contain a social message?
5. What are the connotations of the word "dusky" in line 12?

Topic for Writing

1. The poem has many references to black history. A paper could discuss these historical aspects.

MOTHER TO SON (p. 1130)

This is the first of the poems in this selection in which Hughes speaks through another voice, in this instance an old woman worn down with her life but "still climbin'."

Questions for Discussion

1. What is the poem's extended metaphor?
2. What kind of real staircase does Hughes describe in the poem? Where would he have seen a staircase like it?
3. Why would we say that the line "Life for me ain't been no crystal stair" is an understatement?
4. What is the woman telling her son in lines 18–19?

Topic for Writing

1. Relate some of the images of the real staircase metaphor to life experiences the woman may have had.

I, Too (p. 1130)

1. Is this poem, like "Mother to Son," an extended metaphor?
2. Who is Hughes referring to as the other person who sings America when he writes "I, too"?
3. The class could discuss the shift in emphasis from "I, too, sing America" to "I, too, am America."
4. Is there a specific connotation of the word "company" in this context, or is it meant only metaphorically?

Topic for Writing

1. An important political movement of the 1960s emphasized that "black is beautiful." Students could discuss the similarities between this poem and these attitudes and examine whether this poem might have been one of the movement's sources.
2. Students could discuss whether they believe that the "tomorrow" of which Hughes speaks in the poem has finally arrived.

Bound No'th Blues (p. 1131)

Hughes was one of the first writers to apply the structure of a blues song to poetry. He has, however, written this poem in six-line stanzas that make it difficult to see immediately its relationship to the blues. Students might find it helpful if the instructor wrote the poem out in the way a blues song is usually sung. This is the first stanza of Hughes's poem written as a blues song:

> Goin' down the road, Lawd, goin' down the road.
> Down the road, Lawd, way way down the road.
> Got to find somebody to help me carry this load.

This is a typical blues verse:

> Woke up this morning with a heavy achin' head,
> Lawd, woke up this morning with a heavy achin' head,
> Nothin' but the blues, hangin' 'round my bed.

The essence of a blues verse is that the first two lines present a physical situation and the third line presents an emotional reaction to that situation. Blues songs are very seldom narrative. A blues song is usually — as in Hughes's poem — a series of associative verses that develop a single emotional theme.

In this poem Hughes uses the image of a Mississippi town as unfit for a "hoppin' toad." A well-known folk/blues song describes the water in Michigan as tasting "like sherry wine," while down south in Mississippi the water "tastes like turpentine." Again, Hughes is using another voice, this time a rural black voice speaking in dialect, and he has captured the speech patterns with unerring accuracy.

Questions for Discussion

1. How does Hughes avoid the repetition that is inevitable in a blues song?
2. What is the situation and the emotional reaction to the situation of each of the stanzas? What single emotional theme do the stanzas develop?
3. What is the political import of the last stanza?
4. Students could discuss how these lines would be scanned for meter if the poem was sung as a blues song.
5. What are some of the changes in diction and syntax Hughes has made to capture the flavor of vernacular speech?

Topic for Writing

1. The class could collaborate on writing a blues song of their own.

SONG FOR A DARK GIRL (p. 1132)
HOUSE IN THE WORLD (p. 1132)

The strong social protest in "Song for a Dark Girl" is implicit in Hughes's use of the last line of the popular southern song "Dixie" as the opening line of each stanza. The instructor could emphasize the intent of the poet here by singing this line from the song as the poem is read aloud. "Song for a Dark Girl" expresses Hughes's rage at southern racial violence, and "House in the World" is as close as he would get to despair about the racial prejudices he faced.

Questions for Discussion

1. What statement is Hughes making with the phrase "white Lord Jesus" in line 7 of "Song for a Dark Girl"?
2. Why does he repeat the word "naked" in the last two lines of the poem?
3. What is the term for the figure of speech in the last lines? What is Hughes describing specifically?
4. Is there a contradiction in the term "white shadows" in "House in the World"? Does Hughes mean shadows in the denotative sense here, or is there a connotative meaning?
5. What does he mean by the term "house"?
6. In "Song for a Dark Girl" Hughes contrasts black and white; in "House in the World" the contrast is between dark and white. The class might discuss whether they think Hughes implied any difference in his use of "black" or "dark."

Topic for Writing

1. A paper could contrast and discuss other poems where quotation is used to express a specific political meaning, as it is in "Song for a Dark Girl."

FLORIDA ROAD WORKERS (p. 1132)

In this poem Hughes presents us with another of his large cast of speakers, this time a worker building a road in Florida. Although this is a masculine voice, it is not in the same vernacular dialect as the blues singer of "Bound No'th Blues." The poem is as freely structured as "Mother to Son," but here the voice is distinctly masculine. Students should also note that in this poem Hughes describes class differences rather than racial differences, a shift in theme that was to become stronger in the poems he wrote a short time later as the depression deepened.

Questions for Discussion

1. In lines 6 and 7, what might be some of the reasons that Hughes breaks out of dialect?
2. The phrases "fly by on," "sweep over," and "light and civilization to travel on" are all metaphorical. What is the larger social metaphor of the poem?
3. Who is Buddy? Is it anyone specific named in the poem?
4. Although we hear the poem as written in black dialect, could this be the voice of any worker looking at the job he is doing? Could it be a woman's voice? Why or why not?
5. What is the compensation the worker feels he is getting for his work on the road?

Topics for Writing

1. Discuss the social-class differences the poem describes in terms of the year in which it was written.
2. Compare the speech of the old woman in "Mother to Son" with the speech in "Florida Road Workers" and discuss what terms or phrases suggest the sex of the speaker.

GOOD MORNING REVOLUTION (p. 1133)
COLUMBIA (p. 1135)

These are two of Hughes's most specifically political poems. During the McCarthy era, so much controversy was generated by this aspect of Hughes's writing that he omitted them from his collected poems. "Good Morning Revolution" is particularly interesting because its vernacular dialect is no longer exclusively African American but could be working-class American. In this poem Hughes seems to suggest that the issues of economic revolution are larger than issues of race.

Questions for Discussion

1. "Good Morning Revolution" is a direct address to an inanimate object. What is the term for this figure of speech?
2. What is Hughes suggesting in line 27, "And struts all over the earth"?
3. To what is he alluding with the interjection "Great day in the morning" in line 43?
4. What elements in the poem's dialect suggest that its speaker is working class? Is there anything in the poem that suggests that the speaker is African American?
5. Discuss who might be the speaker of "Columbia." Could this be Hughes's own voice this time?

6. What are some of the specific differences of diction and syntax between this poem and "Good Morning Revolution"?
7. What is the denotative allusion of "Columbia," and what are its connotations?
8. Who is the person that Columbia personifies?
9. What is the meaning of the word "middies" in line 15? What allusion is Hughes making?
10. What is the allusion in lines 18–19?
11. Why does Hughes specifically name India, Africa, Manchuria, and Haiti in the poem?

Topics for Writing

1. CONNECTIONS Students could compare these poems with poems by other political activists, including Allen Ginsberg and Lawrence Ferlinghetti.
2. Students could discuss the different "voices" of these poems in the context of Hughes's other dialect poems in the anthology.
3. The political attitudes Hughes expresses in these poems are different from his later political poetry. A paper could analyze the differences and be the basis for a class discussion.

PERSONAL (p. 1136)
LITTLE LYRIC (*OF GREAT IMPORTANCE*) (p. 1136)
MERRY-GO-ROUND (p. 1136)
DOWN WHERE I AM (p. 1136)

In these later poems there is a note of ironic humor, and even the anger now has a wry resignation. Hughes still feels the humiliation of racism and discrimination but now seems to be lacking the weapons to fight this injustice — a situation he had not anticipated when he wrote his confident political poems of the early 1930s.

Questions for Discussion

1. What is "Jim Crow" in "Merry-Go-Round"?
2. "Merry-Go-Round" and "Down Where I Am" are written in different voices. Which words or phrases in the first poem suggest the speaker's youth, and which in the second poem suggest the speaker's age?
3. What does Hughes mean by "Climbin' that hill" in line 10 of "Down Where I Am"?
4. Discuss the metaphor of line 13, "I'm gonna plant my feet."

Topics for Writing

1. Students could discuss the implication of the poem title "Personal."
2. "Merry-Go-Round" is a humorous poem, despite the seriousness of the subject. A short paper could analyze its humor.
3. Discuss the social implications of the imagery of "door," "up there," and "that hill" in "Down Where I Am."

THEME FOR ENGLISH B (p. 1137)

In this poem Hughes presents us with still another of his personas, this time a young African American university student. Although Hughes also studied briefly in New York, the poem is clearly not a description of his own experience. Students should note that in this poem it is not only race that is the decisive issue but also age and social role, as the older white man is the student's instructor.

Questions for Discussion

1. Do you think the instructor gave the class assignment as a poem? Why do you think Hughes turned it into a poem?
2. Why does the student describe the way back to his room in such detail in lines 11–15? Is this part of the assignment, "let that page come out of you"?
3. What is the "you" that ends line 18?
4. Is the instructor as liable as the student to like "Bessie, bop, or Bach"? Who is Bessie? What is bop?
5. In lines 34–35, Hughes uses the term "sometimes" to describe the instructor's feelings and "Nor . . . often" to describe the student's feelings. What difference in attitude is Hughes implying here?
6. In lines 37–38, "As I learn from you, / I guess you learn from me — ," is the student uncertain about how much the instructor is learning from him because of racial differences, or is it because he feels the instructor is older?
7. What is the student saying in line 40, "Somewhat more free"?
8. The class could discuss what grade they would give the student for his paper.

Topics for Writing

1. The poem raises important issues of acculturation and cross-cultural identity, which the student sums up in line 33, "That's American." A student paper could discuss some of these issues.
2. A paper could analyze the elements of speech and the details that create a young persona in the poem.

DREAM DEFERRED (p. 1138)

In this poem Hughes speaks in his own voice, and the message is as determined in its opposition to racism as it was in his earliest poems.

Question for Discussion

1. The class could discuss the implications of the strong images of the poem: "fester like a sore" or "stink like rotten meat."

Topic for Writing

1. As a class assignment, students could discuss whether they think this poem is a prophecy or a description of the racial situation as Hughes experienced it.

(text pp. 972, 973, 984)

RANDALL JARRELL

Next Day (p. 972)
The Death of the Ball Turret Gunner (p. 984)

NEXT DAY

The comments in the text and Peter Schmitt's discussion of the poem in the commentary section (p. 1307) should clarify any difficulties students might have in understanding the poem.

Questions for Discussion

1. Why has a supermarket made the woman feel her sadness over her friend's death even more intensely?
2. Does Jarrell intend the irony of the names of the brands of soap?
3. What is the woman saying about her own sexuality in lines 20–27?
4. Does she mean lines 24–25 ironically?
5. What is she revealing in lines 29–31?
6. Is her comment in line 55, "Really, no one is exceptional," bitter or resigned?

Topics for Writing

1. Although the poem is spoken by a woman, it was written by a man. Female students might comment on whether they feel that Jarrell's writing accurately reflects a woman's emotions.
2. Although "My Last Duchess" and "Next Day" are both dramatic monologues, the text explains the differences between them. Students might find it interesting to compare them, in terms of the differences described in the text.
3. The supermarket in this poem could also be taken to symbolize many things in the woman's life. Students could discuss the symbolism here and decide the extent to which Jarrell intended the supermarket to be understood in these terms.

THE DEATH OF THE BALL TURRET GUNNER

This short poem is Jarrell's best-known work. Much of the effect is its laconic, antiheroic stance. Nothing in the poem is what the reader would expect from a poem about war. The central figure has been dropped into the state, the way an animal is dropped, and the state becomes not a home but the belly of the turret where he crouches. He is not like a person but like an animal, with fur instead of skin. The final line, with its flat description, is the final deflation of any myth of the heroism of war. Although the poem, of course, is not autobiographical, Jarrell served England with the United States Air Force during World War II, and in the poem that opens *Little Friend, Little Friend*, a book about his life in wartime, he refers to his fellow pilots as "other murderers."

Questions for Discussion

1. What is Jarrell describing in the phrase, "my wet fur froze"?
2. What does he mean by the phrase "loosed from its dream of life"?
3. What is he telling us with his images of the "dream of life," "I work," and "nightmare fighters"?

Topics for Writing

1. Many sociologists have written that without the social conditioning that young men receive through film, television, and books, they would not be so willing to sacrifice their lives in war. Students might consider how this poem would or would not influence someone's decision to go into military service.
2. Students might want to compare the attitude expressed in this poem with two well-known antiwar novels of World War II, Joseph Heller's *Catch-22*, and Kurt Vonnegut's *Slaughterhouse Five*, both of which center on pilots or bombing raids.

LOUIS JENKINS

How to Tell a Wolf from a Dog (p. 961)

Poetry is where you find it, and if students open their eyes and ears to poetry, they will be surprised to find how much of it there is around them. "How to Tell a Wolf from a Dog" offers us all a little comic relief. The joke is in the title, and it seems so obvious: Why do you need a poem to tell you the difference between a wolf and a dog? For that matter, unless you are ecology-minded, why would you even *need* to tell the difference between a wolf and a dog?

Like Robert Bly, Jenkins lives in Minnesota and has been writing prose poems for twenty-five years. It is a poetic form he takes with great seriousness. In his introduction to his 1995 collection *Nice Fish*, which contains "How to Tell a Wolf from a Dog," he writes, "The form of the prose poem is the rectangle, one of our most useful geometric shapes. Think of the prose poem as a box . . . . The box is made for travel, quick and light. Think of the prose rectangle as a small suitcase. One must pack carefully, only the essentials, too much and the reader won't get off the ground. Too much, and the poem becomes a story, a novel, an essay, or worse."

Questions for Discussion

1. Jenkins's poem is meant to be humorous, but it is also a complicated comment on our human relationship to nature. What is he saying with his comparison?
2. Does he want us to see the wolf as a symbol of all endangered natural species?
3. Some of the images of the poem refer to the world of business and regular employment. What are they? What is Jenkins saying about them?
4. What is he saying about the wolf in the first sentence, he "carries his head down, tail down"? Is this also an image that could be used to describe unemployed men and women?
5. Are the characteristics Jenkins attributes to the dog all characteristics we regard positively?
6. Would the poem be described as ironic?

Topics for Writing

1. **CONNECTIONS** Compare the concern for the earth's natural species in this poem with Robert Bly's "The Dead Seal near McClure's Beach" (p. 960).

2. **CONNECTIONS** Compare this poem to the description of the dog in Lawrence Ferlinghetti's poem "Dog" (p. 1092) and Hjalmar Söderberg's story "A Dog without a Master" (p. 617).

Ben Jonson

To the Memory of My Beloved, The Author, Mr. William Shakespeare, and What He Hath Left Us (p. 1005)

Some students may be aware of the century-long controversy over who might have written the plays of William Shakespeare. The heart of the argument is that some English critics, usually from the upper classes, decided that Shakespeare's plays were too good to have been written by someone from the lower classes who had never been to college. Several men, most of them from the educated nobility, have been suggested as the real author of Shakespeare's plays.

Anyone who tries to deny that Shakespeare wrote the plays, however, has to explain this poem, which was written by another great playwright who knew Shakespeare well. Several Elizabethan documents mention Shakespeare and praise his writing, but this is the most detailed and eloquent description of his success as a dramatist, and it was printed as an introduction to the first publication of the plays only a few years after Shakespeare's death.

Students will notice that Jonson doesn't hesitate to show off his own learning, as he names in lines 29–30 the earlier Elizabethan dramatists Shakespeare superseded and in lines 33–35 and 51–52 the classical dramatists of Greece and Rome. He is also careful, in line 74, to remind his readers that the plays were a success with Queen Elizabeth and King James. Although writers can be fiercely jealous of one another, this is one of the most generous tributes one writer has ever paid a rival. One of the reasons for Jonson's generosity is expressed in lines 41–43. With Shakespeare, England has a dramatist all of Europe admires, and as an Englishman, Jonson shares in the pride of this achievement.

Questions for Discussion

1. In the first seventeen lines of the poem, Jonson describes some of the mistaken reasons that others have used for writing a poem like this. What reasons does he give when he says that he couldn't write from ignorance, blind affection, or malice?
2. What does Jonson mean in line 22, when he writes, "Thou art a monument, without a tomb"?
3. In lines 59–63 Jonson describes how a writer revises his work. What does he conclude about this?
4. What does Jonson mean in line 73, "when flights upon the banks of the Thames"?

Topics for Writing

1. **CONNECTIONS** Three other poems are included in the "Address and Tribute" section of Chapter 15 (pp. 1004–1008). Students could compare Jonson's poem to any or all of them.

2. The other three poems in the "Address and Tribute" section are about writers who had died many years before the poem was written. Students could analyze whether it would be easier or more difficult to write about a contemporary.

3. Almost four hundred years have passed since Jonson wrote his tribute to William Shakespeare. Students could look at current critical views about Shakespeare to determine if our feelings about his plays have changed.

JOHN KEATS

To Autumn (p. 903)

A Thing of Beauty (p. 917)

Ode on a Grecian Urn (p. 934)

When I have fears that I may cease to be (p. 949)

On First Looking into Chapman's Homer (p. 999)

Ode to a Nightingale (p. 1139)

Bright star, would I were steadfast as thou art — (p. 1141)

As they read John Keats's poetry, students should remember that the work of every creative artist — writer, composer, painter — divides into different periods, and within each period the artist works through a series of closely related ideas and concepts. With Keats there is only one creative period — the brief time of less than three years between his first mature poetry and his illness and death from tuberculosis. Because the poems all come from this one period, students will find that there are themes, ideas, images, concepts, and even ways of structuring the poems that flow through them all. These selections include the first of Keats's major poems, the sonnet "On First Looking into Chapman's Homer," written in 1816, when he was twenty-one; a section from his second book, *Endymion*, from 1817; three poems from 1819, his most richly productive year ("To Autumn," "Ode to a Nightingale," and "Bright star, would I were steadfast as thou art —"); and "Ode on a Grecian Urn," which was finally completed in 1820, a year before his death.

ON FIRST LOOKING INTO CHAPMAN'S HOMER

Keats's creative months were so few that it's almost meaningless to think of early or late work, but "On First Looking into Chapman's Homer" is the first of his writing that is distinctly in his own voice. Here is the sensitivity to every nuance of rhythm and to the verbal tone of each word, the delicate balance between homage to classical literature and Keats's excited discovery of the new lyric style of poetry, the subtle technical mastery of meter and accent, and the rapture — almost a childish excitement — at beauty that has just been revealed to him. Students will find these elements are present in some way in each of the poems. The comments in the text explain the circumstances of this sonnet. We know that Keats wrote it at dawn in less than two or three hours, hurrying from a night of reading

(text pp. 903, 917, 934, 949, 999, 1138–1142)

with a friend, and somehow the poem feels like a dawning day, even if the only image that might apply is "I felt like some watcher of the sky."

Questions for Discussion

1. When he writes that "Much have I travell'd in the realms of gold" in the first line, is Keats writing metaphorically? What is he telling us about himself in this image?
2. What is he describing in the first four lines of the poem?
3. What is the "wide expanse" of line 5?
4. What do we call the figure of speech in his phrase "its pure serene" in line 7?
5. Could the correct name of the Spanish explorer who first saw the Pacific Ocean, Balboa, be inserted in the line to replace "stout Cortez"? Why was the poem never corrected?

Topic for Writing

1. One of the dominant themes of the poem is the importance of classical literature to young readers like Keats. A student paper could discuss this influence on Keats's writing.

A THING OF BEAUTY

As they are reading Keats's poetry, students should also read "Oatmeal" (p. 1008), Galway Kinnell's tribute to Keats. It will remind readers that Keats wasn't only the sensitive young man of the poems. He was a London cockney who got into a lot of fights in school. The poetry was written under the shadow of Keats's poverty, hopeless love, and growing illness.

His book *Endymion* was attacked so savagely by the critics that some of his friends felt that his disappointment hastened his death. In letters written at the time, however, Keats agreed that the book did have serious problems: it was too long and too ambitious for a poet so inexperienced. The opening line of this excerpt from it, however — "A thing of beauty is a joy forever" — has become a standard quotation. In this line and the two that follow, Keats states his great theme, that beauty lives forever: "It will never / pass into nothingness." And unlike the difficulties of his own life, beauty will keep a bower for him, a bower of "sweet dreams, and health, and quiet breathing." It was tuberculosis that had killed Keats's brother as he sat at the bedside trying to nurse him, and Keats would die of it himself. "Health, and quiet breath" would mean everything to him. Beginning with "Such the sun" in line 13, Keats, for the next eleven lines, describes the things that for him are beautiful. He uses similar images of nature in many of his poems that followed.

Questions for Discussion

1. How does line 5 reflect Keats's personal situation?
2. What is he suggesting in the image in lines 6–7, "are we wreathing / A flowery band to bind us to the earth"?
3. In lines 12–13 he writes that many things can lift us out of depression. What are some of these things that he mentions in the next twelve lines?
4. What is he saying about literature in lines 22–25?

5. What is the term for the figure of speech he uses in lines 23–24? What is being compared?
6. What is he saying about eternity in line 26 to the end of the verse?

Topics for Writing

1. Students could discuss the personification of nature in this and other Keats poems.
2. Students could discuss the pantheism of this and other Keats poems.

WHEN I HAVE FEARS THAT I MAY CEASE TO BE

The sonnet "When I have fears that I may cease to be" is a direct expression of Keats's fear that his illness would not give him time to write the "high-piled books" he had dreamed of. It is, also, one of the most uncomfortable of his major poems, as if he can't bring himself to come to a more open expression of his despair. He stays within the sonnet form, even if it forces him into the verbally stiff end rhyme of "think" and "sink." Images like "fair creature of an hour" or "the fairy power / Of unreflecting love" are standard fare of the period and express little of the passion and despair that he was pouring into his letters to Fanny Brawne, the young woman he loved. The sense of rapture at the books he might have written, however, reminds the reader of his belief in the meaning of beauty.

Questions for Discussion

1. What does Keats mean by the word "gleaned" in line 2? What do we call this figure of speech? How does "gleaned" anticipate the phrase "full-ripened grain" in line 4?
2. In line 8 he describes "the major hand of chance." What is he saying about a writer's creative act?
3. In lines 9 and 11 he used clichés, "fair creature of an hour" and "the fairy power / Of unreflecting love." The class might discuss why he might have used them here.
4. In the last line, is Keats suggesting that he thinks nothing will last of love and fame?

Topic for Writing

1. Students might discuss Keats's concept of art and literature as "Huge cloudy symbols of a high romance."

ODE TO A NIGHTINGALE

With "Ode to a Nightingale" Keats expresses again all of his major themes: beauty, its eternal freshness, and the contrast with the pain and death of mortal life. It is a complex poem. In musical terms it would be described as polyphonic. Its themes are presented; new themes take their place; then ideas return and are presented in new forms. As always with Keats, the opening phrase is immediately effective: "My heart aches." If the reader has trouble with lines 3 and 4, they mean that Keats feels as though a minute ago he drank some sort of depressant and he is drifting off to dreamland. Paradoxically, he insists that his heart aches not out of envy for the nightingale's "happy lot" but out of an excess of happiness that the bird "In some melodious plot . . . singest of summer with full-throated ease." The second verse hints at the death he handled so gingerly in "When I have fears." This time he will take the draught, a wine, that he felt he might have drunk (the "hemlock" mentioned in the poem's opening lines), and leave the world.

In the first two stanzas Keats presents the reader with some of the same images of natural beauty that he arrayed in "A Thing of Beauty," but in the third stanza they are contrasted with what he knows of life's realities, its "weariness, the fever." Line 26, "Where youth grows pale, and specter-thin, and dies," must refer to his brother, consciously intended or not. The fifth stanza is one of Keats's most startling poetic passages. He can't see where he is walking, as it is night, but even in the darkness he can guess what flowers and wild growth are "at his feet," and his description once again presents the natural images of the excerpt from *Endymion* and the whole of "To Autumn," which was written in these same months.

In the sixth stanza Keats returns to his own death, the theme of "When I have fears," but these lines are free of the sonnet's borrowed diction, and they repeat his dream of a moment with "no pain." In the next stanza he insists that the nightingale's song is immortal. He ignores the reality of any single nightingale's death. The song will be continued by another nightingale. It is the song — beauty — that is immortal. Then to end the poem suddenly he brings the reader back to the poem's opening, "My heart aches." This verse begins, "Forlorn," and in a few words he is back in the drowsy, half-forgetful state of the poem's first lines. Was it all a dream? He leaves us with the confused suggestion "Do I wake or sleep?"

Questions for Discussion

1. Could Keats's suggestion of the use of an opiate in "Ode to a Nightingale" be compared with Coleridge's use of opium in "Kubla Khan" (p. 1056)?
2. Is the poet awake or dreaming?
3. In the first stanza he suggests that his heart is aching, but aching with "being too happy." Is this a contradiction? How is the contradiction clarified in the final stanza?
4. There is a seeming paradox in line 6, "But being too happy in thine happiness." Is this like the paradox of an Elizabethan "conceit"?
5. What is Keats asking for in the beginning of the second stanza? Is this like the opiate he describes in the first stanza, or are their effects different?
6. Who is he saying will fade away in the first line of the third stanza?
7. Is he saying that only human beings experience mortality in the rest of the stanza?
8. What is the inference in line 27, "but to think is to be full of sorrow"?
9. In line 33, what is Keats telling us about "Poesy"?
10. Why is he contemplating suicide in the sixth stanza?
11. Ruth, in line 66, is the first reference in the poem to something other than nature or the poet's own feelings. Why is she an appropriate symbol here?
12. What is Keats saying in line 72, "the fancy cannot cheat so well"?

Topic for Writing

1. **CONNECTIONS** This poem is close in subject matter and theme to Percy Bysshe Shelley's "To a Sky-Lark" (p. 1191). Students could examine the two poems' similarities and differences.

Bright star, would I were steadfast as thou art —

Keats is calmer at the thought of his death in the sonnet "Bright star, would I were steadfast as thou art —, " and now he has found an image to express his tenderness and his love. He will live forever with his head on his loved one's breast, hearing her soft breath — or he will die with the beauty of the moment.

Questions for Discussion

1. How does this poem fit the usual definitions of the sonnet?
2. In the opening lines of the poem, is Keats asking for eternal life?
3. In line 5, what does he mean by the waters "at their priestlike task"?
4. This is a love poem. What does he ask of eternity for himself?
5. The term "sweet unrest" in line 12 is a common phrase from Elizabethan love poetry. Do you think Keats intended the allusion?
6. What is he saying in the sonnet's final line?

Topic for Writing

1. Many of Keats's themes — for instance, the fear of death and the dream of eternity — appear in "When I have fears" and "Bright star." Students could explicate the references to these themes in the two sonnets.

To Autumn

The imagery of "To Autumn" is discussed in the text. Students should also read Sidney Lea's commentary on the poem for a discussion of its "democratic" perspective (p. 1280). It was the last of Keats's great odes from 1819, and there is a calmness about the poem, as though, for a moment, Keats no longer felt the need to wrestle meanings or interpretations from what he was feeling and experiencing.

Questions for Discussion

1. What is Keats saying about the season and the sun in line 2?
2. What do we call the figure of speech he uses in line 12, "Who has not seen thee oft amid thy store"?
3. What would we call the figure of speech of the rest of the verse, lines 12–20?
4. How would you paraphrase the description of autumn in this verse?
5. In line 23, is Keats speaking of the songs of spring in a real or metaphoric sense? What would he refer to as "real" spring songs?
6. What image is he describing in line 25, "barred clouds bloom the soft-dying day"?
7. Lines 27–29 evoke a striking picture of a cloud of gnats. What poetic devices does Keats use to bring this picture to life?
8. A class discussion could develop a personified image of a different season of the year and a different kind of human occupation or interest.

Topics for Writing

1. Keats's poetry is rich in assonance and alliteration. Students could analyze the opening lines of "To Autumn" for these elements.
2. The personified image of the poem is autumn as farmworker. It would be interesting to describe what we can tell of the worker's daily tasks from the details in the poem.

ODE ON A GRECIAN URN

The fullest expression of Keats's themes is the famous "Ode on a Grecian Urn." For more than a hundred years it was one of the best-known poems in the English language. Today's students are probably not so familiar with it, but its ideas and poetic idiom had an immeasurable influence on English and American poetry until the social turmoil that followed World War I threw so many of the poem's values into question. In the poem Keats contrasts his theme of the eternity of beauty with the turmoil of everyday life. What the vase depicts is life's "mad pursuit," "struggles to escape," and "wild ecstasy," but the vase itself is a "still unravished bride of quietness." The poem's sexual undertones — for instance, the description of the unfulfilled embrace in lines 16–20 and the images of physical passion in lines such as 26–27, "For ever warm and still to be enjoyed, / For ever panting and for ever young" — lend it an even more intense poignancy.

The beauty Keats describes in the poem is almost beyond our comprehension. He writes in lines 11–12, "Heard melodies are sweet, but those unheard / Are sweeter." And because the beauty is depicted on the vase, it will be eternal. Students have usually accepted the poem's last lines without question, but commentators on the poem have argued over whether there is a contradiction between the opening of the poem, in which the poet addresses the vase, and these final lines, in which the vase addresses humankind. Keats doesn't seem to have felt any contradiction himself. There is a more difficult problem of interpretation in line 45. Does the description "Cold Pastoral!" contradict the message of warmth and beauty Keats presents in the rest of the poem? The colon in the line suggests that he means the term as a description of eternity, the word immediately preceding the colon, but it is an ambiguous image. For most students the final lines will present no difficulties, even if they don't agree with Keats's message.

Questions for Discussion

1. What does Keats mean by the term "Sylvan historian" in line 3?
2. The class could discuss the meaning of lines 11–12, "Heard melodies are sweet, but those unheard / Are sweeter; therefore, ye soft pipes, play on."
3. In line 14, what is Keats referring to as "spirit ditties of no tone"?
4. What is he describing in line 30, "a burning forehead, and a parching tongue"?
5. The class could discuss possible interpretations of "Cold Pastoral!" in line 45. Is it eternity Keats is describing?
6. What is he suggesting about the power of art in line 44, "Thou, silent form, dost tease us out of thought"?
7. What does he mean in line 47 when he refers to the urn as "a friend to man"?
8. The class could discuss the ideas expressed in the poem's final two lines.
9. A class discussion could be structured around the moral implications of Keats's statement that "Beauty is truth — truth beauty."

Topics for Writing

1. Keats uses the word "beauty" throughout his poetry. Students could compare the various ways he uses the concept of beauty in different poems.
2. **CONNECTIONS** Students might want to compare the idea of line 19 in "Ode on a Grecian Urn," that the beauty of the woman depicted on the vase cannot fade, with the sentiments in Andrew Marvell's "To His Coy Mistress" (p. 910).

3. An interesting paper could interpret Emily Dickinson's "I died for Beauty — but was scarce" (p. 1073) in terms of the last lines of Keats's poem.

GALWAY KINNELL

The Man Splitting Wood in the Daybreak (p. 958)
Oatmeal (p. 1008)
The Deconstruction of Emily Dickinson (p. 1350)

Kinnell was born in Providence in 1927 and has had a successful career as a poet; he received Fulbright, Guggenheim, MacArthur, and Rockefeller grants and won the Pulitzer prize for his poetry in 1983. Like many other American poets whose subject matter is the experience of nature and the daily tasks on a small farm, Kinnell has spent much of his life in the classroom as a university professor.

THE MAN SPLITTING WOOD IN THE DAYBREAK

Students will find a discussion of "The Man Splitting Wood in the Daybreak" in the text. They should also notice the poem's interpolations of random facts — the comment that societies in which divorce will soon be possible fear that marriages will fly apart in the way that the wood Kinnell is splitting flies apart, or the description of the way a willow seems to "weep" when it is split. These asides mirror the way most people's minds work when they are performing mundane tasks like splitting wood. Our minds keep us entertained with a variety of thoughts and associations.

Questions for Discussion

1. What is the extended metaphor of the poem? Discuss how Kinnell carries this metaphor through to the poem's final lines.
2. The poem's actual theme is mortality and death. What images does Kinnell use to present this theme?
3. Discuss the asides he presents in lines 7–10. Do they have immediate associations with his task of splitting wood?
4. What is he describing in line 13?
5. Because he is writing in open form, Kinnell has no need to use the difficult image "the unperplexed / looking-back of the numerals" in line 15. Why does he present the image this way?
6. Is line 20 meant as irony or paradox?

Topic for Writing

1. Analyze the imagery of lines 4–7 to discuss how Kinnell makes the reader feel the strength and speed of the ax blows.

OATMEAL
THE DECONSTRUCTION OF EMILY DICKINSON

Although Kinnell writes in the modern open form he uses more structured techniques to achieve the intensity and the allusive power of traditional verse. He also feels himself part of this poetic tradition, and in the description of his imaginary breakfast with John Keats, he not only manages to give us a fresh and lively glimpse of what Keats must have been like, but he also offers a shrewd commentary on one of Keats's most beautiful but complex poems, "Ode to a Nightingale."

"The Deconstruction of Emily Dickinson" is Kinnell's pained outcry against the trend of deconstructive criticism that was in vogue for several years. Like many writers, Kinnell despised this theory, as it excluded both the writer and the writer's text from any kind of coherent discussion of the process of creating the text. As he sheepishly admits in the poem, however, he is helpless to protect Dickinson from "all that Humbug," and what he imagines as Dickinson's response to his own ineptitude is silence.

Questions for Discussion

1. Although the ostensible subject of these poems is Kinnell's meeting with John Keats and his attempt to defend Emily Dickinson, each poem has an underlying theme. Discuss these themes.
2. Is the imagery of line 19 in "Oatmeal" — "and the way here and there a line . . . " — a modern metaphor, or is Kinnell paraphrasing Keats's poetic style?
3. The denotative meaning of "amnion" is the innermost membrane enclosing the fetus before birth. What is Kinnell saying with line 28, "maybe there is no sublime, only the shining of the amnion's tatters"?
4. Is the awkwardness Kinnell describes in himself in "The Deconstruction of Emily Dickinson" genuine, or is it only a device to give him the opportunity to present several thoughts about Dickinson and her critics?
5. What is Kinnell telling us about the professor in his image "He kissed his lips together"?
6. Despite Kinnell's passionate defense of Dickinson, does he find any allusion in her poem that intimates she was thinking of a "slave auction"? Is this a personal interpretation that Kinnell has imposed on her poem?
7. Why does Kinnell tell us that he has disappointed the women in the class (lines 54–57)? Does he imply that they would rather have had a role in defending the woman poet?
8. Why does Kinnell give the professor the final word in their discussion?

Topics for Writing

1. Analyze the means Kinnell has used in "Oatmeal" to present us with a living portrait of John Keats.
2. The classroom experience Kinnell narrates in "The Deconstruction of Emily Dickinson" could be read as an acknowledgment of a writer's feeling of helplessness before the weight of established authority. Discuss the elements in the poem that support this reading.

Yusef Komunyakaa

Boat People (p. 993)

Yusef Komunyakaa was born in 1947 in Bogalusa, Louisiana. His military service in Vietnam in 1969 and 1970 is one of the major themes of his work. He teaches at the University of California at Irvine.

Questions for Discussion

1. Discuss how Komunyakaa's tone changes from the first to the second stanza.
2. Explore his use of color in the poem.

Topic for Writing

1. **CONNECTIONS** In a two-page essay, have students compare Anna Akhmatova's depiction of prisoners in "Instead of a Preface" (p. 990) and "Dedication" (p. 990) to Komunyakaa's depiction of boat people.

D. H. LAWRENCE

Mountain Lion (p. 1143)
Snake (p. 1144)

D. H. Lawrence's poetry will not present any comprehension problems for students, especially if they have read his short fiction. "Mountain Lion" makes clear the intense awe and veneration Lawrence felt for the natural world. In line 5 he describes men as "The only animal in the world to fear!" Lawrence had a strong streak of misanthropy, and he allows it to come out in these poems. In the final stanza of "Mountain Lion" he writes that he can see no reason that the lion was killed; the world contained room enough for both the lion and himself. He says that if a "million or two of humans" were to be killed, he would never miss them, but "what a gap in the world" he feels with the death of the lion.

In "Snake" Lawrence again encounters the natural world. Instead of a dead lion it is a poisonous snake, alive and well in a water trough in the Sicilian mountains. Lawrence has come to the trough to get water, and although he understands that this kind of snake is dangerous and realizes that he should kill it, he is fascinated with its languid strength. He challenges himself to kill it, accusing himself of cowardice, of a lack of manliness, but he only wants to talk to the snake. Finally, as the snake is gliding away, he throws a log at it. As the poem ends he regrets that with that act he has missed his chance with "one of the lords of life."

Questions for Discussion

1. Why does Lawrence change the syntax in the description of the spruce trees and the balsam at the beginning of line 2 of "Mountain Lion"?
2. What is his meaning in line 5, "The only animal in the world to fear"?
3. What is he describing with the image "snowy inwardness" in line 12?
4. Why does everyone smile foolishly when the two groups meet in lines 18–20? Is it embarrassment or self-consciousness?
5. Students might want to discuss Lawrence's idea in line 45 that the earth could spare "a million or two of humans."
6. In "Snake," what is the name of the figure of speech Lawrence uses in line 14?
7. In line 20, does the phrase "burning bowels of the earth" refer to the nearby volcano?
8. Why does Lawrence say that he feels "honoured" in line 33? Is feeling honored at the sight of something beautiful in nature a common human emotion?

9. Why does Lawrence finally throw a log at the snake?
10. What does he mean in line 65, "I despised myself and the voices of my accursed human education"?
11. In line 70 why does he speak of the snake as having been in exile?
12. Why does he say he missed his chance with "one of the lords of life" (line 71)?

Topic for Writing

1. Students could relate Lawrence's expressed reverence for nature in these poems with the responsibility for nature that is advocated by today's environmental movement.

DENISE LEVERTOV

The Well (p. 933)

Levertov was born in England in 1923, the daughter of a Hassidic Russian immigrant who became an Anglican minister. Deeply influenced by the poetry of Tennyson, she began publishing her poetry when she was still a teenager. Her first book, *The Double Image*, appeared in 1946. Two years later she married an American and moved to New York, where she discovered the poetry of William Carlos Williams and other American modernists. In the 1960s her poetry was often directed against the war in Vietnam, but in this late poem from 1987 she looks back to her adolescence.

Questions for Discussion

1. The phrase "a dangerous / gleam of steel" in line 7 can be read in several ways. What are some of them?
2. Levertov's description of the moon in line 12 is decidedly unromantic. How does this compare with images of the moon in other poems in the anthology?
3. What is Levertov saying about sleep in the phrase "sunk in the well" in line 16?
4. In the last two lines she writes, "if not beautiful / filled with some other power." Is she suggesting that beauty has power? What could be the "other power" she mentions?

ROBERT LOWELL

Skunk Hour (p. 1147)
For the Union Dead (p. 1149)
Epilogue (p. 1150)

One of the strengths of Robert Lowell's poetry is its clarity and precision. Students will find that although the concepts Lowell presents have several dimensions, he doesn't end a poem until each of these elements has been integrated into the overall structure. Students should read his commentary on "Skunk Hour" (p. 1286) for insight into the care and creative thought that are continual in his writing. Students might also find it useful to read Elizabeth Bishop's "Armadillo" (p. 1027), the poem that "Skunk Hour" is answering. Lowell's poem is structured like a letter: The language has been tightened in some lines, and there's a literary quality to others, but the poem is, in a very uncomplicated way, a reply to Bishop.

"For the Union Dead," unlike "Skunk Hour," depicts a moment in Lowell's consciousness. He is first at the site of the old South Boston Aquarium, where he remembers pressing his hand against the glass as a child. Now he presses his hand against the fence of a building site on Boston Common, a park in Boston's business district. A parking garage is under construction, and the work is disturbing the memorial to an African American regiment that was led by Robert Shaw, a young white Bostonian, during the Civil War. The 54th Massachusetts Regiment was defeated by Confederate forces, who refused to accept their surrender and killed everyone they could seize, including the commanding officer. Students may be familiar with the film *Glory* (1989), which dramatizes the regiment's development and eventual massacre at Fort Wagner, South Carolina, or they might have seen the regiment and its fate documented in the television series *The Civil War*. At the time the poem was written, the regiment's story had been almost forgotten. As Lowell wrote, the memory of it "sticks like a wishbone / in the city's throat."

Although the poem represents a moment in Lowell's consciousness, he is sorting through images to show connections and relationships. On television he sees African American schoolchildren defying school segregation; in a store window he sees a photograph of the atomic explosion that destroyed Hiroshima; and as the poem ends he remembers the old aquarium where he began, only what he now sees are cars with fish fins, and the memory of the "cowed, compliant fish" is replaced with the "savage servility" of the new city.

"Epilogue" can be interpreted as Lowell's plea to himself to give his poetry even more truth, even more clarity. He suggests that, with poetry, the "poor passing facts" of life, the human figures in the images and memories we have of our lives, can be given a "living name."

Questions for Discussion

1. What is Lowell telling us about his emotional state in lines 31–36 of "Skunk Hour"?
2. Why does he title the poem "Skunk Hour"?
3. Is the phrase "Sahara of snow" in line 2 of "For the Union Dead" an oxymoron?
4. In line 8 of the poem, what does Lowell mean by "cowed, compliant fish"?
5. Are the African American regiment and its colonel the subject of the poem? What is the subject of the poem?
6. Does Lowell's description in lines 59–60 of the faces he is seeing on television serve as a comparison with the faces in the memorial that he describes in line 22?
7. In "Epilogue," what is Lowell telling us about poetry in his description of the effect of a Vermeer painting?

Topics for Writing

1. Students could relate Lowell's references to the African American regiment with the actual events.

2.   In "Epilogue," Lowell writes that he wants to "make / something imagined, not recalled." Students could discuss this inference that these two kinds of writing are quite different.

Related Commentaries

Robert Lowell, "An Explication of 'Skunk Hour,'" p. 1286.
Robert Lowell, "On Robert Frost," p. 1357.
Robert Lowell, Foreword to Plath's *Ariel*, p. 1369.
Louis Simpson, "On Lowell's 'Skunk Hour,'" p. 1315.

ARCHIBALD MACLEISH

Ars Poetica (p. 874)

The New Critical methods of the 1950s that swept the record of American poetry clean of the great women poets of the 1920s also dismissed the politically committed poets of the 1930s, among them such writers as Archibald MacLeish. MacLeish was not only one of the decade's most widely read and influential poets, but he also won the Pulitzer Prize three times — twice for poetry (in 1932 for *The Conquistador* and in 1952 for his *Collected Poems*) and in 1958 for his play *J.B.*, based on the Book of Job. He served as Librarian of Congress from 1939 to 1944 and held several important administrative positions in the government during World War II. Among his other writing are the radio plays that spoke out against the rise of European fascism — *The Fall of the City*, first broadcast in 1937, and *Air Raid*, broadcast in 1938.

MacLeish was born in Illinois in 1892. He served as an artillery captain in France in World War I and after the war briefly practiced law before deciding to become a poet. A younger brother was killed in aerial combat in 1918, which had a strong effect on MacLeish's writing. He was the Boylston Professor of Poetry at Harvard University from 1949 to 1962. He died in 1982, shortly before his ninetieth birthday.

"Ars Poetica" is still one of MacLeish's most popular poems, as much for its skilled use of language as for its insistence that the art of poetry is ultimately beyond analysis. Students may have difficulty with some of the poem's imagery, but a discussion developed around the following questions should assist them.

Questions for Discussion

1.   Why does MacLeish use a Latin phrase for the poem's title?
2.   What would we call the image of the first line: tactile? auditory? visual?
3.   Does MacLeish use the same kind of image in lines 2–3?
4.   Discuss the choice of diction in lines 5–6. What is MacLeish suggesting about the art of poetry in his word choice here? Does this relate to his choice of a Latin phrase for the poem's title?
5.   Discuss the syntactical changes in lines 13–14, "Leaving, as the moon behind the winter leaves, / Memory by Memory the mind."
6.   What is MacLeish saying in lines 17–18, "A poem should be equal to: / Not true"?

7. In lines 20 and 22, what is the name for the figure of speech MacLeish is using?

8. Have the class discuss what they think MacLeish means with the poem's last two lines, "A poem should not mean / But be."

ANDREW MARVELL

To His Coy Mistress (p. 910)

Students should have no trouble understanding this poem. The only image that presents any difficulty is the phrase "slow-chapt" in line 40. "Chap" is an archaic word derived from the German; it means jaw, and Marvell is using it as a contrast to the verb "devour" in the line before. He is saying that he and his mistress would do better to eat up time quickly than to wait for time to chew slowly. Most of the poem is skillfully handled, but these two lines are clumsy, and if students have difficulties visualizing the image here it is as much Marvell's fault as their own.

"To His Coy Mistress" is usually described as a carpe diem poem, and students might be asked to look at Robert Herrick's "To the Virgins, to Make Much of Time" (p. 888) as a classic example of the concept. Certainly this is a theme in "To His Coy Mistress," but Marvell introduces it only as an attempt to seduce his hesitant mistress. He is so impatient with her that the reader gets the impression that if this idea doesn't work he'll try something else. Not only is Marvell impatient ("Had we world enough and time"), but he is also annoyed ("this coyness Lady were no crime"), jeering ("For Lady you deserve this state"), and insulting ("your quaint honor"). As he begins to run out of ideas, all he can think of to promise the woman is that they will share physical enjoyment like "am'rous birds of prey," which is almost an oxymoron. He doesn't even offer her any real sexual pleasure. His metaphor for her first sexual encounter is "tear our pleasures with rough strife," and although "iron gates of life" could be interpreted to mean the adversities of life, it can also be interpreted to mean the difficulties of piercing the hymen. The poem's last two lines seem to suggest that something will be shared out of the experience, but it seems mostly to be an image of days filled with sex, which Marvell assumes the woman will also enjoy. Certainly he doesn't offer her anything else.

The instructor might ask students also to read the next poem in this group, Lady Mary Wortley Montagu's "The Lover: A Ballad" (p. 911). She responds to arguments like the ones presented by Marvell with arguments of her own, defending a woman's right to choose her lovers for reasons other than time being short. When she writes "I loathe the lewd rake," it is clearly someone like Marvell she is describing.

Regardless of how one interprets Marvell's poem, it is still one of the most subtle and sophisticated seduction poems in English. Students might want to compare it with John Donne's "The Flea" (p. 1079), which is certainly far less skillfully written. Even in today's world, the poem is a vivid example of masculine impatience and persuasiveness. Students should also read X. J. Kennedy's commentary on the poem (p. 1277). Kennedy provides detailed background information on Marvell and examines some of the mythological sources of the poem's imagery.

Questions for Discussion

1. What does Marvell mean by the phrase "our long love's day" in line 4?
2. There is a double meaning in Marvell's use of the term "vegetable love" in line 11. What is he telling the reader by using it? How does it contrast with animal love?
3. In line 24, Marvell speaks of "eternity" as a vast desert, whereas in Christian theology "eternity" is usually regarded as the ultimate in pleasure — as unity with God. What is Marvell's intention in this image?
4. What is he suggesting to his mistress in the phrase beginning in line 26, "Nor, in thy marble vault, shall sound / My echoing song"?
5. The class could discuss what they think Marvell is saying in the last two lines of the poem.

Topic for Writing

1. Students could discuss the concept of carpe diem and try to identify a modern equivalent of the term.

EDNA ST. VINCENT MILLAY

God's World (p. 889)
What lips my lips have kissed, and where, and why (p. 950)
First Fig (p. 1151)
Recuerdo (p. 1152)
I too beneath your moon, almighty Sex (p. 1152)

Students usually have little difficulty with the poetry of Edna St. Vincent Millay. Her books have been continuously in print since the 1920s, when she was one of the most discussed and certainly one of the most widely read poets in America.

The fervor of her early poem "God's World" should be compared with the ecstatic writing of Gerard Manley Hopkins, and also with the poems of H.D. Like H.D., Millay is overwhelmed by the glory of nature. Although she is able to contain her rapture in traditional forms, she is moved to express her emotion in lines such as "Here such a passion is / As stretcheth me apart." Conversely, in "First Fig" and "Recuerdo," both of which were written three years later, she is rueful and almost cynical, not with the world of nature but with her personal world of relationships and disappointments. There is a tenderness in "Recuerdo," in which she describes a night spent with a lover riding back and forth in New York harbor on the Staten Island Ferry.

For many of Millay's readers and critics, her sonnets were her highest poetic achievement. She wrote in the Italian form, although the last sextet often contains variations on this form. In the openness of these poems, in the frankness with which she wrote about her sexuality, Millay could be called the first confessional poet. The first two lines of "I too beneath your moon, almighty Sex" and its last line — "And lust is there, and nights not spent alone" — along with the opening lines of "What lips my lips have kissed" scandalized some of Millay's readers and attracted many others. Although their modern frankness sometimes seems to struggle against the sonnet's Victorian confines, Millay's sonnets are written with considerable skill and are an important addition to this poetic form.

GOD'S WORLD

Questions for Discussion

1. What physical image does Millay present in the first line? There is a difference between the verbs she uses in the first line and in line 7, "hold" and "get." What emotional difference is being implied?
2. What is Millay telling us about herself in line 4? Is it the woods and the autumn day that "ache and sag / And all but cry"?
3. Explain what Millay means by the sentence beginning in line 11, "Lord, I do fear / Thou'st made the world too beautiful this year."
4. What is she telling us about her ecstatic mood in the poem's last two lines?

Topics for Writing

1. **CONNECTIONS** Students could compare Millay's ecstatic emotions in "God's World" with poems by Gerard Manley Hopkins and H.D.
2. **CONNECTIONS** Students could compare Millay's descriptions of nature in "God's World" with John Keats's evocations of nature in "To Autumn" (p. 903).

FIRST FIG
RECUERDO

Questions for Discussion

1. "First Fig" is Millay's sly answer to a common phrase describing someone who is living life much too hastily. What is the phrase?
2. What is Millay saying about herself in her answer?
3. How does "Recuerdo" relate to the theme of "First Fig"?
4. The meter of "Recuerdo" is complex. How would the first stanza be scanned?

Topic for Writing

1. Students could discuss "First Fig" and "Recuerdo" in relation to the concept of carpe diem.

WHAT LIPS MY LIPS HAVE KISSED, AND WHERE, AND WHY
I TOO BENEATH YOUR MOON, ALMIGHTY SEX

Questions for Discussion

1. In "What lips my lips have kissed," what is Millay describing in lines 4–5, "ghosts that tap and sigh / Upon the glass and listen for reply"? Is she remembering or imagining?
2. What is she telling us about her lovers, the "unremembered lads," in lines 7–8?
3. Millay is saying several things in the poem's last two lines, "summer sang in me / A little while, that in me sings no more." What are some of these things?

4. In "I too," with what image is Millay describing herself in the first two lines?
5. What does she mean with the phrase in lines 4–5, "to vex / With tittering chalk"?
6. What is she telling us about her neighbors in line 6, "neighbors sitting where their mothers sat"?
7. Is there a contradiction between the reason that Millay built her "tower" ("To Beauty") and the materials she used to build it?

Topics for Writing

1. **CONNECTIONS** Students could discuss the changes in women's lives in the 1920s that made poetry like Millay's possible, comparing it with the poetry of Victorian women and with the poetry of women today. Poets to consider include Elizabeth Barrett Browning, Emily Dickinson, Sylvia Plath, Sharon Olds, and Anne Sexton, all of whom are included in the anthology.
2. "What lips my lips have kissed" contains many images of loss. Students could describe these images and relate them to the poem's theme.
3. Using the image of "the Tower" in "I too," students could explicate Millay's allusion to the construction of a self-image.

JOHN MILTON

When I consider how my light is spent (p. 949)
On the Late Massacre in Piedmont (p. 981)

These two sonnets do not represent the epic scope and grandeur of Milton's long, complex masterpieces, *Paradise Lost* and *Paradise Regained*, but they are written with the same conscious authority and sure command of language. During his long and controversial life, Milton was indulged, angry, and beset by tragedy. It was only during his final years, when he was blind and bitter and almost impoverished, that he began dictating his great poems to his daughters, and here is where his life took on an epic dimension.

Milton was born in London in 1608 and lived until 1674. His wealthy father was sympathetic to his son's intellectual interests, so after earning his bachelor's and master's degrees at Cambridge University, Milton spent six additional years studying and traveling. With the consolidation of the Puritan Commonwealth following the execution of Charles I in 1649, Milton became fully engaged in the turmoil that had uprooted English society and was named secretary to the Commonwealth protector, Oliver Cromwell.

Midway through his term of office, Milton was suddenly left blind after years of acute eyestrain, but he continued to serve Cromwell with the aid of assistants. When the Commonwealth collapsed and Charles II was restored to the throne in 1660, Milton was imprisoned and eventually fined and his property confiscated. Until this moment, he had written several longer poems that showed the promise of his later work, but much of his writing during his years under Cromwell was confined to prose pamphlets arguing political questions. His great poems were composed despite his blindness and the difficulty of dictating work of such daunting complexity to his daughters. There is nothing in the writing, in fact, to suggest that his powers were impaired by his affliction.

The sonnet "When I consider how my light is spent" is about Milton's blindness; he insists that even though he is unable to do what he had hoped, his life is still given to God, who may use him in any way he wishes. The sonnet ends with the famous line "They also serve who only watch and wait." "On the Late Massacre at Piedmont" was written in anger when the Holy Roman Empire's troops killed members of a free-thinking religious group in the Piedmont Valley in northern Italy.

Questions for Discussion

1. How do the rhyme schemes of the two sonnets differ?
2. What is Milton saying in line 11 of "When I consider"? Is he saying, in lines 12 and 13, that God already has so many doing his bidding that Milton's services are not needed?
3. In the last line of "On the Late Massacre," what is Milton describing with the term "Babylonian"?

Topics for Writing

1. **CONNECTIONS** Compare Milton's sonnet on his blindness with that of John Keats on his fear of death, "When I have fears that I may cease to be" (p. 949).
2. In "On the Late Massacre," Milton asks God to avenge the slaughter of the peasants whose views of Christ differed from the Catholicism enforced by the Holy Roman Empire. Discuss Milton's description of the slaughtered peasants and their religious faith.

JANICE MIRIKITANI

Recipe (p. 986)

Janice Mirikitani is a third-generation Japanese American, born in 1942. She lives in San Francisco, where she works as a poet, choreographer, and community activist.

Questions for Discussion

1. What is Mirikitani protesting in this poem?
2. Comment on her use of details. What is the effect of focusing on this process, these items?

Topic for Writing

1. Have each student write a "recipe" poem about his or her own ethnicity.

LADY MARY WORTLEY MONTAGU

The Lover: A Ballad (p. 911)

Although Lady Montagu's poem was written almost 250 years ago, most women today would agree with her argument. Students may find it takes more than one reading to find all the meanings, but there should be no problems with interpretation. The poet is defending a woman's decision to remain chaste until she finds a man who will treat her with respect, discretion, and honor. She is not a hard moralist but admits that "I hate to be cheated." When she finds the right man, then "he may be rude, and yet I may forgive." Lady Montagu's poem is written with wit and style, and although it makes some of the classical allusions characteristic of Augustan poetry, there is an easy familiarity to the language. It was not until feminist critics examined the literary traditions they were expected to inherit that poems such as this one began to be read and discussed again.

Students will find it interesting to read this poem in relation to the one by Andrew Marvell that precedes it in the anthology. Lady Montagu answers all of Marvell's impatient arguments with skill and intelligence.

Questions for Discussion

1. How would you describe the men the poet doesn't want to be with?
2. What is she saying about herself in line 6, "Nor is Sunday's sermon so strong in my head"?
3. Explain the meaning of line 16, "For I would have the power though not give the pain."
4. What is the poet saying, in line 31, about the things that make us feel we are alive?
5. In lines 36–40, is she really insisting that no one will meet her standard, or has she already suggested in the poem that it is possible she will find a man to suit her?
6. What does she mean by line 41, "I never will share with the wanton coquette"?

Topics for Writing

1. Students could paraphrase the poem in modern terms and discuss its relevance to women's lives today.
2. **CONNECTIONS** Students could compare the attitudes toward love expressed in Andrew Marvell's "To His Coy Mistress" (p. 910) and Lady Montagu's poem and decide which poem seems the more valid in terms of today's morality.

MARIANNE MOORE

Poetry (p. 875)
The Fish (p. 1153)
The Mind Is an Enchanting Thing (p. 1154)

Elizabeth Bishop's commentary, "Efforts of Affection" (p. 1236), will introduce students to Marianne Moore as a person; Moore's responses in her interview with poet Howard Nemerov (p. 1289) will introduce them to her as a writer, giving them some insight into how she constructs her poems. Her admission that "I like end-stopped lines and depend on rhyme, but my rhymes are often hidden and, in being inconspicuous, escape detection" could give students the impression that her writing is less adventurous than it is, but as they read her poetry they will recognize its originality.

The comments in the text should help students read and interpret "Poetry." "The Fish," as students will quickly find, isn't about a fish and has no connection to Elizabeth Bishop's poem with a similar title. Moore's poem is a description of the turmoil at the edge of the sea, where a cliff meets the water and the sea creatures tangle against one another. If the poem has an obvious subject, it is the cliff itself, which Moore introduces in the fourth stanza. The poem is a series of brilliant images, beginning with "wade / through black jade," the poet's metaphor describing the fish swimming in shallow dark water. The rhymes are obvious, despite Moore's comment that she often conceals them, and part of the poem's startling effect is the abrupt rhyme of single words and even partial words used as perfect rhymes. Her lines are, as she said, end-stopped, but for her a line can be a single syllable long.

Like "The Fish," "The Mind Is an Enchanting Thing" is a series of images. Each image in the poem presents us with a new aspect of the mind's powers. Students will probably not be familiar with Walter Gieseking's performances of Scarlatti's keyboard sonatas, but the simile of the opening lines — "like the glaze on a / katydid wing" — is a visual equivalent of the music's sound. The stanza form is similar to that used in "The Fish," but there is an additional line (six lines instead of five), the opening line is three stresses in length, and the rhyme joins the first and third lines instead of the first and second. As she often did, Moore uses unusual words in this poem. "Apteryx" is defined in a footnote to the poem, and students should consult their dictionaries for "regnant." The poem, which is about the mind, is itself an ingenious example of the mind's capabilities.

Questions for Writing

1. In the first two lines of "Poetry" — "I, too, dislike it; there are things that are important beyond all / this fiddle" — what is Moore telling us about poetry?
2. When she includes critics in her list of creatures we don't understand, what is she telling us about her opinion of critics?
3. What is she telling us about "business documents and / school books" in line 23?
4. In "The Fish," what is Moore describing in lines 8–9, "The barnacles which encrust the side / of the wave"?

5.   What is she telling us, in the fourth stanza of "The Fish," with her image of the sea driving an iron wedge into the cliff's iron edge?
6.   In "The Mind Is an Enchanting Thing," what is she suggesting in the complex series of images in the second stanza? How might this stanza be paraphrased?
7.   Why does Moore return to the music of Scarlatti in the final stanza? Is this an example of the poet herself submitting "confusion to proof"?

Topics for Writing

1.   Students could discuss Moore's phrase "Imaginary gardens with real toads in them" in line 23 of "Poetry."
2.   Students could suggest some reasons that Moore shortened "Poetry."
3.   Students could describe the images of the mind's power in "The Mind Is an Enchanting Thing."

Related Commentaries

Elizabeth Bishop, "Efforts of Affection: A Memoir of Marianne Moore," p. 1236.
Marianne Moore, "Some Answers to Questions Posed by Howard Nemerov," p. 1289.

Pat Mora

Border Town: 1938 (p. 985)

Pat Mora was born in El Paso, Texas, in 1942. She is Mexican American, and her poetry often includes Spanish words and phrases to emphasize her belief in the importance of a bilingual culture. She studied at the University of Texas at El Paso and now lives in Cincinnati.

Questions for Discussion

1.   Why does Mora begin and end the poem as she does?
2.   What does "the farmer in the dell" symbolize?

Topic for Writing

1.   Students could write a one- to two-page essay about Mora's use of the nursery rhyme "The Farmer in the Dell."

Sharon Olds

The Elder Sister (p. 1156)
Summer Solstice, New York City (p. 1157)

Sharon Olds's language is so immediately accessible, so close to everyday speech, that students may not be conscious of the artistic choices that shape the diction and syntax of these two poems. In "The Elder Sister," Olds's initial choice has been to strip the poem of any sentimentality or any association with any other poem about the relationship between sisters. Olds expresses love for her sister in terms that no poet has used before. The entire poem is built on physical images, beginning with her sister's birth — a birth that left her sister with "the long hollow cheeks of a Crusader." The body continues to be the focus of the poem's images — the developing breasts and pubic hair — and as Olds begins to see her sister in a new way, as a protector, she also expresses this feeling in bodily images — wrinkles, clenched jaw, frown lines. Then, in a simile that relates to the earlier image of the Crusader and resonates from it, she describes her sister as a shield and the marks she sees on her sister's face as the blows from which her sister has protected her. The resolution of the poem — that her sister's body held before her has been the shield that allowed Olds to escape from her own childhood — is a revelation for which the rest of the poem has skillfully prepared us.

In "Summer Solstice, New York," the language is as direct, but much of the poem's imagery is built on actions outside the body. The poem contains some of Olds's most imaginative figures of speech. In line 6, the social agencies that are summoned into action at emergencies are called "the huge machinery of the earth." In line 18, the edge of the roof where the man is threatening to jump is described as "the lip of the next world." Mingled with these images are images of birth and the body, which Olds brings to a resolution by comparing the way the police handle the man after he has abandoned his suicide attempt with the way a woman would handle a child who has been lost. In the poem's last lines she catches the emotions we feel at that brief moment when something frightening or threatening ends and we can begin to live again: Cigarettes the policemen had lit "burned like the / tiny campfires we lit at night / back at the beginning of the world."

Despite the cliché that "no one reads poetry," Sharon Olds's poems have found a steadily growing audience. *The Dead and the Living*, the collection from which "The Elder Sister" is taken, was reprinted sixteen times in the first eighteen months after its publication.

Questions for Discussion

1. Explain what Olds means in lines 27–29 of "The Elder Sister" — "as a / hostage protects the one who makes her / escape."
2. In "Summer Solstice," what is Olds telling us about summers in New York City?
3. What is she saying about the policeman's feelings as he puts on his bullet-proof vest in line 10 of "Summer Solstice"?

Topics for Writing

1. Students could discuss the relationship between sisters, using "The Elder Sister" as a point of departure.
2. In "Summer Solstice," Olds mingles images of birth and death. Students could discuss the attitudes these images are expressing.

Marge Piercy

The woman in the ordinary (p. 1158)
Putting the good things away (p. 1159)

Piercy's themes of anger and anticipation — "acid and sweet," as she describes them in "The woman in the ordinary" — are conveyed with such immediate language that students should have no trouble interpreting her poems. "The woman in the ordinary" is a series of images depicting the woman who is waiting within the body of every young girl — waiting "like a hand grenade set to explode" and "like goldenrod ready to bloom."

"Putting the good things away" is a gentle poem to the memory of Piercy's mother, in which the poet attempts to understand the source of her own anger. Each poem contains strong images — for instance, "a Christmas card virgin with glued hands" (line 11 of "The woman") and "where old dreams / whistle on bone flutes" (lines 29–30 of "Putting the good things away") — but Piercy's is a spare, winnowed poetry in which the emotions, not the language, give the lines their form.

Questions for Discussion

1. In the opening line of "The woman in the ordinary," what is Piercy saying about a woman's identity? How would the reader explain lines 3–4?
2. Lines 5–7 are a rich weave of figures of speech. The class could discuss some of the ways the poet has used language in these lines.
3. What does Piercy mean by the phrase "glued hands" (line 11)? What are its emotional implications?
4. What is Piercy describing in line 12, "fishes for herself in other's eyes"?
5. In "Putting the good things away," what is she saying about her mother in the verse that begins with line 29, "in the heart where old dreams"?
6. What is she saying about herself in the verse that begins with line 49, "Her anger annealed me"? What is the meaning of the word "annealed" here?
7. In the poem's last line, is Piercy speaking for her mother or making a judgment of her mother?

Topic for Writing

1. **CONNECTIONS** Both Marge Piercy and Sharon Olds (p. 1156) describe the changes within an adolescent girl's body. Students could compare their descriptions and discuss why earlier women's poetry did not contain such descriptions.

Sylvia Plath

Students will find considerable help in approaching Sylvia Plath's poetry in the text's biographical note and casebook commentaries. Students should be encouraged to look at Plath's poetry from every possible angle and to be open-minded when interpreting meaning. Plath was a poet who took chances, and students will more fully understand and respond to her work if they take chances in their own reading of it.

A Winter's Tale (p. 1163)
Black Rook in Rainy Weather (p. 1164)
Ella Mason and Her Eleven Cats (p. 1165)

Plath wrote these poems as an apprentice, and they show her developing skills and her nascent creative independence. Like John Keats, her career was short, but she crammed much poetic development into that brief time. Only five years passed between the tentative skills of "A Winter's Tale" to the mastery of the *Ariel* poems. For this period of her writing, students should read the excerpt from her *Journals* (p. 1368) and Anne Sexton's memoir of their meetings in Robert Lowell's poetry class in Boston (p. 1370).

Questions for Discussion

1. Is "A Winter's Tale" an ironic poem? Which images suggest that it is, and which suggest that it isn't?

2. What is the image of line 11, "Haloes lustrous at Sirius"? What is the term for this figure of speech?

3. With the interjection "Lord, the crowds are fierce!" in line 15, Plath seems to be addressing someone. Is there anything in the poem that could identify this person?

4. Students should try to paraphrase the first ten lines of "Black Rook in Rainy Weather."

5. With "Although, I admit, I desire, / Occasionally, some backtalk / From the mute sky" (lines 11–13), is Plath explaining her religious beliefs? Why does she use four commas to separate the first six words of this passage?

6. There are many hints that this is a religious poem. Have the class discuss these hints.

7. What is Plath saying in line 32, when she confesses to fearing "total neutrality"?

8. "Ella Mason and Her Eleven Cats" is a brilliant example of the effective use of near or slant rhyme. Have the class list these rhymes, including those of the fifth lines of each stanza, which extend the pattern of rhyme from stanza to stanza.

9. Do the last lines of each stanza function as a refrain? What does this tell us about Plath's concept of the rest of the poem?

10. Discuss the imagery in lines 7–8, "Rum and red-faced as a water-melon, her voice / Long gone to wheeze and seed."

11. Describe the alliteration of line 41, "That vain jades sulk single down bridal night." What does the line mean? What earlier line in the poem clarifies its meaning? Is the noun "jade" a modern or dated usage? What is Plath telling us by her choice of diction with this word?

Topic for Writing

1. **CONNECTIONS** Lines 27–32 of "Black Rook," beginning with "I only know that a rook . . . ," expresses the same wonder at the world's beauty as the poems of Gerard Manley Hopkins, H.D., and Edna St. Vincent Millay. Students could compare a poem by each of these writers with the emotions Plath expresses in this poem.

Morning Song (p. 1166)
Mirror (p. 1167)
The Bee Meeting (p. 1167)

"Morning Song" is the first poem in the *Ariel* collection, and although it describes a familiar domestic scene — a young mother at home with her first child — it does so in a series of startlingly original images. As a sustained image, "Mirror" is one of Plath's most skilled and controlled poems, with many levels of meaning. All of these poems are tied to the events of her domestic life, but in "The Bee Meeting," her sense of her surroundings begins to take on surreal overtones. This group of poems displays many of the characteristics of confessional poetry, a form that Robert Lowell initiated in his 1959 collection *Life Studies* and Anne Sexton was to take to further limits in the years after Plath's suicide. Students might find it helpful to read Denise Levertov's discussion of confessional poetry (p. 1373).

Questions for Discussion

1. What is the meaning of the first line of "Morning Song": "Love set you going like a fat gold watch"?
2. What is the term for the figure of speech in the phrase "your bald cry" in line 2?
3. What does Plath mean in line 10, "your moth breath"?
4. What is the term for the figure of speech she uses in line 16, "swallows its dull stars"?
5. In "Mirror," what does the mirror mean when it refers to itself as "a little god, four-cornered" in line 5?
6. What does the mirror mean when it calls the candles or the moon "liars" in line 12?
7. In "I am important to her" of line 15, what is the mirror saying about the woman?
8. What do the poem's last two lines mean?
9. What does "The Bee Meeting" describe?
10. What is Plath saying in line 6, "I am nude as a chicken"? What do the villagers do to help her?
11. Describe the image she presents with the verb "scarves" in line 36.
12. What does she mean by "The mind of the hive" in line 37?
13. How does line 53, "I am the magician's girl who does not flinch," contrast with Plath's description of herself at the beginning of the poem? What is she saying about her neighbors?

Topics for Writing

1. Students could analyze the details in "Morning Song" and discuss what the poem tells us about Plath's daily life.
2. The poet pretends that the "Mirror" has no "preconceptions." It swallows everything, "unmisted by love or dislike." Students could discuss whether a person would be as objective in his or her observations as Plath has described the mirror to be.
3. **CONNECTIONS** "The Bee Meeting" was influenced by poems Plath had received from her friend Anne Sexton. Students could analyze the Sexton poems in the anthology and show how they might have affected Plath's poem.

THE APPLICANT (p. 1169)

This poem is perhaps best approached as a feminist statement in which Plath's anger is expressed through bitter irony. Students should read the poet's own guarded explanation of the poem's meaning on p. 1162.

Questions for Discussion

1. What is the sex of the applicant? Why did Plath choose this sex for her poem?
2. Who could be the person interviewing the applicant? Does Plath even clarify this individual in the poem?
3. What is the applicant seeking? What details in the poem make this clear?
4. Does Plath intend irony when she has the interviewer ask the same question — "Will you marry it?" — for both a suit and a woman?
5. What is the allusion in line 6, "Stitches to show something's missing"?
6. What is Plath describing in line 16, "To thumb shut your eyes at the end"?
7. Line 18, "We make new stock from the salt," alludes to the Old Testament. What is the allusion?
8. Consider Plath's description of a woman in lines 31–35. What is "A living doll" referring to?
9. What is the meaning of the penultimate line, "it's your last resort"?

Topic for Writing

1. Students could analyze the feminist perspective of the poem and compare it with other feminist documents of the early 1960s.

DADDY (p. 1170)

Before students read these *Ariel* poems, they might find it helpful to read the commentaries by Robert Lowell (p. 1369), who both influenced and was influenced by Plath, and by Joyce Carol Oates (p. 1375), whose writing also shares some of Plath's visceral intensity. The *Ariel* poems have been analyzed and discussed many times, but this should not inhibit students. They should reread Plath's comment on "Daddy" (p. 1163) before beginning their analysis of this poem.

"Daddy" inspired many later woman poets to address their fathers in verse, but Plath's is still the most raw and brutal poem of them all. The pain and anger are so sharp that it is hard to believe that Plath's father died when she was eight years old and in many ways she never really remembered him. "Daddy" is her creation of her father, not her memory of him.

Questions for Discussion

1. What does Plath mean by the first line, "You do not do, you do not do / Any more"?
2. What is the symbolism of her description of her father as a "black shoe" and herself as a "white foot"?
3. The abrupt "Achoo" at the end of the first stanza is meant as sardonic humor. What are some other instances in the poem when she is being grimly humorous? Why does she use humor in the poem? Is this what could be termed "black humor"?
4. To what is Plath referring with the phrase "Chuffing me off like a Jew" in line 32?

5.   Consider the various implied meanings in line 58–59, "At twenty I tried to die / And get back, back, back to you." Do the emotions of these lines contradict Plath's other statements about her father in the poem?

6.   Whom could she be describing in line 72, "The vampire who said he was you"?

Topic for Writing

1.   Plath imagines herself as a Jew in "Daddy." Students could analyze the associations she develops through this Jewish identity.

LADY LAZARUS (p. 1172)

This poem continues and extends some of the images and themes of "Daddy," including an image of a foot, although here it's the poet's right foot turned into a paperweight. The theme of "Lady Lazarus" is Plath's recoveries from near death — first from illness when she was a child, then from her first suicide attempt when she was twenty, and now, at thirty, when she is recovering from what she considers a third near death, which is probably her separation from her husband: "I am only thirty / And like the cat I have nine times to die." Only a few months later she found out that she was not like a cat, and finally she achieved death.

Questions for Discussion

1.   What is the emotional source for the Nazi concentration camp imagery of the first lines?

2.   As "Lady Lazarus," Plath is saying that she has returned to life. Does she identify what she nearly died from this time? What in the poem supports the idea that she could be speaking metaphorically of her separation from her husband?

3.   In lines 10–21 she describes her resurrection from the dead. Does she identify the enemy she addressed in line 11? Who seems to be the enemy?

4.   In lines 25–34 she describes her return to life as a circus act. What does she mean by "The big strip tease" in line 29?

5.   Consider the implications of lines 37–38, "I meant / To last it out and not come back at all."

6.   What does the class make of Plath's conception of dying as an "art" in line 43?

7.   Describe some of the emotions Plath might be feeling in line 46, "I do it so it feels like hell."

8.   Is the enjambment of line 53, which ends with the word "brute," as though Plath were referring to a person, intentional?

9.   Does Plath mean her father by "Herr Doktor" in line 65? Is she alluding to the concentration camp analogy of "Daddy"?

10.   How would the class interpret the poem's last three lines, which seem to suggest a different motivation for Plath's self-resurrections?

Topic for Writing

1.   Students could discuss the influence of the Holocaust on Plath's poetry. (This will require some biographical research.)

Words (p. 1174)
Edge (p. 1175)

With these poems Plath is reaching the end of her strength, and in "Words" she even questions her language, which has been her one weapon. She concludes the poem by acknowledging that other forces in her life have had more power over her than "Words dry and riderless." In "Edge," Plath seems to have reached some resolution, as though certain that this time she will finally succeed at dying. The poem transcends the anger that flared up in "Daddy" and "Lady Lazarus": it is calm, accepting, and — perhaps most important — unafraid.

Questions for Discussion

1. In "Words," is Plath using "axes" as a metaphor for words? What is she suggesting with this comparison?
2. What does she claim for the power of words in the first five lines?
3. What is the image of lines 6–7, "The sap / Wells like tears"?
4. In line 11 Plath transmutes a rock dropped into the water to a skull. What does this comparison suggest? Discuss the alliteration of line 13. How important are these effects to the poem's theme?
5. What visual image do lines 16–17 evoke? Why does Plath use the word "indefatigable" in line 17?
6. In lines 19–20, is she saying that words, after all, have had little effect on her life?
7. What does Plath mean by the title "Edge"?
8. How is the allusion in line 4, "The illusion of a Greek necessity," related to Plath's expressed acceptance that she will die?
9. What is the association in line 5, "her toga"?
10. Why does Plath write "dead child" in line 9? Does this mean she is intending to kill her children along with herself, or does it imply a metaphorical death as she draws her memory of them into herself as she dies?
11. What does she mean with the image of the last line?

Topics for Writing

1. Students could relate Plath's fatalistic philosophy in "Words" ("fixed stars / Govern a life") to "The illusion of a Greek necessity" in "Edge."
2. **CONNECTIONS** Both Christina Rossetti (p. 1184) and Emily Dickinson (p. 1075) also wrote poems about their own deaths. Students could compare and contrast these three poems.

Edgar Allan Poe

The Bells (p. 895)

Students will probably be familiar with Edgar Allan Poe through his short fiction or through the film versions of some of his best-known tales. Poe was well known as a poet during his lifetime, and "The Bells," "The Raven," and other of his verse have been frequently anthologized for many years. Although students may be deafened by all the clanging in the poem, it is subtly written. Each stanza echoes the sound of different kinds of bells. In the first stanza it is sleigh bells; in the second, wedding bells; in the third, alarm bells; in the fourth, steeple bells. The final group of lines, beginning with "To the Paean of the bells," is a clamoring return of all the bells of the poem.

Questions for Discussion

1. Compare the first three lines of each stanza. What is the rhyme scheme that Poe repeats in each?
2. Each of the stanzas uses different sounds and language to depict its own kind of bell. Discuss the language of each stanza in terms of the bell it describes.
3. An often-discussed aspect of the poem is Poe's repetition of the word "bells" seven times in the penultimate line of each stanza. What prepares us, in the poem's metric structure, for seven repetitions of the word?
4. In his short fiction, Poe was a master of horror and the macabre. How is this evident in the third stanza?
5. Consider lines 74 and 75: "How we shiver with affright / At the melancholy meaning of the tone!" What is Poe depicting here?
6. Is there a contradiction between his description in line 88, "They are Ghouls," and line 92, "And his merry bosom swells"?
7. In Poe's time, there was much interest in purported discoveries of Viking ruins in Massachusetts. Is his use of the term "Runic" (line 96), which refers to Viking carved inscriptions, a poetic device with symbolic meaning, or is it a trendy mention of a popular subject?

Topics for Writing

1. The poem is filled with alliteration and assonance. Students could identify and discuss examples of these techniques.
2. Students could compare the images in each of the four stanzas to show how Poe presents each type of bell.
3. Contemporary readers were fascinated by the poem's varied rhythms. Analyze the meter of each stanza and discuss why Poe varied the length and the pattern of the lines.

Ezra Pound

In a Station of the Metro (p. 964)
A Pact (p. 1007)
The River-Merchant's Wife: A Letter (p. 1176)
From *Hugh Selwyn Mauberley (p. 1177)*

The shrewd assessment of Pound's language by his friend and fellow poet William Carlos Williams (p. 1329) should help students to make sense of these poems. Pound's "On the Principles of Imagism" (p. 1297) is also enlightening, offering a glimpse into his complex personality. His imagist poem "In a Station of the Metro" is discussed in the text. "A Pact" is a simple but sincere tribute to Walt Whitman for creating a new kind of poetry.

Although "The River-Merchant's Wife: A Letter" is from a Chinese poem by Li Po, it should be considered a free version rather than a direct translation. The poem's opening line, "While my hair was still cut straight across my forehead," shows Pound's sensitivity to detail, giving the reader an immediate sense of the speaker as a young girl. The poem is about a Chinese girl, but we recognize that same haircut in young girls everywhere. The parallel structure of lines 2 and 3, ending with "pulling flowers" and "playing horse," effectively presents us with the contrast between a girl and a boy. The shift of syntax in line 7, "I married my Lord you," manages to communicate her awe at the prospect of their marriage and yet her familiarity with her new husband simply by reversing the expected word order. Students will find many more examples of Pound's instinctive skills throughout the poem.

In contrast, the segment from *Hugh Selwyn Mauberley* is such a thicket of allusion and reference that students should read the footnotes before the poem. They should also note any phrases that are still unclear in their reading and go back over the poem again. This is a sardonic, brilliant, raging poem in which Pound brings one period of his life to a close. The poem is autobiographical not only in its details but in its barely concealed blending of disdain and anger. Pound was offended by the modern world, and the poem could be considered his effort to keep this unsightly, intrusive world at a distance. Developments such as the new art of film elicit his judgment in line 43 that his own age can only achieve "a tawdry cheapness."

The fourth and fifth stanzas attracted the most attention when the poem was first published. In the fourth he describes the young men who had gone off to World War I only a few years before, mocking their deaths with a rephrasing of the well-known Latin motto, *Dulce et decorum est, pro patria mori*, which translates as "It is a sweet and fitting thing to give one's life for one's country." "Non 'dulce,'" Pound writes, "non 'et decor'": It wasn't sweet, and it wasn't fitting.

For college students and young rebels between the two world wars, Pound's description of European civilization as "an old bitch gone dead in the teeth" struck a deep chord, but part of the poem's effect was how much it drew from the literary traditions of this dead civilization. There is the comforting familiarity of the *abab* rhyme scheme and the four-line stanzas. The rhythm is free from the constraints of regular meter, but many of the lines have a pattern of four stresses. The classical references would be familiar to any educated person of the time, but the context in which Pound presented them made them new. Students will be able to find definitions for the unfamiliar words and phrases, but the poem is essentially of its time: Only Pound's contemporaries could sense how much the poem was shaped and directed by the poet's passionate love of the past.

Questions for Discussion

1. In "A Pact," Pound writes that Whitman "broke the new wood, / Now is the time for carving." What does Pound mean by the "new wood"? What poetic means does Pound seem to have taken from Whitman's "new" way of writing?

2. The narrator of "The River-Merchant's Wife: A Letter" says in line 25, "They hurt me. I grow older." What does she mean?

3. What might she be expressing in her thoughtful qualification of how far she will go to meet her husband? Is she afraid? Young?

4. What is Pound referring to in line 6 of the excerpt from *Hugh Selwyn Mauberley*, "a half savage country"? What does he mean?

5. What is he describing in line 13, "His true Penelope was Flaubert"?
6. In the second section of the poem, Pound writes that the vulgar world in which he finds himself contains no true feeling or appreciation of art. Is this something that was true for Pound's time, or is it a feeling that many artists and writers experience?
7. Why might Pound have chosen the diction of lines 33 and 35, using an "etc" to end line 33 and putting the word "replaces" in quotation marks at the end of line 35?
8. What is the reason for his derisive adjective "tin wreath" in line 60?
9. The mood of the poem changes in the fourth section, beginning with line 61. Has anything prepared us for his genuine despair at the waste of life in the war?
10. What does Pound mean by the image "laughter out of dead bellies" in line 86?

Topics for Writing

1. Some critics at the time felt that Pound's relentless presentation of his classical knowledge owed to his insecurity at being an American living in Europe. Students could discuss this theory in relation to some of Pound's ideas about poetry and art in general.
2. Many people were offended by *Hugh Selwyn Mauberley's* proposition that the young men's deaths owed to their belief in "old men's lies." Students could discuss this reaction to the poem and consider whether it was justified.
3. **CONNECTIONS** Many of the poem's antiwar sentiments echo the emotions of Randall Jarrell's "The Death of the Ball Turret Gunner" (p. 984). Students could compare the two poets' attitudes toward war.

JUDITH RODRIGUEZ

Eskimo Occasion (p. 908)

Judith Rodriguez is an Australian writer who was born in 1936. Her work is published by the University of Queensland Press.

Question for Discussion

1. What "occasion" is the poem built around? Why has Rodriguez surrounded it with these "eskimo" images?

Topic for Writing

1. Have students think of another mundane occasion and write a poem about it, using grand mythic images as Rodriguez does.

Theodore Roethke

The Waking (p. 957)
Big Wind (p. 1181)
My Papa's Waltz (p. 1182)
Elegy for Jane (p. 1182)

The Waking

"The Waking" is a brilliant example of Roethke's skill with traditional verse forms. The text discusses the villanelle (p. 957), which is the poem's form. Despite the complexities of its structure, the poem is a somber meditation on the poet's mortality, which he introduces with the paradox of the opening line, "I wake to sleep." The form of the poem, however, with its repetitions and dancelike rhythms, gives it a lightness that almost contradicts its underlying melancholy.

Questions for Discussion

1. Although presented in a complicated verse form, "The Waking" is simply a description of waking up. What are some of the details Roethke mentions as part of the waking?
2. Why might Roethke have used the paradox of the opening line, "I wake to sleep"?
3. What is he telling us in line 5, "I hear my being dance from ear to ear"?
4. In lines 7–8, what is he telling us about how he wakes up?
5. What does he mean by the phrase in line 17, "What falls away is always"?

Topic for Writing

1. Students could discuss the modern paradoxes in "The Waking" and how they contrast with the older poetic forms that the poem suggests.

Big Wind
My Papa's Waltz
Elegy for Jane

Students will immediately notice the detail in Roethke's poetry. Lines 6–16 of "Big Wind" describe each step that the narrator and his father take in their effort to save the roses in their nursery from a wild storm. The simile of the first line of "Elegy for Jane," "the neckcurls, limp and damp as tendrils," carefully describes the young girls' hair. Roethke's art, however, is much more subtle than a listing of details. "Big Wind" changes with the words "she rode it out" in line 21 to an extended metaphor that continues until the poem's conclusion. The greenhouse is transmuted into a ship, and the poem becomes a vivid description of a ship battling a storm. Students will notice how the active verbs that describe the struggle against the wind ("ploughing," "bucking," "flailing," "flinging") slow down to "veering," almost come to a halt with "wearing themselves out" and "whistling thinly," and then stop when the storm blows itself out (the verb of the penultimate line is in a simple past tense, "sailed").

The childhood memory "My Papa's Waltz" is written in a different style, again demonstrating Roethke's subtle artistry. The story is told directly: The narrator's father had come home drunk one night and waltzed around the kitchen with him — in front of his disapproving mother — and then put him to bed. To turn this small anecdote into a poem, Roethke has written it as a modest lyric ballad, in four-line stanzas of iambic trimeter, rhyming *abab*. He demonstrates his skill by using feminine rhymes in lines 2 and 4 of the first and third stanzas, and masculine rhymes in these lines in the alternating stanzas.

The poem's emotional effect is achieved with the first line, "The whiskey on your breath," and as the young boy is put to bed the last line, "Still clinging to your shirt" — still hugging his father. Despite the confusion, awkwardness, and discomfort that he feels, the boy still loves his father. To reassure readers of the poem's intentions, Roethke has the boy call his father "papa," and in line 5 he uses the verb "romped," with its connotations of pleasant play.

The emotional resolution of "Elegy for Jane" comes in the final line, as the poet admits to having no right to mourn his student like this, he being neither her father nor her lover. Still, he has already established his distance from her with the same kind of detail-rich metaphor of "Big Wind." In "Elegy," his young student, in line 5, becomes a small bird. He describes her as three birds — a wren in line 5, a sparrow in line 14, and a pigeon in line 19 — but the images all depict a bird's nervous movements, and the reader is conscious that the poet had physically come no closer to her than he would come to any small bird.

Questions for Discussion

1. In "Big Wind," what is Roethke describing in the first four lines?
2. In lines 21–29, he is comparing the greenhouse with a ship. What are some of the details he uses in his comparison? What is the term for this figure of speech?
3. What is the connotation of the last line, "Carrying her full cargo of roses"?
4. In "My Papa's Waltz" Roethke creates a word in the phrase "Could not unfrown itself." What does he mean by this? In an alteration in the poem's simple diction he uses the word "countenance" instead of "face" to describe his mother watching them. Why did he do this?
5. Does the poem's language imply that this is a happy or an unhappy memory?
6. What can we infer about the age of the boy from the language Roethke uses?
7. In "Elegy for Jane," what is meant by the term "pickerel smile" in line 2?
8. Consider the image of line 3, "the light syllables danced for her." What does this mean?
9. The poem describes Jane as a wren, a sparrow, and a pigeon. What are some of the details that Roethke associates with these bird metaphors?
10. What consolation do "The sides of wet stones" offer in line 16?

Topics for Writing

1. "Big Wind" features a very skillful sequence of verbs. Students could discuss the structure of the poem through its verbs — their connotations as well as their tense.
2. Students could analyze the imagery of small birds in "Elegy for Jane" and compare the birds' shyness with the shyness of the small deer in Sir Thomas Wyatt's "They Flee from Me" (p. 887).

CHRISTINA ROSSETTI

I wish I could remember that first day (p. 949)

Song (p. 1183)

After Death (p. 1184)

Up-Hill (p. 1184)

Although none of Christina Rossetti's other writing caused as much critical debate as her long poem *Goblin Market*, her shorter lyrics had a wide readership during her lifetime. Her brief, careful poems have gone through periods of relative neglect, but the purity and subtle skills of her lyrics have assured her a larger role as today's readers reevaluate nineteenth-century writing. Her themes and poetic idiom were not at all uncommon, but in lines such as "Haply I may remember / And haply may forget," from "Song," she displays a unique poetic voice. "After Death" is unusual in that the poem's narrator has died and does not respond to the person who has come in the room to stand by her body. Modern biographers have learned through letters and papers that Rossetti intensely loved a man who was unaware of her passion and who was secretly married to someone else. The poem could be read as an unconscious metaphor of her "death" to this man who did not love her.

Questions for Discussion

1. In "Song," is Rossetti expressing an indifference to love in the lines "And if thou wilt, remember, / And if thou wilt, forget"? What is her meaning in this seeming disinterest?
2. The "nightingale" in line 11 could be an allusion to Keats's "Ode to a Nightingale." Do you think this was Rossetti's intention?
3. What is she describing in lines 13–14, "And dreaming through the twilight / That does not rise nor set"?
4. "I wish I could remember" seems to describe a real moment in Rossetti's life. Is this a moment that lovers often try to recall?
5. An unusual emphasis occurs in line 2, when the poet writes, "your meeting me." Was this change in syntax only for the sake of the rhyme, or did she intend to imply something different?
6. What is she describing in lines 7–8, "the budding of my tree / That would not blossom yet for many a May"?
7. "Up-Hill" is often read as a prayer. What elements make it useful in this capacity?
8. Is "Up-Hill an expression of Christian faith? What images suggest this?
9. What is Rossetti saying about life in the question of the opening line?

Topics for Writing

1. The popular appeal of short lyric poems such as Rossetti's has long contributed to the role that poetry plays in our culture. Students could discuss the place of the short, personal lyric poem in literature.
2. Rossetti's poems share many of the themes of Emily Dickinson's. Students could select one poem by Rossetti and one by Dickinson that address similar ideas or express similar sentiments and analyze how each poet uses language, style, and structure to develop this theme.

Tadeusz Rozewicz

Pigtail (p. 991)
What Happens (p. 992)

Tadeusz Rozewicz was born in Poland in 1921 and was prolific as a poet and playwright. His work has been consistently committed to the struggle for social justice and — in his writings about the Holocaust — atonement. He said in an interview in 1976, "I tend to find any old newspaper of more interest than the finest poetry edition."

Questions for Discussion

1. Discuss the hair metaphors in "Pigtail." What sort of transformation of them takes place as the poem progresses?
2. Explain the significance of the title "What Happens." What is Rozewicz saying "happens"?

Topic for Writing

1. Have students compare and contrast Rozewicz's tones in these two poems.

Muriel Rukeyser

The Sixth Night: Waking (p. 873)

On first reading, students may not realize that the sixth night to which Rukeyser is referring is the sixth night that God has labored in the book of Genesis. Adam and Eve are asleep under a tree, and with the word from God, "Let meanings move," suddenly there is the beginning of poetry. Rukeyser is suggesting that once you begin to question the basis of your experience, you will need poetry.

Questions for Discussion

1. What does Rukeyser mean by "first green night of their dreaming"?
2. Why is "Tree" capitalized?
3. Does the rhetoric of "Let meanings move" echo other phrases from Genesis?

Topics for Writing

1. Rukeyser is emphasizing that poetry plays an important role in naming and defining our experience and our world. Students could discuss this concept of poetry's role.
2. Poetry is one of humankind's oldest forms of creative expression. Students could analyze why poetry begins so early in our common experience.

MARY JO SALTER

Welcome to Hiroshima (p. 988)

Mary Jo Salter was born in 1954 and has traveled and lived in Japan. She teaches at Mount Holyoke College.

Question for Discussion

1. What is Salter's point about history and the atomic bomb in this poem? Discuss in particular how she conveys the synthesis of past and present.

Topic for Writing

1. Have students write an essay or poem about a visit to a historical war site, such as Gettysburg or the Alamo, or to a memorial commemorating participation in a war, such as the Vietnam Veterans Memorial in Washington, D.C. Have them emphasize how the sense of history emerges in response to the setting.

ANNE SEXTON

All My Pretty Ones (p. 1185)
The Starry Night (p. 1187)

Anne Sexton's commentary on Sylvia Plath, "The Barfly Ought to Sing" (p. 1370), will tell students as much about Sexton as it does about Plath. We in fact learn more about Sexton than she reveals in "All My Pretty Ones," a poem about her father — for instance, that she was a pimply, boy-crazy adolescent who flunked most classes in high school. In "'Some Tribal Female Who Is Known but Forbidden'" (p. 1270), critic Richard Howard emphasizes that Sexton's work is based almost entirely on her own experience. If you are a writer like Sexton, he says, "You must begin somewhere, though, generally with your life, above all with your life when it seems to you to welter in a particular exemplary status." Students will find that these two poems contain no generalizations, no larger political or religious issues: Sexton's life is her subject.

The subject of "All My Pretty Ones" is Sexton's father and her relationship to him. He has just died, and she is going through the things he left behind. Because the faces in a photo album mean nothing to her, she throws it away. What swells up in the poem is Sexton's anger at her father's drunkenness, and yet there is also the suggestion that he failed her in other ways. In a different group of photos Sexton sees him living a life that is seemingly successful, but none of the photos she describes includes herself. As she says of him in lines 39–40, he was "my drunkard, my navigator, / my first lost keeper." "All My Pretty Ones" is written in a flat, hard, almost unpoetic language, but Sexton has framed it in ten-line stanzas of loose iambic pentameter, with a rhyme scheme of *ababcdcdee*.

"The Starry Night" describes a Van Gogh painting that moves Sexton so strongly that she feels she wants to die in just the way the night is depicted in the painting. She wants to disappear into the emotional vortex of the painter's vision. The painting itself was inspired by a Walt Whitman poem, so with Sexton's poem the response of writer to painter to writer has come full circle. The first two stanzas end with the same balladlike refrain, "Oh starry starry night! This is how / I want to die," and there is a rhyme between the third and seventh lines. The last stanza, however, seems to lose itself in the poet's emotional turmoil, and the poem ends with the despairing image "no flag, / no belly, / no cry."

Questions for Discussion

1. "All My Pretty Ones" is a line from Shakespeare's *Macbeth*, but the reference is to slain children, not dead parents. Why do you suppose Sexton chose this for her title? Does this explain the reference "Whether you are pretty or not" in line 49?
2. What is she telling us in line 17, "time meanwhile / has made it unimportant who you are looking for"?
3. In line 24 she tells us that President Hoover is "wriggling his dry finger" at her. What does she mean with the phrase? What is the name for the figure of speech she is using?
4. What does the poet mean by the words she uses to describe her father in lines 39–40?
5. What does she mean by line 48, "Only in this hoarded span will love persevere"?
6. In "The Starry Night," why does Sexton say that the drowned woman slips *up* into the sky?
7. What might the term "The old unseen serpent" mean in line 10?
8. How would you paraphrase the poem's last lines, "no flag / no belly, / no cry"?
9. In his commentary on Sexton's poetry, Richard Howard writes, "Hers is the truth that cancels poetry." What is he saying about her writing?

Topics for Writing

1. **CONNECTIONS** The anthology contains other examples of poets responding to paintings — for instance, W. H. Auden's "Musée des Beaux Arts" (p. 1022) and Lawrence Ferlinghetti's "In Goya's greatest scenes we seem to see" (p. 1094). Students could analyze the ways in which the paintings are used in each of these poems and discuss why poets sometimes write about paintings.
2. **CONNECTIONS** Sexton's friend and fellow poet Sylvia Plath also wrote a poem about her father, "Daddy" (p. 1170). Students could compare the two poems and discuss the imagery each poet uses in her description.

WILLIAM SHAKESPEARE

That time of year thou mayst in me behold (p. 945)
Shall I compare thee to a summer's day? (p. 1188)
When to the sessions of sweet silent thought (p. 1189)
Let me not to the marriage of true minds (p. 1189)
My mistress' eyes are nothing like the sun (p. 1189)

Students will find biographical information and critical discussions of William Shakespeare in the casebook on *Hamlet* in Part Three. They should also read Erica Jong's commentary, "Devouring Time: Shakespeare's Sonnets" (p. 1275).

In her essay, Jong describes the sonnets as "the 152 best poems in our language," but it took more than two hundred years for Shakespeare's verse to be so highly regarded. The sonnets were originally published in 1609; there was another edition in 1640; they appeared again in a collection of Shakespeare's writing in 1766, published in response to a new interest in the comedies. In 1789, when the publisher issued a new edition of the collected writings, he omitted the sonnets, saying, "the strongest Act of Parliament that could be framed would fail to compel readers into their service." It was not until the nineteenth century that the sonnets came to be regarded as an irreplaceable part of our literary heritage.

Most commentators on the sonnets agree that they were written in the 1590s, at the time when Shakespeare was writing his lighter plays. They have little of the darkness of his late tragedies, although, as Jong points out, they share the Elizabethan obsessions of time and mortality. Many efforts have been made to trace a story in the sonnets, and there have been almost as many efforts to prove that someone else besides Shakespeare wrote them. Some of the difficulty with these interpretations, however, is that we generally read the sonnets in modernized versions, in which spelling, punctuation, and sometimes even words themselves have been altered. In this original form, it is more obvious that many stylistic differences exist between the poems, indicating that they were written over a period of years. There is in fact no suggestion that they were written or intended to be read as a story.

Shakespeare was a writer capable of assuming many guises and adopting many styles. The style of the sonnets is largely derived from Henry Howard, the earl of Surrey, who developed the form of the sonnet that Shakespeare used; from Sir Philip Sidney, whose sonnet sequence *Astrophel and Stella* was published in 1582; and from Edmund Spenser, one of the most important poets of the generation just preceding Shakespeare's and whose sonnet sequence *Amoretti* was published in 1595. The power of Shakespeare's sonnets lies in his refusal to comply with the thematic conventions that his predecessors had developed. He expands the sonnet's emotional limits beyond the realm of courtly love and into contemplations of mortality and the nature of time. His technical brilliance takes the sonnet into dimensions of rhetorical inquiry that no poet before him had attempted.

THAT TIME OF YEAR THOU MAYST IN ME BEHOLD

Questions for Discussion

1. Scan the sonnet and discuss its metrical form and rhyme scheme. This same form will fit the other sonnets as well.
2. Discuss the sonnet's extended metaphor.
3. The sonnet contains several metaphors for death. What are they?
4. What is the meaning of the phrase "Bare ruined choirs" in line 4?
5. What is Shakespeare saying about night in line 7?
6. What is he saying about love in line 13? Paraphrase this line.

Topic for Writing

1. **CONNECTIONS** Discuss the meaning of carpe diem in terms of this sonnet. Compare it to another carpe diem poem — for instance, Robert Herrick's "To the Virgins, to Make Much of Time" (p. 888).

SHALL I COMPARE THEE TO A SUMMER'S DAY?

Questions for Discussion

1. Nature is present in many guises throughout the sonnet. Discuss which references to nature are images, and which are metaphors.
2. What is the term for the figure of speech represented by "death" in line 11?
3. What claim is Shakespeare making for poetry in the last two lines? Is this claim unique to this sonnet? Why would he use images that were part of the common poetic vocabulary of his time?

Topic for Writing

1. In the second line of the sonnet, Shakespeare praises his mistress for being "temperate." Discuss why the Elizabethans valued this as a virtue in women.

WHEN TO THE SESSIONS OF SWEET SILENT THOUGHT

Questions for Discussion

1. What mood is Shakespeare describing in the first line of the sonnet?
2. The first line is a classic example of alliteration. Discuss the alliteration of this and other lines in the sonnet.
3. What does Shakespeare mean by "old woes new wail" in line 4?
4. In lines 6–12, describe what happens to the poet in his mood.
5. Paraphrase lines 10–12.

Topic for Writing

1. Analyze and discuss how Shakespeare's unhappiness is manifested while he is in this mood.

LET ME NOT TO THE MARRIAGE OF TRUE MINDS

Questions for Discussion

1. In the sonnet's concept of "the marriage of true minds," is Shakespeare denying physical love? What does he mean by the phrase?

2. What qualities of love does Shakespeare describe in the sonnet?
3. Discuss the conceit of line 4.
4. What does Shakespeare mean by "his bending sickle's compass come" in line 10?

Topics for Writing

1. Read Erica Jong's paraphrase in the commentary and write a similar paraphrase for this sonnet.
2. **CONNECTIONS** Compare the concept of eternal love in this sonnet and the sonnet by E. E. Cummings, "goodby Betty, don't remember me" (p. 951).

My mistress' eyes are nothing like the sun

Questions for Discussion

1. Could this sonnet be described as an antilove poem? What saves it from this?
2. Is this list of the mistress's attributes a conscious rebuttal of the clichés of the courtly sonnet? What was Shakespeare intending by writing in this manner?
3. Is the sonnet meant to be humorous?
4. Discuss the meaning of the last line.

Topic for Writing

1. Write a modern antilove poem, using contemporary images in the way that Shakespeare used images in his sonnet.

PERCY BYSSHE SHELLEY

When Passion's Trance Is Overpast (p. 917)
Ode to the West Wind (p. 935)
Ozymandias (p. 1191)
To a Sky-Lark (p. 1191)

Students may not want to read the entire excerpt from Shelley's "A Defence of Poetry" in the commentary section (p. 1311), but many of the essay's passages suggest a theory and a response to poetry that can help readers gain a fuller understanding of Shelley's writing. The first paragraph begins with "A poem is the very image of life expressed in its eternal truth" and ends with "Poetry is a mirror which makes beautiful that which is distorted." "Poetry is ever accompanied with pleasure," Shelley writes. "All spirits on which it falls, open themselves to receive the wisdom which is mingled with its delight. . . . Poetry is indeed something divine. It is at once the centre and circumference of knowledge; it is that which comprehends all science, and to which all science must be referred. It is at the same time the root and blossom of all other systems of thought; it is that from which all spring, and that which adorns all; and that which, if blighted, denies the fruit and the seed, and withholds from the barren world the nourishment and the succession of the scions of the tree of life." Few poets or critics have expressed a more exalted view of poetry and its powers.

OZYMANDIAS

For an intensive discussion of this poem, students should read "Shelley in Ruins: The Appeal of 'Ozymandias'" (p. 1303), the commentary by poet Sherod Santos. Although complex, Santos's essay gives a good overview of the poem's themes.

Questions for Discussion

1. "Ozymandias" is written in an irregular rhyme scheme that does not entirely fit either the Italian or the English models of the sonnet. What other characteristics of the sonnet do we find in the poem?
2. In line 5, what is Shelley depicting with the phrase "sneer of cold command"?
3. Discuss some of the possible interpretations of line 8, "The hand that mocked them, and the heart that fed."

Topic for Writing

1. The poem is usually interpreted as a parable of the futility of human vanity and pride. Students could discuss the reasons for this interpretation.

ODE TO THE WEST WIND

The form of the poem, terza rima, is discussed in the text. In a note to the poem, Shelley said that it was largely composed in a forest outside of Florence on a windy, tempestuous day in which a thunderstorm eventually erupted.

"Ode to the West Wind" is long and complex, but students should not have any difficulty following Shelley's thought if they read the poem carefully, section by section. The generally accepted structural interpretation is that the first three sections conceive of the autumn wind as a dark presence bringing death to the earth. Throughout the poem the forceful wind is personified: The first section ends with the words "Destroyer and Preserver"; in the second section the wind is described as "Thou Dirge / Of the dying year" (lines 23–24); and the closing lines of the third section describe the wind's voice reaching even to the plants in the depths of the ocean, which on hearing the wind's voice "suddenly grow grey with fear, / And tremble and despoil themselves." Also, each of the sections ends with an invocation to the wind, "O hear!," which has the sound of a supplicant before an almighty power.

The last two sections suggest a life that is contained within the wind, beginning with Shelley's realization that the wind has the power to save him from difficulties and disappointments. He opens the fourth section, beginning at line 43, with the wish "If I were a dead leaf thou mightest bear," and the lines are carried forward with the dream that the wind could lift him and carry him in his "sore need." The images rush to a climax with Shelley's pained outcry "I fall upon the thorns of life! I bleed!" The entire section is an invocation to the wind, but the tone of Shelley's pleading has changed. He now identifies with the wind; he is no longer a supplicant. In the last line he has become "One too like thee: tameless, and swift, and proud."

In the final section, beginning at line 57, the wind becomes a life-giving force, capable of scattering Shelley's thoughts to the world, just as it scattered the leaves in the first stanza. The wind, by scattering his words, will be a trumpet of prophecy to the slumbering earth. On a first reading, the last image of "O Wind, / If winter comes, can Spring be far behind?" may seem simply to describe the change of seasons from the dying of autumn to the rebirth of spring. But as Shelley has made clear in the preceding lines, he now sees the wind as the deliverer of his words to the earth's people. "Spring" is not only the natural season; it is also a spring of Shelley's words.

Students will also better understand the poem if they are aware that it is essentially written in two modes. Through his continuous reading and his passionate commitment to poetry, Shelley was exceptionally learned, and at the time he was writing, the new concept of Romantic poetry was still being formed. Although the mood of the first three sections is wild and driven, their structure and style are essentially of the late Augustan mode. Augustan poetry used elevated diction and personification, was preoccupied with large general truths, made extensive literary and classical reference, and avoided openly expressed subjective emotion. All of this describes the first three sections of "Ode to the West Wind." Beginning with the fourth section, however, the poem suddenly shifts into the personal and the subjective. It is now in the Romantic mode. One of the poem's achievements is its successful fusion of the two modes.

Questions for Discussion

1. What is Shelley describing with the image "Pestilence-stricken multitudes" in line 5?
2. What is he telling the reader about the wind in the first three stanzas?
3. In the image of line 11, "Driving sweet buds like flocks to feed in air," he is using two interconnected figures of speech. What are they?
4. In the second section, what is Shelley suggesting when he writes that the leaves are spread on the stream of the wind?
5. What does he mean with his image, in lines 24–25, that the night will be "the dome of a vast sepulchre"?
6. In line 29 he says that the wind has wakened the Mediterranean "from his summer dreams." What is he telling us?
7. Who is the dreamer he describes in lines 33–34? What does he mean by "the wave's intenser day"?
8. What is Shelley describing with the image "Cleave themselves into chasms" in line 38?
9. What is he telling us about his childhood in lines 48–51?
10. What is he telling us about his life now in line 55?
11. What is he asking the wind to do when he asks it to make him its lyre?

Topics for Writing

1. Students could discuss the elements of the Augustan or neoclassical style in the poem's first three sections.
2. The final section, beginning with the line "Make me thy lyre," presents the poet as the instrument of the wind. Students could explicate Shelley's meaning in this section.
3. Leaves appear as symbol and metaphor throughout the poem. Students could analyze what this leaf imagery suggests about Shelley's poetic methods.

To a Sky-Lark

"To a Sky-Lark" is so compelling in its imagery and syntax that it is possible to read the poem through to the end without questioning its themes, even as the reader senses them within the poem's structure. Shelley would have considered this judgment the highest praise. He was one of the most technically accomplished of the Romantic poets, and all his skill and imagination are displayed in this poem's form. To convey his sudden surprise at the lark's song, he has written the poem in short bursts of words, alternating them with longer phrases as a musical contrast. The stanzas consist of five lines — the first four in trochaic trimeter, then, in a swift modulation, the final line doubles in length to hexameter, and the stresses shift from trochaic to iambic. So that the fifth line will still be heard as part of the stanza, it rhymes with lines 2 and 4, and there is an enjambment between lines 4 and 5. The best way to appreciate Shelley's finesse is to read the poem aloud. The stanza is heard as one long phrase, like the song of the skylark.

The poem's central theme is the idea that nature contains a joy and purity that humans can never know, and although the poem's effect is of a single long song, it is skillfully structured so as to outline Shelley's argument. In the first six stanzas he describes the lark's song and the bird's presence overhead, even if he cannot see it. Then line 32 asks, "What is most like thee?" In the following five stanzas, beginning with "Like a Poet hidden" at line 36, he answers the question by comparing the skylark to a poet, a maiden, a glow-worm, a rose, and the sound of rain on the grass. Each of them is described as unnoticed by the world, or the small space around them, until the song, love, light, scent, or sound they generate attracts attention. Ending the last of these stanzas in lines 59–60, however, Shelley makes it clear that nothing compares with the skylark's song: "All that ever was / Joyous, and clear and fresh, thy music doth surpass."

In the next stanza, beginning with line 61, the poet asks the bird to teach humankind its melodies, as nothing he has ever heard matches their beauty. He follows this with four stanzas, beginning with "Chorus Hymeneal," which examine the songs of humans and ask what it is the bird sees and feels, as its song is so much richer than any human expression. In the often quoted stanza beginning with line 86, "We look before and after . . . ," Shelley sums up those characteristics of human nature that keep us from happiness. In the final stanzas he laments that even if we should learn to overcome our hate, pride, and fear, we still couldn't match the skylark's joy, and in the last line he implores the bird to teach him "half the gladness" that the bird is feeling — in which case the world would listen to him, as he stands listening to the skylark.

Questions for Discussion

1. What is Shelley saying in the poem's second line, "Bird thou never wert"?
2. What are some of the connotations of line 15, "Like an unbodied joy whose race is just begun"?
3. Lines 18–20 describe the lark as being an unseen presence. What simile is Shelley using to tell us this?
4. The precision of Shelley's depiction of sunrise in the fifth stanza, beginning with line 21, indicates that he has seen the sun rise many times. What details make us realize this?
5. Each of the four stanzas that compare the skylark to other things, beginning at line 36, opens with the word "like." What is the term for these kinds of comparisons?

6. What is the "hidden want" that Shelley feels in line 70?
7. How would you explain what Shelley is telling us in lines 91–95?
8. What is the meaning of the phrase "Scorner of the ground!" in line 100?
9. In the final stanza, lines 101–105, what is Shelley asking of the skylark for his own poetry?

Topics for Writing

1. The musicality of the lark's song is suggested by the musicality of the poem's first stanza. Students could discuss Shelley's use of assonance, alliteration, rhyme, and near rhyme in this stanza.
2. Students could examine the famous verse "We look before and after..." and discuss the view of human nature that Shelley presents.

WHEN PASSION'S TRANCE IS OVERPAST

"When Passion's Trance Is Overpast" was published after Shelley's death. On its most obvious level, it is a lyric poem lamenting how little is left of the love between a man and a woman after their initial infatuation has passed. In the second stanza he maintains that he would even accept a relationship that stopped short of complete sexual union if only she would love him again as she did before. In the final stanza he says sorrowfully that everything in nature comes back to life in the spring, except life and love. The actual circumstances of the poem are transparently visible through the lines. His young wife, Mary, after repeated pregnancies and the deaths of all but one of their children while still babies, refused to continue sleeping with him. Shelley had become interested in the wife of a friend who was staying with them in Italy, and he was writing longer, questioning poems to her. The despair in the line "When passion's trance is overpast" was as much for himself as it was for Mary and their marriage.

Questions for Discussion

1. Why does the poet speak of passion as a "trance"? Was this a common description in classic poetry? Is it something we would say today?
2. What is the hope Shelley expresses in the first stanza?
3. What does he mean by his description of his feelings "and burn and be / The secret food of fires unseen" in lines 8–9?
4. What does he mean when he says that everything in nature will revive in the spring except life and love, but that these two "move / And form all others"? Is there a contradiction in these two statements?
5. Would a close reading of the poem suggest that Shelley is angry as he writes? Would some other emotion serve as a better description?

CHRISTOPHER SMART

From *Jubilate Agno* (p. 937)

Smart wrote his free-verse masterpiece *Jubilate Agno* while confined in an insane asylum for "an excessive devotion to prayer," as such behavior was then termed. Written over a period of several years in notebooks Smart was allowed to keep in the asylum, the poem is about Jeoffry, the cat Smart was permitted to keep during his confinement. The poem is also, however, written in praise of the Divine Spirit that the cat represents.

Born in 1722, Smart had been a brilliant Latin scholar and poet — educated at Cambridge, with an active role in London's literary life — before suffering an emotional breakdown. He was confined from 1756 to 1763. After his release, he managed to publish some less unconventional poetry, but he was unable to support himself and died in a debtor's prison in 1771. *Jubilate Agno* was not published until 1939, but Smart was immediately recognized as close in spirit to William Blake, and the poem influenced many contemporary writers, especially the Beat poets.

Questions for Discussion

1. What in Smart's verse tells us that this is a religious poem?
2. What elements of the poem suggest a prayer?
3. What does Smart describe his cat doing as a service to him?
4. Is the line "For he can tread to all the measures upon the music" a description of something the cat can do, or is it a metaphor for a spiritual response in the cat?

Topic for Writing

1. **CONNECTIONS** Allen Ginsberg named this poem as one of his sources of inspiration. Compare the form of this poem with the meter and line length of the excerpt from Ginsberg's *Howl* (p. 1110).

STEVIE SMITH

Not Waving but Drowning (p. 885)

Stevie Smith, as both a poet and novelist, seems so much a part of London that it's a surprise to realize that she wasn't born there. She was born in Hull, in the west of England, as Florence Margaret Smith in 1903, but moved to London when she was three, and died there in 1971. She worked all her life as the private secretary to the managing directors of a large British magazine publisher, and she titled her first novel, published in 1936, *Novel on Yellow Paper*, as she'd written much of it in the office on the lined yellow sheets of her stenography pad. Her first collection of poems, *A Good Time Was Had by All*, was published the next year. Smith was very popular as a reader of her wry, witty writing on the BBC Radio, and her books had a wide audience. "Not Waving but Drowning" is based on a newspaper story Smith had read about a group of friends who, while picnicking on the beach, waved cheerily back to one of their group who had swum too far out and was desperately signaling for help.

Questions for Discussion

1. Is the drowned man accusing his companions of letting him drown?
2. In line 7, are the man's companions attempting to justify themselves?
3. In line 9, what is the drowned man saying about his life?

Topics for Writing

1. Smith has taken a simple news story and transformed it into an allegory of the victim's life. Discuss how she has done this.

2. Smith wrote this poem using both traditional and modern means, and the poem achieves the spontaneity of open-form verse within the stanza structure and a rhyme scheme of closed verse. Discuss how she accomplished this, analyzing the poem's meter and rhythm, including the notable half-rhyme of "moaning"/ "drowning."

GARY SNYDER

Milton by Firelight (p. 1195)
How to Make Stew in the Pinacate Desert (p. 1196)

Snyder's poetry is meant to be easily understood, and the only difficult allusion is the ironic quotation from John Milton that opens "Milton by Firelight." Before the end of the stanza, Milton's reference to the story of Adam and Eve is dismissed as "a silly story." Although Snyder begins the poem with a quotation from one of the classic English poets, he does not seem to be concerned with literary tradition: What does concern him is the destruction of the environment. As he writes in lines 22–24, in ten thousand years the mountains where he lives, the Sierras, will be "dry and dead, home of the scorpion." In line 25, Snyder alludes to Milton's poem again, stressing that there will be nothing so dramatic in the destruction of the Sierras, there will be "No paradise, no fall." In its reference to Milton, however, the poem can also be read as a meditation on one of the oldest forms of classic poetry, even though Snyder's language and context are entirely modern.

"How to Make Stew in the Pinacate Desert" has a subtitle, "Recipe for Locke & Drum," and this describes the poem. It is a recipe for cooking stew over an open fire in the Arizona desert with two close friends, Drummond and Locke Hadley. The commentary by Samuel Charters (p. 1245) suggests that the poem could also be read as a nature ceremony or ritual.

Questions for Discussion

1. Although the title tells us a great deal about "Milton by Firelight," it is necessary to read the entire poem to understand what Snyder is describing. If we make the association between lines 1–2 and lines 31–32, what is the scene of the poem, and why does Snyder begin with the lines from Milton? What is he alluding to in that particular quotation?

2. What does he mean by the phrase "our lost general parents" in line 11?

3. What is he alluding to in line 25, "No paradise, no fall"?

4. What is Snyder implying in line 28, "Man, with his Satan"?

5. What is Snyder saying about cattle in line 4 of "How to Make Stew"?

6. Should bisquick in line 5 and budweiser beer in line 29 have been capitalized? Why might Snyder have written them the way he did?

7. Line 10 suggests a ceremonial significance with the phrase "something free." What could Snyder have meant by this phrase?

8. What is he telling us with the description "black pot" in line 35?

Topic for Writing

1. "Milton by Firelight" can be described as a meditation, and "How to Make Stew" can be read as a ceremony. Students could relate the poems to some of humankind's oldest rituals.

GARY SOTO

Mexicans Begin Jogging (p. 1197)
Walking with Jackie, Sitting with a Dog (p. 1198)

Students will immediately recognize that "Mexicans Begin Jogging" is an ironic comment on the situation of immigrants — legal and illegal — along the border between the United States and Mexico. In the poem Soto pretends that none of the problems needs to be taken seriously. The title itself is a sardonic joke on Anglo-Americans' obsession with health and fitness. The "running" Soto describes is a rush by Mexicans to flee from the Border Patrol, but the effort is presented as mere exercise. Soto uses strong images to reinforce the dilemma: He works "under the press / of an oven yellow with flame"; as he runs through the streets he becomes the "wag to a short tail of Mexicans." The harsh reality that the people to whom he is running for protection work in the fields in the summer as laborers is emphasized by the metaphor in line 16, they "paled at the turn of an autumn sky."

"Walking with Jackie, Sitting with a Dog" is an affectionate portrait of a morning during the narrator's childhood when he and a friend go walking on a Saturday morning, when it's "as early as it's ever going to get." It is a simple moment, but Soto uses figures of speech and shifts of diction and syntax to turn his simple description into a poem. His mother's shouts that he should not go outside become the poetic phrase "a strained / Voice," in lines 4–5, using metonymy to substitute his mother's voice for the description of her objections to their going out. In a use of synecdoche, girls become "all legs." The most startling simile is his description "We grin / like shovels," and the most suggestive image is the assertion that "we're brothers / To all that's heaved over fences" in lines 15–16. Just as he maintained in "Mexicans Begin Jogging" that he could go into the next century "on the power in a great, silly grin," in this poem he insists that nobody ever has to struggle to stay alive because there is always something to eat — "oranges now and plums four months away."

Questions for Discussion

1. Why does Soto tell the story of "Mexicans Begin Jogging" as a joke?
2. Do any lines in the poem suggest that this might not be a joke?
3. What is Soto saying about the sociologist's description of Mexicans in line 18?
4. In "Walking with Jackie, Sitting with a Dog," what does he mean by line 20, "The scattered newspaper, cartwheeling across / A street, is one way to go"?
5. Why does the sun, in lines 24–25, mean "little"?

Topics for Writing

1. Students could discuss whether it was necessary for Soto to use irony in "Mexicans Begin Jogging."
2. Consider whether "Walking with Jackie, Sitting with a Dog" contains anything that would make the experience described specifically Mexican American.

WALLACE STEVENS

Thirteen Ways of Looking at a Blackbird (p. 966)

A useful approach to this enigmatic poem might be to gather thirteen critical ways of looking at "Thirteen Ways of Looking at a Blackbird." Here are three responses to the poem that may shed some light on its opacities.

HELEN VENDLER

Like other American poets influenced by the *chinoiserie* of Imagism, Stevens turned for a time from Western models to Eastern ones, and wrote his set of serial "views" after the manner of Chinese and Japanese painters, calling his set "Thirteen Ways of Looking at a Blackbird." In writing this poem, Stevens discovered his affinity for the aspectual poem — a series of variations on a theme.... Each of the "parts" of [the poem] is equally valid. Visual experience, measuring the world by eye, thus becomes the equable model (since we do not privilege one glance over another) for modern perception and cognition alike. Implication, innuendo, eccentricity of perspective, and summary aphorism become the condensed vehicles for Stevens's multiple "ways of looking." (From *Voices and Visions* [New York: Random House, 1987], p. 134)

HAROLD BLOOM

As the color black becomes [in the poem "Domination of Black"] the color or trope of *ethos* or Fate, so in "Thirteen Ways" it also serves as the emblem of Ananke, of Fate conceived as Necessity, where again Emerson is the likeliest origin for Stevens. Section VIII seems to me the revelation of the poem's disjunctiveness:

> I know noble accents
> And lucid, inescapable rhythms:
> But I know, too,
> That the blackbird is involved
> In what I know

What the poet knows is poetry, *materia poetica* and poetry being the same thing for Stevens. But there is no *materia poetica* without the domination of the blackbird, for the blackbird is Stevens's first thinker of the First Idea. And so he mixes in everywhere, including the union of a man and a woman. He is our knowledge, to use Stevens's very

American idiom, not just that it is snowing, but that it is going to snow. (From *Wallace Stevens* [Ithaca, N.Y.: Cornell University Press, 1977], p. 105)

WILLIAM BURNEY

"Thirteen Ways of Looking at a Blackbird" . . . begins and ends in the snow; and the permanence of the blackbird in this otherwise destructive element makes it the chief instance of a persona who has indeed a mind of winter. This poem — perhaps the most systemic exercise in epistemology that Stevens ever indulged in — . . . deserves careful explication. The poem begins in a cold, sublime setting. The speaker, or looker, is moved or disturbed by the eye of the blackbird. The rhythms are arranged to make "eye" a prolonged utterance to correspond with a prolonged and fascinated attention to it. The speaker is made self-conscious by the little blackbird's eye; he is not so much looking at the blackbird as being looked at by it. (From *Wallace Stevens* [New York: Twayne, 1968], p. 32)

Perhaps just as helpful is an unsigned comment by a *Time* magazine reviewer in 1953: "Few living poets can be as vivid and as vague, both at once."

Wallace Stevens was born in 1879, studied law at Harvard University and New York Law School, and, after an unsuccessful attempt to set up his own practice, became a legal counsel for the Hartford Accident and Indemnity Company in 1916. He remained with the company for the rest of his life, becoming a vice president in 1934. He was already writing poetry as a student, and he continued to write throughout his long business career. Stevens's bibliography might give the impression that his literary career began with the publication of his first book, *Harmonium*, in 1923, but this book and much of his other work until the late 1930s was published by coterie presses in small editions that failed even to sell their few hundred copies.

Although his work began to be available in larger editions after World War II, Stevens has pretty much remained a poet's poet: Outside of the academic world he is largely read and studied by other poets, and it is these other poets who have made "Thirteen Ways" so important. Reprinted in popular anthologies since the 1940s, it has strongly influenced young poets both in Europe and America, and it continues to fascinate new writers. Perhaps the poem is more accessible to poets because they don't have to try to understand it: They can simply let its juxtapositions, inferences, inflections, and innuendos work on their imaginations.

Stevens's *Collected Poems* appeared in 1955, the year of his death, and it won both the Pulitzer Prize and the National Book Award.

Question for Discussion

1. Students should read the text's linked sequence of four haikus by Bashō (p. 962). What similarities and differences are there between the style of Stevens's poem and that of the haiku sequence?

Topic for Writing

1. Have students choose any subject and, in the style of Stevens, write poems expressing their own thirteen ways of looking at it.

WISLAWA SZYMBORSKA

The Terrorist, He Watches (p. 992)

Wislawa Szymborska was born in Poland in 1923. She is a prolific writer and has published several collections of poetry, much of it deeply involved in social and feminist issues. She won the Nobel Prize for Literature in 1996.

Questions for Discussion

1. Discuss Szymborska's depiction of the terrorist. What does she convey to us about his reactions to those he watches?
2. Why does the poet continually present specific moments of time? What effect does she achieve by doing so?

Topic for Writing

1. **CONNECTIONS** In a one- to two-page essay, have students compare Szymborska's terrorist with Carolyn Forché's colonel (p. 989).

GENEVIEVE TAGGARD

With Child (p. 890)

Taggard was born in 1894 in a small town in Washington State and attended the University of California, where she edited the literary magazine. After living a brief period in New York City, where she helped found the literary magazine *The Measure*, she began teaching, first at Bennington College and then at Sarah Lawrence College. She died in New York in 1948.

Taggard was one of the talented group of women poets who were important figures in the American literary scene of the 1920s and 1930s — a group that included Edna St. Vincent Millay, Elinor Wylie, and Louise Bogan. "With Child," from Taggard's first collection, *For Eager Lovers* (1923), is a pioneering poem by a woman describing the physical aspects of pregnancy.

Questions for Discussion

1. To whom is the poem addressed?
2. Why does Taggard describe herself as a "worn" beast? What does she mean by "velvet-footed"?
3. In line 13, what does she mean by "Earth's urge, not mine"?
4. Discuss the contrasts between her depiction of herself as a young woman in the first stanza and the moods and attitudes of her unborn child in the final lines.

Topic for Writing

1. **CONNECTIONS** Compare Taggard's poem with Louise Glück's poem about her "experience" of her mother's pregnancy, "For My Mother " (p. 1118).

ALFRED, LORD TENNYSON

Ulysses (p. 1199)
Break, Break, Break (p. 1201)

Students will find Richard Wilbur's commentary, "Tennyson's Voyage of the Mind" (p. 1326), an illuminating analysis of the sources and poetic style in "Ulysses." "Break, Break, Break," written a year later, also laments the death of Tennyson's friend Arthur Hallam. The rhythm of the poem's first line evokes the sound of the sea crashing against rocks, but with its somber, repeated tones, it also evokes the sound of tolling funeral bells. Tennyson was one of the most rhythmically dextrous of the Victorian poets, and this brief lyric features continuing shifts in line length and stress, from the three strong beats that begin the poem to the fluid mixing of feet in the third line of each stanza.

Questions for Discussion

1. In line 4, Ulysses describes the country's laws as "unequal." It is unusual for a ruler to say this about his own country's laws; could this be one of the reasons for his discontent?
2. What is he saying about himself in line 11, "I am become a name"?
3. Why would anyone who has traveled widely use the phrase that Ulysses does in line 18, "I am part of all that I have met"?
4. Ulysses seems to be dismissing everyday life as meaningless in his image in line 24, "As though to breathe were life." Is this a reasonable interpretation?
5. In line 33, Tennyson begins the second long section of the poem with the words "This is my son." Is it ever made clear in the poem to whom he is speaking? Could the poem also be interpreted as a soliloquy?
6. In line 42, what does Tennyson mean by "household gods"?
7. What is he describing in line 58, "Push off, and sitting well in order smite / The sounding furrows"?
8. The class could discuss what sounds each student hears in the opening line of "Break, Break, Break."
9. In the second and third stanzas of the poem, Tennyson seems to be alluding to the three stages of life with "fisherman's boy," "sailor lad," and "stately ships." Was this interpretation intended?
10. Is there a contradiction in line 15, which speaks of the "tender grace" of "a day that is dead"?

Topics for Writing

1. Richard Wilbur, in his discussion of "Ulysses," contrasts Ulysses as the central figure and speaker in the poem with Ulysses as he was portrayed by Homer and also by Dante in the *Divine Comedy*. Ulysses, as far as we can tell, is only a figure in Homer's imagination. Students could discuss how a character in a writer's imagination can become the subject of a broader analysis of human nature.
2. "Break, Break, Break" can be read as a personal expression of Tennyson's grief at the death of a friend or as an expression of the grief that anyone feels in the presence of death. Students could analyze the poem in these terms.
3. "Break, Break, Break" is a marvel of versification. Students could examine the metric shifts within each line and the poem's overall pulse.

Dylan Thomas

In My Craft or Sullen Art (p. 1202)
Do Not Go Gentle into That Good Night (p. 1202)

Dylan Thomas's poetry was written for what could be described as a musical instrument — his own voice. He was one of the great readers of poetry, and recordings of his readings probably sold even more copies than his books. If students have the opportunity to listen to such a recording, they will immediately understand the methods of his poetry. If no recordings are available, certainly the poems should be read aloud in class.

The meter of Thomas's poetry is always flexible, and at the same time it is obvious to the listener. The basic meter of "In My Craft or Sullen Art" is trochaic tetrameter, but Thomas doesn't hesitate to add syllables or to use trimeter, as in line 9, which can be scanned as an awkward four-stress unit but read aloud as three. It is always Thomas's ear that makes the final decision. "In "Do Not Go Gentle into That Good Night" the basic meter is iambic pentameter, but the final line of the first stanza, repeated in three other stanzas, is heard as hexameter.

Each of the poems is a tour de force of rhyme. The rhyme scheme of "In My Craft" seems almost to be random but there is careful repetition in the two stanzas, even though the second is two lines shorter. The rhyme pattern of the first stanza is *abcdebdecca*. The second stanza repeats the rhymes of the first five and the last four lines, so it is *abcdeecca*. We hear the rhymes but not as an intrusive pattern. What we hear is the return of the *a* rhymes at the beginning and ending of each stanza — "art" / "heart" and "apart" / "art" — and the repeated *c* rhymes in the penultimate two lines of each stanza — "stages" / "wages" and "ages" / "wages." One of the challenges of musical composition is keeping listeners aware of where they are in the piece, and Thomas mastered this art as successfully as any poet ever has. "Do Not Go Gentle into That Good Night" is a villanelle, and students should read the section in the text (p. 957) that explains the villanelle's structure.

To match the poetry's rich musicality, Thomas used imagery that some critics consider forced or extravagant but that is nonetheless part of the effect of his poems when they are performed. Images such as "from the raging moon I write / On these spindrift pages" (from "In My Craft or Sullen Art") may seem overblown in classroom analysis, but the spoken words can be very moving. In the same poem we hear the allusion to Shakespeare — "strut . . . on the ivory stages" — reminding the reader of Macbeth's soliloquy, "Tomorrow and tomorrow." We also hear the irony of lines 4–5, "the lovers lie abed / With all their griefs in their arms." Lovers in bed embracing would be expected to be embracing their joys. Instead, Thomas is referring to love's dark side, its grief. Musical composition demands that if you do something unexpected, you should repeat it so that the listener will know the effect was intended. In line 17–18 Thomas repeats his image of "lovers, their arms / Round the griefs of the ages" so that his audience will be sure they heard him correctly.

"Do Not Go Gentle into That Good Night" is, on the surface, an exhortation to live fully and bravely up to the moment of death. Each of the kinds of men he names — wise men, good men, wild men, and grave men — should rage with regret that they didn't make more of their lives. The poem could also be read, however, as Thomas's attempt to justify his uncontrolled wildness to his dying father, or his dismay and fear that his father is so near death. The power of the poem comes from these emotional undercurrents.

Questions for Discussion

1. What is Thomas saying about poets in the first two lines of "In My Craft or Sullen Art"?
2. What does he mean by "common wages" in line 10?
3. What is he saying about some people in lines 12–13, "the proud man apart / From the raging moon"?
4. What is he saying about love in the two images of lovers in bed with their arms about their griefs?
5. In "Do Not Go Gentle into That Good Night," what does Thomas mean in line 5, "Because their words had forked no lightning"?
6. What is the contradiction he suggests in lines 10–11?
7. In line 17, is he asking his father to curse him, or bless him, or both?
8. What does he tell the reader about death in the term "that good night"?

Topics for Writing

1. In "In My Craft or Sullen Art" Thomas makes a distinction between a writer's craft and art. Students could discuss whether such a distinction exists.
2. Students could take examples from other love poems in the anthology and discuss Thomas's description, in line 18, of love as "griefs of the ages."
3. In his descriptions of different types of men in "Do Not Go Gentle into That Good Night," Thomas contrasts the ambitions and dreams of each kind of man with the disappointment of these men's actual achievement. Students could explicate the disappointments Thomas finds here.

ANNE WALDMAN

Our Past (p. 1203)
Marianne Moore (p. 1206)
To the Censorious Ones (p. 1206)

Waldman could be called a "vernacular" poet, as her language displays few "literary" overtones. "Our Past" is a direct, emotionally engaged account of a love affair that has ended unhappily. The poem is narrated with the simple expressiveness of a friend telling a story. The person to whom the narrator is telling the story is her lover, although it is clear that he is not present, and her poem is a kind of letter that will never be sent. Students should have no difficulty understanding it.

"Marianne Moore" describes a reading by the poet (see pp. 1153–1154), who was an important role model for generations of American women poets. In the poem Waldman has consciously or unconsciously adopted some of Moore's mannerisms. Words and phrases like "twilight beacon," "alchemist's stone," "askance," and "inexorably" echo Moore's vocabulary, and Waldman's explanation of her use of the word "it" in line 12 suggests Moore's precise sense of context. Waldman's assumption of some of Moore's ways of writing is the most sincere tribute one poet can pay another.

Waldman is a very popular performer and has won the All-American Poetry Slam Competition. Many of her performance pieces, such as her well-known "Fast Talking Woman," are long and are much more effective in performance. "To the Censorious Ones," however, is shorter, and its women's "chorus" is usually a success with audiences. By the term "censorious" Waldman means the negative criticism and denigration that some men have historically used to prevent women from achieving an equal role in society. In lines 17–18 she names some of the attitudes that men have scorned women for adopting: iconoclasm, bravado, and derision of patriotic rituals and military ceremonies. The poem is also an unmistakable allusion to the myth of Pandora and the box containing the world's ills, which was never supposed to be opened.

Questions for Discussion

1. Why does Waldman title the poem "Our Past" when what she describes is her own experience of the affair?
2. What do the many described trips and brief meetings tell us about Waldman's life?
3. In line 49 she writes, "You were having a public life. I felt you were turning into me." What is she saying about herself?
4. What does the dead bird in line 54 symbolize?
5. What is Waldman saying about the relationship in the last line?
6. In "Marianne Moore," what does Waldman mean by the terms "twilight beacon" and "alchemist's stone" in line 2?
7. What does she mean in lines 5–6, "A claim on us / Not negotiable"?
8. Why does she use the word "impasse" in line 14? Does she mean it humorously?
9. What does she mean by the phrase "music inexorably owned"?
10. In "To the Censorious Ones" Waldman uses the terms "Men of War" and "Censorious Ones" to address the men in the poem, then in line 8 she addresses them as "big boys." What does she suggest by this change?
11. In line 13 she describes the "hermetic" texts men tried to suppress. Why have men wanted these texts buried?
12. In line 20 she uses the term "dark fantasies." Is it the men's fantasies she is referring to?
13. Waldman's poem alludes to the myth of Pandora's box, but how is the contents of the box Waldman opens different from that of Pandora's?

Topics for Writing

1. Students could discuss whether the freedom described in the relationship of "Our Past" reflects Waldman's life as a poet or whether the poem reflects a new independence for women in emotional relationships.
2. Students could analyze the role Marianne Moore's poetry has played in the development of American women poets, using the examples of Elizabeth Bishop and Anne Waldman.

(text pp. 1203–1207)

Suggested Readings

Ann Charters. *The Portable Beat Reader*. New York: Viking/Penguin, 1992. 421–424.

ALICE WALKER

How Poems Are Made / A Discredited View (p. 879)

Alice Walker was born in 1944 in Eatonton, Georgia, the daughter of a poor African American farmer. She graduated from Sarah Lawrence College in 1965 and began teaching writing and African American literature in southern black colleges. She has been successful as a poet, novelist, essayist, and writer of short fiction (see p. 697 for her story "Roselily"). Her novel *The Color Purple* was an international best-seller and was made into an equally successful film. She currently lives in San Francisco.

Although much of Walker's work focuses on the African American experience and the oppression of women, this is a simple, thoughtful reflection on the way a poem can come to its writer.

Questions for Discussion

1. What is Walker saying about her emotions in the first stanza?
2. What is the rhythmic change in lines 5–8? Could it be intended as a crooning, half-chanted interjection?
3. Why does Walker suggest that "leftover love . . . runs and hides"? What could it be ashamed of?
4. In line 16 , does she mean — in the phrase "upbeat memories" — that her memories are positive?
5. What does she mean by "The flagged beats of the running/ heart" in lines 17–18?
6. What is she describing in lines 20–23?

Topics for Writing

1. Walker uses the term "gradually" to describe how she comes to understand how poems are made. Discuss what she is telling the reader about the poetic process with the word "gradually."
2. Discuss what Walker means by describing a poem as a "place" she can bring things to.

PHILLIS WHEATLEY

To the Right Honourable William, Earl of Dartmouth (p. 1208)

On Being Brought from Africa to America (p. 1209)

Phillis Wheatley's poems were published when she was about twenty, and because some time had passed since their writing, we have to conclude that she was only a teenager when she wrote them. Although in her own time the wonder was that a woman from Africa could write any kind of poetry at all, the wonder for readers today is that she was such an extremely precocious, talented young poet. Wheatley's poems are written in the high Augustan style, and in these two examples she reveals her mastery of the style's elevated vocabulary and complex structuring. If she had lived longer her poetry would certainly have become more individual, but the writing she did have time to complete demonstrates a high level of accomplishment.

"To the Right Honourable William, Earl of Dartmouth" mixes flattery and supplication as Wheatley thanks the North American secretary of state, which was Dartmouth's position in the English government, for a slackening of the tight string of laws and regulations that bound the colonies to England, and asks, in line 33, that he renew his favors. The poignancy of the poem is felt in the fourth stanza, when she addresses Dartmouth personally as an African American woman who has experienced slavery. As she writes in line 30, "can I then but pray / Others may never feel tyrannic sway?" In her shorter poem, "On Being Brought from Africa to America," Wheatley again speaks in the personal voice of someone who has been a slave, and she goes as far as she dares to admonish those who are prejudiced against her, reminding them that as fellow Christians, "Negros" may also be welcomed into heaven.

Questions for Discussion

1. Is "To the Right Honorable" a political poem? What is its message to the earl of Dartmouth?
2. What does Wheatley mean by the phrase in line 25, "Afric's fancy'd happy seat"?
3. Who does she mean by the term "that soul" in line 28?
4. In the first two lines of "On Being Brought" the poet describes herself as fortunate to have been brought from Africa. Why does she say this?
5. What is meant by "diabolic die" in line 6?

Topic for Writing

1. Wheatley expresses her feelings about being brought from Africa in both of these poems, emphasizing different aspects of the experience in each. Students could compare her feelings in the two poems and describe the differences.

Related Commentaries

Michael S. Harper, "On Black American and African Writing," p. 1265.
Robert Hayden, "On Negro Poetry," p. 1266.

WALT WHITMAN

Out of the Cradle Endlessly Rocking (p. 1210)
Beat! Beat! Drums! (p. 1215)
By the Bivouac's Fitful Flame (p. 1215)
When I Heard the Learn'd Astronomer (p. 1216)
A Noiseless Patient Spider (p. 1216)
Good-bye My Fancy! (p. 1216)

The instructor will find two commentaries on Whitman in Chapter 18, as well as a section from Whitman's introduction to the first edition of *Leaves of Grass*, as it was published in 1855. Students might empathize with the commentary by poet Robert Creeley (p. 1250), who recalls the difficulty he had reading Whitman's poetry when he was a student himself. Ezra Pound's response to Whitman (p. 1300) is particularly interesting because it reflects the opinion of most intellectuals of the modernist period. Whitman's introduction to his first collection of poems (p. 1323) is more of a celebration of poetry and his dream of a national culture than it is an explanation of his new poetic idiom, but it will help students to understand some of the attitudes and emotions beneath his writing.

OUT OF THE CRADLE ENDLESSLY ROCKING

The poem, one of Whitman's greatest achievements, first appeared (under the title "A Child's Reminiscence") on the front page of the *Saturday Press* on December 24, 1859, as a Christmas present to its readers. There have been many "readings" of the poem, often straining to tie it to something hidden or misunderstood in Whitman's life, or to interpret it as a metaphor for some emotion that Whitman was unconscious of himself, but this takes away something that students should never forget when they read Whitman's poetry. To borrow a term from the poet Gary Snyder, this takes away his "writerliness." The poem was first and foremost written by Whitman to become part of a new edition of *Leaves of Grass*, and if there are whispers from Whitman's unconscious as he composed it, they are only one of the elements in the poem's texture. The poem yields much more if it is read as the front-page Christmas offering of a popular magazine. There on the page is a memory of a childhood experience that impelled Whitman to write poetry and taught him the meaning of death.

A more immediate challenge to students reading the poem for the first time will certainly be its length. Poetry is so often concentrated, and the largest thoughts can be presented in a handful of lines. Students will find, however, that Whitman's most important poems will take more of their time. The poem's exposition — the preliminary section in which Whitman explains that he is going to recall something from his childhood — is itself more than twenty long lines. What Whitman tells us is that one September night — "the Ninth-month midnight" — when he was a boy, he crept out of bed and went to the shore of Long Island Sound, which was just behind the farmhouse where he lived. This opening explanation is spread through the twenty lines, and the richness of the poetic material makes it difficult to follow. Each line might be the point when the poem starts, and so many of the lines have a haunting beauty of their own — for instance, "Out of the cradle endlessly rocking" or "From under that yellow half-moon late-risen and swollen as if with tears" or "From the thousand responses of my heart never to cease."

Whitman's reminiscence begins at line 23, "Once Paumanok." The previous May he had discovered two migratory birds that had flown north from Alabama and were nesting on the shore. He went to watch them every day — "never too close, never disturbing them." In line 32 we hear for the first time one of the birds singing — it is a melody Whitman describes as an aria, and for him an opera aria was the highest form of music. Then one morning he notices that the female bird has failed to come back to the nest, and she never returns. For the rest of the summer the boy could hear the male bird lamenting the loss of his mate. Lines 52–54 sing the first notes of the bird's mournful song. Whitman remembers that he could hear the bird at night, when he stole carefully down to the beach in the darkness, staying out of the moonlight so that the bird would not see him. In the darkness the boy could see Long Island Sound, and he describes it in his unforgettable metaphor for the waves in line 66, "the white arms out in the breakers tirelessly tossing." He stood by the water, the wind "wafting" his hair, listening.

The bird's sorrowing aria is fifty-nine lines long, but in the whole structure of the poem its length balances Whitman's act of remembering. The song ends, and as the boy stands at the shore, the mournful sound of the surf suddenly tells him that the song could have been for him. His description for himself is now "outsetting bard," which means that he is setting out to be a poet. In lines 144–147 he says,

> Demon or bird! (said the boy's soul,)
> Is it indeed to your mate you sing? or is it really to me?
> For I, that was a child, my tongue's use sleeping, now I have heard you,
> Now in a moment I know what I am for . . .

His destiny has now been assured, and in lines 158–59 he wants to know what last secret has been withheld from him. The sea, "Delaying not, hurrying not," whispers to him as he stays that night on the beach, whispers over and over the word "death." In the final short section Whitman reaffirms that his own "song" was awakened from that hour, and in the penultimate line we learn the meaning of the first line of the poem, "Out of the cradle endlessly rocking." The cradle is the sea, endlessly in motion, "some old crone rocking the cradle," that whispers to him. Was the cry of the sad, lonely bird in the long aria a veiled cry for something or someone that Whitman had lost and that he could only express in his poem? Alterations in the manuscript drafts suggest that other meanings might have been intended, but there is really no way to know more than what he has told us in the poem.

Questions for Discussion

1. The poem's first fifteen lines all begin with prepositions — "out," "down," "up," "out," and "from." What does Whitman mean by them?
2. In line 10, what is he describing about the moon? Is this appearance of the moon something students have seen themselves?
3. In line 13 he uses the phrase "thence-roused words," which will be one of the poem's major themes. What does Whitman mean by the phrase?
4. What do the flock of birds in lines 15–17 represent?
5. Why does Whitman use the word "aria" for the bird's song?

6. Many critics have pointed out the sexual imagery of the first eight lines of the bird's song, beginning at line 71. Might this be an unconscious projection of Whitman's own emotions?

7. In line 99 he describes the bird's song as a "carol." Why has he changed the word he uses for the bird's melody?

8. In line 139 he suggests that he has never cried before. What is he telling us about his childhood?

9. In line 150 he says that the bird in its solitary singing is "projecting me." What does he mean by this?

Topics for Writing

1. The poem contains many images of the sea as a mother, and the title describes the rocking movement of the waves. Students could discuss this imagery of the sea, particularly comparing the differing ways in which Whitman describes the sea as "mother."

2. Students could explicate Whitman's references to finding his own poetic voice during those nights on the beach.

3. The boyhood memory that begins the poem is overlaid with Whitman's mature understanding of what the experience of hearing the bird meant to him as a boy. Students could discuss which elements of the poem are derived from the boy's memory and which come from the older man's reflections.

BEAT! BEAT! DRUMS!
BY THE BIVOUAC'S FITFUL FLAME
WHEN I HEARD THE LEARN'D ASTRONOMER

Whitman was never satisfied with the form of *Leaves of Grass*, and in each of the editions he published during his lifetime he rearranged and rewrote the poems, often changing titles and sometimes dropping poems entirely. The poems of the "Drum-Taps" section of *Leaves of Grass* were published as a separate book in the spring of 1865, and for some time Whitman considered them as separate from the rest of his poetry. Certainly the original group of *Drum-Taps* poems are different stylistically. They are generally shorter; the subject is no longer Whitman and his optimistic dream of a new American society; and the poems have a clear focus in his everyday experiences as a hospital aide in Washington, D.C., nursing the wounded of the Civil War battles that were being fought often within hearing of the city.

Drum-Taps was also rearranged after its first publication, but it was tragic circumstances and not any uncertainty about the book that caused Whitman to alter it. The book was published a few weeks before Lincoln's murder, and during the days of national mourning and the funeral procession across America with Lincoln's body, Whitman wrote his elegy "When Lilacs Last in the Dooryard Bloom'd" and his shorter dirge "O Captain! My Captain!" He then had them printed and bound into the remaining copies of the book. *Drum-Taps* was a small, brown book, somber in appearance and different in many ways from *Leaves of Grass*. Although it is less challenging than the larger book, it is Whitman's most artistically consistent volume. Characteristically, when Whitman incorporated the poems into subsequent editions of *Leaves of Grass*, he rearranged the order, dropping some of the poems, and the final "Drum-Taps" group in the larger book doesn't have the clear focus of the smaller collection as it was originally published.

"Beat! Beat! Drums!" is one of the best known of the *Drum-Taps* poems, vividly capturing the first moments of the war, when it burst on the country with the clamor that Whitman describes. His habit of lists, which he used in many of his long poems, works effectively here, as the thunder of the drums and bugles reaches everyone in the churches and the schools, the bridegroom and the farmer, the people in the cities and on the streets. In the second stanza he describes the things that the clamor of the drums and bugles will stop, including sleep, business, and singing, and if these things don't stop then he admonishes the drums to "rattle quicker, heavier" and the bugles to "wilder blow." In the third stanza he commands the drums and bugles to stop for no one, not for the timid, the weeper, the person who is praying, the old, the child, the mother — not even for the dead, as he tells the drums and bugles to shake the wooden supports that were put up under coffins. Students will notice how the rhythms differ from the longer lines of "Out of the Cradle Endlessly Rocking." The lines clatter with onomatopoeia, and they are written in much tighter rhythms than those in "Out of the Cradle." Even the longer lines, such as 5 and 6, divide in the middle, so that they are heard as short, abrupt phrases.

"By the Bivouac's Fitful Flame" is one of the book's many short poems that foreshadow a number of the characteristics of modern verse. There is none of the framing within a generalization or a moral conclusion that was so typical of nineteenth-century poetry. "By the Bivouac" could be considered the prototype of an imagist poem, and it may have been just such a poem that caused Ezra Pound in his essay to admit that although he tried to dismiss Whitman, "when I write of certain things I find myself using his rhythms." The scene in the poem has a dreamlike quality, but Whitman was drawing on personal experience of the life of a soldier in the field. He had spent time in a bivouac with his brother, who was with a regiment close to Washington, D.C. As he did in the opening section of "Out of the Cradle Endlessly Rocking," Whitman delays telling the reader what the poem is about until nearly the end. He describes a procession winding around him as he sits by a campfire outside of a tent; then just as he is about to tell us what the procession is, he breaks off and describes the dark scene, the night camp barely stirring. In one strong image he seems to see the bushes and trees watching him as he sits there on the ground. As in the other *Drum-Taps* poems, the descriptive lines are short, and the scene is distinctly sketched. In the penultimate line he tells us that what he feels winding around him is a procession of thoughts of home.

Although Whitman opened himself to every kind of experience, he was impatient with learned explanations of his experience. There were so many things, he knew, that couldn't be contained within formal explanations or studied responses. "When I Heard the Learn'd Astronomer" is the clearest expression of these feelings, and it is one of Whitman's most frequently anthologized poems. In the poem he describes trying to listen to an astronomer explain the stars with "figures . . . ranged in columns" and "charts and diagrams," but the lecture, despite much applause, makes him "tired and sick," and in his quiet protest he goes out into the night and stares up "in perfect silence at the stars." Many students will have stood in the darkness themselves and experienced Whitman's wonder at the night sky.

Questions for Discussion

1. "Beat! Beat! Drums!" has many examples of alliteration. What are some of the more obvious ones?

2. In the second line Whitman could have used the definite article "the" in the phrase "through doors," which would have given the first half of the line a regular trochaic meter. Why do you think he didn't?

3. Whitman takes on the role of enthusiastic encourager as he exhorts the drums and bugles to sound the war alarms. Does this suggest that he welcomed the Civil War, or that he is only being swept along in the excitement of the moment?

4. Why does he change the "beat" to "thump" in his call to the drums in the last line?

5. There is also considerable alliteration in "By the Bivouac's Fitful Flame." What examples can students find in the first two lines?

6. How does the line structure of this poem differ from that of "Beat! Beat! Drums!"?

7. What figure of speech is Whitman using in his image of the shrubs and trees watching him?

8. Line 4 begins with five even stresses in iambic meter, then the line breaks before the last phrase. What is the term for the break?

9. Many of Whitman's poems, even the shorter ones, contain lists. What does he list in "When I Heard the Learn'd Astronomer"?

10. What does he contrast with the applause in the hall?

11. Why does he use the word "unaccountable" in line 5?

Topics for Writing

1. In "Beat! Beat! Drums!" the list of people and occupations Whitman is telling the drums to arouse is a cross section of the society of his time, complete with its peaceful farmers, scholars, lawyers, and speculators. Students could describe what this list might include to present a cross section of today's society.

2. Students could discuss which elements of "By the Bivouac's Fitful Flame" point the way to modernist poetry.

3. There is a strong streak of anti-intellectualism in the American character. Students could examine the nature of this anti-intellectualism in terms of "When I Heard the Learn'd Astronomer."

A Noiseless Patient Spider

In this short poem written after his experience of the war years, Whitman identifies with the small patient spider that he watches sending out threads from its body, waiting for them to catch on to something. He feels that his soul is doing the same thing, sending out messages, waiting for them to connect. One of the most marked differences between Whitman's worldview and that of most of his contemporaries is Whitman's refusal to assume that beyond himself and his consciousness there is a God. The spider is exploring "vacant vast space;" Whitman is sending out his signals in "measureless oceans of space." This poem has been interpreted as an expression of religious feelings because of the term "my soul," but Whitman could also be seeking a comrade, a companion, and what his soul is seeking is a bridge to this other soul.

Questions for Discussion

1. What things does Whitman list in this poem?

2. Why, in line 4, does he repeat the word "filament" three times instead of simply writing the plural of the word?
3. Is he saying in the poem that he feels as isolated as the spider?
4. Is his isolation spiritual or physical?
5. What does he mean by the word "them" in line 8? Is it clear what connections he is seeking?
6. What interpretations do the terms "ductile anchor" and "gossamer thread" suggest? What is Whitman telling us emotionally about these terms?

Topic for Writing

1. Students could compare the images of the spider and Whitman's soul, emphasizing the feelings of isolation expressed for each.

GOOD-BYE MY FANCY!

After a thorough reshaping of *Leaves of Grass* for a new edition in 1881, Whitman left the order and the text of the poems unchanged but continued to write short poems, despite the effects of a severe stroke. He collected the new poems into slim volumes that he published as "annexes," so it was clear that, unlike the *Drum-Taps* poems, these were part of his larger work. "Good-bye My Fancy!" was the title poem of the last of the annexes. It is a poem of farewell, but it is certainly one of the most joyous farewell poems ever written. The self-portrait Whitman had presented in all of the versions of his book had been of the rough comrade who absorbed life, lived it fully, and held on to it with joy and delight. His poem of good-bye is a last glimpse of this self-portrait. By his "Fancy" does he mean someone he has loved, the person that any of us has loved, or the creative impulse that gave him his poetry? Students might want to discuss what the poem seems to say about this.

Questions for Discussion

1. What are some possible interpretations of the word "fancy," particularly in reference to lines 16–17?
2. What hope does the poet hold out for the future?
3. What does Whitman mean when he suggests in lines 15–16 that he and his fancy might "learn something," or that they might find the "true songs"?
4. What is he telling us with the line "Yet let me not be too hasty"? What is he specifically referring to in the previous line?
5. In line 17, what does he mean by the term "mortal knob"?
6. Whitman adds the word "hail" to the last line. Why does he do so?

Topics for Writing

1. Students could describe their views of the way death is treated in this poem. Does Whitman present any Christian ideas of heaven and eternity?
2. The poem seems to develop its ideas as it goes. Students could discuss how Whitman's thoughts and feelings change as he is writing.

A Note on Whitman's Sexuality

In the classroom the instructor may be questioned about Whitman's sexuality. Was he homosexual? As we use the word today, no. Did he have some kind of same-sex experience as a young man? Perhaps, but the mid-nineteenth century was a different world from ours. Marriage was almost impossible unless there was some sort of economic security, and relationships with young women of middle-class background were severely circumscribed by guardians, religious scruples, and the lack of adequate methods of contraception. The cities thronged with prostitutes, and gonorrhea and syphilis were widespread and virtually incurable. The list of nineteenth-century authors who ended their lives insane from the effects of syphilis is discouragingly long. Whitman does write specifically about mastur-bation, but he feels, like most reformers of his time, that it is an evil practice that destroys the body, the mind, and the soul. In one poem, "Spontaneous Me," as David S. Reynolds points out in *Walt Whitman's America: A Cultural Biography* (1995), Whitman writes of nocturnal emission with some consciousness that the young man might experience "strange, half-welcome pangs, visions, sweats," but the man at the same time feels "red, ashamed, angry."

Perhaps because of the prohibitions surrounding sexual expression there were compensations in intense friendships between men and between women. The words that Whitman uses can, in themselves, confuse his readers. "Lover" meant someone for whom there were strong feelings of friendship. "Orgy" was simply a word for party. Because of the crowding and inadequate housing, it was very common for a man to share a bed with another man — or sometimes two or three other men — just as it was common for women to sleep together. If these men were sincere friends, there was usually an embrace and some kisses. If anything more happened, between young men it was often mutual masturbation. In our society a same-sex experience is interpreted to mean that the parties are gay or lesbian. In Whitman's time it was simply considered an expression of one's irrepressible sexual urges.

But what do we know of any same-sex relationships that Whitman might have had? The truth is, nothing. As Reynolds points out, "His sister Mary had five children: although next to nothing is known about her, we know for certain five more things about her sex life than about Walt's" (p. 197). Did Whitman feel a strong emotional attachment to a man, and did he have strong homoerotic desires? This seems certain from the poetry. His friends when he was younger, however, were heterosexual, and a letter from a woman at the time seems clearly to indicate that they had made love the night before. In Washington in the mid-1860s he developed an intense emotional relationship with a working man named Peter Doyle, who was young enough to be Whitman's son. In a diary entry in 1870 he castigates himself for his intense feelings for Doyle, saying specifically that Doyle feels differently. They were physically close, but it seems from his diary note that Doyle would not permit anything beyond the conventional expressions of friendly affection common at the time. The longest poetic expression of one man's love for another in nineteenth-century literature is Tennyson's elegy for his friend Arthur Hallam, *In Memoriam*, but contemporary readers did not assume that the relation-ship was sexual.

This still leaves the questions as to why Whitman is so widely considered to have been homosexual, and why his poetry has such a central place in the gay literary consciousness. In his own time, and for years thereafter, the difficulty most middle-class readers had with Whitman was what they considered were his hopeless wallowings in sexual relationships with women. When an English writer, Arthur Symonds, questioned Whitman closely about what Symonds and other European writers felt were homosexual suggestions in the "Calamus" section in the third edition of *Leaves of Grass*, Whitman was stunned. He blustered and exaggerated in his denial, but there is no mistaking his dismay. What gay and lesbian communities have found in Whitman is a portrayal of love that is so open and so free that there is room for any expression of love. Whitman is the only major poet from the past whose work does not exclude the possibility of a love that crosses sexual boundaries. For this, and for the ambiguity of the love he expresses in some of his major poems, he will continue to be a voice that the homosexual community feels speaks for them.

Suggested Reading

Reynolds, David S. *Walt Whitman's America: A Cultural Biography.* New York: Vintage Books, 1995.

WILLIAM CARLOS WILLIAMS

The Red Wheelbarrow (p. 965)
Classic Scene (p. 966)
Tract (p. 1218)
Spring and All (p. 1219)
This Is Just to Say (p. 1220)
The Dance (p. 1220)

William Carlos Williams's poetry emphasizes the personal, the local, and the domestic. Of the major modernist poets (H.D., Eliot, Pound, and Stevens), he is the least "literary." His poems contain no hidden motifs, symbolic inferences, or complex allusions. As he said of his own aims, "no ideas, but in things," and he described a poem as "a small machine made out of words."

TRACT

"Tract" can be read as its title suggests. *The Oxford Pocket Dictionary* defines a tract as "a short treatise, especially one on a religious subject." Williams's poem is a treatise instructing his neighbors on how to bury their dead. Williams spent much of his career as a writer striving to achieve an idiom and expression that would be purely American, but in this poem, ironically, he is trying to convince his neighbors to imitate burial customs of the French countryside and to do away with the conventional American parade of limousines led by a flower-filled hearse.

Questions for Discussion

1. What does Williams mean in the first stanza when he says that his neighbors "have it over a troop / of artists" and that they "have the ground sense necessary"?
2. What is he telling people in asking for a weathered wagon or a rough dray?
3. What is he suggesting about the dead person in line 44, "even flowers if he had come to that"?
4. Why, in lines 46–57, does he insist that the driver shouldn't ride on the wagon?

5. What does he mean when he writes "us" in line 65, and what does he mean by the phrase "money in your pockets"?

Spring and All

This poem first appeared in a book Williams paid to have published in the south of France, *Spring and All*. It consists of short prose paragraphs, poems, works-in-progress, opinions, and reflections. There is no order or structure to the book, and its mood reflects Williams's disappointment at what he felt was his failure as a writer. At this point he had no publisher, except for coterie literary magazines, and he paid for what books he did publish. He was also furious at the success of T. S. Eliot's *The Waste Land*, which had appeared the previous year. It is possible that Williams had the opening lines of Eliot's poem, "April is the cruelest month / Breeding lilacs out of the dead land," somewhere in his mind when he wrote "Spring and All." Certainly the theme of Williams's poem is suggested by these lines from *The Waste Land*: "What are the roots that clutch, what branches grow / Out of this stony rubbish?"

This poem is one of Williams's best, perhaps his finest single lyric. Its theme is one of poetry's oldest — the renewal of life that comes with spring — but Williams more than delineates what is there before his eyes. In the first thirteen lines he makes the reader conscious of this moment of early spring as it lives in his or her own memory. The adjectives of lines 14–15 — "lifeless," "sluggish," "dazed" — come as a natural extension of the bleakness the poet sees in the raw day. There is some ambiguity in the word "they," which begins (at line 16) what could be termed the poem's second half. It is not until line 20 that the poet begins to name what he means by the word: "they" are the plants that come alive out of the devastation of winter. In the poem's unforgettable last lines, Williams describes these plants as "rooted," taking a new grip on the earth as they waken.

In the last images, or in the earlier description of the new growth entering the world "naked, / cold, uncertain," it is impossible to forget that Williams was a pediatrician who delivered thousands of babies into the world.

Questions for Discussion

1. Is there any symbolic meaning to the words "contagious hospital," or is that simply the road Williams was driving that day?
2. Why does he use the noun "waste" in line 5?
3. In the first section the colors of the earth are "brown" and "muddy." What colors does Williams contrast these with later in the poem?
4. In line 19, what does he mean by saying that the wind is "familiar"?
5. In line 23, what does the word "it" refer to?

Topic for Writing

1. Students could compare the descriptions of spring in Williams's poem and in T. S. Eliot's *The Waste Land*.

The Red Wheelbarrow

"The Red Wheelbarrow" was also included in *Spring and All* and was reprinted in a pamphlet of experimental poetry that was published in Europe the next year. In *Modern American Poetry, 1865–1950,* Fred Moramarco presents a plausible reading of this much discussed poem:

> His famous poem, "The Red Wheelbarrow," much anthologized and overexplained, is nonetheless an excellent example of his poetry. . . . It shows his sharpness of visual perception — the way he looks at the world with a painter's eye. The simple and direct message of the poem is the importance of observing carefully, of opening our eyes to the physical world around us. . . . Apart from the first two lines, this little machine made of words is a nearly pure imagist poem that calls the reader's attention to a simple but precisely composed scene. The first two lines create a tension and tease us with an unsupported assertion — "so much depends / upon" — and the reader expects some important religious, scientific, or philosophical statement to follow. Instead there follows a simple painterly description of a bucolic scene. I say "painterly" because Williams constructs this poem almost as if it were a painting, isolating color, shape, object, texture, and relationship. Notice how the poem's scene unfolds, word by word — *red, wheel, barrow,* and so on — until the whole picture comes into view like a developing photograph. Once the picture comes into focus, the reader cannot help but refer back to the beginning of the poem and ask why it is that so much depends on these things. So much depends, Williams seems to be saying, on paying attention to the colors, shapes, textures, and relationships between the objects that are right in front of you, and what happened to be in front of him when he conceived this poem was a red wheelbarrow and some chickens. He took what was "close to the nose" and put it in a poem that invites the reader to do the same. (From Alan Shucard, Fred Moramarco, William Sullivan, *Modern American Poetry, 1865–1950* [Amherst: U of Massachusetts P, 1990], p. 153)

Question for Discussion

1. What does Williams achieve with the phrase "glazed with rain"?

CLASSIC SCENE

This poem was written in the 1930s, and it is impossible not to associate it with the decade's industrial images — mills, railroads, factories, the new scenery of the photographs of Walker Evans, Margaret Bourke-White, and Charles Sheeler. Williams wrote about the work of many artists, and he also contributed articles to small magazines that emphasized the new problems of labor and industry. Students will notice the personification of the building and chimneys in the first lines. It is also impossible not to relate the term "squalid shacks" to the social criticism of the period, when much writing was directed at America's massive unemployment and social upheaval.

Questions for Discussion

1. Why does Williams title this poem "Classic Scene"?
2. Why is he so specific about naming the material of the chimneys?
3. Why does he use the word "passive" in the last line?
4. Explain the personification of the poem.

(text pp. 965, 966, 1217–1221)

Topics for Writing

1. Students could discuss the elements that make this an imagist poem.
2. Students could analyze the ways in which the colors Williams uses in the poem relate to painting.

THIS IS JUST TO SAY

Williams is supposed to have left this note for his wife, Flossie, on the kitchen table. It is one of his most popular poems, probably because it evokes an image of emotional closeness and warm domesticity. Few modern poets have described anything in their lives as so comfortable and so ordinary, and at the same time — as he tells the reader that the plums were "so sweet / and so cold" — so filled with wonder.

Topic for Writing

1. This poem could just as well be written in prose form, as a note. Students could discuss whether it would still be a poem.

THE DANCE

If students have studied W. H. Auden's poem "Musée des Beaux Arts," they have already read another poet's response to a painting by Pieter Brueghel the Elder. Williams was not literary, but he had considered a career as a painter when he was young, and his eye continually sought out the visual. This is a peasant dance, and Williams has unconsciously used a different vocabulary — words like "squeal," "blare," and "tweedle" and archaic phrasing such as "rollicking measure" and "prance as they dance."

Questions for Discussion

1. Why does Williams repeat the word "round" in the opening lines, then repeat it again when he describes the bellies of the dancers?
2. What figure of speech is Williams using by describing the bagpipes with words like "squeal," "blare," and "tweedle"?
3. What does he mean by "whose wash they impound" in line 6?
4. In line 9 he uses the term "Fair Grounds." Is this a conscious anachronism?
5. What does Williams mean in line 9, "those / shanks must be sound"?

Topic for Writing

1. **CONNECTIONS** Students could compare "The Dance" with W. H. Auden's "Musée des Beaux Arts" (p. 1022).

Related Commentaries

Ezra Pound, "On the Principles of Imagism," p. 1297.
William Carlos Williams, "Ezra Pound's Language," p. 1329.

WILLIAM WORDSWORTH

I Wandered Lonely as a Cloud (p. 915)
My Heart Leaps Up (p. 916)
We Are Seven (p. 925)
Nuns Fret Not (p. 947)
Ode: Intimations of Immortality (p. 1222)

Students should read Wordsworth's Introduction to the second edition of his *Lyrical Ballads* in Chapter 18 (p. 1330). This essay not only provides insights into Wordsworth's writing, but it also includes the poet's lengthy justification of the use of natural speech and idioms in poetry. If students substitute "ordinary, everyday life" for "low and rustic life" and "ordinary people" for "these men," they will realize that Wordsworth was anticipating much of today's poetry. We accept our ordinary language for the very reasons Wordsworth suggested — because we believe this language to be "a more permanent, and a far more philosophical language, than that which is frequently substituted for it by poets," by which he means a poetic language created by an educated elite.

WE ARE SEVEN

Although Wordsworth proposed a poetic style based on rural speech, he was too close to the Augustan age to free himself entirely from its poetic idiom. It was his longer odes in a neoclassical style that attracted early readers. The rural ballads and short pieces he wrote in an idiom closer to folk vernacular were largely ignored, although the best of them have an emotional directness that some of his more philosophical poetry lost. The ballad "We Are Seven" is the earliest of Wordsworth's poems in this selection. It is from the first edition of *Lyrical Ballads,* and its theme is closest to what he proclaimed in the Introduction of 1802, "The principle object, which I proposed to myself in these poems was to choose incidents and situations from common life." Stylistically, the poem is very close to a folk ballad. It is written in four-line stanzas rhyming *abab,* with alternating lines of iambic tetrameter and trimeter. Its sentimental depiction of the little girl's unwavering faith is also close to the folk tradition.

Questions for Discussion

1. In Wordsworth's time the term "cottage girl" had a specific connotation. What did Wordsworth mean by it?
2. Before this century, infant mortality was high, and it was common for families to lose many young children. Is this familiarity with death the reason for the little girl's acceptance of the loss of her brother and sister, or is the reason her religious faith?
3. What does she say in the poem that suggests that her religious faith helps her to deal with death?
4. What is the little girl suggesting in line 37, "Their graves are green"?

Topic for Writing

1.   **CONNECTIONS** Students could compare this "literary" ballad with the folk ballads in the text (pp. 921–24), examining how the author's anonymity or familiarity affects our understanding of the work.

MY HEART LEAPS UP
I WANDERED LONELY AS A CLOUD

These are two of Wordsworth's best known short lyrics, each written after the ballad "We Are Seven." His subject is no longer "incidents and situations from common life." Instead, he is writing of his own emotional response to the beauty of nature. Students will remember the later section in his Introduction to *Lyrical Ballads*, when he declares that "all good poetry is the spontaneous overflow of powerful feelings," which precisely characterizes "My Heart Leaps Up." The next paragraph of the Introduction includes the statement that poetry "takes its origin from emotion recollected in tranquility," which is a precise characterization of "I Wandered Lonely as a Cloud."

Written in 1802, the same year as the Introduction, "My Heart Leaps Up" describes Wordsworth's immediate, spontaneous response to the beauty of a rainbow. He feels the same excitement now as he did when he was a child, and he says that if he doesn't feel this same excitement when he grows old and sees a rainbow, then "let me die." In one of his most famous lines, "The Child is father of the Man" (line 7), he looks back to the days when he was a child and wishes he might always feel the same response to God and nature. In "I Wandered Lonely as a Cloud," written two years later, he looks back and remembers the dazzling beauty of a bank of wild daffodils in bloom that he saw along a lake shore. He says that now when he is resting or thinking he will suddenly remember the beautiful sight and will feel the same pleasure. It is this that he meant by "emotion recollected in tranquility."

Questions for Discussion

1.   In "My Heart Leaps Up," what is Wordsworth saying with line 7, "The Child is father of the Man"? Could he mean that the child is the father's instructor?
2.   What does he mean by the term "natural piety" that ends the poem?
3.   In "I Wandered Lonely as a Cloud," what figure of speech is Wordsworth using in line 12, "Tossing their heads in sprightly dance"? What is the comparison?
4.   In line 22 he describes the "bliss of solitude." What does this tell us about Wordsworth?

Topics for Writing

1.   Students could discuss the ways in which two comments from Wordsworth's Introduction — "All good poetry is the spontaneous overflow of powerful feelings" and that poetry "takes its origin from emotion recollected in tranquility" — are illustrated by these two poems.
2.   Students could discuss the concept of "natural piety" introduced in the last line of "My Heart Leaps Up."
3.   In "I Wandered Lonely as a Cloud," Wordsworth uses the word "dance," "dancing," or "dances" in each of the poem's four stanzas. Students could describe what he means by each use of the word.

NUNS FRET NOT

The theme of this sonnet is described in the text (p. 947). "Nuns Fret Not" was written after the two lyric poems, when Wordsworth had moved another step from the fervors of his youth; he even suggests in the sonnet that he has felt "the weight of too much liberty." In the lines that present the "blithe and happy" workers and students, however, he makes it clear that he still believes in the superior qualities of a simple life.

Questions for Discussion

1. Is this an Italian or an English sonnet?
2. What does Wordsworth mean by his description of the bees?
3. What is he suggesting by the phrase "brief solace" in the last line?

Topics for Writing

1. **CONNECTIONS** Students could compare Wordsworth's idea of a sonnet, as a "scanty plot of ground," with Rita Dove's introduction to her collection of sonnets included in Chapter 18 (p. 1252).
2. Students could examine Wordsworth's idea that "the prison, unto which we doom / Ourselves no prison is."

ODE: INTIMATIONS OF IMMORTALITY

The instructor might find this interpretation by David Daiches helpful in beginning a classroom discussion of this long and difficult poem:

> In the "Immortality Ode" Wordsworth gave the most complete account of the balance sheet of maturity as he saw it: in a poem whose very fabric is remembered perception giving way to reflection, he charts the course of the developing sensibility.... The naive freshness of the child's awareness gives way to the more sober vision of the man; mediated by love, the child's perceptions in a strange world take on a meaning which, as he grows up, finally emerges as the recognition of profound human significance in nature.... [I]t is a record of the profit and loss of growing up. The poet is only born when the child's bliss gives way to the man's more sober but profound sensibility, which works through "relationship and love" rather than mere animal sensations. The poem is thus one of Wordsworth's most central and illuminating works. (From *A Critical History of English Literature*, vol. 4 [London: Secker & Warburg, 1971], p. 881)

The epigraph to "Ode" is from Wordsworth's "My Heart Leaps Up," which students may have already read and discussed. If students read the text's introductory note to "Ode" carefully, they noted that its first four stanzas were written together, and that Wordsworth had difficulty completing the poem. These first four stanzas express a joy and spontaneity that Wordsworth seldom achieved in his other writing: the form of the stanzas themselves conveys this spontaneity. The stanzas are irregular in length: the first two are each nine lines long, then, as though he couldn't contain his running thoughts, Wordsworth makes the third eighteen lines long, and the fourth grows to twenty-two. Although there is a basic iambic rhythm to the lines, they are irregular in length and follow no regular rhyme scheme.

The poem's central theme appears in the fifth stanza, beginning with the line "Our birth is but a sleep and a forgetting," and a classroom discussion could help clarify Wordsworth's thesis. The first four lines contain the theme that he develops through the rest of the poem. He says in these lines that our earthly life is only an interruption in the divine life that all beings experience before birth. As he writes in lines 64–65, "trailing clouds of glory do we come / From God, who is our home." Then, in Daiches's phrase, life becomes a "record of the profit and loss of growing up." The child loses the memory of his or her divinity, slowly, inexorably, as he or she grows older.

Questions for Discussion

1. Could the first five lines be described as pantheistic?
2. What is Wordsworth saying in line 16, "sunshine is a glorious birth"?
3. Why, in line 22, does he think of himself as "alone"?
4. How would 26, "No more shall grief of mine the season wrong," be paraphrased?
5. In lines 39–40, what is Wordsworth saying about his own response to the day?
6. What "tale" is he learning from the trees and the grass, and how does this relate to his central theme?
7. In line 72, what is he suggesting when he describes the young person as "Nature's Priest"?
8. In lines 82–84 he describes the role of a child's nurse as a keeper, and the child as an inmate. Is he saying the nurse is playing a negative role in the child's life?
9. What are some of the things the child is foreseeing in his "dream of human life"?
10. In lines 106–107, is Wordsworth suggesting that the child spends his life imitating what he sees of life around him? As Wordsworth has expressed the theme of the poem, would this be a step away from the child's divine memory?
11. Who is the "Thou" of line 108?
12. In line 155 Wordsworth speaks of "truths that wake, / To perish never." Are these truths the faith that was to be challenged a generation later by scientific discoveries?
13. What does Wordsworth mean by the images of "splendor in the grass" and "glory in the flower"?
14. In line 199, "Another race hath been," is he saying that a life has been lived? And in "other palms are won," does he mean that there have been rewards for this life?
15. What does he mean when he writes in the last line that thoughts can be too deep for tears?

Topics for Writing

1. Students could discuss the metaphor of the heaven that precedes childhood as an "immortal sea," which Wordsworth describes in lines 161–167.
2. **CONNECTIONS** Students could compare the image of lines 167–168, "And see the Children sport upon the shore, / And hear the mighty waters rolling everywhere," with the image of the waters drawing down the shore and signaling the poet's loss of faith in Matthew Arnold's "Dover Beach" (p. 1018).

3. Students could interpret the poem's last two lines in terms of something they have strongly experienced.
4. Students could analyze whether the poem could have been written in the same way, or written at all, after the questioning of religious faith that occurred in England only a generation later.

Related Commentary

William Wordsworth, From the Introduction to *Lyrical Ballads*, p. 1330.

LADY MARY WROTH

In this strange labyrinth how shall I turn? (p. 948)

Although few women of her time were educated, Lady Mary Wroth was from one of England's important literary families, and she was given a liberal education. Her uncle was the poet Sir Philip Sidney, and her aunt was the countess of Pembroke, also a poet and translator. Wroth was one of the circle of poets around Ben Jonson, and during the years of her marriage to Sir Robert Wroth, Jonson often visited them at their estate of Penhurst. She was born about 1587, and her death date is probably 1651. Her own title was countess of Montgomery. Wroth was a prolific author, highly regarded in court circles for her prose romances and her poetry. Her sonnet sequence *Pamphilia to Amphilanthus* is the only one written by an Elizabethan woman.

"In this strange labyrinth how shall I turn?" is one of a "crown" of sonnets, a poetic form brought, with the sonnet itself, from Italy. In a crown of sonnets, the last line of the first sonnet is repeated as the first line of the second sonnet, and the circle continues until, with the fourteenth sonnet, the last line of the final sonnet is the first line of the opening sonnet. Wroth's sonnet is filled with the conceits and paradoxes of Elizabethan poetry. Her writing is less complex and convoluted than John Donne's, but it is considerably more knotted than the limpid songs of Ben Jonson. In this sonnet she is trying to decide which "pass," or path, to take, when what she really desires is to follow the path to love.

"The thread of love" in the final line alludes to the thread that Ariadne gave to Theseus to unwind behind him so that he could find his way out of the labyrinth after he had killed the Minotaur and return to her. Everyone in Wroth's courtly circle of friends would have immediately understood the allusion.

Questions for Discussion

1. What is the form of Wroth's sonnet, English or Italian?
2. What are the reasons she presents for not going to the right, the left, forward, or back?
3. In line 12, "travail" is a pun on the word "travel," and she is suggesting that to travel might be the best decision for her. Has she decided where she will travel?
4. Despite all its complexities, the sonnet seems relatively lighthearted. What does Wroth intimate in the phrase "troubled sense" in line 13?
5. Is it love that draws her, in the final lines?

(text p. 948)

Topic for Writing

1.   **CONNECTIONS**   This is a sonnet by an Elizabethan woman. Compare it with Shakespeare's "Shall I compare thee to a summer's day?" (p. 1188) in terms of the two sonnets' descriptions of women.

SIR THOMAS WYATT

They Flee from Me (p. 887)

As they read "They Flee from Me," students should also read Christopher Merrill's introduction to Wyatt and the metrical complexities of this poem in Chapter 18 (p. 1287). Although the poem's final stanza ends ambiguously, it is one of the most frequently anthologized early English love lyrics. Much of the lyric poetry of Wyatt's century — and for some centuries to follow — used a highly formalized, allusive poetic diction for lyric poems about love, but the moment in which the woman the narrator loves slips off her gown and takes him in her arms is described in language as immediate, as expressive, and as direct as any love poem written today.

Questions for Discussion

1.   Analyze the rhyme scheme of the first stanza. Is it used consistently for the other stanzas?
2.   Although, as Merrill points out in his commentary, the meter of various lines is irregular, the shifts of stress in some of these lines are justified by Wyatt's use of a caesura. Discuss the lines in which these are used, among them lines 4, 16, and 18.
3.   Nothing in the poem identifies what the poet sees in his mind with the image of "they" in the first stanza, the wild creatures that "stalked in his chamber." Some commentators have suggested that the image Wyatt has in his mind is wild deer. What details elsewhere in the poem are suggestive of deer?
4.   What is Wyatt saying in line 6, "To take bread at my hand"? Is this a metaphor for a physical action or for an emotional exchange?
5.   Consider lines 19 and 20 in terms of the end of the relationship. The narrator is given leave to go; is it willing on his part? Is the word "newfangledness" saying that the woman is going on to new lovers?

Topic for Writing

1.   The poem's last two lines can be read as ironically sarcastic or as resignedly accepting of the inevitable end of a brief relationship. Discuss the possible meanings of "served" and "deserved" and decide if the poem ends in anger or resignation.

WILLIAM BUTLER YEATS

Yeats sometimes referred to himself as "the last Romantic," by which he meant the last of the poets of the Romantic school, and students will find much in his poetry to remind them of that earlier group of writers. By the time Yeats began to write, however, a century had passed since the Romantics' technical innovations were new, and their idiom had been sifted and resifted until the force of discovery, the excitement with the new idiom and language, had sunk under the weight of repetition. If students have read Keats, Wordsworth, Shelley, and Blake, they will find that Yeats, as a young poet, often used imagery and language reminiscent of the Romantics, but with little of their imaginative power. It was a conscious choice that some critics have termed "self-conscious romanticism." In "Symbol as Revelation," an essay written in 1890, Yeats explained the poetic method that he shared with several other younger London poets, among them his friends Arthur Symonds, Lionel Johnson, and Ernest Dowson:

> We would cast out of serious poetry those energetic rhythms, as of a man running, which are the invention of the will with its eyes always on something to be done or undone; and we would seek out those wavering, meditative, organic rhythms, which are the embodiment of the imagination, that neither desires or hates, because it has done with time, and only wishes to gaze upon some reality, some beauty. . . . The form of sincere poetry, unlike the form of popular poetry, may indeed be sometimes obscure, or ungrammatical . . . but it must have the perfections that escape analysis, the subtleties that have a new meaning every day.

Their new poetry was to look back at the old, but as he also wrote in the essay, the gift of poetry that Yeats's generation inherited was not intended "to mirror our own excited faces, or the boughs waving outside the window." Although Yeats's style became sharper and more clearly defined in later years, he kept to his dictum to write poetry that would not show his excited face or describe the tree limbs outside his window.

Between the 1890s and World War I, while Yeats and his group were developing their aesthetic, the younger modernist poets were sweeping away the last of the Romantic tradition with their experiments in free verse, imagism, poetic diction, and theme. Yeats responded by rewriting a number of his earlier poems to eliminate some of the "wavering rhythms" he had previously advocated. For a short period he employed Ezra Pound as a secretary, but he fired Pound when he discovered that the younger poet was rewriting some of the poems Yeats was giving him to submit to publications in an attempt to make them more modern.

When he was in his late forties, Yeats began to write in a much stronger and more direct style. His life had seen so many disappointments that the tone of regret lingered, but he could be specific about political questions other than Irish independence, and he was able to address larger social issues. One of the considerations for the awarding of the Nobel Prize for Literature is the writer's commitment to a more just society, and Yeats's writing — as a poet, playwright, and activist fighting for Irish freedom — certainly qualified him for the prize, which he won in 1924.

At the end of Yeats's life, his poetry was dominated by his belief in spiritualism, and he developed a system of symbols based on the messages he believed he was receiving from spirits. Students should read W. H. Auden's poem "In Memory of W. B. Yeats" (p. 1022), which expresses the respect many poets felt for Yeats at the time of his death.

THE LAKE ISLE OF INNISFREE (p. 1227)

Yeats's father, the painter Jack Yeats, had read parts of Henry David Thoreau's *Walden* to him when he was a boy, and Yeats had always had a dream of living, like Thoreau, in a cabin beside a lake. The immediate inspiration for this poem was something Yeats glimpsed when he was walking in London. In his *Memoirs* he wrote, "I was going along the Strand, and passing a shop window where there was a little ball kept dancing by a jet of water, I remembered waters about Sligo and was moved to a sudden emotion that shaped itself into 'Lake Isle of Innisfree.'"

"The Lake Isle of Innisfree" became Yeats's most popular poem, which made him uncomfortable, as he had reservations about the sententiousness of the opening lines.

Questions for Discussion

1. The theme of the poem — a longing to return to a simple country life — is familiar, and Yeats has no new insight to add to the long inventory of poems with this theme. The poem's meter, however, is complicated. Students should scan the poem and discuss its unusual line lengths.
2. The use of a comma to mark the caesura in seven of the poem's nine long lines divides the lines into two units of three stresses each, and the two lines that lack the comma, lines 6 and 10, divide metrically into the same three-stress units. Discuss Yeats's possible reasons for writing the poem in the long lines he has chosen, instead of shorter lines that would emphasize the poem's implied meter. What effect would a shorter line length have on Yeats's rhyme scheme?
3. Discuss the use of alliteration in lines 4 and 10. Would the choice of the word "lapping" be classed as onomatopoeia?
4. Is Yeats describing a real cabin in line 2?
5. All of the nature images in the poem are clichés. Why did Yeats choose to fill the poem with these familiar phrases?
6. The phrase "Nine bean rows" in line 3 is a conscious allusion to Thoreau's *Walden*. Are there any other images that allude to Thoreau's Walden experience?
7. Describe what Yeats is saying with the last line, "deep heart's core."

Topic for Writing

1. The poem is a reverie about an imagined life in nature that has no reality. Discuss the contrasts between Yeats's imaginary country life and the realities of country life.

WHEN YOU ARE OLD (p. 1228)

Although students will not find many hints of strong emotion in the poetry Yeats wrote when he was young, for much of his life he was passionately and hopelessly in love with a young Irish actress named Maude Gonne. In his *Memoirs*, published posthumously in 1972, he recalls his first meeting with her:

> I was twenty-three years old when the troubling of my life began. I had heard from time to time in letters . . . of a beautiful girl who had left the society of the Vicegeral Court for Dublin nationalism. In after years I

persuaded myself that I felt premonitory excitement at the first reading of her name. Presently she drove up to our house in Bedford Park
with an introduction from John O'Leary to my father. I had never
thought to see in a living woman so great beauty. It belonged to
famous pictures, to poetry, to some legendary past. A complexion like
the blossom of apples, and yet face and body had the beauty of
lineaments which Blake calls the highest beauty because it changes
least from youth to age, and a stature so great that she seemed of a
divine race. Her movements were worthy of her form, and I understood at last why the poet of antiquity, where we would but speak of
face and form, sings, loving some lady, that she paces like a goddess.

Gonne was in fact as beautiful as Yeats describes her and had an immense
vitality. She was also as strongly committed to the cause of Irish independence as
he was, and he was powerless to end his hopeless love for her, despite the
flamboyance of her personal life and his own sexual inexperience and timidity. In
"When You Are Old" he tries to remind her that when she is old and no longer
beautiful she should remember that there was one man, himself, who loved her for
something besides her beauty. He loved her for her "pilgrim soul." Yeats's poems
are often filled with melancholy and regret, and in the last stanza he passes on some
of his usual emotions to her. When she thinks of him, he says, *she* will feel regret.

Questions for Discussion

1. What does Yeats mean by "the pilgrim soul in you" in line 7?
2. What is the term for his image of love hiding his face in the last two lines?
3. What is he suggesting with the phrase "a crowd of stars" in the final line?

The Wild Swans at Coole (p. 1228)

This poem was written almost thirty years after "The Lake Isle of Innisfree,"
when Yeats's poetic idiom was much more concentrated. The poem is still gray,
with Yeats's usual mood of autumnal regret, but the language is free of the
Romantic clichés that had numbed much of his early poetry. According to the
anthologist and critic Louis Untermeyer, "With . . . 'The Wild Swans at Coole' a
change in tone is immediately apparent. The idiom is sharper, the imagery sparser.
The language, no longer richly colored, is almost bare of ornament, the tone
pitched on a conversational plane. . . . One likes to believe that it was the later work
that won Yeats the Nobel Prize for Literature in 1924" (in *Modern British Poetry*
[New York: Harcourt Brace, 1950], p. 108).

Coole Park was the ancestral home of Lady Gregory, Yeats's patron and a
close friend. He first saw Coole Park in 1897, and in 1916, when the poem was
written, he walked by the lake again to see the wild swans.

Questions for Discussion

1. The class could scan the poem and compare its meter with "The Lake Isle of
   Innisfree" and "When You Are Old." What are the differences between the
   meter of this mature poem and Yeats's earlier writing?
2. What are the differences in his use of rhyme?
3. The poem's language is free of the clichés of "The Lake Isle of Innisfree."
   What words and phrases does Yeats use to describe the scene before him?
   Are these images a direct response to what he is seeing?

4. What is he describing with the phrase "bell beat of their wings" in line 17?
5. Yeats has made several shifts of context in lines 15–18 to maintain the form of the stanza. What would these lines' usual word order be?
6. In the fourth stanza, beginning with "Unwearied still, lover by lover," is Yeats implying that, unlike the swans, he is weary now?
7. What is he saying about the swans in the phrase "Passion or conquest" in line 23? Is the poet envious of the swans?
8. Yeats seems to be returning to his older, less concentrated style in line 26, when he refers to the swans as "Mysterious, beautiful." What is he suggesting with this shift in context? Does he intend the image to reinforce the swans being a metaphor for his own dreams and desires?

Topics for Writing

1. Compare "The Lake Isle of Innisfree" and "The Wild Swans at Coole" in terms of their meter and rhyme. Discuss how Yeats perceived the differences between them.
2. Discuss the use of assonance and alliteration in the poem.

THE SECOND COMING (P. 1229)

Some poems can be read without placing them in a historical context, but this poem needs to be considered in terms of 1919, the year it was written. In 1919 a violent civil war was raging in Russia between the armies of the new Communist government and the reactionary armies of the Right, who were aided by international brigades from more than forty nations. Communist insurgents in Berlin staged a near coup that was put down with brutal repression. In Ireland the first fighting had begun between the small bands struggling for independence from Britain and British soldiers and their loyalist allies. It could have been any or all of these events, along with the prolonged horror of World War I, against which Yeats was reacting in "The Second Coming," one of his most overtly political poems. He is so engaged in this poem that its form is rough, with ambiguities that are difficult to interpret.

In his own notes to this poem, Yeats identified "Spiritus Mundi" as "a general storehouse of images which have ceased to be the property of any personality or spirit." A "gyre" can be defined as a shortened version of the word "gyration," which would clarify the image of the opening lines as a hunting falcon on a widening gyration beyond the voice of the falconer. An interpretation of this would be humankind losing touch with God or Christ. Yeats, however, felt the poem had a mystical symbolism based on a gyre, which Richard J. Finneran explains as "one-half of a symbol which consists of two intertwined cones, the base of each being the apex of the other. The movement of the gyres in opposite directions suggests the inherent conflict in existence" (in *The Collected Poems of William Butler Yeats* [New York: Macmillan, 1989], p. 493).

The poem alludes to the Christian doctrine that the Second Coming of Christ will occur on the Day of Judgment, when the world ends. To Yeats, it seemed that the world was already ending in a flood of violence, as he indicates in the famous lines "Things fall apart; the center cannot hold." It is difficult to know precisely what Yeats meant by the "rough beast" that was going to be born in Bethlehem, as Christ had been, but it could be interpreted as a metaphor for anarchy itself, rather than any specific cause.

Questions for Discussion

1. What is the form of the poem? Why did Yeats choose this form for a poem with this subject?
2. Discuss the different interpretations of the first line.
3. Is "Mere anarchy" in line 4 an example of understatement, or is "mere" meant as an adjective that would diminish the importance of "anarchy"?
4. What is Yeats saying in lines 7–8 about the situation facing the societies of the world?
5. Could line 14 be interpreted as an allusion to the statue of the Sphinx?
6. What does Yeats mean by his image of the beast in lines 14–17?
7. Explain the image of line 20.

Topics for Writing

1. Yeats writes in the poem that the anarchy he sees rising around him is a prophecy of a Second Coming. Discuss the images he uses to describe this anarchy.
2. Explain the meaning of lines 7–8, "The best lack all conviction, while the worst / Are full of passionate intensity," and discuss their relevance to current social problems.

SAILING TO BYZANTIUM (P. 1229)

In "The Lake Isle of Innisfree," Yeats dreamed of fleeing his difficult life in London for an imagined freer life in the country. In "Sailing to Byzantium" he dreams again of leaving a harsh reality, but this time it is the reality of growing old, and he will leave it to sail to the city of Byzantium (now the city of Istanbul). In the eleventh century, Byzantium was the rich and highly civilized capital of the Holy Roman Empire of the East and the holy city of the Greek Orthodox religion.

In the final lines of "Sailing to Byzantium," Yeats claims for himself, after his reincarnation, the role of a golden "form," a mechanical bird on a golden bough that will sing of the past, the present, and the future — which certainly can be interpreted as an allusion to Yeats's role in this life as a poet. In a note to the poem Yeats write, "I have read somewhere that in the Emperor's Palace at Byzantium was a tree made of gold and silver and artificial birds that sang."

Many images in the poem, however, present more difficulties. The critic Cleanth Brooks Jr. summarized his interpretation of the poem in an essay published in 1934:

> The poet's own country is a land of natural beauty, beauty in the body. But his own body is old. The soul must, therefore, sing the louder to compensate for the old and dying flesh. . . . But there is no singing school for the soul except in studying the works of the soul. "And therefore" he has sailed to Byzantium, for the artists of Byzantium do not follow the forms of nature but intellectual forms, ideal patterns. He appeals to them to "Consume my heart away; sick with desire / And fastened to a dying animal" and by severing him from the dying world of the body, to gather him into what is at least "the artifice of eternity." (From "A Note on Symbol and Conceit," *American Review* [May 1934])

Questions for Discussion

1. Discuss Yeats's use of rhyme and half-rhyme in the poem.
2. What is Yeats alluding to with "That" in the first line? Would the poem have been clearer if he had used the word "This"?
3. What is he saying about the world's creatures in the phrase "commend all summer long" in line 5?
4. Discuss his meaning in lines 7–8, "Caught in that sensual music all neglect / Monuments of unageing intellect."
5. Discuss Yeats's meaning in "A tattered coat upon a stick" in line 10. What is the term for this figure of speech?
6. The class could paraphrase the second stanza to clarify its meaning.
7. What is Yeats saying about his heart in lines 21–23? Is he telling us that his heart is separate from his body?
8. What is the meaning of line 25, "Once out of nature"?

Topics for Writing

1. In line 8 Yeats writes of "Monuments of unageing intellect." Analyze his meaning and list some examples of these monuments.
2. Discuss Yeats's concept of reincarnation as he presents it in this poem.
3. **CONNECTIONS** Read W. H. Auden's poem "In Memory of W. B. Yeats" (p. 1022) and select passages from Yeats's poetry that would illustrate what Auden has written about him.

AL YOUNG

Birthday Poem (p. 985)

Al Young, in describing his childhood, remembers that he "grew up in homes where the verbal jam session was a floating and usually festive experience." He was born in Mississippi in 1939 and how lives in Palo Alto, California, where he teaches and writes fiction, poetry, and drama.

Question for Discussion

1. The last line comes as something of a surprise; discuss what sort of bliss Young might be referring to. What is the significance of ending the poem in this manner?

Topic for Writing

1. Ask students to write a "birthday poem" about their parents or heritage.

PART THREE

DRAMA

SOPHOCLES

Oedipus the King (p. 1419)

Sophocles' audiences would have been familiar with the general outline of the Oedipus legend. Such knowledge is necessary for students to recognize the series of dramatic ironies and foreshadowings contained in the play. Because of a prophecy that their son will kill his father and marry his mother, Laius, king of Thebes, and his wife, Jocasta, pin their newly born son's feet together and send him to be abandoned in the mountains. Pitying the infant, the shepherd entrusted with this task gives him to a fellow shepherd who passes him on to Polybos, king of Corinth, and his wife, Merope. The couple, being childless, raise Oedipus as their own. In adulthood Oedipus hears the same prophecy given to Laius, that he will kill his father and marry his mother and, believing Polybos and Merope to be his parents, leaves Corinth to avoid such a fate. On his travels he is forced off the road by a chariot and treated uncivilly by its occupant. In his anger he kills both servants and passenger, who is (unbeknownst to him) his father, Laius. Oedipus continues on to Thebes, liberating it from the evil Sphinx by answering her riddle and being rewarded by marriage to the widowed Jocasta and becoming king. They have four children together and prosper for some years until fortune takes a turn. Sophocles begins his play at this point in Oedipus's life. Thebes is suffering from a plague and Oedipus is determined to save the city by uncovering the cause.

At the start of the play Sophocles shows us Oedipus at the height of his power. The central action of the play is Oedipus's determination to save his city. As the play progresses he gradually discovers his own damnation, ironically, by his own relentless insistence to uncover the truth. In a single day he falls from sovereignty and fame to a self-blinded degradation. The chorus draws from this the moral that one should never take good fortune for granted, but to see this as Sophocles' isolated theme would be an oversimplification. The students' first impression of Oedipus should be mostly positive through observing his paternal care for his people. He is truly concerned and wishes to help. But they should also perceive behind this a proud feeling of superiority that will contribute to his downfall. The Greeks called this pride "hubris." It was such, perhaps, that led to Oedipus's violent response against the chariot that pushed him from the road. Though Laius was insulting to Oedipus, his response was out of proportion, and he should be made to recognize his guilt. The Priest reminds us that although the people admire Oedipus greatly, he is still a man and not a god. Lest we forget, Sophocles points out the important role and power of the gods in the Parodos. Between each scene he has the chorus offer a commentary on events, directing both the mood and the audience's response.

Sophocles wishes us to consider the moral issues behind human action and to recognize the powers that operate on human affairs. Oedipus is in conflict throughout the play; on the surface this seems to be against the plague, then Tiresias, then Creon, but the central conflict of the play is between Oedipus and the gods. This leads us to the play's twin areas of interest: Oedipus's character and Oedipus's fate. What Sophocles so cleverly shows is how intricately these two aspects of the narrative are woven. Oedipus is neither wholly virtuous nor wholly blameless but is presented as a complex being who offers the audience an intellectual and moral challenge. He is partly a victim of fate and the "savagery of God," but his spirited character leads him to make errors that contribute to his downfall.

Students may find Tiresias a problematic figure, as we are shown slight motivation for what he chooses to divulge and when (Why not denounce Oedipus when he first came to Thebes? Why not tell him the truth clearly now?). It may help to remember that, as a mouthpiece for the gods, he may act, therefore, as inexplicably as they. Oedipus's rage at Tiresias is partly justified by his noble determination to learn the truth that Tiresias, at first, refuses to tell.

Oedipus's suspicion of Creon is less easy to justify. At times Oedipus's fury is both precipitous and unreasonable, and his eventual suffering is partly justified as a punishment for such behavior. He holds on for some time to his belief that Tiresias's words are a plot against him, for this is an easier belief than accepting what is really indicated: that Oedipus has failed to escape the prophecy of the gods. Sophocles has Creon's defense underline his character and offer a clear contrast to Oedipus. Where Oedipus's vanity insists on his being number one, Creon is satisfied with being number three. Creon is not a man to take risks; he waits and does nothing decisive that has not been corroborated by the gods. Supporting those same community values of reason, order, and compromise that the chorus voices, he lives the safe life that men like Oedipus proudly eschew, and therein lies Oedipus's magnificence and his downfall.

The "shadow memory" that Jocasta's words spark from Oedipus marks the change from total blindness to the truth to the beginnings of "sight." Despite Jocasta's insistence that all prophecy is false, both she and Oedipus are forced to recognize the untruthfulness of such a defense. Sophocles shows that disbelief is as difficult as belief when we learn Polybos is dead without being killed by his "son," and yet Oedipus still fears a marriage to Merope. Ironically, it is the giving of the prophecy itself that has ensured its completion; had Oedipus not been told he was in danger of killing his father, he may never have left Corinth in order to do so. Just as the Sphinx had destroyed herself when Oedipus had answered her riddle, so, too, must Oedipus destroy himself when he finally solves his own. The two prongs of the gold pins with which he blinds himself recall the two prongs that Laius had struck out against him; thus, Sophocles relates this expiation directly to Oedipus's sin of patricide.

One of Sophocles' major contributions to drama was his introduction of a third actor. This changes the whole dynamic of the play, allowing for far more dramatic interaction between the various characters. Thus, for example, we can have the Scene 2 confrontation between Oedipus and Creon interrupted and resolved by Jocasta and the ironic remeeting of the messenger and shepherd before the man they had jointly worked to save as an infant and now provide the very information that will destroy him. *Oedipus* can be viewed as an ideal tragedy. Indeed, of all the plays he had seen or read, Aristotle chose *Oedipus* as the basis for many of his conclusions concerning the nature of tragedy. Oedipus is neither a criminal who would lose our sympathy nor a saint whose treatment might lead us to outrage. He is a noble protagonist who encounters misfortune and brings misfortune on others, as Aristotle suggests, not through "vice" or "depravity" but by "error and frailty."

Caught in a tragic dilemma, Oedipus can either shirk his duty as king or try to rid the city of plague, but, for him, either course would be ruinous. We must watch as a successful ruler is gradually devastated and, through this experience, finally exhibits his extraordinary human spirit by accepting responsibility for events as he blinds himself in order to perform the required penance to save Thebes. Watching his downfall induces our pity and fear; his misfortunes are really out of proportion to his faults and yet these faults make him human enough for us to recognize in his downfall our own vulnerability. With Oedipus's spirited response, however, Sophocles ensures we are not left in despair; Oedipus has courageously confronted powerful forces (both internal and external) with a dignity that reveals the depth and breadth of the human spirit in the face of defeat. Whereas comedy likes to show people at their worst, tragedy allows them to be at their best and so offers us hope for the future of humanity.

Susan C. W. Abbotson

Questions for Discussion

1. Aside from determining the central action of the play, what important information do we learn from the Prologue concerning the character of Oedipus, the people of Thebes, and the nature of the gods?
2. Tracing the instances of "dramatic irony" that occur throughout the play, what do you feel their function might be?
3. What can be determined about Oedipus's character from his treatment of Tiresias and Creon? How does this relate to the events at the three-way crossroads?
4. Why does Oedipus so quickly decide that Creon has been plotting against him?
5. How far is Creon's defense against Oedipus's charges borne out by his words and actions in the play?
6. What functions do the chorus serve?
7. What are the chorus's views and beliefs and how do they differ from those of Jocasta? Can we accept the moral the chorus asserts at the close?
8. To what extent are the things that happen to Oedipus his own fault or the fault of others? Is he ever able to choose a course of action?
9. How true is the messenger's declaration that what has occurred was "evil not done unconsciously, but willed"?
10. What would have happened if Oedipus had died according to his birth parents' plan?
11. Why does Oedipus blind himself instead of committing suicide as Jocasta does?
12. Although the situations and characters of *Oedipus the King* were devised long ago, in what ways are they still relevant in today's society?

Topics for Writing

1. On whom should we blame the misfortunes that occur in *Oedipus the King*: Laius and Jocasta? Oedipus? the shepherd who saved Oedipus as a child?

Tiresias? the gods? fate? Sophocles? Write an essay that considers these possibilities and reaches some kind of conclusion.

2. Tracing the images of light and dark, sight and blindness, knowledge and ignorance throughout *Oedipus the King*, show how these relate to one another and what Sophocles intends for his audience to conclude by their use.

3. Imagine that you are a psychiatrist who has conducted a series of interviews with Oedipus. Write what you consider to be a professional assessment of his character and condition, giving recommendations for future treatment.

4. Write the story line for what you think might be the modern day equivalent of this play. Try to follow the dynamics of *Oedipus the King* as closely as possible.

5. **CONNECTIONS** How far is an understanding of the nature of tragedy important in any interpretation of *Oedipus the King*? In what ways does William Shakespeare's *Hamlet* also fulfill this criteria of tragedy? Does Shakespeare tend to support or contradict Sophocles' assumptions?

6. **CONNECTIONS** Discuss the parallels between *Oedipus the King* and any one of the following: August Strindberg's *Miss Julie*, Henrik Ibsen's *A Doll House*, and Tennessee Williams's *The Glass Menagerie*.

Suggested Readings

Bloom, Harold, ed. *Sophocles' "Oedipus Rex."* New York: Chelsea, 1988.

Edmonds, Lowell. *Oedipus: The Ancient Legend and Its Later Analogues.* Baltimore: John Hopkins UP, 1985.

Gardiner, Cynthia P. *The Sophoclean Chorus: A Study of Character and Function.* Iowa City: U of Iowa P, 1987.

Hogan, James C. *A Commentary on the Plays of Sophocles.* Carbondale: Southern Illinois UP, 1991.

Keogh, J. G. "O City, City: Oedipus in the Waste Land." *Antigonish Review* 69–70 (1987): 89–112.

Knox, Bernard M. *Oedipus at Thebes: Sophocles's Tragic Hero and His Time.* New York: Norton, 1971.

O'Brien, Michael John, ed. *Twentieth Century Interpretations of "Oedipus Rex": A Collection of Critical Essays.* Englewood Cliffs, NJ: Prentice-Hall, 1968.

Rudnytsky, Peter. *Freud and Oedipus.* New York: Columbia UP, 1987.

Seale, David. *Vision and Stagecraft in Sophocles.* Chicago: U of Chicago P, 1982.

Segal, Charles. *"Oedipus Tyrannus": Tragic Heroism and the Limits of Knowledge.* New York: Twayne, 1993.

Senior, W. A. "Teaching Oedipus: The Hero and Multiplicity." *Teaching English in the Two-Year College* (December 1992): 274–79.

Sophocles. *The Theban Plays.* New York: Knopf, 1994.

Verhoeff, Han, and Harly Sonne. "Does Oedipus Have His Complex?" *Style* 18 (1984): 261–83.

Nō Drama

Kantan (p. 1465)

Nō plays, such as *Kantan*, are built around a dream vision of the central "shite" (pronounced *shee-tay*) character. This play's fusion of music, dance, mask, costume, and poetic language combine to offer its audience a truth about the world. The play is a piece of "performance art," and reading it on the page will give students only a vague idea of how it would play on the stage. Students will need to imagine the surrounding spectacle created by the ornate costumes, masks, and lengthy songs and dances. The text is also full of allusions to other works and legends, which may be lost to many students. Even so, the young seeker should be a familiar literary figure, and the play's spiritual message is direct enough to be comprehended, regardless of whether every allusion is recognized. In Nō, the form of the piece is considered more important than the meaning, so students should pay close attention to how characters and events are presented to the audience. They should be aware of the "wordless" events of the play, such as mime and dance, that are as important as the dialogue. The twin aims of this play, as with all Nō drama, are to lead the audience to greater pleasure and greater knowledge; each performance is meant to entertain as well as to educate.

Kantan is set in China, although its location bears little importance beyond emphasizing the great distance Rosei has traveled on his quest. As in most Greek drama, the plots of Nō plays are usually based on tales that were well-known to the original audiences. *Kantan* is based on a familiar Japanese legend, in which a young man goes out to seek his fortune. Characters, symbolic objects, and settings have antecedents in other Nō plays (for example, the quester and pillow in *Taiheiki* or the dream palace in *Heike monogatari*). Such similarities indicate the strength of cultural connection in Nō drama, which strives not so much to innovate as to build on an established tradition. Yet *Kantan* does show some originality in that it has altered the usual quest story line by having the young man seeking wisdom and enlightenment rather than success or great wealth. In this the play shows its strong religious background, based in Buddhist thought, which exhibits a concern with spiritual and psychological wholeness. The play's action asserts the need to renounce attachments to worldly objects of desire and the life of the senses. Earthly life is not a thing one should seek to hold onto, for it is better to move through the world as speedily as possible to get closer to nirvana. This is the lesson the young man Rosei must learn. Playing the role of a shite, Rosei will learn to eschew earthly attachments, under the watchful gaze of the Envoy, who plays the role of a "waki."

The action of the play is simple. At the start, Rosei is traveling to find a well-known sage to give him advice. The word *Buddhism* means enlightenment and comes from the Sanskrit word *buhd*, which means "to know." What Rosei seeks is knowledge. He meets the female Innkeeper, a peasant named Ryosen'o, who allows Rosei to sleep on a magic pillow which has been given to her by a Buddhist monk. The magic of this pillow is that anyone who sleeps on it will awaken to truth. Sleeping on the pillow, Rosei dreams he attains worldly glory, but on awakening he sees the vanity of such thoughts and goes home. His quest is ended and he no longer needs to seek the sage, for he has gained the answer to all the questions he ever had.

We are introduced to two central props right at the start of the play: a structure representing the "palace" and the pillow of Kantan. These props will eventually encapsulate the central opposition in the play between worldly goods (palace) and spiritual truth (pillow). The playwright strives for no sense of tension between the characters or mystery regarding the pillow's powers. Straight away Ryosen'o announces both what the pillow does to those who sleep on it and the fact that she will freely offer the use of it to any passing traveler. Students should note that Ryosen'o tells us that the pillow will indicate "the truth of past and future" alone, as the present is of no great concern to spiritual people. Sleeping on the pillow is a kind of "test," which we should realize by Ryosen'o's warning: "Take heed, good people! I will have him in to stay!" It is a test Rosei must undergo and survive. Not everyone is brave enough to face or cope with the truth, but Rosei willingly accepts the test as it is the truth for which he has been searching.

Rosei has not followed a Buddhist path, and he begins the play feeling insecure and dissatisfied. "Lost on the journey of this dreary life," he treads "the path of dreams," searching for a holy sage to give him guidance. The way in which he describes his life should give students an early clue to the reality/dream inversion this play will eventually assert. Life, which we have supposed to be real, becomes the dream, as it is both transient and largely inconsequential when equated with the larger, spiritual scheme of Buddhism. Rosei's background as a non-Buddhist is emphasized through repetition, as are all the important pieces of information in the play. Rosei's quest into the mountain heights has been a lengthy one, and he is a long way from home. As he tells us, "The home I knew so well / vanishes behind me in the clouds." This complete separation from all the worldly things he must have left behind in that home is a necessity if he is to achieve enlightenment. The asperity of his journey has begun to prepare him for the changes he will soon be making in his lifestyle, although his basic needs for food and shelter have been met without difficulty. So far, however, he has shed the objects of his earthly life unwittingly; he must learn to make this a conscious choice.

Ryosen'o, who is an "ai" figure, offers Rosei her pillow willingly and tells him of its magic. The pillow's powers offer little surprise to Rosei, who has already heard about its existence. With the pillow's aid, Rosei will now be able to find truth for himself. The emphasis on learning for himself is important, for lessons of experience have far greater impact than something we are told by another. At this point in the play, Rosei alludes to *Eguchi*, a tale in which a Buddhist monk seeking shelter from the rain comes to a brothel where a harlot points out to him that his reproaches toward those who refuse him shelter are entirely unjustified. If, as a Buddhist, he has given up earthly concerns, then he should neither crave shelter for his earthly body nor be upset when he is refused. Here too, while seeking shelter from the rain, Rosei will learn the truth from an unexpected and lowly quarter.

When Rosei covers his face with a fan, it is an indication that he now sleeps. The Envoy enters and appears to disturb him with a message that he is to be the next king of So. We are left uncertain for a short while as to whether Rosei is awake or asleep at this point. The ambiguity underlines the assertion in Buddhist theology that all we regularly term "real" is only another kind of dream. The Envoy has brought a "jewelled palanquin," a style of covered litter, to carry Rosei to his new palace. Rosei takes up the offer without hesitation, for, being unskilled in Buddhist asceticism, he cannot resist the attraction of such worldly riches. The lure of wealth's gleam and sparkle will be constantly repeated; but one should not forget that a sparkle, as well as being attractive, can also dazzle and blind one to the truth. Rosei enters the palanquin and readily accepts what are patently unnecessary riches.

The imperial palace, which is likened to the "Cloud-Dragon Hall" and "Abo Palace" of secular legends, is rich with gold, silver, and jewels. Both setting and inhabitants are described as shining with richness. The place is compared, significantly, with Buddhist palaces called the "City of Glory" and the "Fair Citadel." This is asking for a comparison between the physical and the spiritual. We should recognize that such a comparison can only be false, just as the light that emanates from those jewels will turn out to be false. The only true en*light*enment will come from Buddhism rather than any earthly source. Being "walled in the four directions," Rosei's palace may seem like a trap, but to stay or to leave is up to the individual. In this way, it becomes your desires that hold you trapped within the walls. Rosei is surrounded by his wealth, which is reflected in the mountains and suns of gold and silver. Such a sight is unnatural, and it is evident that something is not right in this kind of existence.

Fifty days pass without any change, and Rosei finds himself tempted by the opportunity to remain in this environment for a thousand years. He even generously passes around the cup of elixir so that all might share in his longevity. Meanwhile, we should realize that much time is passing and little is being achieved in the palace, apart from drinking and dancing. Night and day merge and lose their meaning as timelessness destroys all distinctions, and thereby identity. Rosei joins in the dance, caught in the brilliance of his dream, but as he dances, the dream turns to confusion. As days and seasons begin to whirl and speed up alongside the dance, no one can tell whether it is day or night or what season it is. This cannot be natural or good, and we see that fifty years "melt away to nothing" in such a place. There is nothing lasting in a life of the brute senses; these people should be cultivating their spirits rather than their physical desires. The glories themselves are finally divest of meaning as we realize that the palace and its wonders are only a dream and not truly substantial. So, too, the play tells us, is life.

Rosei rushes to lay his head on the pillow before he awakes, to ensure that he will know the truth at this moment. The pillow itself has acted as the sage Rosei had been seeking, and it has allowed him to uncover the truth he sought. Rosei wakes up and recognizes the transience of all physical riches and faces the more lasting reality of the simple millet for his meal — a necessity while he remains alive on the earth. He recalls his dream and considers its meaning. He recognizes that the lowly lodging in Kantan can provide for a person's physical needs as fully as the palace he has left. Therefore, to desire such palaces is a waste of time and resources. Our lives are just brief flashes in the larger scheme of time, so it is wise not to waste them in the worthless pursuit of physical acquisition and pleasure. It is better to invest that time in spiritual matters. What Rosei learns is the ironic fact that it is physical objects that are truly insubstantial and spiritual things that have substance. This realization leads Rosei to embrace the Three Treasures and become a Buddhist. The three real treasures are not jewels but Buddha, his teaching, and the fellowship of monks. Rosei recognizes that the treasures of his dream palace are worthless, for they are transient. At the end of earthly life, he cannot take such treasures with him as he can the incorporeal, spiritual treasures of Buddhism.

SUSAN C. W. ABBOTSON

Questions for Discussion

1. Why is Rosei traveling? For what is he really searching?
2. Why is Rosei dissatisfied with his life?
3. Why does the playwright emphasize the distance Rosei has come from his home?
4. What do each of the following represent: the palace, the pillow, the elixir of life, and the millet? How do they contrast with one another?
5. What roles do the Innkeeper and the Envoy play? How is each presented? How do they assist Rosei in arriving at the truth?
6. What is significant about the way the land of So and its riches sparkle? How valuable are the riches of So? What is more valuable?

315

7. Why is the city walled in? How far are the people who live there free to come and go?
8. At what point do we realize that this is Rosei's dream? Why are we kept uncertain if he is awake or asleep?
9. What does Rosei achieve during his fifty years as king of So? Why does he accept the position so readily at first and then later reject it?
10. Why does Rosei need to rush near the end to replace his head on the pillow?
11. What happens to time during Rosei's dream, and how should this be interpreted?
12. What is the truth that Rosei learns?

Topics for Writing

1. During much of *Kantan*, the central character is asleep and dreaming. What does the play tell us about the nature of dreams? Why is Rosei's dream so important, and what is its message?
2. *Kantan* is full of symbols that underline the central beliefs of its writer and direct the audience toward the play's final message. What are these symbols and how do they operate?
3. Decide what you feel is the central message of *Kantan* and write a poem describing this theme, linking together as many of the play's symbolic items and events that you can.
4. **CONNECTIONS** How should one behave in order to get the best out of life? This is an issue over which many of us tend to disagree. What do we mean by "best," and what are the barriers that prevent some of us from achieving an ideal life? Consider the quality of the lives depicted in *Kantan* and Eugene O'Neill's *Bound East for Cardiff*, Arthur Miller's *Death of a Salesman*, or Marsha Norman's *'night, Mother*. For each play, describe the quality of the characters' lives as they appear in the plays, and define what you believe each author considers to be the ideal life. With which author do you most agree, and why?
5. **CONNECTIONS** Both *Kantan* and Samuel Beckett's *Krapp's Last Tape* show a central character seeking enlightenment. What is each author's view on the nature of enlightenment? Do both Rosei and Krapp reach true enlightenment? How does each character achieve enlightenment (or not), and what is his response to what he learns?

Suggested Readings

Hare, Thomas B. "Apples and Oranges: The Construction of Character in Greek Tragedy and Noh Drama." *Par-Rapport: A Journal of the Humanities* 5–6 (1982–83): 3–12.

———. *Zeami's Style: The Noh Plays of Zeami Motokiyo*. Stanford, CA: Stanford UP, 1986.

Johnson, Martha. "Reflections of Inner Life: Masks and Acting in Ancient Greek Tragedy and Japanese Noh Drama." *Modern Drama* 35 (1992): 20–34.

Lai, Sheng Chuan. "Mysticism and Noh in O'Neill." *Theatre Journal* 35 (March 1983): 74–87.

Lamarque, Peter. "Expression and the Mask: The Dissolution of Personality in Noh." *Journal of Aesthetics and Art Criticism* 47 (1989): 157–68.

Menta, Ed. "Beckett in a Noh light: An Analysis of Selected Plays of Samuel Beckett Using Critical Principles of the Japanese Noh Theatre." *Theatre Studies* 35 (1990): 50–63.

Takahashi, Yasunari. "The Theatre of Mind: Samuel Beckett and the Noh." *Encounter* 58 (April 1982): 66–73. See commentary on p. 2026.

Toyoichiro, Nogami. "The Monodramatic Principle of the Noh Theatre." Translated by Chiedo Irie Mulhern. *Journal of the Association of Teachers of Japanese* 16 (1981): 72–86.

Wang, I. Chun. "Life-Is-a-Dream Theme: Pillow/Dream in Chinese and Japanese Drama." *Tamkang Review* 18 (Autumn 1987–Summer 1988): 277–86.

William Shakespeare

Hamlet, Prince of Denmark (p. 1474)

On the surface, *Hamlet* is a "revenge tragedy" in the tradition of Thomas Kyd's *Spanish Tragedy*. The conventional pattern of such revenge tragedies depicts a ghost who calls for vengeance and a revenger who pretends to be insane at least part of the time and who eventually dies having completed his revenge. Shakespeare enriches this formula by making his revenger, Hamlet, an unusually complex figure and by exploring many themes beyond the act of revenge — themes ranging from suicide to the meaning of life. Students may approach this play from numerous angles and should consider a variety of the issues Shakespeare raises: How far do appearances deceive? Can truth ever fully be known? What is the nature of evil? How far should we accept human frailty and changeability? What makes an effective ruler? How does the notion of honor affect how we live, how far do guilt or innocence matter in a potentially predetermined universe? In what ways are our lives ruled by Providence or our own natures?

The character of Hamlet and the difficulties he has in pursuing the revenge the ghost has demanded constitute the core of the play. Students should consider not only the evident changes and developments in Hamlet's character during the play but also the character of Hamlet before we first meet him. This can be pieced together from comments made by other characters and by clues dropped by Hamlet himself. Such a Hamlet was considered the "rose of the fair state" and equally adept as a courtier, soldier, and scholar. The Hamlet we initially meet has undergone a profound change and is evidently suffering from dark suspicions and depression. His father's death and mother's hasty remarriage have severely shaken his view of the world. By focusing on his only unguarded speech (when he talks in soliloquy), we can trace his development through despair, self-disgust, and, finally, self-knowledge. His first soliloquy is disjointed, full of whirling accusations and dismay. As time progresses his speeches become more ordered and orderly as he matures and comes to terms with the world in which he must live (and die). Hamlet's drive to know recalls that of Oedipus, and it is, ultimately, as destructive as Oedipus's — of both self and others. As with Oedipus, it is useful to consider what might be Hamlet's "tragic flaw," but beware of oversimplifying his character. Samuel Coleridge suggests that Hamlet suffers from an "overplus of the meditative faculty," an interpretation that could lead to a discussion regarding how an individual's will to act can be smothered by thinking too much about the action; Hamlet's difficulties, however, go deeper than this.

Old Hamlet's ghost provokes the first in a series of problems for Hamlet: Is this an authentic spirit or a devil sent to tempt him? Despite a "prophetic" feeling that the ghost speaks the truth, Hamlet has initial doubts over its authenticity, which is one reason he insists on getting further proof of its accusations. The ghost has been "prompted to [his] revenge by heaven and hell" — that is, by a sense of divine justice but also by anger. As it is impossible to disconnect the two, the act of revenge is both a moral and immoral choice.

Hamlet cannot ignore the moral problem of revenge that makes it difficult to redress a crime without becoming a criminal oneself. He is not afraid to die, but he is afraid of damnation — maybe even of the act of killing. But once he has firm proof that Claudius poisoned his father, he has no choice but to kill his uncle to restore his family honor. Honor and duty are powerful motivations in the play and strip many characters of their freedom of choice. Laertes must avenge his father and sister; to ensure this, he is drawn into using a deceit he would normally reject. Ophelia rejects Hamlet and spies on him out of duty to her father. Even Gertrude's obtuseness can be explained by her sense of duty to husband and monarch.

Students should be encouraged to make comparisons between the various kings and young men they see and hear about. Shakespeare intends for the characters of Old Hamlet, Old Fortinbras, Fortinbras, Laertes, and Horatio to act as foils to Hamlet. Young Hamlet is as unlike his father as Fortinbras is to his. Whereas Fortinbras and Old Hamlet are men of passion, warriors who do not hesitate to throw themselves into conflict and justify it with notions of honor, Hamlet is caught between passion and judgment, which he thoughtfully recognizes are frequently at odds. He admires Horatio for his judgment, seeing him as a man who lives by reason and who refuses to allow passions to sway him. Yet can one live a full life by living in such a way? Horatio is ever on the periphery of action: He survives to tell the tale, but he is not a player. The death of Hamlet's father paralyzes Prince Hamlet, while both Fortinbras and Laertes actively counter the deaths of their fathers: Fortinbras, through "noble" battle, ends with the crown of Denmark; Laertes, through dishonest schemes, ends with death. The way one acts makes a difference.

The fight between Hamlet and Laertes over Ophelia's grave announces that Hamlet has changed since his voyage to England — he is readier for action, just as he had seized the opportunity to change ships. When Hamlet declares, "There's a divinity that shapes our ends / Rough-hew them how we will" (5.2.10–11), he has reached an important understanding. Although he has been unable to make sense of it, he can now accept that he must let fate guide him, for it is something he cannot fight. All he can do is to attempt to live with honor, despite fate's demands. Hamlet fails in this as long as he fails to avenge his father. Shakespeare seems to suggest that man must simply accept whatever fate throws at him and try always to do his best. Hamlet's new maturity convinces us that he will now be able to meet such a challenge. Hamlet finally kills Claudius, not with a plan but on the spur of the moment, after witnessing the poisoning of his mother and Laertes's confession pointing out the king's additional treacheries. Claudius dies quickly with all his sins upon his head, unable to expiate himself, and Old Hamlet is avenged in full. That Hamlet must also die is an issue related, perhaps, to the nature of evil.

The very fact that a ghost walks the battlements is, as Horatio recognizes in the opening scene, an indication that something is wrong in Denmark. Throughout the play we find striking images of corruption, decay, and death: This is the real and dirty world of Denmark. The evil, initiated by Claudius in killing his brother, reaches out to touch everyone, and Hamlet, as avenger, becomes the direct and indirect cause of further deaths and even the object of revenge himself. In order to purge Denmark of evil, Hamlet becomes a part of that evil and so must die along with anyone else who is contaminated to restore the state to health. The difference between his death and that of Claudius is that his is a noble sacrifice, whereas Claudius's is merely an ignoble end. That Hamlet insists Horatio remain alive to tell his tale and to ensure that he is remembered honorably is an indication of this important distinction.

Claudius should not be viewed as a straightforward villain. Students should note that on the surface what he says often appears reasonable. It is only when we view his words in light of the guilt and suspicions we know he has that we can recognize his more selfish and even sinister purposes. Claudius enjoys the pomp and show of kingship but is neither a fool nor a tyrant, despite Hamlet's criticisms. He consults his council and rules practically, negotiating rather than fighting. There is no doubt he committed a serious crime to gain this position and his conscience troubles him, but in refusing to give up what he has gained he cannot repent. He recognizes Hamlet's popularity and cannot treat him too harshly if he is to maintain control (a control revealed to be tenuous, as the people take Laertes's side against him). He must eliminate Hamlet, however, once he realizes that Hamlet knows his guilty secret. Claudius's initial plan of sending Hamlet to England to be executed is thwarted by the pirate attack on the ship. Hamlet returns to Denmark unscathed, so Claudius expediently manipulates Laertes to assist in Hamlet's killing, displaying an enviable capacity for instant action. Like Macbeth, Claudius discovers that one crime can only lead to another and, in Shakespeare's ordered world, can only end in the perpetrator's death.

There has been much discussion regarding whether Hamlet plays at being mad or actually becomes mad, which fuels the debate over "appearance" but neglects the simple expedience of the decision to put on an "antic disposition." Hamlet's realization of danger is real, and his "madness" does help protect him (as it did the original Hamlet in the tale on which Shakespeare based his play). Polonius is long-winded (in his first speech it takes him thirty-two words to say "yes") but it is a mistake to dismiss him as a fool. Polonius is the king's chief minister and minion, adept at intriguing and spying, even on his own son. Polonius makes most sense when his character is read as a purely political figure. Thus, ethics and morality only feature in his nature insofar as they are politically expedient. At one point, Hamlet likens him to Jephthah, who sacrificed his own daughter (2.2.359), and we see Polonius quite willing to use his daughter to gain information on a man who is threatening his king.

Ophelia should gain our sympathy as a victim. She is treated cruelly by Hamlet, who uses her to get at Gertrude and Claudius, and further used by her father as a spy against her former lover. Her entire life has been guided by men, but when their support disappears — after Polonius has been killed by Hamlet and Laertes remains in France — she collapses. The world of *Hamlet* is male dominated, and the women are given little opportunity for independence, which raises the question of whether or not they can be held responsible for their behavior. The men of the play seem to think not: The ghost, like Hamlet, is more concerned over Gertrude's incest than losing the crown, but both blame Claudius for Gertrude's actions. After all, their reasoning goes, she is only a weak woman from whom little more could be expected!

An uncut performance of *Hamlet* would run for six hours, and although any performance nowadays will have been cut, students should be aware that there are no irrelevancies here. Every line contributes to our understanding of not just Shakespeare's time but our own time as well, for the human issues *Hamlet* explores have not changed as much in four hundred years as we would sometimes like to believe.

SUSAN C. W. ABBOTSON

Questions for Discussion

1. In what ways does the ghost influence Hamlet's decisions? Can Hamlet trust it? Should he?
2. What are the women's lives like at Elsinore? Are Ophelia or Gertrude responsible for what happens to them?
3. In what way can Laertes and Fortinbras be said to be "foils" to Hamlet's character?
4. Hamlet enjoys mocking Polonius, but is Polonius really a fool? Does he deserve to die? Do you believe that any of the characters who are killed deserve to die? If so, why?
5. Why does Hamlet so often delay killing Claudius? Why not kill him when he is praying?
6. Although it is a tragedy, there are many comic moments in *Hamlet*. What types of humor does Shakespeare seem to use and when and why do such moments occur?
7. What is the difference between blank verse and prose and why does Shakespeare switch between the two? In speaking to Horatio, Rosencrantz and Guildenstern, the audience, Claudius, Gertrude, and the Players, does Hamlet use verse or prose? What does his choice tell us about these relationships? Do any other characters alternate between verse and prose like this?
8. What are the functions of the theatrical troupe and its performance? How is "acting" a relevant issue to the play as a whole?
9. To what degree can Claudius be seen as simply evil? Does he not have any redeeming personal qualities? Is Claudius a bad king? Would Hamlet have made a better one if he had been elected?
10. Why does Shakespeare have Hamlet's return to Denmark take place in a graveyard? Has Hamlet changed while he has been away?
11. Under what circumstances could Hamlet be called both a hero and a villain? Who is ultimately responsible for the "unfortunate" events that occur in the play — events such as Hamlet losing the crown, Polonius's murder, Ophelia's suicide, Laertes' trickery, Hamlet's death?
12. Do you consider *Hamlet* to be ultimately optimistic or pessimistic?

Topics for Writing

1. How necessary is Fortinbras? Many productions of *Hamlet* have chosen to eliminate the character. Discuss how such an omission affects the dynamics of the play and explain how you feel this character ought to be presented.
2. By analyzing the language, logic, and presentation of Hamlet's main soliloquies, outline the developments they exhibit of his growing control and understanding. In what ways can we say that the Hamlet at the close of the play is different from the Hamlet at the start?
3. Compare and contrast two different productions of *Hamlet*. You may select from the number of film, television, or audio cassette recordings available or, if possible, go see a live performance. Giving reasons, include an assessment of which version you think Shakespeare would have preferred.

4. After reading Tom Stoppard's "Encore" *Hamlet*, write a version of *Hamlet* that will take ten minutes to perform from beginning to end and yet encapsulate the longer play. Consider the key developments in each of the five acts and include any lines that you feel are integral to the play's meaning. Other speeches can be paraphrased in whatever idiom you choose. You may leave out certain characters but do not add any.

5. **CONNECTIONS** Compare the character of Claudius in *Hamlet* to that of Oedipus in Sophocles' *Oedipus the King*. Which seems more suited to being an effective ruler and why?

6. **CONNECTIONS** Compare and contrast the suicidal impulses of Hamlet and Jessie from Marsha Norman's *'night, Mother*. Explore how far this impulse can be said to be springing from similar concerns.

Suggested Readings

Bevington, David M, ed. *Twentieth Century Interpretations of "Hamlet": A Collection of Critical Essays*. Englewood Cliffs, NJ: Prentice, 1968.

Bradley, A. C. *Shakespearean Tragedy*. New York: Penguin, 1991.

Cantor, Paul. *Shakespeare: "Hamlet."* Cambridge: Cambridge UP, 1989.

Dean, Leonard F., ed. *Shakespeare: Modern Essays in Criticism*. New York: Oxford UP, 1967.

Dion, Gregg. "Fortinbras, Our Contemporary." *Theatre Studies* 38 (1993): 17–27.

Hopkins, Lisa. "'That's Wormwood': Hamlet Plays His Mother." *Hamlet Studies* 16 (1994): 83–85.

Jones, Ernest. *Hamlet and Œdipus*. New York: Norton, 1949.

King, Walter N. *Hamlet's Search for Meaning*. Athens: U of Georgia P, 1982.

Lupton, Julia Reinhard. *After Oedipus: Shakespeare in Psychoanalysis*. Ithaca, NY: Cornell UP, 1993.

Maher, Mary Z. *Modern Hamlets and Their Soliloquies*. Iowa City: U of Iowa P, 1992.

Prosser, Eleanor. *Hamlet and Revenge*. 2d ed. Stanford, CA: Stanford UP, 1972.

States, Bert O. *"Hamlet" and the Concept of Character*. Baltimore: John Hopkins UP, 1992.

Wofford, Susanne L., ed. *Hamlet*. Case Studies in Contemporary Criticism Series. Boston: Bedford–St. Martin's, 1994.

Wood, Robert E. *Some Necessary Questions of the Play: A Stage-Centered Analysis of Shakespeare's "Hamlet."* Lewisburg, PA: Bucknell UP, 1994.

HENRIK IBSEN

A Doll House (p. 1579)

Seen by many as the unofficial "father of modern drama," Henrik Ibsen had a career that went through many phases. *A Doll House* is a pioneer work that attempts to portray controversial social issues in a realistic manner without recourse to melodrama or sentimentality. John Gassner describes Ibsen as "too radical" for the nineteenth century but "too conservative" for the twentieth. It is true that by today's standards Nora's rebellion may not seem so major, but in 1879 it was considered downright immoral to suggest that a woman could be capable of abandoning both husband and children. By showing Torvald's romanticized marriage to be an empty dream, Ibsen was exploding the conventional, sentimental Victorian ideals of the "little woman" and the "angel in the house." As Gassner suggests, Nora's leaving to pursue "self-fulfillment" challenges the traditional "sanctity of marriage" in its innate plea for "female emancipation." Students, however, should be warned against solely considering the issue of women's rights within the play, for Ibsen is not so narrowly focused. *A Doll House* asks us to consider issues of hypocrisy, pseudo-respectability, human nature, and the "life-lie" that go beyond gender. For Ibsen, the "life-lie" is an individual's greatest offense against himself and others. It occurs when we do not allow ourselves to live according to our true natures but hide behind idealizations and deceits: Both Nora and Torvald are guilty of this.

George Bernard Shaw's *The Quintessence of Ibsenism* (1891) did much to bring Ibsen to critical attention. Defining idealism as that which masks realities that are too unpleasant to face, and realism as that which unmasks the truth for the general audience, Shaw saw himself and Ibsen as "realists," for both liked to engage in the stripping away of masks. Shaw also introduced the idea of the "discussion play" as opposed to the "well-made play." A "well-made play" creates suspense through meticulous plotting that gradually releases information toward a final dénouement; both Shaw and Ibsen felt this to be artificial. A "discussion play" can be equally well-crafted, but it leads to an unresolved discussion that supersedes the demands of plot and allows the audience to judge events for themselves. The heated controversies surrounding *A Doll House* indicate that this is an effective, early example of a "discussion play." That Ibsen intended to disturb his audience and make them think is without question; that he does so without resorting to diatribe, and with such a well-crafted and entertaining piece, is a measure of his genius.

The realism of Ibsen's work goes beyond mere set detail, although that is an important aspect of how he wished his plays to be produced. Ibsen tries to create psychologically real people in commonplace social situations. One should not ignore his use of symbolism, but it does not negate the sense of reality he generates. The furnishings of the Helmers' "doll house" are an early indication of the owner's consumer mentality, where appearances count most. From its piano, etchings, and "well-bound" books to its stove and comfortable chairs, it is on the surface an ideal setting. But is it a real home or just the doll house of the title? The two doors to the room will symbolize Nora's eventual options: One leads to Torvald's inner sanctum and the other to the outside world. Ibsen's symbols do not intrude so much as help point to what lies beneath the surface. Nora's desire for macaroons ensures we understand she is yet a child who needs to grow up; she is, after all, a willing "doll." The stripped and disheveled Christmas tree indicates the extent to which Nora has been shattered, though she continues to uphold a veneer of gaiety in front of others. The fact that Torvald will not even allow Nora to read the mail, locking it in a box to which only he holds a key, shows how far he has kept her apart from the outside world in order that she may remain under his total control.

Initially, Nora does deserve the incessant diminutives Torvald heaps on her, although one may resent the intellectual disdain such objectifications imply. She virtually twitters as she throws things around, leaving them for servants to pick up, and coyly flirts with her husband and childishly plays with her children: She *is* a "little lark," "a little squirrel," "a little featherbrain." Her frivolous world is in stark contrast to Torvald's cautious, ordered world of business. He naturally prefers the sanctuary of his study or of work, merely using his wife as an occasional diversion or entertainment. But his world will be shown to be as remote and cold as Norway itself, a strict world of men and law in which women are allowed no footage. As Nora develops we see her being related, in contrast, to the warmer, more passionate climes of Italy. It is to Italy she takes Torvald after showing some spirit in defying the male world and procuring the necessary funds. It is an Italian dance, the tarantella, that Ibsen uses to indicate her feminine growth and development into a woman. When Nora threatens to burst out as a woman in the tarantella, Torvald feels compelled to control her and quiet her down, although, to his consternation, his attempts are less than effective. It is a growth he will not be able to comprehend or prevent.

Although Nora is initially naive, she is not stupid, and Ibsen has prepared us from the start for her hidden depths. Students should note the difference between the way she talks to her husband and the way she talks to Dr. Rank or Mrs. Linde. Although she banters with all three, it is on different levels, and with different awarenesses. She is capable of both manipulating her husband, playing up to his expectations of her as a "feather-head" and fooling him: He thought her to be making Christmas decorations when she was really engaged in copying to make some extra cash. She eats macaroons in defiance of his commands and openly denies it to him. She has a spirit that has not yet been crushed, albeit the only independence she can achieve is through deceit and lying. Although Nora plays the childish role Torvald demands of her, we know that inwardly she resents it. We see this in the pride she displays over her "adult" actions of getting the money and independently working to repay it. The fact that the law actually prohibited a woman from borrowing money without a male relative's consent is important to recognize. Norway is a patriarchal society, and it will not be easy for Nora to combat it alone. It is an incredibly brave action she takes in leaving at the play's end.

Nora wins our sympathy through her generous spirit and because of her domineering husband. Her generous nature is indicated from the start as she overtips the porter and earnestly tries to assist her old friend, Mrs. Linde. Her spending is noticeably on others and not on herself. Even the crime she has committed was done to restore her husband's health. He had thoughtlessly refused to raise the money they needed for the trip the doctor recommended, preferring instead to risk leaving his wife and newborn child without a husband and father. Nora's marriage has no pretense of equality — Torvald simply cannot envisage such a relationship. He selfishly runs their lives according to his own whims and does not feel it necessary to consider his wife's feelings. Nora is aware that their marriage is based on appearances and realizes she may need something to keep Torvald's interest once her looks have faded. What Ibsen is telling us is that a true marriage needs a deeper bond than Torvald and Nora have managed to create. Nora has invested a great deal into her marriage, far more than Torvald could ever envisage, but she has invested unwisely and will be forced to recognize this sad fact.

We may ask why Nora decides to admit the forgery to Krogstad; he is only guessing and has no firm proof. Is it an act of defiance betraying her inner strength or simple naïveté? Her natural impulse is for truth rather than deception, thus she instinctively answers Torvald's questions about Krogstad honestly and ensures Torvald's unfortunate decision to fire Krogstad. In her dealings with Krogstad, Nora finds herself swiftly out of her depth; she is too innocent and inexperienced in the ways of the world. She is unable to offer the appropriate defense, appealing instead to idealistic notions of honor and sensibility. She has some awareness of the power relations of the male world, but not enough to judge accurately how to deal with Krogstad. Torvald is similarly incompetent in his dealings, as he is too concerned with his ego to judge clearly. While we can sympathize with Nora's failings, it is harder for us to sympathize with Torvald, who misjudges through pompous pride rather than ignorance.

We see the irony as Torvald snobbishly condemns Krogstad, unaware that his condemnation is going straight to the heart of his wife. Torvald's own respectability is not so pure; we know that he turned a blind eye to his father-in-law's criminal practices and even helped to clear him. He can only afford to live the life he does because of sacrifices his wife has made — sacrifices he could never even acknowledge. He dismisses Krogstad not because of the man's reputation but for purely personal reasons; thus he invalidates any idea of merit being integral to a man's success. When Nora calls him "narrow-minded," she is blurting out a truth. Torvald *is* a hypocrite, and his emotionless calculations make him scarcely human.

Although a minor character, Dr. Rank performs a number of functions, one of which is as a foil to Torvald. In contrast to Torvald, he treats Nora with respect and an undemanding love. As a cynic, his commentary on the world is a realistic vision of its amorality. The morally corrupt do tend to fare better than the scrupulously honest, as the world itself is not concerned with honesty, just the appearance of it. Rank's father contracted syphilis from extramarital liaisons, and his son has congenital syphilis from which he will soon die. Thus he becomes an emblem of the way the older generation's depravity can continue to affect future generations. Similarly, Nora is right when she realizes that she must change before she can be a fit mother. She does not wish her children to suffer the same blindness and restrictions that have dominated her generation.

The scene in which Rank declares his love touches on many issues in the play. Confessing his love to Nora lifts a huge burden from Rank's shoulders, and after this he is noticeably buoyant, despite his impending death. This underlines the necessity for truth-telling, as secrets are a heavy burden. In addition, we gain further evidence that Nora is not so unaware of reality. Nora knew of Rank's love all along and is annoyed at his confession. Whilst this love remained unspoken, she could pretend that it did not exist; after all, this is a world in which appearances take precedence over truths. Rank is a man with whom Nora has talked and behaved more openly, having been able to set aside her doll persona. By treating her as a real human being, he has been able to give her the companionship Torvald could not. Nora's fine sensibility is underlined by her refusal to take Rank's money once he has altered their relationship by declaring his passion. Although we may be initially surprised at her refusal, her impulse is the right one, reinforced by the realization that Krogstad will not allow her to buy back the bond.

Mrs. Linde, meanwhile, can be seen as a foil to Nora. While Nora married into an idealized dream of love, Mrs. Linde first married because she felt responsible for her family. She gave up her true love for the financial security of a richer man who subsequently lost his money and died, leaving her to go out into the world and work to support her mother and younger brothers. Though harsh, this has perhaps been the making of Mrs. Linde; she has gained self-respect from her achievements. She is now a woman who can bind herself to a man she respects without losing that independence. Her misfortune has allowed her to tap her own hidden resources, and she may be the lead Nora must learn to follow.

Krogstad, the man Mrs. Linde once loved, is far more human than Torvald. He did not rest on scrupulous sensibilities when his family's well-being was at stake, a decision Ibsen does not actually condemn. Although Krogstad initially appears to be the villain of the piece, Ibsen will turn the tables on us. Krogstad is scarred by life and knows the way of the world — that it is essentially corrupt and run by appearances. Respectability is a must for certain advancements in society, but it need only be a surface affair and is something that can be acquired rather than won with honor. Both Krogstad and Mrs. Linde have suffered in life and both have learned from these blows to become attuned to the real ways of the world and be supremely practical people. In an interesting gender reversal, Mrs. Linde proposes to him as she persuades him that they need each other equally — and we cannot fault the honesty of this. Indeed, they exhibit the qualities on which a true marriage should be based: mutual honesty and respect rather than concealment and false-hood. Thus the woman who married for money and the man with the dubious reputation defeat our expectations as they turn out to be the examples of how to behave. Krogstad even takes pity on Nora and returns the bond so that he might be worthy of his new wife. Indeed, it is Nora and Torvald who have done everything wrong.

Torvald's image of Nora is romantic fantasy: No human being could really be like that. Indeed, it restricts Nora from being human as it denies her her own personality. She finally learns to reject Torvald's "doll-like" image of her as she realizes that this rejection is the only way she can reclaim her humanity. Torvald helps her in this decision by his reaction to her dealings with Krogstad: He completely condemns her, does not consider her altruistic motives, and only considers how he will be affected. Nora realizes that she has been the victim, also, of a romantic dream, having expected her husband to stand by her and even to nobly take the blame. She now realizes that such "a wonderful thing" is only fantasy. She needs to enter the real world so that she can discover how it operates and discover an identity for herself. Torvald tries to rekindle his dream world when he is assured there is no longer any threat from Krogstad, but Nora refuses to allow this retreat. She insists they face each other honestly. She recognizes her own fault in having allowed first her father and then Torvald to use her as a plaything, but she concludes that theirs is the greater fault for expecting her to fulfill such a role and for not allowing her to be any more than that. Torvald offers to teach her now but it is too late: She has lost respect for him. We must also seriously doubt that he even has the ability to teach her, as he still has lessons himself to learn. He does offer to change, and she rightly judges that this can only happen if she leaves.

Susan C. W. Abbotson

Questions for Discussion

1. What can be assessed from a careful consideration of how the Helmers' home and home life are depicted?
2. In what ways does Nora change in each of the three acts? In what aspects does she remain constant? How is the Nora at the close of the play a better or worse person than she is at the start?
3. How does Torvald treat his wife? What lies at the heart of this treatment?
4. What kind of deceits does Ibsen suggest can be condoned and what deceits does he condemn? Is motivation an issue?
5. What is the function and significance of the following images: the maca-roons, the Christmas tree, the children's presents, the tarantella, the letter box, the whole idea of dolls and doll houses?

6. What is the role and function of Dr. Rank? How does his relationship with Nora contrast with her marital relationship?
7. What are the roles and functions of Krogstad and Mrs. Linde?
8. For which of the characters in the play can we feel any sympathy and why?
9. How would having Nora stay instead of leave change the way we perceive the messages of the play?
10. What aspects of this play seem to you to be particularly realistic and what aspects are not?
11. Could this be called a comedy or a tragedy? Does the play exhibit elements of either of those genres?
12. What do you think might happen next to these characters?

Topics for Writing

1. Contrast the relationship of Krogstad and Mrs. Linde to that of Torvald and Nora Helmer. You need to trace what we know of the changes each relationship goes or has gone through and assess which one Ibsen seems to prefer.
2. Using *A Doll House* as evidence, what does Ibsen seem to suggest about the nature of women and how they should be treated within the home and society in general?
3. Imagine one year has passed and Nora returns home to visit her husband and children. Write a short story or play scene that illustrates this meeting. Consider how both Torvald and Nora may or may not have changed in the passing year.
4. **CONNECTIONS** Looking at *A Doll House* and Anton Chekhov's *The Bear*, consider what Ibsen and Chekhov seem to suggest about the nature of love.
5. **CONNECTIONS** Compare *A Doll House* with either Arthur Miller's *Death of a Salesman* or August Strindberg's *Miss Julie* and assess how far each can be considered realistic *and* tragic. Bear in mind the respective playwright's views on the nature of both realism and tragedy.

Suggested Readings

Ahmad, Shaiuddin, and Angela Gawel. "The Politics of Money: Incomplete Feminism in *A Doll's House*." *Dalhousie Review* 70 (1990): 170–90.

Davies, H. Neville. "Not Just a Bang and a Whimper: The Inconclusiveness of Ibsen's *A Doll's House*." *Critical Quarterly* 24.3 (1982): 33–43.

Fjelde, Rolf, ed. *Ibsen: A Collection of Critical Essays*. Englewood Cliffs, NJ: Prentice, 1965.

Johnston, Brian. "Three Stages of *A Doll House*." *Comparative Drama* 25.4 (1991–92): 311–28.

Lebowitz, Naomi. *Ibsen and the Great World*. Baton Rouge: Louisiana State UP, 1990.

Lyons, Charles R., ed. *Critical Essays on Henrik Ibsen*. Boston: G. K. Hall, 1987.

McFarlane, James. *Ibsen and Meaning: Studies, Essays, and Prefaces 1953–87*. Norwich, CT: Norvik, 1989.

Quigley, Austin E. "*A Doll's House* Revisited." *Modern Drama* 27 (1984): 584–603.

Shafer, Yvonne, ed. *Approaches to Teaching Ibsen's "A Doll's House."* New York: MLA, 1985.

———. *Henrik Ibsen: Life, Work, and Criticism*. Fredericton, NB: York, 1985.

Templeton, Joan. "*The Doll House* Backlash: Criticism, Feminism, and Ibsen." *PMLA* 104 (January 1989): 28–40.

Young, Robin. *Time's Disinherited Children: Childhood, Regression, and Sacrifice in the Plays of Henrik Ibsen*. Norwich, CT: Norvik, 1989.

AUGUST STRINDBERG

Miss Julie (p. 1633)

August Strindberg's own unhappy upbringing may be at the root of his objections to conventional authority, and he rejects not only the traditional stage techniques of his time but also the traditional beliefs and conventions of his society. *Miss Julie* exhibits many important dramatic innovations from its attempt to create realistic dialogue that mimics everyday speech to its refusal to destroy the illusion of reality with scene breaks, to its inclusion of music and ballet to utilize the actors' talents. Furthermore, its very situation — an illicit affair between a young lady and her father's valet — though considered shocking, was one that clearly grew out of the real world. Students should recognize that Strindberg is attempting to create a realistic setting by the detailed stage directions he supplies. He wishes us to view his characters as we would real-life people, considering their motives and beliefs from various perspectives.

Strindberg makes it clear in his Foreword to *Miss Julie* that he had intended to create a drama that manifests his naturalist beliefs. Strindberg recognizes the basic conflicts of life as drastically polarized between love and hate, life and death. The Darwinian principle of the survival of the fittest is the sole deciding factor regarding who fails or succeeds within personal relationships or class conflicts. Strindberg sees the aristocracy as decaying and bound for destruction by natural law and the lower classes, by the strength of their ambition, inevitably taking control. It is as though the aristocracy have nowhere left to go and so it is only the lower classes who can have any sense of direction.

Strindberg warns us against taking sides in the conflict between Miss Julie, last representative of a failing aristocracy, and Jean, the ruthless, amoral manipulator of the future. Each character is portrayed with apparent contradictions to convey the real complexity of human lives. Jean both despises and reveres the upper classes; he criticizes Miss Julie for being no better than an animal and yet dreams of one day becoming a count. Miss Julie wishes to be as one with the common folk and yet insists on judging herself by aristocratic standards. Miss Julie and Jean are both victimizers and victims, depending from what perspective you wish to view them. Each dreams, quite literally, of escaping the class to which he or she was born, yet each is incapable of such an act. Strindberg wishes us to recognize the good and bad in both his central characters but not to be misled that their goodness or badness will be deciding factors in their survival. Strindberg sees the concept of moral justice as a human construct, not one that necessarily applies to the natural world. Indeed, one can see that it is the traditionally better side of Miss Julie's character — her sense of honor and nobility — that destroys her, whereas it is Jean's worse, more selfish and brutal side that allows him to survive. What Strindberg wishes us to recognize is that the fates of both these characters have been determined by a number of factors created by their heredity, their environment, and the individual elements of chance. Such issues as morality or justice have little place in the modern world.

Jean declares, "When the gentry try to behave like the common people — they become common." Jean believes that by behaving like the gentry he will become gentry. He has educated himself to recognize fine food and wine, learned to dance and to speak French. Yet Strindberg forces us to wonder how deep Jean's refinement really goes. For Jean, these "refinements" are merely a means to an end. He easily allows his "baser" instincts to lead him when he deals with Miss Julie, first seducing and then betraying her. On a Darwinian level we are all animals, and Strindberg is aware that refinement in anyone is little more than a veneer. Is Miss Julie's "refinement" any more secure when we consider her willingness to be seduced? Jean has the upper hand in their relationship, owing to both his class and his gender. Being lower class, he has no scruples of honor or nobility to get in the way of his ambitions, and he lies and manipulates with ease. As a man he has the sexual advantage of living in a time when a woman's reputation is destroyed by extramarital sex, whereas a man's is more likely developed. Also, the woman runs the further danger of pregnancy, which would betray her illicit act to the world, while the male may remain anonymous unless he chooses to acknowledge his participation.

Miss Julie is unsure of what she wants to do with her life. Her mother's efforts to turn her into a man-hater, if not a man, have not been wholly successful. They have set up antipathies within Miss Julie that precipitate her erratic behavior as she tries to satisfy her conflicting desires. Unable to change, she remains perpetually dissatisfied with both her class and her gender. The servants reluctantly put up with her intrusion on their celebrations, believing they do not have the power to refuse. It is an act she would not have dared had her father been home. In Jean, however, she meets someone who recognizes his own potential for power, and it is a power that ultimately leads to her destruction. Jean vacillates between playing the part Miss Julie demands of him — that of a romantic lover — and the part closer to his true nature — that of a ruthless entrepreneur. It is the latter role that will dominate as he finally sends her to commit suicide, not out of a sense of pity so much as to save his own skin.

Whether Jean or Miss Julie are capable of love is purely speculative. Rather than view each other directly as human beings, each seems to construct an ideal of the other that is gradually shattered. At base, Jean appears too practical and Miss Julie's romantic dreams are shown to be as false as the picture she paints of Lake Como. For both, love seems more a weapon each uses to try to dominate the other. The risks Miss Julie takes to assert her independence are great. Jean uses his sexuality to bargain with her until he discovers that she does not actually have the cash he needs to start his hotel. She tries to bargain with him but has nothing he really wants. As a man, Jean can brutally demean her as a "whore" and she has no defense. In that kitchen she is way out of her element and is battling Jean on his "home turf." She is bound to lose, and her ultimate destruction is complete. She pretends for a while that she may be capable of lowering herself to become the wife of an innkeeper, but she is finally forced to recognize her true nature. In this recognition lies the seed of her stature as a tragic protagonist as she bravely accepts her doom and her fate.

Susan C. W. Abbotson

Questions for Discussion

1. What impression does Jean immediately give us of Miss Julie and her behavior, and how far is this borne out when we first meet her?
2. Why has Miss Julie's engagement been broken off and what lies behind her "training" session?
3. What are the differences and similarities in the way Jean treats Miss Julie and Kristine? Do both women treat Jean in the same way?

4. What are the essential differences between Jean and Miss Julie, Jean and Kristine, and Miss Julie and Kristine?
5. What does it mean to be a member of the upper or lower class? What demands do each have of its membership?
6. Does Jean ever tell the truth? If so, what do you believe that truth to be? Is Miss Julie more truthful?
7. What is the symbolism behind Diana (Miss Julie's dog), Miss Julie's bird, and the kitchen setting?
8. How far can Miss Julie's parents be said to be "characters" in this play? How do their actions influence the drama?
9. What are the functions of the peasants' intrusion? In what way is the song they sing significant?
10. Does Miss Julie love Jean, or is she using the idea of love to hide from certain truths? Does Jean love anyone?
11. For whom do you feel the most sympathy in the play and why? Could any of the characters behave differently from the way they do, or is their behavior, throughout, determined by their nature? What do Strindberg's views on gender appear to be?
12. Why does Miss Julie commit suicide and why does Jean need to tell her to do so?

Topics for Writing

1. Critics see Strindberg's *Miss Julie* as a realistic play. What aspects of the play do you feel contribute to this feeling of realism?
2. To what extent can the conflict between Jean and Miss Julie be said to be solely a class issue?
3. At the close of the play Miss Julie exits to commit suicide. Imagine that before doing so she has time to write a detailed letter to explain why she feels compelled to do this. Based on the events of the play and what you learn about Miss Julie's character, write this letter. You should indicate to whom Miss Julie is writing, as it may color what she decides to say.
4. **CONNECTIONS** Both *Miss Julie* and Henrik Ibsen's *A Doll House* deal with gender relationships and pass comment on the treatment and possibilities of women in the nineteenth century. Strindberg ends with his heroine committing suicide, and Ibsen has his heroine leave home. To what extent are the actions of Miss Julie and Nora decided by the views of Strindberg and Ibsen on the character and place of women? Which playwright do you feel has the greater insight and sympathy over gender issues?
5. **CONNECTIONS** Both Miss Julie and William Shakespeare's Hamlet have unusual relationships with their parents — relationships that influence their actions and beliefs. Outline these relationships and explain how far the fates of Hamlet and Miss Julie have been determined by their parents.

Suggested Readings

Bertin, Michael, ed. *The Play and Its Critic: Essays for Eric Bentley.* Lanham, MD: UP of America, 1986.

Blackwell, Marilyn Johns, ed. *Structures of Influence: A Comparative Approach to August Strindberg.* Chapel Hill: U of North Carolina P, 1981.

Chaudhuri, Una. "Private Parts: Sex, Class, and Stage Space in *Miss Julie.*" *Theatre Journal* 45 (1993): 317–32.

Napieralski, Edmund. "*Miss Julie*: Strindberg's Tragic Fairy Tale." *Modern Drama* 26 (1983): 282–89.

Robinson, Michael, ed. *Strindberg and Genre*. Norwich, CT: Norvik, 1991.

Sprinchorn, Evert. *Strindberg as Dramatist*. New Haven, CT: Yale UP, 1982.

Stockenstrom, Goran, ed. *Strindberg's Dramaturgy*. Minneapolis: U of Minnesota P, 1988.

Tornquvist, Egil, and Barry Jacobs. *Strindberg's Miss Julie: A Play and Its Transpositions*. Norwich, CT: Norvik, 1988.

ANTON CHEKHOV

The Bear (p. 1661)

The Bear, in a fashion reminiscent of Alexander Pope's great satires, unveils a comical battle of the sexes that begins in words and moves toward a potentially physical conflict as the two characters prepare to duel. Smirnov's criticisms of fashionable women and their behavior are as comical as they are true; the humorous delivery serves to deflect possible offense. Popova is allowed to respond in defense of her sex and be equally satirical of male roles and expectations in her society. Each passes judgment on the faults of the other's gender by basing his or her assessments solely on personal experience. In this way, both authenticate their opinions through valid experiences while also showing the audience that there is more to both genders than either will allow.

As the Russian actor and producer Constantin Stanislavsky has suggested, "The poetic power of Chekhov's plays does not manifest itself at the first reading. After having read them, you say to yourself: This is good, but . . . it's nothing special, nothing to stun you with admiration. Everything as it should be. Familiar . . . truthful . . . nothing new. . . . Yet as you recollect some phrases and scenes, you feel you want to think about them longer. . . . You want to re-read it — and then you realize the depths hidden under the surface. . . . Chekhov is inexhaustible because, despite the everyday life which he appears to depict in his plays, he is really talking all the time not of the accidental and specific, but of the Human."

Although *The Bear* does not have the length of one of Chekhov's later, more serious plays, students should not dismiss it as an inconsequential sketch. Although Chekhov called it a "joke" and a "vaudeville," which imply a farcical work with little substance, we should not forget the tremendous acclaim and financial success the play achieved. Furthermore, it exhibits the onset and early development of Chekhov's dramatic techniques that did help to revolutionize the art of the theater. Moving away from sensational or sentimental melodrama, Chekhov focuses our attention on "real life" as it is lived by ordinary people.

Besides its brevity and easy humor, *The Bear* illustrates many of Chekhov's innovative trademarks. It may not contain the stronger vein of tragedy with which his later plays were imbued, but it has its serious side nonetheless. Popova and Smirnov are both failures in many ways, and the futility of their lives could at any moment defeat them. Popova is torn between resentment over her unfaithful, deceased husband and the tedium of the life of mourning and self-denial she has resolved to lead. Smirnov's anger and cynicism arise from both his serious financial problems and his unfortunate past relationships with women. Although the play appears cheerful on the surface, Chekhov was too honest a writer not to ensure that harsh truths remained just beneath that pleasant surface. His characters are genuine human beings involved in everyday life and must deal with all of its confusions.

There are a number of means by which Chekhov achieves his lifelike effect. One is by choosing an everyday event on which to base the action. What could be more mundane than a debt collection? In *The Bear* we witness a local landowner, Smirnov, attempting to reclaim a debt from the widow Popova and, against his better judgment, falling in love with her. This is not so much a romantic "falling in love" as a realistically contradictory and messy development. Dialogue is very important and Chekhov allows his characters to converse in a repetitive, disconnected, and at times, illogical fashion, as people often do in everyday life. In his choice of characters he celebrates ordinariness. Neither Smirnov nor Popova are strict stock characters, and both surprise us. Each has his or her own individualized merits and faults. While Popova has both spirit and courage, especially in the way she faces up to Smirnov, she is also both proud and vindictive. Smirnov is full of life but needs a little more self-discipline. With neither character behaving fully in the right or wrong, Chekhov allows his audience to decide with whom they will have the most sympathy.

Smirnov's honesty and his energy are his best features. Initially, he intrudes on Popova's posturing as the "mourning, heartbroken widow" with his "loud ring." His bombastic entrance is full of life and colorful language to contrast with Popova's lifeless seclusion and romantic clichés. Chekhov allows us to laugh at his lack of refinement while also admiring his lack of artifice. With his shouting and breaking of chairs he manages to shatter Popova's unnecessary seclusion and awaken her to the possibilities of life with a man who genuinely admires and loves her. Her allegiance to her late husband, depicted by her desire to give his horse, Toby, some extra oats (possibly a pun on her husband's evident tendency to "sow his wild oats"), is clearly broken by the end of the play. Gruff and direct, Smirnov is the most obvious candidate for the "bear" of the title. His directness allows him to see through Popova's artifice and to finally admit his own attraction to her, which has been building as the scene progresses. His growing attraction is subtly conveyed through a series of asides by which he acknowledges her beauty, her dimples, and her manner. It is, however, important to notice that it is, finally, not her outward beauty that wins his heart but her inner spirit.

Chekhov ensures we will not be deceived by appearances as he makes it evident that Popova's mourning is out of revenge rather than respect or love. Her feelings toward her late husband are rightly bitter; he was negligent and unfaithful. Her decision to sacrifice the rest of her life to revenge, by being everything her husband was not, is clearly a misguided one that needs to be prevented. Popova has allowed herself to be trapped by her own romanticized view of her position. She may be constant and faithful, but is this life she leads true to her nature? She has the spirit to match Smirnov, and though she calls him a brute, we should recognize that her behavior is, in many ways, more brutish when it is less honest. Her posturing nearly leads to her downfall, but luckily Smirnov is able to spark the "bearish," more natural side of her nature, and through this she wins herself a better husband. For all his temper, we know that Smirnov is a better man than her first husband; his single-mindedness may be translated into faithfulness and his financial dealings into generosity. Their future marriage may be full of arguments, but it promises to be more equal, more honest, and more lively than Popova's last marital experience.

The idea of freedom is central to all of Chekhov's work, especially freedom from lies. His goal was always the truth. The minor character of Luka provides the audience with a practical, no-nonsense voice of truth. As he tells Popova, "You're young, pretty, blooming with health — all you need is to live and enjoy yourself to the full." He knows her protracted mourning is an unnatural way to behave, whatever society's expectations. Chekhov saw the Russia of his day as a prison that confined people within its rules and social conventions. He encouraged people to escape such confinement.

Behind the satire in *The Bear* we can glimpse evidence of numerous gender restrictions that force both men and women to act unnaturally or cruelly toward each other. Chekhov derives much humor from having Smirnov refuse to treat Popova as his society demanded that one should treat a woman. We should not ignore Popova's ability to rise to that challenge, proving certain limitations in her society's view of women. The climax of the play, with the preposterous duel and subsequent change of heart of both characters as they end in an embrace, may seem improbable on one level, but it is, nevertheless, an honest reflection of the true nature and needs of both Popova and Smirnov.

Susan C. W. Abbotson

Questions for Discussion

1. What kind of man was Popova's late husband? How did he treat Popova?
2. Why is Popova mourning so intensely? Is this correct behavior on her part?
3. What is the function of Luka in the play? Why is his character necessary?
4. What is the relationship between Luka and his mistress? Does this tell us anything about Chekhov's views regarding class?
5. Why does Smirnov say what he does about women? What have his experiences with women been like? Whose fault has this been?
6. In what ways is Smirnov like a bear? Is this shown to be a good or bad aspect of his character?
7. Can anyone else in the play be seen as "bear-like"? What kind of animal might describe Popova's character?
8. What is the importance and function of Toby? How does he symbolize Popova's shifting affections?
9. What is it about Popova that wins Smirnov's affection?
10. What is it about Smirnov that wins Popova's affection?
11. In what ways is the relationship between these two realistic?
12. What expectations and aspects of social life is Chekhov satirizing in *The Bear*?

Topics for Writing

1. Although on the surface a farce, *The Bear* does convey some serious points. What appear to be the central messages and themes behind the foolery?
2. When do Popova and Smirnov make you laugh and why? Consider the techniques Chekhov uses to create humor in *The Bear*.
3. Assume that either Popova or Smirnov keeps a diary. Considering the character of whichever one you have chosen and the events that have just occurred, write a detailed entry to cover the day on which *The Bear* takes place. Do not simply relate what happens, but convey a sense of your character's thoughts of and reactions to the day's events.
4. **CONNECTIONS** *The Bear* is often called a "farce," whereas Edward Albee's *The Sandbox* is an early example of "absurdist drama." Compare and contrast

the ways in which Chekhov and Albee create humor within their plays to produce such laughter. At what or at whom is each playwright getting us to laugh?

5. **CONNECTIONS** Compare and contrast the ways in which *The Bear* and August Strindberg's *Miss Julie* present the following aspects and describe the effect of their use: the relationship of masters/mistresses to their servants, monologues, realistic dialogue, symbols.

Suggested Readings

Eekman, Thomas A., ed. *Critical Essays on Anton Chekhov*. Boston: G. K. Hall, 1989.

Emeljanow, Victor, ed. *Chekhov: The Critical Heritage*. London: Routledge, 1981.

Friedland, Louis S., ed. *Letters on the Short Story, the Drama, and Other Literary Topics*. London: Bles, 1924.

Jackson, Robert L., ed. *Chekhov: A Collection of Critical Essays*. Englewood Cliffs, NJ: Prentice, 1967.

Kirk, Irina. *Anton Chekhov*. Boston: Twayne, 1981.

Magarshak, David. *Chekhov the Dramatist*. New York: Hill, 1960.

Miles, Patrick, ed. *Chekhov on the British Stage*. Cambridge: Cambridge UP, 1993.

Pitcher, Harvey J. *The Chekhov Play: A New Interpretation*. New York: Barnes, 1973.

Wellek, René, and Nonna D. Wellek. *Chekhov: New Perspectives*. Englewood Cliffs, NJ: Prentice, 1984.

Williames, Lee J. *Anton Chekhov the Iconoclast*. Scranton, PA: U of Scranton P, 1989.

Susan Glaspell

Trifles (p. 1673)

This play is not about murder so much as marriage. Glaspell leaves us in no doubt that Minnie Wright killed her husband, but John Wright's death only provides the occasion of the play. Its focus is on the differing male and female reactions as they search for a motive. Glaspell contrasts male and female perspectives throughout the play and engages our sympathy firmly on the side of the women. While the men vainly seek signs of violent rage, the women, with growing empathy, are able to recognize the signs of quiet desperation under which many women of their time were forced to live. We are asked to witness Mrs. Wright's life rather than Mr. Wright's death, and we are shown that the true "crime" has been the way she was being subjugated and "destroyed" by her marriage. We never see Minnie Wright; we learn about her only through others' comments. This dramatic method serves the dual function of allowing her to avoid particularity and so serve as a symbol of all women trapped in loveless marriages, as well as ensuring that our attention is focused on the reactions of those others.

The play's opening firmly sets the scene. The gloomy kitchen is where Minnie Wright struggled to stay sane, and the domineering men immediately take charge while the women remain on the periphery. We learn that John Wright said little and demanded the same from his wife. We can also recognize that he is not so different from these other men, who clearly see women as a subservient group whose concerns hold little importance. Thus in their search for hard evidence to convict Mrs. Wright, they will repeatedly overlook the existing evidence that the women uncover, dismissing such as mere "trifles." Mrs. Hale's early defense of

Mrs. Wright against the belittling comments of Mr. Henderson foreshadows her growing sympathy and complicity with the "murderess."

Once a woman marries she loses her former identity, along with her maiden name, and becomes subsumed by her husband: Note how even the sheriff calls his wife "Mrs. Peters." The lives of Mrs. Peters and Mrs. Hale may not be quite as dreary as the life Mrs. Wright evidently led, but, as women, they are aware of the limitations that a patriarchal society has placed on their gender. Their husbands are a little more communicative, and both women have children to distract them, but their days are no less yoked to the home and the demands of those husbands. Standing in the kitchen, the center of every farm wife's existence, Mrs. Hale and Mrs. Peters soon piece together the clues to events that continue to elude the men. Before marriage, Minnie Foster had been singing and full of life; placed within the confines of her marriage, however — symbolized by the house she lives in "down in a hollow" where you "don't see the road" and the concentric bars of the log cabin pattern of her quilt and the canary cage — she has had all the life strangled out of her. Her husband destroyed Minnie Foster, just as he destroys her canary. Her revenge, knotting a rope around his neck while he slept, eventually appears just. Mrs. Hale leads Mrs. Peters to a full understanding of the situation as she removes the clues they discover, unpicking the erratic stitching in the quilt and putting the dead bird in her pocket.

Having known Minnie from the past and being a neighbor who had neglected to visit for over a year, Mrs. Hale accepts her own guilt in not having helped Minnie. Guided by Mrs. Hale, both women now take on that responsibility by removing evidence and lying to Mr. Henderson, the county attorney, about how the canary died. Mrs. Hale's final retort, "We call it — knot it, Mr. Henderson," becomes layered with significance. The words themselves sound defiant against Henderson's facetious tone, and she mocks him with the evidence that she and Mrs. Peters have found and that even now he continues to miss — the knot around Mr. Wright's neck being clearly related to such a quilting knot. The emphatic "*We* call it," further suggests the "knot" or bond that has been tied between these women and Minnie against the men. Glaspell wishes us to recognize the potential strength bestowed on the women who forge such bonds — a strength that comes with unity. It is a strength that will allow them not only to withstand male subjugation but also, we hope, begin to forge an independent female identity.

As Barbara Ozieblo points out in *The Provincetown Players*, however, "Although Glaspell condones the breaking of those codes of behavior which strangle women, she does not alienate the men who make them up." *Trifles* is not antimale so much as an attempt to awaken audiences to the dilemmas of womanhood. Feminism was still in its infancy, and even its supporters were at times ambivalent as to where it might lead. The rebellion of Glaspell's women is consequently minimal; Minnie is safely locked away in prison. Mrs. Hale and Mrs. Peters may protect her, but they do not speak openly to the men in her defense.

Susan C. W. Abbotson

Questions for Discussion

1. How do you explain the play's title?
2. How does the setting of the play contribute to our understanding of Minnie Wright's position?
3. How does the entrance of the characters distinguish between the men and the women?

4.   How can Hale's description of Minnie Wright as she sits in her rocking chair be interpreted from a female point of view rather than the male one that Hale provides?
5.   Is there any doubt that Minnie Wright killed her husband? In what ways might her trial be affected if Minnie Wright was facing a court at the close of the twentieth century rather than at its start?
6.   How should we interpret the behavior of Mr. Henderson, the county attorney? Why is Mrs. Hale so annoyed by him?
7.   In what ways can Mrs. Peters be said to be a "foil" to Mrs. Hale?
8.   What are the main differences between Minnie Foster and Minnie Wright?
9.   Is Mr. Wright so very different from the other men we witness in this play?
10. Why do the men miss all the real evidence, and why do the women cover it up?
11. Why do we never see either of the Wrights directly?
12. In what ways is Minnie Foster related to the canary?

Topics for Writing

1.   Is Mr. Wright really so very wrong? We are told John Wright was not a bad man, "he didn't drink, and kept his word. . . and paid his debts." Minnie Wright's murder of her husband would be condoned by feminist critics, like Catherine Belsey, as a "defiance of patriarchy." Was it a "crime" for Minnie to strangle her husband or simple justice?
2.   In what ways does the ironic title of the play shape its meaning? Explain the full significance of the title as well as the symbolism of the house, quilt, bird cage, and bird.
3.   The play ends with the suggestion that Minnie Wright may just manage to "get away with murder." Write a play script or short story depicting the trial that will be taking place and include as many of the characters from the play as possible. Consider how the time period in which this play takes place will be an influential factor regarding what occurs during this trial.
4.   Write the diary of Minnie Foster/Wright from just before she met John Wright up until she is taken to jail.
5.   **CONNECTIONS** How does *Trifles* compare to the short story "Jury of Her Peers," and in what ways has Glaspell changed the emphases of her account?
6.   **CONNECTIONS** Compare the differences that are portrayed between the lives of men and women in *Trifles* and August Strindberg's *Miss Julie* or Henrik Ibsen's *A Doll House*.

Suggested Readings

Alkalay-Gut, Karen. "'Jury of Her Peers': The Importance of *Trifles*." *Studies in Short Fiction* 21 (1984): 1–9.
Bach, Gerhard. "Susan Glaspell: Provincetown Playwright." *Great Lakes Review* 4 (1978): 31–43.
Ben-Zvi, Linda, ed. *Susan Glaspell: Essays on Her Theater and Fiction*. Ann Arbor: U of Michigan P, 1995.
Dymkowski, Christine. "On the Edge: The Plays of Susan Glaspell." *Modern Drama* 31 (1988): 91–105.
Makowsky, Veronica. *Susan Glaspell's Century of American Women: A Critical Interpretation of her Work*. New York: Oxford UP, 1993.
Mustazza, Leonard. "Generic Translation and Thematic Shift in Susan Glaspell's *Trifles* and 'A Jury of Her Peers.'" *Studies in Short Fiction* 26 (1989): 489–96.

Noe, Marcia. *Susan Glaspell: Voice from the Heartland.* Macomb: Western Illinois UP, 1983.

Smith, Beverly A. "Women's Work — *Trifles*? The Skill and Insights of Playwright Susan Glaspell." *International Journal of Women's Studies* 5 (1982): 172–84.

Waterman, Arthur E. *Susan Glaspell.* New York: Twayne, 1966.

Zehfuss, Ruth E. "The Law and the Ladies in *Trifles.*" *Teaching English in the Two-Year College* (February 1992): 42–44.

Eugene O'Neill

Bound East for Cardiff (p. 1685)

Bound East for Cardiff was the first O'Neill play to appear on stage, and it is a seminal one. On the surface, *Bound East for Cardiff* tells the brief tale of a sailor's death after a careless fall aboard an eastbound tramp steamer. The way in which that tale is told, however, makes this a far more complex production. The Provincetown Players had declared an intention to create a new kind of theater along classical Greek lines that could be called "American." To this end they sought out new playwrights such as O'Neill. As in Greek tragedy, *Bound East for Cardiff* has little plot but is centered on discussion and the occasional "speech." The group of sailors surrounding the central relationship between Driscoll and Yank can be seen as a kind of chorus. We are guided by their reactions and responses. O'Neill allows no doubt that Yank will die; he is fated to do so. The only question is how he will die: Will he attain a perception that allows his death to be ennobling? Yank becomes the seed for a new kind of tragic hero, to whom Arthur Miller will pay attention in *Death of a Salesman.* He is a common man whose heroism lies in the dignity he maintains, despite the forces working against him.

Clearly influenced by Strindberg's naturalism, O'Neill attempts a similar dissection of the human soul, revealing those harsh truths we mostly choose to ignore. The lessons of this brief play will be illuminating rather than uplifting. The men in *Bound East for Cardiff* respond to the threat of death with instinctive awe and dread. Death is something we all must face, although each of us struggles to avoid such a truth. O'Neill's own bouts with tuberculosis and an earlier suicide attempt had heightened his awareness of the transience of life.

To O'Neill, realism means more than a realistic setting or true-to-life characters; it means something that has spiritual truth. At times his characters are not fully fleshed out, but they offer moments of what O'Neill calls "truth behind the real," against which the plausibilities of realism become irrelevant. His concern as a dramatist, as he wrote in a letter to drama critic George Jean Nathan, was to illuminate "even the most sordid and mean alleys of life" with a "poetical vision." One might view Yank's life as sordid or even clichéd. As an itinerant sailor, he has been drunk and involved in fights from coast to coast and he has even killed a man. As he approaches death, however, he is able to engage our sympathy as a human being.

Through an intricate blend of realism and expressionism, O'Neill creates a production in which the mood and setting clearly take precedence over the action. The atmosphere O'Neill strives to create is essential to our understanding of the play. The confined space in which these sailors live, along with the constant fog, dirt, and tobacco smoke, all convey that sense of darkness, squalor, and constric- tion that O'Neill believes *is* life. This is the stifling world of unattainable desires in which most people live, although we try to ignore that fact. The constricted atmosphere also helps to underline the inevitability of Yank's death, as he has nowhere else to go. The surrounding clutter offers a suggestion of people living all together in a jumble. They survive together, sharing similar hopes and dreams, and they all will die, just like Yank, when their time comes. Cocky's opening tale of being seduced by a "cannibal" is partly a colorful exaggeration to convey Cocky's own nature, but it also provides an initial contrast to the stark surround- ings and increasingly dark mood with its laughter and exotic location. The crew's joviality is soon broken by Yank's groans, and the descent into gloom emphasizes the encroaching nature of death. Their silence as Yank's dying presence becomes felt informs the audience of Yank's fatal condition without the need for verbal exposition.

O'Neill intends us to see beyond the realistic picture of life on the sea to a more symbolic idea of what such a life represents. We are all, in some way, lost and lonely wanderers through the confusions and hardships of the sea of life. Our lives are as isolated and insecure as the lives of the sailors we meet. We may make the occasional friendship, as do Driscoll and Yank, which will serve to brighten our lives, but we go alone to our graves. To O'Neill the sea represented a mighty natural force — an indication of the forces against which humanity is destined to pit itself. Although the conflict had already begun in Europe when this play was produced, O'Neill pointedly sets *Bound East for Cardiff* in the years prior to World War I. For O'Neill, the political or social concerns of his time are too small a canvas on which to paint. The war does not interest him as much as issues of life and death as they apply to all people at all times. His interest, he has declared, is not in the "relation between man and man" but "between man and God." The God he envisions is as powerful as He is inscrutable; the man, as tragic as he is self- deluded.

O'Neill's sailors are individual characters from scattered origins, indicated by their different accents. We quickly recognize Cocky, the boasting, loud- mouthed Cockney; Scotty, the close Scotsman; Driscoll, the boozy, warm-hearted, and irresponsible Irishman; Olson, the colder, more measured Swede; and Yank, who is a generous American shipmate, though prone to bouts of violence. Collec- tively they give an idea of the pervasive reach of the sea and all such global powers. Many of these personalities will reappear in later O'Neill plays, for they represent what their author felt to be common types of men. Although students may have some problem understanding their dialects, they should note that the rendering of such colloquial accents in this fashion not only assists in swiftly defining characters through their ethnicity (using racial stereotyping), but it was also innovative for the time, particularly in a tragic piece.

The crew are all very scornful of the captain, making it clear that O'Neill intends there to be a sense of "us and them" between the men and the officers. Such a class system is perhaps unavoidable, but O'Neill takes pains to show that both classes in their own way are well-meaning, though unable to fully understand the other's point of view. In a sense they cannot understand in order to preserve their own identity and security. The sailors are united in the common bond of their class; they have identity as "us" only when they preserve the right to see the officers as "them." The comradeship this allows supports them through their abject lives. Their comradeship is the only thing they can depend on in this world. The captain is unable to perform the miracles his crew demands: He is only human and does not have control over life and death. He does his best to make Yank comfortable, he allows Driscoll to stay and neglect his watch, and he shows genuine concern. He cannot, however, address Yank with any sense of comradeship.

The sailor's life is one of constant movement, without security or fixity. It is a dangerous way to live, although we are allowed to recognize its passing rewards as Yank and Driscoll happily recount some of their adventures. It is however, movement with little real progression, and they have little to show for it at the end. They fantasize about how much better it might have been if they had stayed on land, but we should realize that this is no answer. A farmer's life is no less fraught with difficulty, and farmers most likely dream of being sailors. We all make choices and create our own lives; we must learn to live (and die) with the lives we have chosen. The fog grows thicker as Driscoll and Yank reminisce, possibly suggesting that the past is not the place to go for clear sight. Memories are usually clouded and not necessarily accurate. For the truth one must look to the present, however bleak that might be.

The shipwreck that Yank and Driscoll underwent on the *Dover* emphasizes the difficulties and dangers that come with a life on the sea. We are made to realize that our grasp on life is tenuous, that death can come at any time. The shipwreck also provides us with the sense that Yank has been living on borrowed time: He has avoided death once, but such luck rarely happens twice. We know what the outcome will be on this occasion. This earlier survival, however, allows us to consider Yank's stamina; he is no weakling and will not give in to death easily. This time the powers against him are too big to overcome, but it takes a while for Yank to accept this. The fact that he does accept his fate should be admirable, for it allows him to die with a measure of dignity. Yank's desire to die on deck with a view of the moon and stars could suggest a desire to unite with the greater universe. A recognition of one's insignificant presence in the greater scheme may make it easier to let go. It is also easier to die when one is not entirely alone, and so Yank insists that Driscoll stay with him as the ship's bell marks time and anticipates his death knell.

Students may wish to consider the significance of the title, which indicates a reversal of the traditional pioneering "go West, young man." These sailors are heading back to their origins — a journey into their truer, more primal natures. This is a journey, however, blanketed by fog. Fog is used throughout the play (as it has appeared in other of O'Neill's plays) as a symbol, an image of something indistinct and uncertain. The fog frustrates our vision and aspirations alike. We proceed in this world blindly, the fog created partly by our own inability to see what destinies await us. At the close the fog significantly lifts, perhaps not from our eyes as much as from the dying eyes of Yank.

The "pretty lady in black" whom Yank sees as he dies is an interesting inversion of the usual death figure of a skeletal and imposing male figure. The image implies that death may be a welcome release, providing a comforting embrace. Yank has informed us that he wishes he had settled down with a good woman: Perhaps he now has his wish. It is the last we hear from Yank. Driscoll's following prayer, reinforced by Cocky's awed response of "Gawd blimey," indicates that the only available haven for those scared by death may be religion. It is a religion, however, that cannot protect you when your time comes. It was not until a few years later that O'Neill suffered a religious crisis as he asked himself whether it was possible to live without religion. For Driscoll, at least, it still offers itself as a comfort in times of stress.

SUSAN C. W. ABBOTSON

Questions for Discussion

1. What is the mood of the play, and how is it created? Is *Bound East for Cardiff* a realistic or an expressionistic play?
2. In what ways is the play's setting integral to its meaning? What is the play about? What is the significance of the play's title?
3. How does O'Neill convey a sense of the inevitability of Yank's impending death?
4. What is the function of the steam whistle that repeats throughout the play?
5. How does the image of the fog operate during the play? What does it represent?
6. Why does O'Neill present such a variety of nationalities among his crew? What is the crew's function as a group?
7. What type of men are Yank and Driscoll? What is their friendship based on?
8. Would Yank and Driscoll have been better off as farmers?
9. What is the captain like? Are the crew fair in their remarks about him?
10. What does O'Neill seem to be saying about the nature of life and death? How does he want us to view Yank's demise?
11. What is the significance of the "pretty lady dressed in black" whom Yank sees as he finally expires?
12. What is the significance of Driscoll resorting to pray after Yank's death and Cocky's final declaration of "Gawd blimey"? What is O'Neill saying about people's religious beliefs?

Topics for Writing

1. O'Neill has stated that he tries to write about "the relation between man and God" rather than "the relation between man and man." Does *Bound East for Cardiff* do this? Compare and contrast the characters of Driscoll and Yank. Consider why they are such good friends and how each views the issues of life and death?
2. Is *Bound East for Cardiff* just a play about a dying seaman or does it concern itself with deeper issues? At what point does expressionism take over from realism? Use close details to support your answer.
3. Imagine that Cocky has a sister and is writing a letter home about the events of the past couple of days. Also consider what the captain may have been writing in his ship's log. Following these formats, write two pieces that illustrate the different perceptions and perspectives of these two characters.
4. **CONNECTIONS** In what ways is the tone and form of *Bound East for Cardiff* reminiscent of a Greek tragedy like Sophocles' *Oedipus the King*?
5. **CONNECTIONS** Both Eugene O'Neill and Tennessee Williams employ many symbols and fatalistic images in their works. Referring to *Bound East for Cardiff* and *The Glass Menagerie*, illustrate how each playwright does this. What do you see as the message each is trying to convey through such imagery? In comparing these two plays, which do you feel is the more successful and why?

Suggested Readings

Ackerley, Chris. "Lowry and O'Neill: Cows and Pigs and Chickens." *Malcolm Lowry Review* 19–20 (1986–87): 129–30.

Bagchee, Shyamal, ed. *Perspectives on O'Neill: New Essays.* Victoria: U of Victoria, 1988.

Bogard, Travis. *Contour in Time: The Plays of Eugene O'Neill.* New York: Oxford UP, 1988.

Bogard, Travis, and Jackson R. Bryer, eds. *Selected Letters of Eugene O'Neill.* New Haven, CT: Yale UP, 1988.

Estrin, Mark W., ed. *Conversations with Eugene O'Neill.* Jackson:UP of Mississippi, 1990.

Gelb, Arthur, and Barbara Gelb. *O'Neill.* New York: Harper, 1973.

Hirsch, Foster. *Eugene O'Neill: Life, Work, and Criticism.* Fredericton, NB: York, 1986.

Jiji, Vera. "Reviewers' Responses to the Early Plays of Eugene O'Neill: A Study in Influence." *Theatre Survey* 24 (1988): 69–86.

Kobernick, Mark. *Semiotics of the Drama and the Style of Eugene O'Neill.* Amsterdam: Benjamins, 1989.

Martine, James J., ed. *Critical Essays on Eugene O'Neill.* Boston: G. K. Hall, 1984.

Maufort, Marc, ed. *Eugene O'Neill and the Emergence of American Drama.* Amsterdam: Rodopi, 1989.

Moorton, Richard F. Jr., ed. *Eugene O'Neill's Century: Centennial Views on America's Tragic Dramatist.* Westport, CT: Greenwood, 1991.

Stroupe, John H., ed. *Critical Approaches to O'Neill.* New York: AMS, 1988.

Williams, Gary Jay. "Turned Down in Provincetown: O'Neill's Debut Reexamined." *Eugene O'Neill Newsletter* 12 (1988): 17–27.

SAMUEL BECKETT

Krapp's Last Tape (p. 1696)

At the age of twenty-four, Krapp began recording a tape every year on his birthday, reviewing a previous year before making the new tape. He is now turning sixty-nine and begins the day by listening to a tape he made thirty years previously, at which time he had just listened to a tape from about ten years before. Thus the audience receives a picture of Krapp's life and development from his twenties to the end of his sixties — we learn what decisions have affected this man's life to reduce him to his current poverty and isolation. In Krapp's sparse world we witness a great range of tone and style, from humor to dry narrative, and emotions running the gamut from passionate conviction to weary disdain. Yet this wealth of life experience has been trapped within those tapes, which will be lost, for Krapp has no one left with whom to share his experience. At thirty-nine, Krapp had seen himself "at the . . .crest of the wave," and his decision to reject love and life seemed to be an amazing insight, but at sixty-nine he views this moment, instead, as the turning point leading toward his current empty existence. By sixty-nine, Krapp has lost much of his earlier fire, passion, and interest in the future; he is now concerned only with the past. What Krapp does in this play, like Jessie in Marsha Norman's *'night, Mother,* is attempt one final evaluation of his life before he dies.

Krapp begins his birthday routine by selecting a tape from a previous year. This is done apparently at random for its contents seem a mystery, even when he reads his notes. And yet, as he listens to the tape he made on his thirty-ninth birthday, he seems to be seeking a particular memory. The tape marks a turning point in Krapp's life when he believed he had found access to dark areas of his life that he then determined to make the central focus of his writing. The current Krapp now dismisses this moment with mockery and contempt, preferring instead to recall the girl he had decided, at this past point, to abandon. At thirty-nine he had an epiphany and relates the events of "that memorable night" on his birthday tape, "when suddenly I saw the whole thing." It is a vision in which the sixty-nine-year-old has lost interest. He fast-forwards the tape at the point that his younger self is about to relate what he saw, and he misses the revelation. Krapp is looking for something else, which has taken on a greater importance. The moment at which he finally arrives is an encounter with a girlfriend while out boating. He had ended their relationship all those years ago, and the final image he relates is of the pair of them stuck in the weeds and unmoving while all around them life continues on. This turns out to have been the moment when his life truly became stuck, and he ceased to move for good.

Although *Krapp's Last Tape* is less overtly comic than many absurdist works, it remains true to the essential tenets of absurdist drama that Beckett helped to pioneer. The aim of theater of the absurd is to depict lives not so much as ridiculous as devoid of purpose and without recognizable meaning. Krapp's attempt to fix his own humanity with his constant recordings is necessarily limiting rather than illuminating. As each Krapp mocks and rejects his earlier selves, he eradicates another part of his selfhood until he is left with just an empty shell. Krapp's whole life becomes a process of embrace and rejection, in which he gradually destroys all the positive value of the initial embrace. As he removes himself further and further from others and the world, so he removes himself from himself, to a point where he can no longer communicate even with himself, and his whole life becomes a silence. For Beckett, the extent to which we can communicate with others is a measure of how much we can make of our brief lives. Man is by nature a poor communicator, however, not the least because the means by which we communicate — words — are so slippery. Language becomes necessary *and* impotent; it both allows and prevents communication. In *Krapp's Last Tape*, just as in *Waiting for Godot*, Beckett depicts a breakdown of "purpose to life" where all that is left is a futile struggle against meaninglessness. Krapp ceases to "live" because he is unable to create effective values to live by. Despite his desire to undercover meaning, his whole life has been a reduction of meaning, as he has grown farther and farther apart from his fellow human beings.

Beckett was interested in traditional Japanese dramatic forms, and *Krapp's Last Tape* can be seen as reminiscent of such Nō plays as *Kantan*. Through his tapes, Krapp becomes both "shite" and "waki," with his sixty-nine-year-old self taking on the role of the "waki" who must witness the vision of his younger "shite" self. Krapp has sought the same enlightenment that Rosei sought in *Kantan*. At thirty-nine, he gave up what he believed to be the worldly objects that were preventing him from attaining enlightenment. This action, however, was not only selfish and intent on self-aggrandizement in ways that any enlightened Buddhist would reject, but it was also false. Krapp continued to indulge in all the worldly pleasures he had formerly enjoyed: bananas, alcohol, and sex. What he has given up are people and the emotions that had linked him to people. Any insight he has had becomes meaningless, for there is no one left with whom it can be shared. Rosei does not embrace solitude as much as a simple, modest life, in which fellowship is one of the Three Treasures he must preserve. At sixty-nine, Krapp undergoes another enlightenment, but there can be no joy in his discovery that his whole life has been as wasteful as those of the people who had abided in Rosei's dream palace. Krapp has nothing to take with him into the next life, as he has failed to develop his spiritual nature.

Krapp changes during this short play; at the end he cuts a different figure from what we saw at the start. He begins with clownish actions and ends motionless, staring into space and listening to silence as if there is nothing left to say. This silence may denote his death. The title of the play is deliberately ambiguous, for the word *Last* could hold a variety of meanings. We witness Krapp attempting to make what may be his *final* tape, because he now sees the pointlessness of the exercise and has run out of things to say, or he is about to die and will never reach his seventieth birthday. He begins the tape for his sixty-ninth year but throws it away before it is completed. If this is his last tape, then it is an incomplete one — a fitting testimony for a man whose whole life appears to be incomplete. The title could even refer to the tape Krapp had made at thirty-nine, when he still had a capacity for love and life. This was, perhaps, the last tape Krapp recorded that had any meaning. The decisions he made at that time have gradually eradicated any subsequent meaning from his life.

The importance of setting the play "in the future" is manifold. There is a practical element in that when this play was written, the tape recorder was a new invention and Beckett needed to set the play in the future, at a time when it was realistic for Krapp to have been making tapes for forty-six years. But it also helps to underline Krapp's relation to us all and ensure that he is not relegated to the past, where he can be deemed irrelevant to our current lives. Furthermore, the time frame carries the suggestion that the play might only offer a possible future, which may be changed before we travel too far on the path Krapp has chosen. The single character we see on stage, alone with his tape recorder, captures the essence of Krapp's whole life in a way the audience may understand better than Krapp himself. His excremental name is undoubtedly intentional, implying the quality of the man. He clearly has no regard for his own appearance, which is grimy and decrepit, indicating the state of his inner spirit and his lack of self-respect.

Krapp begins the play as a clown figure with his purple nose, white face, and baggy, ill-fitting clothes, performing a "routine" with his banana peel. We are soon forced to see the direct contrast between this comic appearance and his tragic inner life. The potential humor of the opening is quickly deflated as we learn of the alienation toward which this man's ego has forced him; his is a life of waste and loss. Every one of Krapp's felt experiences has been of loss — of his father, mother, lovers, and finally himself. Krapp at sixty-nine is a picture of humanity reduced to nothingness as he has stripped himself of all connection to others — which is what makes us human after all — in his quest for something that simply cannot be known. His evidently restricted senses of sight and hearing are indicative of the restricted life he has forced himself to lead. His shabby and ridiculous outer appearance has become a mere reflection of his impoverished, shabby and ridiculous inner life now that he has wasted his potential. As we learn more about him, we begin to see his long and barren life filled with meager pleasures — alcohol, bananas, occasional sex, and an obsession with words — which are his only distractions in the dark hole he now inhabits. Ironically, his whole life has been an attempt to resist the pleasures of the flesh, and yet that is all with which he is finally left. Set apart from work, love, family, religion, and companionship, Krapp's few remaining pleasures have become meaningless even to him.

Krapp's life can be judged by the objects with which he surrounds himself — his bananas, locked desk, detailed ledger, and numerous tapes. These objects converge to conjure up a picture of a cold and faintly ridiculous figure. He eats a banana, first placing it in his mouth and stroking it as a deliberately ridiculous and phallic gesture that, when he finally bites into it, suggests the extent to which he has emasculated himself. He has purposefully cut himself off from a life of love, care, and companionship. He drops the banana skin on the floor and later nearly slips on it in classic vaudeville fashion. This underlines the image of him as a foolish clown and shows the insecurity of the ground on which he treads. The locked drawers on a desk that no one else is present to see highlight Krapp's repressed character. He has spent a lifetime locking emotions away. All he has left in life is in these drawers — his final tape and a number of bananas — which may turn out to be equally worthless. His ledger is highly organized, perhaps as a stay against the chaos of the fuller life he has denied himself. His tapes are an intrinsically lifeless substitute for human companionship.

Krapp has exchanged a "real" life of feeling for a "reel" life of mechanization. Because the earlier Krapp is only on tape, rather than a figure on the stage, he is dehumanized. We see how Krapp's misguided impulses have created a flawed human being who has become like his tape-recordings — prone to repetition and eventual silence. His behavior is mechanistic, his body a faulty machine beyond repair — a condition symbolized by his lifetime problem with constipation. Krapp talks back to his machine, but he cannot really communicate; it is, after all, only a machine. His reactions and responses cannot affect the other speaker; all he can do is to switch himself on or off. His taped voice, likewise, cannot communicate with him as it is only a mechanical voice from the past and no longer exists. His rituals are the only remaining way he has of announcing his existence. By the end of the play, however, he has lost both the desire and capacity for even these empty rituals, and so he must cease to exist.

Because *Krapp's Last Tape* only has one actor on stage, it could be viewed as a monologue or soliloquy. Because of the tape, however, and because of Krapp's active interaction with that tape, the play becomes more of a dialogue. The three Krapps we learn about are different characters, despite their similarities. There is a connection between Krapp and his earlier selves; he exhibits consistent behavior patterns and responses. This is not, however, an image of communication but one that illustrates an intrinsic lack of development and growth. Krapp's thirty-nine-year-old self dismisses an earlier self for indulging in alcohol, sex, and bananas — indulgences we see he has yet to give up at sixty-nine. His continual constipation acts as a reflection of the self-involved way in which he has led his whole life. Each time Krapp listens to a younger self, he mocks and ridicules the man he once was. His reaction, at times, borders on surprise, as if he no longer understands his former selves. This suggests a reversal of the very process he is seeking to advance — instead of progressing toward greater knowledge, he is regressing into ignorance. Instead of discovering meaning in his recordings, he is confronted with the errors that have led to his current isolation, alienation, and life of futility.

Though he indulges in the same things he did in his twenties, we see that his sixty-nine-year-old self does so in a more reclusive manner. He drinks at home by himself, instead of at a bar. We are given reminders that his knowledge has lessened over the years — such as his inability to understand vocabulary he has used in earlier times. "Viduity" takes on resonance as he re-explores its meaning and brings to mind the important difference between "being" and "remaining." In our eyes he becomes a kind of "vidua-bird," dressed in black and mourning his own wasted life.

At thirty-nine he had wished his mother's speedy death as he had found the emotions of coping with loss too exhausting. Out by the weir when his mother was dying, Krapp threw a ball to a dog; this ball becomes an emblem of his mother and how easily he tossed her away rather than cope with the pain of her death. It seemed, at the time, a tidier way to live, but tidy lives are empty ones. By trying to avoid all emotion — be it good (love) or bad (suffering) — Krapp ends up escaping life rather than death. At thirty-nine, he shows growing signs of his move toward isolation as he doesn't talk to the people in the park. He is already becoming the uninvolved observer, always on the periphery of life. This is a position he now realizes is wholly unsatisfying, for life is involvement, emotion, and risk. Krapp shows an obsessive concern with eyes in the play, especially female eyes. They seem to confirm Krapp's existence for him. When they gaze on him, they offer the possibility of connection and companionship. Yet throughout his life he has turned all eyes away, rejecting every chance of "love" and connection. Even the recording he made in his late twenties recalled the eyes of a woman he had then admired but left.

Students should notice a distinct contrast between the strong and pompous voice of Krapp at thirty-nine and the cracked tones and halting diction of Krapp at sixty-nine. His voice, just like his life, has dried up. When he begins to record the tape for his sixty-ninth birthday, Krapp cannot complete it, for he runs out of words. Instead, he returns to his "farewell to love" and becomes lost in regret. He describes his thirty-nine-year-old self as a "stupid bastard" and denigrates him as he recognizes the major mistakes he has made. He never should have chosen to ignore the larger world and concentrate on himself in the way he did. In retrospect, he can find no justification, as this concentration has achieved nothing and led him to a dead end. His great book only sold seventeen copies. He is left with mere words, which have become empty of meaning. He is utterly alone and "burning to be gone." His sex, these days, is solely with prostitutes as he has terminated all his past relationships. He has reached the end of his recording project as he has nothing left to record. His life no longer has any point — and it was he himself who reduced it to such a state. At thirty-nine he believed he was making the right decision to rid himself of all "distractions" and cannot see how he can ever regret such a decision; when he is sixty-nine we see that regret. The past thirty years have been a total waste, because those distractions of which he has rid himself were his life, and he has lost them for good. There truly is nothing left to say as the tape runs on in silence. We are left, finally, with a stark and chilly image of Krapp, isolated in an encroaching darkness, bleakly registering his lonely failure by complete silence.

Susan C. W. Abbotson

Questions for Discussion

1. How significant is Krapp's physical appearance? Does he change or develop in any way during the play? How does he appear at the start and at the close of the play?

2. What are the similarities and differences between Krapp in his twenties, at thirty-nine, and sixty-nine? At which age does Krapp seem to have been the wisest? happiest? best?
3. Why exactly did Krapp withdraw from the world? What did he hope to achieve, and how far has he fulfilled his earlier ambitions?
4. What reasons might Beckett have had for setting the play in the future?
5. Describe the significance in the play of the following: bananas, female eyes, black rubber ball, alcohol, images of light and dark.
6. What does Beckett intend for us to understand by the title of this play?
7. What is the point of Krapp's recordings? How does he use them? What is his attitude each time to his earlier selves?
8. How does Beckett want us to respond to Krapp? Does Beckett see Krapp as having created his own fate? Should we feel sorry for Krapp?
9. Is Krapp, at sixty-nine, any more aware of the conditions of life than he has been in the past? At what periods in his life could Krapp be seen as an enlightened individual?
10. Has Krapp, at any point in his life, allowed himself to be fully human? In what ways has his attitude toward his own humanity and that of others been manifested?
11. Does Krapp grow more aware of his condition during the play, or is he just having an existing belief confirmed?
12. Does anything in the play finally have any meaning?

Topics for Writing

1. How far can *Krapp's Last Tape* be called either a tragedy or a comedy?
2. In what ways is this play clearly a product of theater of the absurd?
3. Write a tale in which you describe how an independent observer might view Krapp's life story, basing it on what we learn from his tapes.
4. **CONNECTIONS** How does Beckett adapt traditional Nō form to *Krapp's Last Tape*? Make a comparison between *Krapp's Last Tape* and *Kantan*, which takes into consideration character, plot, tone, setting, and message.
5. **CONNECTIONS** *Krapp's Last Tape* and Marsha Norman's *'night, Mother* both appear to be making an analysis of a person's life and the choices they have made. Compare the lives of Krapp and Jessie, deciding which life seems to have achieved the most. Explain your choice fully, and indicate which of Krapp and Jessie's choices have been the most valid.

Suggested Readings

Bishop, Ryan, and Walter Spitz. "'Run On in Silence': Language, Dialogue, and Failed Rituals in Beckett's *Krapp's Last Tape*." *Language and Literature* 15 (1990): 57–78.

Campell, Sue Ellen. "*Krapp's Last Tape* and Critical Theory." *Comparative Drama* 12 (1978).

Catanzaro, Mary F. "The Voice of Absent Love in *Krapp's Last Tape* and *Company*." *Modern Drama* 32 (1989): 401–12.

Doherty, Francis. "*Krapp's Last Tape*: The Artistry of the Last." *Irish University Review* 12 (1982).

Dukore, Bernard F. "*Krapp's Last Tape* as Tragicomedy." *Modern Drama* 15 (1973).

Esslin, Martin. *The Theatre of the Absurd*. New York: Doubleday, 1961.

Gordon, Lois. "*Krapp's Last Tape*: A New Reading." *Journal of Dramatic Theory and Criticism* 5 (1990): 327–40.

Knowlson, James, ed. *Samuel Beckett: "Krapp's Last Tape."* London: 1980.

Menta, Ed. "Beckett in a Noh Light: An Analysis of Selected Plays of Samuel Beckett Using Critical Principles of the Japanese Noh Theatre." *Theatre Studies* 35 (1990): 50–63.

Scholz, Amiel. "The Dying of the Light: An Actor Investigates *Krapp's Last Tape.*" *Theatre Research International* 16 (1991): 39–53.

Sherman, Rob. "Shadows of the Evening: Narcissus, Doubles, and Failed Rituals in Beckett's *Krapp's Last Tape.*" *Theatre Studies* 38 (1993): 45–55.

Smith, Joseph H., ed. *The World of Samuel Beckett.* Baltimore: John Hopkins UP, 1991.

Takahashi, Yasunari. "The Theatre of Mind: Samuel Beckett and the Noh." *Encounter* 58 (April 1982): 66–73. See commentary on p. 2026.

Tennessee Williams

The Glass Menagerie (p. 1704)

Students should not view *The Glass Menagerie* as realistic drama but as a memory play, as all we are shown is related through the lens of Tom Wingfield's guilty memory after he has abandoned his mother and crippled sister by going off to sea in search of adventure. Williams's staging captures this nostalgic mood with dim lighting, recurring musical themes, and screen images. Williams warns us that memory tends to distort, omitting or exaggerating details, and is an emotional rather than logical response to events. What we witness is a replay of Tom's earlier life as he recalls the formative moments of his past. The play is autobiographical in that Thomas "Tennessee" Williams's early life followed a similar pattern: living in poverty with an absent father, dominated by a strong mother, wasting his talents working in a shoe factory and feeling guilt over neglecting his shy sister, Rose (who had been given a lobotomy in the absence of his protection). Just as Eugene O'Neill tries to explain and exorcise his family-related guilt in *Long Day's Journey into Night*, so does Williams in *The Glass Menagerie*, and both come to the same conclusion. Fear and guilt are inescapable, crippling, and reducing, but they are not things from which one can escape by physically running away. They are psychological and will travel with you.

Williams does not allow Tom to shoulder sole blame but insists we recognize how much others contribute to his torment. Amanda, Laura, and Tom are individually imprisoned, each isolated from the others in fantasy worlds of their own creation. Amanda is trapped in memories of the South and her childhood, possibly more imagination than fact, but both have now vanished in reality. She dresses in her old clothes in an effort to recapture her illusions and will sacrifice her daughter's potential happiness by co-opting Jim as if he were one of her own suitors. She cannot let go of the past because she cannot face the fact that her husband left her, and so she dwells on her memory of a happy and opulent life on a southern plantation before that occurred. An unforgiving woman whose son must always be the first to apologize after a row, Amanda can never forgive her husband for leaving. She lives in a fake world of sentimental illusion because reality would destroy her. She will not come to terms with her present urban dwelling and the poverty in which the family now lives. On the rare moments

Amanda is forced to face reality she is drained of vitality until she can retreat again into her nostalgia.

Laura, crippled and shy, hides, behind her difference from her mother, in a world created for her by her records and glass animals. Her records are old and in their antiquity create a euphoric past where she can be happy. Through her glass creatures she can create a safe and innocent world where she is in charge, in contrast to the scary, confusing world she glimpses outside her room. She effectively retires from life, and her awakening with Jim is only transitory. Neither the outside world nor her mother can accept her extreme sensitivity, but she does not reject the world so much as it rejects her. The only place she has left to live is in her fantasy world. Her home life has been gradually whittled away as first her father leaves and then Tom. Outside of her fantasy world she is utterly dependent, so much so that she must even ask her mother what it is she should be wishing for on the moon.

Tom feels trapped in a routine job that is crushing his sensitive spirit and desire to be a writer, but he cannot quit because he feels responsible for his family. Amanda constantly takes pains to remind him of this responsibility to keep him there. At work he is as isolated as Laura is at home, and home, to Tom, is a nailed-up coffin in which he has no life. He tells Laura about a stage magician he went to see who was able to get out of a nailed-up coffin and wishes that he too had this ability to escape. Tom cannot leave the home as cleanly as his father did, and his only escape is into dreams of adventure stimulated by the movies. Tom is aware that the movies are not real, but he tells himself that they might be as he can see no other form of escape. What he really wants is to live someone else's life as he has no idea what to do with his own.

When Tom finally does leave, it is only a physical escape, for he cannot psychologically leave his family behind. After the initial sense of freedom, disillusionment sets in and turns to guilt as his imagination transforms innocent and unconnected items into cruel reminders of his poor sister. Then Tom becomes totally trapped, a prisoner of his own remorse. Tom's only release is that of death, suggested in the play's closing image of the candles being extinguished. This is an ambiguous allusion to both the brief candle of life that Shakespeare has extinguished in *Macbeth* and to the home fire to which Tom can never return: The death could be Tom's or Laura's.

Tom's feelings of guilt for Laura are greater than Amanda's because he sees Laura's difficulties, whereas Amanda ignores them in order to avoid such guilt. Amanda is, in fact, in danger of seeming a monster. She relies on Tom as the family provider and so refuses to allow him any freedom, even though she knows he is unhappy. She dominates him as one would a small child by treating him like a small child, for allowing him the mind of an adult might lead to rebellion. As an adult, Tom does try to rebel, but Amanda quells such moments by reminding him of his particular responsibility to Laura. She forces her illusions on them and manipulates them to create her own ideal environment. Through dramatic posturing she ensures their guilt and uses that to force them both into doing what she wants.

Laura is as easily broken as her glass; her mother's attempts to relive her own youth through Laura completely desiccate Laura's last shreds of self-confidence. Amanda continually expects too much of Laura, especially because she refuses to acknowledge any of her daughter's problems. Yet Williams insists that there is "much to admire in Amanda," and we should include love and pity in our judgment of her. She is admirable in her endurance, for her life has not been easy. She was abandoned by her husband and left to rear two children on her own, one of whom needs special treatment. At the end of the play "her silliness is gone and she has dignity and tragic beauty" as she comforts her daughter. Amanda's use of "we" and "us" rather than "you" when talking of Laura denotes the strong bond she has forged with her daughter's future — she intends to hold onto Laura for life, but we need not see anything sinister in that, as Laura at least has someone to look after her. Amanda has been a failure all her life and tries to make up for this by organizing everyone around her and forcing them to be successes. What goes wrong with this plan is her limited imagination; she cannot accept the roads her children would choose and tries to manipulate them onto roads of her choosing — roads that are entirely unsuitable. Laura's job as a secretary and Tom's in the shoe factory are both utterly antagonistic to their natures.

This is not just a family tale, however, and Williams wishes us to consider what he believes are the root causes behind success and failure in people's lives. Occasional references to the outside world suggest that the Wingfields are not the only people to be leading illusory lives, for people ignore Spain's troubles and the impending world war by living lives of apparent gaiety. Even Jim as a representative of this outer world exudes a lost sense of promise and is not entirely honest. He enjoys Tom's company largely because he allows him to live on his past glories, having known him since his high school glory days. Jim's rise to fame has been restricted and quelled in the real world, but, like Amanda, he refuses to give in. He has the self-confidence that Tom lacks, so maybe he will make it. Meanwhile, he boosts that confidence by playing along with Amanda and drawing Laura out for a brief moment before getting cold feet and escaping down that fire escape in a way Tom can only dream about.

SUSAN C. W. ABBOTSON

Questions for Discussion

1. Considering Williams's production notes, how does he intend the screens, music, and lighting in the play to operate? Do you think they are effective?
2. How does the play's setting — with its alleyway, fire escape, and glowing photograph — contribute to its meaning?
3. How important is the use of memory in this play, and how does it affect the events we witness and the way the story is told?
4. How does Amanda control and manipulate her children and to what ends?
5. Why does Tom spend so much time at the movies? Why does he find his job so difficult? How is he like his father?
6. According to what we are shown and told in the play, what are the differences between northern and southern values and ways of life?
7. Why is Laura unable to complete her secretarial course? What do we learn about Laura from where she chooses to go when she pretends to go to typing school? Why is the spotlight on her when Amanda and Tom are arguing?
8. Why is Amanda so concerned to get Laura a husband? Is there any irony in this?
9. What motivates Jim's behavior, and does he help Laura or set her back? How is he different from the Wingfields? Is he any more likely to succeed?
10. How does the symbol of the unicorn (whole and broken) work? Why does Laura give it to Jim? What other objects and events in the play appear to be symbolic?

11. How far has Tom achieved his dreams of escape and adventure by the end of the play?
12. How do the glimpses we get of events in the outside world relate to the play? In what ways can this play be said to be about failure and its consequences?

Topics for Writing

1. Analyze the images of imprisonment and escape in *The Glass Menagerie* and discuss how they relate to the central characters.
2. How far can the women in this play be considered "sympathetic" characters?
3. How would this play be different if it was related from one of the other characters' memories? Select your character and provide a commentary to frame one of the play's scenes in the same way Williams uses Tom throughout the play. You should consider how this scene might have affected your character and how this character might choose to color his or her memory.
4. Decide what you feel is the central message of *The Glass Menagerie* and write a poem describing this theme, linking together as many of the play's symbolic items and events as you can.
5. **CONNECTIONS** Memory is central to both *The Glass Menagerie* and Samuel Beckett's *Krapp's Last Tape*. Describe how it influences each production and what Williams and Beckett believe to be the power and importance of memory.
6. **CONNECTIONS** Williams based his play *The Glass Menagerie* on an earlier story he had written, "Portrait of a Girl in Glass." Compare and contrast these two versions, considering how the characters are presented and what seem to be the author's central concerns.

Suggested Readings

Arnott, Catherine, ed. *Tennessee Williams on File*. New York: Methuen, 1985.
Griffin, Alice. *Understanding Tennessee Williams*. Columbia: U of South Carolina P, 1995.
Hirsch, Foster. *A Portrait of the Artist: The Plays of Tennessee Williams*. Port Washington, NY: Kennikat, 1979.
Jones, John H. "The Missing Link: The Father in *The Glass Menagerie*." *Notes on Mississippi Writers* 20 (1988): 29–38.
Leverich, Lyle. *Tom: The Unknown Tennessee Williams*. New York: Crown, 1995.
Levy, Eric. "'Through the Soundproof Glass': The Prison of Self-Consciousness in *The Glass Menagerie*." *Modern Drama* 36 (1993): 529–37.
Mann, Bruce. "Tennessee Williams and the Rose-Garden Husband." *American Drama* 1 (Fall 1991): 16–26.
Parker, R. B., ed. *"The Glass Menagerie": A Collection of Critical Essays*. Englewood Cliffs, NJ: Prentice, 1983.
Spoto, Donald. *The Kindness of Strangers: The Life of Tennessee Williams*. Boston: Little, 1985.
Stanton, Stephen S. *Tennessee Williams: A Collection of Critical Essays*. Englewood Cliffs, NJ: Prentice, 1977.
Thompson, Judith J. *Tennessee Williams' Plays: Memory, Myth, and Symbol*. New York: Lang, 1987.
Usui, Masami. "'A World of Her Own' in Tennessee Williams' *The Glass Menagerie*." *Studies in Culture and the Humanities* 1 (1992): 21–37.
Williams, Tennessee. *Memoirs*. Garden City, NY: Doubleday, 1975.

Arthur Miller

Death of a Salesman (p. 1752)

Death of a Salesman covers the last twenty-four hours of Willy Loman's life. A victim of both a heartless capitalist society and his own misguided dreams, Willy's eventual suicide is presented with tragic dimensions. We learn of past events leading up to this moment by seeing Willy's memories acted out on the stage. The transitions between current action and memory are fluid, and occasionally the two occur simultaneously; some students will find this confusing. Writing in a style that has become known as "subjective realism," Arthur Miller carefully blends a realistic picture of a salesman's home and life in the postdepression years of the early 1940s with the subjective thoughts that are going through its protagonist's head. He achieves the same blend of realism and expressionism that O'Neill had attempted in *Bound East for Cardiff*, and he develops it into a full-length play. Willy doesn't have flashbacks so much as immediate experiences in which time has clearly been dislocated. "The past," Miller suggests in his autobiography, "is a formality, merely a dimmer present, for everything we are is at every moment alive in us." The concepts of past and present are presented to the audience through careful staging and the suggestive use of scrims and lighting.

Miller's strong sense of moral and social commitment runs throughout the play. Heavily influenced by Ibsen, Miller follows a similar style of dramaturgy and displays the same zeal regarding social issues. The aims of *Death of a Salesman* are twofold. Miller wanted to write a social drama confronting the problems of an ordinary man in a conscienceless, capitalistic social system, and also to write a modern tragedy adapting Aristotelian theory to allow for a common man as tragic protagonist. Students should read the commentaries in which Miller explains why he feels Willy Loman is a tragic figure. We should not allow Willy's domestic situation to blind us to his tragic stature. Miller ties his definition of heroism to a notion of personal dignity. Willy is heroic because he strives to be free and to make his mark in society despite the odds against him. Although he is destroyed in the process, he is motivated by love, and his destruction allows for learning to take place. Through Willy's sacrifice, Biff is able to accept his father's love while recognizing the emptiness of the dream Willy espoused. Willy Loman had accepted at face value overpublicized ideas of material success and therein lies his tragedy. His downfall and final defeat illustrate not only the failure of a man but also the failure of a way of life.

From the start of the play students should recognize that Linda is very worried and Willy is very tired. For all of Willy's talk, this is a couple at the end of their tether. Willy is like a wounded animal near the end of its life, trying to die with dignity in a world that has passed him by. His whole life has been a sell-out, his sons have turned out badly, and his relationship with Biff has been soured. Willy recalls his idealized past both as an escape and an attempt to discover what went wrong. He searches for the answer to a question he has asked all his life: How do you become successful? Willy has convinced himself that the answer is to be well-liked, and he passes this belief onto his two sons. Miller makes it clear, however, that being well-liked has little to do with success. In this world people get ahead through hard work (Charley and Bernard), inheritance (Howard), or sheer luck (Ben). Neither Howard nor Ben waste any time trying to be liked, and both are depicted as selfish, brusque, and rude.

Related by his recording device to cold technology, Howard foreshadows the hard-hearted businessmen who will decimate their work forces as cheaper automation takes over. Howard has not worked for his success; he merely inherited it from his father. He has no time for his father's old salesman and does not even listen to what Willy tries to tell him. Howard represents an uncaring and exploitative business world — a world in which being well-liked holds no relevance. He has used Willy up and now dismisses him without a qualm. His only evidence of humanity is his uneasiness at having to witness Willy's reaction to this dismissal.

When the real world forces its attention on Willy in this way, he swiftly retreats to his dreamworld, where he can seek Ben's advice. Ben, as a self-made man, tells his tale of finding a fortune in the African jungle as if it were some kind of solution, but it is merely a boast. Ben was a selfish man, and he survives the jungle by plundering it. Willy and Ben's father had left a wife and two young sons to seek success in Alaska and was never heard from again. Ben similarly ignores family responsibility as he follows his father's footsteps. Ben's hardness has helped him to survive, and he has chanced on a fortune by luck. Willy could never do what Ben has done, and so Ben's advice is useless to him. Willy blames Linda for holding him back from going with his brother, but would he have taken that risk if he had been free? He is too fearful of the risk one must take to achieve things in the way Ben did. He is right to be scared; the chances of such success are small. Willy, also, cannot be as selfish as his brother. He is not the perfect father, but he does love his family and accepts the responsibilities their existence demands.

Charley, on the other hand, is successful, content, and a nice guy. Charley is satisfied with moderate success without feeling compelled to be the best, and he doesn't take any short-cuts but relies on steady, hard work. He recognizes that one's humanity has nothing to do with one's level of success. Charley passes on his values to his offspring just as Willy does. As children, Biff and Happy idolized their father and looked down on Bernard for his more cautious lifestyle and belief in work. Students should recognize, however, that Bernard represents an ideal in the play. He works for his success and it is well-earned, but it is not the be-all of his existence. This is the lesson Willy needs to learn but refuses to accept. Willy's sons look to him for guidance, but he feeds them unrealistic dreams. His wife supports and loves him, but he has an affair. Willy fails socially, as a salesman, and personally, as a husband and father, because he has no strong value system.

As a youth, Biff was led to believe that because he was "well-liked," he could get away with anything. He begins to steal — a football from school, lumber for the house, a crate of balls from Bill Oliver. Willy is desperate that Biff should succeed in life, and so, instead of punishing him, he condones the thefts and makes excuses. Willy neglects to instill in his son the moral values a parent should teach a child. Biff appears successful in high school as a football player, but he reaps no benefit from this as he never goes to college. Initially he had planned to retake the math course he needed to get into college, but he catches his father with a mistress. At this point Biff's self-confidence dissipates as he loses respect for his father. As a result, his belief in the fantasies his father has fed him cannot be maintained. Out in the real world, away from the destructive influence of his father, Biff begins to recognize his own true nature. He takes some time to learn, spending a stretch in jail, but he eventually replaces his father's dream with one of his own. Whether or not Biff can achieve his dream of working with the land is not as important as the fact that it is more suited to his nature. Biff has gained self-knowledge and in recognizing his own mediocrity and insignificance, he may be able to build himself a happier life. It would have been better for Willy to work at something he was happy doing, like carpentry, instead of trying to be the number-one salesman.

Happy does not reach the same level of awareness as his brother. Since his childhood Happy has admired both his father and his older brother. His brother left home, but Willy remained as a role model, and Happy has become a pale imitation of his father. He is a dreamer, although his dreams are more selfish than his father's, and more limited. He has no depth, living a shallow life that he pretends is a lot more glamorous than it really it. He isn't really happy, but he pushes his inner discontent to one side. Bereft of even the few decencies Willy retains, such as a conscience and a sense of responsibility, Happy cuts an entirely disreputable figure. Despite his supposed love and respect for his father, Happy has no compunction about leaving Willy behind in a bar when he is clearly distressed. Happy has no dignity or honor; he takes bribes from manufacturers and he sleeps with the fiancées and wives of men higher in the firm than he, possibly to get even with them for being more successful than he will ever be. What is worse, his faith in his father's dream remains undiminished at the close.

Linda's central importance seems to be as a voice of protest and outrage against what is happening to her husband. She insists that "attention must be paid" to Willy and his suffering. As Linda recognizes, Willy is a human being, and it *is* a terrible thing that happens to him. Dreams, illusions, and self-deceptions feed the action of this play; Linda, in contrast, seems very much planted in reality with her concerns over house payments, mending work, insurance premiums, and her husband's care. She knows exactly what her sons are, and she makes no bones about telling them, especially when they hurt her husband.

Despite Linda's clear sight, however, she allows her family's dreams to flourish; she even encourages them. Why she does this is partly due to the ambivalent nature of such dreams. When Biff is led to dream that he and Happy can start a business on a loan from Bill Oliver, we see the family revitalized and Willy gain the strength to go and ask for a better job. For a time the dream is clearly less destructive than reality. But to feed the dream Biff has to reinvent not only his own abilities but also his relationship with Mr. Oliver. Such dreams can never be fulfilled, as they are based on lies. Although the dream may grant strength while it is maintained, as soon as reality intrudes the dream is shattered and lays the dreamer open to harsh disillusionment. But the question remains: Is it possible to live in dreams?

Linda tries to protect Willy from the truth, and his own blinkers assist in his own deception; it is difficult to judge their decisions. Charley tells us, "A salesman is got to dream," and seems to suggest that Willy had no other option. When Biff insists that the truth be told, Willy cannot listen and misses the point, fixating instead on the single element of Biff's love for him, which he then uses as justification for suicide. Miller ensures that even the consequences of this act remain as ambivalent as the dream that provoked it. We are given no assurance that Biff will accept the money, and there is great uncertainty that the insurance company will pay out.

Students will need to read the lengthy setting and character descriptions, as they offer valuable clues for interpretation. Willy is presented as living in a claustrophobic, urban setting indicative of the harsh life he has chosen. His home is surrounded by apartment houses that emanate a threatening orange glow.

When memory takes over, this glow gives way to a more dreamlike background with shadowy leaves and music, evoking a happier, pastoral era. At the close of the play, however, we see the looming "hard towers" of the apartment building dominating the setting once more. Without Willy's memories, the dream of a happier, Edenic life cannot exist in this city.

Many of Willy's activities can be seen as highly symbolic. He plants seeds just as he plants false hopes: Both will die and never come to fruition, largely because the house has become too hemmed in by the city. The front porch constructed out of stolen lumber is indicative of how their lives, as well as their house, have been built on something false. Willy does not fit into the modern world of machinery, and the values he espouses, where deals are made with a smile and a handshake, are clearly those of a bygone age. To illustrate this point, Miller frequently depicts Willy's uneasy relationship with such machinery as his car, his refrigerator, and Howard's recording machine.

The names of characters can also provide insights. Willy is a childish version of the more adult William, indicating an intrinsic immaturity in his nature. The Loman men all need to grow up and find true direction in their lives, especially Willy with his unrealistic dream of wanting everyone to like him. The surname Loman has been read as indicating Willy to be a low man, common and insignificant. Miller, however, declares that this was unintentional, for he picked the name subconsciously from a movie he had once seen: *The Testament of Dr. Mabuse.* For Miller, the name "Lohmann" evokes the voice of a "terror-stricken man calling into the void for help that will never come." Meanwhile, Biff seems to indicate an abrasive nature and someone who will have to fight to get what he wants, whereas Happy invokes a happy-go-lucky personality — even though we learn it is a deluded happiness.

Miller describes salesmen as "actors whose product is first of all themselves, forever imagining triumphs in a world that either ignores them or denies their presence altogether. But just often enough to keep the game going one of them makes it and swings to the moon on a thread of dreams unwinding out of himself." The "Death of a Salesman" is initially that of Dave Singleman. Willy idealizes Singleman's death but views it bluntly: The man passed away on a train still trying to make that big deal, and despite the many who attended his funeral, he died alone. A salesman must always be on the move, and such a life inevitably wears you down. Singleman was a salesman of the past who could still manage to get by on being liked; Willy attempts to emulate Singleman's life in a less sentimental age. Working against greater odds, Willy runs out of steam, and it is *his* death with which the play ends. His funeral is not nearly so well attended, indicating a society in which people are accorded less importance, which seems finally to invalidate Willy's insistence on personality being the key to success.

SUSAN C. W. ABBOTSON

Questions for Discussion

1. What kind of relationships do Willy and Charley have with their sons? What values do they teach to their offspring? Whom do you think is the better father and why?
2. Why is David Singleman so important to Willy? What is the life of a salesman? What does Willy sell?
3. What were Willy's father and brother really like? Does Ben have the answer that Willy is looking for? How did Ben get rich?

4. Why is Bernard so much more successful than Biff and Happy? What are the differences between Bernard and Howard?

5. What sort of woman is Linda Loman? How far can she be held responsible for what happens to her husband?

6. What are the turning points in Biff and Willy's relationship?

7. Does Willy Loman ever fully face the truth about his own life and the lives of his two sons? Do either of his sons?

8. Describe the significance of the following: the surrounding apartment houses, the flute music, Willy's seeds, the porch, Willy's reactions to machines, the jungle Ben goes into, and the names of the Loman men.

9. How is Willy's suicide foreshadowed in the play? Will the insurance company pay out?

10. What is Miller saying about the nature of the American Dream and capitalism? Is Willy's death inevitable? Does the play support or reject Willy's beliefs?

11. Though Willy is ordinary in many ways, what qualities does he possess that make him special and worthy of our sympathy?

12. Is Willy a tragic hero? What does he do that determines your answer to this question?

Topics for Writing

1. Arthur Miller insists that he does not condemn the capitalistic system as a whole but only those elements of it that appear false or hypocritical. How does *Death of a Salesman* support or refute this assertion?

2. Harold Clurman has suggested that "the father in Miller's work is a recurrent figure regarded with awe, devotion, love, even when he is proved lamentably fallible and when submission to him becomes painfully questionable. The father is a godhead because he is the giver and supporter of life; he is expected to serve as an example of proper conduct, of 'good.' . . . He gives identity and coherence to our being, creates value." Bearing this quote in mind, describe Willy's relationship with his two sons and decide whether or not he is a good father.

3. The ending of *Death of a Salesman* is intentionally ambiguous. What do you think may happen to the Lomans after Willy's suicide? What lessons have they learned or failed to learn? Write a short story that explores these questions and attempts to answer them.

4. **CONNECTIONS** Arthur Miller is very concerned about how tragedy should be presented. After reading his essay "Tragedy and the Common Man," illustrate the essential difference between Greek and modern tragedy using *Death of a Salesman*, Sophocles' *Oedipus the King*, and Eugene O'Neill's *Bound East for Cardiff*.

5. **CONNECTIONS** In *Death of a Salesman* and *A Raisin in the Sun*, Arthur Miller and Lorraine Hansberry both show an interest in the needs and difficulties of families. By comparing and contrasting the Lomans and the Youngers, outline what those needs and difficulties appear to be. Is there such a thing as a perfect family? Does either playwright suggest how this ideal might be accomplished?

Suggested Readings

Aarnes, William. "Tragic Form and the Possibility of Meaning in *Death of a Salesman*." *Furman Studies* 29 (1983): 57–80.

Anderson, M. C. *"Death of a Salesman*: A Consideration of Willy Loman's Role in Twentieth Century Tragedy." *Crux* 20 (May 1986): 25–29.

Bigsby, C. W. E. *Modern American Drama, 1945–1990*. Cambridge: Cambridge UP, 1992.

Bigsby, Christopher, ed. *Arthur Miller and Company*. London: Methuen, 1990.

Bloom, Harold, ed. *Arthur Miller's "Death of a Salesman."* New York: Chelsea, 1988.

———. *Willy Loman*. New York: Chelsea, 1990.

Burgard, Peter J. "Two Parts Ibsen, One Part American Dream: On Derivation and Originality in Arthur Miller's *Death of a Salesman*." *Orbis Litterarum* 43 (1988): 336–53.

Carson, Neil. *Arthur Miller*. London: Macmillan, 1982.

Centola, Steven R., ed. *The Achievement of Arthur Miller: New Essays*. Dallas: Contemporary Research, 1995.

Corrigan, Robert W., ed. *Arthur Miller: A Collection of Critical Essays*. Englewood Cliffs, NJ: Prentice, 1969.

Martin, Robert A., ed. *Arthur Miller: New Perspectives*. Englewood Cliffs, NJ: Prentice, 1982.

Martine, James J., ed. *Critical Essays on Arthur Miller*. Boston: G. K. Hall, 1979.

Miller, Arthur. *The Theatre Essays of Arthur Miller*. Edited by Robert A. Martin. New York: Viking, 1978.

———. *Timebends: A Life*. New York: Grove, 1987.

Murphy, Brenda. *Miller: "Death of a Salesman."* New York: Cambridge UP, 1995.

Roudané, Matthew C., ed. *Conversations with Arthur Miller*. Jackson: UP of Mississippi, 1987.

Weales, Gerald, ed. *"Death of a Salesman": Text and Criticism*. New York: Viking, 1967.

Edward Albee

The Sandbox (p. 1823)

In *The Sandbox*, Mommy and Daddy bring Grandma to the beach to die. They show no affection for her and are eager to get on with their own lives. Their lives, ironically, are so empty that they may as well be as dead as they desire Grandma to be. Although Grandma is initially unhappy about their actions, she allows the Angel of Death to claim her and so escapes their restrictive world. Albee disagrees with critics who have accused him of being obsessed with death and insists that his true interest is in life and the degree to which people are willing to live it fully. He wants people to participate more fully in their own lives.

Like O'Neill, Albee is concerned with people's capacity to delude themselves as to truth and to hide in the unrealistic dreams they have created. Like O'Neill, Albee has had to defend himself against charges of nihilism and pessimism. He responds in the same fashion, by stating that his work is merely truthful. The world contains many hypocrites like Mommy and Daddy, mouthing their cant and empty platitudes as they pursue selfish, denaturing dreams. Mommy and Daddy are incapable of learning and have become monstrous through their callousness, but Albee hopes his audience will learn by witnessing their mistakes.

Albee felt that American theater had become staid and stagnant in the 1960s. He wished to revitalize the art by breaking down conventions and involving his audience in the theatrical experience in new ways. Albee has always believed that drama should engage rather than offer an escape. His aim is to disrupt the social conventions on which many of his audiences depend. Being part of his audience is meant to be an uncomfortable experience. His advice to people watching his plays is "to stop thinking and react emotionally." In *The Sandbox*, naturalism and realism are set aside as Albee explores new techniques. The play contains many elements that are common within theater of the absurd: repetitive and clichéd speech to illustrate the essential emptiness of the lives of the speakers, incongruous setting and properties to disconcert the audience, characters who are types rather than individuals and who view their own existence as fictional rather than real. Although influenced by theater of the absurd, Albee's plays are a uniquely American version of this tradition.

The intention of theater of the absurd, outlined by European playwrights such as Samuel Beckett and Eugène Ionesco, was to present a vision of the meaninglessness of life and the helplessness of individuals caught in an absurd world. Modern life was to be depicted as senseless, useless, and devoid of purpose, and there was nothing left for us to do but to laugh at it. But Albee cannot accept that there is nothing one can do that will be meaningful. Ultimately, he still believes in the validity of reason (things can be proved, events can have meaning) and refuses to accept that the universe is irreversibly absurd. Some critics see this as a failure of nerve; others recognize it as a fundamental optimism in Albee's nature. What sets him apart from European absurdists are his morality and his social responsibility. His work is satirical more than purely absurd. His attacks are virulent, and the scenes he creates are often horrific, but in the end he loves the humanity he satirizes. Like Jonathan Swift, Albee exposes human follies by magnifying them so that they will not be missed. By recognizing these follies as our own, we are meant to rectify them. Albee asks his audience to do far more than laugh.

Belgian critic Gilbert Debusscher declares that the purpose of *The Sandbox* is "to decry accepted ideas, stereotyped attitudes, convenient sentiments — in brief, the clichés of daily life and language. The two idols Albee attacks are the family and death." As an adopted child whose mother alienated and eventually disowned him, Albee felt in a strong position to attack the sanctity of what he saw as the myth of the American family. Mommy and Daddy are the American family stripped down to the barest bones, and what remains is not attractive. We witness as they first deposit their aging mother on the beach to die, and then completely disassociate themselves from the event. How different is this from abandoning such a relative in an old-age home? In the past, society respected its elderly and kept them close at hand; nowadays, we peripheralize them and attempt to distance ourselves from their inevitable deaths. But Grandma's death is more than a telling picture of how we treat the elderly: it indicates the death of a type of person in America — the pioneer.

Albee portrays three generations in this short play. Grandma, born in the nineteenth century, represents the old pioneer spirit. Her bright eyes and sharp tongue symbolize the fire and energy such people have within them. Grandma has led a hard life. She married young, was widowed early, and had to raise her daughter alone. She deplores the way her society has descended into hypocrisy and false notions of duty. She resents the restrictions her daughter has placed on her by taking her away from the freedom of the farm to live with her in the enclosed city. Her childish behavior as she sits in the sandbox where her family have dumped her is an indication of the condition to which her family have reduced her. It is a condition from which she desperately needs to escape. Her only avenue of escape turns out to be through death.

She has lost the capacity to communicate directly with her daughter and son-in-law; to their ears she makes unintelligible baby sounds. She can only demonstrate her disgust and resistance to them nonverbally, by throwing sand at Mommy. Though she cannot speak to Mommy and Daddy, she can to the audience and to the Young Man, which indicates that the lack of communication is not in the speaker but in the listeners. As Mommy and Daddy have ceased to recognize Grandma as an adult, they have ceased to hear her as one.

Grandma's attraction to the Young Man is twofold. It is partly toward the idea of the American Dream which his apparent perfection represents and toward which the pioneers had striven. It is also toward the death and consequent release he comes to represent. Although on the surface she only pretends to die to get rid of her daughter, she is secretly attracted to the release real death offers. Her decisions to speed things up by summoning the dark and to shovel sand over herself in an act of self-burial betray her inner desire to attain death. In the end she goes with easy resignation as the Young Man politely claims her. She believes that death is offering her the respect and comfort for which she has been longing.

Mommy and Daddy are entirely twentieth-century creatures who have lived through two world wars and an economic depression. Together they represent many of the faults Albee sees in contemporary middle-aged, middle-class society. They are symbolic American parents who are imprisoned by their own stereotypical thinking and clichéd language. They show themselves to be completely devoid of human feeling or compassion. They survive, but at what cost? Mommy survives by trampling on others; Daddy, by kowtowing to Mommy. Mommy leads, and Daddy passively follows, as he is unable to act without her guidance. He has no remaining spirit and is the opposite of Grandma, who objects, as best she can, to everything. Because their lives have been emptied of all spirit and feeling, Mommy and Daddy have nothing "new" left to say. Neither can truly enjoy life; for them it has become an empty routine, although they continue to keep up appearances.

There is irony behind their titles of Mommy and Daddy for they are a sterile couple who have no child (they had adopted one in Albee's earlier play, *The American Dream*, but Mommy mutilated the child to a point where it died). They have brought to the beach the opposite of a child — an old lady about to die. They are the opposite of how parents should behave, as they callously leave their ward to die in a sandbox grave. Mommy's pretense at sorrow over her mother's death is made evident by her swift mood swing from despair to breezy optimism — both equally empty.

Despite his surface simplicity, the Young Man's character contains disturbing contradictions. As well as representing the fate and condition of the American Dream, he is both an example of the younger generation and the emissary of death in the play. What is it that he wants to do with his life as a typical youth? For most of the play he performs mindless calisthenics to tone and display his already perfect body. Obsessed with his appearance, he has centered his hopes on a career that will feed this obsession in the fake world of the movies. He is certainly no actor, but that will not matter in a world where only appearances count. His evident vacancy and inability to remember even a simple line indicate his inner emptiness; his beauty is a superficial and deceiving appearance.

He represents what remains of the American Dream — a dangerously shallow and empty shell. While his calisthenics depict his apparent vitality, they also mark him as the Angel of Death in their suggestion of "the beating and fluttering of wings." Eugene O'Neill subverts the idea of death by presenting it as a young woman; Albee does it by presenting death as a virile young man. Both are asking us to take a closer look at death's place in all of our lives. By depicting the Angel of Death and the representative of the American Dream (both titles having the same initials) within the same body, Albee suggests that the American Dream that this Young Man represents can lead only to the grave.

The Musician is initially called onto the stage by Mommy. She asks him to play as they bring Grandma in, and then she tells him to stop. After Grandma throws the sand at her, Mommy asks him to play again. Grandma asks him to stop as she finds his music annoying. He stops for a while but continues once "night falls," although only quietly, as Grandma has requested. Stopped again as Mommy leaves, he finally plays for the Angel of Death, and his music is allowed the last "word." The Musician appears to represent time itself, with his playing marking the passage of time. His on/off performance indicates how time passes in most of our perceptions — not smoothly and comfortingly but in fits and starts. Both women try to control him and direct his actions, and on the surface they appear to have some success. But their control can only be temporary. At the close, he, just like death, cannot be stopped.

Behind *The Sandbox*, as in many of Albee's plays, is an assertion of the need for the individual to acknowledge the nature of reality and the necessity for genuine human relationships. There is also a concern with what Albee saw as the collapse of American idealism. As he told Edward Kosner, he is concerned with what he calls "the substitution of artificial values for real values, the acceptance for content, the slow drift of accommodation." As social criticism that refuses to pull any punches, *The Sandbox* attempts to combat such a dynamic.

Susan C. W. Abbotson

Questions for Discussion

1. What is the importance of the setting in this play? Why does it take place at a beach? What does the sandbox represent?
2. What is the relationship between the family characters? Who has the most control?
3. Mommy and Daddy's speech is full of repetitions and clichés. What does their manner of speech tell us about their characters? How do you read their reactions to Grandma's "death"?
4. How many generations of Americans are depicted in the play, and how do they differ from one another?
5. What is the role and function of the Musician?
6. Why are the names Mommy and Daddy ironic?
7. What is the difference between the way Grandma "speaks" to Mommy and Daddy and to the Young Man? How do you account for this difference?
8. Although Albee tells us that the Young Man is the Angel of Death, what else does he represent? What is his relationship to the concept of the American Dream?

9. How do the Young Man and Grandma respond to each other?
10. What does the off stage rumble signify?
11. Why does Albee have his characters behave as actors who comment on stage technique, give lighting cues, and forget their lines? What does this indicate about the lives of these people?
12. Why does the spirited Grandma accept her death so easily at the close?

Topics for Writing

1. What is the American Dream and how is it presented in *The Sandbox*? Which of the characters seems to have the greatest capacity for happiness? Give evidence from the play to support your response.
2. Considering both the form and the apparent aims of *The Sandbox*, how would you categorize the play? How far can it be described as either theater of the absurd or social satire?
3. What do we learn of the home life of Mommy, Daddy, and Grandma? Imagine that you are a social worker who has visited this home. Write a report that describes what you might have witnessed and offer recommendations to alleviate the situation.
4. **CONNECTIONS** Compare the three generations Edward Albee dramatizes in *The Sandbox* with the three ages of Krapp depicted in Samuel Beckett's *Krapp's Last Tape*. Are there historical reasons to account for the differences between the generations/ages, or are they differentiated by character traits alone?
5. **CONNECTIONS** Both *The Sandbox* and Marsha Norman's *'night, Mother* can be seen as plays centered on death. Each playwright considers the nature of death and how it is viewed by society. Why do Grandma and Jessie accept their own deaths? In what ways do Edward Albee's and Marsha Norman's outlooks differ and coincide?

Suggested Readings

Amacher, Richard E. *Edward Albee*. Boston: Twayne, 1982.

Bigsby, C. W. E., ed. *Edward Albee: A Collection of Critical Essays*. Englewood Cliffs, NJ: Prentice, 1975.

Esslin, Martin. *The Theatre of the Absurd*. New York: Doubleday, 1961.

Gabbard, Lucina P. "Edward Albee's Triptych on Abandonment." *Twentieth Century Literature* 28 (Spring 1982): 14–33.

Guo, Jide. "Albee and the Theater of the Absurd." *Foreign Literature Studies* 33.3 (1986): 32–38.

Kolin, Philip C. *Conversations with Edward Albee*. Jackson: UP of Mississippi, 1988.

Kolin, Philip C., and J. Madison Davis. *Critical Essays on Edward Albee*. Boston: G. K. Hall, 1986.

McCarthy, Gerry. *Edward Albee*. New York: St. Martin's, 1987.

Roudané, Matthew C. *Understanding Edward Albee*. Columbia, SC: U of South Carolina P, 1987.

Shull, Kathleen R. "Albee's Humanistic Enterprise: *The Sandbox* and *The American Dream*." *North Dakota Quarterly* 51 (1983): 116–28.

Stenz, Anita Maria. *Edward Albee: The Poet of Loss*. New York: Mouton, 1978.

Wasserman, Julian N., ed. *Edward Albee: An Interview and Essays*. Houston: U of St. Thomas, 1983.

LORRAINE HANSBERRY

A Raisin in the Sun (p. 1829)

Much of *A Raisin in the Sun*'s plot was drawn directly from Hansberry's own experience. Attempts were made to dissuade her family from settling in what was perceived as a white area, and while growing up Hansberry had seen the increasing tension between wanting to assimilate and maintaining pride in one's own culture. But the fact is, *A Raisin in the Sun* explores a variety of topics, from family dynamics and the generation gap to black identity and women's rights. Robert Nemiroff rightly describes the play as presaging a "revolution in black and women's consciousness." He insists that the play has not grown less relevant with the passing of time, as the issues with which it deals remain prevalent in American society. Hansberry's cast does not just depict relationships defined by race and gender but includes characters of different classes, ages, and nationalities, so that we can consider universal issues surrounding class, generations, and national development besides the more obvious issues of race and gender. It is the play's ability to maintain *and* to go beyond its author's racial identity that makes it so effective.

The aspirations, relationships, and desires of the Younger family are universal, and they make the Youngers recognizably human to an audience who would have been unused to seeing African Americans realistically depicted on stage. These universal aspects also raise key issues regarding relationships between spouses, generations, and human beings in general. A number of critics have seen color as almost irrelevant to the plot and declare Hansberry to be a universalist rather than a racial activist, when in fact she is both. If Hansberry had been overtly radical it is likely that the play would never have been produced. By submerging her racial commentary, Hansberry was able to get the play performed and to prove that African Americans had a place on Broadway and should no longer be dismissed. She writes about a black family who are specific — we can only universalize them because they are so realistic. It would be wrong to downplay the Youngers' race, which is central to their existence. The Youngers are not just middle class but African American middle class, and the stakes in their struggle to make good are intensified by this fact.

Some critics have accused Hansberry of embracing white middle-class ideas and advocating assimilation. This assessment is unfair to Hansberry and her play. *A Raisin in the Sun* is as wary of assimilation as it is of finding all the answers in Africa. Both are extremes that do not fully satisfy any African American. An effective value system for African American families becomes problematic as they need to find a balance between African tradition and American experience. African Americans face what Bernard Bell calls "a biracial and bicultural identity." This suggests a "double-consciousness" that must allow mutually exclusive identities to be held in balance. Neither Africanness nor Americanness should be neglected, as each has something essential to offer. This consciousness creates some of the apparent contradictions within the play, such as the conflict between Mama's matriarchal rule (African) and Walter's patriarchal expectations (American). Hansberry does not wish us to take sides but to consider the potential within each tradition. Hansberry's opening description tells us that she wants the set to reflect "indestructible contradictions." It is, possibly, the ability to live with such contradictions that makes the Younger family so durable.

Although the Youngers' furniture seems ordinary and worn, in their home it evokes a sense of hope and pride. The audience should realize that even this modest apartment has been a hard-won achievement. Life for the Youngers is a constant struggle to keep ahead and to keep up appearances as they scramble to become part of the middle class. Hansberry wishes us to consider the dangers of becoming so involved with appearances that we neglect what lies beneath — qualities of love, dignity, and unselfish sacrifice. These are concepts that Walter and Beneatha, especially, need to understand. All the characters in the play are so centered on their own dreams that their vision is restricted, and they fail to recognize one another's dreams. As the play progresses we see the Youngers learn to recognize and accept one another's dreams and so strengthen the family as a unit.

The differences between Joseph Asagai and George Murchison are important, as is Beneatha's choice between them. While Asagai is the complete African, George is the assimilated American. George is not a character to emulate, as he refuses to recognize either the equality of women, wanting Beneatha as his "little woman," or the importance of his African heritage, dismissing it as irrelevant. He knows facts about Africa but has lost touch with its spirit and strength. Because of his wealth, he is satisfied with the status quo and so selfishly refuses to change. Such individual selfishness is antagonistic to African American development as a whole. George may have wealth, but he has no real identity of his own, and he lacks the vibrancy we see in Asagai's secure ethnic identity.

Asagai is showing the rich tradition of Africa not just to Beneatha but also to the audience. In the 1950s, when this play was first produced, his sophistication would have been at odds with many people's limited perception of Africans as savages. Yet we should recognize that Asagai is unable to recognize what might be seen as "American aspects" of Beneatha's character, for his experience is entirely African. Asagai cannot accept Beneatha's drive for independence, although he admires her spirit. In his own way he wishes to dominate her as much as George does. Beneatha needs to find her *own* identity, which will lie somewhere between the Americanness of George and the Africanness of Asagai.

Asagai does point Beneatha toward a central truth of the play — that every individual must make his or her own life. If you do not use your own resources, then what you receive will never truly belong to you. Life is a struggle that must be embraced as any gain necessarily includes risk. The future is never guaranteed, but to maintain your dignity, you must strive to pursue what you feel is right. Asagai wants to take Beneatha to Africa, but his impulse is selfish. Beneatha's home is in America, and America needs her spirited input. We never learn if she accepts his invitation to go to Africa, but we should hope she refuses. Beneatha will not find her identity solely in Africa, because she is also American. Beneatha dresses as a Nigerian, but she has no idea of what being a Nigerian means, for it takes more than clothing and hairstyles to become assimilated.

Students may ask the extent to which Beneatha's interest in African culture is just a fad — as her excursions into photography, acting, horse-riding, and the guitar seem to have been. Yet we can view each of these hobbies not as a waste but as a part of the necessary process of finding and expressing oneself. Beneatha is right to suggest that African Americans need a better understanding of Africa as an important part of their heritage, but she must not ignore the fact that they live in America, and this, too, is a part of their heritage. Beneatha and Walter's exhibition of their African roots shows an important pride, but they also need to have pride in their American-born family and to recognize what their strength has achieved in six generations.

Beneatha has lessons to learn beyond her academic education, including a need for tact and a respect for her elders and their beliefs. Her ambitions rely heavily on financial support from her family, and their sacrifice, if made, should be acknowledged. Walter limits her by her gender, feeling she should be satisfied with being a nurse or a wife rather than being a doctor. Her spirit allows her to rise above his opinion. Beneatha wants to be independent, and it is this aspect of her dream that places her even beyond the understanding of Mama and Ruth. Mama and Ruth are not against female independence, but they do not see how it can be practically possible at this time, and it is a question Hansberry leaves open to debate. Mama and Ruth do teach Beneatha an important lesson about love — a truth that, in her immaturity, she has not realized: Love is not necessarily peaceful or easy, but like life itself, it is a constant struggle if it is to have any meaning.

At the start, Ruth seems prematurely aged and tired, ready to give in and accept the meager life she has. She has momentarily lost her passion to strive further up the social ladder. Ruth dislikes risks and wants a safe life, but safety allows for little progress. Although the rest of her family still have the energy and desire to want more, she has been worn down by hard work. She has borne a large burden, nurturing and providing for her family with little reward.

Ruth's resignation is in direct contrast to Walter's intensity: A fire burns within him, even if it is still immature and its flames are only nervous and fitful. His "erratic" quality sets him apart, differentiating him from the ordinariness and predictability that are beginning to crush Ruth's spirit. Ruth and Walter are at odds; she has given up and become indifferent to the outside world, whereas Walter refuses to give up his desire to be a part of that wider society. This is indicated by his interest in the newspaper. Ruth's dormant strength returns, however, as she refuses to give up the house that Mama buys. We learn that this has been her dream as much as Mama's, and she is able to reinforce Mama's slipping spirit. Evidently, some advances need more than individual strength, which underlines the importance of family connections. The Youngers live in a ghetto neighborhood, and Mama and Ruth's desire to move is valid: The kids chase rats in the street, and the apartment is not only cramped but infested with cockroaches. A better home will allow them more room to grow. The urgency of this move is emphasized by the discovery that Ruth will be having another child.

Mama's key attributes are her strength and her clear sense of direction. It was her and her husband's combined strength that brought the family this far. Hansberry is fully aware that black progress in America will not happen overnight but will be a lengthy process, just as it is for any social group forced to begin with next to nothing. Equality will take generations of struggle — each generation contributing a little bit to the progress. Mama's plant, which she so doggedly preserves, underlines both her desire to grow and refusal to give in. It also represents her dream — to have a house with a garden. The "Scarlett O'Hara" hat that Travis gives Mama is an indication of her development: In owning property, she has become akin to the mistress of the plantation rather than one of the slaves who worked there. Having provided a house, Mama needs to give her family space to grow. She initially declares, "We working folk not business folk," and so dismisses Walter's business dreams without fair consideration. She wants the family to progress, but she may selfishly want to be the instrument of change. Mama must allow her children control of their own lives. Still, although Mama is the head of the family at the start, it may not be so much a role she demands as one she must take, as Walter has yet to grow into it. Beneatha calls Mama a tyrant, but after putting a deposit on the house, Mama soon gives her son control of the family fortune, which he consequently wastes. This underlines the important lesson that control or respect cannot be given; it must be earned.

Whether or not Walter is the central character of the play is debatable. Although his growth toward manhood is important, so, too, is Beneatha's search for selfhood. In a way, privileging Walter's development over Beneatha's is an acceptance of the very male supremacy Hansberry questions. The check that Walter hopes for is not his but his mother's; an insurance policy paid out on his father's death. Taking this money will not assert his manhood, for this is something he needs to achieve by his own resources. It is, perhaps, hard for him to live under his mother's roof, but he must earn his own way out. At the start of the play Walter is more talk than action, and Ruth is wise not to get sucked into his dreams; she has heard them too often, seen too little done to achieve them, and has little time for dreams. Walter's early assertions of control seem ridiculous as he still thinks like a boy, without regard for his responsibilities. He defies his wife by giving Travis money, but then he has to borrow money from his wife for his car fare. Walter's view of Africa is a romanticized one, as he performs his tribal dance, but it allows us to see the inner potential in Walter, which has become buried by so much empty talk.

There is a strong critique of money throughout the play. Walter is obsessed with money and getting on, and he is slow to realize what manhood really requires. Although Walter seems at first to be empowered by money, we come to realize that his true empowerment comes from his denial of money and insistence on dignity. Like Arthur Miller, Hansberry suggests that capitalism gets in the way of the real system of love under which people should live their lives. Walter erroneously believes that life is money, but Mama knows that freedom is more important, having been closer to a generation that had none. It is what one does with that freedom that will determine one's life. Walter needs to respect the past and his parents' achievements, but it is now his turn to achieve, and Mama must allow him the freedom to develop self-respect. It is Mama's self-respect that provides the roots of her strength. Mama allows Walter real control not when she gives him money but when she allows him the freedom to choose what to do about the house. If Walter were to accept Lindner's money, it would be a major regression for the whole family. He would be playing the black stereotype from which they are striving to escape and ruin any chance of self-respect for the future.

Karl Lindner interrupts Walter's naive optimism and provides a reality check. Lindner's characterization is subtle: Awkward and soft-spoken, he seems to offer little threat by himself. We should recognize, however, the larger community and power behind such a figure. Viewing his discomfort, we realize that what he is asking is wrong. Even he seems to realize this, but he cannot surmount his own prejudices. He uses platitudes to mask what he is doing, but no one is ultimately fooled. His commentary on empathy is ironically something of which he is incapable. How, we should ask, is the Youngers' hard-working background any different from those folk in Clybourne Park? How can Lindner be anything other than a complete racist? Walter's instinct to eject this man from his home is right, and this action will be more empowering than the money he got from Mama. Walter begins his second confrontation with Lindner fairly sheepishly, but he draws strength as he continues — partly from within himself and his own pride and partly from his family and a recognition of the dignity he owes them for their sacrifices. It is at this moment that we see the man in Walter: Now he can give orders to others and expect them to follow as he has finally earned their respect.

There are dark aspects of the play which should not, finally, be overlooked. One such aspect (which may be seen as realism, although it has engendered some criticism) is Hansberry's depiction of how little black solidarity exists, with the inclusion of such unhelpful characters as Willy Harris and Mrs. Johnson. While Willy runs off with Walter's money, Mrs. Johnson's appearance as a gossipy, unhelpful neighbor further underlines the inability of many blacks to assist one another. Mrs. Johnson seems probably motivated by jealousy, not wanting the Youngers to rise above her. In this way she is as guilty as George of wanting to keep the status quo. Beneatha is right to compare Mrs. Johnson to the Ku Klux Klan: Both are destructive to black development in America.

Hansberry also ensures that we realize how potentially dangerous it will be for the Youngers to move to Clybourne Park. It would be a mistake to see this play as having a "happy ending." Hansberry purposefully leaves us uncertain as to what will happen next. Even Mama's emotion at the end, being inarticulate, remains ambivalent: Is it from pride of her son's growth, or could it indicate an element of fear toward the dangerous unknown into which her family is going? What indignities might the Youngers be forced to suffer in Clybourne Park, where they are clearly not welcome? What will Beneatha decide to do with her life, and will her gender restrict her choices? What these stage characters have achieved so far is only a fragment of what they will need to ensure true equality in our society for both African Americans and women.

SUSAN C. W. ABBOTSON

Questions for Discussion

1. To what degree does the Langston Hughes poem at the start help to explain the play's action and characters? Are all the options it suggests considered in the play? Whose dreams are being deferred?

2. What are the "indestructible contradictions" that Hansberry suggests should be evident in the set design, and why are they so important? In what ways could this whole play be said to rest in contradictions?

3. In what ways are the characters of Ruth, Beneatha, and Mama (Lena) different? Which would you say is the strongest? What is the play saying about women's consciousness and rights in the 1950s?

4. What are the similarities and differences between George Murchison and Joseph Asagai? How far is their nationality accountable for their differences? Whom do you feel would make the better partner for Beneatha?

5. The character of Mrs. Johnson did not appear in early productions of the play. What does her character add? In what ways can she be compared to Willy Harris?

6. How is Karl Lindner presented? How are we supposed to react to his character?

7. At what point does Walter Lee become the true "Head of the House"?

8. What kind of man was Walter Senior? How far does his insurance money create or solve problems? What is Hansberry's attitude toward wealth?

9. What kind of relationship exists between Walter and Ruth? How does each relate to their son, Travis? What is the importance of children in this play?

10. Explain how the following symbols operate in the play: Mama's plant,

Mama's gardening hat, Walter's liquor store, Ruth's unborn child, the house in Clybourne Park, Walter's two dances.

11. What will life be like for the Youngers in Clybourne Park? To what extent is the ending of this play "happy"?

12. To what extent are Hansberry's views in the play on race and gender still applicable in today's society?

Topics for Writing

1. All the characters in *A Raisin in the Sun* are caught up in dreams of a better future. What is each character's dream and how does he/she plan/hope to achieve it? In what ways do some of these dreams conflict? Whose dreams do you believe to be the most important, and why?

2. What are the racial issues in *A Raisin in the Sun* and how are they portrayed? Give reasons for your decision on whether or not "race" is the play's central issue.

3. Write a letter from one of the Youngers to a close friend in which you describe their interpretation of the play's final scene. What happens to the family when they move to Clybourne Park? Try to be true to the characters as they are depicted in *A Raisin in the Sun*.

4. **CONNECTIONS** *A Raisin in the Sun* and Arthur Miller's *Death of a Salesman* both portray families who are struggling to survive and progress in a society that seems antagonistic to their dreams. In describing the forces operating on each family, decide to what extent these forces are internal or external and how this might affect our judgment of the families.

5. **CONNECTIONS** *A Raisin in the Sun* paints a picture of what life is like for African Americans living in America, whereas David Henry Hwang's *As the Crow Flies* looks at the lives of an elderly Asian couple. In what ways are the dreams, lives, and problems of each of these minority groups shown to be intrinsically the same or different? How far have either accepted what we call the American Dream?

Suggested Readings

Barthelemy, Anthony. "Mother, Sister, Wife: A Dramatic Perspective." *Southern Review* 21 (1985).

Brown, Lloyd W. "Lorraine Hansberry as Ironist: A Reappraisal of *A Raisin in the Sun*." *Journal of Black Studies* 4 (1974).

Carter, Steven R. *Hansberry's Drama: Commitment and Complexity*. Urbana: U of Illinois P, 1991.

Cheney, Anne. *Lorraine Hansberry*. Boston: Twayne, 1984.

Cooper, David O. "Hansberry's *A Raisin in the Sun*." *Explicator* 52 (1993): 59–61.

McKelly, James C. "Hymns of Sedition: Portraits of the Artist in Contemporary African-American Drama." *Arizona Quarterly* 48 (1992): 87–107.

Nemiroff, Robert, ed. *To Be Young, Gifted, and Black: Lorraine Hansberry in Her Own Words*. Englewood Cliffs, NJ: Prentice, 1969.

Seaton, Sandra. "*A Raisin in the Sun*: A Study in Afro-American Culture." *Midwestern Miscellany* 20 (1992): 40–49.

Washington, J. Charles. "*A Raisin in the Sun* Revisited." *Black American Literature Forum* 22 (1988): 109–24.

Wilkerson, Margaret B. "*A Raisin in the Sun*: Anniversary of an American Classic." *Theatre Journal* 38 (1986).

WOODY ALLEN (AND MARSHALL BRICKMAN)

Two Monologues from Annie Hall *and* Manhattan *(p. 1897)*

Pauline Kael has called Woody Allen "the spirit of the seventies incarnate" in his obsessions with self, identity, and the desire for acceptance. Though sometimes criticized for such "pathological narcissism," Allen's concerns are shared by many of his contemporaries, which may partly account for his popularity. Many of us quickly identify with Allen and his characters, because we, too, live shaky lives, unable to form satisfying relationships, constantly traumatized by fears of intimacy or the inevitable apocalypse. Vincent Canby describes Allen as "the poet of America's emotionally disenfranchised, urban, upwardly mobile males who seek fame, fortune and girls they can relate to. Like all artists, he's a bit schizoid. He's a participant in the American Dream but never for a moment isn't he standing a little to one side, watching himself."

The elements of self-critique and humor that imbue Allen's pathology should make us aware that the writer may not take himself quite as seriously as some of his staunchly adverse critics believe. Barbara Schapiro suggests, however, that although Allen is aware of his psychological problems, this does not negate their continued existence, and although his detached self-awareness is often humorous, it may also be seen as symptomatic of a "deeper narcissism of which he may not fully be aware." Whatever we choose to believe, what is certain is that Woody Allen's work has the power to make us laugh and to make us think.

Allen's personality does dominate all of his characters, not just the "nebbish" male leads he assigns himself. Every character we witness in his movies will talk in the same broken, wise-cracking style as if to accentuate his or her inner insecurity and sense of fragmentation. Yet it is dangerous to judge any single character as purely autobiographical, whatever the surface similarities. To do so detracts from the skill with which Allen has carefully created these personas. Students will need to look carefully at the way in which Allen presents both Alvy Singer and Ike Davis. The very nature of monologues, with their direct address, can often lead the listener to implicitly believe every word he or she hears. An audience should maintain caution, however, considering not only what is being said but how it is being said; also, the audience should look for what is not said. Ensure that a critical distance is maintained, at least initially, while that which lies within and behind the words the characters choose is deciphered.

Allen's concerns do extend beyond himself. He exhibits what is often described as a postmodern spirit in his explorations of alienation, fragmentation, and mechanization. Allen sees American culture in dire trouble and seeks to remedy this by at least drawing attention to the fact, as he offers up the more unattractive aspects of this culture to close scrutiny. Exploring feelings, and ways to translate them into powerful and recognizable images, is one of Allen's primary objectives. Allen sees society as suffering from a widespread religious disappointment and a profound realization of the emptiness of most objects with which people surround themselves; such beliefs are as hard to bear as they are to accept. He suggests that, given this predicament, we are left with two choices: accept on sheer faith that life is not meaningless, or create some kind of social structuring that can offer the individual a chance at real fulfillment. People, Allen declares, have "got to give up the immediate, self-gratifying view" and work toward achieving a more honest and ethical culture.

On a personal level, Allen's characters fluctuate between idealistic, self-absorbed fantasies and expressions of contemptuous self-loathing. As social creatures they view other folk with the same ambivalence. Allen dramatizes city life as verbal communication, cerebral rather than physical, owing to confinements of time and space. And yet verbal communication is one of the trickiest things going. Language, with its ability to externalize and distort, is a slippery creature. Allen enjoys exploring its curves and forcing us to confront the difficulties we all face when attempting to express ourselves honestly and truthfully.

Annie Hall and *Manhattan* mark for Allen a move away from his earlier, more cartoonish comedies, as they seek to introduce real, human characters. Allen talks of how he tried to cut down on the potential for laughter in both movies in order not to distract his audience entirely from the more serious concerns he was trying to address. Allen has developed a way to address serious topics in the comic mode without becoming ponderous. While *Annie Hall* is more concerned, in its concentration on Annie, with the predicament of the contemporary woman, *Manhattan* can be seen as a companion piece that concentrates its attention and sympathy on the man.

Annie Hall has been called a "comedy about urban love and incompatibility." In this opening monologue, Alvy begins a free wheeling, self-deprecating search for the truth about why his affair with Annie Hall went sour. Annie, we will later discover, is as emotionally tangled and confused as Alvy, which largely answers this question. Annie left him because he was too insecure to fully commit to her; although he lets her move in with him, he insists that she maintain her own flat. Alvy never fully understands this, but we do, as we get to know his chronically suspicious, determinedly depressive nature. Alvy is simply overawed by the sheer complexity of "life, the universe, and everything," which ultimately freezes him into an endless cycle of uncertainty and noncommitment.

One should note how Alvy makes no attempt to tell us his story chronologically; he skips around from one aspect to another as each slips into his mind. He suggests that his intention is to create some kind of orderly explanation for what has taken place between him and Annie, but the very method by which he pursues this aim seems to resist, either consciously or subconsciously, any such order. Is this because he is secretly scared by what he might find? Isolated events become important to Alvy because they are the ones he has chosen to talk about. The audience must be guarded, however, for all too often the recollection begins to take precedence over the reality. Alvy wavers between reaching for the truth or a self-perpetuating fantasy with which he may find it easier to live. We should carefully analyze everything Alvy tells us. His opening jokes declare his predisposition to think ill of life and others, while wistfully wishing it might be otherwise. He translates his life and worries into jokes as a means of coping with them. Having recently turned forty, he is a prime example of a man undergoing a mid-life crisis.

Alvy's obsession with his own possible future indicates both his selfishness and his profound uncertainty. Things happen to Alvy, and he is never sure why, and that bothers him. He wants to know answers in a world that only seems to pose more questions. What might help him arrive at a better understanding would be to look beyond himself in these issues. He introduces his concern about why he and Annie broke up, but note how far his speech is centered on the first-person singular pronoun "I." He decides, quite typically, that it must have something to do with him. Telling us nothing more about Annie at this point, he goes straight into recounting his own life story. Through this account, the audience will learn why they broke up, but it is uncertain that Alvy ever becomes fully aware.

Manhattan attempts to offer a realistic, though highly subjective, view of life in New York City in the 1970s. Through this, Allen is attempting to explore what he sees as the contemporary human condition. The city is a place of dreams and squalor, which can fascinate, uplift, and destroy those who choose to live in it. It is a place where fashion can affect more lives than illness, catastrophe, or drugs. *Manhattan* is essentially a film about love and relationships, and it explores how a man can gain some control over his own life in such a milieu. What happens is not nearly as important as how it happens and what that tells us about the sad frustration of many people's lives. In Ike, Allen tries to capture what it means to be a contemporary male who is utterly mixed up — caught between vulnerability and corruption, innocence and fear, selfishness and the desire to connect with others. Behind his apparently comic moments of self-realization, Ike displays a quiet anguish.

On the surface, Ike's opening monologue appears to be a humorous attempt at uncovering a strong, individual voice with which to tell his tale. As a kind of interior dialogue with himself, we hear Ike create a sequence of identities that he then considers accepting or rejecting. Each attempt provokes laughter as he plays so obviously with increasingly reductive and ridiculous stereotypes. He begins with the voice of uncritical nostalgia, a man who adores New York without qualification because he simply refuses to recognize its current reality. This is quickly rejected for the voice of someone a little more savvy and street smart; he does not want to make himself too vulnerable. Having devolved into the hackneyed verbiage of a hard-boiled detective, he realizes that this, also, is not suitable.

He now tries to affect sincerity, and in the affectation he loses all sense of authenticity as he becomes a preachy editorializer bemoaning the decay of contemporary culture from a platform of self-imposed superiority. Instantly recognizing his own insincerity, he tries an angrier denunciation of the very society he had begun describing so uncritically. Having run the gamut of extremes, he finally settles for what is, in all likelihood, the most unrealistic self-description of all: a self-confident, successful womanizer. He decides to keep this persona, but it is one so obviously fake that it should put us instantly on guard against anything we further hear from this character. Ike's choice undermines the very authenticity he supposedly had been seeking and believes himself to have achieved. It is comic because of the obvious gap between this self-image and reality. Although we have yet to see Ike, we know Allen, who is playing the character, and the lady-killer image does not fit. Allen has exposed the character's inner desires and vulnerability, and the audience, knowing the truth, can laugh with a sense of its own superiority. Deep down, Ike may also know the truth, but for the moment he grasps the dream over the reality with great enthusiasm: "I love this."

It should be borne in mind, also, that in the movie this monologue is given as a voice-over. While Ike talks, the screen shows a series of New York scenes, while a Gershwin tune plays in the background. The choice of black and white images, coupled with such music, evoke the more romantic image of New York with which Ike begins, but from which he swiftly moves on. The images attempt to fit the subsequent descriptions, but the music remains the same, which suggests an underlying insincerity in Ike's changing identities. The images grow spasmodically incongruous to the monologue as Ike strives, unsuccessfully, to get beyond his opening, overly romanticized stance. The music swells and the sequence speeds up to an explosive ending, with an ambiguous burst of fireworks. This may pretend to valorize Ike's "success" in finding a satisfactory identity, but it can also be seen as a distracting image of fragmentation, mocking that success and showing its falsity. As the film progresses we will discover how far from a heroic adventurer and successful Lothario Ike really is. Instead, he will reveal what he really is — an insecure and undecided figure who is buffeted around by an increasingly fragmented and fractious society.

Although Ike does appear to find a satisfactory partner by the end of the movie, their age gap of twenty-five years is hardly conducive to our being able to believe in the lasting future of their relationship. Furthermore, she is about to embark on a six-month trip abroad without him. It is an ending imbued with the same romanticism we glimpse at the start of the movie, but it is, perhaps, this romanticism that is the key to Ike's having been able to continue functioning in such a world.

Susan C. W. Abbotson

Questions for Discussion

1. What things does Alvy choose to tell jokes about? Is there any significance in his choice of topics?
2. What is Alvy's view of the world he lives in? What is Alvy's view of himself? What does Alvy see happening in the future to himself? to society? What is Alvy most frightened of?
3. How would you describe Alvy's character? What is his most prominent characteristic?
4. Is there any significance in the order in which Alvy chooses to tell us things? If his central concern is to understand his relationship with Annie Hall, why not begin with that? What is the point behind his trying to analyze why he and Annie broke up? Why is Alvy so insecure about women?
5. What clues about Alvy's character does this opening speech offer that might explain why he and Annie broke up?
6. What is the effect of the broken speech both Alvy and Ike use?
7. In what ways are Alvy and Ike similar or different? Do you prefer one character to the other? Why?
8. How would you define the different identities Ike tries out in this monologue? From where might he be getting the ideas for these identities? Which identity do you feel is closest to the real Ike? Which seems the farthest away?
9. What is the effect of the way Allen makes this monologue a kind of interior dialogue between Ike and the identities he is attempting to create?
10. What kind of place is New York City? Why is it so hard for Ike to describe? What elements of his description of the city seem to be constants?
11. What is the effect of Ike declaring about his final, settled identity, "I love this"? What does this tell us about Ike?
12. To what extent do you believe Alvy and Ike to be products of their time? Do you share any of their evident worries? Why? In what ways might they be referred to as postmodern characters?

Topics for Writing

1. Both Alvy Singer and Ike Davis write jokes for a living, but it is possible to read between the lines of their wise-cracking personas and uncover strong, subconscious concerns and fears. Outline what these concerns and fears

might be, and explain how Woody Allen manages to convey them in this monologic form.

2. View these opening scenes as they appear in the movies *Annie Hall* and *Manhattan*. Outline in what ways the inclusion of the visual and any other sound effects contributes to your reading of Alvy and Ike and their two monologues.

3. Write a short monologue using the same style by which Woody Allen creates Alvy Singer and Ike Davis. You may like to base it on your own experiences, fears, and concerns, or you may prefer to create a fictional persona. Don't just tell random jokes; try to address some specific contemporary concerns.

4. **CONNECTIONS** In what ways is the character Kugelmass, in Woody Allen's "The Kugelmass Episode," the same or different from Alvy Singer and Ike Davis in the two monolgues? Compare, also, Allen's depiction of the type of world in which each of these characters lives. How do the demands of the different genres of cinema and short fiction affect the manner in which Allen writes?

5. **CONNECTIONS** Compare the two characters portrayed in Woody Allen's two monologues with the janitor in August Wilson's *The Janitor*. Both writers create characters through whom they voice certain social concerns. What concerns are raised by each monologue, and how are they conveyed? Which writer do you feel is the more effective? Why?

Suggested Readings

Allen, Woody. *Woody Allen on Woody Allen*. New York: Grove, 1995.

Blansfield, Karen C. "Woody Allen and the Comic Tradition in America." *Studies in American Humor* 6 (1988): 142–53.

Brown, Devin. "Powerful Man Gets Pretty Woman: Style Switching in *Annie Hall*." *SECOL Review* 16.2 (1992): 115–31.

Canby, Vincent. "*Annie Hall*: Allen at His Best." *New York Times*, 21 Apr. 1977, sec. 3, p. 22.

Didion, Joan. "Letter from Manhattan." *New York Review of Books*, 16 Aug. 1979, 13, 18–19.

Feldman, Seth. "Taking Woody Allen Seriously." *Canadian Review of American Studies* 14 (1983): 353–57.

Girgus, Sam B. *The Films of Woody Allen*. New York: Cambridge UP, 1993.

Gittelson, Natalie. "The Maturing of Woody Allen." *New York Times Magazine*, 22 Apr. 1979, 30–32, 102, 104–105, 107.

Knight, Christopher J. "Woody Allen's *Manhattan* and the Ethicity of Narrative." *Film Criticism* 13.1 (1988): 63–72.

Lax, Eric. *Woody Allen: A Biography*. New York: Knopf, 1991.

McCann, Graham. *Woody Allen: New Yorker*. London: Polity, 1990.

Morris, C. "Woody Allen's Comic Irony." *Literature Film Quarterly* 15 (1987): 175–80.

Schapiro, Barbara. "Woody Allen's Search for Self." *Journal of Popular Culture* 19.4 (1986): 47–62.

Schatz, Thomas. "*Annie Hall* and the Issue of Modernism." *Literature Film Quarterly* 10 (1982): 180–87.

Yacowar, Maurice. *Loser Take All: The Comic Art of Woody Allen*. New York: Ungar, 1979.

Ziv, Avner, and Anat Zajdman, eds. *Semites and Stereotypes: Characteristics of Jewish Humor*. Westport, CT: Greenwood, 1993.

AUGUST WILSON

The Janitor (p. 1901)

August Wilson is perhaps best known for his declaration that he intends to write a play to show the state of African Americans for each decade of the twentieth century. This short play is not intended to be a part of that cycle, but it certainly relates to the same issues the longer plays explore: how far the past influences and impinges on the present; how important the notion of a secure, personal identity is to individual contentment; how African Americans have been historically viewed and treated in American society; how the social treatment of African Americans has affected the ways in which they view themselves; what strategies African Americans should adopt to improve their lot in America. Basing his viewpoint on valuable personal experience, the janitor, Sam, touches briefly on every one of these issues.

Sam may act as a mouthpiece for many of Wilson's views, but he does so within the confines of his own authentic persona. Wilson wants the monologue delivered "with the literacy of a janitor" — that is, in a colloquial diction in keeping with the speech of a typical janitor and not that of some academic in janitor's clothing. Wilson's mother, Daisy Wilson, had worked as a janitor in order to support her family after her husband left her with five children. Daisy taught her son to recognize stereotypes and the dangers of such, just as she taught him about the exclusionary class tactics that society uses to keep the poor in their place. Many of Wilson's plays show underprivileged, underrepresented members of society and allow them, finally, a voice. Such working-class individuals as Sam are usually kept silent at the fringes of society, trapped in menial jobs and wrongly taught that this is both their place and their measure. Wilson presents a picture of the potential such people might have if society allowed them to voice an opinion and gave them the attention they deserve. People cannot be expected to contribute to society if they are never allowed the opportunity or means to do so. Wilson gives Sam both the time and an audience before which he can express his concerns and opinions, and the resulting experience should warn us to give more attention to such people in the future.

Sam begins by sweeping the stage but soon surprises us by proving himself to be more than the broom-sweeping automaton to which society is trying to reduce him. Although not as schooled as those who have had the privilege of higher education, this man has evident intellect and wisdom. He notices that the forthcoming conference, for which he is preparing the stage, is to be on youth. He "nods his approval," for Sam is fully aware that the youth are the future of any nation and need to be given attention. He pauses in his work to imagine what he would say at such a conference. His fifty-six years of life experience have taught him some life lessons he feels may be useful to the nation's youth. By so doing, he consciously steps beyond the confines of his menial task and rises above the lowly social expectations of his occupation. The suggestion that a simple janitor possesses sufficient imagination to do such a thing should warn us that what we are about to hear may defy our narrow expectations.

Aware that this occasion will be attended by well-educated, economically superior members of his race, it seems as if Sam begins by trying to speak on what he feels will be their level. He charges his speech with flowery poetical diction, the "biggest" words he can think of, and quotes Shakespeare. This attempt at sophistication fails, for instead of a polished speech, his wisdom almost gets buried under cliché, and his advice is hard to follow. It is not that he is unable to understand poetry, "big" words, and Shakespeare, but that it is unnatural for him to communicate in this way. He innately knows this as he starts to translate his own word choices for the audience — he translates *resilience* into the more everyday "its bounce back," and he evokes Popeye to help explain Shakespeare.

"Youth is sweet before flight" carries the suggestion that our best hope is in the young, whose lives are as yet unspoiled and full of promise. As Sam points out, however, though youth is a time of potential we should be prepared for its passing and not fooled into thinking it will last forever. What is important are the youths' expectations. While Popeye insists "I am what I am" and is fixed by that single definition, Sam believes these youths should not allow themselves to be defined so simply. "I am not what I am" implies the fluid potential to become anything. Although it is better to keep oneself open to possibility, such freedom always carries danger, because one's position can change for the better or for the worse. People are inevitably defined, in part, by their past, what they "have been," but this by no means diminishes their potential for future change if they accept that past.

As Sam proceeds, his stilted poetic diction becomes more fluid as it takes on the resonance and style of a preacher, with its repetitive speech patterns and open concern for the audience. Sam no doubt attends a local community church, and such religious images as a river, Jacob and the angel, and Gabriel blowing his horn come readily to mind. He begins to truly warm to his task as he warns his audience not to make the mistake of setting the past aside. By this point he means more than the individual's past, but the past of a whole race. Like many other African Americans, Sam has suffered by forgetting the "names of the gods" of his African ancestry. These should be remembered, and through that memory a firm identity and pride may be forged, which can provide a sense of security in an antagonistic world.

Sam has lived through many changes but is also aware of all that has not changed for African Americans. Born in the 1920s, and a survivor of all that has happened to African Americans since, he has seen the violent black nationalism of the 1960s come and go. The 1980s have the potential to be different, but only if people try to make them so. Jacob wrestled with the angel and through courage won an identity: that of Israel. He became the representative of a people who were offered a future of promise. Sam expects no less commitment from each African American, and the time to face such battles is in the strength of their youthful prime.

Sam has warned the youths not to waste their potential by losing touch with who they are and what they would like to become. Time inexorably passes and those who do not actively pursue better lives will wake up one day to a sad existence. "Ain't nobody innocent," he tells them, "We are all victims of ourselves." It is no use heaping blame for their positions on others, for it is their own responsibility to do something with their lives. Too often have African Americans allowed themselves to be treated as second-class citizens and been dominated by their own self-induced subservience.

Sam teaches an important lesson of responsibility as he succinctly conveys his realization that life is process. Every decision one makes throughout life has consequences that the person must be prepared to accept, "just like reaping and sowing." People should decide with care, to try to create the best of all possible lives. A poor decision has unfortunate and often painful consequences, which must be borne by whoever makes the decision. This is an integral part of living a responsible life, facing up to even unpleasant responsibilities, because to avoid them will cause harm. Sam asks the nation's youth to think carefully before they proceed. Life is long, energy is finite, and each of them holds his or her own future within his or her own hands. He warns them against cynicism, against blaming others for their own faults, against fighting the natural way of the world. He asks them, instead, to remember their heritage, to maintain self-pride, and to learn from their experiences so that they will not make the same mistake twice. Unfortunately, he gets cut off before he can give any further advice.

His disarmingly honest and perceptive vision of life would probably better serve the soon to be gathered youth than the indubitably pat and pretentious speeches to which they will be forced to listen. Wilson shows Sam emerging from the cocoon of a lowly, disregarded menial worker to the pinnacle of a feeling, thinking man, with something of importance to pass on to American youth. At the close of the piece he is returned once more into his cocoon by the attention of his unfeeling white boss, Mr. Collins, who tells him to "quit wasting time and get this floor swept." Sam instantly drops his effective public-speaking persona and becomes once again the inarticulate menial he is expected to be by such men as Collins: "Yessuh, Mr. Collins. Yessuh," he intones as he gets on with the sweeping.

The impersonal title, *The Janitor*, suggests the inhumanely reductive way in which such people tend to be regarded by society. The fact that many such menial jobs tend to be filled by blacks or other minorities in a similar low economic class, reducing Sam to his job title, represents society's casual dismissal of racial minorities and provides a fitting focus for the struggles of both class and race. While Mr. Collins may represent the insensitive white overseers who have tried to keep minorities "in their place" for centuries, we see in Sam's short-lived rebellion the wasted potential of such minorities. Sam is an untapped source of knowledge and inspiration, which has been ignored for too long.

SUSAN C. W. ABBOTSON

Questions for Discussion

1. What is the significance of the impersonal title of this piece? How would the effect be changed if it was called *Sam*?
2. What do we learn about Sam as a character? What has his life been like?
3. What issues regarding the lives of African Americans does Sam seem to be raising?
4. How many types of diction does Sam use in this piece, and what key elements define them? Why does Sam adopt these different speaking styles?
5. Why does a man like Sam work as a janitor? How does society usually perceive janitors? What other occupations are commonly held by minorities in the low economic bracket? What is the significance behind these types of jobs, and what opportunities do they allow the people who hold them?
6. Why is it so important that this is to be a conference for youths? What does Sam mean by the phrase "Youth is sweet before flight"? How does America tend to treat the idea of youth, and does this jar at all with what Sam is saying?
7. What is the link between Shakespeare and Popeye? What is the effect of putting these two names in juxtaposition?

8. What does Sam mean when he tells us, "Ain't nobody innocent," and, "We are all victims of ourselves"?

9. What gods' names have been forgotten, and why is this important? What is the significance of the various religious images Sam invokes? What does he intend them to represent?

10. Overall, what is Sam telling youths to do, and what is he telling them not to do? How do you think this speech might differ from the speeches the youths will be hearing at the conference?

11. Why does Wilson have Mr. Collins tell Sam to get back to work at the end? What is the significance of Sam's response to Mr. Collins?

12. Could this monologue be spoken by a white actor? How would this change the impact of the piece?

Topics for Writing

1. Using *The Janitor* as evidence, what does August Wilson seem to believe is problematic with American attitudes toward race and class?

2. Write a close analysis of *The Janitor*, marking the different phases through which Sam's speech goes and fully explaining the significance behind each of these changes. What, in the end, is the core of Sam's advice, and how is it borne out by his life?

3. Consider what other occupations are commonly held by minorities in the low economic bracket. Choose one such occupation and give the person doing this job the opportunity to speak his or her mind in a short monologue. You may wish to try to write in a colloquial form, but if inauthentic it could be very distracting; use a style of speech with which you feel comfortable and in command.

4. **CONNECTIONS** What differences or similarities do you see in the way African Americans are portrayed in Lorraine Hansberry's 1950s play *Raisin in the Sun* and August Wilson's 1980s play *The Janitor*? Has society's treatment of African Americans changed? Has the "African American" image of self changed? What social factors may be attributing to your answers of the preceding questions?

5. **CONNECTIONS** Compare August Wilson's *The Janitor* to either Samuel Beckett's *Krapp's Last Tape* or Woody Allen's monologue from *Manhattan*. Each could be described as a monologue in which the protagonist undergoes a change of outlook. In what ways does each writer indicate these changes? Consider not only the text itself but also its surrounding semiotics: movements, setting, lighting, properties, and so forth.

Suggested Readings

DiGaetani, John. *A Search for a Postmodern Theater: Interviews with Contemporary Playwrights*. New York: Greenwood, 1991.

Elkins, Marilyn. *August Wilson: A Casebook*. New York: Garland, 1994.

Harrison, Paul Carter. "August Wilson's Blues Poetic." In *Three Plays, August Wilson*. Pittsburgh: U of Pittsburgh P, 1991.

Nadel, Alan, ed. *May All Your Fences Have Gates: Essays on the Drama of August Wilson*. Iowa City: U of Iowa P, 1994.

Pereira, Kim. *August Wilson and the African-American Odyssey*. Chicago: U of Chicago P, 1995.

Plum, Jay. "Blues, History, and the Dramaturgy of August Wilson." *African American Review* 27 (1993): 561–67.

Reed, Ishmael. "A Shy Genius Transforms the American Theater." *Connoisseur* 217 (Mar. 1987): 92–97.

Savran, David, ed. *In Their Own Words: Contemporary American Playwrights.* New York: Theatre Communications Group, 1988.

Shafer, Yvonne. "August Wilson: A New Approach to Black Drama." *Zeitschrift fur Anglistik und Amerikanistik* 39 (1991): 17–27.

Shannon, Sandra. *The Dramatic Vision of August Wilson.* Washington, DC: Howard UP, 1995.

Wilson, August. "A Conversation with August Wilson." By Mark Rocha. *Diversity: A Journal of Multicultural Issues* 1 (Spring 1993): 24–42.

———. "Interview." By Kim Powers. *Theatre* 16.1 (Fall 1984): 50–55.

Marsha Norman

'night, Mother (p. 1904)

Marsha Norman has stated that all theater is about wanting things you can or cannot have and do or do not get. It is on these terms that we are asked to view Jessie Cates and her decision to commit suicide. We listen as Jessie prepares her Mama to accept her impending demise. Norman refuses to sentimentalize the play's issues, which strengthens its impact. This is no early death because of terminal illness but a conscious ending of a life. Jessie is a middle-aged epileptic who, since her divorce, has been living with her mother. She has recently come to a realization of how unhappy her life actually is. Students should note that "it is only in the last year" that Jessie "has gained control of her mind and her body." Her decision to commit suicide reflects a need to take control of her life — the loss of control being symbolized, to some extent, by her epilepsy. We are not witnessing a debate so much as an explanation; Mama cannot make Jessie change her mind. Jessie's attempt to rationalize her decision is not for herself but for her mother. Her effort results in a moment of connection and, possibly, understanding, between the two characters. Having lived in the same house as virtual strangers without honest communication, these two women are finally speaking directly to each other, without prevarication.

The house the Cateses live in is relatively comfortable, though isolated. Norman takes great pains in her opening directions to insist that her set and characters should be both specific *and* universal. Everything should be portrayed with sufficient detail for it to be realistic but not too extraordinary. Despite specific aspects, these are intrinsically, ordinary women. Norman wants us to view them as "normal" women undergoing difficulties that are not as extraordinary as many would like to believe, although they are aspects of life that many try to ignore. Norman forces us to face the full implications of such lives.

Like Samuel Beckett, Norman tends to place her characters in a critical situation to see how they survive and what choices they make. She, too, focuses on the helplessness, isolation, and pain of being human. Despite the ordinary quality of the Cateses' lives, Norman uses them to explore complex issues of life, death, and personal choice. Mama conjures up the accepted clichés by which we tend to regard suicide: Suicidal people are overly upset, retarded, deranged, abnormal. Such complacent responses are now subverted as Jessie is presented as being none of the above. Norman makes her appear calm, intelligent, rational, and essentially ordinary. By this, Jessie's suicide becomes more shocking because its impulse becomes evident in many of our lives: We can no longer separate ourselves from those who commit suicide as if they have no connection to our "normal lives."

Norman makes the bedroom door the focal point of the set so that we won't lose sight of Jessie's aim — to go into that room and kill herself. The door is described as a point of both "threat and promise" that encompasses the extreme possibilities of Jessie's act. We are not allowed to expect a dramatic turnaround or rescue. Jessie is merely explaining her decision to her mother, and, of course, to the audience. The decision to die has been made before the play begins. The play shows why she has come to this decision and how her mother reacts. Although Jessie tells her mother of her plan to commit suicide in advance, this is neither a cry for help nor an indication that she wishes to be stopped. Norman does not want us to doubt for a moment that Jessie will commit suicide and that she will do it successfully; her father's gun will "definitely work." Jessie has waited until she feels well before going through with her suicide plans, and her desire to kill herself cannot be attributed to her illness, but goes far deeper. It is not a spur of the moment decision.

Norman establishes familiarity with a realistic set and colloquial speech and the mundane activities we see Jessie performing. She then strips all of this away when Jessie announces her decision to kill herself. It is now a struggle between the two characters for control. Jessie has the advantage of surprise, but Mama rallies and tries to bring reason, threats, bribes and diversions to bear. She mocks Jessie, suggesting her suicide will fail as she will "miss" or "wind up as a vegetable." What she has not grasped is that Jessie already feels as though she is a vegetable. The usual dependencies of mother and daughter are upturned as Mama, with her love of candy and moments of petulance, seems more the child, while Jessie nurtures and cares for Mama in a way this mother has never been able to do for her daughter. Mama wheedles, untruthfully insists she needs Jessie, and offers to change what she believes are the reasons for Jessie's decision. Everything she thinks and does is wrong, and all of her ploys are merely efforts to maintain her own control.

The inadequacy of Mama's responses should be apparent as she tries to change Jessie's mind by offering to buy new dishes or rearrange the furniture — such ephemera cannot give Jessie's life the meaning it lacks. All of Mama's efforts are ineffective, as Jessie refuses to give up her control; her decision has already been made. Mama even tries to take responsibility for the suicide onto herself, but Jessie cannot allow this for it would eliminate its whole point. "It doesn't have anything to do with you!" she declares — and she is right. Mama sees this, finally, as she acknowledges Jessie's autonomy. "I thought you were mine," she declares, now seeing her mistake; no human being can belong to anyone but themselves. Jessie has finally claimed ownership of herself.

Jessie's decisive, competent actions contrast with her appearance, which is "vaguely unsteady." Her paleness suggests the paucity of her life spirit. Jessie's control is only psychological, and she is forever threatened by a physical betrayal. For this reason alone, her current sense of determination and control offers her something she cannot afford to ignore. It gives her a "peaceful energy" and "sense of purpose" she has lacked all her life. Always a loner, Jessie has long been misunderstood by others. People, including her own family, tend to avoid contact, for she makes them uncomfortable. She never leaves the house; they even have their groceries delivered. Her mother is largely a stranger to Jessie, despite the familiarity that has come from living together in a regular routine. Jessie's life has become little more than a series of lists and schedules. The house is filled with Mama's clutter rather than a joint mess, for Jessie's presence has left no mark. This indicates how little of Jessie actually remains. The working clock is an important part of the set. Jessie is minutely aware of time; it is something precious to her, and she does not wish to waste any. Her efficiency is a further indication of this. A competent household organizer, she displays equal organization in planning her suicide. Jessie has been planning the event carefully for some time, canceling the papers, stockpiling supplies for her mother, and working out every detail, even down to what her mother will do next.

An important and troubling aspect of Jessie's suicide is that she *doesn't have to do it* — she does it by choice. Norman is not advocating suicide as a common answer for people: It is merely the right path for Jessie. Jessie makes a conscious choice in order to escape what has become an empty life. She describes it in terms of choosing to get off the bus early as she knows the scenery will no longer be changing. Given the person she has become, there is no future of progress or change, so she may as well end it now rather than live on without hope. In doing so she takes charge. Jessie's isolation is repeatedly stressed. No one wishes to employ her, and even her own family fail to recognize her needs. The only person with whom she felt any camaraderie, her father, died some time ago, so she has nothing to do on a Saturday night but tend to her mother.

Jessie no longer feels alive: She is "cold" all the time and longs for the "dark and quiet" of death. She is tired of having other people rule her life and wants control for herself. She has logically eliminated every reason she might have had for remaining alive: She no longer believes she is of any use to her husband, son, brother, or mother; she has no impact on their lives as she herself has no real existence. She does not care for them anymore than she cares for herself. "I'm just not having a very good time and I don't have any reason to think it'll get anything but worse. I'm tired. I'm hurt. I'm sad. I feel used." Mama insists on a rational reason, and this, apparently, is it. Jessie's belief and action is not meant to be an answer for others; it is what Jessie believes is true for her. All she has left that is her own is her life, and she declares her right to say "no" to it. She embraces death as her only remaining choice.

Jessie has lost her selfhood, and suicide is her attempt to regain it. She is finally having a say about her life: Even if what she finally says is no, the decision and control is hers alone. Yet Norman still allows us to sympathize with Mama as a survivor with her guilt as she mourns the loss of her daughter. Part of the play's strength comes from Norman allowing us to sympathize with both Jessie and Mama. As Leslie Kane suggests, "We are Thelma [Mama] trying to understand, placate, compromise, escape guilt, rely on reason and logic, and deny death. And we are Jessie wanting freedom from suffering, fighting against vulnerability, affirming individual choice and dignity." Both Jessie and Mama are special people in their own ways.

Mama has led a selfish life, and it is initially hard to sympathize with her character. Like her son, Dawson, she withdraws into her own world and concentrates on herself when communicating with others becomes too difficult. She loves her family, but, not having the strength to help them, she allows that love to dissipate into thoughtlessness and evasion. She is more concerned with what outsiders might think than what her family itself might be feeling. Accustomed to manipulating others to create a comfortable existence for herself, she has mostly shunned the truth; it would be too discomforting to face. Mama is domineering and likes to be in control; it annoys her when things don't happen her way. She has become reliant on Jessie for assistance with the daily chores of life — indeed, she has Jessie do everything. She gives orders and Jessie obeys without demur.

Norman ensures that we see the essential emptiness not only of Jessie's life but also that of Mama's, even though these lives appear comfortable. This is a truth Mama likes to avoid, but it sneaks out on occasions, such as when Mama points out that "we don't have anything anybody'd want, Jessie. I mean, I don't even want what we got, Jessie." Jessie agrees: "Neither do I," she says, which is central to her decision to kill herself. Neither woman has a life which satisfies, but where Jessie is now willing to face up to that truth, Mama insists on avoiding it. We can, gradually, feel sorry for Mama as we learn of her loveless marriage and her suppressed guilt and jealousy. She does love Jessie and has done her meager best for her, but, being human, she does not have all the right answers. Such human fallibility allows us to sympathize with, rather than condemn, her failings.

The final communication Mama has with Jessie means a lot to her, as it has given her a moment of contact with her daughter, perhaps for the first time in her life. They each admit things that they had previously kept secret, which allows them to grow closer with the bond of shared understanding. Both are able to confess and unburden themselves of various failures and jealousies. Mother and daughter finally manage not only authentic communication but also intimacy. Such a moment gives Mama something to live for. Her life, in many ways, has been as empty as Jessie's, yet she chooses to live — just as rationally as Jessie chooses to die. As she tells us, "I don't know what I'm here for, but then I don't think about it."

Mama becomes even admirable on deeper reflection. She indicates a deceptively profound knowledge of what makes life bearable and significant when she discusses her friend Agnes. "Agnes likes a feeling of accomplishment," she declares. Also there is Agnes's desire to keep her life full, to give it meaning, and to experience occasional change. Just as Agnes may burn down a house before it falls down in order to remain in control, so, too, does Jessie destroy herself before she falls down. Agnes is a force of life and is held in contrast to Jessie's death force — which is why she stays away from Jessie. Mama, too, is a life force. She can survive, as do many of us, by inventing stories to make her life less boring. Jessie is left with only stark truths and an incapacity to create any more fictions to make life livable. She has irrevocably lost herself and sees no point in continuing. Mama finally sees the truth of this: "Who am I talking to? You're gone already, aren't you?" Mama accepts Jessie's reasons in the end, but as an agent of life she cannot let her go without a struggle.

Jessie's whole family is clearly dysfunctional. None of the family members truly like each other. Christmas, with all its associations of family closeness, is marked as a turning point in Jessie's decision. It has allowed her to see all the more clearly how little family connection she really has. In a way, these characters represent an unpleasantly typical, modern community. Each person is alone, for no one is capable of real communication.

The playwright is suggesting that we live in a culture where there is little remaining interaction between parents and children — indeed, between people in general. It is hard for anyone to have a meaningful conversation as the mundane aspects of life start to stifle and weigh people down. Living together, Jessie and

Mama are in a position to be close friends, and yet they have to struggle to rise above the mundane aspects of their lives before they can pursue any meaningful conversation. An important aspect of the play is that, for the first time in their lives, Mama and Jessie do communicate, truthfully.

The wider society Norman has created is a male world where men have more control and say in their lives; Mama and Jessie's store account has to be in Dawson's name, and Jessie has to get him to order her bullets. But for all their control, men are presented as a sorry lot, with none of Jessie or Mama's saving graces. Mama's husband was a supremely indifferent man who rarely spoke to his wife. Jessie's husband, Cecil, disappointed by his wife's abilities, deserted her for another woman. Jessie's brother, Dawson, is as selfish as his mother; he takes things without asking, and although he comes when called, he performs his familial duties with little real thought or consideration. Jessie's son, Ricky, has turned into a drug addict and petty thief, and Jessie firmly believes he is on the way to becoming a more serious criminal. But it is the women's relationship that is the play's focus.

SUSAN C. W. ABBOTSON

Questions for Discussion

1. Is there any point in the play where we are allowed to think that Jessie should not or will not commit suicide? Why does Jessie want to die?
2. At what point in her life does Jessie feel that things have gone wrong for her? Whom does she blame? What is Jessie trying to do this last night of her life?
3. In what ways is the impact of *'night, Mother* reliant on Jessie being portrayed as both ordinary and reasonable?
4. How far can Mama (Thelma) be held to blame for any of Jessie's problems? Is anyone else to blame?
5. How does the setting of the play contribute to its message? Why is the door of the bedroom made into a focal point?
6. In what ways can the action of Jessie's suicide be compared to Agnes burning down a house? In what ways are Jessie and Agnes different? In what ways are Jessie and Mama different?
7. How are men portrayed in the play? Are women portrayed any differently?
8. How far does Mama finally accept Jessie's reasoning?
9. What, in Norman's belief, gives people a reason to live?
10. What does Mama mean when she says "I thought you were mine"?
11. Is it Jessie's right to say "No"? Does Norman expect her audience to accept Jessie's decision?
12. Should we feel happy, sad, or disgusted at Jessie's suicide?

Topics for Writing

1. To what extent is the play a comment on how our society treats epileptics, or should we see this condition as representative of a more general spiritual malaise?
2. Is suicide ever the answer? Discuss the pros and cons of Jessie's decision to die. Use as evidence what the play teaches us about Jessie's life. Decide whether or not you support or condemn her decision, and give firm reasons for what *you* decide.
3. Imagine that this play never took place and Jessie has decided, instead, to write her mother a detailed suicide note. Either write that note or write a

monologue during which we witness Mama reading and reacting to this note.

4. **CONNECTIONS** *'night, Mother* and Samuel Beckett's *Krapp's Last Tape* both deal with death and the importance of connections between people. In what ways are the characters, lives, and decisions of Jessie and Krapp similar or different?

5. **CONNECTIONS** Both *'night, Mother* and Arthur Miller's *Death of a Salesman* can be seen as offering assessments of people's lives. Compare the life of either Jessie or Mama to that of either Willy Loman or Linda Loman. Which do you feel has led the more satisfying life and why? Try and identify the social beliefs and forces against which each must strive.

Suggested Readings

Beard, Sherilyn. "An Interview with Marsha Norman." In *Southern California Anthology*. Los Angeles: U of South California P, 1985.

Demastes, William W. "Jessie and Thelma Revisited: Marsha Norman's Conceptual Challenge in *'night, Mother*." *Modern Drama* 36 (1993): 109–19.

Forte, Jeanie. "Realism, Narrative, and the Feminist Playwright." *Modern Drama* 32 (1989): 115–27.

Greiff, Louis K. "Fathers, Daughters, and Spiritual Sisters: Marsha Norman's *'night, Mother* and Tennessee Williams's *The Glass Menagerie*." *Text and Performance Quarterly* 9 (1989): 224–28.

Kintz, Linda. *The Subject's Tragedy: Political Poetics, Feminist Theory, and Drama*. Ann Arbor: U of Michigan P, 1992.

Nightingale, Benedict. "Or Not to Be." *Canadian Forum* (April 1985): 38.

Pearlman, Mickey, ed. *Mother Puzzles: Daughters and Mothers in Contemporary American Literature*. Westport, CT: Greenwood, 1989.

Schleuter, June, ed. *Modern American Drama: The Female Canon*. Rutherford, NJ: Farleigh Dickinson UP, 1990.

Spencer, Jenny S. "Norman's *'night, Mother*: Psycho-Drama of Female Identity." *Modern Drama* 30 (1987): 364–75.

Stone, Elizabeth. "Playwright Marsha Norman: An Optimist Writes about Suicide, Confinement, and Despair." *Ms.* 12 Jul. 1983, 56–59.

CHRISTOPHER DURANG

For Whom the Southern Belle Tolls (p. 1937)

Christopher Durang is well known for his tendency to burlesque and parody other writers. The title *For Whom the Southern Belle Tolls* recalls the John Donne phrase "for whom the bell tolls," which Ernest Hemingway used as the title of his Spanish Civil War novel. With its evident delight in playing against gender expectations, *For Whom the Southern Belle Tolls* faintly mocks the macho pretensions of Hemingway's characters, but the real target here is Tennessee Williams's *The Glass Menagerie*. *For Whom the Southern Belle Tolls* seems to hold up a fun house mirror to Williams's play, which becomes twisted and distorted to hilarious yet meaningful ends. The fact that Williams's work withstands such treatment is testament to both the original play's power and Durang's own sneaking respect.

It is possible to enjoy *For Whom the Southern Belle Tolls* without knowing *The Glass Menagerie*; its central theme regarding parent-child relationships is universal. Far more can be gained, however, by a person who has close knowledge of *The Glass Menagerie*. Students need to compare more than the characters and plot lines; they should analyze the serious concerns of each playwright and measure how far they might coincide rather than work at odds. A parodist is often seriously engaged in the same subjects as the writer parodied. The bite of the humor is not always directed at the artist but sometimes at the public, who have refused to learn from the original work. Just like Williams, Durang is concerned about people's fears of engagement with a world full of dangers, about the strangulating nature of family ties, and about the pain of sexual disorientation and social intolerance. Unlike Williams, Durang has finally lost patience with Laura and has come to find her dependency and sensitivity intensely annoying. It is his version of this character who bears the brunt of his mockery.

With an inventive imagination, Durang embraces his subjects with great audacity, using what Howard Stein refers to as his "twin gifts — originality and an anarchic spirit." Stein comments that "laughter for Durang not only affords relief but a temporary refuge which might well be the only remaining source of salvation." Such an agenda allies him to the absurdist tradition of Edward Albee. Durang uses laughter as a response to the grave and inherently tragic in order to contain and control such forces. Common targets for Durang are the myths of the happy American family and the joys of parenting. *For Whom the Southern Belle Tolls* depicts the dysfunctional Wingvalley family, a group of people who appear to genuinely hate each other. The mother is only counting the days when she will finally be rid of her ridiculous child and be able to live a relatively normal life.

Durang enjoys playing with gender expectation and sex-role reversal. Williams's Laura becomes the terribly fey Lawrence, and the "gentleman caller" is no longer Jim but Gin, or Ginny, a "feminine caller" who is anything but feminine. Further irony is derived from having a girl, who is rather butch, teach Lawrence, who is a bit of a wimp, to swagger and shout like a man. His scrambling of genders within the play is an effective way of showing his audience just how restricted our gender expectations truly are. For all our supposed liberalism, homosexuality still maintains the power to shock. Thus Tom picks up sailors down at the X-rated movie theater and brings home a lesbian to meet his brother. Tom's suggested homosexuality is not a major issue, but it is based on the knowledge that the original Tom was autobiographical and that Williams was homosexual. It is a sign that attitudes have become more open in the fact that Durang can present Tom in this way — which is something censorship would not have allowed Williams to do in the 1940s.

Durang also enjoys showing his audience the absurdity of the theater itself in its inescapable artifice — an artifice built, in part, on such ambiguous things as words. Through Ginny's poor hearing, effective communication through words alone becomes an impossibility; "popular" becomes "popsicle," "machinery" becomes "scenery," "souvenir" becomes "queer," and everything said becomes nonsense. In this and other ways, such as the confusion over who wears glasses owing to the indeterminate personal pronoun, Durang seems to be making a comment on the slippery nature of language itself and how much we depend on something so easily disrupted. At another time, Durang plays with the stage conventions of soliloquy by having Amanda actually hear Tom's speech and ask him who he is talking to out on the porch. Durang also twists certain theatrical

(text pp. 1937–1948)

motifs from *The Glass Menagerie* in order to draw attention to the entirely subjective manner by which such operate. Why does it matter whether a shy, incapacitated child collects glass animals or glass swizzle sticks? What is it about the latter that makes us instantly laugh when we have accepted so readily the intrinsic seriousness of the former? In this way we are made aware of the intrinsic fallibility of all such subjective symbols.

Durang is very aware that the success of his plays is often dependent on how they are played. Audiences become quickly bored with one-dimensional characters, and Durang is wary of actors who tend to overact in his plays, in a misguided attempt to match his exaggerated style. He prefers them, instead, to uncover the truthful psychological underpinnings of his characters, so that they can play them beyond a single dimension. It is through this that the comedy gains its more serious undercurrents.

Durang's Amanda, who is outwardly impatient and rude toward her maladjusted offspring, partly reflects a contemporary dismissal of Williams's overly sensitive creatures. Amanda Wingvalley is more forthright and less histrionic than Amanda Wingfield. She faces the unpleasantness of her life directly and makes no bones about stating her disgust with her children. She wishes Lawrence to marry so she can be free of him for good, not so that he will be able to provide for her in the future. Unlike her predecessor, Amanda Wingvalley is no persuader and manipulator but responds directly to what she sees as the torments of her life. When Lawrence defies her, she responds with unveiled threats rather than the use of any subtle wiles. She neither denies nor supports her children's peculiarities. She strives for sympathy not from her children, as does Amanda Wingfield, but from the audience. Durang would like us to feel some sympathy for this woman, who is unable to pursue other possibilities in life owing to the encumbrance of her impossible son, Lawrence.

Although not without the charm and manners of the old southern aristocracy that define Amanda Wingfield, this Amanda is decidedly modern in outlook and able to drop the Southern pose whenever necessary. She drinks gin and tonic, not mint juleps or lemonade. She swears, she mocks, and even plays a trick on her guest to get rid of her, by pretending she has a similar hearing problem. Her one reminiscence of the past seems closer to an advertisement for self-esteem than any heartfelt nostalgia; she is a woman who is looking toward the future, however blank that may be. The psychological truths she voices make her situation, in reality, a dark one, which can become comic only through the correct tone and timing of the actress playing her part.

Rather than the frail, otherworldly Laura that haunts Williams's imagination, Lawrence is a sulky, sallow youth whose affectations become ridiculous. Durang does not wish him to be too effeminate, despite Amanda's jibes, but "'soft' in soul and aura." It is a softness that is ultimately as reductive as it is destructive. As a male, Lawrence's oversensitivity can be seen as less socially defensible. Also, because he is more forthright than his predecessor, openly admitting his problems, his claims to shyness and sensibility seem far less convincing. There are repeated suggestions that all of his ailments are fake, which make him even less sympathetic.

Durang describes Lawrence as "a hypochondriac, but he does believe in his ailments. He treasures his ailments." He uses his ailments to escape from a world he finds terrifying, but Durang makes it hard to feel sympathy by making him more cowardly than pathetic. Lawrence has inner strength, as seen in some of his ripostes to his mother, but he chooses not to fight for a place in the outer world. Unlike her counterpart, Jim, Ginny purposefully breaks the glass piece handed to her and shows no remorse or sympathy. It seems it is impossible for anyone to have lasting patience with Lawrence, which is how Durang wishes the audience to react.

Tom has become, at first glance, a rather crude figure. Decisive and physical in a way that would appall Williams's Tom, this Tom breaks down doors and openly denounces, rather than attempt to protect, his sibling. "You know the stupid fuck won't open the door, so why don't you let him alone about it? [To GINNY] My kid brother has a thing about answering doors. He thinks people will notice his limp and his asthma and his eczema." Desperate to leave a home anyone in their right mind would want to leave, Tom is in the process of applying to everything from the merchant marines to the Ballet Trockadero. But despite his crudity and confused sexuality, Tom has an inner humanity that allows him to feel genuine emotions. His angry argument with his mother seems honestly motivated. Also, in his lengthy monologue, Durang allows Tom to catch the lyricism of Williams's Tom in a close parody of the character's pursuing guilt, before he deflates the moment with a self-serving reference to how he can use this experience to write a play. Nevertheless, the audience is able to catch, for a brief moment behind the jokes, a sense of the true pathos, sensitivity, and sadness of lives like these.

Ginny has, like Jim, been taking a public speaking course that has led her to be, rather than an efficient speaker, simply loud. Coupled with the increasingly evident fact that she is almost deaf, we find that Ginny is ironically unable to communicate, as she cannot hear what is said to her and responds tangentially to what she falsely believes she has heard. Ginny no longer calls the siblings "blue roses" and "Shakespeare" for any significant reason other than her bad hearing. It is significant that Ginny never acknowledges her own deafness; she either makes her own twisted sense of what has been said or believes that the person has not spoken clearly enough. When people react in confusion to what she has said she never notices; she just carries on in her own world in which everything is fine. This is the key to her character, because Ginny, just like Jim, is essentially a happy, contented soul, in direct contrast to the Wingvalleys, even if this is achieved partly through ignorance. Although momentarily angry at Lawrence and Amanda, she soon regains her composure. She exits by saying that she had a good time, and meaning every word.

Durang has none of Williams's real southern nostalgia — to him, the South means eating pigs feet and endless, meaningless conversation. It is hard to sympathize with any member of this family, for they are all essentially selfish, mean-spirited individuals with little saving grace other than that we have been able to laugh at them and their plight. The point is that this is no longer the America of Tennessee Williams — an America still able to recall a past gentility, an America in which homosexuality could not be openly named, an America in which people still had dreams. This is a modern America where everyone is out for himself, where sexuality is openly but often exploitatively discussed, where people are filled with the rage and despair that Amanda reads about in the paper. The star they finally wish on is, ironically, no ethereal shooting star but the *Evening Star*, a tacky, sensationalist "rag" that just about sums up the world they have to live in. The play closes with a touch of pathos as we realize the emptiness of such people's lives, when all they have left to hope for is "some more swizzle sticks."

The appeal of a play like *For Whom the Southern Belle Tolls* may partly be the joy many of us derive from seeing established icons brought down to earth and grandiose reputations deflated. It also, however, asks us to re-examine the original play and what it said, which can prevent it from being taken for granted. *For Whom the Southern Belle Tolls* does not seek to destroy *The Glass Menagerie* but to compliment it. It works best at those moments when it produces a blurring between the satire and its source. Such moments allow us to recognize the similarities between the concerns of the two writers, despite the overall, differing tone of their work. For fleeting moments, Durang does catch the lyricism of Williams's play, and it is such moments that allow us to consider that this may be more than an extended joke at Williams's expense. Although Durang may seem to dismember and ridicule *The Glass Menagerie*, he is also acknowledging that it contains something worth remembering.

SUSAN C. W. ABBOTSON

Questions for Discussion

1. Considering not only the characters but also the plot, the themes, the symbols, and the overall message, in what ways does *For Whom the Southern Belle Tolls* compare and contrast with *The Glass Menagerie*?
2. How would you describe each of the characters in this play? What are their individual strengths and limitations? Which character seems most content, most self-aware, most sympathetic, least sympathetic? Why?
3. How would you describe the family relationships in the play?
4. Why does Amanda Wingvalley want Lawrence to marry or go to work? Are her intentions different from those of Amanda Wingfield?
5. Does Ginny know that she is hard of hearing? Why is this important?
6. Is there anything really wrong with Lawrence? How does the answer to this affect how we view him?
7. What tricks does Durang play with gender and sexuality in the play? Why does he do this?
8. How does Durang use language in the play? What games does he play, and what may be the point of such tricks?
9. How does Durang draw attention to the artifice of theater in his play and why?
10. What aspects of the play seem to be typical of absurdist drama?
11. What does Durang seem to believe is wrong with modern American society? How does he use his parody to show this?
12. In what ways is Durang's America different from that of Williams? What might account for this?

Topics for Writing

1. Nancy Franklin suggests that in *For Whom the Southern Belle Tolls* "Durang turns outsiderness inside out, releasing his characters from their raw, tender feelings by sending them over the top, to a place where they, and we, feel no pain." How far do you agree or disagree with this statement?
2. Just as Tom Stoppard wrote altered versions of *Hamlet*, Christopher Durang's *For Whom the Southern Belle Tolls* is clearly informed by Tennessee Williams's *The Glass Menagerie*. In what ways does Durang support or betray Williams's essential concerns?
3. Consider the ways in which *For Whom the Southern Belle Tolls* parodies *The Glass Menagerie*. Write a short parody based on an episode taken from any

one of the other plays in this anthology. In writing a parody you will need to consider both the style and concerns of the original and what kind of statement you wish your version to convey.

4. **CONNECTIONS** Consider Christopher Durang's *For Whom the Southern Belle Tolls* and Edward Albee's *The Sandbox* as absurdist works. What appears to be the central social issue each play addresses? Which is the more successful in conveying its playwright's deeper concerns? Which of these plays, do you believe, works more effectively as an absurdist drama? Why?

5. **CONNECTIONS** Christopher Durang's *For Whom the Southern Belle Tolls* and Woody Allen's two monologues both attempt to deal with serious issues within a comic framework. What makes such a technique successful or unsuccessful? What does each playwright believe to be wrong within American society, and how do these works convey this?

Suggested Readings

Brantley, Ben. "The First of a Menagerie of Amandas." *New York Times*, 4 Jun. 1994, 11, 14.

———. "Plays That Cast an Irreverent Eye over Two Revered Playwrights." *New York Times* 14 Nov. 1994, C11–12.

Canby, Vincent. "For Limping Parody, Durang to the Rescue." *New York Times*, 4 Dec. 1994, sec. 2, pp. 5, 8.

Denby, David. "Chris Durang — Funny Baby." *Vogue*, February 1984, 358, 423.

Dieckman, Suzanne. "Metatheatre as Antitheatre: Durang's *Actor's Nightmare.*" *American Drama* 1.2 (1992): 26–41.

Durang, Christopher. "Introduction." In *Christopher Durang Explains It All for You*, ix–xx. New York: Grove, 1983.

Franklin, Nancy. "Sturm Und Durang." *New Yorker*, 28 Nov. 1994, 153–55.

DAVID HENRY HWANG

As the Crow Flies (p. 1950)

Hwang is best known for his 1988 play *M. Butterfly*, but the short play *As the Crow Flies*, written two years earlier, succinctly touches on many of the writer's key concerns regarding ethnicity, gender, and theatrical form. Students should be encouraged to see the humor in this short play, which may best be realized by having them act it out in class. Hwang uses humor, such as Mrs. Chan's smart logic over the goldfish, or her ridiculously forgetful husband, to allow his audience some degree of comfort so that they will be more receptive to his more serious underlying messages. He does not aim to unsettle his audience in the way that absurdists such as Edward Albee try to do.

As the Crow Flies partly explores the relationship that David Henry Hwang suggests may have existed between his grandmother and her servant. Attention is centered on the female relationship and bond between Mrs. Chan and her cleaner, Hannah, to show the strategies by which each has survived a harsh life. Through its symbolism, it also examines a belief of Hwang's that "there's more to the world than we perceive with our five senses." Like his early mentor, Sam Shepard, Hwang likes to explore the mythical states that underlie reality. Sandra becomes an "angel of death" who tries to prepare the feisty Mrs. Chan — who has surrounded herself with elaborate rituals to keep death at bay — for the next world.

Hwang is very interested in how people of different cultures and genders perceive and react to one another. He sees racism as something that can deeply affect people's personalities. A question he enjoys asking is "What does it mean to grow up in America with a color that's not Caucasian?" As we can see by Mrs. Chan and Hannah, it means, amongst other things, isolation, a splintering of the personality, and unrewarding hard work. Like August Wilson, Hwang feels it is important to ascertain and take pride in one's individual ethnic identity rather than attempt to assimilate. With a secure ethnic identity, it is easier for each individual to contribute positively to the larger society, and a multicultural society is stronger than a monocultural one. The best American society would be one where people's differences are as apparent and welcomed as the common humanity that ultimately holds them together. Mrs. Chan and Hannah are products of two very different cultures, and each, we discover, has drawn strength from her own self-affirming ethnicity/identity. Through the telling of their individual histories, however, they, and the audience, come to recognize the intrinsic similarities between their lives.

Hwang's interest in Japanese literature and Asian theatrical forms has a clear bearing on As the Crow Flies. Through its form, sense of cultural connection, and philosophy, As the Crow Flies shows a relation to Nō plays such as Kantan. Both are symbolic, not realistic, dramas wherein the audience must discover their own meaning in the symbols they are shown. As in Kantan, Hwang's characters move easily between dialogue and direct monologue; their actions are carefully choreographed; and the playwright's aim is to entertain as well as to provide insight. As in Kantan, the characters' beliefs, superstitions, and attitudes are governed by their cultural backgrounds. The Buddhist philosophy underpinning Kantan — that death is a welcome release and relief from earthly struggles — reappears in As the Crow Flies.

Mrs. Chan, despite her advancing years, is a forceful, self-confident lady. Her stoicism, as much as her fighting spirit and indomitable will, has enabled her to cope with a series of dislocations from China to the Philippines to America. Meanwhile, her cleaner separates her public and private identities to the extent that she appears as two totally separate characters: Hannah, an elderly, industrious, submissive servant, and Sandra, a younger, more forceful, pleasure-seeker. Hwang's plays often center on diametrically opposed characters between whom, as David Savran points out, "the conflict builds to a climactic confrontation at which point he who appeared most vulnerable becomes, through an ironic reversal usually brought about by the revelation of withheld information, the victor." In As the Crow Flies we see this in the way Hannah, the lowly cleaner, quite literally takes the self-confident Mrs. Chan's place by the end of the play and sits in her chair. But the image is an ambiguous one; Mrs. Chan has left, presumably to die, but is she being displaced or replaced by Hannah? Has this been an act of aggression or solidarity? Hwang, perhaps, wishes us to see it as both.

Hwang's writing shows a distinct preference for collision over integration, which is exhibited most forcefully in his strong desire to uncover the relationships between things rather than fuse them together. One such conflict is that which exists between the differing values of the East and the West. Mrs. Chan is a representative of the East and Hannah/Sandra of the West. Though by the close of the play we are made to see how each has been chasing the same "crow," each has necessarily pursued it in a different way: Hannah by ironically remaining on the spot, and Mrs. Chan by being constantly on the move. The difference is a result of the opportunities their respective cultures have offered them.

At the start of the play Mrs. Chan is perceived to be the more successful of these two women. She dominates their early conversation, with Hannah being little more than a "yes man." Mrs. Chan is placed center stage on her "throne," which lies midway between doors that lead to either the inner refuge of her house or the uncertainty of the outside world. Mrs. Chan lives in a fairly opulent home with her devoted, if not entirely dependent, husband. Her cleaner, Hannah, by contrast, lives in a small apartment with a series of unfaithful husbands who treat her as a meal ticket. Hannah's apparent age is partly due to a life of hard work in which she has garnered no apparent improvement in her living conditions. When she separates herself from this work she becomes Sandra, who is apparently twenty years younger.

Mrs. Chan easily accepts and appears to understand Hannah's explanation of her dual identity, drawing on her own experiences to show how she has witnessed such splits in her own culture. It is ambiguous, however, as to whether she relates the story of her uncles, who are split into anywhere from six to eight different identities, in an effort at "one-upmanship" or to make Hannah feel at ease. Still, she is fully conversant with the ways in which the pressures of varied social roles can force a character to splinter into entirely separate personalities. Mrs. Chan's strength partly derives from her refusal to see anything as impossible, which, in turn, allows her to keep an open mind, giving her the flexibility to cope with anything that happens. Her remaining strength, however, comes from her ability, also, to be inflexible and insist on a structured life determined by certain rules.

Mrs. Chan uses rules and rituals to order her life and create a sense of security. Rules create something one can rely on in a changing world — a point against which one can orient oneself — but one must have a strong personality to enforce and insist on such rules. Mrs. Chan uses a number of traditional Chinese rituals to create an orderly world where she believes she can both outwit and control "ghosts." She offers Hannah strength and protection by seeking to control her alter ego, Sandra, by such rules. She defines Sandra as an outside figure and Hannah as an inside figure, thus attempting to restrict Sandra's access to her house.

Maxine Hong Kingston's *The Woman Warrior* suggests how the Chinese embrace a different understanding of ghosts than is common in the West. To call someone a ghost is often synonymous with acknowledging them as unfamiliar or unknown. Although it is instinctual to fear the unknown, to fear a ghost will give it power over you. Ghosts cannot be avoided, but sometimes they can be fought in the same way one fights ignorance — by learning something about what it is you are fighting. At first Sandra seems a ghost to Mrs. Chan, but as the two women begin to connect, she becomes more human in aspect and less threatening. Through her ministrations she, in fact, allows Mrs. Chan to peacefully accept that larger unknown — death.

Mrs. Chan's husband, P.K., is a man who has lost the capacity to remember anything and has become entirely dependent on his wife to keep him vicariously grounded in some kind of reality. In a way, by holding on to his golf clubs and living in his own little dream world where he can still drive the Eldorado and play golf, P.K. survives longer than his wife. But he is living in the past, and such a life can have little vitality. Mrs. Chan refuses to live in the past, and such a choice makes her more vital but also more vulnerable to the future. How P.K. will cope with his wife leaving at the close is left open, but if his evident dependency is anything to go by, he will not last long without her.

In the ten years that Mrs. Chan has lived in America Hannah has been her cleaner, and yet it is not until the entry of Sandra that Mrs. Chan is finally brought to realize just how much she has in common with her servant. Sandra comes into her home disturbing her rules, and although she refuses to offer her any hospitality, Sandra forces Mrs. Chan to recognize the type of woman Hannah is and just how much she and Mrs. Chan have in common. Both have lived lives full of exploitation, hard work, and unfair calamity, and, most important, both have survived intact. Mrs. Chan has done this by refusing to dwell on the past and forever fighting for a better future. Refusing to see any dwelling she has lived in as a home, she has been able to withstand being evicted. She sees herself as a spirit who was "born traveling" and has never been at rest. Her mother, in giving her portable wealth in the form of jewelry, has taught her to only keep that which can easily go along with you when you move on. But there comes a time when there is nowhere left to run, and Mrs. Chan is gradually brought to face this fact. Mrs. Chan has remained aware of the world around her in order to be able to struggle with death when it comes — not because she fears it so much as her great spirit cannot allow her life to end. She uses her family responsibilities and cultural rituals to protect her and to hold her to life, but in the end they will not be enough. One needs more than sheer willpower to avoid death.

Hannah, as opposed to Mrs. Chan, has partly survived owing to her fixity, her strong sense of home being the only permanent aspect of her life. Her husbands have come and gone, and she has worked like a mule all her life for people who are better off than she. It is little wonder that she has less spirit than Mrs. Chan, but she is a survivor nonetheless. Her survival is also due to her ability to separate her identity in order to find some freedom and release through her alter ego, Sandra. Mrs. Chan resists when Sandra calls her house a home, because she has always avoided the fixity of calling her residence a home. She sees in that one word the end of her running, which will make her vulnerable to death. Stuck in her chair, however, it is evident that for all her talk, Mrs. Chan is tired of running and has run out of strength.

The crow at which she has been staring out of the window is a complicated and central symbol in the play. "As the crow flies" is a common adage to describe the shortest distance between two fixed points — but to which fixed points is Hwang referring? These women come from either side of the globe, but finally discover how close they are, despite their differences. This would suggest that the best road toward understanding is one that strips away all unnecessary clutter and goes directly to the human heart. Or Hwang may be referring to the points of birth and death we all must experience, with life being a brief interlude between. The actual existence of two points, rather than a single one, implies the necessity in all our lives to recognize difference while still allowing communication to take place.

Sandra describes how two children (most likely Mrs. Chan and Hannah) have been chasing the crow all of their lives. The darkening terrain they enter suggests the old age toward which we all must go. Both have kept up the chase all of their lives, despite hardships and various setbacks, through self-determination and faith. Their lives have passed in constant work. It should, therefore, be a relief to come to the end of the crow's flight and finally have time to "pause" and feel "pleasure."

The crow itself appears emblematic of life, hope, and even death. It embraces all metaphysical aspects. It also becomes the scent of home and the rest and safety such a place offers. As Mrs. Chan listens to Sandra she finally gains the strength to rise from her chair and leave the room — she goes outside, into the unknown. The image of her dress rising evokes the idea of ascendancy and her spirit rising to heaven, with her white slip beneath suggesting an angelic goodness, as well as connecting her to Hannah, who wears an identical slip. The words of Mrs. Chan and Sandra/Hannah in this closing section seem to flow into one another as the bond between them is finally recognized and forged, further strengthened by the fact that Hannah takes over the vacant chair. Hwang may be suggesting that Mrs. Chan can move on to her final destination knowing that someone is there to continue caring for those who still live.

Susan C. W. Abbotson

Questions for Discussion

1. Do you see any aspects of Mrs. Chan's character that seem particularly Chinese and others that seem particularly American?
2. How would you describe the relationship between Mrs. Chan and her husband, P.K.? What are the differences between the ways that Mrs. Chan and P.K. appear to live their lives?
3. How would you describe the relationship between Mrs. Chan and Hannah? Does this relationship change at all during the play? Why?
4. What do we know of the past lives of Mrs. Chan and Hannah? In what ways have these past lives been different or the same?
5. What are the differences between Hannah and Sandra? Why does Hannah appear to be so much older than her alter ego? Are there any similarities? What does Sandra appear to be representing in the play?
6. How does Mrs. Chan see herself, and what is her attitude toward death? Does this attitude change in the course of the play?
7. What does Mrs. Chan think ghosts do? In what ways are the "ghosts" Mrs. Chan talks about the same or different from what you have been taught to believe about ghosts? Can you explain this?
8. Why does Mrs. Chan stay sitting in her chair throughout most of the play, and what is the significance of her finally standing? Why does Hannah sit in Mrs. Chan's chair, and what might this signify?
9. Where do you think Mrs. Chan goes to at the close of the play? What evidence can you give to support your belief?
10. What will happen to P.K. without his wife?
11. What is the significance of the play's title?
12. What might the figure of the crow represent in the play?

Topics for Writing

1. Outline what you see as the differences and similarities between the characters of Mrs. Chan and Hannah/Sandra. Support your outline with details from the play. Consider, also, to what extent each woman's ethnicity might be a contributing factor in the aspects of character that you reveal.
2. Discuss the symbolic aspects of *As the Crow Flies*. By considering a variety of possible readings, explain which you believe to be the most fitting.

3. Write a monologue in the character of P.K. that covers the events of this play as if he had witnessed everything that took place. In doing this, bear in mind how the play presents his character and consider how such a character might seek to describe and explain such events.

4. **CONNECTIONS** What do you see as the possible points of comparison between David Henry Hwang's *As the Crow Flies* and *Kantan*? Both plays come out of Asian traditions although they were written many years apart. In what ways does that tradition appear to have changed or stayed the same over the years? Use details from both plays to illustrate your answer.

5. **CONNECTIONS** Both *As the Crow Flies* and *The Janitor* deal with issues concerning the pressures of being a minority in American society. What does each play appear to offer as a solution to these pressures? How do David Henry Hwang and August Wilson believe minority groups should think and behave?

6. **CONNECTIONS** In both David Henry Hwang's *As the Crow Flies* and Edward Albee's *The Sandbox* we are shown grandmothers who face an "angel of death" figure. Compare and contrast these figures of death and the ways in which the grandmothers react to them. Also, consider in what ways the lives of the two grandmothers have been the same or different and how this might be affecting their response to death.

Suggested Readings

Christon, Lawrence. "Playwright Balances Life's Improbabilities." *Los Angeles Times,* 12 Feb. 1986, sec. 6, pp. 1, 4.

DiGaetani, John. *A Search for a Postmodern Theater: Interviews with Contemporary Playwrights.* New York: Greenwood, 1991.

Gerard, Jeremy. "David Hwang Riding on the Hyphen." *New York Times Magazine,* 13 Mar. 1988, 44–45, 88–89.

Hwang, David Henry. "Evolving a Multicultural Tradition." *MELUS* 16.3 (1989–90): 16–19.

Kingston, Maxine Hong. *The Woman Warrior.* New York: Knopf, 1976.

Maufort, Marc, ed. *Staging Difference: Cultural Pluralism in American Theatre and Drama.* New York: Lang, 1995.

Savran, David, ed. *In Their Own Words: Contemporary American Playwrights.* New York: Theatre Communications Group, 1988.

Skloot, Robert. "Breaking the Butterfly: The Politics of David Henry Hwang." *Modern Drama* 33 (1990): 59–66.

Street, Douglas. *David Henry Hwang.* Boise: Boise State UP, 1989.

APPENDIX OF AUDIOVISUAL RESOURCES

The films and videos marked with an asterisk (*) are available for rental from member institutions of the Consortium of College and University Media Centers. For further information, consult the *Educational Film & Video Locater*, published by R. R. Bowker.

Fiction

MARGARET ATWOOD

Atwood and Family
30 min., color, 1989.
Beta, VHS, 3/4" U-matic cassette, 16-mm film.
Atwood talks about her life and work.
Distributed by the National Film Board of Canada.

TONI CADE BAMBARA

Interview with Toni Cade Bambara and Kay Bonetti [recording]
1 cassette (90 min.).
The author discusses her writing style and political concerns. Part of the Women's Studies Series.
Distributed by American Audio Prose Library.

RAYMOND CARVER

Readings and Interview [recording]
2 cassettes (120 min.).
Distributed by American Audio Prose Library.

JOHN CHEEVER

The Swimmer
94 min., color, 1968.
Starring Burt Lancaster, Janet Landgard.
Directed by Frank Perry.

ANTON CHEKHOV

Anton Chekhov: A Writer's Life
37 min., color and b/w, 1974.
Beta, VHS, 3/4" U-matic cassette, 16-mm film.
A biographical portrait of the writer.
Distributed by Films for the Humanities and Sciences.

The Lady with the Pet Dog
86 min., b/w, 1960.
Beta, VHS.
In Russian, with English subtitles.
Starring Iya Savvina, Alexei Batalov, Alla Chostakova.
Directed by Joseph Heifitz.
Distributed by Facets Multimedia, Inc.

KATE CHOPIN

Kate Chopin's "The Story of an Hour"
24 min., color, 1982.
1/2" open reel (EIAJ), 16-mm film.
A dramatization of the story, with an examination of Chopin's life.
Distributed by Ishtar.

STEPHEN CRANE

The Open Boat
29 min., b/w, 1965.
Distributed by Michigan Media.

"The Red Badge of Courage" and Other Stories [recording]

6 cassettes (6 hours, 39 min.), 1976.
Includes title story, "The Mystery of Heroism," "The Open Boat," and "The Bride Comes to Yellow Sky."
Distributed by Listening Library.

LOUISE ERDRICH

Interview [recording]

1 cassette (50 min.).
Erdrich and her husband, Michael Dorris, discuss the centrality of a Native American identity to the author's work.
Distributed by American Audio Prose Library.

WILLIAM FAULKNER

*Barn Burning

41 min., color, 1980.
Beta, VHS, 16-mm film.
With Tommy Lee Jones. Same program available in "The American Short Story Series II" on manual p. 397.
See local retailer.

The Long Hot Summer

118 min., color, 1958.
Beta, VHS.
A film adaptation of "Barn Burning." Directed by Martin Ritt. With Paul Newman, Orson Welles, Joanne Woodward, Lee Remick, Anthony Franciosa, Angela Lansbury, and Richard Anderson.
See local retailer.

The Long Hot Summer

172 min., color, 1986.
Beta, VHS.
A made-for-TV version of "Barn Burning." Directed by Stuart Cooper. With Don Johnson, Cybill Shepherd, Judith Ivey, Jason Robards, and Ava Gardner.
See local retailer.

*A Rose for Emily

27 min., color, 1983.
Beta, VHS, 3/4" U-matic cassette, 16-mm film.
Distributed by Pyramid Film and Video.

William Faulkner: A Life on Paper

120 min., color, 1980.
Beta, VHS, 3/4" U-matic cassette.
A documentary biography. With Lauren Bacall, Howard Hawks, Anita Loos, George Plimpton, Tennessee Williams, and Jill Faulkner Summers (the author's daughter).
Distributed by Films, Inc.

*William Faulkner's Mississippi

49 min., color and b/w, 1965.
Beta, VHS, 3/4" U-matic cassette.
Deals with Faulkner's life and works.
Distributed by Benchmark Films.

GABRIEL GARCÍA MÁRQUEZ

A Very Old Man with Enormous Wings

90 min., color, 1988.
Directed by Fernando Birri. With Birri, Daisy Granados, Asdrubal Melendez, and Luis Alberto Ramirez. Available in Spanish and English.
See local retailer.

*Gabriel García Márquez: Tales Beyond Solitude

59 min., color.
VHS, 3/4" U-matic cassette.
Profiles the Colombian author. Features footage from his life and clips from films on which he has worked.
Distributed by Home Vision Cinema.

CHARLOTTE PERKINS GILMAN

The Yellow Wallpaper
15 min., color, 1978.
Produced by International Institute of Television.
Distributed by Indiana University Instructional Support Services.

NATHANIEL HAWTHORNE

Favorite Stories by Nathaniel Hawthorne, Vol. 1 [recording]
2 cassettes (2 hours, 30 min.).
Read by Walter Zimmerman and John Chatty. Includes "Dr. Heidegger's Experiment" and "The Minister's Black Veil."
Distributed by Jimcin Recordings.

Great Short Stories [recording]
1 cassette (57 min.), 1973.
Distributed by The Mind's Eye.

The Minister's Black Veil [recording]
1 cassette (82 min.).
Read by Walter Zimmerman and John Chatty. Includes "Young Goodman Brown."
Distributed by Jimcin Recordings and Books on Tape.

Nathaniel Hawthorne: Light in the Shadows
23 min., color, 1982.
Beta, VHS, 3/4" U-matic cassette, 16-mm film, special order formats.
A background of the author's life and works, especially *The Scarlet Letter* and *The House of the Seven Gables*.
Distributed by the International Film Bureau.

Young Goodman Brown
30 min., color, 1972.
Beta, VHS, 3/4" U-matic cassette, 16-mm film.
Distributed by Pyramid Film and Video.

ERNEST HEMINGWAY

Ernest Hemingway: A Life Story
Part 1, 11 cassettes, Part 2, 10 cassettes (1 hr., 30 mins. per cassette).
Read by Christopher Hunt. Draws from Hemingway's diaries, letters, and unpublished writings as well as personal testimony from the people who played a part in the author's life.
Distributed by Blackstone Audio Books.

Ernest Hemingway: Grace Under Pressure
55 min., color, 1978.
Beta, VHS, 3/4" U-matic cassette.
A biography of the author using photographs, newsreels, and film clips.
Distributed by Films for the Humanities and Sciences.

Hemingway
54 min., b/w, 1962.
Beta, VHS, 3/4" U-matic cassette, 16-mm film.
A biography using rare stills and motion picture footage. Narrated by Chet Huntley.
Distributed by CRM Films.

Hemingway: Up in Michigan, the Early Years
28 min., color, 1986.
Beta, VHS, 3/4" U-matic cassette.
A literary biography of the writer.
Distributed by Centre Communications.

SHIRLEY JACKSON

The Lottery
18 min., color, 1969.
Distributed by Encyclopaedia Britannica.

SARAH ORNE JEWETT

A White Heron
26 min., color, 1978.
Distributed by Learning Corp. of America.

CHARLES JOHNSON

In Black and White: Charles Johnson
27 min., color, 1992.
VHS.
Johnson describes his literary objective: to explore classic metaphysical questions from East and West against the backdrop of American life and history.
Distributed by California Newsreel.

See also **"In Black and White: Conversations with African American Writers"** on manual p. 398.

JAMES JOYCE

"The Dead" & Other Stories from "Dubliners" [recording]
2 cassettes (2 hrs., 15 min.).
Distributed by Audio partners.

James Joyce
80 min., color, 1989.
Beta, VHS, 3/4" U-matic cassette, 8-mm film.
A biography of James Joyce. Discusses influence of Harriet Weaver and Sylvia Beach.
Distributed by Films for the Humanities and Sciences.

James Joyce's Women
91 min., color, 1983.
Beta, VHS.
Actors portray Joyce's wife plus Molly Bloom and two other of his female characters. Adapted and produced by Fionnula Flanagan. With Flanagan, Timothy E. O'Grady, Chris O'Neill.
See local retailer.

The Dead
82 min., color, 1988.
Beta, VHS.
John Huston's adaptation of the short story. With Anjelica Huston, Donal McCann, Helena Carroll, Cathleen Delaney.
See local retailer.

FRANZ KAFKA

The Trials of Franz Kafka
15 min., b/w, 198?.
Beta, VHS, 3/4" U-matic cassette.
Kafka's life and times, told in his own words. Narrated by Kurt Vonnegut.
Distributed by Films for the Humanities and Sciences.

D. H. LAWRENCE

The Rocking-Horse Winner
30 min., color, 1977.
Starring Kenneth More. Adapted by Julian Bond. Directed by Peter Modak.
Distributed by Learning Corp. of America.

The Rocking-Horse Winner
91 min., b/w, 1949.
Starring John Mills, Valerie Hobson. Directed by Anthony Pelessier.
Distributed by Budget Films, Films for the Humanities and Sciences, and Films, Inc.

*D. H. Lawrence
30 min., color, 1984.
VHS, 16-mm film.
A biographical portrait of the writer. Includes his views on war and censorship. Part of the "Famous Authors" series.
Distributed by Britannica Films.

*D. H. Lawrence as Son and Lover
52 min., color, 1985.
Beta, VHS, 3/4" U-matic cassette.
A biography culled from the
writer's letters, essays, and
autobiographical pieces.
Distributed by Films for the
Humanities and Sciences.

The Horse Dealer's Daughter
30 min., color, 198?.
VHS. Close captioned.
Distributed by Monterey Home
Video.

GUY DE MAUPASSANT

The Necklace
23 min., color, 1979.
Available on film.
Distributed by FilmFair Communications.

*"The Necklace"
22 min, color, 1981.
VHS, 16-mm film.
Distributed by Barr Entertainment.

***"The Necklace" by Guy de
Maupassant**
20 min , color, 1980.
Beta, VHS, 3/4" U-matic cassette,
16-mm film.
A contemporary setting of the
classic story.
Distributed by Britannica Films.

Maupassant's Best Known Stories
[recording]
2 cassettes (1 hour, 38 min.).
Includes "The Necklace," "In the
Moonlight," "Piece of String,"
"Babette," "Wedding Night,"
and "Passion."
Distributed by Cassette Works.

HERMAN MELVILLE

*Bartleby
28 min., color, 1969.
Beta, VHS, 3/4" U-matic cassette,
16-mm film.
Distributed by Britannica Films.

*Bartleby: A Discussion
28 min., color, 1969.
Beta, VHS, 3/4" U-matic cassette,
16-mm film.
A commentary by author Charles
Van Doren.
Distributed by Britannica Films.

Bartleby, the Scrivener
60 min., color, 197?.
Beta, VHS, 3/4" U-matic cassette.
Distributed by Maryland Public
Television.

**Herman Melville: Bartleby, the
Scrivener**
59 min., color, 1987.
Beta, VHS, 3/4" U-matic cassette.
Distributed by Films for the
Humanities and Sciences.

*Herman Melville
22 min., color, 1978.
Beta, VHS, 3/4" U-matic cassette,
16-mm film. Ancillary materials
available.
Part of the Authors Series of
biographies.
Distributed by Journal Films, Inc.

***Herman Melville: Consider the
Sea**
28 min., color, 1982.
Beta, VHS, 3/4" U-matic cassette,
16-mm film, special order
formats.
Deals with the author and his
relationship with the sea. Major
works discussed include *Moby-
Dick*, *Billy Budd*, and "Bartleby,
the Scrivener."
Distributed by the International
Film Bureau.

***Herman Melville: Damned in
Paradise**
90 min., color, 1986.
Beta, VHS, 3/4" U-matic cassette.
Documents Melville's personal and
intellectual history.
Distributed by Pyramid Film and
Video.

*Herman Melville: "November in My Soul"
27 min., color, 1977.
Beta, VHS, 3/4" U-matic cassette, 16-mm film.
A portrait of the author's life and writing. Narrated by John Cullum.
Distributed by Phoenix/BFA Films.

BHARATI MUKHERJEE

Bharati Mukherjee: Conquering America
30 min., color, 1994.
VHS.
In this interview with Bill Moyers, Mukherjee discusses America's newest immigrants and the building resentment and tensions between our country's various cultures.
Distributed by Films for the Humanities and Sciences.

JOYCE CAROL OATES

Smooth Talk
92 min., color, 1985.
A film adaptation of "Where Are You Going, Where Have You Been?" starring Laura Dern and Treat Williams. Directed by Joyce Chopra.
Distributed by Vestron Video, Inc.

Joyce Carol Oates [recording]
1 cassette (29 min.), 1989.
The author talks about her writing habits.
Distributed by New Letters on the Air.

TILLIE OLSEN

I Stand Here Ironing [recording]
1 cassette (77 min.).
Includes title story, "Oh Yes," and "Yonnondio."
Distributed by American Audio Prose Library.

EDGAR ALLAN POE

Edgar Allan Poe: Terror of the Soul
1 hour, color, 1995.
Beta, VHS.
A biography revealing Poe's creative genius and personal experiences through dramatic recreations of important scenes from his work and life. Includes dramatizations of Poe classics such as "The Tell-Tale Heart" performed by Treat Williams, John Heard, and Rene Auberjonois.
Distributed by PBS Video.

With Poe at Midnight
60 min., color, 1979.
Beta, VHS, 3/4" U-matic cassette.
Examines the interaction between Poe's life and work.
Distributed by Media Concepts Press.

LEO TOLSTOY

The Death of Ivan Ilych
29 min., color, 1978.
Part of the Begin with Goodbye Series.
Distributed by Mass Media Ministries.

JOHN UPDIKE

John Updike
30 min., b/w, 1966.
16-mm film.
Discusses Updike's beliefs and attitudes. The author reads selections from his works.
Distributed by Indiana University Instructional Support Services.

Selected Stories by John Updike [recording]
2 cassettes (2 hrs., 49 min.), 1985.
Updike reads six unabridged stories: "A & P," "Pigeon Feathers," "The Family Meadow," "The Witnesses,"

"The Alligators," and "Separating."
Distributed by Random Audiobooks.

What Makes Rabbit Run?
29 min., color, 1986.
VHS, 16-mm film.
Updike reads from his works and discusses his life.
Distributed by Barr Entertainment.

*Writers: John Updike
30 min., b/w, 1966.
3/4" U-matic cassette, 16-mm film, special order formats.

An interview with the writer.
Distributed by Indiana University Instructional Support Services.

RICHARD WRIGHT
Almos' a Man
39 min., color, 1977. Available on film or videotape.
A film adaptation of "The Man Who Was Almost a Man." Starring LeVar Burton. Directed by Stan Lathan.
Distributed by Perspective Films.

Fiction: General Resources

*The American Short Story Series I
45 min./program, color, 1978.
Beta, VHS, 3/4" U-matic cassette, 16-mm film. Ancillary materials available.
Includes nine film adaptations of short stories that appeared on PBS: "Parker Adderson, Philosopher," "The Jolly Corner," "The Blue Hotel," "I'm a Fool," "Soldier's Home," "Bernice Bobs Her Hair," "Almos' a Man," "The Displaced Person," and "The Music School."
Distributed by Coronet/MTI Film & Video.

*The American Short Story Series II
50 min./program, color, 1980.
Beta, VHS, 3/4" U-matic cassette, 16-mm film.
Eight programs: "The Golden Honeymoon," "Paul's Case," "The Greatest Man in the World," "Rappaccini's Daughter," "The Jilting of Granny Weatherall," "The Sky is Grey," "The Man that Corrupted Hadleyburg," and "Barn Burning." With Geraldine Fitzgerald, Brad Davis, and Tommy Lee Jones.
Distributed by Coronet/MTI Film & Video.

*The Authors Series
22 min./program, color, 1978.
Beta, VHS, 3/4" U-matic cassette, 16-mm film.
Programs deal with biographical information as related to the creative process. Five programs: James Fenimore Cooper, Stephen Crane, Emily Dickinson, Henry James, and Herman Melville.
Distributed by Journal Films.

Dialogue
20 min., b/w, 198?.
Beta, VHS, 3/4" U-matic cassette.
Mr. and Mrs. Alfred A. Knopf remember the authors they worked with, including John Updike and Albert Camus.
Distributed by Phoenix/BFA Films.

Exploring the Short Story: For Entertainment and Comprehension

37 min., color, 1976.
Beta, VHS, 3/4" U-matic cassette.
Ancillary materials available.
Deals with character, plot, setting, style, theme, and point of view.
Distributed by the Center for Humanities, Inc.

Great American Short Stories, Vol. I [recording]

7 cassettes (90 min. each), 1981.
Includes "Bartleby, the Scrivener," "The Minister's Black Veil," and 14 others.
Distributed by Jimcin Recordings and Books on Tape.

Great American Short Stories, Vol. III [recording]

7 cassettes (90 min. each), 1984.
Includes "The Bride Comes to Yellow Sky," "The Birthmark," and 15 others.
Distributed by Jimcin Recordings and Books on Tape.

In Black and White: Conversations with African American Writers

30 min approx./program, color, 1992.
VHS.
Interviews with African American writers: Alice Walker, August Wilson, Charles Johnson, Gloria Naylor, John Wideman, and Toni Morrison.
Distributed by California Newsreel.

A Movable Feast

30 min./program, color, 1991.
VHS.
Hosted by Tom Vitale. Profiles of eight writers: (1) Allen Ginsberg; (2) Joyce Carol Oates; (3) Li-Young Lee; (4) Sonia Sanchez; (5) T. Coraghessan Boyle; (6) T. R. Pearson; (7) Trey Ellis; (8) W. S. Merwin.
Distributed by Acorn Media.

*The Short Story

20 min., color, 1962.
16-mm film.
A history of the American short story.
Available through Consortium.

Women in Literature, The Short Story: A Collection [recording]

5 cassettes (7 hrs., 30 min.), 1984.
Includes "The Story of an Hour" and other works by Chopin, Edith Wharton, Willa Cather, Mary E. Wilkins Freeman, Sarah Orne Jewett, George Sand, Frances Gilchrist Wood, and Selma Laerloff.
Distributed by Jimcin Recordings and Books on Tape.

*The Writer in America

29 min./program, color, 1979.
Beta, VHS, 3/4" U-matic cassette, 16-mm film.
Interviews with eight contemporary writers: (1) Eudora Welty; (2) Ross MacDonald; (3) Janet Flanner; (4) John Gardner; (5) Toni Morrison; (6) Wright Morris; (7) Robert Duncan; (8) Muriel Rukeyser.
Distributed by Coronet/MTI Film & Video.

Poetry

ANNA AKHMATOVA

Anna Akhmatova: Selected Poems [recording]
1 cassette (60 min.).
Akhmatova reads her poems in
Russian. Includes transcript.
Distributed by Interlingua VA.

The Anna Akhmatova File
65 min., color, 1989.
Beta, VHS.
Documentary of the Russian Poet.
Russian with English subtitles.
Distributed by Facets Multimedia,
Inc.

MATTHEW ARNOLD

Treasury of Matthew Arnold [recording]
1 cassette.
Distributed by Spoken Arts.

See also **"Literature: The Synthesis of
Poetry," "Palgrave's Golden
Treasury of English Poetry"**
and **"Victorian Poetry"** (film
and recording) on manual pp.
418–424.

W. H. AUDEN

The Poetry of W. H. Auden, Part I [recording]
1 cassette (50 min.), 1953.
Part of the YM-YWHA Poetry
Center Series.
Distributed by Audio-Forum.

The Poetry of W. H. Auden, Part II [recording]
1 cassette (59 min.), 1966.
Part of the YM-YWHA Poetry
Center Series.
Distributed by Audio-Forum.

W. H. Auden [recording]
1 cassette (48 min.).
Read by the poet.
Distributed by Spoken Arts.

*W. H. Auden and the Writers of
the 1930s [recording]*
1 cassette (59 min.), 1953.
Read by Stephen Spender.
Distributed by Audio-Forum.

W. H. Auden Reading [recording]
1 cassette.
The poet reads his work.
Distributed by Caedmon/
HarperAudio.

W. H. Auden Remembered [recording]
1 cassette (56 min.).
Read by Heywood H. Broun and
Stephen Spender. From the
Broun Radio Series.
Distributed by Audio-Forum.

See also **"The Poet's Voice"** and
**"Caedmon Treasury of Modern
Poets Reading Their Own
Poetry"** and **"20th Century
Poets Reading Their Work"** on
manual p. 418–424.

JOHN BERRYMAN

See **"The Poet's Voice"** on manual
p. 422.

ELIZABETH BISHOP

*Delmore Schwartz, Richard
Blackmur, Stephen Spender,
and Elizabeth Bishop*
1 cassette.
Distributed by the Library of
Congress.

See also **"Voices and Vision"** on
manual p. 424.

WILLIAM BLAKE

*Essay on William Blake

52 min., color, 1969.
3/4" U-matic cassette, 16-mm film,
special order formats.
A profile of the poet.
Distributed by Indiana University
Instructional Support Services.

William Blake: Selected Poems
[recording]

2 cassettes (180 min.), 1992.
Includes "The Tyger" and "A
Poison Tree."
Distributed by Blackstone Audio
Books.

William Blake: The Marriage of
Heaven and Hell

30 min., color, 1984.
3/4" U-matic cassette.
Dramatizes the life of Blake and his
wife Catherine. With Anne
Baxter and George Rose.
Distributed by Modern Talking
Picture Service.

The Poetry of William Blake
[recording]

1 cassette.
Distributed by Caedmon/
HarperAudio.

Poetry of William Blake [recording]

1 cassette.
Distributed by Spoken Arts.

*William Blake

26 min., color, 1973.
16-mm film.
Hosted by Kenneth Clark. Focuses
on Blake's drawings and
engravings.
Distributed by Pyramid Film and
Video.

William Blake: Something About
Poetry [recording]

1 cassette (22 min.), 1969.
Distributed by Audio-Forum.

William Blake

30 min.
VHS.
A Dramatization of Blake's inner
world.
Distributed by Insight Media.

William Blake

57 min., color, 1976.
Beta, VHS, 3/4" U-matic cassette,
special order formats.
A biographical portrait.
Distributed by Time-Life Video.

See also **"Introduction to English
Poetry"** and **"Romantic
Pioneers"** on manual pp. 420
and 422.

ROBERT BLY

Robert Bly I & II [recording]

1 cassette (60 min.), 1979, 1991.
Distributed by New Letters on the
Air.

Robert Bly: Booth and Bly, Poets

30 min., color, 1978.
1/2" open reel (EIAJ), 3/4" U-
matic cassette.
A four-part series of workshops
and readings by the poets.
Distributed by Nebraska Educational Television Network.

Robert Bly: An Evening of Poetry
[recording]

2 cassettes.
Distributed by Sound Horizons.

Robert Bly: Fairy Tales for Men
and Women [recording]

90 min., 1987.
Bly applies psychoanalytical
analysis to poetry.
Distributed by Ally Press.

Robert Bly: For the Stomach —
Selected Poems, 1974 [record-
ing]

64 min.
Bly reads his poetry.
Distributed by Watershed Tapes.

Robert Bly: The Human Shadow
   [recording]
   2 cassettes.
   Distributed by Mystic Fire.

Robert Bly: A Man Writes to a
   Part of Himself
   57 min., color, 1978.
   3/4" U-matic cassette, special
      order formats.
   Poetry and conversation with the
      writer.
   Distributed by Intermedia Arts of
      Minnesota.

Robert Bly: Poetry East and West
   [recording]
   140 min., 1983.
   Bly gives a poetry lecture, accom-
      panied by the dulcimer.
   Distributed by Dolphin Tapes.

Robert Bly: Poetry in Motion
   30 min., color, 1981.
   Beta, VHS, 3/4" U-matic cassette.
   Video biographies of three poets:
      Robert Bly, Frederick Marfred,
      and Thomas McGrath.
   Distributed by Intermedia Arts of
      Minnesota.

The Poetry of Robert Bly [record-
   ing]
   1 cassette (38 min.), 1966.
   Part of the YM-YWHA Poetry
      Series.
   Distributed by Audio-Forum.

Robert Bly: Poetry Reading — An
   Ancient Tradition [recording]
   2 cassettes (150 min.), 1983.
   Bly talks about the oral tradition in
      poetry.
   Distributed by Dolphin Tapes.

Robert Bly: Selected Poems
   [recording]
   2 cassettes (131 min.), 1987.
   Distributed by Ally Press.

Robert Bly: The Six Powers of
   Poetry [recording]
   1 cassette (90 min.), 1983.
   A lecture from the San Jose Poetry
      Center.
   Distributed by Dolphin Tapes.

See also **"Moyers: The Power of the**
   Word" on manual p. 421.

GWENDOLYN BROOKS

*Gwendolyn Brooks
   30 min., b/w, 1966.
   3/4" U-matic cassette, 16-mm film,
      special order formats.
   Brooks talks about her life and
      poetry.
   Distributed by Indiana University
      Instructional Support Services.

Gwendolyn Brooks I & II [record-
   ing]
   1 cassette (60 min.), 1988, 1989.
   Distributed by New Letters on the
      Air.

Gwendolyn Brooks Reading Her
   Poetry [recording]
   1 cassette.
   Distributed by Caedmon/
      HarperAudio.

See also **"The Harlem Renaissance**
   and Beyond" on manual p. 420.

ELIZABETH BARRETT BROWNING

Elizabeth Barrett Browning:
   Sonnets from the Portuguese
   [recording]
   1 cassette.
   Performed by Katherine Cornell
      and Anthony Quayle.
   Distributed by Caedmon/
      HarperAudio.

Elizabeth Barrett Browning:
Sonnets from the Portuguese
[recording]
1 cassette.
Read by Penelope Lee.
Distributed by Spoken Arts.

See also **"Victorian Poetry"** (recording) on manual p. 423.

ROBERT BROWNING

Robert Browning: My Last
Duchess & Other Poems
[recording]
1 cassette.
Distributed by Caedmon/
HarperAudio.

Robert Browning: Selected Poems
[recording]
4 cassettes (360 min.).
Read by Frederick Davidson.
Distributed by Blackstone Audio
Books.

The Poetry of Browning [recording]
1 cassette.
Distributed by Caedmon/
HarperAudio.

*Robert Browning — His Life and
Poetry
21 min., color, 1972.
Beta, VHS, 3/4" U-matic cassette,
16-mm film, special order
format.
A dramatization of Browning's life
and several of his poems,
including "My Last Duchess."
Distributed by International Film
Bureau.

Treasury of Robert Browning
[recording]
1 cassette.
Distributed by Spoken Arts.

See also **"Victorian Poetry"** (recording) on manual p. 423.

ROBERT BURNS

Robert Burns: Love and Liberty
38 min., color, 1985.
Beta, VHS, 3/4" U-matic cassette.
Burns's lyrics are sung and read
aloud.
Distributed by Films for the
Humanities and Sciences.

Robert Burns: Love Songs [recording]
1 cassette.
Distributed by Spoken Arts.

Robert Burns: The Poetry of
Robert Burns & Border
Ballads [recording]
1 cassette.
Distributed by Caedmon/
HarperAudio.

See also **"Palgrave's Golden Treasury**
of English Poetry" on manual
p. 421.

GEORGE GORDON, LORD BYRON

Lord Byron: Selected Poems
[recording]
2 cassettes (180 min.).
Read by Frederick Davidson.
Distributed by Blackstone Audio
Books.

The Essential Byron [recording]
1 cassette.
Unabridged edition.
Distributed by Listening Library.

The Poetry of Byron [recording]
1 cassette.
Distributed by Caedmon/
HarperAudio.

Treasury of George Gordon, Lord
Byron [recording]
1 cassette.
Distributed by Spoken Arts.

See also **"English Literature: Romantic Period," "English Romantic Poetry," "Palgrave's Golden Treasury of English Poetry,"** and **"The Young Romantics"** on manual pp. 418–424.

Amy Clampitt

Amy Clampitt: The Dahlia Gardens [recording]
1 cassette (56 min.), 1986.
Distributed by Watershed Tapes.

Lucille Clifton

Lucille Clifton [recording]
1 cassette (29 min.), 1989.
Distributed by New Letters on the Air.

Lucille Clifton: The Place for Keeping [recording]
1 cassette (45 min.).
Distributed by Watershed Tapes.

Samuel Taylor Coleridge

Samuel Taylor Coleridge: The Fountain and the Cave
57 min., color, 1974.
Beta, VHS, 3/4" U-matic cassette.
A biography of the poet, filmed on location. Narrated by Paul Scofield.
Distributed by Pyramid Film and Video.

The Poetry of Coleridge [recording]
1 cassette.
Distributed by Caedmon/ HarperAudio.

Samuel Taylor Coleridge: The Rime of the Ancient Mariner & Other Poems [recording]
1 cassette.
Distributed by Spoken Arts.

Samuel Taylor Coleridge: The Rime of the Ancient Mariner & Other Great Poems [recording]
2 cassettes.
From the Cassette Bookshelf Series.
Distributed by Listening Library.

See also **"English Romantic Poetry," "Palgrave's Golden Treasury of English Poetry,"** and **"Romantic Pioneers"** on manual pp. 418–424.

Countee Cullen

The Poetry of Countee Cullen [recording]
1 cassette.
Distributed by Caedmon/ HarperAudio.

See also **"The Harlem Renaissance and Beyond"** and **"Modern American Poetry"** on manual pp. 420 and 421.

E. E. Cummings

E. E. Cummings Reading His Poetry [recording]
1 cassette.
Distributed by Caedmon/ HarperAudio.

E. E. Cummings Reads [recording]
1 cassette (60 min.), 1987.
From The Poet Anniversary Series.
Distributed by Caedmon/ HarperAudio.

E. E. Cummings Reads His Collected Poetry, 1920–1940, & Prose [recording]
2 cassettes (79 min.).
Distributed by Caedmon/ HarperAudio.

E. E. Cummings Reads His Collected Poetry, 1943–1958 [recording]
2 cassettes.
Distributed by Caedmon/ HarperAudio.

**E. E. Cummings: The Making of a
      Poet*
24 min., 1978.
Beta, VHS, 3/4" U-matic cassette.
A profile of cummings told in his
      own words.
Distributed by Films for the
      Humanities and Sciences.

*E. E. Cummings: Nonlectures
      [recordings]*
6 cassettes.
(1) I & My Parents; (2) I & Their
      Son; (3) I & Selfdiscovery; (4) I
      & You & Is; (5) I & Now & Him;
      (6) I & Am & Santa Claus.
Distributed by Caedmon/
      HarperAudio.

*Poems of E. E. Cummings [record-
      ing]*
1 cassette (60 min.), 1981.
Part of the Poetic Heritage Series.
Distributed by Summer Stream.

*E. E. Cummings: Twentieth-
      Century Poetry in English:
      Recordings of Poets Reading
      Their Own Poetry, No. 5
      [recording]*
Distributed by the Library of
      Congress.

See also **"Poetry for People Who Hate
      Poetry," "Inner Ear, Parts 5 and
      6,"** and **"Caedmon Treasury of
      Modern Poets Reading Their
      Own Poetry"** on manual pp.
      418–424.

H.D. [HILDA DOOLITTLE]

H.D.: Helen in Egypt [recording]
1 cassette (39 min.).
Part of the Archive Series.
Distributed by Watershed Tapes.

EMILY DICKINSON

**Emily Dickinson: The Belle of
      Amherst*
90 min., color, 1980.
Beta, VHS, 3/4" U-matic cassette.
With Julie Harris.
Distributed by Cifex Corporation.

**Emily Dickinson: A Certain Slant
      of Light*
29 min., color, 1978.
Beta, VHS, 3/4" U-matic cassette,
      16-mm film.
Explores Dickinson's life and
      environment. Narrated by Julie
      Harris.
Distributed by Pyramid Film and
      Video.

*Emily Dickinson: Magic Prison —
      A Dialogue Set to Music*
35 min., color, 1969.
Beta, VHS, 3/4" U-matic cassette,
      16-mm film.
Dramatizes the letters between
      Dickinson and Colonel T. W.
      Higginson. With an introduc-
      tion by Archibald MacLeish and
      music by Ezra Laderman.
Distributed by Britannica Films.

*Emily Dickinson: Poems and
      Letters [recording]*
2 cassettes.
Distributed by Recorded Books.

*Emily Dickinson: Selected Poems
      [recording]*
4 cassettes (360 min.), 1993.
Read by Mary Woods.
Distributed by Blackstone Audio
      Books.

*Emily Dickinson: Seventy-Five
      Poems [recording]*
2 cassettes (75 min.).
Distributed by Recorded Books.

*Poems and Letters of Emily
      Dickinson [recording]*
1 cassette.
Distributed by Caedmon/
      HarperAudio.

*Emily Dickinson
22 min., color, 1978.
Beta, VHS, 3/4" U-matic cassette.
A film about the poet and her
poems. Part of the "Authors"
series.
Distributed by Journal Films Inc.

Emily Dickinson [recording]
1 cassette.
Distributed by Recorded Books.

Emily Dickinson Recalled in Song
[recording]
1 cassette (30 min.).
Distributed by Audio-Forum.

Poems by Emily Dickinson
[recording]
2 cassettes (236 min.), 1986.
Distributed by Audio Book
Contractors.

Poems of Emily Dickinson [record-
ing]
1 cassette.
Distributed by Spoken Arts.

See also **"Inner Ear, Parts 3 and 4,"**
"Introduction to English
Poetry," "Voices and Vision,"
and **"With a Feminine Touch"**
on manual pp. 418–424.

John Donne

Essential Donne [recording]
From the Essential Poets Series.
Distributed by the Listening
Library.

John Donne
40 min., color.
VHS.
Discusses the poet's life and works.
Distributed by Insight Media.

John Donne: Love Poems [record-
ing]
1 cassette.
Distributed by Recorded Books.

John Donne: Selected Poems
[recording]
2 cassettes (180 min.), 1992.
Read by Frederick Davidson.
Distributed by Blackstone Audio
Books.

The Love Poems of John Donne
[recording]
1 cassette.
Distributed by Caedmon/
HarperAudio.

Treasury of John Donne [recording]
1 cassette.
Distributed by Spoken Arts.

See also **"Metaphysical and Devo-**
tional Poetry" and **"Palgrave's**
Golden Treasury of English
Poetry" on manual p. 421.

T. S. Eliot

*The Mysterious Mr. Eliot
62 min., color, 1973.
Beta, VHS, 3/4" U-matic cassette,
16-mm film.
A biographical film about the poet.
Distributed by Insight Media and
CRM Films.

T. S. Eliot: Selected Poems [record-
ing]
1 cassette (49 min.), 1971.
The author reads his poetry,
including "The Waste Land."
Distributed by Caedmon/
HarperAudio.

T. S. Eliot: Twentieth Century
Poetry in English: Record-
ings of Poets Reading Their
Own Poetry, No. 3 [record-
ing]
Distributed by the Library of
Congress.

T. S. Eliot and George Orwell
[recording]
1 cassette (41 min.), 1953.
Read by Stephen Spender.
Distributed by Caedmon/
HarperAudio.

T. S. Eliot Reading "The Love Song of J. Alfred Prufrock" *[recording]*
1 cassette.
Distributed by Caedmon/ HarperAudio.

T. S. Eliot Reading "The Wasteland "& Other Poems
1 cassette.
Distributed by Caedmon/ HarperAudio.

See also **"Modern American Poetry," "The Poet's Voice," "Voices and Vision," and "Caedmon Treasury of Modern Poets Reading Their Own Poetry"** on manual pp. 418–424.

CAROLYN FORCHÉ

Carolyn Forché *[recording]*
1 cassette (29 min.), 1989.
Distributed by New Letters on the Air.

Carolyn Forché: Ourselves or Nothing *[recording]*
1 cassette (58 min.), 1983.
Distributed by Watershed Tapes.

ROBERT FROST

Afterglow: A Tribute to Robert Frost
35 min., color, 1989.
Beta, VHS, 3/4" U-matic cassette.
Starring and directed by Burgess Meredith.
Distributed by Pyramid Film and Video.

Robert Frost *[recording]*
1 cassette, 1981.
Includes "The Pasture" and "Stopping by Woods on a Snowy Evening."
Distributed by the Library of Congress

*Robert Frost: A First Acquaintance
16 min., color, 1974.
Beta, VHS, 3/4" U-matic cassette, 16-mm film.
An examination of Frost's life through his poems.
Distributed by Films for the Humanities and Sciences.

Frost and Whitman
30 min., b/w, 1963.
Beta, VHS, 1/2" open reel (EIAJ), 3/4" U-matic cassette, 2" quadraplex open reel.
Will Geer performs excerpts from the two poets' works.
Distributed by New York State Education Department.

An Interview with Robert Frost
30 min., b/w, 1952.
Beta, VHS, 3/4" U-matic cassette.
Bela Kornitzer interviews Frost, who reads from his poetry.
Distributed by Social Studies School Service.

*Robert Frost: A Lover's Quarrel With the World
40 min., b/w, 1970.
Beta, VHS, 3/4" U-matic cassette, 16-mm film.
A documentary film on Frost's philosophic and artistic ideas.
Distributed by Phoenix/BFA Films.

*Robert Frost
10 min., color, 1972.
Beta, VHS, 3/4" U-matic cassette, 16-mm film.
A biographical sketch of the poet.
Distributed by AIMS Media Inc.

Robert Frost in Recital *[recording]*
1 cassette.
Distributed by Caedmon/ HarperAudio.

Robert Frost Reads [recording]
1 cassette (60 min.), 1987.
From The Poet Anniversary Series.
Distributed by Caedmon/
HarperAudio.

Robert Frost Reads His Poems
[recording]
1 cassette (55 min.), 1965.
Distributed by Audio-Forum.

Robert Frost Reads His Poetry
[recording]
1 cassette (48 min.).
Distributed by Recorded Books.

Robert Frost Reads "The Road
Not Taken" & Other Poems
[recording]
1 cassette.
Distributed by Caedmon/
HarperAudio.

*Robert Frost's New England
22 min., color, 1976.
Beta, VHS, 3/4" U-matic cassette,
16-mm film, special order
formats. Ancillary materials
available.
Explores some of Frost's poetry
relating to New England and its
seasons.
Distributed by Churchill Media.

Robert Frost: Twentieth Century
Poetry in English: Record-
ings of Poets Reading Their
Own Poetry, No. 6 [record-
ing]
Distributed by the Library of
Congress.

See also **"Literature: The Synthesis of
Poetry," "Modern American
Poetry," "Poetry by Ameri-
cans," "The Poet's Voice,"
"Voices and Vision," and
"Caedmon Treasury of Modern
Poets Reading Their Own
Poetry"** on manual pp. 418–424.

ALLEN GINSBERG

Allen Ginsberg [recording]
1 cassette (29 min.), 1988.
The author talks about the Beat
movement and his ongoing
battle against censorship.
Distributed by New Letters on the
Air.

Allen Ginsberg: First Blues
[recording]
Recorded in the 1970s these songs
represent Ginsberg's earliest
experiments combining impro-
vised text with music.
Distributed by Poet's Audio
Center.

The Life and Times of Allen
Ginsberg
83 min., color, 1993.
VHS.
Chronicles the life of the poet with
commentary from Abbie
Hoffman, Ken Kesey, Jack
Kerouac, Joan Baez, and others.
Distributed by First Run/Icarus
Films.

See also **"Fried Shoes, Cooked
Diamonds," "A Moveable
Feast," "The Poet's Voice,"
"Potpourri of Poetry," "Spoken
Arts Treasury of American
Jewish Poets Reading Their
Poems, Vol. VI,"** and **"Poets in
Person"** on manual pp. 418–424.

THOMAS HARDY

The Poetry of Thomas Hardy
[recording]
1 cassette.
Distributed by Caedmon/
HarperAudio.

See also **"Introduction to English
Poetry," "Romantics and
Realists,"** and **"Victorian
Poetry"** (recording) on manual
pp. 418–424.

ROBERT HASS

Robert Hass: A Story about the Body [recording]
1 cassette, 1988.
Distributed by Watershed Tapes.

GEORGE HERBERT

See **"Introduction to English Poetry"** and **"Metaphysical and Devotional Poetry"** on manual pp. 420 and 421.

ROBERT HERRICK

See **"Palgrave's Golden Treasury of English Poetry"** on manual p. 421.

GERARD MANLEY HOPKINS

The Poetry of Gerard Manley Hopkins [recording]
1 cassette.
Distributed by Caedmon/ HarperAudio.

Gerard Manley Hopkins: The Wreck of the Deutschland [recording]
1 cassette.
Distributed by Audio-Forum.

See also **"Romantics and Realists"** and **"Victorian Poetry"** (recording) on manual p. 423.

A. E. HOUSMAN

A. E. Housman: A Shropshire Lad & Other Poetry [recording]
1 cassette.
Distributed by Caedmon/ HarperAudio.

See also **"Romantics and Realists"** and **"Victorian Poetry"** (recording) on manual p. 423.

LANGSTON HUGHES

*Langston Hughes
24 min., color, 1971.
Beta, VHS, 3/4" U-matic cassette, 16-mm film.
A biographical sketch of the poet.
Distributed by Carousel Film & Video.

Langston Hughes: Dream Keeper and Other Poems [recording]
1 cassette, 1955.
Distributed by Smithsonian/ Folkways Recordings.

Langston Hughes: The Making of a Poet [recording]
1 cassette (30 min.).
Read by the poet.
Distributed by National Public Radio.

Langston Hughes: Poetry & Reflections [recording]
1 cassette.
Performed by the author.
Distributed by Caedmon/ HarperAudio.

Langston Hughes Reads and Talks about His Poems [recording]
1 cassette
Includes "The Negro Speaks of Rivers" and "Dream Boogie."
Distributed by Spoken Arts.

The Poetry of Langston Hughes [recording]
2 cassettes.
Performed by Ruby Dee and Ossie Davis.
Distributed by Caedmon/ HarperAudio.

The Voice of Langston Hughes: Selected Poetry and Prose [recording]
1 cassette or CD (38 min.).
Selections from the years 1925– 1932. The author reads poetry from "The Dream Keeper and Other Poems," "Simple Speaks His Mind" and he narrates his

text from "The Story of Jazz," "Rhythms of the World," and "The Glory of Negro History." Distributed by Smithsonian/ Folkways Recordings.

Langston Hughes: Simple Stories [recording]
1 cassette.
Performed by Ossie Davis.
Distributed by Caedmon/ HarperAudio.

See also **"Harlem Renaissance: The Black Poets," "The Harlem Renaissance and Beyond," "Modern American Poetry,"** and **"Voices and Vision"** and **"20th Century Poets Reading Their Work"** on manual pp. 418–424.

RANDALL JARRELL

Randall Jarrell: The Bat Poet [recording]
1 cassette.
Distributed by Caedmon/ HarperAudio.

The Poetry of Randall Jarrell [recording]
1 cassette (67 min.), 1963.
Part of the YM-YWHA Poetry Center Series.
Distributed by Audio-Forum.

Randall Jarrell Reads and Discusses His Poems Against War [recording]
1 cassette.
Distributed by Caedmon/ HarperAudio.

See also **"The Poet's Voice"** on manual p. 422.

JOHN KEATS

*John Keats — His Life and Death
55 min., color, 1973.
Beta, VHS, 3/4" U-matic cassette, 16-mm film.

Extended version of "John Keats — Poet" (see below). Explores the poet's affair with Fanny Browne and the events surrounding his death. Written by Archibald MacLeish.
Distributed by Britannica Films.

*John Keats — Poet
31 min., color, 1973.
Beta, VHS, 3/4" U-matic cassette, 16-mm film.
A biography of the poet, with excerpts from his letters and poems. Written by Archibald MacLeish.
Distributed by Britannica Films.

John Keats: Selected Poems [recording]
2 cassettes (180 min.), 1993.
Read by Frederick Davidson.
Distributed by Blackstone Audio Books.

John Keats: Odes [recording]
1 cassette.
Distributed by Audio-Forum.

The Poetry of Keats [recording]
1 cassette.
Distributed by Caedmon/ HarperAudio.

Treasury of John Keats [recording]
1 cassette.
Distributed by Spoken Arts.

See also **"English Literature: Romantic Period," "Palgrave's Golden Treasury of English Poetry,"** and **"The Young Romantics"** on manual pp. 418–424.

GALWAY KINNELL

Galway Kinnell I & II [recording]
1 cassette (60 min.), 1982, 1991.
Distributed by New Letters on the Air.

The Poetry of Galway Kinnell
[recording]
1 cassette (33 min.), 1965.
Part of the YM-YWHA Poetry
Center Series.
Distributed by Audio-Forum.

The Poetry & Voice of Galway
Kinnell [recording]
1 cassette.
Distributed by Caedmon/
HarperAudio.

See also **"Moyers: The Power of the**
Word" on manual p. 421.

D. H. LAWRENCE

Poems of D. H. Lawrence [record-
ing]
1 cassette (36 min.).
Distributed by Spoken Arts.

DENISE LEVERTOV

Denise Levertov [recording]
1 cassette (29 min.), 1983.
The author reads her poems and
discusses political activism and
the responsibility of a writer.
Distributed by New Letters on the
Air.

Denise Levertov: The Acolyte
[recording]
1 cassette (63 min.), 1985.
Distributed by Watershed Tapes.

*Poetry: Denise Levertov and
Charles Olson
30 min., b/w, 1966.
3/4" U-matic cassette, 16-mm film,
special order formats.
An introduction to the two poets'
work.
Distributed by Indiana University
Instructional Support Services.

The Poetry of Denise Levertov
[recording]
1 cassette (37 min.), 1965.
Part of the YM–YWHA Poetry
Center Series.
Distributed by Audio-Forum.

See also **"Spoken Arts Treasury of**
American Jewish Poets
Reading Their Poems, Vol. V"
(recording) on manual p. 423.

ROBERT LOWELL

*Poetry — Richard Wilbur and
Robert Lowell
30 min., b/w, 1966.
3/4" U-matic cassette, 16-mm film,
special order formats.
Interviews with the two poets.
Distributed by Indiana University
Instructional Support Services.

The Poetry of Robert Lowell
[recording]
1 cassette (28 min.), 1968.
Part of the YM-YWHA Poetry
Center Series.
Distributed by Audio-Forum.

Robert Lowell: Twentieth Century
Poetry in English: Record-
ings of Poets Reading Their
Own Poetry, Nos. 11 and 32–
33 [recording]
Distributed by the Library of
Congress.

See also **"Voices and Vision"** on
manual p. 424.

ARCHIBALD MACLEISH

Archibald MacLeish Reads His
Poetry [recording]
1 cassette.
Distributed by Caedmon/
HarperAudio.

Archibald MacLeish: Twentieth
Century Poetry in English:
Recordings of Poets Reading
Their Own Poetry: Nine
Pulitzer Prize Poets, No. 29
[recording]
Distributed by the Library of
Congress.

See also **"Caedmon Treasury of Modern Poets Reading Their Own Poetry"** on manual p. 419.

ANDREW MARVELL

Andrew Marvell: Ralph Richardson Reads Andrew Marvell [recording]
1 cassette.
Distributed by Audio-Forum.

See also **"Metaphysical and Devotional Poetry"** on manual p. 421.

EDNA ST. VINCENT MILLAY

Edna St. Vincent Millay: Renascence
60 min., color.
A biography of the poet.
Distributed by Films for the Humanities and Sciences.

Poems of Edna St. Vincent Millay [recording]
1 cassette (60 min.), 1981.
Part of the Poetic Heritage Series.
Distributed by Summer Stream.

Poetry of Edna St. Vincent Millay [recording]
1 cassette.
Distributed by Caedmon/ HarperAudio.

See also **"With a Feminine Touch"** on manual p. 424.

JOHN MILTON

*Milton
28 min., color, 1989.
Beta, VHS, 3/4" U-matic cassette.
Looks at Milton's sonnets to his wife Katherine and *Paradise Lost*.
Distributed by Films for the Humanities and Sciences.

*Milton and 17th Century Poetry
35 min., color, 1989.
Beta, VHS, 3/4" U-matic cassette.
A study of Milton and other metaphysical poets.
Distributed by Films for the Humanities and Sciences.

Milton by Himself
27 min., color, 1989.
Beta, VHS, 3/4" U-matic cassette.
A biography constructed from Milton's autobiographical writings.
Distributed by Films for the Humanities and Sciences.

Milton the Puritan: Portrait of a Mind [recording]
10 cassettes (900 min.).
Distributed by Books on Tape.

The Poetry of John Milton [recording]
1 cassette.
Distributed by Caedmon/ HarperAudio.

Treasury of John Milton [recording]
1 cassette.
Distributed by Spoken Arts.

See also **"Palgrave's Golden Treasury of English Poetry"** and **"Introduction to English Poetry"** on manual pp. 419 and 420.

MARIANNE MOORE

Marianne Moore Reading Her Poems & Fables from La Fontaine [recording]
1 cassette.
Distributed by Caedmon/ HarperAudio.

Marianne Moore Reads Her Poetry [recording]
1 cassette (22 min.), 1965.
Distributed by Audio-Forum.

See also **"Inner Ear, Parts 3 and 4,"**
"Modern American Poetry,"
"The Poet's Voice," "Voices
and Vision," and **"Caedmon**
Treasury of Modern Poets
Reading Their Own Poetry" on
manual pp. 418–424.

SHARON OLDS

Sharon Olds [recording]
1 cassette (29 min.), 1992.
Distributed by New Letters on the
Air.

Sharon Olds: Coming Back to Life
[recording]
1 cassette (60 min.).
Distributed by Audio-Forum.

See also **"Moyers: The Power of the**
Word" on manual p. 421.

MARGE PIERCY

Marge Piercy: At the Core [record-
ing]
1 cassette (58 min.), 1977.
Distributed by Watershed Tapes.

SYLVIA PLATH

Sylvia Plath: The Bell Jar
113 min., color, 1979.
Beta, VHS.
Based on Plath's
semiautobiographical novel.
See local retailer.

Sylvia Plath
4 programs (30 min. each), color,
1974.
VHS, 1/2" open reel (EIAJ), 3/4"
U-matic cassette, 2" quadraplex
open reel.
A biographical examination of the
poet and her work.
Distributed by New York State
Education Department.

Sylvia Plath [recording]
1 cassette (48 min.), 1962.
A historic reading of 15 poems
recorded the month before the
poet's suicide.
Distributed by Poet's Audio
Center.

Sylvia Plath: Letters Home
90 min., color, 1985.
Beta, VHS, 3/4" U-matic cassette.
Staged version of Plath's letters to
her mother.
Distributed by Films for the
Humanities and Sciences.

Sylvia Plath, Part I: The Struggle
30 min., color, 1974.
Beta, VHS, 1/2"open reel (EIAJ),
3/4" U-matic cassette,
2"quadraplex open reel.
A dramatization of Plath's poetry
by The Royal Shakespeare
Company.
Distributed by New York State
Education Department.

Sylvia Plath, Part II: Getting
There
30 min., color, 1974.
Beta, VHS, 1/2" open reel (EIAJ),
3/4" U-matic cassette, 2"
quadraplex open reel.
Plath's poems are set to music by
Elizabeth Swados and per-
formed by Michele Collison.
Distributed by New York State
Education Department.

Sylvia Plath Reading Her Poetry
[recording]
1 cassette.
Distributed by Caedmon/
HarperAudio.

Sylvia Plath Reads [recording]
1 cassette (60 min.), 1987.
From The Poet Anniversary Series.
Distributed by Caedmon/
HarperAudio.

See also "The Poet's Voice," "Voices and Vision," and "With a Feminine Touch" on manual pp. 418–424.

EDGAR ALLAN POE

Edgar Allan Poe: The Raven, The Bells and Other Poems [recording]
1 cassette.
Distributed by Spoken Arts.

See also "With Poe at Midnight" and "Edgar Allan Poe: Terror of the Soul" on manual p. 396 and "Poetry by Americans" on manual p. 422.

ALEXANDER POPE

Treasury of Alexander Pope [recording]
1 cassette.
Distributed by Spoken Arts.

See also "English Literature: Eighteenth Century" and "Restoration and Augustan Poetry" on manual pp. 419 and 422.

EZRA POUND

Ezra Pound Reading Cantico Del Sole, Canto Ninety-Nine & Other Poems [recording]
2 cassettes.
Distributed by Caedmon/ HarperAudio.

*Ezra Pound: Poet's Poet
29 min., b/w, 1970.
Beta, VHS, 3/4" U-matic cassette, 16-mm film.
A profile of Pound and his influence on later poets.
Distributed by Films for the Humanities and Sciences.

See also "Modern American Poetry," "The Poet's Voice," "Voices and Vision," and "Caedmon Treasury of Modern Poets Reading Their Own Poetry" on manual pp. 418–424.

THEODORE ROETHKE

The Poetry of Theodore Roethke [recording]
1 cassette (36 min.).
Part of the YM-YWHA Poetry Center Series.
Distributed by Audio-Forum.

Theodore Roethke [recording]
1 cassette (48 min.), 1972.
A posthumous collection of Roethke reading his poetry.
Distributed by Caedmon/ HarperAudio.

Theodore Roethke: Twentieth Century Poetry in English: Recordings of Poets Reading Their Own Poetry, No. 10 [recording]
Distributed by the Library of Congress.

Words for the Wind: Read by Theodore Roethke [recording]
1 cassette, 1962.
Distributed by Smithsonian/ Folkways Recordings.

See also "The Poet's Voice" on manual p. 422.

ANNE SEXTON

Anne Sexton Reads Her Poetry [recording]
1 cassette.
Distributed by Caedmon/ HarperAudio.

The Poetry of Anne Sexton [recording]
1 cassette (35 min.), 1964.
Part of the YM-YWHA Poetry Center Series.
Distributed by Audio-Forum.

WILLIAM SHAKESPEARE

*William Shakespeare: Poetry and Hidden Poetry
53 min., color, 1984.
A micro-examination of Shakespeare's poetry and its hidden meanings. Produced by the Royal Shakespeare Company.
Distributed by Films for the Humanities and Sciences.

Selected Sonnets by Shakespeare
40 min., color, 1984.
Beta, VHS, 3/4" U-matic cassette.
Features readings by Ben Kingsley and Jane Lapotaire.
Distributed by Films for the Humanities and Sciences.

Selected Sonnets of Shakespeare [recording]
1 cassette.
Distributed by Spoken Arts.

William Shakespeare: The Sonnets [recording]
1 cassette.
Distributed by Recorded Books.

William Shakespeare Sonnets [recording]
2 cassettes (120 min.).
Distributed by Caedmon/HarperAudio.

William Shakespeare's Sonnets
150 min., color, 1984.
Beta, VHS, 3/4" U-matic cassette.
An in-depth look at fifteen of Shakespeare's sonnets. With Ben Kingsley, Roger Reese, Claire Bloom, Jane Lapotaire, A. L. Rowse, and Stephen Spender.
Distributed by Films for the Humanities and Sciences.

See also **"Poetry for People Who Hate Poetry," "England: Background of Literature," "Introduction to English Poetry," "Medieval and Elizabethan Poetry,"** and **"Palgrave's Golden Treasury of English Poetry"** on manual pp. 418–424.

PERCY BYSSHE SHELLEY

The Poetry of Shelley [recording]
1 cassette.
Distributed by Caedmon/HarperAudio.

Treasury of Percy Bysshe Shelley [recording]
1 cassette.
Distributed by Spoken Arts.

See also **"English Literature: Romantic Period," "English Romantic Poetry," "Introduction to English Poetry,"** and **"Palgrave's Golden Treasury of English Poetry"** on manual pp. 418–424.

GARY SNYDER

*Gary Snyder: Poetry—Phillip Whalen and Gary Snyder
30 min., b/w, 1966.
3/4" U-matic cassette, 16-mm film, special order formats.
Interviews with the two poets.
Distributed by Indiana University Instructional Support Services.

Gary Snyder: This Is Our Body [recording]
1 cassette (61 min.), 1989.
Distributed by Watershed Tapes.

See also **"Inner Ear, Parts 5 and 6"** on manual p. 420.

GARY SOTO

Gary Soto I & II [recording]
1 cassette (60 min.), 1982, 1992.
The author reads his work and talks about the recent rise of Chicano Literature.
Distributed by New Letters on the Air.

See also **"Poets in Person, No. 7"** (recording) on manual p. 422.

WALLACE STEVENS

Wallace Stevens Reads [recording]
1 cassette (60 min.), 1987.
Part of The Poet Anniversary Series.
Distributed by Caedmon/ HarperAudio.

Wallace Stevens Reading His Poems [recording]
1 cassette.
Distributed by Caedmon/ HarperAudio.

See also **"Inner Ear, Parts 3 and 4," "Modern American Poetry," "The Poet's Voice," "Voices and Vision,"** and **"Caedmon Treasury of Modern Poets Reading Their Own Poetry"** on manual pp. 418–424.

ALFRED, LORD TENNYSON

Treasury of Alfred, Lord Tennyson [recording]
1 cassette.
Read by Robert Speaight. Includes "Ulysses," "The Lotus Eaters," and "The Charge of the Light Brigade."
Distributed by Spoken Arts.

See also **"England: Background of Literature," "Palgrave's Golden Treasury of English Poetry,"** and **"Victorian Poetry"** (recording) on manual pp. 418–424.

DYLAN THOMAS

*The Days of Dylan Thomas
21 min., b/w, 1965.
Beta, VHS, 3/4" U-matic cassette, 16-mm film.
A biography of the poet.
Distributed by CRM Films.

Dylan Thomas [recording]
4 cassettes.
Distributed by Caedmon/ HarperAudio.

Dylan Thomas
25 min., color, 1982.
Beta, VHS, 3/4" U-matic cassette.
A portrait of the poet.
Distributed by Films, Inc.

*A Dylan Thomas Memoir
28 min., color, 1972.
Beta, VHS, 3/4" U-matic cassette, 16-mm film.
A character study of the poet.
Distributed by Pyramid Film and Video.

Dylan Thomas Soundbook [recording]
4 cassettes.
Read by the author.
Distributed by Caedmon/ HarperAudio.

Dylan Thomas Reading "And Death Shall Have No Dominion" & Other Poems [recording]
1 cassette.
Distributed by Caedmon/ HarperAudio.

Dylan Thomas Reading His Poetry [recording]
2 cassettes.
Distributed by Caedmon/ HarperAudio.

Dylan Thomas Reading "Quite Early One Morning" & Other Poems [recording]
1 cassette.
Distributed by Caedmon/ HarperAudio.

Dylan Thomas Reading "Over Sir John's Hill" & Other Poems [recording]
1 cassette.
Distributed by Caedmon/ HarperAudio.

Dylan Thomas Reads a Personal Anthology [recording]
1 cassette.
Distributed by Caedmon/ HarperAudio.

An Evening with Dylan Thomas [recording]
1 cassette.
Distributed by Caedmon/ HarperAudio.

Dylan Thomas: In Country Heaven — The Evolution of a Poem [recording]
1 cassette.
Distributed by Caedmon/ HarperAudio.

Dylan Thomas: A Portrait
26 min., color, 1989.
Beta, VHS, 3/4" U-matic cassette.
A biographical film.
Distributed by Films for the Humanities and Sciences.

Dylan Thomas: An Appreciation [recording]
1 cassette.
Distributed by Audio-Forum.

Dylan Thomas: Under Milkwood [recording]
2 cassettes (90 min.).
Distributed by S & S Audio.

The Wales of Dylan Thomas
Color, 1989.
Images of Wales in Thomas's poetry, prose, and drama.
Distributed by Films for the Humanities and Sciences.

See also **"Caedmon Treasury of Modern Poets Reading Their Own Poetry"** on manual p. 419.

Walt Whitman

Walt Whitman: Crossing Brooklyn Ferry & Other Poems [recording]
1 cassette.
Distributed by Caedmon/ HarperAudio.

The Democratic Vistas of Walt Whitman [recording]
1 cassette (22 min.), 1968.
By Louis Untermeyer. Part of the Makers of the Modern World Series.
Distributed by Audio-Forum.

*Walt Whitman: Endlessly Rocking
21 min., color, 1986.
Beta, VHS, 3/4" U-matic cassette.
Shows a teacher's unsuccessful attempts to interest her students in Whitman.
Distributed by Centre Communications.

Walt Whitman: Frost and Whitman
30 min., b/w, 1963.
Beta, VHS, 1/2" open reel (EIAJ), 3/4" U-matic cassette, 2" quadraplex open reel.
Will Geer performs excerpts from the two poets' works.
Distributed by New York State Education Department.

Walt Whitman: Galway Kinnell Reads Walt Whitman [recording]
1 cassette (59 min.).
Kinnell reads excerpts from "Song of Myself," "I Sing the Body Electric," and several shorter poems.
Distributed by Sound Rx.

Walt Whitman: The Living Tradition
20 min., color, 1983.
Beta, VHS, 3/4" U-matic cassette.
Allen Ginsberg reads Whitman's poetry.
Distributed by Centre Communications.

Walt Whitman: Memoranda During the War: From Specimen Days [recording]
240 min.
Distributed by Recorded Books.

Walt Whitman: Orson Welles Reads "Song of Myself" [recording]
1 cassette.
Distributed by Audio-Forum.

*Walt Whitman: Poet for a New Age
29 min., color, 1972.
Beta, VHS, 3/4" U-matic cassette, 16-mm film.
A study of the poet.
Distributed by Britannica Films.

Readings of Walt Whitman [recording]
1 cassette, 1957.
Distributed by Smithsonian/ Folkways Recordings.

Treasury of Walt Whitman: Leaves of Grass, I & II [recording]
2 cassettes (92 min.).
Unabridged edition.
Distributed by Spoken Arts.

Walt Whitman: Twentieth Century Poetry in English, Nos. 13–17 [recording]
From the Leaves of Grass Centennial Series.
Distributed by the Library of Congress.

*Walt Whitman
10 min., color, 1972.
Beta, VHS, 3/4" U-matic cassette, 16-mm film, open captioned.
Readings and a discussion of Whitman's life. Hosted by Efrem Zimbalist Jr.
Distributed by AIMS Media Inc.

Walt Whitman
12 min., color, 1989.
Beta, VHS, 3/4" U-matic cassette.
Examines Whitman's poetic language.
Distributed by Films for the Humanities and Sciences.

*Walt Whitman's Civil War
15 min., color, 1988.
Beta, VHS, 3/4" U-matic cassette.
Discusses Whitman's perspective on the war.
Distributed by Churchill Media.

See also **"Poetry by Americans"** and **"Voices and Vision"** on manual pp. 422 and 424.

William Carlos Williams

William Carlos Williams Reads His Poetry [recording]
1 cassette.
Distributed by Caedmon/ HarperAudio.

William Carlos Williams: People and the Stones: Selected Poems [recording]
1 cassette (60 min.).
Distributed by Watershed Tapes.

See also **"Inner Ear, Part 1," "The Poet's Voice," "Voices and Vision,"** and **"Caedmon Treasury of Modern Poets Reading Their Own Poetry"** on manual pp. 418–424.

William Wordsworth

William Wordsworth: Selected Poems [recording]
2 cassettes (180 min.).
Read by Frederick Davidson.
Distributed by Blackstone Audio Books.

The Poetry of Wordsworth
[recording]
1 cassette.
Distributed by Caedmon/
HarperAudio.

Treasury of William Wordsworth
[recording]
1 cassette.
Distributed by Spoken Arts.

*William Wordsworth: William
and Dorothy*
52 min., color, 1989.
Beta, VHS, 3/4" U-matic cassette.
Explores Wordsworth's poetry and
his troubled relationship with
his sister. Directed by Ken
Russell.
Distributed by Films for the
Humanities and Sciences.

*William Wordsworth
28 min., color, 1989.
Beta, VHS, 3/4" U-matic cassette.
An examination of the poet's work
set against the Lake District,
subject for many of the poems.
Distributed by Films for the
Humanities and Sciences.

*William Wordsworth and the
English Lakes*
15 min., color, 1989.
Beta, VHS, 3/4" U-matic cassette.
Looks at Wordsworth's use of
language.
Distributed by Films for the
Humanities and Sciences.

See also **"English Literature: Roman-
tic Period," "English Romantic
Poetry," "Introduction to
English Poetry," "Palgrave's
Golden Treasury of English
Poetry," "Romantic Pioneers,"
and "The Young Romantics"**
on manual pp. 418–424.

THOMAS WYATT

See **"Medieval and Elizabethan
Poetry"** and **"Palgrave's
Golden Treasury of English
Poetry"** on manual pp. 420–421.

WILLIAM BUTLER YEATS

*Dylan Thomas Reads the Poetry
of W. B. Yeats & Others*
[recording]
1 cassette.
Includes readings of Yeats, Louis
MacNeice, George Barker,
Walter de la Mare, W. H.
Davies, D. H. Lawrence, and W.
H. Auden.
Distributed by Caedmon/
HarperAudio.

*The Love Poems of William Butler
Yeats*
30 min., b/w, 1967.
Beta, VHS, 1/2" open reel (EIAJ),
3/4" U-matic cassette, 2"
quadraplex open reel.
Selections from the poet's works.
Distributed by New York State
Education Department.

*Poems by W. B. Yeats and Poems
for Several Voices*
1 cassette, 1973.
Includes "Sailing to Byzantium"
and features poems by Thomas
Hardy, Robert Graves, and
Gerard Manley Hopkins.
Read by V. C. Clinton-Baddeley,
Jill Balcon, and M. Westbury.
Distributed by Smithsonian/
Folkways Recordings.

Poems of William Butler Yeats
[recording]
1 cassette.
Distributed by Spoken Arts.

*The Poetry of William Butler
Yeats* [recording]
1 cassette.
Distributed by Caedmon/
HarperAudio.

*William Butler Yeats et al.:
    Treasury of Irish Verse, Folk
    Tales, & Ballads [recording]*
6 cassettes (294 min.), 1986.
Distributed by Spoken Arts.

*William Butler Yeats: Twentieth
    Century Poets Read Their
    Works [recording]*
6 cassettes (270 min.), 1986.
Distributed by Spoken Arts.

W. B. Yeats [recording]
1 cassette (49 min.), 1953.
Read by Stephen Spender.
Distributed by Audio-Forum.

*Yeats Country
19 min., color, 1965.
VHS, 3/4" U-matic cassette, 16-
    mm film.

Juxtaposes Yeats's poetry with
    scenes of the Ireland he wrote
    about.
Distributed by International Film
    Bureau.

Yeats Remembered
30 min.
VHS.
Biographical film using period
    photographs and interviews
    with the poet and his family.
Distributed by Insight Media.

See also **"Caedmon Treasury of
    Modern Poets Reading Their
    Own Poetry," "Introduction to
    English Poetry," and "20th
    Century Poets Reading Their
    Work"** on manual pp. 418–424.

Poetry: General Resources

*Anthology of Contemporary
    American Poetry [recording]*
1 cassette, 1961.
Includes poems by John Ciardi,
    Richard Ebhardt, Theodore
    Roethke, Howard Nemerov,
    Galway Kinnell, Donald Justice,
    May Swenson, Richard Wilbur,
    Karl Shapiro, and others.
Distributed by Smithsonian/
    Folkways Recordings.

*Anthology of Negro Poets [record-
    ing]*
1 cassette, 1954.
Includes the poetry of Langston
    Hughes, Sterling Brown, Claude
    McKay, Countee Cullen,
    Margaret Walter, and
    Gwendolyn Brooks.
Distributed by Smithsonian/
    Folkways Recordings.

*Anthology of 19th Century
    American Poets [recording]*
1 cassette.
Includes Longfellow, Holmes,
    Whittier, Lowell, Emerson, Poe,
    and Whitman.
Distributed by Spoken Arts.

Birthright: Growing Up Hispanic
59 min., color, 1989.
VHS, Beta, 3/4" U-matic cassette.
Focuses on the achievements of
    Hispanic American writers.
    Includes the work of Alberto
    Ríos and Judith Ortiz Cofer.
Distributed by Cinema Guild.

*Caedmon Treasury of Modern
    Poets Reading Their Own
    Poetry [recording]*
2 cassettes (95 min.).
Includes T. S. Eliot, W. B. Yeats, W.
    H. Auden, Edith Sitwell, Dylan
    Thomas, Robert Graves,
    Gertrude Stein, Archibald
    MacLeish, E. E. Cummings,
    Marianne Moore, Stephen

Spender, Conrad Aiken, Robert Frost, William Carlos Williams, Wallace Stevens, Ezra Pound, Richard Wilbur, and others.
Distributed by Caedmon/ HarperCollins.

Conversation Pieces: Short Poems by Thomas Hardy, Housman, Auden, Keats, & Others
1 cassette, 1964.
Distributed by Smithsonian/ Folkways Recordings.

*England: Background of Literature
11 min., color, 1962.
Beta, VHS, 3/4" U-matic cassette, 16-mm film, special order formats.
Presents the works of English writers against the backgrounds that inspired them: Shakespeare, Dickens, and Tennyson.
Distributed by Coronet/MTI Film & Video.

*English Literature: Eighteenth Century
14 min., color, 1958.
Beta, VHS, 3/4" U-matic cassette, 16-mm film, special order formats.
Treats the work of Addison and Steele, Pope, Swift, and others.
Distributed by Coronet/MTI Film & Video.

*English Literature: Romantic Period
13 min., color, 1957.
Beta, VHS, 3/4" U-matic cassette, 16-mm film, special order formats.
Includes selections from Wordsworth, Byron, Shelley, Keats, and others.
Distributed by Coronet/MTI Film & Video.

*English Literature: Seventeenth Century
13 min., color, 1958.
Beta, VHS, 3/4" U-matic cassette, 16-mm film, special order formats.
Examines works by Jonson, Pepys, and others.
Distributed by Coronet/MTI Film & Video.

English Romantic Poetry: Coleridge, Shelley, Byron, Wordsworth [recording]
3 cassettes.
Distributed by Recorded Books.

*Fried Shoes, Cooked Diamonds
55 min., color, 1982.
Beta, VHS, 3/4" U-matic cassette.
Documents a summer at the Jack Kerouac School of Poetics at the Naropa Institute in Boulder, Colorado. Features such poets from the Beat generation as Allen Ginsberg, Gregory Corso, William S. Burroughs, Peter Orlovsky, and Timothy Leary.
Distributed by Centre Communications, Inc. and Mystic Fire.

Great Poets of the Romantic Age [recording]
6 cassettes (270 min.), 1986.
Distributed by Spoken Arts.

*Haiku
19 min., color, 1974.
Beta, VHS, 3/4" U-matic cassette, 16-mm film.
An overview of this poetic form.
Distributed by AIMS Media Inc.

*Harlem Renaissance: The Black Poets
20 min., color, 198?.
Beta, VHS, 3/4" U-matic cassette, 16-mm film.
Discusses this era, including an examination of Georgia Douglas Johnson, Fenton Johnson, W. E. B. DuBois, and Langston Hughes.

Distributed by Carousel Film & Video.

The Harlem Renaissance and Beyond
31 min., 1989.
VHS.
A still-image program with excerpts from Countee Cullen, Langston Hughes, Claude McKay, Gwendolyn Brooks, Alice Walker, and Richard Wright.
Distributed by Insight Media.

Inner Ear, Part 1 [recording]
1 cassette (60 min.).
Includes the poetry of Carl Sandburg and William Carlos Williams.
Distributed by National Public Radio.

Inner Ear, Parts 3 and 4 [recording]
1 cassette (60 min.).
Emily Dickinson, Marianne Moore, and Wallace Stevens.
Distributed by National Public Radio.

Inner Ear, Parts 5 and 6 [recording]
1 cassette (60 min.).
E. E. Cummings and Gary Snyder.
Distributed by National Public Radio.

*Introduction to English Poetry
28 min., color, 1989.
Beta, VHS, 3/4" U-matic cassette.
Introduces students to English verse, with readings from Chaucer, Shakespeare, Herbert, Milton, Swift, Blake, Wordsworth, Shelley, Emily Brontë, Dickinson, Hardy, Yeats, and Ted Hughes.
Distributed by Films for the Humanities and Sciences.

Literature: The Synthesis of Poetry
30 min.
VHS.

Hosted by Maya Angelou, who reads some of her own work as well as the poetry of Frost, Sandburg, and Arnold.
Distributed by Insight Media.

Medieval and Elizabethan Poetry
28 min., color, 1989.
Beta, VHS, 3/4" U-matic cassette.
Examines trends of the period, focusing on John Skelton, Thomas Wyatt, Tichborne, Nashe, Walter Raleigh, Marlowe, Drayton, and Shakespeare.
Distributed by Films for the Humanities and Sciences.

*Metaphysical and Devotional Poetry
28 min., color, 1989.
Beta, VHS, 3/4" U-matic cassette.
Looks at the works of John Donne, George Herbert, and Andrew Marvell.
Distributed by Films for the Humanities and Sciences.

Modern American Poetry
45 min., 1989.
VHS.
Hosted by Helen Vendler. Deals with poets from between the World Wars: Eliot, Pound, Stevens, Cullen, Hughes, Frost, Moore, and Crane. Focuses on development of an American, as distinct from European, voice.
Distributed by Insight Media.

A Moveable Feast
8 programs (30 min. each), color, 1991.
VHS.
Features profiles of contemporary writers: (1) Allen Ginsberg; (2) Joyce Carol Oates; (3) Li-Young Lee; (4) Sonia Sanchez; (5) T. Coraghessan Boyle; (6) T. R. Pearson; (7) Trey Ellis; (8) W. S. Merwin.
Distributed by Acorn Media.

Moyers: The Power of the Word

6 programs (60 min. each), color, 1989.

Beta, VHS, 3/4" U-matic cassette.

Bill Moyers talks with modern poets: James Autry, Quincy Troupe, Joy Harjo, Mary Tallmountain, Gerald Stern, Li-Young Lee, Stanley Kunitz, Sharon Olds, William Stafford, W. S. Merwin, Galway Kinnell, Robert Bly, and Octavio Paz.

Distributed by PBS Video.

Palgrave's Golden Treasury of English Poetry [recording]

2 cassettes.

Includes Marlowe, Shakespeare, Barnefield, Wyatt, Lyly, Donne, Herrick, Dryden, Waller, Lovelace, Milton, Gray, Rogers, Burns, Goldsmith, Keats, Wordsworth, Byron, Shelley, Coleridge, Tennyson, Arnold, and Crashaw.

Distributed by Caedmon/ HarperAudio.

Poems from Black Africa [recording]

1 cassette.

Many poets and poems from Africa, including oral traditions from various parts of the continent (Nigeria, South Africa, Ghana, and others).

Distributed by Caedmon/ HarperAudio.

Poetic Forms [recording]

5 cassettes (300 min.), 1988.

Includes the list poem, the ode, the prose poem, the sonnet, the haiku, the blues poem, the villanelle, the ballad, the acrostic, and free verse.

Distributed by Teachers & Writers Collaborative.

*Poetry: A Beginner's Guide

26 min., color, 1986.

Beta, VHS, 3/4" U-matic cassette.

Interviews contemporary poets and examines the tools they use.

Distributed by Coronet/MTI Film & Video.

*Poetry by Americans

4 programs (10 min. each), color, 1988.

Beta, VHS, 3/4" U-matic cassette, 16-mm film.

Robert Frost, Edgar Allan Poe, James Weldon Johnson, and Walt Whitman. Narrated by Leonard Nimoy, Lorne Greene, Raymond St. Jacques, and Efrem Zimbalist Jr.

Distributed by AIMS Media Inc.

*Poetry for People Who Hate Poetry

3 programs (15 min. each), color, 1980.

Beta, VHS, 3/4" U-matic cassette, special order formats.

Roger Steffens makes poetry accessible to students. Three programs: (1) About words; (2) E. E. Cummings; (3) Shakespeare.

Distributed by Churchill Media.

Poetry in Motion

90 min., color, 1982.

Laser optical videodisc.

A performance anthology of 24 North American poets, including Ntozake Shange, Amiri Baraka, Anne Waldman, William Burroughs, Ted Berrigan, John Cage, Tom Waits, and others. Performed by Ntozake Shange, Amiri Baraka, and Anne Waldman.

Distributed by Voyager Company.

The Poet's Voice [recording]
6 cassettes.
From the tape archive of the Poetry
Room, Harvard University.
Includes John Ashbery, W. H.
Auden, John Berryman, T. S.
Eliot, Robert Frost, Allen
Ginsberg, Randall Jarrell,
Robinson Jeffers, Marianne
Moore, Sylvia Plath, Ezra
Pound, Theodore Roethke,
Wallace Stevens, and William
Carlos Williams.
Distributed by Watershed Tapes.

*Poets in Person: A Series on
American Poets & Their Art
[recording]*
7 programs (30 min. each), 1991.
Thirteen poets in conversation,
reading their poems, discussing
their lives, work, and the
changing styles in contemporary American poetry: (1) Allen
Ginsberg; (2) Karl Shapiro,
Maxine Kumin; (3) W. S.
Merwin, Gwendolyn Brooks; (4)
James Merrill, Adrienne Rich;
(5) John Ashbery, Sharon Olds;
(6) Charles Wright, Rita Dove;
(7) Gary Soto, A. R. Ammons.
Distributed by Modern Poetry.

*Potpourri of Poetry — from the
Jack Kerouac School of
Disembodied Poetics,
Summer 1975 [recording]*
1 cassette (60 min.), 1975.
Allen Ginsberg, Dianne DiPrima,
John Ashbery, Ted Berrigan,
Philip Whalen, and others.
Distributed by Watershed Tapes.

**Restoration and Augustan
Poetry*
28 min., color, 1989.
Beta, VHS, 3/4" U-matic cassette.
Discusses the age of satire in
England, including the Earl of
Rochester, John Dryden,
Jonathan Swift, and Alexander
Pope.

Distributed by Films for the
Humanities and Sciences.

*Romantic Pioneers
28 min., color, 1989.
Beta, VHS, 3/4" U-matic cassette.
Readings of poems by Christopher
Smart, William Blake, William
Wordsworth, and Samuel
Taylor Coleridge.
Distributed by Films for the
Humanities and Sciences.

*Romantics and Realists
28 min., color, 1989.
Beta, VHS, 3/4" U-matic cassette.
Discusses Thomas Hardy, Gerard
Manley Hopkins, A. E.
Housman, and Rudyard
Kipling.
Distributed by Films for the
Humanities and Sciences.

*Serenade: Poets of New York
[recording]*
1 cassette, 1957.
Read by Aaron Kramer, Maxwell
Maxwell, Bodenheim.
Distributed by Smithsonian/
Folkways Recordings.

*Spoken Arts Treasury of American
Jewish Poets Reading Their
Poems [recording]*
7 cassettes.
Includes the work of Dorothy
Parker, Philip Levine, Anthony
Hecht, Denise Levertov, Allen
Ginsberg, and John Hollander.
Distributed by Spoken Arts.

*A Survey of English and American
Poetry*
16 programs (28 min. each), color,
1987.
Beta, VHS, 3/4" U-matic cassette.
A history and anthology of
English-language poetry.
Programs include: (1) Introduc-
tion to English Poetry; (2) Old
English Poetry; (3) Chaucer; (4)
Medieval to Elizabethan Poetry;
(5) The Maturing Shakespeare;

(6) Metaphysical and Devotional Poetry; (7) Milton; (8) Restoration and Augustan Poetry; (9) Romantic Pioneers; (10) William Wordsworth; (11) The Younger Romantics; (12) Victorian Poetry; (13) American Pioneers; (14) Romantics and Realists; (15) The Earlier Twentieth Century; (16) The Later Twentieth Century.

Distributed by Films for the Humanities and Sciences.

Teaching Poetry

30 min., color, 1990.
VHS.

A new approach to teaching poetry. Includes discussion questions and homework assignments.

Distributed by Video Aided Instruction.

20th Century Poets Reading Their Work [recording]

6 cassettes.

Includes William Butler Yeats, Stephen Spender, Langston Hughes, W. H. Auden, Richard Wilbur, and James Dickey.

Distributed by Spoken Arts.

*Victorian Poetry

28 min., color, 1989.
Beta, VHS, 3/4" U-matic cassette.

An examination of works by Alfred Tennyson, Emily Brontë, Christina Rossetti, Elizabeth Barrett Browning, Matthew Arnold, and Algernon Swinburne.

Distributed by Films for the Humanities and Sciences.

Victorian Poetry [recording]

3 cassettes.

Includes John Henry, E. B. Browning, Edward Fitzgerald, Alfred, Lord Tennyson, W. M. Thackeray, Robert Browning, Edward Lear, Charlotte Brontë, Emily Brontë, A. H. Clough,

Charles Kingsley, George Eliot, Matthew Arnold, George Meredith, Dante Gabriel Rossetti, Christina Rossetti, Lewis Carroll, James Thomson, Algernon Charles Swinburne, Thomas Hardy, Gerard Manley Hopkins, Coventry Patmore, Robert Bridges, William Ernest Henley, R. L. Stevenson, Oscar Wilde, A. E. Housman, Francis Thompson, George Santayana, Arthur Symons, and Rudyard Kipling.

Distributed by Caedmon/HarperAudio.

*Voices and Vision

13 programs (60 min. each), color, 1988.
Beta, VHS, 3/4" U-matic cassette.

A series exploring the lives of some of America's best poets. Hosted by Joseph Brodsky, Mary McCarthy, James Baldwin, and Adrienne Rich. Programs include: (1) Elizabeth Bishop; (2) Hart Crane; (3) Emily Dickinson; (4) T. S. Eliot; (5) Robert Frost; (6) Langston Hughes; (7) Robert Lowell; (8) Marianne Moore; (9) Sylvia Plath; (10) Ezra Pound; (11) Wallace Stevens; (12) Walt Whitman; (13) William Carlos Williams.

Distributed by the Annenberg/CPB Collection.

West Coast: Beat & Beyond

60 min., color, 197?.
Beta, VHS.

A portrait of Jack Kerouac and the Beat generation.

Distributed by Facets Multimedia, Inc.

With a Feminine Touch

45 min., color, 1990.
VHS.

Readings from Emily Dickinson, Anne Brontë, Charlotte Brontë,

Emily Brontë, Sylvia Plath, and Edna St. Vincent Millay. Read by Valerie Harper and Claire Bloom.
Distributed by Monterey Home Video.

The Young Romantics
28 min., color, 1989.
Beta, VHS, 3/4" U-matic cassette.
Features the work of John Keats, William Wordsworth, and Lord Byron.
Distributed by Films for the Humanities and Sciences.

Drama

EDWARD ALBEE

The Sandbox
10 min., 1965.
16-mm.
Distributed by University of Southern California Department of Cinema.

The Problems of Literary Creativity [recording]
1963.
Princeton Symposium on World Affairs (T4073–1–4). Albee in discussion with Arnold Gingrich, Bernard Malamud, and Robert Penn Warren.

Problems of the Contemporary Artist [recording]
1963.
Princeton Symposium on World Affairs (T4073–12). Further discussion between Albee, Gingrich, Malamud, and Penn Warren.

WOODY ALLEN (AND MARSHALL BRICKMAN)

Annie Hall
93 min., 1977.
VHS.
Directed by Woody Allen. With Woody Allen, Diane Keaton.
Distributed by Intervision.

Manhattan
96 min., 1979.
VHS.
Directed by Woody Allen. With Woody Allen, Diane Keaton, Meryl Streep, Mariel Hemingway.
Distributed by Warner.

NŌ DRAMA

The Style of the Classic Japanese Noh Theater
17 min.
VHS.
With Sadayo Kita.
Distributed by Insight Media.

Acting Techniques of the Noh Theater of Japan
30 min., 1980.
VHS.
With Akira Matsui.
Distributed by Insight Media.

The Tradition of Performing Arts in Japan
35 min., 1990.
VHS.
Distributed by Insight Media.

SAMUEL BECKETT

Krapp's Last Tape [recording]
1986.
Part of the "Sound of Modern Drama" series.
Distributed by Spoken Arts.

Krapp's Last Tape
54 min., 1971.
VHS.
Directed by Alan Schneider. With
Jack MacGowran.
Distributed by Pennebaker
Associates, Insight Media.

Beckett Directs Beckett: A Trilogy
Tape 3, 46 min., 1990.
VHS.
With Richard Cluchey.
Distributed by Smithsonian
Institution Press Video Division,
Insight Media.

Samuel Beckett: Silence to Silence
80 min., 1989.
VHS, 3/4" U-matic cassette.
Distributed by Films for the
Humanities and Sciences.

Waiting for Beckett: A Portrait of Samuel Beckett
86 min., 1993.
VHS.
Distributed by Insight Media.

ANTON CHEKHOV

The Cherry Orchard, Part I: Chekhov, Innovator of Modern Drama
21 min., 1968.
VHS, 16-mm, 3/4" U-matic
cassette.
Distributed by Britannica Films.

Anton Chekhov: A Writer's Life
37 min., 1974.
VHS, 16-mm, 3/4" U-matic
cassette.
Distributed by Films for the
Humanities.

SUSAN GLASPELL

Trifles
21 min., 1979.
VHS, 16-mm.
Adapted from the story by Susan
Glaspell.
Distributed by BFA Films/
Columbia.

Trifles
22 min., 1981.
VHS, 3/4" U-matic cassette.
Distributed by Centre Communications.

LORRAINE HANSBERRY

A Raisin in the Sun
127 min., 1982.
VHS.
Directed by Daniel Petrie. With
Sidney Poitier, Claudia McNeill,
and Ruby Dee.
Distributed by Columbia Home
Entertainment.

A Raisin in the Sun
171 min., 1989.
VHS.
Directed by Bill Duke. With Danny
Glover and Esther Rolle. An
"American Playhouse" produc-
tion.
See local retailer.

A Raisin in the Sun [recording]
With Ossie Davis and Ruby Dee.
Distributed by Caedmon/
HarperAudio.

A Raisin in the Sun
9 min., 1969.
16-mm.
Introduction to racial issues in the
play.
Distributed by Phoenix/BFA
Films.

Black Theatre Movement from "A Raisin in the Sun" to the Present
130 min., 1979.
16-mm.
Distributed by Consortium

Lorraine Hansberry: The Black Experience in the Creation of Drama
35 min., 1975.
VHS, 3/4" U-matic cassette.
Distributed by Films for the
Humanities.

Henrik Ibsen

A Doll's House
89 min., 1959.
VHS.
With Julie Harris, Jason Robards Jr., Hume Cronyn, and Christopher Plummer.
Distributed by MGM/UA Home Video.

A Doll's House
63 min., 1968.
VHS, 3/4" U-matic cassette.
Distributed by Encyclopaedia Britannica Educational Corporation.

A Doll's House
85 min., 1973.
VHS.
Directed by Patrick Garland. With Claire Bloom, Anthony Hopkins, Denholm Elliot, Anna Massey, Edith Evans, and Ralph Richardson.
Distributed by Films Inc.

A Doll's House
98 min., 1973.
VHS, 16-mm.
Directed by Joseph Losey. With Jane Fonda, Edward Fox, Trevor Howard, and David Warner.
Distributed by Insight Media, Prism Entertainment, and Starmaker Entertainment Inc.

A Doll's House: Oppression and Emancipation of Women
41 min., 1973.
VHS.
Directed by Hillard Elkins. With Claire Bloom and Anthony Hopkins. Edited version.
Distributed by AIMS Media, Inc. and Insight Media.

A Doll's House, Part I: "The Destruction of Illusion"
34 min., 1968.
VHS, 16-mm, 3/4" U-matic cassette.
With Norris Houghton.
Distributed by Britannica Films.

A Doll's House, Part II: "Ibsen's Themes"
29 min., 1968.
VHS, 16-mm, 3/4" U-matic cassette.
With Norris Houghton.
Distributed by Britannica Films.

Arthur Miller

Death of a Salesman
115 min., 1951.
16-mm.
Directed by Laslo Benedek. With Frederick March, Kevin McCarthy, and Mildred Dunnock.
Distributed by numerous rental agencies.

Death of a Salesman [recording]
1966.
With Lee J. Cobb and Mildred Dunnock.
Distributed by Caedmon/ HarperAudio.

Death of a Salesman [recording]
1986.
With Paul Douglas.
Distributed by The Mind's Eye.

Death of a Salesman
135 min., 1986.
VHS.
Directed by Volker Schlöndorff. With Dustin Hoffman, John Malkovich, and Charles Durning.
Distributed by Lorimar Home Video and Insight Media.

Arthur Miller: Part 1
50 min., 1964.
16-mm.
Interview with Arthur Miller.
Distributed by Films, Inc.

Private Conversations on the Set of "Death of a Salesman"
82 min., 1985.
VHS.
PBS documentary.
Distributed by Insight Media.

Marsha Norman

'night, Mother
97 min., 1987.
VHS.
Directed by Tom Moore. With
Sissy Spacek and Anne
Bancroft.
Distributed by MCA Home Video

William Shakespeare

Hamlet
153 min., 1948.
VHS, 16-mm.
Directed by Laurence Olivier. With
Olivier, Basil Sydney, Jean
Simmons, Stanley Holloway,
Christopher Lee, and Peter
Cushing.
Distributed by Learning Corpora-
tion of America.

Hamlet
115 min., 1969.
VHS, 16-mm.
Directed by Tony Richardson. With
Nicol Williamson.
Distributed by Learning Corpora-
tion of America.

Hamlet
150 min., 1979.
VHS, 3/4" U-matic cassette.
Directed by Derek Jacobi. With
Jacobi.
Distributed by Time-Life Videos.

Approaches to Hamlet
45 min., 1979.
VHS, 16-mm, 3/4" U-matic
cassette.
Narrated by John Gielgud. With
Gielgud, Laurence Olivier, John
Barrymore, and Nicol
Williamson.
Distributed by Films for the
Humanities and Sciences.

Discovering Hamlet
53 min., 1990.
VHS, 3/4" U-matic cassette.
Narrated by Patrick Stewart.
Distributed by PBS Video.

Hamlet: The Age of Elizabeth, I
30 min., 1959.
VHS, 16-mm, 3/4" U-matic
cassette.
Distributed by Britannica Films.

Hamlet: What Happens in Ham-let, II
30 min., 1959.
VHS, 16-mm, 3/4" U-matic
cassette.
Distributed by Britannica Films.

Shakespeare's Theater
1995.
CD-ROM.
Distributed by Insight Media.

Sophocles

Oedipus Rex
90 min., 1957.
VHS, 16-mm.
Directed by Tyrone Guthrie. With
Douglas Campbell, Douglas
Rain, Eric House, and Eleanor
Stuart. Based on William Yeats's
translation.
Distributed by Insight Media.

Oedipus the King
45 min., 1975.
VHS, 16-mm, 3/4" U-matic
cassette.
With Anthony Quayle, James
Mason, Claire Bloom, and Ian
Richardson.

Distributed by Films for the
Humanities and Sciences.

Oedipus the King
120 min., 1987.
VHS, 3/4" U-matic cassette.
With John Gielgud, Michael
Pennington, and Claire Bloom.
Distributed by Films for the
Humanities and Sciences.

Oedipus Rex: Age of Sophocles, I
31 min., 1959.
VHS, 16-mm, 3/4" U-matic
cassette.
Distributed by Britannica Films.

*Oedipus Rex: The Character of
Oedipus, II*
31 min., 1959.
VHS, 16-mm, 3/4" U-matic
cassette.
Distributed by Britannica Films.

AUGUST STRINDBERG

Miss Julie
90 min., 1985.
VHS.
Directed by Alf Sjöberg. With
Anita Björk and Ulf Palme. The
1951 Swedish film with sub-
titles.
Distributed by Embassy Home
Entertainment.

Miss Julie
105 min.
VHS.
Royal Shakespeare Company
production.
Distributed by Insight Media.

*Drama: Play, Performance,
Perception: 14 — Miss Julie*
60 min., 1978.
VHS, 3/4" U-matic cassette.
Directed by Richard Callanan.
With Patrick Stewart and Lisa
Harrow.
Distributed by Films, Inc.

TENNESSEE WILLIAMS

*Tennessee Williams Reads from
"The Glass Menagerie" and
Others [recording]*
46 min., 1989.
Recorded by Tennessee Williams
in 1952.
Distributed by Caedmon/
HarperAudio.

The Glass Menagerie
134 min., 1987.
VHS.
Directed by Paul Newman. With
Joanne Woodward, Karen Allen,
and John Malkovich.
Distributed by MCA Home Video
and Insight Media.

The Glass Menagerie [recording]
60 min., 1980.
Abridged version. With Helen
Hayes and Montgomery Clift.
Distributed by The Mind's Eye.

*In the Country of Tennessee
Williams*
30 min., 1977.
VHS, 3/4" U-matic cassette.
Distributed by New York State
Education Department.

AUGUST WILSON

August Wilson: Writing the Blues
30 min., 1988.
VHS, 3/4" U-matic cassette.
Interview with Bill Moyers.
Distributed by Films for the
Humanities and Sciences.

*In Black and White: Conversa-
tions with African American
Writers. Part 5: August
Wilson*
22 min., 1992.
VHS.
Directed by Matteo Bellinelli.
Distributed by Insight Media.

DIRECTORY OF DISTRIBUTORS

Acorn Media
7910 Woodmont Avenue
Suite 350
Bethesda, MD 20814
(301) 907–0030
(800) 999–0212

AIMS Media Inc.
9710 DeSoto Ave.
Chatsworth, CA 91311–9409
(818) 773–4300
(800) 367–2467

Ally Press
524 Orleans St.
St. Paul, MN 55107
(612) 291–2652

American Audio Prose Library
P.O. Box 842
Columbia, MO 65205
(314) 443–0361
(800) 447–2275

Annenberg/CPB Collection
P.O. Box 2345
South Burlington, VT 05407–2345

Applause Productions
85–A Fernwood Lane
Roslyn, NY 11576
(516) 365–1259
(800) 253–5351

Arcus Films
1225 Broadway
New York, NY 10001

Audio Alternatives
P.O. Box 405
Chappaqua, NY 10514
(914) 238–5943

Audio Book Contractors
P.O. Box 40115
Washington, DC 20016
(202) 363–3429

Audio Bookshelf
174 Prescott Hill Road
Northport, ME 04849
(800) 234–1713

Audio Brandon Films
See *Films, Inc.*

Audio-Forum
Jeffrey Norton Publishers
96 Broad St.
Guilford, CT 06437
(203) 453–9794
(800) 243–1234

Audio Literature
P.O. Box 7123
Berkeley, CA 94707
(800) 841–2665

Audio Partners
Publishers Group West
P.O. Box 8843
Emeryville, CA 94662
(510) 658–3453
(800) 788–3123

Bantam Audio Publishers
A division of Bantam Doubleday
Dell
1540 Broadway
New York, NY 10036-4094
(212) 354-6500
(800) 223-6834

Barr Entertainment
12801 Schabarum Ave.
P.O. Box 7878
Irwindale, CA 91706
(818) 338–7878

Benchmark Films
569 North State Road
Briarcliff Manor, NY 10510
(914) 762–3838
(800) 438–5564

BFA Educational Media
2211 Michigan Ave.
Santa Monica, CA 90404

Blackstone Audio Books
P.O. Box 969
Ashland, OR 97520
(503) 776–5179
(800) 729–2665

Books in Motion
E. 9212 Montgomery
Suite 501
Spokane, WA 99206
(509) 922–1646
(800) 752–3199

Books on Tape
P.O. Box 7900
Newport Beach, CA 92658
(714) 548–5525
(800) 626–3333

Britannica Films
310 South Michigan Ave.
Chicago, IL 60604
(800) 621–3900

Budget Films
4590 Santa Monica Blvd.
Los Angeles, CA 90029

Caedmon/HarperAudio
P.O. Box 588
Dunmore, PA 18512
(717) 343–4761
(800) 242–7737
(800) 982–4377 (in Pennsylvania)

California Newsreel
149 Ninth Street
Suite 420
San Francisco, CA 94103
(415) 621–6196

Carousel Film & Video
260 Fifth Ave.
Suite 405
New York, NY 10001
(212) 683–1660
(800) 683–1660

Cassette Works
125 North Aspen
Azusa, CA 91702
(818) 969–6699
(800) 423-8273

Center for Humanities, Inc.
Box 1000
Mount Kisco, NY 10549
(914) 666–4100
(800) 431–1242

Centre Communications
1800 30th St.
Suite 207
Boulder, CO 80301
(303) 444–1166
(800) 886–1166

Chivers North America
1 Lafayette Road
P.O. Box 1450
Hampton, NH 03842–0015
(603) 926–8744
(800) 621–0182

Chelsea House Publishers
Division of Main Line Book Co.
P.O. Box 914
Brommall, PA 19008
(610) 353–5166
(800) 848–2665

Churchill Media
6901 Woodley Ave.
Van Nuys, CA 91406–4844
(818) 778–1978
(800) 334–7830

Cifex Corporation
1 Teconic Hills Center
Southampton, NY 11968
(516) 283–4795

Cinema Guild
1697 Broadway
Suite 506
New York, NY 10019
(212) 246–5522
(800) 723–5522

Classic Films Museum, Inc.
4 Union Sq.
Dover-Foxcroft, ME 04426

Columbia Records
550 Madison Avenue
New York, NY 10022-3211
(212) 833-8000

Coronet/MTI Film & Video
P.O. Box 2649
Columbus, OH 43216
(614) 876–0371
(800) 321–3106

CRM Films
2215 Faraday Ave.
Carlsbad, CA 92008–7295
(619) 431–9800
(800) 421–0833

Crossroads Video
15 Buckminster Lane
Manhasset, NY 11030
(516) 365–3715
(516) 741–2155

Crown Publishers
See *Random Audiobooks*

Direct Cinema Limited, Inc.
P.O. Box 10003
Santa Monica, CA 90410
(310) 396–4774
(800) 345–6748

Dolphin Tapes
P.O. Box 71
Esalen Hot Springs
Big Sur, CA 93920
(408) 667–2252

Drama Classics Video
P.O. Box 2128
Manorhaven, NY 11050
(516) 767–7576
(800) 892–0860

Durkin Hayes Publishing
1 Colomba Dr.
Niagara Falls, NY 14305
(716) 298–5150
(800) 962–5200
Canadian address:
3375 North Service Road
Unit B7
Burlington, ON
CANADA L79 3G2
(905) 335–0393

Encyclopaedia Britannica Educational Corp.
425 North Michigan Ave.
Chicago, IL 60611

Facets Multimedia, Inc.
1517 W. Fullerton Ave.
Chicago, IL 60614
(800) 331–6197

FilmFair Communications
10621 Magnolia Blvd.,
North Hollywood, CA 91601

Films for the Humanities and Sciences
12 Cerrine Road
Monmouth Junction, NJ 08852
(609) 275–1400
(800) 257–5126

Films, Inc.
5547 North Ravenswood Ave.
Chicago, IL 60640–1199
(312) 878–2600
(800) 323–4222

First Run/Icarus Films
153 Waverly Place
New York, NY 10014
(212) 727–1711
(800) 876–1710

Gallaudet University Library
Gallaudet Media Distribution
800 Florida Ave. NE
Washington, DC 20002
(202) 651–5579
(202) 651–5440

Home Vision Cinema
5547 North Ravenswood Avenue
Chicago, IL 60640–1199
(312) 878–2600
(800) 826–3456

IASTA
310 West 56th St., #1B
New York, NY 10019
(212) 581–3133

Indiana University Instructional Support Services
Franklin Hall, Room 0001
Bloomington, IN 47405–5901
(812) 855–2853

Insight Media
2162 Broadway
New York, NY 10024
(212) 721–6316
(800) 233–9910

Interlingua VA
2615 Columbia Pike
P.O. Box 4132
Arlington, VA 22204
(703) 920-6644

Intermedia Arts of Minnesota
425 Ontario St. SE
Minneapolis, MN 55414
(612) 627–4444

International Film Bureau
332 S. Michigan Ave.
Suite 450
Chicago, IL 60604–4382
(312) 427–4545
(800) 432–2241

Ishtar
14755 Ventura Blvd.
Suite 766
Sherman Oaks, CA 91403
(800) 428–7136

Jimcin Recordings
P.O. Box 536
Portsmouth, RI 02871
(401) 847–5148
(800) 538–3034

Journal Films, Inc.
1560 Sherman Ave.
Suite 100
Evanston, IL 60201
(312) 328–6700
(800) 323–5448

Kit Parker Films
P.O. Box 227
Carmel Valley, CA 93924

Kultur
195 Highway #36
West Long Branch, NJ 07764
(908) 229–2343
(800) 458–5887

Learning Corporation of America
See *Coronet/MTI Film & Video*

Library of Congress
orders to:
Superintendent of Documents
P.O. Box 371954
Pittsburgh, PA 15250–7954
(202) 783–3238

Listening Library
1 Park Ave.
Old Greenwich, CT 06870
(203) 637–3616
(800) 243–4504

Maryland Public Television
11767 Owings Mills Blvd.
Owings Mills, MD 21117
(410) 356–5600

Mass Media Ministries
2116 N. Charles St.
Baltimore, MD 21218

McGraw-Hill Films
1221 Avenue of the Americas
New York, NY 10020

Media Concepts Press
331 North Broad St.
Philadelphia, PA 19107
(215) 923–2545

Media Guild
11722 Sorrento Valley Rd., Suite E
San Diego, CA 92121
(619) 755–9191
(800) 886–9191

Michigan Media
University of Michigan
400 Fourth St.
Ann Arbor, MI 48109

The Mind's Eye
P.O. Box H
Novato, CA 94949
(415) 883–7701
(800) 227–2020

Modern Poetry
60 W. Walton Street
Chicago, IL 60610
(312) 255–3703

Modern Talking Picture Service
4707 140th Avenue North
Suite 105
Clearwater, FL 34622
(813) 541–7571
(800) 243–6877

Monterey Home Video
28038 Dorothy Drive
Suite 1
Agoura Hills, CA 91301
(818) 597–0047
(800) 424–2593

Mystic Fire
P.O. Box 9323
South Burlington, VT 05407
(800) 292–9001

National Broadcasting Company
30 Rockefeller Plaza
New York, NY 10112
(212) 664–4444

National Film Board of Canada
16th floor
1251 Avenue of the Americas
New York, NY 10020–1173
(212) 586–5131

National Public Radio
Audience Services
635 Massachusetts Avenue NW
Washington, DC 20001
(202) 414–3232

Nebraska Educational Television Network
Public Affairs Unit
1800 N. 33 St.
Lincoln, NE 68583
(402) 472–3611

New Dimensions Radio
P.O. Box 569
Ukiah, CA 95482
(707) 468–5215
(800) 935–8273

New Letters on the Air
University of Missouri at Kansas City
5100 Rockhill Rd.
Kansas City, MO 64110
(816) 235–1168

New York State Education Department
Media Distribution Network
Room C–7, Concourse Level
Cultural Education Center
Albany, NY 12230
(518) 474–1265

Paramount Home Video
5555 Melrose Ave.
Hollywood, CA 90038

PBS Video
1320 Braddock Place
Alexandria, VA 22314–1698
(703) 739–5380

Perspective Films
65 East South Water St.
Chicago, IL 60601

Phoenix/BFA Films
2349 Chaffee Drive
St. Louis, MO 63146
(314) 569–0211
(800) 221–1274

Poet's Audio Center
P. O. Box 50145
Washington, DC 20091–0145
(202) 722–9105

Pyramid Film & Video
P. O. Box 1048
Santa Monica, CA 90406
(800) 421–2304

Random Audiobooks
400 Hahn Rd.
Westminster, MD 21157
(800) 733–3000

Recorded Books
270 Skipjack Rd.
Prince Frederick, MD 20678
(301) 535–5590
(800) 638–1304

ROA Films
1696 N. Astor St.
Milwaukee, WI 53202

The Roland Collection
22D Hollywood Avenue
Hohokus, NJ 07423
(201) 251–8200

SL Film Productions, Inc.
P. O. Box 41108
Los Angeles, CA 90041

S & S Audio
795 Abbot Blvd.
Fort Lee, NJ 07024
(201) 224–3100
(800) 734–4758

Smithsonian/Folkways Recordings
Office of Folklife Programs
955 L'Enfant Plaza, Suite 2600
Smithsonian Institution
Washington, DC 20560
(202) 287–3262

Social Studies School Service
10200 Jefferson Blvd.
Culver City, CA 90232–0802
(310) 839–2436
(800) 421–4246

Spoken Arts
801 94th Ave. N.
St. Petersburg, FL 33702
(813) 578–7600
(800) 726–8090

Sound Horizons
250 W. 57th St.
Suite 1517
New York, NY 10107
(212) 956–6235
(800) 524–8355

Sound Rx
See *Audio Alternatives*

Sound Photosynthesis
P.O. Box 2111
Mill Valley, CA 94942–2111
(415) 383–6712

Sounds True
735 Walnut Street
Boulder, CO 80302-5032
(303) 449-6229
(800) 333-9185

Summer Stream
P.O. Box 6056
Santa Barbara, CA 93160
(805) 962–6540

Tapes for Readers
4410 Lingan Road
Washington, DC 20007
(202) 338–1215

Teachers & Writers Collaborative
5 Union Square W.
New York, NY 10003
(212) 691–6590

Time-Life Video
Customer Service
1450 East Parham Rd.
Richmond, VA 23280
(800) 621–7026

Twyman Films, Inc.
329 Salem Ave.
Dayton, OH 45401

University of California Extension Media Center
2000 Center Street
Suite 400
Berkeley, CA 94704
(510) 642–0460

University of Washington Educational Media Collection
Kane Hall, DG–10
Seattle, WA 98195
(206) 543–9909

University of Wyoming Audiovisual Services
Box 3273
Laramie, WY 82071
(307) 766–3184

Vestron Video, Inc.
P. O. Box 4000
Stamford, CT 06907

Video Aided Instruction
P.O. Box 332
Roslyn Heights, NY 11577
(800) 238–1512

Video Yesteryear
Box C
Sandy Hook, CT 06482
(203) 426–2574
(800) 243–0987

Voyager Company
1 Bridge Street
Irvington, NY 10533
(914) 591–5500
(800) 446–2001

Water Bearer Films
205 West End Ave.
Suite 24H
New York, NY 10023
(212) 580–8185
(800) 551–8304

Watershed Tapes
Dist. by Inland Book Co.
P.O. Box 120261
East Haven, CT 06512
(203) 467–4257
(800) 243–0138

Westcoast Films
25 Lusk St.
San Francisco, CA 94107

WNET/Thirteen Non-Broadcast
356 West 58th St.
New York, NY 10019
(212) 560–2000

CASE STUDIES IN CONTEMPORARY CRITICISM
Series Editor: Ross C Murfin, *University of Miami*

■ innovative and widely adopted literary reprint series ■ each volume reprints an authoritative text of a classic literary work together with 5 critical essays representing 5 contemporary critical approaches ■ each critical essay has been especially written or edited for undergraduates and is preceded by an introduction (with bibliography) to that critical perspective ■ the work itself is preceded by an introduction providing important biographical and historical contexts and followed by a survey of critical responses since publication

"Every student needs to hear a chorus of critical voices, to broaden the teacher's inevitably limited vocal range. The Case Studies in Contemporary Criticism series provides that chorus in the best possible form."

— Wayne C. Booth, *University of Chicago*

HOWARDS END
E. M. Forster
Edited by
Alistair M. Duckworth,
University of Florida
Sept. 1996/paper
500 pages/$8.50 net

Psychoanalytic Criticism: J. H. Stape
Cultural Criticism: Peter Widdowson
Feminist & Gender Criticism: Elizabeth Langland
Marxist Criticism: Judith Weissman
Deconstruction: J. Hillis Miller

THE SECRET SHARER
Joseph Conrad
Edited by Daniel R.
Schwarz, *Cornell University*
Jan. 1996/paper
256 pages/$8.00 net

Psychoanalytic Criticism: Daniel R. Schwarz
Reader-Response Criticism: James Phelan
The New Historicism: Michael Levenson
Feminist Criticism: Bonnie Kime Scott
Deconstruction: J. Hillas Miller

Also Available:

JANE EYRE
Charlotte Brontë
Edited by Beth Newman, *Southern Methodist University*
1996/paper/646 pages/$7.50 net

Feminist Criticism: Sandra M. Gilbert
Psychoanalytic Criticism: Dianne F. Sadoff
Deconstruction: Nina Schwartz
Cultural Criticism: Elsie Michie
Marxist Criticism: Susan Fraiman

WUTHERING HEIGHTS
Emily Brontë
Edited by Linda H. Peterson, *Yale University*
1992/paper/467 pages/$7.50 net

Psychoanalytic Criticism: Philip K. Wion
Feminist Criticism: Margaret Homans
Deconstruction: J. Hillis Miller
Marxist Criticism: Terry Eagleton
Cultural Criticism: Nancy Armstrong

CASE STUDIES IN CONTEMPORARY CRITICISM

Series Editor: Ross C Murfin, *University of Miami*

"Editions of major literary texts have often pretended that in the ideal world readers would all agree on the work's significance and effect. The Case Studies in Contemporary Criticism series acknowledges that the reading experience will be greatly affected by the reader's own assumptions and methods and that major texts are precisely the sites of critical contestation and difference. The series enables students to plunge immediately into a wide range of diverse and often conflicting interpretations. The well-prepared materials make it clear that great literature demands, and often repays, passionate and sustained intellectual commitment."

— Stephen Greenblatt, *University of California, Berkeley*

Also Available:

THE WIFE OF BATH
Geoffrey Chaucer
Edited by Peter G. Beidler, *Lehigh University*
1996/paper/306 pages/$6 net
The New Historicism: Lee Patterson
Marxist Criticism: Laurie Finke
Psychoanalytic Criticism:
    Louise O. Fradenburg
Deconstruction: H. Marshall Leicester, Jr.
Feminist Criticism: Elaine Tuttle Hansen

THE AWAKENING
Kate Chopin
Edited by Nancy A. Walker, *Vanderbilt University*
1993/paper/343 pages/$7 net
Feminist Criticism: Elaine Showalter
The New Historicism: Margit Stange
Psychoanalytic Criticism:
    Cynthia Griffin Wolff
Deconstruction: Patricia S. Yaeger
Reader-Response Criticism:
    Paula A. Treichler

HEART OF DARKNESS
Joseph Conrad
Second Edition
Edited by Ross C Murfin, *University of Miami*
1996/paper/315 pages/$7 net
Reader-Response Criticism: J. Peter Rabinowitz
Feminist and Gender Criticism: Johanna M. Smith
Deconstruction: J. Hillis Miller
The New Historicism: Brook Thomas
Cultural Criticism: Patrick Brantlinger

GREAT EXPECTATIONS
Charles Dickens
Edited by Janice Carlisle, *Tulane University*
1996/paper/641 pages/$7.50 net
Psychoanalytic Criticism: Peter Brooks
Deconstruction: Edward W. Said
Feminist Criticism: Hilary Schor
Gender Criticism: William A. Cohen
Cultural Criticism: Jay Clayton

THE SCARLET LETTER
Nathaniel Hawthorne
Edited by Ross C Murfin, *University of Miami*
1991/paper/371 pages/$6.50 net
Psychoanalytic Criticism: Joanne Feit Diehl
Reader-Response Criticism: David Leverenz
Feminist Criticism: Shari Benstock
Deconstruction: Michael Ragussis
The New Historicism: Sacvan Bercovitch

CASE STUDIES IN CONTEMPORARY CRITICISM

Series Editor: Ross C Murfin, *University of Miami*

"The series is splendidly useful, authoritative in Professor Murfin's introductory material, and immensely useful in showing the active practice of the spectrum of major kinds of criticism."

— J. Hillis Miller, *University of California, Irvine*

Also Available:

THE DEAD
James Joyce

Edited by Daniel R. Schwarz, *Cornell University*

1994/paper/248 pages/$6 net

Psychoanalytic Criticism: Daniel R. Schwarz
Reader-Response Criticism:
    Peter J. Rabinowitz
The New Historicism: Michael Levenson
Feminist Criticism: Margot Norris
Deconstruction: John Paul Riquelme

A PORTRAIT OF THE ARTIST AS A YOUNG MAN
James Joyce

Edited by R. B. Kershner, *University of Florida*

1993/paper/404 pages/$6.50 net

Psychoanalytic Criticism: Sheldon Brivic
Reader-Response Criticism:
    Norman N. Holland
Feminist Criticism: Suzette Henke
Deconstruction: Cheryl Herr
The New Historicism: R. B. Kershner

THE TURN OF THE SCREW
Henry James

Edited by Peter G. Beidler, *Lehigh University*

1995/paper/313 pages/$6.50 net

Reader-Response Criticism: Wayne C. Booth
Deconstruction: Shoshana Felman
Psychoanalytic Criticism: Stanley Renner
Feminist Criticism: Priscilla L. Walton
Marxist Criticism: Bruce Robbins

HAMLET
William Shakespeare

Edited by Susanne L. Wofford, *University of Wisconsin — Madison*

1994/paper/418 pages/$6.50 net

Feminist Criticism: Elaine Showalter
Psychoanalytic Criticism: Janet Adelman
Deconstruction: Marjorie Garber
Marxist Criticism: Michael D. Bristol
The New Historicism: Karin S. Coddon

FRANKENSTEIN
Mary Shelley

Edited by Johanna M. Smith, *University of Texas at Arlington*

1992/paper/358 pages/$7 net

Reader-Response Criticism:
    Mary Lowe-Evans
Psychoanalytic Criticism: David Collings
Feminist Criticism: Johanna M. Smith
Marxist Criticism: Warren Montag
Cultural Criticism: Lee E. Heller

THE HOUSE OF MIRTH
Edith Wharton

Edited by Shari Benstock, *University of Miami*

1994/paper/498 pages/$7.50 net

Cultural Criticism: Lillian S. Robinson
Marxist Criticism: Wai-chee Dimock
Feminist Criticism: Frances L. Restuccia
Deconstruction: Margot Norris
Psychoanalytic Criticism:
    Ellie Ragland Sullivan

Bedford Books
For exam copies, call 1–800–446–8923

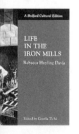

The Bedford Shakespeare Series

Series Editor: Jean E. Howard, *Columbia University*

Each volume provides: ■ an authoritative edition of a widely taught play ■ thematically arranged historical and cultural documents (modernized and annotated) — such as maps, illustrations, facsimiles of quartos and the first folio, excerpts from conduct books, legal writings, statutes, popular ballads, homilies, and playhouse records ■ a general introduction, glosses for the play, and an introduction to each thematic unit ■ a headnote and annotations for each document ■ illustrations, a bibliography, and an index.

"As pedagogical tools, the plays so annotated and accompanied by primary historical materials promise to be immensely useful."

— Linda Gregerson, *University of Michigan — Ann Arbor*

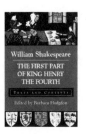

**William Shakespeare
THE FIRST PART
OF KING HENRY
THE FOURTH
Texts and Contexts**

Edited by Barbara Hodgdon,
Drake University

1997/paper
419 pages/$7.50 net

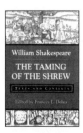

**William Shakespeare
THE TAMING OF THE
SHREW
Texts and Contexts**

Edited by Frances E. Dolan,
Miami University

1996/paper
347 pages/$6.50 net

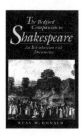

**THE BEDFORD
COMPANION
TO SHAKESPEARE
An Introduction with
Documents**

Russ McDonald, *University of
North Carolina at
Greensboro*

1996/paper
371 pages/$8.00 net

Forthcoming:

**William Shakespeare
MACBETH
Texts and Contexts**

Edited by William Carroll, *Boston
University*

**William Shakespeare
A MIDSUMMER NIGHT'S DREAM
Texts and Contexts**

Edited by Gail Kern Paster, *George
Washington University*

**William Shakespeare
OTHELLO
Texts and Contexts**

Edited by Kim Hall, *Georgetown University*

**William Shakespeare
ROMEO AND JULIET
Texts and Contexts**

Edited by Dympna Callaghan, *Syracuse
University*

Bedford Books
For exam copies, call 1–800–446–8923

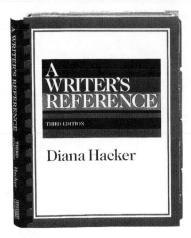